The Camellia House
The Drake

Pig

Tropical Bounty
LAMA HO'OHUIHUI 'IA
Proud Bird Cocktail
Beachcomber Chi Chi
Tahitian Coffee • Rum • Scotch • B
Canadian • Beachcomber Mai Tai
Gin • Vermouth • Sherry • Mixes •
Champagne
"ALOHA KAKAHIAKA"
LAMA HO'OHUIHUI 'IA
Tahitian Coffee
Bloody Mary
Screwdriver
Champagne
WAI A ME HUA'AI
Chilled Tomato or
Kauai Guava Juice
Kula Breakfast Fruit
'AI A MA'ONA
Eggs Benedict on Iania English M
Tenderloin Steak, Ulupalakua
PALAOA
Freshly heated Croissants
and Assorted Muffins, Maika'i
Butter, Momona
MEA INU
Kona Coffee • Tea • Sanka
Coca-Cola • Sprite • Fresca
Canada Dry • Quinine • Club Soda

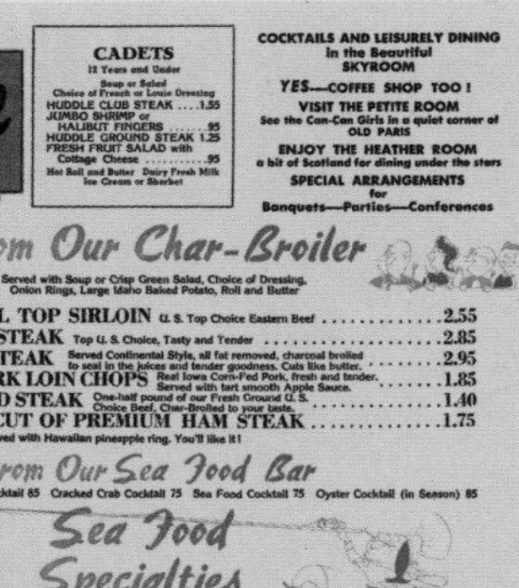
CADETS
12 Years and Under
Soup or Salad
Choice of French or Louie Dressing
HUDDLE CLUB STEAK 1.55
JUMBO SHRIMP or
HALIBUT FINGERS 95
HUDDLE GROUND STEAK 1.25
FRESH FRUIT SALAD with
Cottage Cheese 95
Hot Roll and Butter Dairy Fresh Milk
Ice Cream or Sherbet
COCKTAILS AND LEISURELY DINING
in the Beautiful
SKYROOM
YES—COFFEE SHOP TOO!
VISIT THE PETITE ROOM
See the Can-Can Girls in a quiet corner of
OLD PARIS
ENJOY THE HEATHER ROOM
a bit of Scotland for dining under the stars
SPECIAL ARRANGEMENTS
for
Banquets—Parties—Conferences
From Our Char-Broiler
Served with Soup or Crisp Green Salad, Choice of Dressing, Onion Rings, Large Idaho Baked Potato, Roll and Butter
PECIAL TOP SIRLOIN U. S. Top Choice Eastern Beef 2.55
K CUT STEAK Top U. S. Choice, Tasty and Tender 2.85
NON STEAK Served Continental Style, all fat removed, charcoal broiled to seal in the juices and tender goodness. Cuts like butter. 2.95
UT PORK LOIN CHOPS Real Iowa Corn-Fed Pork, fresh and tender. Served with tart smooth Apple Sauce. 1.85
ROUND STEAK One-half pound of our Fresh Ground U. S. Choice Beef, Char-Broiled to your taste. 1.40
NTER CUT OF PREMIUM HAM STEAK 1.75
d tender. Served with Hawaiian pineapple ring. You'll like it!
From Our Sea Food Bar
Lobster Cocktail 85 Cracked Crab Cocktail 75 Sea Food Cocktail 75 Oyster Cocktail (in Season) 85
Sea Food Specialties
Served with Cole Slaw, French Fries, Tartar Sauce, Lemon, Roll and Butter
RIMP, FRENCH FRIED Fresh from Mexican waters—Louisiana sauce. 1.25
ALLOPS We use the best of the frozen to assure supply and our uniform quality. 1.25
N SWORDFISH Center cut, Char-Broiled. In the mood for fish? This is it. 1.65
N HALIBUT FINGERS Crisp, golden brown and tasty. 1.15
TION SEA FOOD PLATE Shrimp, Scallops, Halibut Fingers. 1.45
CHINOOK SALMON STEAK Broiled to Perfection 1.55
Desserts
Our Chef's Specials
TY:
memade Individual Pies 35
nd Fresh Strawberry
pped Cream or
ream
NENTIAL
..............40
..............25
e Cream/5c Extra
RRY
..............45
CAKE 20
Drinks
COFFEE (Apffel's) 10
POT OF TEA 15
MILK 15
BUTTERMILK 15
HOT CHOCOLATE ..20
ICED TEA 15
ICED COFFEE 15
SANKA OR POSTUM 15
Our Famous Spicy Chili and Beans 50c
Loaded with Choice Beef. Served with toasted bun, garnished.
HUDDLE SIZE 85c
¼ lb. of Choice Beef Burger. Smothered with our Special Spicy Chili and Beans and chopped onions. Served with toasted bun, garnished.
DELICIOUS OYSTER STEW 75c
Pacific oysters from deep blue waters. The most nutritious of foods. Floating islands of butter. Salted crackers.
POOR BOY SANDWICH 80c
¼ lb. of Burger topped with Cheese, Chili and Beans, salad. Kosher dill pickle, carrot curl, lettuce and tomato. Coffee or tea.

Billy Rose's
CASA MAÑANA

islander

ORIGINAL POODLE DOG
117 MASON STREET
BETWEEN EDDY AND ELLIS
SAN FRANCISCO, CALIFORNIA

La Conga

THE WORLD FAMOUS
COTTON CLUB

"BOTTOMS UP"
ICE SHOW

HOTEL
El Rancho
VEGAS
EL RANCHO VEGAS
WESTERN AMERICA'S FINEST

LUNCHEON

PLANTATION

CHILDREN'S
MENU

Les Comiques
AMERICA'S HAPPIEST INSTITUTION
HOLLYWOOD PLAZA HOTEL

International
Casino
MENU

RESTAURANT
LONGCHAMPS
MENU

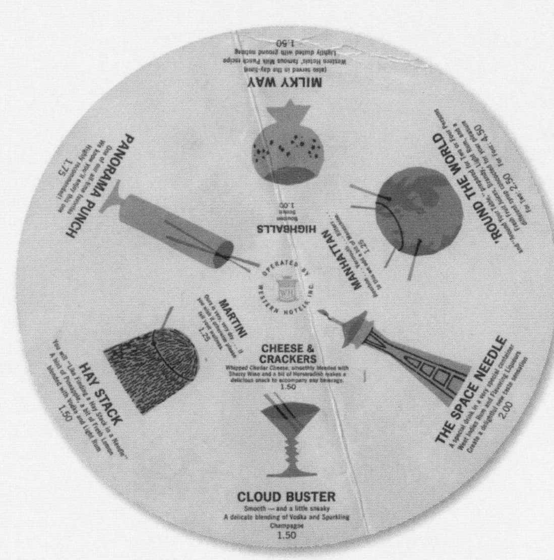
MILKY WAY
'ROUND THE WORLD
PANORAMA PUNCH
HIGHBALLS
MANHATTAN
MARTINI
CHEESE & CRACKERS
1.50
HAY STACK
THE SPACE NEEDLE
CLOUD BUSTER
Smooth — and a little sneaky
A delicate blending of Vodka and Sparkling Champagne
1.50

WHITNEY BROS
PIE SHOP
THE HOME OF TASTY PIES & FRESH FROZEN ICE CREAM

ATOMIC

SUPPER
HOTEL
PENNSYLVANIA

Mocambo

WILSHIRE AT GLENDON, WESTWOOD VILLAGE

Menu Design In America

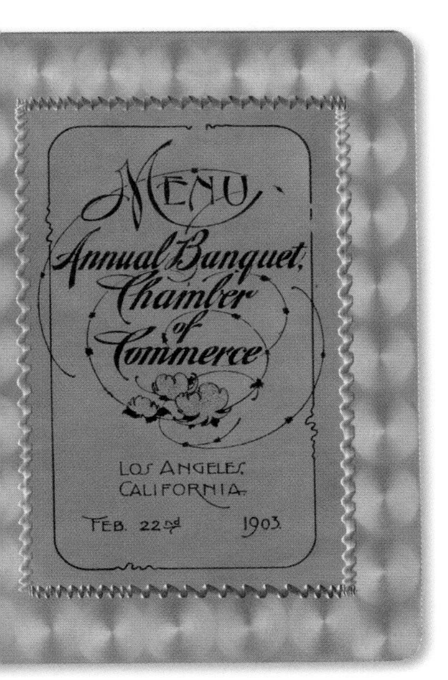

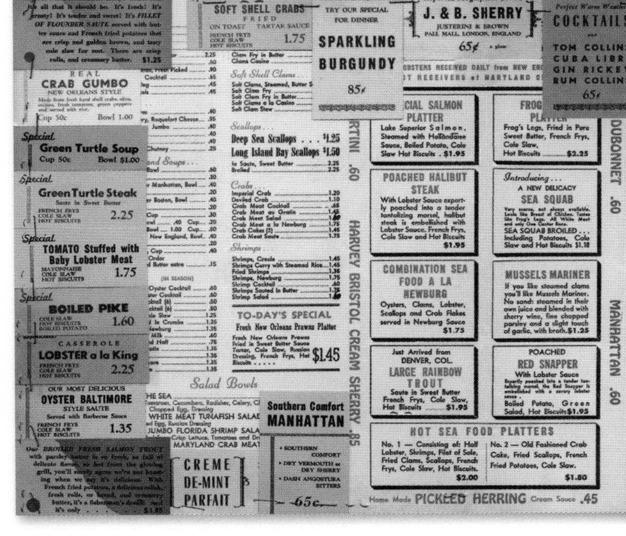

AMERICA'S FINEST BARBECUED CHICKEN AND RIBS
Rudy's
PALM SPRINGS NEWEST, MOST UNIQUE RESTAURANT
Rudy's

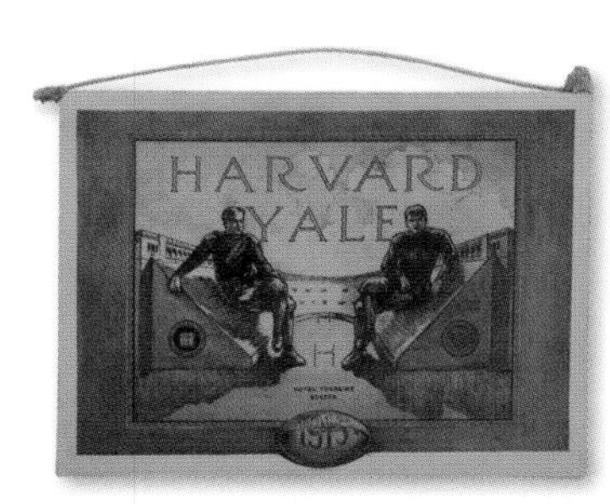
HARVARD
YALE

CHURCHILL'S

SINGAPORE
MAXEY'S SPA

Menu

BILL OF FARE
St. Louis, Cairo, Memphis & New-Orleans Passenger Packet
M. S. MEPHAM
Breakfast from 7½ to 9 A.M.
Dinner from 1 to 2½ P.M.
Supper at 6 P.M.
JAMES ABBEY Steward.

KON-TIKI

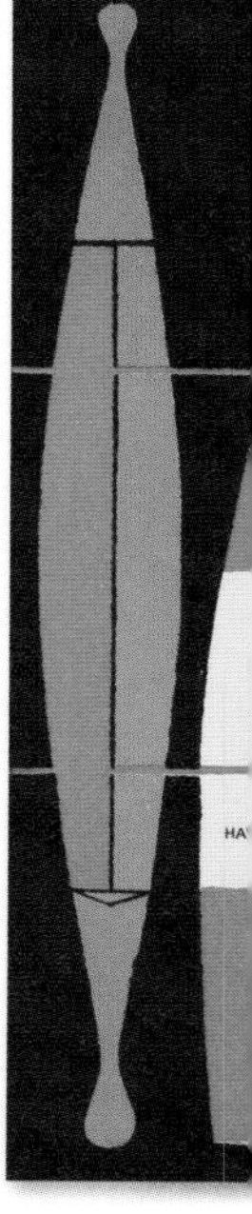

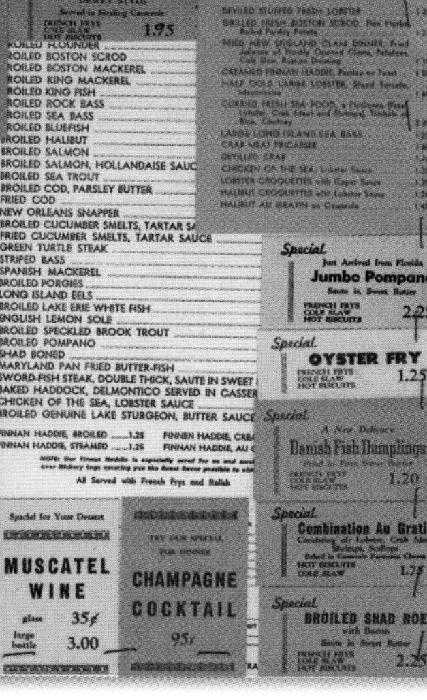
Special
CRAB MEAT
DEWEY STYLE
Served in Sizzling Casserole
FRENCH FRYS
COLE SLAW
HOT BISCUITS
1.95
To Day's Fish Specials
ROILED BOSTON SCROD
ROILED BOSTON MACKEREL
ROILED KING MACKEREL
ROILED KING FISH
ROILED ROCK BASS
ROILED SEA BASS
ROILED BLUEFISH
BROILED HALIBUT
BROILED SALMON
BROILED SALMON, HOLLANDAISE SAUC
BROILED SEA TROUT
BROILED COD, PARSLEY BUTTER
FRIED COD
NEW ORLEANS SNAPPER
BROILED CUCUMBER SMELTS, TARTAR SA
FRIED CUCUMBER SMELTS, TARTAR SAUCE
GREEN TURTLE STEAK
STRIPED BASS
SPANISH MACKEREL
BROILED PORGIES
LONG ISLAND EELS
BROILED LAKE ERIE WHITE FISH
ENGLISH LEMON SOLE
BROILED SPECKLED BROOK TROUT
BROILED POMPANO
SHAD BONED
MARYLAND PAN FRIED BUTTER-FISH
SWORD-FISH STEAK, DOUBLE THICK, SAUTE IN SWEET
BAKED HADDOCK, DELMONTICO SERVED IN CASSER
CHICKEN OF THE SEA, LOBSTER SAUCE
BROILED GENUINE LAKE STURGEON, BUTTER SAUCE
All Served with French Frys and Relish
Special
Just Arrived from Florida
Jumbo Pompano
Saute in Sweet Butter
FRENCH FRYS
COLE SLAW
HOT BISCUITS
2.25
Special
OYSTER FRY
1.25
Special
A New Delicacy
Danish Fish Dumplings
1.20
Special
Combination Au Gratin
HOT BISCUITS
COLE SLAW
1.75
Special
BROILED SHAD ROE
with Bacon
Saute in Sweet Butter
2.25
MUSCATEL
WINE
glass 35¢
large bottle 3.00
CHAMPAGNE
COCKTAIL
95¢

MARIO'S
PIZZA
HOUSE
COLUMBUS
GRANT
BROADWAY
JOHN'S RENDEVOUS
EL MATADOR
FIOR D'ITALIA
VANESSI'S
FINOCCHIO'S
NEW JOE'S
HOUSE OF PISCO
JULIUS' CASTLE
XOCHIMILCO
JAI ALAI
NORMANDIE

the Pan Lad
charcoal broiler

BRIGHT
ANGEL
LODGE
Coffee Shop
Fred Harvey
GRAND CANYON
NATIONAL PARK
ARIZONA

Good
morning!
WHAT'S GOOD ABOUT IT?
WALT DISNEY'S STUDIO RESTAURANT
BURBANK CALIFORNIA

Jim Heimann [Ed.]
Steven Heller
John Mariani

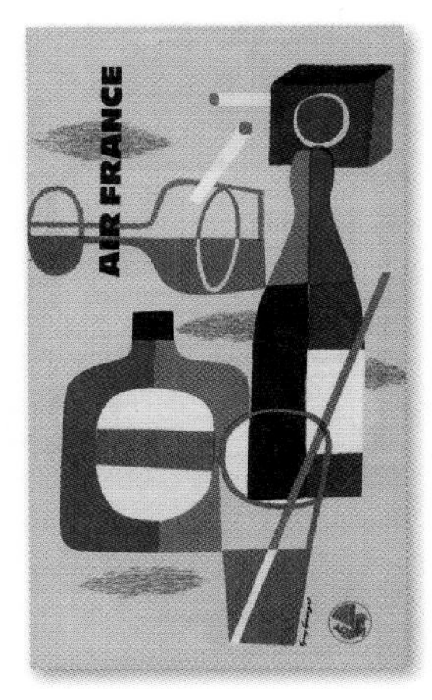

Menu Design In America

A Visual and Culinary History of Graphic Styles and Design 1850–1985

el nuevo
Salón Imperial

The Informal Cocktail Lounge and Dining Room of the Motion Picture Industry
OF YOUR HOST . . "Sugie"
SUGIE'S Original
Tropics
NATIONALLY FAMOUS
Beverly Hills . . . California
WE HAVE NO BRANCHES ANYWHER

WE PREPARE Kentucky Fried Chicken FOR ANY SIZE GROUP UP TO 5,000!

MR.CHOW
PORTRAIT OF MR. CHOW
DAVID HOCKNEY 1969
BEVERLY HILLS 213-278-9911
N.Y. 212-751-9030 LONDON 01-589-7347
MR. CHOW SAYS
AVERAGE CONTENTS 35

Little Tommy Tucker
Sings for his supper
What will he eat? Why,
Brown Bread and Butter.
This is the way we clean our teeth,
Clean our teeth, clean our teeth,
This is the way we clean our teeth,
Early every morning.

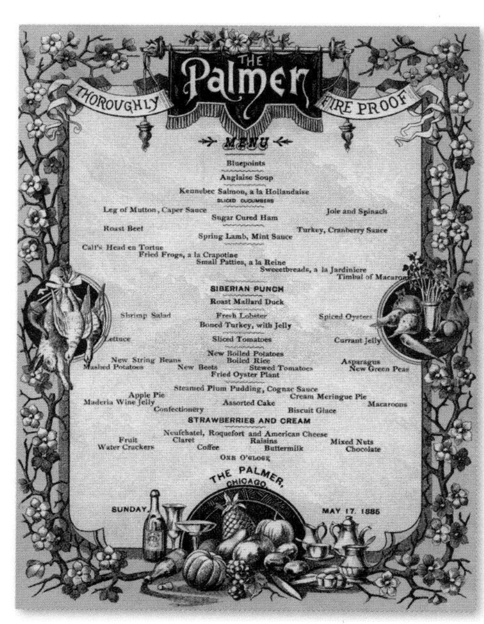

THE Palmer
THOROUGHLY
FIRE PROOF
MENU
Bluepoints
Anglaise Soup
Kennebec Salmon, a la Hollandaise
SLICED CUCUMBERS
Leg of Mutton, Caper Sauce
Sugar Cured Ham
Joie and Spinach
Roast Beef
Spring Lamb, Mint Sauce
Turkey, Cranberry Sauce
Calf's Head en Tortue
Fried Frogs, a la Crapotine
Small Patties, a la Reine
Sweetbreads, a la Jardiniere
SIBERIAN PUNCH
Roast Mallard Duck
Shrimp Salad
Fresh Lobster
Spiced Oysters
Boned Turkey, with Jelly
Sliced Tomatoes
Currant Jelly
New Boiled Potatoes
New String Beans
Boiled Rice
Asparagus
New Beets
Stewed Tomatoes
New Green Peas
Fried Oyster Plant
Steamed Plum Pudding, Cognac Sauce
Apple Pie
Cream Meringue Pie
Maderia Wine Jelly
Assorted Cake
Macaroons
Confectionery
Biscuit Glace
STRAWBERRIES AND CREAM
Neufchatel, Roquefort and American Cheese
Fruit
Claret
Raisins
Mixed Nuts
Water Crackers
Coffee
Buttermilk
Chocolate
ONE O'CLOCK
THE PALMER, CHICAGO.
SUNDAY,
MAY 17. 1885

HACIENDA
DINE and DANCE

CLUB
BALLYHOO
8373 Sunset Blvd
Hollywood Calif.

HARRY CARPENTER'S
Special
Small Steak
MIXED GREEN SALAD
SHOESTRING POTATOES
TOASTED SESAME BUN
50c
CHICKEN in the STRAW
Every Bite a Tender Delight
SERVED UNJOINTED
WITHOUT SILVERWARE
"The Natural Way"
Butter Drenched Toast.
Honey
50c
ROAST TURKEY PLATE
Dressing, Giblet Gravy, and Cranberry Jelly, Shoestring Potatoes 40
HOT TURKEY SANDWICH
Dressing, Giblet Gravy, Shoestring Potatoes 40
CLUB SANDWICH
(Three-Decker) with Shoestring Potatoes 40
GENUINE ITALIAN SPAGHETTI
With Imported Cheese and Tomato Sauce 30
Three Jumbo French Fried Shrimp
With Our Special Sauce, Generous Portion of Shoestring Potatoes, Well Buttered Toast, All For 30
Special
TOP SIRLOIN STEAK SANDWICH 25
Shoestring Potatoes
LARGE JUICY HOT DOG
LETTUCE, RELISH, MAYONNAISE 15
SOUPS
CARPENTER'S SPECIAL
ASK FOR SELECTION
Cup 10c
Bowl 15c
OLD FASHIONED
Cup 10c
Our Leader !
WITH SPECIAL SAUCE
The Finest
15c
CHICKEN SALAD
SANDWICH
ON GOLDEN BROWN TOAST
FRIED
SHOESTRING POTATOES
ASK FOR OUR PIE LIST

DeMay's
HILL TOP

53 PIER AVENUE HERMOSA BEACH CALIFORNIA FRONTIER 4—9388
Insomniac

WINE LIST
HOTEL
KNICKERBOCKER

PAGE 6 **Louis Martin's, 1911, New York, New York**

Seasoned café operator Louis Martin opened Martin's uptown in 1910 in the Times Square district. Suggestive menus like this drew New York's theater crowd in droves. It was claimed that the restaurant's closing within a year was because he mandated evening dress for men.

Der altgediente Cafébesitzer Louis Martin eröffnete das Martin's 1910 im Viertel am Times Square. Suggestive Speisekarten wie diese zogen die Theaterleute New Yorks scharenweise an. Es wird behauptet, dass das Restaurant schon nach einem Jahr wieder schließen musste, weil Mr. Martin formelle Abendkleidung für Herren vorschrieb.

Louis Martin, gestionnaire aguerri, ouvre le Martin's en 1910 dans le quartier chic de Times Square. Avec des menus éminemment évocateurs, il attire une foule de comédiens et d'amateurs de théâtre. Le restaurant aurait fermé au bout d'un an, peut-être parce que la tenue de soirée était exigée pour les hommes.

PAGE 8 **Southland, 1938, Boston, Massachusetts**

PAGE 10 **The Starlight Roof, the Waldorf-Astoria 1949, New York, New York**

Louis Martin's
42ND ST. & BROADWAY
• NEW YORK •

FOREWORD

Collecting American Menus

by Jim Heimann

Vintage or contemporary, American or international, the menu has become more than a listing of comestibles—it is ephemera that has moved from the restaurant and the banquet table to the collector and the world's leading institutions...

The act of dining is quite simple. Food, service, and a list of available food items are the basics. The menu has gone beyond a mere element of a restaurant to a marketing tool, a branding opportunity, an indicator of cuisine, a barometer of taste, and a highly sought piece of ephemera.

For the most part collectors focus on the golden age of menus, which covers roughly 125 years, starting in the mid-1800s. The criteria for menu collecting is as varied as the number of menus available to collect. Generalists are a minority as most collectors seek out specific categories, be they geographical, restaurant type, or by cuisine. Cocktail, bar menus, and wine lists all have their specialists as do those for coffee shops, diners, and drive-ins. Military-related menus, from banquets to in-the-field meals, have their following, and there are those looking for dishes that can expand their culinary expertise. Autographed menus can demand higher prices if the signature is rare or corresponds to a special event, meal, or restaurant. Often the motivation for collecting is a way to connect with one's past. Each collecting sector claims a Holy Grail, and prices range from the affordable to whatever the market will bear. The Internet has provided the easiest access for the contemporary collector, yet there are those who shun the computer and walk the aisles of flea markets and estate sales looking for their once-in-a-lifetime find.

The printed American menu holds a particular place in the realm of international collecting. Out of sheer diversity and quantity there is little comparison. Although the menu's roots are in Western Europe, as the U.S. dining experience evolved in the 1800s and the number of its restaurants increased exponentially, there were, by the end of the 19th century, an almost infinite amount of menus created, whose design and basic elements rivaled the best of the European tradition. These early examples of culinary ephemera were sought after not only as personal souvenirs to be deposited in scrapbooks, but also for their exquisite design and historical importance. It is perhaps at this juncture that collecting menus accelerated beyond a casual pastime.

American influence on menu design continued into the 20th century as dining reflected the growth of the country. The United States, as an expanding world power, necessitated an abundance of banquets and state dinners. As the culture grew, rich collecting areas developed, including the fields of exploration and aviation. Tributes to early pioneers in these fields warranted fetes such as those for Charles Lindbergh's transatlantic flight in 1927. His three-month postflight tour across the United States resulted in the creation of more than forty banquet menus, a collector's dream. The rise of the automobile additionally created an opportunity for diners to experience cuisines from unfamiliar regions and prompted the collecting of menus from restaurants visited on road trips. The auto also spawned restaurants specific to the roadside, such as diners and drive-ins, contributing to a unique aspect of American eating and another opportunity for the collector.

By the mid-20th century an increasing segment of the menu trade had evolved into a well-defined marketing tool. Designs were produced with the consumer in mind, and food items were strategically placed in a specific hierarchy to attract the attention of the customer and to sell. In the latter part of the 20th century menu engineering became a science, especially when corporations took over a section of the food service industry. The appearance of fast food outlets and chain restaurants tempered the creative menu and at times eliminated it.

As another century has turned, the rise of interest in the culinary arts combined with a surge in the dining experience has sparked an even higher interest in the collecting of menus. Vintage or contemporary, American or international, the menu has become more than a listing of comestibles—it is ephemera that has moved from the restaurant and the banquet table to the collector and the world's leading institutions and museums.

SOUTHLAND
MENU
Boston, Massachusetts

VORWORT

Über das Sammeln amerikanischer Speisekarten

von Jim Heimann

Ob historisch oder aktuell, amerikanisch oder international, die Speisekarte hat sich zu weit mehr als einer Auflistung von Essbarem entwickelt – sie ist ein Sammlerobjekt, das seinen Weg vom Tisch der Speisegaststätte und des Festsaals zu den Sammlern und in die führenden Institutionen und Museen der Welt gefunden hat …

Der Akt des Essengehens ist im Grunde nicht schrecklich kompliziert. Essen, Bedienung und eine Liste der zur Auswahl stehenden Speisen bilden die Grundlage. Die Speisekarte hat sich aber weit über ein reines Hilfsmittel der Restaurants hinaus entwickelt: Sie ist ein Marketinginstrument, ein Hinweis auf die Küche, ein Barometer des Geschmacks und zugleich ein gesuchtes Sammlerobjekt.

Die Sammler konzentrieren sich zum größten Teil auf die goldene Epoche der Speisekartengestaltung, die um 1850 begann und rund 125 Jahre dauerte. Man kann Menükarten nach sehr vielen verschiedenen Kriterien wie Geografie, Art des Restaurants oder der Küche sammeln – Generalisten sind in der Minderheit. Cocktail- und Barkarten sowie Weinlisten haben ihre Liebhaber, genau wie die Karten aus Bistros, Schnellrestaurants und Drive-ins. Einige bevorzugen Speisekarten mit militärischen Themen, vom Bankett bis zum Imbiss auf dem Schlachtfeld; andere sind auf der Suche nach ausgefallenen Gerichten, mit denen sie ihr kulinarisches Repertoire erweitern können. Signierte Speisekarten werden teurer gehandelt, wenn das Autogramm selten ist oder mit einem besonderen Ereignis, Festmahl oder Restaurant in Zusammenhang steht. Der Auslöser für die Sammelleidenschaft ist oft Sehnsucht nach der eigenen Vergangenheit. Die Preise bewegen sich zwischen dem Erschwinglichen und exorbitanten Fantasiepreisen. Das Internet bietet den Sammlern leichten Zugang zu den Objekten ihrer Begierde, doch es gibt auch Kenner, die lieber Flohmarktstände und Nachlassverkäufe absuchen, um den Fund ihres Lebens zu machen.

Die amerikanische Speisekarte nimmt in der internationalen Sammlerszene einen besonderen Platz ein. Auch wenn die Herkunft der Speisekarte in Westeuropa zu suchen ist, schlugen Speisegaststätten in Amerika bereits im 19. Jahrhundert einen ganz eigenen Weg ein. Die Anzahl der Wirtshäuser nahm stark zu und am Ende des 19. Jahrhunderts gab es bereits eine fast unendlich große Menge an Speisekarten, deren Gestaltung und Originalität es mit den besten europäischen aufnehmen konnten. Diese frühen Beispiele waren nicht nur als persönliche Andenken begehrt, sondern auch geschätzt, weil sie exquisit gestaltet waren und historische Bedeutung besaßen.

Der amerikanische Einfluss auf das Speisekartendesign war auch im 20. Jahrhundert stark, als das vermehrte Essengehen den wachsenden Wohlstand im Land zeigte. Die USA waren eine expandierende Weltmacht, was zahllose Staatsbankette und offizielle Abendessen zur Folge hatte. Mit der wachsenden Bedeutung der Esskultur entwickelten sich viele sammelbare Themen, zu denen auch Forschungsreisen und Luftfahrt zählten. Den Pionieren auf diesen Gebieten, wie Charles Lindbergh mit seinem Flug über den Atlantik 1927, wurde mit Festessen Tribut gezollt. Lindberghs dreimonatige Triumphtour durch die USA gab Anlass zu über 40 Banketten, jeweils mit eigener Karte, ein Traum für Sammler. Die Erfindung des Automobils gab den Restaurantbesuchern ganz neue Möglichkeiten, die Kochkünste unbekannter Regionen auszuprobieren und dort Speisekarten zu sammeln. Das Auto führte auch zur Entstehung spezieller, auf Autofahrer ausgerichteter Gaststätten wie Diner und Drive-in, beides amerikanische Erfindungen, die neue Sammelgebiete eröffneten.

Mitte des 20. Jahrhunderts hatte sich ein stetig wachsender Anteil von Speisekarten zu einem effektiven Werbemittel entwickelt. Ihr Design richtete sich an ganz bestimmte Zielgruppen und die angebotenen Gerichte wurden so auf der Karte angeordnet, dass sie die Aufmerksamkeit und den Appetit der Gäste anregten. Ende des 20. Jahrhunderts hatte sich die Gestaltung von Speisekarten zu einer wahren Wissenschaft entwickelt, besonders, als Großunternehmen Teile der Gastronomiebranche übernahmen. Die Ausbreitung von Schnellrestaurants und Restaurantketten verminderte die Kreativität des Speisekartendesigns weitgehend.

Seit der Jahrtausendwende hat ein gesteigertes Interesse an kulinarischen Künsten zusammen mit dem verstärkten Appetit auf gepflegte gastronomische Erlebnisse zu einem noch stärkeren Interesse am Sammeln von Speisekarten geführt. Ob historisch oder aktuell, amerikanisch oder international, die Speisekarte hat sich zu weit mehr als einer Auflistung von Essbarem entwickelt– sie ist ein Sammlerobjekt, das seinen Weg vom Tisch der Speisegaststätte und des Festsaals zu den Sammlern und in die führenden Institutionen und Museen der Welt gefunden hat.

the Starlight Roof
THE WALDORF-ASTORIA

PRÉFACE

Collectionner les menus américains

par Jim Heimann

Vintage ou contemporain, américain ou européen, le menu est devenu bien plus qu'une liste de mets : autrefois support éphémère oublié sur les tables des restaurants et des banquets, il est aujourd'hui précieusement conservé dans des collections privées ou dans les musées les plus prestigieux.

Dîner au restaurant est en soi un acte banal qui repose sur trois « ingrédients » de base : la nourriture, le service et la liste des plats proposés – le menu. Mais au fil du temps, le menu, de simple accessoire gastronomique, est devenu un outil marketing à part entière, la signature d'un chef, le reflet d'une cuisine, un baromètre du goût… et un objet éphémère convoité par les plus grands collectionneurs.

La plupart des « missuphiles » se concentrent sur l'âge d'or du menu, lequel couvre environ cent vingt-cinq ans à partir du milieu du XIXe siècle. Les critères de collection sont aussi variés que les menus eux-mêmes. Parmi les collectionneurs, les généralistes sont une minorité ; la plupart d'entre eux, en effet, s'intéressent à des catégories spécifiques : régions, types d'établissement, spécialités, etc. Cartes de cocktails ou cartes des vins ont également leurs spécialistes, sans oublier les menus des cafétérias, des snacks ou des drive-in. Certains amateurs jettent leur dévolu sur les thèmes militaires – banquets ou simples repas de guerre –, tandis que d'autres sont constamment en quête de mets susceptibles d'enrichir leurs connaissances culinaires. Les menus dédicacés font monter les enchères en fonction de la rareté de la signature ou de la singularité de l'événement, du lieu ou du repas. Souvent le collectionneur est motivé par la quête du souvenir d'un instant perdu. Chaque catégorie a son Saint-Graal et les prix sont très fluctuants. Internet procure un accès simple aux pièces contemporaines mais les collectionneurs peuvent aussi compter sur les marchés aux puces et les ventes aux enchères pour dénicher la perle rare.

Les menus américains imprimés tiennent une place particulière dans les collections internationales. En termes de diversité et de quantité, ils ne souffrent aucune comparaison. Bien que le menu soit originaire d'Europe occidentale, le développement et la fréquentation des restaurants ont si fortement progressé aux États-Unis au XIXe siècle qu'à l'approche du XXe siècle, ses déclinaisons en sont infinies, et ses conceptions et éléments rivalisent avec le meilleur de la tradition européenne. Non seulement convoités comme souvenirs personnels, ces curiosités culinaires éphémères le sont aussi pour leur élégance, leur design et leur valeur historique. À cette époque, collectionner les menus devient bien plus qu'un simple passe-temps.

L'influence américaine sur la conception des menus se poursuit au cours du XXe siècle en même temps que l'évolution de l'offre de restauration reflète la montée en puissance du pays. Les États-Unis, puissance mondiale de premier plan, accueillent alors pléthore de réceptions et de dîners officiels. Tandis que la culture s'étoffe et se diversifie, les collectionneurs s'intéressent à d'autres domaines, dont l'exploration et l'aviation. Les hommages rendus aux pionniers de la première heure légitiment les festivités comme celles organisées après le vol transatlantique de Charles Lindbergh en 1927, dont la tournée à travers les États-Unis sera à l'origine de plus d'une quarantaine de menus créés spécialement – un rêve de collectionneur. L'expansion de l'automobile donne la possibilité à la clientèle de découvrir les gastronomies régionales et l'invite à collectionner les cartes et menus glanés à l'occasion d'étapes gourmandes. La voiture engendre par ailleurs l'apparition de restaurants de bord de route, tels que les snacks et les drive-in, phénomène unique de la gastronomie américaine et opportunité nouvelle pour le collectionneur.

Au milieu de XXe siècle, le menu devient de plus en plus un instrument de marketing répondant à des codes rigoureux. Il est conçu en fonction des attentes du consommateur et l'ordre des plats est hiérarchisé, obéissant à une stratégie commerciale destinée à attirer l'œil du client. Au cours de la dernière partie du XXe siècle, la conception des menus devient une science à part, en particulier depuis que des multinationales contrôlent des pans entiers de l'industrie de la restauration. L'apparition des franchises de restauration rapide et des chaînes de restaurants a grandement porté préjudice à la créativité des menus.

À l'aube du XXIe siècle, le regain d'intérêt pour les arts culinaires et le renouveau gastronomique ont permis de raviver l'engouement pour la collection des menus. Vintage ou contemporain, américain ou européen, le menu est devenu bien plus qu'une liste de mets : autrefois support éphémère oublié sur les tables des restaurants et des banquets, il est aujourd'hui précieusement conservé dans des collections privées ou dans les musées les plus prestigieux.

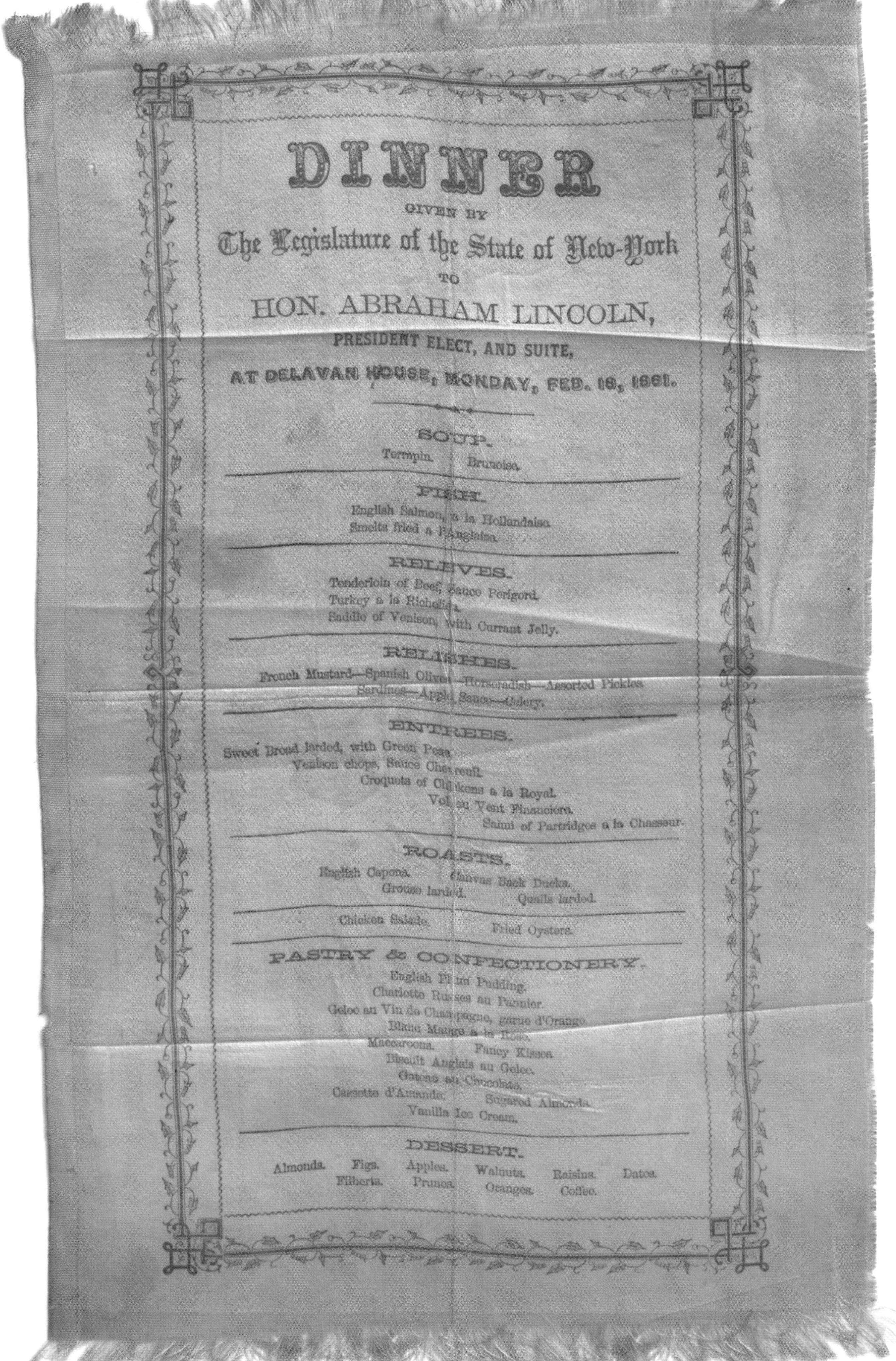

DINNER
GIVEN BY
The Legislature of the State of New-York
TO
HON. ABRAHAM LINCOLN,
PRESIDENT ELECT, AND SUITE,
AT DELAVAN HOUSE, MONDAY, FEB. 18, 1861.

SOUP.
Terrapin. Brunoise.

FISH.
English Salmon, a la Hollandaise.
Smelts fried a l'Anglaise.

RELEVES.
Tenderloin of Beef, Sauce Perigord.
Turkey a la Richelieu.
Saddle of Venison, with Currant Jelly.

RELISHES.
French Mustard—Spanish Olives—Horseradish—Assorted Pickles
Sardines—Apple Sauce—Celery.

ENTREES.
Sweet Bread larded, with Green Peas.
Venison chops, Sauce Chevreuil.
Croquets of Chickens a la Royal.
Vol au Vent Financiere.
Salmi of Partridges a la Chasseur.

ROASTS.
English Capons. Canvas Back Ducks.
Grouse larded. Quails larded.

Chicken Salade. Fried Oysters.

PASTRY & CONFECTIONERY.
English Plum Pudding.
Charlotte Russes au Pannier.
Gelee au Vin de Champagne, garne d'Orange.
Blanc Mange a la Rose.
Maccaroons. Fancy Kisses.
Biscuit Anglais au Gelee.
Gateau au Chocolate.
Cassette d'Amande. Sugared Almonds.
Vanilla Ice Cream.

DESSERT.
Almonds. Figs. Apples. Walnuts. Raisins. Dates.
Filberts. Prunes. Oranges. Coffee.

INTRODUCTION

The American Menu

by Steven Heller

The menu, which does indeed have French origins — as do many things food related — is a functional and fundamentally ephemeral document that evolved comparatively late in the history of French cuisine.

If only some obscure yet eccentric figure from the past, let's call him, "Monsieur Menu" (or rather Georges Laffont Menu, to be exact), was discovered to have conceived the world's first modern menu, a viable origin myth might go something like this:

> *The only living son of a French peasant family from Lot-et-Garonne, at 15 Menu migrated to Paris, where he struggled for years laboring as a lowly plongeur (dishwasher) in the kitchens of the Left Bank. Yet all the while he taught himself the art of cooking the finest of eclectic cuisines. At age 32 he miraculously became the chef for the court of Louis XIV and was a favorite of the courtiers, for whom he hand scribed the culinary offerings of each evening — voilà, le menu!*

Alas, no such person ever existed, that we know of, and the creator of the first menu, whoever he or she may be, is forever lost to posterity. The cosmology of menus is decidedly anonymous — and consequently the quality of the narrative suffers from such anonymity. *Quel dommage!*

Yet there *is* a story to tell, albeit more a patchwork of different strands. The menu, which does indeed have French origins — as do many things food related — is a functional and fundamentally ephemeral document that evolved comparatively late in the history of French cuisine. Claims are made to its initial development in China during the first millennium (perhaps accounting for the birth of the "choose one from column A, one from column B" format), but even if this was true, it was not called a menu. The word itself finds its way to French from the Latin *minutus*, something diminished or made small, as in minuta, and ultimately minute. In France it was used to signify a list or résumé. The menu, therefore, is a résumé of an establishment's offerings.

Early European restaurants or "restaurateurs' rooms," as they were known, did not have menus at the outset. In fact, who needed them? In addition to the lack of such institutions, most people could not afford to dine away from the comfort and security of their homes.

When they did venture out, however, most public eateries were *table d'hôte*, communal tables where dishes were selected by the proprietors, and meals were composed of whatever was roasting over the fire or bubbling in the pot on that particular day (in other words, one took what one got). As more formal restaurants emerged before the French Revolution, menus of daily culinary fare were either orated by the waiter or written on small chalkboards — *à la carte* — which is why selections from the menu are commonly referred to as *à la carte*, or from the card. The chalkboard and its modern equivalents are still quite common, and so are the harried waiters.

The modern menu appeared in the latter part of the 18th century. *Quelle révolutión! Vive la révolutión!*

Rather than the common table (what is now called "family style"), restaurants offered a selection of so-called unseen dishes and specialties of the house. Pricing on this fare also rose upward as food was customized to satisfy the diners' individual desires (mutton with sauce on the side, please!). Menus became invitations to eat. They also became objects of desire.

In *The Invention of the Restaurant: Paris and Modern Gastronomic Culture*, Rebecca L. Spang notes that the actual design of these menus was altered throughout the 19th century and strictly adhered to the typographical inventions of the period — of which, everyone knows, France was a significant wellspring of innovation. With many of the world's great metal-type foundries and poster studios established in Paris, the City of Light was also a printing capital — a city of ink. Paper menus developed from a newspaper-style, single large page with columns of closely packed type in the early part of the 19th century "into a leather-covered booklet held together with a silken cord in midcentury," writes Sprang. Such an elaborate presentation was expensive and fragile, so menus devolved into a single-sheet design with copious illustrations and graphic ornamentation. In Paris, the physical menu was often called a *carte* (which also referred to a map), and in other places it was simply called the "bill of fare." The bill of fare listed the offerings on a menu. Menus were the graphic manifestation of the fare.

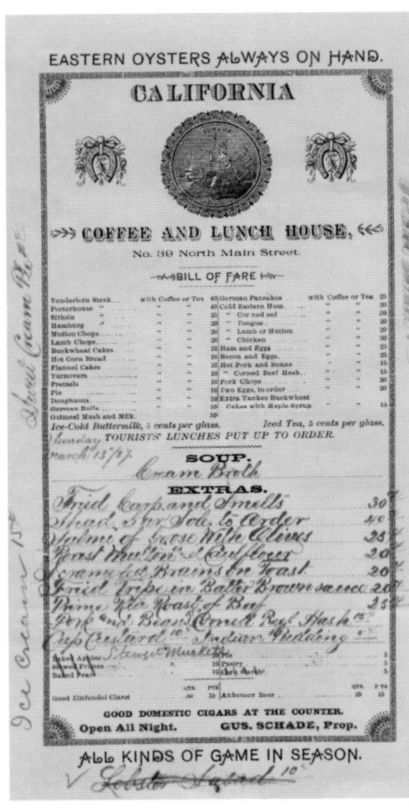
EASTERN OYSTERS ALWAYS ON HAND.

CALIFORNIA

COFFEE AND LUNCH HOUSE,

No. 39 North Main Street.

BILL OF FARE

Tenderloin Steak ... with Coffee or Tea	40	German Pancakes ... with Coffee or Tea	25
Porterhouse "	40	Cold Eastern Ham	20
Sirloin "	25	" Corned eef	20
Hamburg "	20	" Tongue	20
Mutton Chops	20	" Lamb or Mutton	20
Lamb Chops	20	" Chicken	30
Buckwheat Cakes	10	Ham and Eggs	25
Hot Corn Bread	10	Bacon and Eggs	25
Flannel Cakes	10	Hot Pork and Beans	15
Turnovers	10	" Corned Beef Hash	15
Pretzels	10	Pork Chops	20
Pie	10	Two Eggs, to order	20
Doughnuts	10	Extra Yankee Buckwheat	
German Rolls	10	Cakes with Maple Syrup	15
Oatmeal Mush and Milk	10		

Ice-Cold Buttermilk, 5 cents per glass. Iced Tea, 5 cents per glass.

TOURISTS' LUNCHES PUT UP TO ORDER.

SOUP.

Cream Broth

EXTRAS.

Fried Carp and Smelts .30

Baked Apples	10	Pie	5
Stewed Prunes	10	Pastry	5
Baked Pears	10		5

	QTS.	PTS.		QTS.	PTS.
Good Zinfandel Claret	30	15	Anheuser Beer	25	15

GOOD DOMESTIC CIGARS AT THE COUNTER.

Open All Night. GUS. SCHADE, Prop.

ALL KINDS OF GAME IN SEASON.

PAGE 12 **Dinner Given by the Legislature of the State of New York to Honor Abraham Lincoln, Delavan House, 1861, New York**

LEFT **Coffee and Lunch House, 1887, San Francisco, California**

Despite access to Pacific oysters this 24-hour-a-day eatery in San Francisco oddly promotes "Eastern oysters." Also note an early mention of "zinfandel claret," a red wine originally from Croatia introduced to California from the East Coast.

Trotz direkter Nähe zu den Pazifik-Austern stehen in dieser Tag und Nacht geöffneten Gaststätte in San Francisco seltsamerweise „Ostküsten-Austern" auf der Karte. Es findet sich auch eine frühe Erwähnung des „Zinfandel Claret", ein Rotwein aus einer ursprünglich aus Kroatien stammenden Traube, die von der Ostküste aus in Kalifornien eingeführt wurde.

Malgré la proximité des huîtres du Pacifique, ce restaurant de San Francisco ouvert vingt-quatre heures sur vingt-quatre vante les « huîtres de Virginie ». La carte propose un clairet de zinfandel, du nom du cépage venu de Croatie via la côte Est des États-Unis et introduit plus tard en Californie.

Nationalistic bombast to the contrary, not everything culinary belongs to the French. For many tastes, street foods in Asia, Africa, and South America, where menus were unnecessary since the food provided the visual identity, were and are just as delicious as *cuisine française*. Moreover, Americans need not be ashamed of their cuisine, nor their menu production and design. From the Revolutionary War period through the late 18th century, Americans fostered reputable and even inspired chefs. What's more, Americans ate out almost as much as they dined at home. The gastronomical varieties and extravagances may not have equaled those of France, but the entrepreneurial spirit—a critical mass of taverns (though often void of menus) and more opulent eateries (with elaborate menus)—arguably rivaled those official keepers of continental haute cuisine.

There is no definitive date for the first appearance of an American menu. Eighteenth-century taverns and inns mostly had fixed fare for a standard price. But it took the advent of relatively cheap and accessible printing, typography, and engraving techniques to enable "modern" menus to be produced. The first printing press was introduced to the Massachusetts colony in the 1600s, and presses were operated by printing pioneers throughout the century in other Northeastern and Southeastern venues. Press work was limited to newspapers, broadsides, and fliers, but as presses became more plentiful and pressmen more adept, various other printed matter, including menus, emerged, even if only as letterheads on which the daily offerings were written out by hand.

Yet before menus, there were restaurants. In the United States eateries developed in Northeastern cities, like Jullien's Restorator, which opened in Boston in 1794. (Incidentally, the word "restaurant" derives from the Latin *restaurabo*, translated into the French *la restauration*, which in English means "restoration.") The oldest restaurant in continuous operation in the United States, the Union Oyster House, opened in 1826 in Boston and was based on the "shared meal" concept, where diners served themselves from a communal dish. A more formal style of dining, where waiters carried platters of food around the table and diners served themselves, was known as *service à la russe* (a Russian import to France in 1810). For such a method it was not entirely necessary to provide a menu, but since it was a résumé of an establishment's offerings, offering one was the polite—and elegant—thing to do.

As restaurants increased in number as more people could afford to eat out, and as eating became more than a mere necessity of life, but also an integral American entertainment, the menu evolved into an essential tool, art form, and commercial brand. The tool is obvious—what you see is what you can get. The art is more of an extravagance, yet as printing processes (e.g., color, die-cuts, embossing, complex bindings, etc.) progressed, experiments and novelties were routinely introduced. The branding of restaurants derived from the medieval period's branding of merchants and tradesmen. Distinguishing one business from another has been a staple of industry and mercantile trades almost forever, and restaurants, more than many other consumer-targeted establishments, demanded unique identities that underscored the food they served.

Although most menus should not be considered as common advertising or promotion, illuminating the establishment with enjoyable—and memorable—graphics had a beneficial effect. If nothing else, the graphic voice, particularly when either boisterous or quiet, contributed to an establishment's allure and mythology. The function of a menu is clear, but for many they also were the equivalent of luggage labels or dance cards, evidence of a gustatory journey or culinary tripping the light fantastic. The incredible number of custom designs, individual illustrations, and uncanny shapes of those collected in this volume evidence how significant and fashionable this "proof of consummation" was during the late 19th and early 20th centuries.

Menus were frequently retained by consumers. They were souvenirs, taken from meals at state functions, industry congresses, private clubs, large and small weddings, and sea cruises. The personal reasons for hoarding menus could have something to do with status—for instance, proof of being at such tony spots as the Stork Club (which also sold souvenirs to patrons), "21," or Cocoanut Grove. Or for reasons of historical documentation, like attending the reception and dinner

RIGHT Christmas, the Plaza Hotel, 1891, New York, New York

The first Plaza Hotel, on New York's Fifth Avenue across from Central Park, was a modest eight stories, with 400 rooms. It was demolished and replaced in 1910 by the magnificent Beaux Arts Plaza Hotel, now a landmark. This menu dates from Christmastime at the earlier hotel, where in 1882 the first Christmas tree was lit using electricity.

Das erste Plaza Hotel an der New Yorker Fifth Avenue, direkt am Central Park, hatte bescheidene acht Stockwerke und 400 Zimmer. 1910 wurde es wieder abgerissen und von dem heutigen prächtigen Plaza Hotel im Beaux-Arts-Stil ersetzt, einem historischen Monument. Diese Festtagskarte stammt aus dem ursprünglichen Hotel, in dem 1882 der erste Weihnachtsbaum mit elektrischen Kerzen leuchtete.

Le premier Plaza Hotel, sur la Cinquième avenue à New York, en face de Central Park, est un modeste établissement de huit étages et de quatre cents chambres. Il est démoli et remplacé en 1910 par le magnifique Plaza Hotel de style Beaux-Arts, devenu depuis un monument historique. Ce menu date de l'hôtel original, en 1882, lorsque pour la première fois, le sapin de Noël fut éclairé à l'électricité.

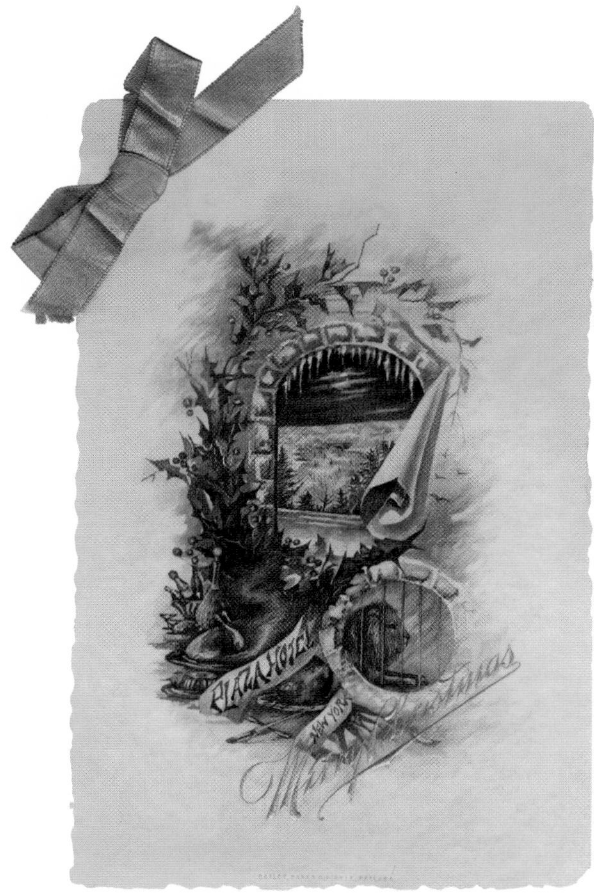

for the *Hindenburg* or *Zeppelin* (before going to war with Nazi Germany). Some were simply so beautifully and stylishly produced—like those from the Rainbow Grill, Casa Mañana, or Cafe Lafayette—that they were a must-steal item. Others stoked a curious fascination, like the Ubangi Club. Yet perhaps the vast majority was collected simply to recall an experience.

How could one forget that glorious time at Red Sails Inn on Fisherman's Wharf? And what better way to remember that special night (or day) than with a menu die-cut in the shape of a sailboat? Who could forget that scrumptious meal at Toed Inn, with its die-cut of the architecture parlante "toad" building (get the pun?), Melrod's "Club Burger" menu in the shape of, you guessed it, a double-decker burger with lettuce, or the Bung Hole, with the menu in the shape of a keg? They fit so nicely into the family scrapbook.

Before the Great Depression, lushly illustrated menus in high- and low-class establishments were very common. The graphic style of the day was art moderne or art deco, and variants on these signature graphic and typographic motifs prevailed (often provided by printers who had different stock-cover artworks available to their customers). Shared conceits developed in menu design. Katson's Drive-In was typical of what is now called vernacular breakfast and lunch layouts—a mélange of white and tinted circles, rectangles, and squares were perfect for framing blue-plate specials, while colored banners, some with small picture "cuts," announced the standard fare. Some menus were specifically pegged to the breakfast crowd—the Northern Hotel's menu cover with two sunny-side-up eggs (eyes) and a strip of bacon as a smile warmed the heart, while Furnace Creek Ranch's crowing rooster at the crack of dawn triggered one's morning appetite. Another specialty menu genre for mixed drinks could make even the staunch teetotaler salivate. The drinks reproduced in Heaven City Hotel's menu seem to light up as though phosphorescent—just think what they do to the head.

Menus were not immune to what today would be charged as politically incorrect—or for that matter downright racist—words and images. Fat Boy Drive-In in Redwood City, California, may be trying to imitate the popular Big Boy chain (which started as Bob's), but big and fat do not have the same meaning. What's more, Big Boy is decidedly more pleasantly cherubic than his obese cousin. Then there is Fat Eddie's, with Eddie in the shape of an overstuffed hamburger—today such a trademark flies in the face of dietary proscriptions. But Fat Eddie and Fat Boy do not even come close to the degree of offense that is projected from Coon-Chicken Inn, one of the most notoriously racist portrayals in menu design. A die-cut of the head of a bellhop with clownishly bulging red lips on a demonic visage was also, in some restaurants, the entryway through which patrons entered. Nonetheless, it was a very popular eating spot. Just when you thought bad taste in eateries couldn't get worse, there was Piccaninny Bar-B-Q, with a black-faced minstrel caricature as mascot. Yet in the guise of humor, menu graphics spared almost no one. Mexicans came in for their share: Pancho's menu shows typically caricatured sombrero-wearing, no-account south-of-the-border neighbors. Stereotypes further abounded on Chinese restaurant menus, from the bamboo-style lettering to the evil-looking Fu Manchu (Yellow Peril) caricature. Italians looked like happy Chef Boy-ar-dees. And women were not exempt from being commodified as body-beautiful, buxom babes on menus for both Jack's and Stan's diners.

The verbal language of menus also developed a distinct cadence and syncopation, not unlike classified newspaper ads, which had to pack a wallop in a small space. Titles were short, sometimes with simple, descriptive qualifiers—"*Thick* Malts and Sundaes"—other times they were a pinch more verbose: "*SuperThick* Malts and *Delicious* Sundaes." Terms like "From Our Char Broiler" and "Soups for the Gourmet" added spice to the imagination. "Menus are the Pavlov's bell of eating out," wrote Sara Dickerman in *Slate* (April 2003). "They are a literature of control. Menu language, with its hyphens, quotation marks, and random outbursts of foreign words, serves less to describe food than to manage your expectations.... [It] doesn't merely entice, it justifies the cost of dining out."

LEFT **University of Illinois, 1898, Urbana-Champaign, Illinois**

OPPOSITE **Grand Hotel L'D, 1901, Yokohama, Japan**

Designed in a Western style, this Japanese menu attests to the growing influence of occidental tastes.

Diese im westlichen Stil gestaltete Speisekarte belegt den wachsenden Einfluss westlichen Geschmacks in Japan.

Conçu dans un style occidental, ce menu japonais témoigne de l'influence croissante d'un goût venu de l'Ouest.

Speaking of managing expectations, former *New York Times* restaurant critic Frank Bruni referred to contemporary menus as literature: "The wordiness of some menus reflects an intense focus on ingredients. . . . The wordiness of other menus has an ethical purpose. The chef wants you to know where he's getting the chicken, how the veal was raised. The chef realizes that you may be making decisions about what you eat based on that information. But the wordiness of yet *other* menus is perhaps best characterized as, well, literary. It represents a kind of a gastronomic cheerleading." The menu as cheerleader is an indelible image. Yet it not only led a cheer, it promised the offerings that triggered the customers' longings.

The language of menus also connoted a level of status (or lack thereof). Haute cuisineries were usually sprinkled with chic-sounding linguistic phrases *comme ça*: *hors d'oeuvres et entre, ou entremets, ou plats du jour, ou Potages* (pardon my French). Of course, other foreign restaurant menus had a surfeit of exotic words that diners would often find hard to pronounce (*schnitzel*, anyone?).

Even native English could be used to titillate: Boston was known for its Brahmin linguistic decorum, which extended into menus. In a letter printed in a social register-script typeface on the back of the "Dinner Bill of Fare" for Jameson & Richardson (1839), potential diners were treated to this very proper sales pitch: "For neatness of arrangement in every particular, and in the discipline of the Waiters, together with the Culinary Department, where the utmost care and skill is requisite for the preparation of food, we can defy competition in this city and elsewhere.... The different relishes of the season are furnished without charge." Some restaurants were very specific when it came to announcing their specialties de la maison. Chicago's the Palmer offered a poetic litany starting with Anglaise soup, Kenseber salmon à la Hollandaise, leg of mutton (and) caper sauce, small patties à la Reine, Siberian punch, biscuit glacé, and strawberries and cream. And if that is not appetizing enough, the Royal Blue Line of the Central Railroad Company noted in its menu, "The management ...has the pleasure of announcing that arrangements have been effected with the Pullman's Palace Car Company for the operation of a Dining Car Service....This service will be strictly first-class and in keeping with the general character of these famous trains." On the menu of March 29, 1881, offered are, among other things, terrapin soup, boiled rock fish in shrimp sauce, sweetbreads — larded — *financière*-style, Siberian sorbet (for the palate), roast redhead duck with currant jelly, charlotte russe, figs in cordial, and Hygeia water. The menu for the Seventeenth Annual Reunion of the Army of Northern Virginia (ANV) from 1892 went *française* all the way with *tortue verte au clair*, *timbales Perigordine*, *pommes de terre persillade*, *terrapene à la Baltimore*, *aspics de foie-gras*, and *petits fours*. *Ooh, la la!*

Diners, burger joints, or, for that matter, luncheonettes, despite the French suffix "-ette," were rarely so haughty. Although sometimes *entrées* and *plats du jour* would sneak through, french fries were never *pommes frites*. In the 1920s the most vernacular of culinary descriptions was the "blue plate special," promoting the day's recommended hot meal. Some say that these "specials" were, in fact, originally served on blue plates, but not for long, though the phrase stuck. California's Pep restaurants announced their specials as though they were B-movie titles: Everything on the menu came with a superlative — and oh, those wonderful prices: "Giant Chocolate Ice Cream Soda (25 cents)," "Big Bowl Chili Beans (30 cents)," and "6 dollar $ize Hot Cakes (50 cents)." Who needs "Chilled Jellied Consommé" when you can have a hamburger and fries (55 cents)?

In addition to verbal language, visual imagery was deliberately used to telegraph attitude — whether a restaurant was hot or cool, old or young, rich or not so rich. Perhaps the most eclectic — indeed erotic — of menus was for a special event in San Francisco (1912), which shows a chromolithograph of a naked blonde woman, bound by the feet and being pulled into a fire place by three satyrs in chef's hats. The title of the menu is « Une poule au pot au Cercle de l'union en l'honneur de MM. Merou, de Chantreau, de Sabla et de Coulon ». ("A Hen to the Jar to the Circle of the Union in honor of MM. Merou of Chantreau of Sandblasted and of Coulon"). Most other illustrations were tamer, representing the aspirations or the realities of an establishment or event.

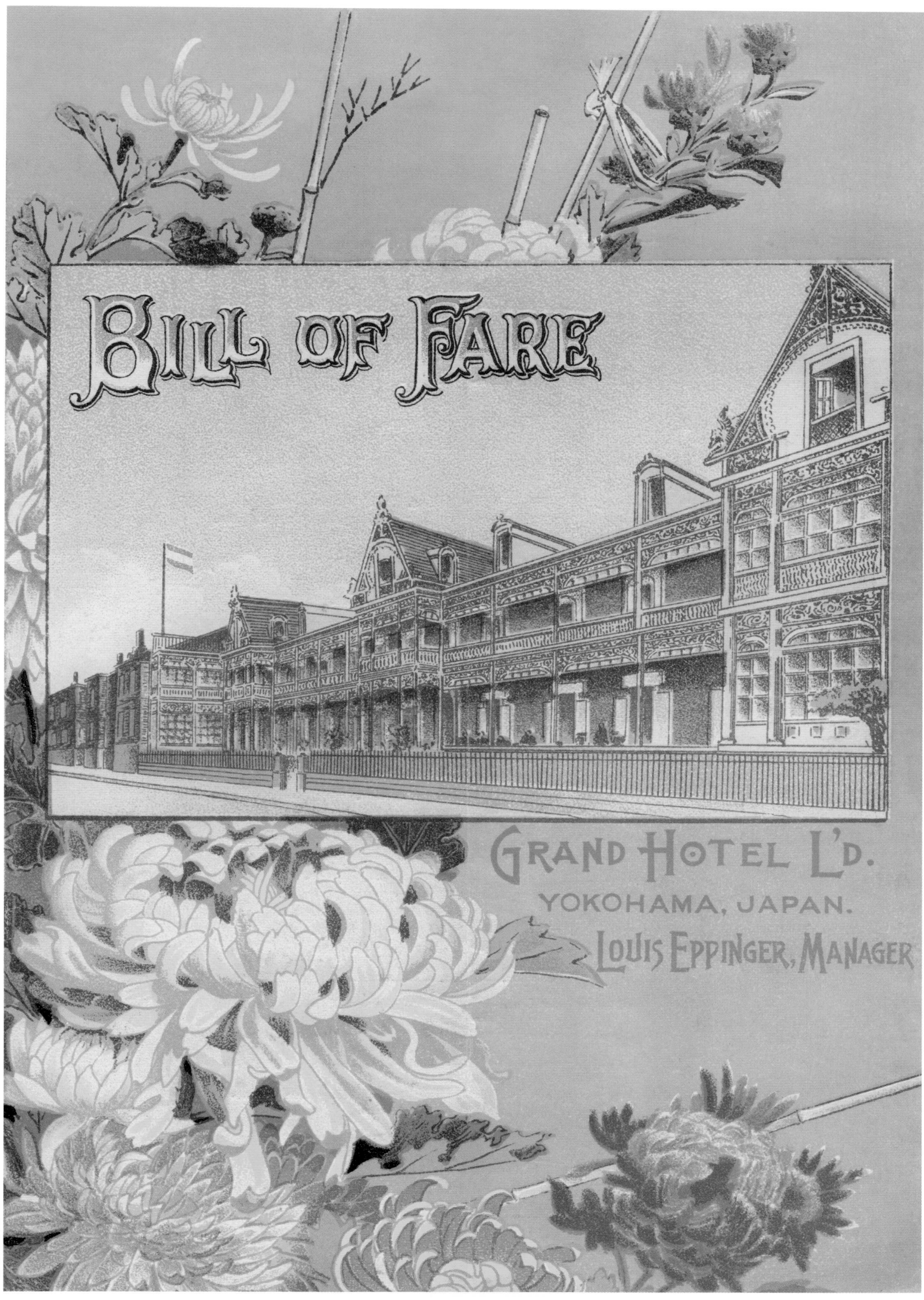
BILL OF FARE
GRAND HOTEL L'D.
YOKOHAMA, JAPAN.
LOUIS EPPINGER, MANAGER

Santa Fe Dining Car Service

BY FRED HARVEY

ASSORTED FRUIT, 20
STEWED PRUNES, 20 ORANGE MARMALADE, 20 PRESERVED FIGS, 20

SHREDDED WHEAT BISCUITS WITH CREAM, 20
ROLLED OATS WITH CREAM, 20
GRAPE NUTS, 20

SLICED TOMATOES, 20

BROILED WHITEFISH, 40
BOILED OR BROILED SALT MACKEREL, 40
CODFISH CAKES WITH BACON, 40

TENDERLOIN STEAK, 70
SIRLOIN STEAK, 70
EXTRA SIRLOIN STEAK, (FOR TWO,) 1.25
PORTERHOUSE STEAK (FOR TWO,) 1,50
CLUB STEAK (FOR TWO,) 1.50
MUTTON CHOPS, 50
BACON, FULL ORDER, 40
BROILED OR FRIED HAM, 40
BACON AND EGGS, 50
HAM AND EGGS, 50
VEAL CUTLET, PLAIN OR BREADED, 40
CALF'S LIVER AND BACON, 40

GARNITURE WITH ABOVE MEAT ORDERS

RASHER OF BACON, 15 TOMATO SAUCE, 15
MUSHROOMS OR FRENCH PEAS, 20
SAUCE BEARNAISE, 25 SAUCE BORDELAISE, 25

BOILED, FRIED, SCRAMBLED OR SHIRRED EGGS, 25
POACHED EGGS ON TOAST, 35
PLAIN OMELETTE, 25; WITH HAM, CHEESE OR JELLY, 35
SPANISH OR MUSHROOM OMELETTE, 40

POTATOES, BAKED OR FRENCH FRIED, 10
HASHED BROWNED OR LYONNAISE, 15
AU GRATIN, 20

HOT ROLLS, 10 CORN MUFFINS, 10
WHEAT CAKES WITH MAPLE SYRUP, 20
DRY TOAST, 10 BUTTERED TOAST, 10
MILK TOAST, 20 CREAM TOAST, 30

COFFEE, PER CUP, 10; PER POT, FOR ONE, 15; PER POT, FOR TWO, 25
COCOA OR CHOCOLATE WITH WHIPPED CREAM, PER CUP, 15
SPECIAL BLEND, YOUNG HYSON OR
ENGLISH BREAKFAST TEA, PER POT, 15
MILK, PER GLASS, 10 CREAM, PER GLASS, 15

OPPOSITE **Santa Fe Dining Car, c. 1910**

RIGHT **Casa Verdugo, c. 1910, Glendale, California**

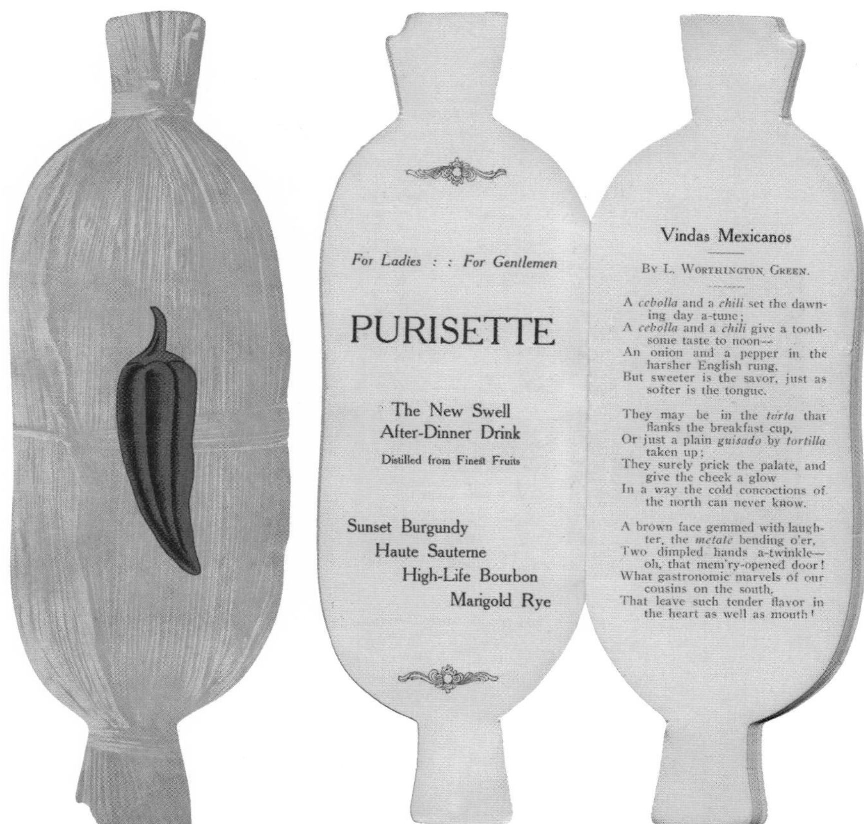

Whatever it meant, it had to have taken the customer's mind off food for a moment.

A considerable amount of graphic innovation could be found in menu design. The nameplate for Bernstein's Fish Grotto, made out of fish forming the letters of "fish" and water filling the word "Grotto," was a clever piece of conceptual typography—and copied by Sea Cave Sea Foods or vice versa. Chinese menus were often illustratively quite elaborate. In addition to the bamboo-style lettering for Forbidden Palace, Lamps of China, Ruby Foo's Den, and Golden Pagoda, the full-color illuminations suggest an exotic quality that was doubtless supplemented by the respective restaurant's décor. In some restaurants, we're told if the menu was too bland, the fare was tainted, too—so it paid to have loud illustrations and demonstrative typography.

Menus were commonly used as advertisements for Acme Ale, Budweiser, and of course Coca-Cola, among many others, who would supply menu templates to local eateries and bars. What better way than this not-so-subliminal promotion to sell a product to hungry and thirsty customers. These menus usually conformed to the mass-market advertisements used to sell their products in newspapers, magazines, and billboards—the one-two-three punch of commercial propaganda. During World War II, menus promoted selling U.S. war bonds through patriotic graphics. For the duration, the New York Central System railway proudly emblazoned the "V" for victory on its menus. Less patriotic but no less American, the menu for Les Comiques in the Hollywood Plaza Hotel promoted the best of the Sunday comics, Tarzan, the Lone Ranger, the Little King, Dagwood and Blondie, and Li'l Abner too.

Holidays were special menu days. The Waldorf-Astoria was known for its annual New Year's versions, often printed in vibrant colors, including embossed silver-metallic inks and flat-color drawings that expressed the joy of the post–World War II years. New Year's Eve at the Congress ushered in the flapper years with stunning art deco illuminations, which was the preferred style of many clubs and cafés operating prior to and during Prohibition. Similarly, the Hotel Taft in New York used every deco conceit—from dancing nymphs to jaggedly composed mountains—for its 1939–40 New Year's menu greeting.

Commissaries at some well-known companies and institutions had their own seasonal menus, but few were as clever as Walt Disney Studio's Restaurant in Burbank, California. Under the red-script heading "Good Morning!" and a clock showing 8:35 sits an exhausted Donald Duck, limply holding his cup of morning coffee. Out of his beak comes, "What's good about it!" Perhaps the relatively cheap prices?

Graphic conventions for menu illustration were often dictated by the unscientific whatever-works principle. Sometimes what is in style—like rampant use of post–World War I art deco or, 50 years later, the restaurant Trident's psychedelicism—is fitting; other times graphic anachronisms abounded, like the naked nymphettes for the menu of South Seas. Often nudity was its own reward, as was the case with Chicago's racy French Casino, Rubenak's Half Way House, and Sutton's Club Lido menus. Unlike other promotional or packaging products, design of a menu did not fill the seats and tables—and market research was irrelevant. At best menus tacitly complemented the "brand" of the restaurant. Which is not to say that some menus were not out of the ordinary. Occasionally, culinary impresarios injected either personal design preferences, like the Paul Klee–inspired marks for the Pan Lad menu, the Joan Miró–inspired mobile fish for Well of the Sea, the jazzy cartoon-style hands for Panza's Lazy Susan, the surrealistic Hungry I, the abstract spear-heads—à la midcentury modern—for the Hotel Sahara's Congo Room, and the colorful planetary New Frontier Hotel. Speaking of the planets, among the most elaborate was the 3-D menu for the Cumberland Hotel's "New Year's Eve Gala 1954," with its Space Age graphic motif and space-girl hostess happily showing off her electronic menu pedestal (not unlike the computer-ized screens in most restaurants today, minus the Flash Gordon accoutrements). Science fiction had appeal, but real graphic futurism, as in the menu for the Airport Roof Restaurant of the Miami International Airport Hotel, suggests the jet age, which has become a new style of future-past.

RIGHT Carte des Vins, Abbaye-Albert, France, c. 1909

OPPOSITE Sunset Inn, 1913, Santa Monica, California

Photography eventually became a staple for showing the bounty available to the consumer. However, most photographs were never as appetizing as illustrations or conceptual type. The carver on the Tick Tock menu is a good shot for a prison yearbook, but as an eatery, no. A clever use, however, was tried by the Coffee Shop of the Hotel Mayflower in Akron, Ohio, in which the word "Luncheon" is photographed in three-dimensional block letters with a real watch between "Lunch" and "eon" spelling "Luncheon." Why these choices were made is one of the mysteries of menu design.

Many creative menus were designed for faux environments. Mike's Ships-a-Hoy, illustrated almost exclusively with retouched color photos, was a landlocked restaurant with seating choices in a multitude of seafaring craft (those prone to seasickness were advised accordingly). Real transportation venues such as railway dining cars, cruise liners, and airplanes—moveable feasts all—were decked out with all kinds of graphic souvenirs from napkins to menus, and some by well-known artists. John Held Jr. drew the cover and inside illustrations for "Speaking of Food," the dining car menu for the New York New Haven and Hartford Railroad. Not to be outdone, the Pennsylvania Railroad, Baltimore & Ohio, and New York Central System provided $1 dinners and threw in the menu for free. The Alaska Steamship Company menu pictured Inuits, while the Great Northern Railway ("Route of the Empire Builder") celebrated Native American chiefs in full garb on its menu (with a special section "for the little folks"). Even the great German poster artist (and Nazi propagandist) Ludwig Hohlwein got into the act with artwork celebrating the 1936 Olympics for the Norddeutscher Lloyd Bremen ship line.

Menus were not easy to elegantly design. The cover was a blank canvas for the artist, illustrator, or typographer—and some did beautifully distinctive work. Others were produced by a printer using stock imagery and typography. Few, if any, were attributed to an individual artist. The best menus had the aesthetic resonance of sheet music, and some were reminiscent of wedding invitations, but most followed the conventions established in the early 20th century—showcase the name of the establishment, use the word "menu," and make certain the layout doesn't confuse the customer. The menu is the hymnal of cuisine and must look the part.

Dining out is a routine fact of life and also a ritualistic one—like Sunday Mass. The menu portion of the experience might be compared to the opening of a hymn or prayer book and selecting the day's offerings. Or, more accurately, it's like opening a gift and being surprised by what is there. Being given the opportunity to choose anything from a bounty of offerings is a special ritual to be sure.

Waiter?!...We're ready to order.

ABOVE LEFT Rector's, 1913, New York, New York

Rector's was Delmonico's main competition in the deluxe dining field. Opened by Charles Rector in 1899, he became a millionaire after opening his namesake restaurant at Broadway between 43rd and 44th Streets. In 1910 he moved it to Broadway and 48th Street, but the restaurant went bankrupt in 1913.

Das Rector's war der Hauptkonkurrent von Delmonico bei den Luxusrestaurants in New York. Charles Rector eröffnete es 1899 zwischen 43rd und 44th Street und wurde damit zum Millionär. Nach dem Umzug 1910 an Broadway und 48th Street ging das Rector's jedoch 1913 Bankrott.

Le Rector's est le principal concurrent du Delmonico dans le domaine de la haute gastronomie. Créé par Charles Rector, il lui apporta la fortune dès son ouverture en 1899, au coin des 43e et 44e rues. En 1910, il emménage au croisement de Broadway et de la 48e rue, mais le restaurant fait faillite en 1913.

PAGE 22 Midnight Frolic, Ziegfeld Roof, New Amsterdam Theatre c. 1918, New York, New York

MENU
SUNSET INN
H·A·Gonden
MANAGER
SANTA MONICA — CALIFORNIA

ZIEGFELD
MIDNIGHT FROLIC

ZIEGFELD
ROOF,
ATOP NEW
AMSTERDAM
THEATRE

A L'ECREVISSE

DÉFENSE D'URINER

EINLEITUNG

Die amerikanische Speisekarte

von Steven Heller

Die Speisekarte stammt tatsächlich aus Frankreich – wie so vieles, was mit dem Essen zu tun hat. Sie ist ein funktionales und grundsätzlich nicht für die Ewigkeit gemachtes Dokument, das relativ spät in der Geschichte der französischen Kochkunst auftauchte.

Würde plötzlich entdeckt, dass eine obskure, aber höchst exzentrische Gestalt aus der Vergangenheit, nennen wir ihn „Monsieur Menu" (oder genauer gesagt Georges Laffont Menu), die erste Speisekarte der Welt erfunden hat, dann ließe sich ein Entstehungsmythos dieser wunderbaren Erfindung schreiben, der ungefähr so klingen könnte:

> *Georges Menu, der einzige überlebende Sohn einer französischen Bauernfamilie aus Lot-et-Garonne, ging im Alter von 15 Jahren nach Paris, wo er jahrelang als von allen missachteter kleiner Tellerwäscher in den Küchen des Rive Gauche schuftete. Doch insgeheim eignete er sich die raffinierteste Kochkunst für die erlesensten Gerichte an. Mit 32 Jahren wurde er wie durch ein Wunder Küchenchef am Hof Ludwigs XIV. und schnell zum Liebling der Höflinge, für die er täglich von Hand die kulinarischen Höhepunkte des Abends aufschrieb – et voilà, le menu!*

Leider hat es diesen Herrn nie gegeben, und der Name des Erfinders oder der Erfinderin der ersten Speisekarte ist nicht überliefert. *Quel dommage!*

Doch die Speisekarte stammt tatsächlich aus Frankreich – wie so vieles, was mit dem Essen zu tun hat. Sie ist ein funktionales und grundsätzlich nicht für die Ewigkeit gemachtes Dokument, das relativ spät in der Geschichte der französischen Kochkunst auftauchte. Angeblich wurde sie zuvor schon im China des 1. Jahrtausends entwickelt, doch selbst wenn dem so wäre, hieße das Produkt noch nicht „Speisekarte" oder französisch „carte" oder „menu" oder englisch „menu". Das Wort „Menü" kommt vom Lateinischen „minutus", etwas Vermindertes oder Kleines, wie die Minute, die „verminderte Stunde". In Frankreich war es eine Liste der Speisenfolge (des Menüs), die ein Lokal seinen Gästen anzubieten hatte.

Anfangs hatten Wirtshäuser in Europa keine Speisekarten. Man brauchte sie schlicht und einfach noch nicht. Die meisten Menschen gerieten nie in die Verlegenheit, außerhalb ihrer vertrauten vier Wände essen zu müssen und hätten sich das auch nicht leisten können. Wenn sie doch einmal ein Gasthaus betraten, dann wurde dort zumeist ein Stammgericht angeboten: Der Wirt bestimmte, was gegessen wurde, nämlich das, was an diesem Tag über dem offenen Feuer geröstet oder im großen Topf gekocht wurde (es wurde eben das gegessen, was auf den gemeinschaftlichen Tisch kam). Vor der Französischen Revolution gab es in Frankreich bereits die ersten formaleren *Restaurants* („Gasthaus eines Restaurateurs"), in denen die Speisefolge des Tages entweder vom Kellner mündlich vorgetragen oder auf kleine Schiefertafeln geschrieben wurde. Auch heute sind solche Tafeln und ihre modernen Entsprechungen noch immer weit verbreitet – und damit auch die genervten Kellner.

Die moderne Speisekarte tauchte irgendwann im ausgehenden 18. Jahrhundert erstmals auf. Nun konnte man „à la carte" dinieren, nach der Karte. *Quelle révolution! Vive la révolution!*

Gaststätten fingen nun an, nicht mehr nur eine Schüssel auf den Tisch zu stellen, aus der sich alle bedienen konnten, sondern eine Auswahl verschiedener Gerichte und Spezialitäten des Hauses anzubieten. Als erstmals die individuellen Wünsche der Gäste berücksichtigt wurden (Hammelkeule, aber die Soße bitte extra!), gingen auch die Preise der Gerichte nach oben. Menü- oder Speisekarten wurden Einladungen zum Essen – und zugleich Objekte der Begierde.

In ihrem Buch *The Invention of the Restaurant: Paris and Modern Gastronomic Culture* beschreibt Rebecca L. Spang, wie stark sich die Gestaltung der Speisekarten im Lauf des 19. Jahrhunderts veränderte und die typografischen Entwicklungen der jeweiligen Zeit widerspiegelte. In Paris waren die wichtigsten Letterngießereien und Plakatdruckereien zu finden: Die Stadt des Lichts war zugleich eine Stadt der Druckerschwärze – die Hauptstadt des Drucks. Die gedruckten Speisekarten sahen anfangs wie eine Zeitungsseite aus und bestanden aus einem großen Blatt mit eng gedruckten Textspalten. „Mitte des 19. Jahrhunderts entwickelten sie sich zu einem in Leder gebundenen Heft, das mit einer Seidenkordel zusammengehalten wurde", schreibt Spang. Eine so aufwendige Präsentation der Speisekarte war teuer und wenig haltbar, deshalb kehrte man zu einer Gestaltung als Einzelblatt mit appetitanregenden Illustrationen und grafischen Ornamenten zurück. In Paris sprach man von „la carte" (das Wort

LEFT **La Tour d'Argent, ca. 1935, Paris, France**

La Tour d'Argent represented an apex in the culinary world. American restaurants aspired to meet its standards and innovations.

La Tour d'Argent stellte einen Höhepunkt der kulinarischen Welt dar, mit dessen innovativen Ideen amerikanische Restaurants zu wetteifern suchten.

La Tour d'Argent représentait le summum de la gastronomie mondiale. Les restaurants américains tentaient de l'égaler et de rivaliser avec ses innovations.

„Karte" kommt vom Material Karton), an anderen Orten nannte man es „bill of fare", also „Küchen- oder Speisezettel". Die Speisekarte entwickelte sich zur grafischen Umsetzung des servierten Essens.

Doch die kulinarische Geschichte ist nicht nationalistisch, und nicht alle Köstlichkeiten der Welt stammen aus Frankreich. Für viele Gaumen war und ist das, was in Asien, Afrika und Südamerika an Straßenständen angeboten wird, genauso köstlich wie *la cuisine française*. Dort waren Speisekarten überflüssig, da das vor den Augen der Gäste gekochte Essen selbst für seine visuelle Präsentation sorgte. Und auch die Amerikaner brauchen sich ihrer nationalen Küche so wenig zu schämen wie ihrer Speisekartengestaltung. Vom amerikanischen Unabhängigkeitskrieg bis zum Ende des 18. Jahrhunderts brachte Amerika bereits versierte und sogar inspirierte Köche hervor. Außerdem neigten Amerikaner schon damals dazu, fast genauso häufig zum Essen auszugehen wie zu Hause zu speisen. Damals gab es in den USA vielleicht noch nicht so viele gastronomische Angebote und Extravaganzen wie in Frankreich, aber zahlreiche Wirtshäuser (oft ohne Speisekarte) und größere Gaststätten (mit umfangreichen Speisekarten) konnten es durchaus mit den offiziellen Hütern der kontinentalen *Haute Cuisine* aufnehmen.

Ein genaues Datum für das erste Auftauchen der Speisekarte in den Vereinigten Staaten gibt es nicht. Gasthöfe und Wirtshäuser des 18. Jahrhunderts besaßen meist ein feststehendes Angebot mit einem Einheitspreis. Doch als die Herstellung von Druckerzeugnissen preiswerter wurde, konnten auch die ersten „modernen" Speisekarten gedruckt werden. Die erste Druckerpresse gelangte schon im 17. Jahrhundert nach Massachusetts; in diesem Jahrhundert waren die Gründerväter des amerikanischen Drucks bereits im Nordosten und Südosten der britischen Kolonie aktiv. Damals konnten nur Zeitungen, Planobogen und Flugblätter gedruckt werden. Doch als es mehr Druckerpressen gab und die Drucker immer geschickter in ihrem Handwerk wurden, kamen weitere Druckerzeugnisse auf den Markt, darunter auch Speisekarten, selbst wenn sie oft nur aus dem Briefkopf der Gaststätte bestanden, unter dem dann die Tagesangebote von Hand hinzugefügt wurden.

Doch lange vor den Speisekarten gab es Restaurants. In den Vereinigten Staaten entstanden in den Städten an der Ostküste schon früh Wirtshäuser wie Jullien's Restorator, das 1794 in Boston eröffnet wurde (das Wort „Restaurant" leitet sich übrigens vom Lateinischen „restaurabo" her – „ich werde euch erquicken"). Das älteste Speiserestaurant der USA, das heute noch bewirtschaftet wird, ist das Union Oyster House, das 1826 in Boston aufmachte. Dort war es noch üblich, dass die Gäste sich selbst aus einem allgemeinen Topf bedienten. Eine formellere Art des Speisens, bei der Kellner Platten mit Essen um den Tisch trugen, von denen sich die Gäste selbst bedienten, wurde als *service à la russe* bezeichnet (eine 1810 aus Russland nach Frankreich gekommene Neuerung). Auch hierfür war eine Speisekarte nicht unbedingt erforderlich, aber da diese das Aushängeschild eines Etablissements und seiner Angebote war, galt es als höflich und elegant, eine solche zur Verfügung zu stellen.

Als sich immer breitere Gesellschaftsschichten eine Mahlzeit außer Haus leisten konnten, nahm die Zahl der Gaststätten ständig zu, und als das Essen sich zu mehr als einer reinen Lebensnotwendigkeit, nämlich zu einer typisch amerikanischen Form der Freizeitgestaltung entwickelte, wurde auch die Speisekarte zu einem wichtigen Medium, zu einer eigenen Kunstform und einem kommerziellen Aushängeschild. Der funktionale Charakter ist offensichtlich: Was man liest, ist das, was man bekommen kann. Der künstlerische Aspekt ist eigentlich ein Luxus, aber als die Druckverfahren raffinierter wurden (Farbdruck, Stanzen, Prägen, komplizierte Arten der Bindung etc.), regte das auch zu vielen Experimenten und Neuerungen in der Speisekartengestaltung an. Dass Restaurants sich ein Image, ein „Aushängeschild" zulegten, leitete sich von den Gildewappen und Händlerzeichen aus dem Mittelalter her. Kaufmanns- und Handwerksbetriebe legten schon immer Wert darauf, sich voneinander zu unterscheiden, und Speisegaststätten brauchten, mehr noch als andere kundenorientierte Einrichtungen, eine unverwechselbare Identität, die darauf hinwies, welche Art von Essen dort angeboten wurde.

Auch wenn die meisten Speisekarten keine Werbeerzeugnisse im eigentlichen Sinn waren, konnte es doch nie schaden, wenn ein

ABOVE Eden-Roc, 1923, Paris, France

S.S. "FUSHIMI MARU"
Commander T. Araki. Saturday, 13th, August, 1932
DINNER
Hors d'Œuvres
Chaudfroid de Poisson
Tomato Mayonnaise Potted Meat on Toast
SOUP
Consomme Meternich Potage Potiron
FISH
Fillet of Gurnet Flamande
EXTRA:— Raw Tunny Fish Japanese Style
(Maguro no Sashimi Osuimono)
Fillet of Beef à l'Athénienne
Epigrammes de Mouton aux Printanier
Haricot Verts Panachée
Plain Rice
Roast Milk Fed Veal with Currant Jelly
Roast Partridge and Straw Potato
Potatoes, Boiled and Browned
Boiled Cabbage
SWEETS
Cabinet Pudding
Ratafia Ice Cream
King Cake
Cheese Biscuits
Assorted Nuts Presserved Chow-chow Dried Figs
Cheese Biscuits
FRUITS:— Apple Orange
Coffee
COLD SIDEBOARD
Roast Sirloin of Beef Bologna Sausage
(COFFEE will be served also in the smoking room)
Time will be put ahead 15 minutes to-night.

ABOVE *S.S. Fushimi Maru*, 1932, Nippon Yusen Kaisha Line

Lokal sich mit hübschen und in Erinnerung bleibenden Illustrationen schmückte. Die Gestaltung der Speisekarten trug zum Reiz und Mythos eines Restaurants bei – insbesondere, wenn sie auffallend schrill oder auffallend minimalistisch waren. Für viele Gäste war die Menükarte das Gegenstück zu Gepäckaufklebern oder Tanzkarten: Andenken an eine Reise des Gaumens oder Souvenir von einem Ausflug in fantastische kulinarische Gefilde. Die unglaubliche Menge individueller Designs, einzigartiger Illustrationen und seltsamster Formen, die für dieses Buch zusammengetragen wurden, zeugt davon, wie weit verbreitet es im ausgehenden 19. und frühen 20. Jahrhundert war, „Beweise des Verzehrs" zu sammeln.

Die Gäste nahmen die Speisekarten regelmäßig mit nach Hause. Sie waren Andenken an Regierungsbankette, Kongressdinner, Privatklubs, große und kleine Hochzeiten und Kreuzfahrten. Die Gründe für das Horten von Menü- und Speisekarten haben vielleicht etwas mit Status zu tun – die Karten könnten zum Beispiel als Beweis dafür dienen, dass man tatsächlich in solch exklusiven Restaurants wie dem Stork Club (wo auch Souvenirs an die Gäste verkauft wurden), dem „21" oder dem Cocoanut Grove gespeist hat. Oder man wollte sie als historisches Zeitdokument besitzen, etwa bei der Teilnahme am Empfang für die Luftschiffe „*Hindenburg*" oder „*Graf Zeppelin*". Manche Karten waren so geschmackvoll und schön – wie die des Rainbow Grill, der Casa Mañana oder des Café Lafayette –, dass man gar nicht anders konnte, als sie in der Handtasche verschwinden zu lassen. Andere waren in ihrer Kuriosität faszinierend – wie die des Ubangi Club. Doch die Mehrzahl wurde wahrscheinlich einfach nur als Andenken an ein schönes Ereignis gesammelt.

Der lustige Abend im Red Sails Inn an der Fisherman's Wharf darf natürlich nicht vergessen werden. Was könnte es für ein schöneres Andenken an den netten Abend geben als die Speisekarte in Form eines Segelboots? Wer würde das köstliche Essen im Toed Inn vergessen, mit der krötenförmig ausgestanzten Speisekarte? Witzig auch die Melrod's Club Burger-Karte in Form eines – Sie haben es erraten – doppelstöckigen Hamburgers mit Salatblatt oder die vom Bung Hole, dessen Karte die Form eines Bierfasses hat.

Vor der Weltwirtschaftskrise waren üppig illustrierte Speisekarten in Gaststätten aller Qualitätsstufen weit verbreitet. Damals waren Jugendstil und Art déco modern, und Varianten der für diese Kunstrichtungen typischen Grafiken und Schriftformen waren vorherrschend (diese wurden oft von den Druckern zur Verfügung gestellt, die ihren Kunden eine Reihe von Druckvorlagen zur Auswahl anboten). Im Speisekartendesign entwickelten sich eigene Trends. Die Karte des Katson's Drive-in war typisch für das, was man heutzutage als Standardlayout für eine Frühstücks- und Mittagskarte bezeichnen würde – eine Mischung aus weißen und farbigen Kreisen, Rechtecken und Quadraten, die perfekt für die Einrahmung des Tagesgerichts geeignet waren, während bunte Banner, manche mit kleinen Bildern darin, das reguläre Angebot vorstellten. Manche Karten waren besonders für die Frühstücksgäste konzipiert – im Northern Hotel sprachen zwei Spiegeleier (als Augen) und ein Streifen Schinkenspeck als Mund den Gaumen an, während der bei Sonnenaufgang krähende Gockel der Furnace Creek Ranch den morgendlichen Appetit anregte. Eine spezielle Karte für Mixgetränke ließ selbst dem standfestesten Antialkoholiker das Wasser im Munde zusammenlaufen. Die auf der Getränkekarte des Heaven City Hotels abgebildeten Cocktails scheinen phosphoreszierend zu glühen – man mag sich nicht vorstellen, was für ein Kater sich nach deren Genuss vermutlich einstellte.

Speisekarten waren in Formulierungen und Darstellungen keineswegs immun gegen das, was man heutzutage politisch inkorrekt oder richtiggehend rassistisch nennen würde. Der Fat Boy Drive-in in Redwood City, Kalifornien, versuchte, die beliebte Schnellrestaurantkette Big Boy (anfänglich noch Bob's) zu imitieren, aber „big" und „fat" sind nun einmal nicht dasselbe. Außerdem ist der liebenswert rundliche Big Boy wesentlich sympathischer als sein eindeutig übergewichtiger Cousin Fat Boy. Und dann gab es noch Fat Eddie's, wobei Eddie die Form eines prall gefüllten Hamburgers hatte – heutzutage würde ein solches Branding sämtlichen Vorstellungen von gesunder Lebensweise widersprechen. Doch Fat Eddie und Fat Boy sind bei Weitem nicht so anstößig wie das Coon Chicken Inn („Hähnchen-

LEFT **The Starlight Roof, the Waldorf-Astoria, 1934, New York, New York**

OPPOSITE **French Casino, c. 1935, Chicago, Illinois**

A startling graphic for the time period exudes a naughty playfulness.

Diese für die Zeit sehr außergewöhnliche Grafik überzeugt durch ihre frivole Verspieltheit.

Ce graphisme surprenant pour l'époque convoque un sens plutôt frivole de l'espièglerie.

braterei Nigger"), das mit einer der rassistischsten Darstellungen in der Geschichte der Speisekarte aufwartete. Der Kopf eines schwarzen Hotelpagen mit clownesk dicken roten Lippen in einer dämonischen Visage bildete in einigen Filialen sogar den Eingang des Lokals. Das tat seiner Beliebtheit jedoch keinen Abbruch. Und wenn man dachte, dass der Geschmack in puncto Außenwerbung nicht mehr schlechter werden könnte, hatte man sich geirrt: Es gab auch noch das Piccanniny Bar B Q („Grill zum drolligen Negerkind"), dessen Maskottchen eine Blackface-Karikatur aus der Minstrel Show war. Unter dem Deckmäntelchen des Humors kam in den Illustrationen praktisch niemand ungeschoren davon. Auch die Mexikaner kriegten ihr Fett weg: Die Karte des Pancho's zeigte meist einen nichtsnutzigen, unter seinem Sombrero schnarchenden Mexikaner. Auf den Karten von Chinarestaurants wimmelte es nur so von Buchstaben in Bambusform bis hin zum finster dreinblickenden Fu Manchu, der personifizierten Gelben Gefahr. Alle Italiener sahen wie der stets fröhlich grinsende *Chef Boy-ar-dee* aus. Und die Frauen erschienen auf den Karten der Schnellrestaurantketten Jack's und Stan's als kurvenreiche Sexobjekte.

Auch die Sprache der Speisekarten entwickelte ihre ganz spezifischen Kadenzen und Synkopierungen, vergleichbar mit den Kleinanzeigen in der Zeitung, die sehr viel Information in gedrängter Kurzform vermitteln mussten. Die Überschriften waren kurz, manchmal angereichert mit einfachen Beschreibungen: „Dicke Eis- und Milchshakes"; ab und zu waren sie ein bisschen geschwätziger: „Superdicke Milchshakes und köstliche Eisbecher". Ausdrücke wie „vom Holzkohlengrill" und „Feinschmeckersuppen" feuerten die Fantasie an. „Speisekarten sind die Glocken des Pawlow'schen Hundes beim Restaurantbesuch", schrieb Sara Dickerman in *Slate* (April 2003). „Sie stellen eine Literatur der Kontrolle dar. Die Sprache der Speisekarten mit den vielen Bindestrichen, Anführungszeichen und willkürlichen Anhäufungen von Fremdwörtern dient weniger der Beschreibung von Essen als der Unterwerfung Ihrer Erwartungen. Die Sprache stimuliert nicht nur, sondern dient vor allem der Rechtfertigung der Ausgaben für den Restaurantbesuch."

Apropos ungewollte Anregung des Speichelflusses – der ehemalige Restaurantkritiker der *New York Times,* Frank Bruni, betrachtete zeitgenössische Speisekarten als Literatur: „Die wortreichen Beschreibungen mancher Karten konzentrieren sich sehr stark auf die Zutaten. Die ausschweifende Prosa anderer Karten hat moralische Hintergründe. Der Küchenchef möchte, dass Sie wissen, wo das Huhn herkommt, wie das Kalb gezüchtet wurde. Er weiß, dass Sie Ihre Entscheidungen über das, was Sie essen, anhand dieser Informationen treffen werden und die ausschweifende Prosa von wieder anderen Karten kann man im Grunde nur als literarisch bezeichnen." Die Speisekarte als Pom Poms schwenkendes Mädchen ist ein durchaus überzeugendes Bild: Die Karte fordert nicht nur zum anschließenden Jubeln auf, sondern löst schon vorher die Sehnsüchte und Wünsche der Speisegäste aus. Die Sprache der Speisekarte transportiert auch einen gewissen Status (bzw. dessen Fehlen). Die Haute Cuisine würzte ihre Karten meist mit *très chic* klingenden französischen Einsprengseln *comme ça: „hors d'œuvres" et „entrée" ou „entremets" ou „plats du jour" ou „potages"*. Andere Restaurantkarten bombardierten die Gäste mit exotischen Ausdrücken, die oft schwer auszusprechen waren (wie wär's mit einem *Babipanggang*?).

Selbst das einheimische Englisch konnte exotisch wirken: Boston war für seine aristokratischen linguistischen Gepflogenheiten bekannt, die sich auch in den Speisezetteln niederschlugen. In einem Brief, der in einer stark nach Oberschicht aussehenden Schriftart auf die Rückseite des „Dinner Bill of Fare" bei Jameson & Richardson gedruckt war (1839), durften Essensgäste folgende distinguierte Eigenwerbung lesen: „Bezüglich der ordnungsgemäßen Abwicklung aller noch so kleiner Einzelheiten und der Disziplin der Kellner, können wir, zusammen mit der Küchenabteilung, die bei der Zubereitung der Speisen äußerste Sorgfalt und Kunstfertigkeit walten lässt, der Konkurrenz hier in der Stadt und andernorts die Stirn bieten … Die verschiedenen pikanten Beilagen der Saison werden kostenfrei zur Verfügung gestellt." Manche Restaurants waren sehr originell, wenn sie die Spezialitäten ihres Hauses beschrieben. Die Speisekarte des Palmer in Chicago las sich wie ein poetisches Langgedicht:

EDOUARDE
SOUVENIR PROGRAM
FOLIES BERGERES
FRENCH CASINO
CLARK AT LAWRENCE
CHICAGO

World Famous
VILLAGE
NUT
CLUB
99 7th Ave. South
In The Heart of
Greenwich Village
NEW YORK CITY
Jontoe

OPPOSITE **Nut Club, c. 1936, New York, New York**

LEFT **Motorliner Kungsholm, Swedish American Line, 1936**

RIGHT **Ming's Drive In Restaurant, c. 1940, Portland, Oregon**

Soup Anglaise, Kenseber-Lachs à la Hollandaise, Hammelkeule mit Kapernsauce, kleine Frikadellen a la Reine, sibirische Bowle, glasierter Biskuitkuchen und Erdbeeren mit Schlagsahne. Als ob das noch nicht appetitanregend genug wäre, fügt die Royal Blue Line der Central Railroad Company auf der Speisewagenkarte hinzu: „Die Geschäftsleitung freut sich bekannt zu geben, dass der Betrieb des Speisewagens der Pullman's Palace Car Company übertragen wurde. Die angebotenen Speisen und Getränke sind ausschließlich erster Klasse und entsprechen dem vorzüglichen Niveau dieser berühmten Züge." Am 29. März 1881 stehen unter anderem Schildkrötensuppe, gekochter Seebarsch in Krabbensauce, in Schmalz gebackenes Kalbsbries-Ragout, sibirisches Sorbet (als Zwischengang), geröstete Ente mit Johannisbeergelee, Biskuitbombe, Feigen in Kräuterlikör und Hygeia-Mineralwasser auf der Karte. Die Speisenfolge beim 17. Bankett der alljährlichen Zusammenkunft der Armee von Nord-Virginia 1892 war ganz französisch: *tortue verte au clair* (Grüne Schildkrötensuppe), *timbales Perigordine* (gegarte Pastete mit Zunge), *pommes de terre persillade* (Petersilienkartoffeln), *terrapene a la Baltimore* (Sumpfschildkröte à la Baltimore), *aspics de foie-gras* (Gänseleberpastete in Aspik) und *petits fours* (kleine Törtchen). *Oh, là, là!*

Normale Gaststätten, Schnellrestaurants und Imbissstuben gaben sich nur selten derart exzentrisch. Auch wenn sich dort bisweilen ein „Entrée" oder ein „Plat du jour" auf die Karte verirrte, wurden die *french fries* niemals *Pommes Frites* genannt. In den 1920er-Jahren war das bodenständigste Angebot das „blue plate special", das warme Tagesgericht. Diese Empfehlung der Küche soll ursprünglich tatsächlich auf blauen Tellern („blue plates") serviert worden sein, eine Sitte, die schnell wieder verschwand, doch der Name hielt sich. Die kalifornischen Restaurants der PEP-Kette boten ihre Gerichte unter Namen an, die an die Titel reißerischer B-Filme erinnern. Alles auf der Karte wurde von einem Superlativ begleitet – und oh, diese herrlichen Preise: „Riesenschokoladen-Eiscremesoda (25 Cent)", „Riesenschüssel Chili con Carne (20 Cent)" und „6 Minipfannkuchen (50 Cent)". Da verzichtet man doch gern auf sein „gekühltes Consommé-Gelee", wenn man „Hamburger und Fritten" für 55 Cent bekommen kann.

Zusätzlich zur Sprache wurde auch die Bebilderung gezielt eingesetzt, um eine bestimmte Attitüde zu signalisieren – ob es sich nun um ein Restaurant für die Schickeria oder Traditionalisten, Junge oder Alte, Reiche oder nicht so Wohlhabende handelte. Die vielleicht ausgefallenste Karte stammt aus San Francisco (1912): Auf der sogar fast pornografischen Karte ist die Chromolithografie einer nackten blonden Frau zu sehen, die an den Füßen gefesselt von drei Satyrn mit Kochmützen in eine offene Kochstelle gezogen wird. Die Überschrift heißt: „Une poule au pot au Cercle de l'union en l'honneur de MM. Merou, de Chantreau, de Sabla et de Coulon" („Ein Huhn für den Topf im Kreis des Verbands zu Ehren der Herren Merou, Chantreau, Sabla und Coulon"). Was die Darstellung zu bedeuten hatte, ist nicht überliefert, aber sie lenkte die Gedanken der Gäste sicherlich kurzfristig vom Essen ab. Meist jedoch waren die Illustrationen wesentlich zahmer und repräsentierten die Idealvorstellungen oder Realitäten eines Etablissements oder Ereignisses.

In der Speisekartengestaltung lässt sich eine beträchtliche Menge innovativen Grafikdesigns entdecken. Der Namenszug von Bernstein's Fish Grotto besteht aus Fischen, die das Wort „Fisch" bilden, und Wasser, mit dem das Wort „Grotto" gefüllt ist: ein cleveres Beispiel konzeptioneller Typografie – das prompt von Sea Cave Sea Foods kopiert wurde, oder umgekehrt. Speisekarten in Chinarestaurants waren oft raffiniert illustriert. Neben den Lettern im Bambusstil beim Forbidden Palace, Lamps of China, Ruby Foo's Den und der Golden Pagoda weisen die vierfarbigen Buchmalereien auf exotische Qualitäten hin, die zweifellos zur Innenausstattung des jeweiligen Restaurants passten. Das Gerücht hielt sich, dass auch das Essen fad schmecke, wenn die Karte langweilig aussähe – es machte sich also bezahlt, wenn man knallige Darstellungen und ungewöhnliche Typografie verwendete.

Es war weit verbreitet, Speisekarten als Werbeflächen für Acme Ale, Budweiser und natürlich Coca-Cola und viele andere Marken zu benutzen. Die Firmen stellten kleinen Gaststätten und Kneipen als Gegenleistung Druckvorlagen für die Speisekarte zur Verfügung. Diese Speisekarten wiederholten im Allgemeinen die Werbeslogans,

SUBWAY CAFE
507
SUBWAY
CAFE
507
NORTH WABASH AVE
LONGEST BAR IN THE WORLD!

OPPOSITE Subway Cafe, 1933, Chicago, Illinois

RIGHT Jimmy Kellys, c. 1938, New York, New York

FAR RIGHT Restaurant Longchamps, 1936, New York, New York

mit denen das Produkt in den Massenmedien angepriesen wurde. Während des Zweiten Weltkriegs wurde auf vielen Menükarten mit patriotischen Abbildungen für den Kauf von amerikanischen Kriegsanleihen geworben. Während des gesamten Krieges strahlte ein stolzes „V" für „Victory" auf den Speisewagenkarten des New York Central Systems. Weniger patriotisch, aber genauso amerikanisch warb die Karte des Les Comiques im Hollywood Plaza Hotel für die besten Comicstrips aus der Sonntagszeitung: Tarzan, Lone Ranger, Der kleine König, Dagwood and Blondie und Li'l Abner.

Zu hohen Feiertagen gab es oft eine besondere Speisekarte. Die alljährlich wechselnde Silvesterkarte im Waldorf-Astoria, oft in leuchtenden Farben gedruckt und mit Silbermetallicfarbe geprägt, war berühmt, weil sie den Glückstaumel der Jahre nach dem Kriegsende wunderbar zum Ausdruck brachte. Auf dem Silvesterball im Congress wurde die Flapper-Ära mit fantastischen Art-déco-Illustrationen eingeläutet. Auch das Hotel Taft in New York folgte immer dem neuesten Art-déco-Trend – von tanzenden Nymphen bis zu zackigen Bergen für den Speisekartengruß zum Jahreswechsel 1939/1940.

Einige Kantinen in bekannten Unternehmen und Institutionen hatten ihre eigenen wechselnden Speisekarten, doch nur wenige waren so clever wie die des Walt Disney Studio Restaurant in Burbank, Kalifornien. Unter dem roten kursiven Schriftzug „Guten Morgen!" und einer 8.35 anzeigenden Uhr sitzt ein erschöpfter Donald Duck, der seinen Morgenkaffee mit letzter Kraft festhält. Aus seinem Schnabel tönt: „Und was soll daran gut sein?" Vielleicht der niedrige Preis?

Die grafischen Konventionen wurden oft sehr laienhaft gehandhabt. Manchmal passte das, was gerade modern war, wie jede Menge Art déco nach dem Ersten Weltkrieg oder 50 Jahre später Psychedelisches im Trident. Aber manchmal wimmelte es nur so von grafischen Anachronismen wie den nackten Nymphchen auf der Karte im South Seas. Aktdarstellungen zogen immer, wie zum Beispiel auf den frivolen Speisekarten des Chicagoer French Casino, im Rubenak's Half Way House oder Sutton's Club Lido. Gelegentlich brachten kulinarische Impresarios ihre ganz persönlichen künstlerischen Vorlieben mit ins Spiel wie die Paul-Klee-Impressionen auf der Karte im Pan Lad, das von Joan Miró inspirierte Fisch-Mobile beim Well of the Sea, die jazzigen, comicartigen Hände im Panza's Lazy Susan, das surrealistische Hungry I, die an Picasso und die 1950er-Jahre erinnernden abstrakten Speerspitzen auf der Karte des Congo Room im Hotel Sahara und die bunten Planetenkonstellationen im New Frontier Hotel. Apropos Planeten: Zu den aufwendigsten Karten gehörte die 3D-Menükarte für die Silvestergala 1954 im Cumberland Hotel mit ihren Motiven aus der Weltraumära und der Raumschiffhostess, die begeistert ihre elektronische Speisekartenkonsole vorführt (die nicht sehr viel anders als die Computerbildschirme aussieht, in die heute die Bestellungen eingetippt werden, abgesehen von den Flash-Gordon-Elementen). Science-Fiction war populär, und die Speisekarte des Airport Roof Restaurant im Miami International Airport Hotel mit ihren futuristischen Grafiken weist auf das „Jet Age" hin, ein weiterer Ausblick auf eine glorreiche Zukunft, die heute bereits wieder Vergangenheit ist.

Irgendwann wurde Fotografie ein allgegenwärtiges Medium, um den Gästen die zur Verfügung stehende Fülle vorzuführen. Allerdings wirkten die meisten Fotos nie so appetitlich wie Zeichnungen oder konzeptionelle Schrifttypen. Der Mann mit dem Fleischsäbel auf der Karte des Tick Tock würde sich vielleicht im Gefängnisjahrbuch gut machen – aber für ein Esslokal nicht. Das Bistro im Hotel Mayflower in Akron, Ohio, versuchte etwas ganz Raffiniertes: Das Wort „Luncheon" (Mittagessen) besteht aus dreidimensionalen Blockbuchstaben mit einer echten Uhr zwischen „Lunch" and „eon". Woher diese Idee kam, ist eines der vielen Mysterien des Speisekartendesigns.

Viele innovative Karten wurden für die Erlebnisgastronomie gestaltet. Mike's Ship-A-Hoy („Mikes Schiff Ahoi"), das fast ausschließlich mit retuschierten Farbfotos ausgestattet war, lag weit weg vom Meer, bot aber Sitzgelegenheiten in einer Vielzahl verschiedener Schiffe an (wer leicht seekrank wurde, wurde vorgewarnt). Echte Transportmittel wie Eisenbahn, Kreuzfahrtschiffe und Flugzeuge – die allesamt fliegende und fahrende Festgelage boten – waren mit grafisch aufwendig gestalteten Souvenirs aller Art bestückt, von

BELOW **Luftschiffbau Zeppelin, Hamburg-Amerika Line, 1934**

Dining was provided on long distance Zeppelin travel, an exclusive transportation option that was short lived.

Auf langen Zeppelinfahrten, einer exklusiven, aber kurzlebigen Transportmöglichkeit, wurde sogar Essen serviert.

Il était possible de se restaurer lors de voyages long-courriers en zeppelin, un moyen de transport très chic, mais qui ne fonctionna guère longtemps.

RIGHT **Liberty Cafe, c. 1945, Albuquerque, New Mexico**

OPPOSITE **Empire Room, the Waldorf-Astoria, 1938, New York, New York**

PAGE 34 **Johore State Pavilion, Golden Gate International Exposition, 1939, San Francisco, California**

Servietten bis Speisekarten, bisweilen von bekannten Designern entworfen. John Held Jr. zeichnete das Cover und die Innenillustrationen für „Speaking of Food“, die Karte für den Speisewagen der New York, New Haven and Hartford Railroad. Da wollten die Pennsylvania Railroad, Baltimore & Ohio und die New York Central System natürlich nicht zurückstehen, boten komplette Mahlzeiten für einen Dollar an und die Karte gab's gratis dazu. Die Alaska Steamship Company bildete Inuits ab, die Great Northern Railway („Route of the Empire Builder“) zeigte Indianerhäuptlinge in voller Zeremonialtracht auf der Karte (die auch eine Spezialabteilung „für die Kleinen“ enthielt). Sogar der bedeutende deutsche Plakatgrafiker (und Nazipropagandist) Ludwig Hohlwein war dabei, mit Illustrationen von der Olympiade 1936 für die Passagierschiffe des Norddeutschen Lloyd in Bremen.

Das elegante Design einer Speisekarte war nicht einfach zu erzielen. Der Einband war eine Leerfläche, auf der sich der Zeichner, Illustrator oder Typograf austoben konnte – einige wunderschöne, bemerkenswerte Arbeiten sind dabei entstanden. Andere Karten wurden jedoch von den Druckereien mit Standardillustrationen und -schrifttypen hergestellt. Selten, falls überhaupt jemals, wurde der Name eines Einzelkünstlers genannt. Die besten Speisekarten besaßen das ästhetische Flair von Notenblättern, manche erinnerten an Hochzeitseinladungen, doch die meisten folgten den zu Anfang des 20. Jahrhunderts etablierten Konventionen: Der Name des Restaurants wird hervorgehoben, das Wort „Speisekarte“ ist zu lesen, und das Layout darf den Gast um Himmels Willen nicht verwirren. Die Speisekarte ist ein Lobgesang auf die Küche eines Gastronomiebetriebes und hat entsprechend auszusehen.

Zum Essen auszugehen ist ein fester Bestandteil des täglichen Lebens, aber auch ein Ritual – wie der Gottesdienst am Sonntag. Ein wenig erinnert die Konsultation der Speisekarte an das Öffnen des Gebet- oder Gesangbuches: Die Auswahl dieses Tages wird getroffen. Oder vielleicht lässt sich das Aufklappen der Karte noch besser mit dem Auspacken eines Geschenks vergleichen: Was wohl drin sein mag? Welch freudige Überraschung! Die Gelegenheit zu bekommen, selbst etwas aus einer großen Fülle herrlicher Angebote auszuwählen, ist zweifellos ein wunderbares Ritual.

Bedienung?!!! ... Wir möchten gern bestellen.

EMPIRE
DINNER
ROOM

جوهر
1939
GOLDEN GATE
INTERNATIONAL
EXPOSITION
SAN FRANCISCO
JOHORE STATE PAVILION

Le menu américain

par Steven Heller

Le menu, qui possède effectivement des origines françaises – comme beaucoup de choses liées à la gastronomie – est un support à la fois fonctionnel et éphémère. Il est apparu assez tard dans l'histoire de la cuisine française.

Si nous découvrions qu'un personnage historique obscur et excentrique – appelons-le « Monsieur Menu » (ou plutôt, soyons précis : Georges Laffont Menu) – avait conçu le premier menu moderne au monde, alors le mythe fondateur pourrait sans doute s'écrire ainsi :

> *Dernier fils encore vivant d'une famille paysanne du Lot-et-Garonne, Menu monta à Paris à l'âge de quinze ans. Il trima des années comme plongeur dans les cuisines de la Rive gauche. Pourtant, parallèlement à ce dur labeur, il apprit sur le tas l'art de la gastronomie la plus raffinée et la plus éclectique. À trente-deux ans, un miracle le conduisit à la cour de Louis XIV où il fut nommé chef de cuisine. Il devint le favori des courtisans pour lesquels, chaque soir, il rédigeait à la main ce qu'il avait concocté pour le souper : « Voici le Menu ! ».*

Malheureusement, à notre connaissance, un tel personnage n'a jamais existé et l'identité du créateur de la première carte est perdue pour la postérité. La genèse des menus reste mystérieuse et le mythe souffre assurément d'un tel anonymat. *Quel dommage !*

Cependant, une histoire *existe* et nous pouvons la conter, même si le récit peut sembler foisonnant. Le menu, qui possède effectivement des origines françaises – comme beaucoup de choses liées à la gastronomie – est un support à la fois fonctionnel et éphémère. Il est apparu assez tard dans l'histoire de la cuisine française. On évoque parfois des origines chinoises datant du premier millénaire (la naissance, qui sait, des plats numérotés ?). Toutefois, même si cela était avéré, il ne pouvait s'appeler « menu », car ce nom bien français vient du latin *minutus*, qui signifie « diminution » ou « réduction », d'où l'unité de temps « minute ». En France, il s'agissait d'une liste ou d'un résumé. Le menu, ainsi, apparaît comme un résumé de l'offre gastronomique proposée par un établissement.

Les premiers restaurants européens, les « tables de restaurateurs » comme on les appelle alors, ne proposent pas de menu. Inutile, car seule une clientèle privilégiée peut se permettre de dîner à l'extérieur, loin du confort et de la sécurité du foyer. Lorsqu'elle s'y aventure, néanmoins, elle se rend principalement dans des *tables d'hôtes* où, autour de tables communes, on la régale de ce qui rôtit au-dessus des flammes ou mitonne dans la marmite, selon l'humeur de l'aubergiste. En d'autres termes, on y mange ce qu'on y trouve ce jour-là. Dans les restaurants plus modernes qui émergent juste avant la Révolution française, les plats sont décrits par le serveur ou sont inscrits sur de petites ardoises ; ils sont proposés *à la carte*. L'ardoise et ses équivalents modernes sont restés de grands classiques, à l'instar du service empressé.

Le menu moderne apparaît à la fin du XVIIIe siècle. *Quelle révolution ! Vive la révolution !*

À la différence de la table commune (restée en usage dans les auberges de type familial), les restaurants offrent un choix de plats inédits et de « spécialités de la maison ». Les prix augmentent car la cuisine est désormais faite pour satisfaire les appétits singuliers (*l'agneau avec la sauce à part, s'il vous plaît !*). Les menus deviennent une invite à la dégustation… des objets de désir.

Dans *The Invention of the Restaurant: Paris and Modern Gastronomic Culture*, Rebecca L. Spang note que la conception des menus évolue au cours du XIXe siècle et colle étroitement aux inventions typographiques de l'époque, dans lesquelles, comme nous le savons, la France a joué un rôle novateur fondamental. Avec certains des affichistes et des fonderies typographiques les plus célèbres du monde, la Ville lumière se révèle être aussi une ville d'imprimerie, une ville d'encre. Le menu en papier inspiré de la presse quotidienne – une pleine page grand format et une typographie resserrée sur plusieurs colonnes – se transforme « au milieu du siècle en un livret de cuir aux feuillets reliés par un cordon de soie », écrit Spang. En raison du coût et de la fragilité d'une telle présentation, le menu évolue ensuite vers une feuille unique aux riches illustrations et ornementations graphiques. En France, le menu, également appelé « carte », est l'expression graphique des mets proposés. Dans d'autres régions du monde, il ne suggère qu'une simple « liste de plats accompagnés de leur prix ».

Boursouflure chauvine mise à part, la gastronomie n'appartient pas uniquement aux Français. Pour de nombreux palais, la cuisine

BELOW **Hotel Astor Roof, New York, New York 1939**

RIGHT **Jimmy Kennedy's Hacienda, c. 1944**

OPPOSITE **Rice Bowl, c. 1936, Los Angeles, California**

In 1938 a new Chinatown opened as a tourist attraction in Los Angeles. With the demise of Prohibition, a restaurant like Rice Bowl could offer cocktails, dancing, and music.

1938 wurde in Los Angeles eine neue Chinatown als Touristenattraktion eröffnet. Nach dem Ende der Prohibitionszeit durfte ein Chinarestaurant wie das Rice Bowl auch Cocktails, Tanz und Musik anbieten.

En 1938, un nouveau Chinatown ouvre à Los Angeles. Il s'agit d'une attraction touristique. Avec la fin de la Prohibition, des établissements comme le Rice Bowl proposent des cocktails, des danses et de la musique.

de rue asiatique, africaine ou sud-américaine – aux menus superflus puisque les mets exposent immédiatement leur identité visuelle – est aussi délicieuse que la *cuisine française*. Les Américains, en outre, n'ont pas à rougir de leur cuisine ni de la conception et du design de leurs menus. Du début de la guerre d'Indépendance jusqu'à la fin du XVIIIe siècle, des chefs renommés, voire inspirés, s'épanouissent aux États-Unis. D'ailleurs, les Américains mangent aussi souvent au restaurant qu'à la maison. Les extravagances et la diversité culinaires des États-Unis n'égalent peut-être pas celles de la cuisine française, mais l'esprit d'entreprise qui y règne, conjugué à l'existence d'une masse critique de tavernes (parfois dépourvues de menus) et de restaurants plus opulents (avec des cartes élaborées), ont permis de rivaliser avec les tenants officiels de la haute cuisine de l'Ancien Continent.

Il n'existe pas de date officielle de la première apparition d'un menu américain. Les tavernes et les auberges du XVIIIe siècle proposent généralement un repas fixe à prix fixe. Mais elles profitent de l'opportunité offerte par l'imprimerie, la typographie et les techniques de gravure, qui deviennent à la fois meilleur marché et accessibles, pour concevoir des menus « modernes ». La première presse typographique est introduite dans la colonie du Massachusetts au XVIIe siècle. Les premiers pionniers imprimeurs se répandent au cours du siècle du nord au sud de la côte Est. Leur travail est d'abord limité aux journaux, aux pamphlets et aux affichettes mais, tandis que le nombre d'imprimeries augmente et que les imprimeurs s'aguerrissent, d'autres productions fleurissent, parmi lesquelles les menus, même s'il ne s'agit que d'une sorte de papier à en-tête sur lequel les plats du jour sont rédigés à la main.

Pour autant, les restaurants ont précédé les menus. Aux États-Unis, ils se développent dans les villes du nord-est, comme le Julien's Restorator, qui ouvre à Boston en 1794. (Le mot « restaurant » vient du latin *restaurabo*.) Le plus ancien restaurant ayant connu une activité continue aux États-Unis, le Union Oyster House, ouvre ses portes en 1826 dans la même ville. Il propose un repas commun et les convives se servent eux-mêmes dans la gamelle collective. Le *service à la russe* est introduit en France dans les années 1810. Plus cérémonieux, des serveurs font le tour de la table en portant les plateaux dans lesquels se servent les commensaux. (Dans de telles circonstances, fournir un menu n'était pas forcément nécessaire, mais comme il s'agissait de la liste des plats, en proposer un semblait à la fois plus raffiné et plus élégant.)

Étant donné que le nombre de restaurants augmente en même temps que le nombre des clients à même de s'offrir un repas à l'extérieur et que se sustenter devient une véritable distraction plutôt qu'un simple besoin vital, le menu fait figure à la fois d'outil pratique (il vous annonce la couleur), de forme d'art et de marque commerciale. L'art tient davantage de l'extravagance, mais au fur et à mesure de l'évolution des procédés (couleur, découpage, embossage, reliures), les expériences et les nouveautés deviennent monnaies courantes. Pour un restaurant, afficher sa propre identité s'inscrit dans la continuité des enseignes des négociants et des marchands du Moyen Âge. Distinguer son activité est à la base de l'industrie et du commerce depuis toujours – ou presque – et les restaurants, plus encore que la majorité des commerces, exigent une identité forte qui souligne la qualité de la nourriture servie.

Bien que la plupart des menus ne puissent être considérés comme de la publicité ou de la promotion, faire connaître un établissement grâce à des graphismes plaisants – et facilement mémorisables – semble offrir des avantages certains. En tout état de cause, la tonalité graphique, démonstrative ou plus réservée, contribue au charme et au mystère de l'établissement. Si la fonction du menu est claire, pour certains clients il est l'équivalent d'une étiquette de bagage ou d'un carnet de bal : des preuves tangibles d'un voyage gustatif ou d'une valse gastronomique. Le nombre incroyable de cartes faites sur mesure, d'illustrations personnalisées, de formes insolites qu'on trouvera dans cet ouvrage montre à l'évidence combien la « preuve de consommation », dans toutes les acceptions du terme, était en vogue à la fin du XIXe et au début du XXe siècle.

Autrefois, les menus étaient fréquemment conservés par les consommateurs. Souvenirs escamotés à l'occasion de cérémonies officielles, de congrès, de soirées en club privé, de croisières, de petits

RICE BOWL
THE OUTSTANDING ORIENTAL CAFE
COCKTAIL
DINE
DANCE
MUSIC
大
華
酒
家
949 SUN MUN WAY
NEW CHINATOWN, LOS ANGELES CAL.

ABOVE **The Bung Hole, c. 1941, Seattle, Washington**

RIGHT **Knight's Diner, c. 1941, Seattle, Washington**

ou de grands mariages…. Thésauriser les menus était sans doute une question de statut: ils valaient preuve de fréquentation des endroits à la mode tels que le Stork Club (qui vendait également des souvenirs à sa clientèle), le «21» ou le Cocoanut Grove. Peut-être les menus servaient-ils aussi à des fins de documentation historique, par exemple comme trace de la participation à la réception et au dîner de lancement du *Hindenburg* ou du *Graf Zeppelin* (avant l'entrée en guerre contre l'Allemagne nazie). D'autres se montraient tout simplement si beaux, si élégants – Rainbow Grill, Casa Manana ou Café Lafayette – qu'on se devait de les subtiliser. Certains suscitaient une étrange fascination – comme celui de l'Ubangi Club. Mais dans la grande majorité des cas, les convives indélicats se les appropriaient simplement pour se remémorer plus tard une expérience particulière.

Comment oublier ces instants merveilleux passés au Red Sails Inn sur le Fisherman's Wharf? Quel meilleur moyen de se souvenir d'un dîner ou d'un déjeuner au bord de l'océan qu'un menu en forme de voilier? Qui pourrait effacer de sa mémoire un repas au Toed Inn, avec son menu découpé à l'image du bâtiment en forme de crapaud (*toad*, homophonie de Toed), ou le menu «Club Burger» du Melrod's qui ressemble – on l'aura deviné – à un double hamburger avec sa feuille de laitue, ou encore The Bung Hole (littéralement, «bonde de fût») et son menu en forme de tonneau? Certes, ils feront de l'effet dans l'album familial…

Avant la crise de 1929, les menus richement illustrés – quelle que soit la catégorie de l'établissement – sont très communs. Le style s'apparente à l'art moderne ou à l'Art déco et les déclinaisons de ces signatures graphiques et de ces motifs typographiques règnent sur le marché (parfois fournis par les imprimeurs qui mettent diverses couvertures à la disposition de leurs clients). La sophistication devient dès lors la règle en matière de conception de menus. La carte du Katson's Drive-In est ainsi typique de la présentation classique du petit déjeuner et du déjeuner: un assortiment de cercles, de rectangles et de carrés blancs et colorés, parfaits pour inscrire le plat du jour, tandis que les plats à la carte sont annoncés dans des bannières de couleur, parfois accompagnées de petites images incrustées. Certains menus sont spécifiquement prévus pour la clientèle du matin: la couverture du menu du Northern Hotel – un visage avec deux œufs sur le plat (les yeux) et une tranche de bacon en guise de sourire – est censé nous réchauffer le cœur, tandis que le coq chantant face au soleil levant sur le menu du Furnace Creek Ranch's nous met en appétit. Les cartes présentant les cocktails pourraient faire saliver le plus sobre des tempérants. Les boissons reproduites sur le menu du Heaven City Hotel semblent briller, comme si elles étaient phosphorescentes: imaginez ce qu'elles réservent à votre cerveau.

Les menus n'échappent pas à des expressions ou des images qu'on trouverait aujourd'hui politiquement incorrectes – voire, parfois, carrément racistes. Le Fat Boy Drive-In de Redwood City en Californie essaie d'imiter la très populaire chaîne Big Boy (connue au début sous le nom de Bob's), mais *big* (gros) et *fat* (gras) n'ont pas la même signification. En outre, Big Boy, le dodu, est assurément plus mignon que son cousin obèse, Fat Boy. Sans oublier Fat Eddie's, avec son Eddie, un hamburger bourré à craquer (aujourd'hui, une telle image de marque va à l'encontre de toutes les prescriptions diététiques). Mais Fat Eddie et Fat Boy n'arrivent pas à égaler le Coon Chicken Inn (littéralement, «Au poulet nègre»), qui offre l'un des portraits racistes les plus célèbres dans l'univers des menus. Dans certains restaurants, d'ailleurs, les clients passaient sans sourciller devant la représentation de ces grooms à l'expression démoniaque et aux grosses lèvres rouges. Il s'agissait pourtant d'endroits très populaires. Alors qu'on pensait avoir atteint le fond du mauvais goût, on découvre le Piccaninny Bar-B-Q (littéralement, «Au négrillon») et sa mascotte: une caricature de chanteur noir. Sous couvert d'humour, les menus n'épargnaient personne. Ainsi les Mexicains en prenaient-ils également pour leur grade: la carte du Pancho dépeignait les voisins méridionaux des Américains comme des bons à rien, des porteurs de sombreros. Les clichés abondaient également dans les restaurants chinois: lettrage style bambou ou représentations du maléfique Fu Manchu (stéréotype du «péril jaune»). Les Italiens, pour leur part, ressemblaient tous au joyeux chef Boyardee, l'incarnation d'une marque de pâtes. Quant aux femmes, elles n'échappaient pas non plus à la marchandisation:

RIGHT Zebra Room, the Town House, c. 1941, Los Angeles, California

FAR RIGHT Gopher Grill, Hotel Saint Paul, 1950, Saint Paul, Minnesota

sur les menus des chaînes de drive-in Jack et Stan, elles apparaissaient uniquement comme des corps de rêve aux formes généreuses.

Le langage des menus a également développé un rythme distinct et syncopé, à l'instar des petites annonces des quotidiens qui doivent trouver place dans un minuscule espace. Les titres sont courts, parfois accompagnés d'un adjectif qualificatif simple et évocateur : « *Thick* Malts and Sundaes » (milk-shakes onctueux et sundaes) ou un peu plus prolixe : « *SuperThick* Malts and *Delicious* Sundaes » (milk-shakes extra-onctueux et sundaes délicieux) ». Des expressions telles que « cuit au feu de bois » ou « soupe spéciale gourmet » titillent l'imagination. « Les menus sont les stimuli pavloviens du repas », écrivait Sara Dickerman dans *Slate* (avril 2003). « Ils incarnent une littérature du contrôle. Le langage de la carte avec ses traits d'union, ses guillemets, ses explosions aléatoires de termes étrangers, décrit moins la nourriture qu'il anticipe nos attentes... Il ne fait pas que séduire, il justifie le coût d'un dîner en ville. »

À propos des attentes des clients, l'ancien critique du *New York Times* Frank Bruni n'a pas hésité à comparer les menus contemporains à la littérature : « Dans certains menus, la phraséologie choisie reflète l'intensité de l'accent mis sur les ingrédients... Pour d'autres, elle poursuit un objectif éthique. Le chef tient à ce que les convives sachent d'où viennent ses poulets et où son veau a été élevé. Il estime qu'ils doivent pouvoir choisir leurs plats en se fondant sur de telles informations. Pour d'autres encore, la phraséologie peut carrément s'apparenter à de la littérature. La carte représente une espèce d'incitation gastronomique, une sorte de *pom-pom girl* culinaire. » Le menu comme *pom-pom girl* : une image qu'on n'oubliera pas de sitôt. Toutefois, il n'incite pas seulement le client, il lui promet l'objet de son désir.

Le langage des menus dénote aussi le prestige (ou son absence). Les menus américains se réclamant de la haute cuisine sont souvent parsemés de phrases qui se doivent de sonner chic : *hors-d'œuvre*, *entremets*, *plats du jour* ou *potages*. Bien entendu, d'autres gastronomies provoquent parfois une indigestion de termes exotiques, souvent difficiles à prononcer (*la* schnitzel, *c'est pour ?*).

La langue anglaise elle-même émoustille parfois les sens : Boston était célèbre pour son décorum linguistique fastueux, qui s'étendait jusque sur les menus. Dans une lettre imprimée dans la police de caractère du bottin mondain et reproduite au dos du menu du Jameson & Richardson (1839), les clients étaient gratifiés d'un argumentaire flamboyant qui pourrait être rendu ainsi : « Au vu de l'ordre irréprochable apporté à nos préparatifs jusque dans les moindres détails, la discipline de nos serveurs, notre cuisine, où le soin et le talent les plus élevés sont exigés dans la préparation de nos plats, nous défions la concurrence dans cette ville et au-delà... Les divers condiments de saison sont mis gracieusement à la disposition des clients. » Certains restaurants faisaient preuve d'une grande précision dans l'énoncé des spécialités *de la maison*. The Palmer à Chicago déclinait ainsi une véritable litanie poétique : soupe anglaise, saumon de Kenseber à la hollandaise, gigot d'agneau et sa sauce aux câpres, bouchées à la reine, punch de Sibérie, biscuit glacé, fraises et crème. Et comme si un tel répertoire ne suffisait pas à aiguiser l'appétit, la Royal Blue Line de la Central Railroad Company complétait sa carte de l'avis suivant : « La direction... a le plaisir de vous annoncer que des dispositions ont été prises avec la Pullman Palace Car Company pour l'ouverture d'un wagon-restaurant... Ce service sera uniquement offert en première classe et respectera la qualité générale offerte par ces célèbres trains. » Sur le menu du 29 mars 1881 sont proposés, entre autres mets : soupe de tortue, rascasse bouillie et sa sauce à la crevette, ris de veau lardés à la financière, sorbet sibérien (pour rincer le palais), canard rôti et sa gelée de groseille, charlotte russe, cordial à la figue et eau minérale Hygeia. Le menu de la 17e réunion annuelle de l'Armée de Virginie du Nord (ANV) de 1892 est en français : « *tortue verte au clair, timbales périgourdines, pommes de terre persillade, terrapene à la Baltimore, aspics de foie gras et petits fours* » (sic).

Les petits restaurants sans prétention, les snacks et même les *luncheonettes* (malgré leur suffixe français) se montraient rarement aussi prétentieux. Si parfois des *entrées* ou des *plats du jour* se faufilaient dans leurs menus, jamais les *french fries* n'y sont devenues des *pommes frites*. D'ailleurs, c'est le *blue plate special* (plat du jour) qu'on retrouve

Town and Country

OPPOSITE **Town and Country, 1956, Chicago, Illinois**

LEFT **Garden Room, the Town House, 1952, Los Angeles, California**

RIGHT **Albert Pick Hotel, 1956, Chicago, Illinois**

le plus souvent dans les descriptions culinaires des années 1920. Certains disent qu'à l'origine, on le servait sur une… assiette bleue. L'expression est restée, pas le contenant. Les restaurants californiens Pep annonçaient les plats du jour comme des films de série B : les superlatifs et – oh ! – des prix incroyables étaient de mise : « Soda et boule géante de glace au chocolat (25 cents) », « Grand bol de haricots rouges (20 cents) », « 6 mini-crêpes de la taille d'un dollar (50 cents) ». Qui voudrait d'un « consommé de poulet en gelée » quand on peut avoir un hamburger et des frites (55 cents) ?

En plus du langage verbal, l'imagerie était employée à dessein pour suggérer l'ambiance et le statut de l'établissement : chaud ou froid, vieux ou jeune, riche… ou pas trop. Peut-être le plus éclectique – voire érotique – des menus fut-il celui créé pour un événement spécial à San Francisco en 1912 : la chromolithographie d'une femme blonde nue, attachée par les pieds, que trois satyres affublés d'une toque de chef ne vont pas tarder à rôtir. Titre de la carte (en français) : « Une poule au pot au Cercle de l'Union en l'honneur de MM. Merou, de Chantreau, de Sabla et de Coulon » (sic). La majorité des illustrations, toutefois, étaient plus ternes et reflètaient uniquement les ambitions ou la réalité d'un établissement ou d'un événement. Quoi qu'il en soit, elles avaient pour but de détourner l'esprit du client pendant un bref instant.

La conception des menus révèle un nombre considérable d'innovations graphiques. L'enseigne du Bernstein's Fish Grotto, où des poissons forment les lettres de « Fish » tandis que de l'eau remplit le mot « Grotto », demeure un exemple ingénieux de typographie conceptuelle. Elle fut d'ailleurs copiée par le Sea Cave Sea foods (ou inversement). Le graphisme des menus chinois est généralement assez élaboré. En plus du lettrage de style « bambou » des Forbidden Palace, Lamps of China, Ruby Foo's Den et autres Golden Pagoda, les enluminures aux couleurs vives suggéraient un exotisme que venait parachever le décor de chaque établissement. Une carte trop terne était, dit-on, annonciatrice de plats avariés. C'est pourquoi de riches illustrations et une typographie exubérante s'avéraient toujours payantes.

Les menus ont également été utilisés comme supports publicitaires par de nombreuses enseignes comme Acme Ale, Budweiser et, bien entendu, Coca-Cola, dont les cartes ont servi de modèles à bien d'autres restaurants et bars du pays. Quel meilleur moyen de vendre un produit à des consommateurs affamés et assoiffés qu'une promotion d'un genre aussi peu subliminal ? Ces menus obéissaient généralement aux canons de la publicité des produits de masse publiée dans les quotidiens, les magazines et sous forme d'affiches – les trois piliers de la propagande commerciale. Pendant la Seconde Guerre mondiale, des menus promouvaient les emprunts de guerre grâce à des illustrations patriotiques. La compagnie ferroviaire New York Central System affichait fièrement le V de la victoire sur tous ses menus. Moins patriotique mais tout aussi américain, le menu du restaurant Les Comiques, logé dans le Hollywood Plaza Hotel, vantait les meilleures bandes dessinées du dimanche : Tarzan, Lone Ranger, Le petit roi, Dagwood and Blondie et Li'l Abner.

Une carte spéciale était préparée pour les jours fériés. Le Waldorf-Astoria était connu pour ses versions du nouvel an, souvent dans des teintes chatoyantes, en particulier des encres métalliques parfois imprimées en relief et des aplats de couleurs qui exprimaient la joie de l'après-Seconde Guerre mondiale. Au Congrès américain, le menu du nouvel an des Années folles était orné d'enluminures Art déco, le style préféré de nombreux clubs et cafés avant et pendant la Prohibition. De la même façon, l'hôtel Taft de New York a usé de tous les ornements Art déco – nymphes dansantes et montagnes escarpées – pour créer son menu du nouvel an 1940.

Quelques restaurants de studios prestigieux proposaient des menus de circonstance, mais rares sont ceux qui étaient aussi ingénieux que celui du Walt Disney Studio's Restaurant à Burbank, en Californie. Sous la bannière rouge annonçant « Good Morning! » et une pendule affichant 8h35, un Donald Duck épuisé tient mollement sa tasse de café. De son bec sort l'exclamation « What's good about it! » (Qu'est-ce qu'il a de bon ?!). Peut-être les tarifs relativement modestes ?

Les conventions graphiques dans le domaine de l'illustration des menus étaient parfois dictées par un principe guère scientifique

ABOVE **House of Chan, c. 1948, New York, New York**

LEFT **The Traders, the Palmer House, 1957, Chicago, Illinois**

OPPOSITE **Tropicana, ca. 1955, Havana, Cuba**

American influences were inevitable in pre-Castro Cuba because of its proximity to the United States as suggested by this menu for the Tropicana nightclub.

Im vorrevolutionären Kuba waren die amerikanischen Einflüsse durch die Nähe zu den USA sehr stark, wie an dieser Speisekarte des Nachtklubs Tropicana abzulesen ist.

Comme on le constate dans ce menu du night-club Tropicana, les influences américaines étaient inévitables à Cuba avant Castro, en raison de la proximité géographique des États-Unis.

obéissant à la formule « Du moment que ça marche ! ». Parfois le style suivait la mode : l'Art déco, endémique après la Première Guerre mondiale ou, cinquante ans plus tard, le psychédélisme. Parfois, les anachronismes abondaient, comme les nymphettes nues du menu du South Seas. Souvent, la nudité se suffisait à elle-même, par exemple sur la carte du French Casino, un établissement plutôt frivole, ou encore sur celles du Rubenak's Half Way House et du Sutton's Club Lido. Contrairement à d'autres supports promotionnels et « emballages marketing », le design d'une carte ne suffit pas à remplir les salles. Dans ce domaine, les études de marché sont inopérantes. Au mieux un menu renforce-t-il implicitement l'« image de marque » de l'établissement. Ce qui ne signifie pas que certains menus n'aient pas été hors du commun. À certaines occasions, des créateurs gastronomiques instillaient leurs préférences esthétiques personnelles, à l'instar des « coups de pinceau » de la carte du Pan Lad, inspirés par Paul Klee, du mobile de poissons du Well of the Sea, inspiré par Joan Miró, des mains style BD du Panza's Lazy Susan, du graphisme surréaliste du Hungry I, des pointes de lance typiques du modernisme des années 1950 du Congo Room de l'hôtel Sahara, ou encore des planètes extravagantes du New Frontier Hotel. Le menu en 3D du Cumberland Hotel imaginé pour le gala du nouvel an 1954 reste l'un des plus élaborés, avec ses motifs « conquête de l'espace » et sa serveuse-astronaute montrant fièrement son ordinateur-menu (pas si éloigné, certes, de l'écran informatique de nos restaurants d'aujourd'hui, hormis l'accoutrement à la Flash Gordon). La science-fiction possède un certain charme, mais le vrai futurisme, comme le montre le menu de l'Airport Roof Restaurant du Miami International Airport Hotel, évoque l'âge de l'avion à réaction, devenu un nouveau style de « futur antérieur ».

La photographie est finalement devenue indispensable pour révéler les trésors réservés à la clientèle. Toutefois, jamais elle n'a été aussi « appétissante » que peuvent l'être des illustrations ou une typographie conceptuelle réussis. Le boucher représenté sur le menu du Tick Tock aurait toute sa place dans l'annuaire d'une prison, mais pas sur la carte d'un restaurant. Toutefois, force est de reconnaître l'artifice ingénieux utilisé pour le menu de la cafétéria de l'hôtel Mayflower d'Akron, dans l'Ohio : le mot *luncheon* (déjeuner) est photographié en lettres tridimensionnelles avec une vraie montre séparant les mots « lunch » (déjeuner) et « eon » (éternité). Le pourquoi d'un tel choix de design demeure un mystère.

De nombreux menus innovants ne reflétaient pas la réalité. Ainsi le Mike's Ship-A-Hoy, dont la carte est réalisée presque entièrement avec des photos couleur retouchées, était un bateau-restaurant ancré sur la terre ferme qui accueillait ses « passagers » dans différents types de décors nautiques (on avertissait d'ailleurs les clients enclins au mal de mer). Les salles de restaurants réellement mobiles – paquebots de croisière, wagons-restaurants, avions de ligne et autres tables de festin ambulantes – étaient agrémentées de petites touches graphiques, depuis les nappes jusqu'aux menus parfois signés par des artistes de renom. John Held Jr. dessina ainsi la couverture et les illustrations intérieures de « Speaking of Food », le menu des wagons-restaurants du New York New Haven and Hartford Railroad. Pour ne pas être en reste, les compagnies ferroviaires Pennsylvania Railroad, Baltimore & Ohio et New York Central System proposèrent des dîners à un dollar et offrirent gracieusement le menu à leurs clients. L'Alaska Steamship Company représentait des Inuits, tandis que la Great Northern Railway glorifiait sur son menu les chefs amérindiens en costume de cérémonie (avec une partie réservée « à nos petits amis »). Le grand affichiste allemand (et propagandiste nazi) Ludwig Hohlwein rentra dans la danse en célébrant les Jeux olympiques de 1936 pour la compagnie maritime Norddeutscher Lloyd Bremen.

Concevoir des menus élégants s'avère une tâche difficile. Partant de la couverture comme une toile blanche offerte à l'artiste, l'illustrateur ou le typographe, d'aucuns y ont signé des œuvres remarquables. Certains menus ont été conçus par des imprimeurs disposant d'un important stock d'images et de typographies. Rares sont ceux que l'on peut attribuer à un unique artiste. Les plus beaux résonnent comme des partitions, d'autres évoquent des faire-part de mariage, mais la plupart suivent les conventions établies au début du XXe siècle : inscrire le nom de l'établissement, employer le mot « menu » et

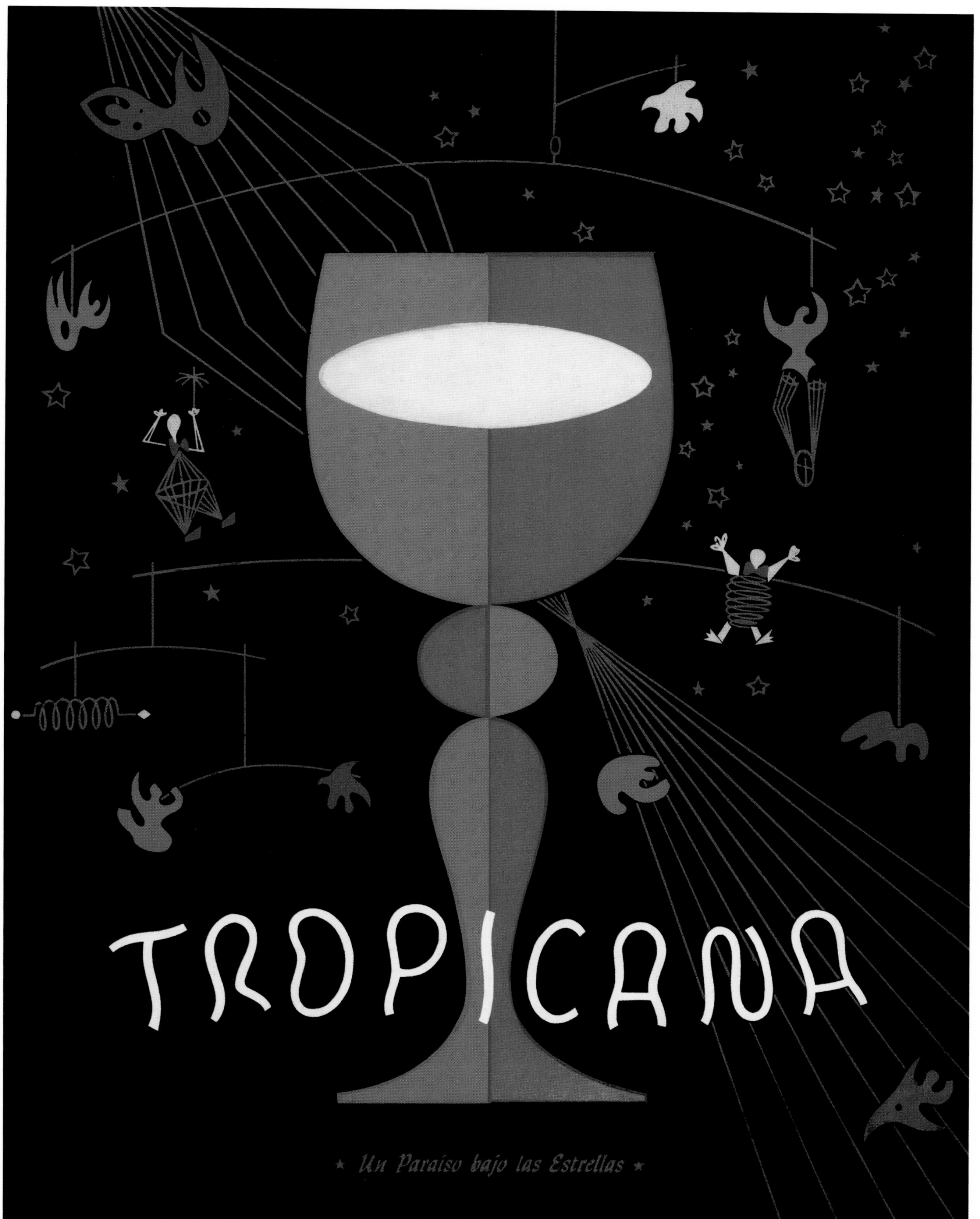
TROPICANA
★ Un Paraíso bajo las Estrellas ★

BELOW Original Jerry's Restaurant, c. 1957

OPPOSITE Orbit Coffee Shop, c. 1962, Los Angeles, California

Space Age graphics were the hallmark of many 1950's coffee shops.

Grafiken mit Raumfahrtelementen waren in den 1950er-Jahren das Markenzeichen vieler Bistros.

Les illustrations «conquête de l'espace» sont caractéristiques de nombreuses cafétérias des années 1950.

PAGE 46 *M. S. Mepham*, St. Louis, Cairo, Memphis, & New Orleans Passenger Packet, 1864

M. S. Mepham Brothers of St. Louis, Missouri, owned several steamers in the mid-19th century, including the *M. S. Mepham*, which plied the Mississippi River from St. Louis to New Orleans, Louisiana. It served the Union side during the Civil War until it burned down on March 4, 1868, in St. Louis.

Die Mepham Brothers aus St. Louis, Missouri, waren Mitte des 19. Jahrhunderts Besitzer mehrerer Dampfschiffe, darunter der *M.S. Mepham*, die den Mississippi von St. Louis bis New Orleans, Louisiana, durchpflügte. Im Amerikanischen Bürgerkrieg wurde sie von den Nordstaaten eingesetzt, bis sie am 4. März 1868 in St. Louis in Flammen aufging.

Les frères M. S. Mepham de Saint-Louis, dans le Missouri, possèdent plusieurs vapeurs au XIXe siècle, dont le *M. S. Mepham* qui sillonne le Mississippi entre Saint-Louis et La Nouvelle-Orléans en Louisiane. Il servira du côté de l'Union pendant la guerre de Sécession jusqu'à son incendie, le 4 mars 1868 à Saint-Louis.

imaginer une présentation qui ne déroute pas le lecteur. Le menu est l'évangile de la cuisine et se doit d'avoir le physique de l'emploi.

Un repas au restaurant est à la fois un rite et un rituel... comme la messe du dimanche. Et la consultation du menu peut être comparée à l'ouverture d'un livre de prières ou de cantiques, et à la sélection de l'offrande du jour. Plus exactement, c'est comme ouvrir un paquet-cadeau et se laisser surprendre par son contenu. Pouvoir choisir ce que l'on désire parmi un trésor d'offrandes demeure à l'évidence une expérience tout à fait unique.

Garçon ! Vous pouvez prendre la commande ?

ORBIT

"Come when you will. We have a welcome for thee"

Breakfast from 7½ to 9 A.M.
Dinner from 1 to 2½ P.M.
Supper at 6 P.M

JAMES ABBEY *Steward.*

MENU

BILL OF FARE.

CITY HOTEL,

TEMPERANCE HOUSE,
BY
BROWN & TUTTLE,
Corner of State and Lake Streets.

Chicago, Oct 11th 1847

SOUP.
Pearl Barley

FISH.

BOILED.
Mutton, Caper Sauce Corned Beef.
~~Ham,~~ Chicken, Tongue.

SIDE DISHES.

ROASTS.
Beef, Lamb,
Pork, Veal,
Chicken, Ducks

VEGETABLES.
Potatoes, Tomatoes Turnips,
Onions, Beets,
Cabbage, Carrots Squash,
Parsnips.

PASTRY.
Pies, Puddings.
Cranberry
Apple Boiled Apple

Breakfast at 7 o'clock. Dinner at 1 o'clock, Tea at 6 o'clock.

TRIBUNE OFFICE PRINT.

LEFT City Hotel, 1847, Chicago, Illinois

Before America had true restaurants, inns and boarding houses offered no menu at all, with everyone eating a common meal. This evolved into a day's offerings scrawled on a chalkboard. With the opening of restaurants in the mid-19th century, menus were rudimentary and, as seen in the City Hotel menu of 1847, changed daily. A temperance house, it served no alcohol and, apparently, only breakfast, lunch ("Dinner"), and tea. It is printed on a simple broadsheet format common to hotels and restaurants of the time.

Bevor es in Amerika richtige Restaurants gab, kannte man Wirtshäuser, die allerdings keine Speisekarten hatten, da jedem Gast dasselbe aufgetischt wurde. Später wurden die Tagesgerichte oft auf eine Tafel geschrieben. Als Mitte des 19. Jahrhunderts in Großstädten wie Chicago die ersten Restaurants aufmachten, gab es nur primitive Speisekarten, die, wie auf dieser vom 11. Oktober 1847 zu sehen, täglich wechselten. Das von Brown & Tuttle geleitete Temperenzlerhaus schenkte keinen Alkohol aus und bot nur Frühstück, Mittagessen („Dinner") und Tee an. Die Karte ist auf einen einfachen Planobogen gedruckt, einem damals für Gastwirtschaften üblichen Format.

Avant l'apparition de vrais restaurants en Amérique, auberges et tables d'hôtes n'offrent pas de menus puisque tout le monde mange le même plat. Plus tard, les propositions du jour sont écrites sur une ardoise. Avec l'ouverture de restaurants au milieu de XIXe siècle dans des villes comme Chicago, les menus restent sommaires et, comme on le voit sur celui du City Hotel en 1847, ils changent quotidiennement. Cet établissement, dirigé par Brown & Tuttle, ne sert pas de boissons alcoolisées ; il propose des petits-déjeuners, des déjeuners et du thé. Il est imprimé sur une feuille grand format jadis commune aux hôtels et aux restaurants.

IRVING HOUSE.

Bill of Fare.

NEW YORK. Saturday, October 12, 1849.

SOUP.
Macaroni.

FISH.
Baked Blackfish, port wine sauce.

BOILED.
Chicken, oyster sauce.
Mutton, caper sauce.
Corned Beef and Cabbage.
Smoked Bacon and Spinach.
Smoked Jole and Spinach
Tongue. Ham.

Cold Pressed Corned Beef.
Cold à la mode Beef.
Cold Roast Beef. Cold Roast Lamb.

ROAST.
Turkeys. Beef. Veal. Geese. Ducks.
Lamb, mint sauce. Chickens.
Ham, champagne sauce. Pork.

ENTREES.
Fricasseed Chicken, with mushrooms.
Breast of Veal, with spinach.
Small Birds, on toast, champagne sauce.
Lamb Chops, breaded tomato sauce.
Tame Ducks, braisés, with olives.
Calf's Head, brain sauce.
Oysters, baked in the shell.
Stewed Pickerels, port wine sauce.
Beef-à-la-mode, with vegetables.
Brains, à la poulette.
Apple Fritters.

GAME.
Saddle of Venison, with currant jelly.

Stewed Tomatoes. Fried Egg Plant.
Baked Sweet Potatoes. Raw Tomatoes.
Baked Stuffed Tomatoes.

PASTRY.
Bread Pudding. Cranberry Pies.
Œufs à'la neige. Apple Pies.
Puffs Napolitaines. Madeleine Cakes.

DESSERT.
Apples. Grapes.
Plums. Raisins. Almonds.
Lemon Ice Cream.

Meals sent to Rooms will be charged extra.

WINE LIST.

MADEIRA.

London Particular	$1 50
Symington's, South Side	2 00
Symington's, Pure Juice	2 00
Stalker's East India	2 50
Stalker's Tinta, or Burgundy Madeira	2 00
March & Benson's, Dry South Side, very fine and delicate	2 50
Stalker's Sercial, fine and high flavored	2 50
Blackburn's, Dry Reserve	3 00
Blackburn's Malmsey or Wedding Wine	3 00
Symington's Bual, fine and delicate	2 50
Stalker's East India	2 00
Superior Old Madeira, 3 years in India	3 50
Blackburn's, Shark, very superior & old	4 00
Charleston Madeira, private stock	4 00
Symington's Diploma Madeira, in Demijohns, extra and old	4 50
Old Madeira, a gentleman's private stock, 25 years in demijohns, bottled in 1815	5 00
J. Oliveira & Co.'s Palhetinho, old, dry and very delicate	4 00

SHERRY.

Table Sherry	$1 50
Symington & Kelly's	2 00
Mansinalla	2 00
Blackburn's, (brown)	2 00
Stalker's, (gold)	2 00
Yrearte, (pale and old)	2 00
Imperial, (very delicate)	3 00
Pemartin, (very delicate)	2 50
Stalker's Amontillado	3 00
Irving, private stock	3 00

PORT.

Symington & Kelly's	~~$2 00~~
Page's Port	2 00
Sandeman & Co.	2 00
Sandeman & Co. (extra and very fine)	2 50

HOCK.

Henkell & Co., Rudesheimer, pints	$1 00
Hockheimer, pints	1 00
Rudesheimer, bottle	2 00
Hockheimer	2 00
Hockheimer, (superior)	2 00
Gusenheim, Rothenberg	2 50
Steinberg, (Cabinet)	3 00
Prince Metternich Castle	5 00
Sparkling Hock	2 00
Sparkling Moselle	2 00

WINE LIST.

CLARET.

St. Julien, bottle	$1 00
St. Julien, pints	0 50
Leoville, bottle	1 50
La Rose	1 50
Mouton	1 50
Chateau Margaux	2 50
Chateau Lafitte, 1841	2 00
Chateau Lateur, 1841	2 50
Margaux, Medoc, pints	0 50
Chateau Lafitte, 1834, bottle	3 00
Chateau Margaux, 1834	3 00

CHAMPAGNE.

Heidseik	$2 00
Iroy	2 00
Cliquot	2 00
Maltese Cross	2 00
Schrider	2 00
De Brimont	2 00
Do., pints	1 00
Bininger's Mumm's Verzenay, bottle	2 50
Do. do., pints	1 25
Lignot	2 00

SAUTERNE.

Bottle	$1 50
Bottle (superior)	2 00
Barsac	2 00
Pints	$1 00

BURGUNDY.

Clos de Vougeot	$2 00
Chambertin	2 00
Sparkling Burgundy	2 00
Pomard	2 00
Volney	2 00

LIQUEURS.

Marachine de Zara	$
Curacoa	
Absynthe	
Annisette	

London Porter	$0 50
" Brown Stout	0 50
Scotch Ale	0 50
Pints	25 cents.

Each Waiter is provided with Wine Cards and Pencil.

CHILDREN TAKING SEATS IN THE LADIES' ORDINARY WILL BE CHARGED FULL PRICE.

W. L. Burroughs, printer, 113 Fulton Street.

RIGHT Irving House, 1847, New York, New York

Dear Sir—

We would most respectfully solicit your attention to our **DINING ROOMS**, at No. 1 Spring Lane, when you have occasion to take a meal away from home.

Our location, being in the central business part of the city, makes it a very desirable place for the man of business who has little time, generally, to spare.

For neatness of arrangement in every particular, and in the discipline of the Waiters, together with the Culinary Department, where the utmost care and skill is requisite for the preparation of food, we can defy competition in this city or elsewhere. Please honor us with a visit and satisfy yourself with the truth of this assertion.

The different Relishes of the season are furnished without charge.

P. S.===Gentlemen dining late, will always find a Fresh Cooked dinner ready at 3 o'clock, P. M.

JAMESON & RICHARDSON,
No. 1 Spring Lane.

Boston, October , 1859.

☞ 40 Lodging Rooms for Gentlemen, by the Day or Week.

(OVER.)

DINNER BILL OF FARE.

SOUPS.

Tomato Soup.	13	Chicken Soup.	13	Brown Soup.	13
Oyster Soup.	13	Mutton Soup.	13	Fish Chowder.	13
Pea Soup.	13	Beef Soup.	13	Clam Chowder.	13
Mock Turtle Soup.	13	Ox-tail Soup.	13		

ROAST.

Turkey.	25	Duck.	38	Veal.	19
Spring Lamb, Mint Sauce.	25	Beef.	19	Beef, a la mode.	19
Chicken.	25	Roast Sirloin Beef.	22	Lamb.	19
Goose, Mongrel.	25	Green Goose.	38	Mutton, Leg.	19
		Pork.	19		

BOILED.

Corned Beef and Vegetables.	19	Calves' Head.	19	Chicken, Oyster Sauce.	25
Leg of Mutton, Caper Sauce.	19	Lobster.	13	Turkey, Oyster Sauce.	25
Bass, Oyster Sauce.	19	Shoulder Pork	19	Ham and Tongue, each.	19

BAKED.

Beef Steak Pie.	19	Pigeon Pie.	25	Oyster Pie.	19
Baked Chicken Pie.	19	Baked Veal Pie.	19	Oyster Patty.	19

ENTREES.

Stewed Pigeons.	25	Pigeon Pot Pie.	25	Dry Toast.	6
Beef Stew.	19	Potted Veal.	19	Fricassee Chicken.	25
Potted Pigeons.	25	Crackers and Milk.	13	Bread and Milk.	13
Hulled Corn and Milk.	13	Butter Toast.	6		

COOKED TO ORDER.

Broiled Chicken.	38	Fried Liver.	15	Fried Ham and Eggs.	19
Smoked Salmon.	19	Stewed Oysters.	13	Pigs' Feet.	15
Rump Steak.	19	Spring Chicken, Broiled.	38	Beef Steak.	13
Pork Steak.	19	Venison Steak.		Fried Sausages.	13
Veal Cutlets.	19	Tenderloin Steak.	31	Boiled or Dropped Eggs.	15
Mutton Chop.	19	Sirloin Steak.	25	Broiled or Fried Tripe.	15
Broiled Shad.	19	Broiled Liver.	15	Fancy Roast.	19

FISH.

Baked Shad.	19	Baked Cod.	15	Smelts.	15
Boiled Bass, White Sauce.	19	Baked Pickerel.	19	Eels.	15
Boiled Salmon.	25	Baked Haddock.	15	Baked Halibut.	15
Fried Perch.	15	Boiled Cod.	16	Baked Salmon Trout.	19
Cod Sounds.	15	Fried Cod.	15	Flounders.	15
Fried Halibut.	15	Broiled Mackerel, salt.	15	Broiled Shad.	19
Boiled Halibut.	15	Mackerel, Fresh.	19		

VEGETABLES.

Asparagus.	6	Celery.	3	Pickles.	
Turnips.	3	Sweet Potatoes.	3	Cold Slaw.	
Cabbage.	3	Cucumbers.	3	Tomatoes.	
Onions.	3	Spinnage.		Pickled Limes.	

PUDDINGS AND PASTRY.

Rhubarb Pie.	6	Cottage Pudding.	6	Baked Indian Pudding.	
Custard Pie.	6	Cracked Wheat Pudding.	6	Tapioca Pudding.	6
Apple Pie.	6	Farina Pudding.	6	Bread and Butter Pudding.	6
Squash Pie.	6	Plum Pudding.	6	Sago Pudding.	6
Mince Pie.	6	Baked Apple Pudding.	6	Suet Pudding.	6
Cranberry Pie.	6	Boiled Apple Pudding.	6	Bird's Nest Pudding.	6
Washington Pie.	6	Sunderland Pudding.	6	Brown Dumpling.	6
Cup Custards.	6	Baked Rice Pudding.	6	Floating Island.	6
Corn Starch Pudding.	6	Boiled Rice Pudding.	6		

DRINKS.

Tea, Coffee and Milk, each.	3	Scotch Ale.	25	Porter.	6
Claret, per glass.	13	London Porter.	25	Cider.	6
Hungarian Wine.	13	Ale.	6		

☞ 40 Lodging Rooms for Gentlemen, by the Day or Week.

SEPARATE BILL OF FARE FOR BREAKFAST AND SUPPER.

Separate Bill of fare

ABOVE **No. 1 Spring Lane, 1859, Boston, Massachusetts**

RIGHT **The Palmer House, 1875, Chicago, Illinois**

Destroyed in the Great Chicago Fire of 1871, the rebuilt hotel, the Palmer House, was much grander—and safer—hence the words "ENTIRELY FIREPROOF" were prominently printed on the menu cover.

Der Neubau des beim großen Brand von Chicago 1871 abgebrannten und dann wieder aufgebauten Hotels Palmer House war sehr viel großzügiger – und feuerfester – als das alte Haus. Auf dem Umschlag der Speisekarte stand deshalb ganz groß: „100 % FEUERFEST".

Détruit lors du grand incendie de Chicago en 1871, l'hôtel Palmer House est reconstruit. Il est plus grand et plus sûr, et le menu s'enorgueillit de l'avertissement suivant: «Construit entièrement à l'épreuve du feu».

PALMER HOUSE.

DINNER--Tuesday, May 25, 1875.

SOUP.

A l'Anglaise. Macaroni.

FISH.

Boiled Lake Trout, Parsley Sauce.
Baked Whitefish, Port Wine Sauce.

BOILED.

Corned Beef.
Chicken, Egg Sauce.
Jole and Spinach.
Sugar Cured Ham.
Leg of Mutton, Caper Sauce.

ROAST.

Beef.
Stuffed Veal.
Turkey, Giblet Sauce.
Loin of Pork, Apple Sauce.
Ham, Champagne Sauce.

COLD.

Smoked Buffalo Tongue. Roast Beef. Corned Beef. Boiled Ham.
Pate of Snipe, with Jelly. Chicken Salad.

RELISHES.

Worcestershire Sauce. Pickles. Olives. French Mustard.
Chow-Chow. Lettuce. Halford Sauce. Horse-radish. Sliced Cucumbers.

ENTREES.

Hashed Lamb, with Poached Eggs.
Fricasse of Turkey Wings.
Baked Pork and Beans.
Salmi of Wild Pigeon.
Croquetties of Rice, Fruit Sauce.
Pork Chops, with Fried Apples.
Frogs, Fried, a la Crapotine.
Macaroni, a l'Italienne.

VEGETABLES.

Mashed Potatoes. Boiled Potatoes. Stewed Parsnips Boiled Rice.
Boiled Onions. Beets. Green Corn. Mashed Turnips.
Spinach. Baked Sweet Potatoes. Stewed Tomatoes. Hominy.
Asparagus.

PASTRY AND CONFECTIONERY.

Tapioca Pudding, Hard Sauce. Steamed Pound Pudding, Brandy Sauce. Rhubarb Pie.
Cocoanut Pie Diamond Rose Cake. Sliced Pound Cake. Chocolate Slices.
Small Queen Cake. Lemon Sponge Drops. Vanilla Ice Cream. Lemon Ice.

DESSERT.

Raisins. English Walnuts. Almonds. Figs. Filberts.
Oranges. Pecans. Pine-apples. Apples.
Coffee.

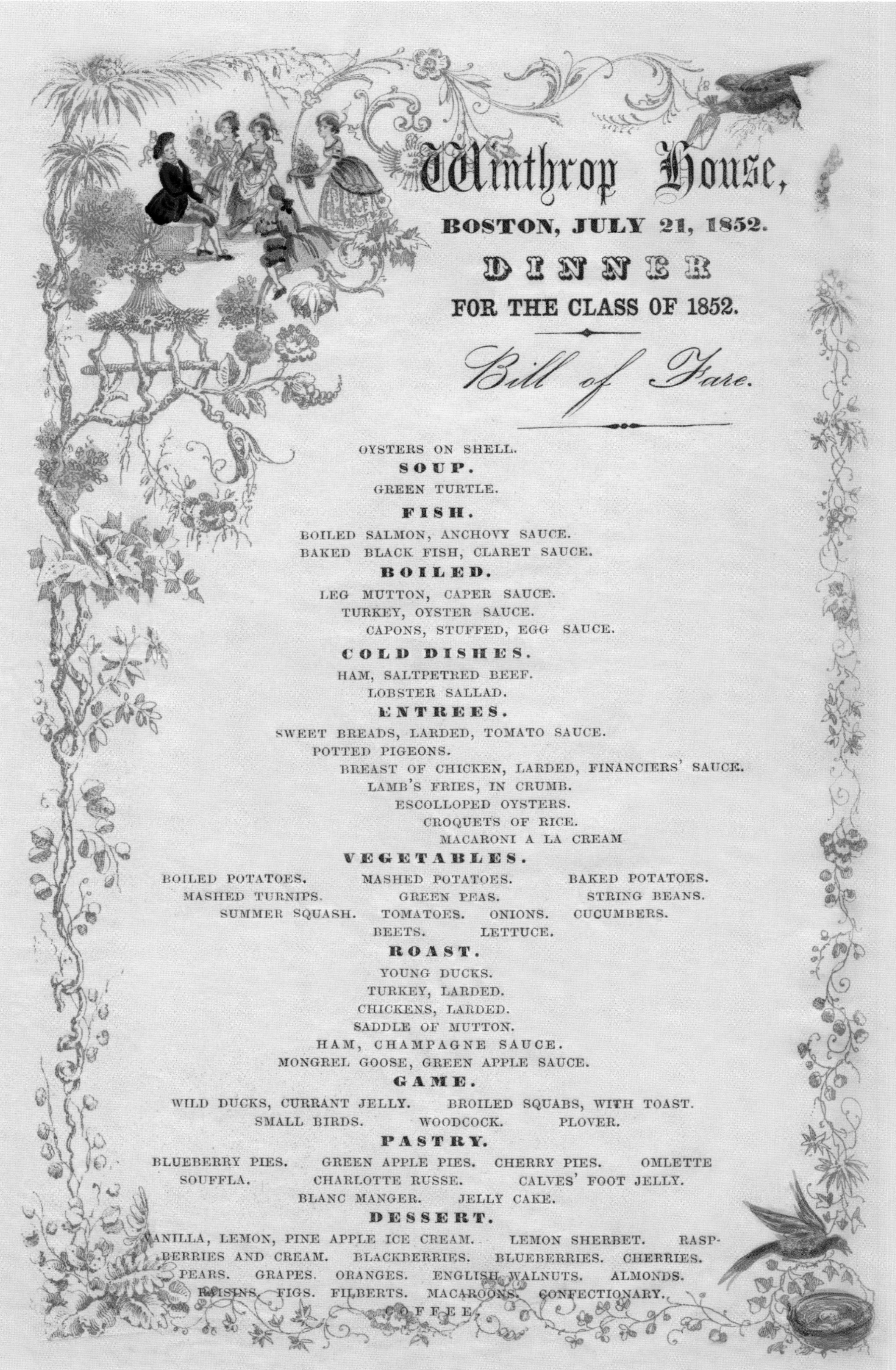

Winthrop House,

BOSTON, JULY 21, 1852.

DINNER

FOR THE CLASS OF 1852.

Bill of Fare.

OYSTERS ON SHELL.

SOUP.

GREEN TURTLE.

FISH.

BOILED SALMON, ANCHOVY SAUCE.
BAKED BLACK FISH, CLARET SAUCE.

BOILED.

LEG MUTTON, CAPER SAUCE.
TURKEY, OYSTER SAUCE.
CAPONS, STUFFED, EGG SAUCE.

COLD DISHES.

HAM, SALTPETRED BEEF.
LOBSTER SALLAD.

ENTREES.

SWEET BREADS, LARDED, TOMATO SAUCE.
POTTED PIGEONS.
BREAST OF CHICKEN, LARDED, FINANCIERS' SAUCE.
LAMB'S FRIES, IN CRUMB.
ESCOLLOPED OYSTERS.
CROQUETS OF RICE.
MACARONI A LA CREAM

VEGETABLES.

BOILED POTATOES. MASHED POTATOES. BAKED POTATOES.
MASHED TURNIPS. GREEN PEAS. STRING BEANS.
SUMMER SQUASH. TOMATOES. ONIONS. CUCUMBERS.
BEETS. LETTUCE.

ROAST.

YOUNG DUCKS.
TURKEY, LARDED.
CHICKENS, LARDED.
SADDLE OF MUTTON.
HAM, CHAMPAGNE SAUCE.
MONGREL GOOSE, GREEN APPLE SAUCE.

GAME.

WILD DUCKS, CURRANT JELLY. BROILED SQUABS, WITH TOAST.
SMALL BIRDS. WOODCOCK. PLOVER.

PASTRY.

BLUEBERRY PIES. GREEN APPLE PIES. CHERRY PIES. OMLETTE SOUFFLA. CHARLOTTE RUSSE. CALVES' FOOT JELLY.
BLANC MANGER. JELLY CAKE.

DESSERT.

VANILLA, LEMON, PINE APPLE ICE CREAM. LEMON SHERBET. RASPBERRIES AND CREAM. BLACKBERRIES. BLUEBERRIES. CHERRIES. PEARS. GRAPES. ORANGES. ENGLISH WALNUTS. ALMONDS. RAISINS. FIGS. FILBERTS. MACAROONS. CONFECTIONARY.

COFFEE.

OPPOSITE Dinner for the Class of 1852, Winthrop House, 1852, Boston, Massachusetts

BELOW Lindell Hotel, 1863, St. Louis, Missouri

The Lindell Hotel opened November 25, 1863, and was called "the largest hotel in the United States" and one of the most expensive, at a cost of $1.5 million. Its banquet hall could hold 3,000 guests. St. Louis was not occupied during the Civil War, but a mysterious fire destroyed the hotel on March 30, 1867. This menu reflects a fairly restrained list of dishes, almost all in the American, rather than French, style. Note the service of prairie chickens, a species of American grouse.

Das Lindell Hotel öffnete am 25. November 1863 seine Pforten, das „größte Hotel der USA" und mit Baukosten von 1,5 Mio. Dollar eines der teuersten. Im Festsaal fanden 3000 Gäste Platz. St. Louis wurde im Bürgerkrieg nicht besetzt, dennoch brannte das Hotel am 30. März 1867 aus ungeklärter Ursache ab. Auf der Karte wird eine nicht allzu große Auswahl an amerikanischen Speisen angeboten, keine französische Küche. Man beachte das *prairie chicken*, eine amerikanische Rebhuhnart.

Le Lindell Hotel ouvre le 25 novembre 1863. Il est baptisé « le plus grand hôtel des États-Unis » et c'est également l'un des plus coûteux avec des travaux estimés à 1,5 million de dollars. Sa salle de réception pouvait accueillir 3 000 invités. Saint-Louis ne fut pas occupé pendant la guerre de Sécession, mais un mystérieux incendie détruisit l'hôtel le 30 mars 1867. Ce menu présente une liste assez sobre de plats, la plupart dans un style américain plutôt que français. On notera la présence de tétras des prairies, une espèce américaine de coq de bruyère.

ABOVE Willards' Hotel, 1862, Washington, DC

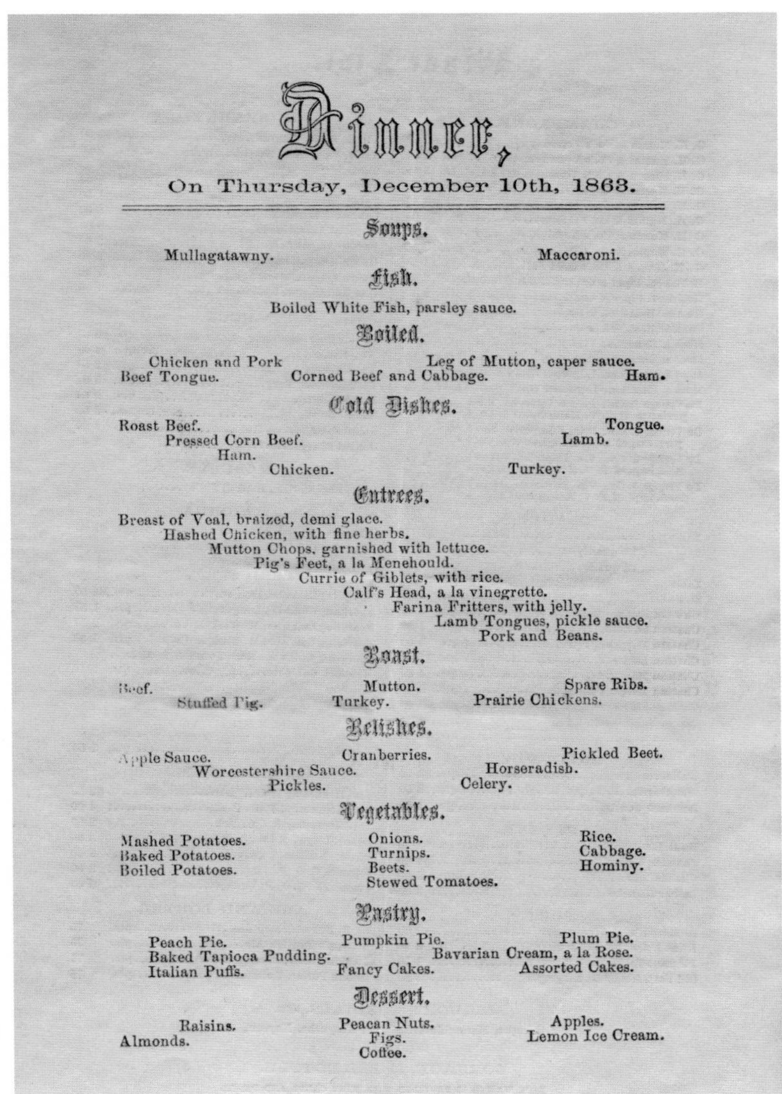

Dinner,

On Thursday, December 10th, 1863.

Soups.

Mullagatawny. Maccaroni.

Fish.

Boiled White Fish, parsley sauce.

Boiled.

Chicken and Pork. Leg of Mutton, caper sauce.
Beef Tongue. Corned Beef and Cabbage. Ham.

Cold Dishes.

Roast Beef. Tongue.
Pressed Corn Beef. Lamb.
Ham.
Chicken. Turkey.

Entrees.

Breast of Veal, braized, demi glace.
Hashed Chicken, with fine herbs.
Mutton Chops, garnished with lettuce.
Pig's Feet, a la Menehould.
Currie of Giblets, with rice.
Calf's Head, a la vinegrette.
Farina Fritters, with jelly.
Lamb Tongues, pickle sauce.
Pork and Beans.

Roast.

Beef. Mutton. Spare Ribs.
Stuffed Pig. Turkey. Prairie Chickens.

Relishes.

Apple Sauce. Cranberries. Pickled Beet.
Worcestershire Sauce. Horseradish.
Pickles. Celery.

Vegetables.

Mashed Potatoes. Onions. Rice.
Baked Potatoes. Turnips. Cabbage.
Boiled Potatoes. Beets. Hominy.
Stewed Tomatoes.

Pastry.

Peach Pie. Pumpkin Pie. Plum Pie.
Baked Tapioca Pudding. Bavarian Cream, a la Rose.
Italian Puffs. Fancy Cakes. Assorted Cakes.

Dessert.

Raisins. Peacan Nuts. Apples.
Almonds. Figs. Lemon Ice Cream.
Coffee.

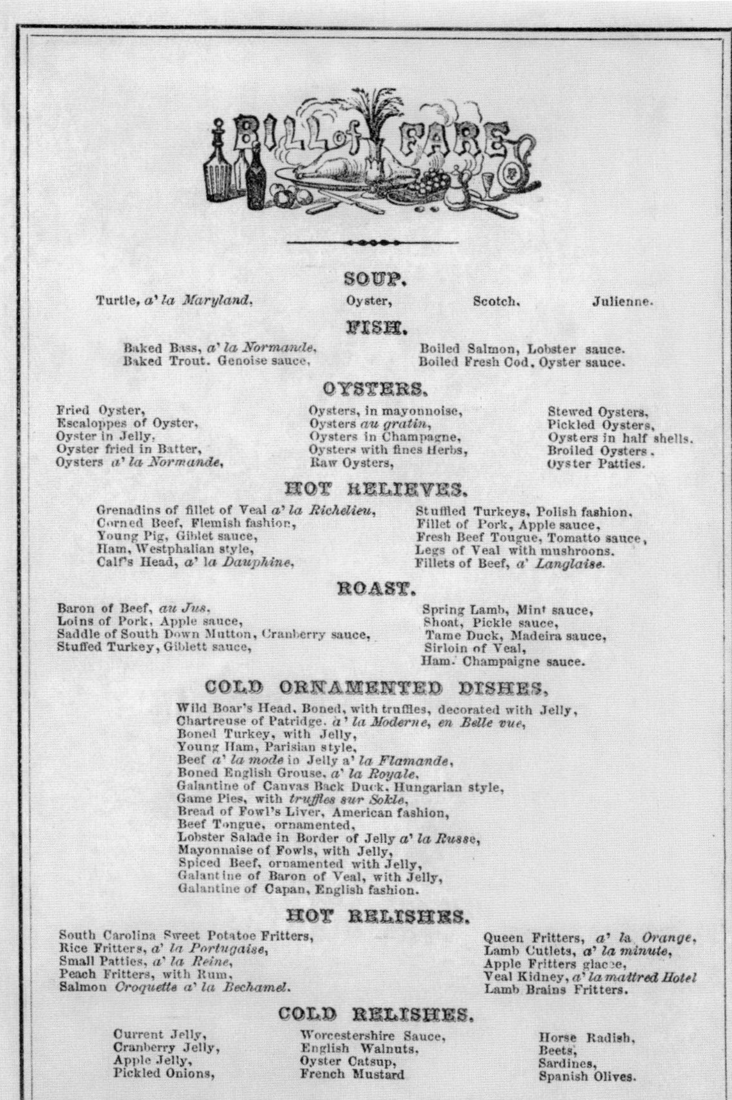

BILL of FARE

SOUP.

Turtle, *a' la Maryland*, Oyster, Scotch. Julienne.

FISH.

Baked Bass, *a' la Normande*,
Baked Trout. Genoise sauce,
Boiled Salmon, Lobster sauce.
Boiled Fresh Cod, Oyster sauce.

OYSTERS.

Fried Oyster,
Escaloppes of Oyster,
Oyster in Jelly,
Oyster fried in Batter,
Oysters *a' la Normande*,
Oysters, in mayonnoise,
Oysters *au gratin*,
Oysters in Champagne,
Oysters with fines Herbs,
Raw Oysters,
Stewed Oysters,
Pickled Oysters,
Oysters in half shells.
Broiled Oysters.
Oyster Patties.

HOT RELIEVES.

Grenadins of fillet of Veal *a' la Richelieu*,
Corned Beef, Flemish fashion,
Young Pig, Giblet sauce,
Ham, Westphalian style,
Calf's Head, a' la *Dauphine*,
Stuffed Turkeys, Polish fashion.
Fillet of Pork, Apple sauce,
Fresh Beef Tougue, Tomatto sauce,
Legs of Veal with mushroons.
Fillets of Beef, *a' Langlaise.*

ROAST.

Baron of Beef, *au Jus.*
Loins of Pork, Apple sauce,
Saddle of South Down Mutton, Cranberry sauce,
Stuffed Turkey, Giblett sauce,
Spring Lamb, Mint sauce,
Shoat, Pickle sauce,
Tame Duck, Madeira sauce,
Sirloin of Veal,
Ham. Champaigne sauce.

COLD ORNAMENTED DISHES,

Wild Boar's Head. Boned, with truffles, decorated with Jelly,
Chartreuse of Patridge. *a' la Moderne, en Belle vue*,
Boned Turkey, with Jelly,
Young Ham, Parisian style,
Beef *a' la mode* in Jelly a' *la Flamande*,
Boned English Grouse, *a' la Royale*.
Galantine of Canvas Back Duck. Hungarian style,
Game Pies, with *truffles sur Sokle*,
Bread of Fowl's Liver, American fashion,
Beef Tongue, ornamented,
Lobster Salade in Border of Jelly *a' la Russe*,
Mayonnaise of Fowls, with Jelly,
Spiced Beef, ornamented with Jelly,
Galantine of Baron of Veal, with Jelly,
Galantine of Capan, English fashion.

HOT RELISHES.

South Carolina Sweet Potatoe Fritters,
Rice Fritters, *a' la Portugaise*,
Small Patties, *a' la Reine*,
Peach Fritters, with Rum,
Salmon *Croquette a' la Bechamel*.
Queen Fritters, *a' la Orange*,
Lamb Cutlets, *a' la minute*,
Apple Fritters glacee,
Veal Kidney, *a' la mattred Hotel*
Lamb Brains Fritters.

COLD RELISHES.

Current Jelly,
Cranberry Jelly,
Apple Jelly,
Pickled Onions,
Worcestershire Sauce,
English Walnuts,
Oyster Catsup,
French Mustard
Horse Radish,
Beets,
Sardines,
Spanish Olives.

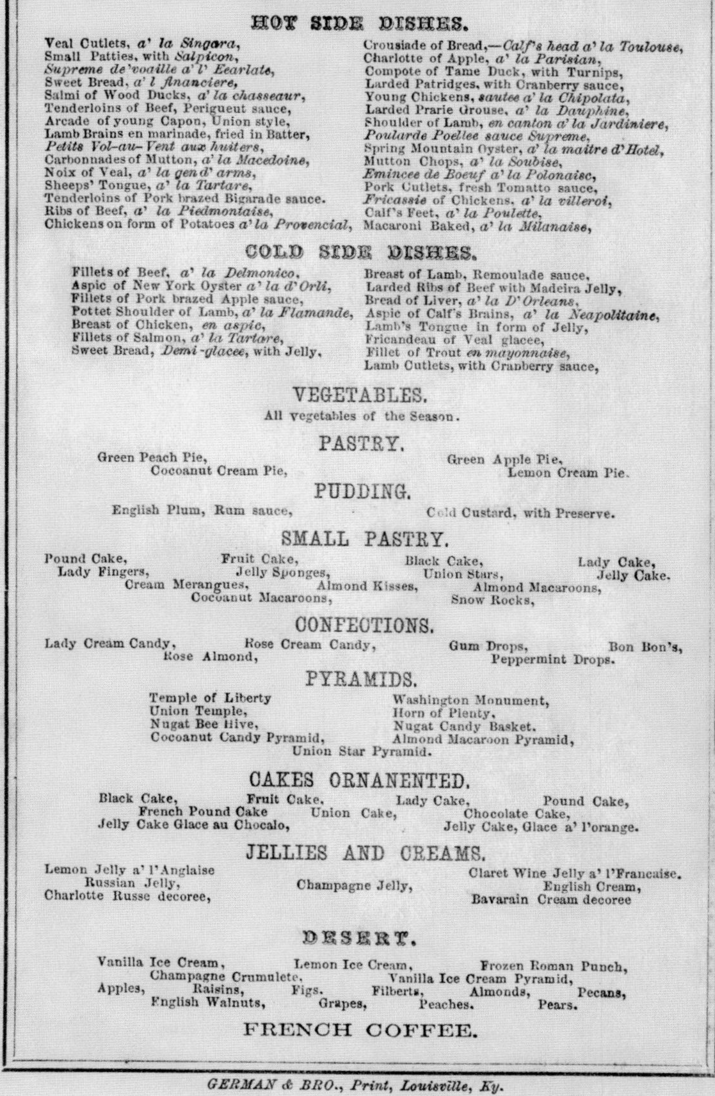

HOT SIDE DISHES.

Veal Cutlets, *a' la Singora*,
Small Patties, with *Salpicon*,
Supreme de'voaille a' l' Eearlate,
Sweet Bread, *a' l financiere*,
Salmi of Wood Ducks, *a' la chasseaur*,
Tenderloins of Beef, Perigueut sauce,
Arcade of young Capon, Union style,
Lamb Brains en marinade, fried in Batter,
Petits Vol-au-Vent aux huiters,
Carbonnades of Mutton, *a' la Macedoine*,
Noix of Veal, *a' la gen d' arms*,
Sheeps' Tongue, *a' la Tartare*,
Tenderloins of Pork brazed Bigarade sauce.
Ribs of Beef, *a' la Piedmontaise*,
Chickens on form of Potatoes *a' la Provencial*,
Crousiade of Bread,—*Calf's head a' la Toulouse*,
Charlotte of Apple, *a' la Parisian*,
Compote of Tame Duck, with Turnips,
Larded Patridges, with Cranberry sauce,
Young Chickens, *sautee a' la Chipolata*,
Larded Prarie Grouse, *a' la Dauphine*,
Shoulder of Lamb, *en canton a' la Jardiniere*,
Poularde Poellee sauce Supreme,
Spring Mountain Oyster, *a' la maitre d'Hotel*,
Mutton Chops, *a' la Soubise*,
Emincee de Boeuf a' la Polonaise,
Pork Cutlets, fresh Tomatto sauce,
Fricassie of Chickens, *a' la villeroi*,
Calf's Feet, *a' la Poulette*,
Macaroni Baked, *a' la Milanaise*,

COLD SIDE DISHES.

Fillets of Beef, *a' la Delmonico*,
Aspic of New York Oyster *a' la d'Orli*,
Fillets of Pork brazed Apple sauce,
Pottet Shoulder of Lamb, *a' la Flamande*,
Breast of Chicken, *en aspic*,
Fillets of Salmon, *a' la Tartare*,
Sweet Bread, *Demi-glacee*, with Jelly,
Breast of Lamb, Remoulade sauce,
Larded Ribs of Beef with Madeira Jelly,
Bread of Liver, *a' la D'Orleans*,
Aspic of Calf's Brains, *a' la Neapolitaine*,
Lamb's Tongue in form of Jelly,
Fricandeau of Veal glacee,
Fillet of Trout *en mayonnaise*,
Lamb Cutlets, with Cranberry sauce,

VEGETABLES.

All vegetables of the Season.

PASTRY.

Green Peach Pie, Cocoanut Cream Pie, Green Apple Pie, Lemon Cream Pie.

PUDDING.

English Plum, Rum sauce, Cold Custard, with Preserve.

SMALL PASTRY.

Pound Cake, Fruit Cake, Black Cake, Lady Cake,
Lady Fingers, Jelly Sponges, Union Stars, Jelly Cake.
Cream Merangues, Almond Kisses, Almond Macaroons,
Cocoanut Macaroons, Snow Rocks,

CONFECTIONS.

Lady Cream Candy, Rose Cream Candy, Gum Drops, Bon Bon's,
Rose Almond, Peppermint Drops.

PYRAMIDS.

Temple of Liberty
Union Temple,
Nugat Bee Hive,
Cocoanut Candy Pyramid,
Washington Monument,
Horn of Plenty,
Nugat Candy Basket.
Almond Macaroon Pyramid,
Union Star Pyramid.

CAKES ORNANENTED.

Black Cake, Fruit Cake, Lady Cake, Pound Cake,
French Pound Cake Union Cake, Chocolate Cake,
Jelly Cake Glace au Chocalo, Jelly Cake, Glace a' l'orange.

JELLIES AND CREAMS.

Lemon Jelly a' l'Anglaise
Russian Jelly,
Charlotte Russe decoree,
Champagne Jelly,
Claret Wine Jelly a' l'Francaise.
English Cream,
Bavarain Cream decoree

DESERT.

Vanilla Ice Cream, Lemon Ice Cream, Frozen Roman Punch,
Champagne Crumulete, Vanilla Ice Cream Pyramid,
Apples, Raisins, Figs. Filberts, Almonds, Pecans,
English Walnuts, Grapes, Peaches. Pears.

FRENCH COFFEE.

GERMAN & BRO., Print, Louisville, Ky.

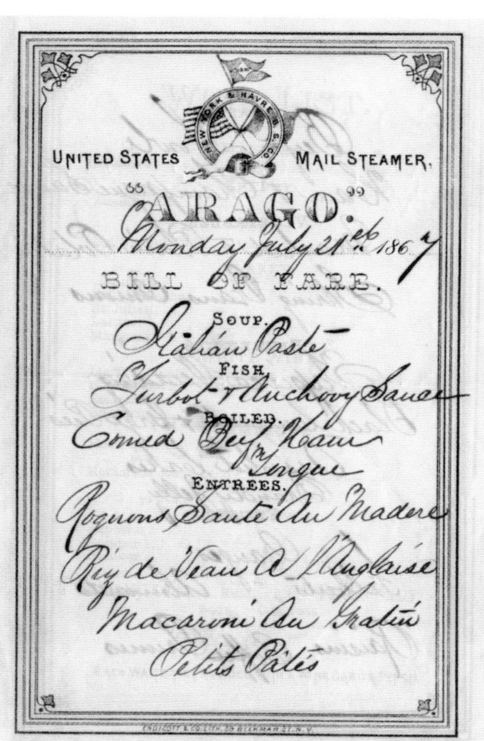

UNITED STATES MAIL STEAMER,

"ARAGO."

Monday July 21st 1867

BILL OF FARE.

SOUP.

Italian Paste

FISH.

Turbot & Anchovy Sauce

BOILED.

Corned Beef & Ham
Tongue

ENTREES.

Rognons Sauté Au Madere
Ris de Veau A l'Anglaise
Macaroni Au Gratin
Petits Pâtés

ABOVE & OPPOSITE Reception Banquet, Louisville Hotel, 1866, Louisville, Kentucky

This menu honors President Andrew Johnson, who took office after Lincoln's assassination, and his cabinet. While the menu is thoroughly in the French culinary style, the sculptural desserts called "pyramids" honor the occasion with names such as "Temple of Liberty" and "Washington Monument."

Dieser Empfang wurde zu Ehren von Präsident Andrew Johnson, der sein Amt nach der Ermordung Lincolns antrat, und seines Kabinetts veranstaltet. Die Speisenfolge ist stark französisch beeinflusst, doch die skulpturartigen „Pyramiden" zum Nachtisch tragen zur Feier des Tages Namen wie „Tempel der Freiheit" und „Washington Monument".

Ce menu rend hommage au président Andrew Johnson et à son cabinet, au pouvoir depuis l'assassinat de Lincoln. Les plats sont typiquement français, mais les desserts sculpturaux, baptisés « Pyramides », font honneur à cet événement spécial. Ils portent des noms tels que « Temple de la liberté » et « Monument à Washington ».

LEFT "Arago," 1867

Reception Banquet
at Louisville Hotel.
Tuesday
Sept. 11th 1866
JOHNSON.
FARRAGUT.
GRANT.
SEWARD.
Complimentary
TO
Prest. Johnson and his Cabinet,
Genl. Grant, Admiral Farragut,
AND OTHER
Distinguished Officers and Citizens.
German Bro, Lith

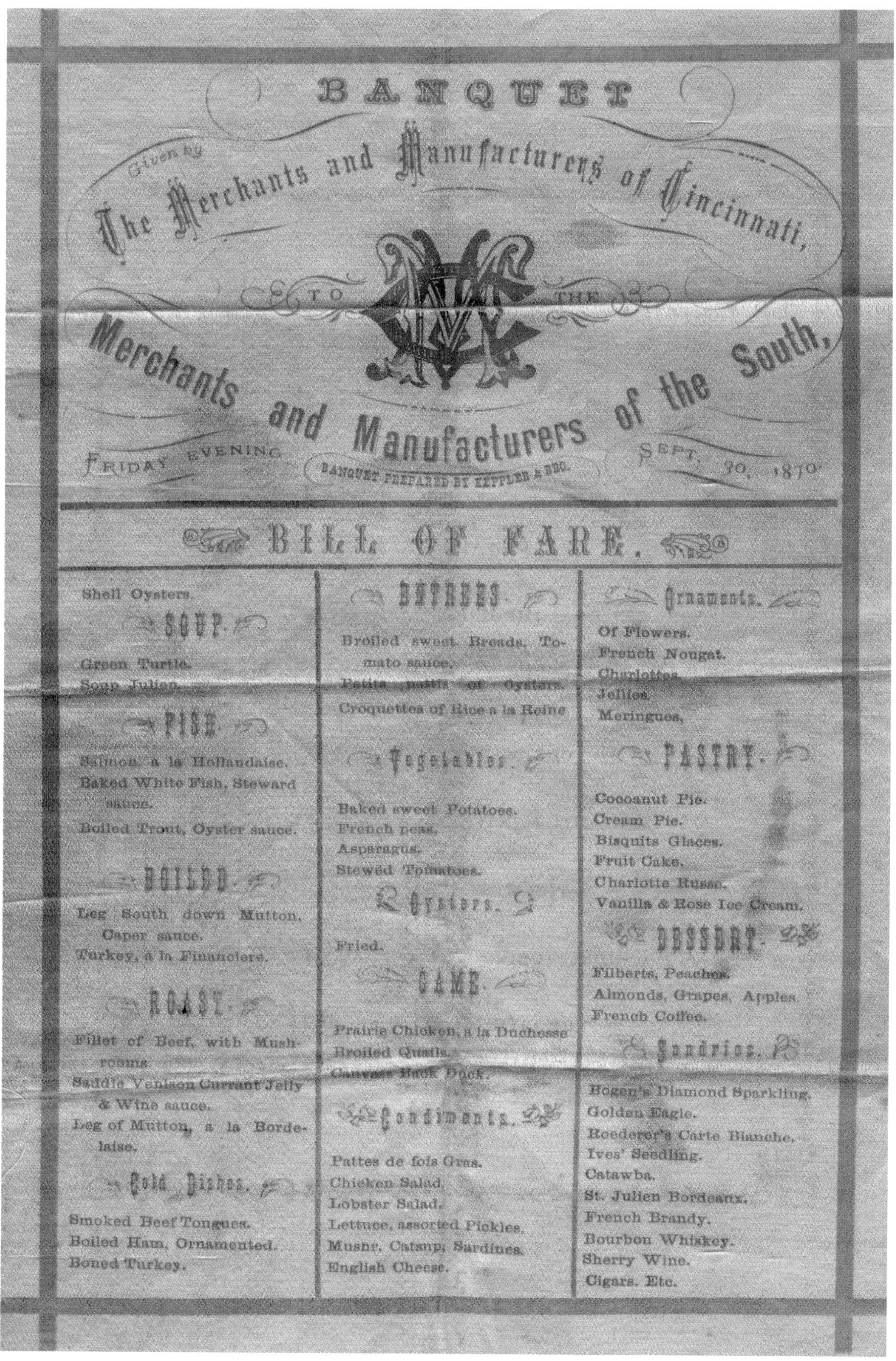

BANQUET

Given by

The Merchants and Manufacturers of Cincinnati,

TO THE

Merchants and Manufacturers of the South,

FRIDAY EVENING SEPT. 30, 1870.

BANQUET PREPARED BY KEPPLER & BRO.

BILL OF FARE.

Shell Oysters.

SOUP.

Green Turtle.
Soup Julien.

FISH.

Salmon, a la Hollandaise.
Baked White Fish, Steward sauce.
Boiled Trout, Oyster sauce.

BOILED.

Leg South down Mutton, Caper sauce.
Turkey, a la Financiere.

ROAST.

Fillet of Beef, with Mushrooms.
Saddle Venison Currant Jelly & Wine sauce.
Leg of Mutton, a la Bordelaise.

Cold Dishes.

Smoked Beef Tongues.
Boiled Ham, Ornamented.
Boned Turkey.

ENTREES.

Broiled sweet Breads, Tomato sauce.
Patits patti's of Oysters.
Croquettes of Rice a la Reine.

Vegetables.

Baked sweet Potatoes.
French peas.
Asparagus.
Stewed Tomatoes.

Oysters.

Fried.

GAME.

Prairie Chicken, a la Duchesse
Broiled Quails.
Canvass Back Duck.

Condiments.

Pattes de fois Gras.
Chicken Salad.
Lobster Salad.
Lettuce, assorted Pickles.
Musnr. Catsup, Sardines.
English Cheese.

Ornaments.

Of Flowers.
French Nougat.
Charlottes.
Jellies.
Meringues.

PASTRY.

Cocoanut Pie.
Cream Pie.
Bisquits Glaces.
Fruit Cake.
Charlotte Russe.
Vanilla & Rose Ice Cream.

DESSERT.

Filberts, Peaches.
Almonds, Grapes, Apples.
French Coffee.

Sundries.

Bogen's Diamond Sparkling.
Golden Eagle.
Roederer's Carte Blanche.
Ives' Seedling.
Catawba.
St. Julien Bordeaux.
French Brandy.
Bourbon Whiskey.
Sherry Wine.
Cigars. Etc.

ABOVE **Faneuil Hall Market, 1876, Boston, Massachusetts**

RIGHT **Christmas Dinner, International Hotel, 1869, San Francisco, California**

BELOW **Acker, Merrall & Condit, 1874, New York, New York**

NET CASH. CURRENCY.

May 11th, 1874.

ACKER, MERRALL & CONDIT,

Importers of

WINES and CIGARS,

Chambers Street and College Place,

And BROADWAY and FORTY-SECOND STREET,

NEW YORK.

TRADE PRICE LIST FOR GOODS IN GLASS.

CHAMPAGNES.

Moet & Chandon's	Qts.	Pts.	L. Roederer's	Qts.	Pts.
Extra Dry Cabinet........	$25 50	$27 50	Carte Blanche...........	$27 00	$29 50
Dry Imperial............	24 50	26 50	Imperial.....	26 00	28 50
Imperial................	24 50	26 50	Cabinet.................	25 50	28 00
Verzenay	22 00	24 00	Dry Sillery.............	24 50	27 00
Dry Sillery.............	22 00	24 00	" Schreider...........	24 00	26 50
			Heidsieck.		
RUINART VERZENAY.....	22 25	24 25	Charles' Extra Dry......	25 50	27 50
DELMONICO.............	25 00	27 00	" Dry Sillery......	21 50	23 50
CLICQUOT..............	25 50	27 50	Heidsieck & Co., Sillery..	21 50	23 50
NAPOLEON CABINET......	23 50	25 50	" Monopole	26 00	28 00
MONTEBELLO	21 50	23 50	Piper & Co..............	24 00	26 00
			Pommery & Greno		
G. H. Mumm's			Carte Blanche...........	28 50	30 50
Extra Dry...............	25 00	27 00	Dry	28 50	30 50
Dry Verzenay...........	23 00	25 00	KRUG & CO............	22 50	25 50
Gold Lack.			Delmonico.		
Half Pints, (4 Doz.)......		28 00	Half Pints, (4 Doz.)......		28 00

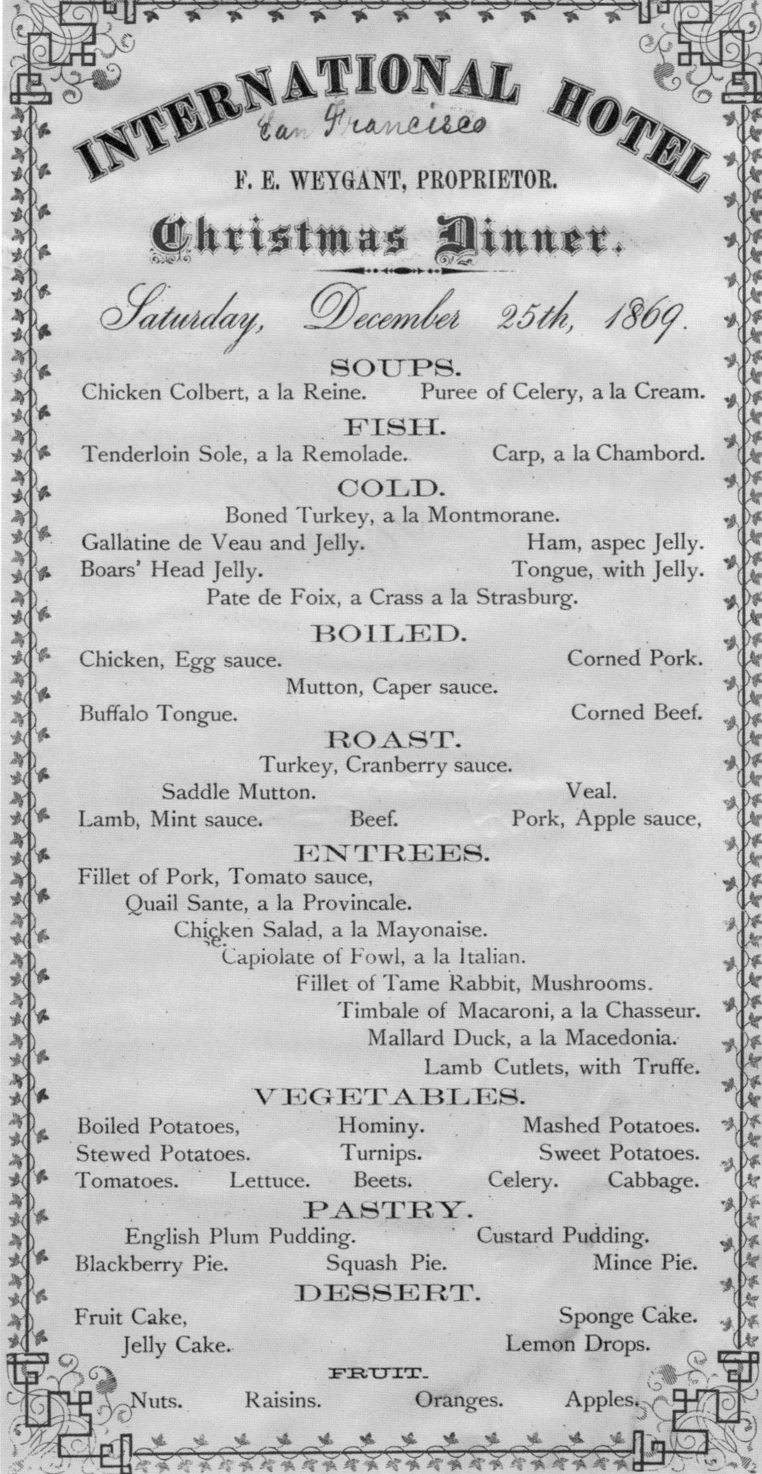

INTERNATIONAL HOTEL

San Francisco

F. E. WEYGANT, PROPRIETOR.

Christmas Dinner.

Saturday, December 25th, 1869.

SOUPS.

Chicken Colbert, a la Reine. Puree of Celery, a la Cream.

FISH.

Tenderloin Sole, a la Remolade. Carp, a la Chambord.

COLD.

Boned Turkey, a la Montmorane.
Gallatine de Veau and Jelly. Ham, aspec Jelly.
Boars' Head Jelly. Tongue, with Jelly.
Pate de Foix, a Crass a la Strasburg.

BOILED.

Chicken, Egg sauce. Corned Pork.
Mutton, Caper sauce.
Buffalo Tongue. Corned Beef.

ROAST.

Turkey, Cranberry sauce.
Saddle Mutton. Veal.
Lamb, Mint sauce. Beef. Pork, Apple sauce,

ENTREES.

Fillet of Pork, Tomato sauce,
Quail Sante, a la Provincale.
Chicken Salad, a la Mayonaise.
Capiolate of Fowl, a la Italian.
Fillet of Tame Rabbit, Mushrooms.
Timbale of Macaroni, a la Chasseur.
Mallard Duck, a la Macedonia.
Lamb Cutlets, with Truffe.

VEGETABLES.

Boiled Potatoes, Hominy. Mashed Potatoes.
Stewed Potatoes. Turnips. Sweet Potatoes.
Tomatoes. Lettuce. Beets. Celery. Cabbage.

PASTRY.

English Plum Pudding. Custard Pudding.
Blackberry Pie. Squash Pie. Mince Pie.

DESSERT.

Fruit Cake, Sponge Cake.
Jelly Cake. Lemon Drops.

FRUIT.

Nuts. Raisins. Oranges. Apples.

OPPOSITE **Banquet Given by the Merchants and Manufacturers of Cincinnati, 1870, Cincinnati, Ohio**

This lavish banquet included oysters shipped by stagecoach along the "Oyster Line." The wines, listed under "Sundries," include domestics from Eastern States, such as Catawba, France's Roederer's champagne and St. Julien Bordeaux.

Bei diesem üppigen Bankett in Cincinnati servierte man auch Austern, die per Postkutsche auf der „Austernlinie" Hunderte von Kilometer weit befördert wurden. Die unter „Verschiedenes" aufgelisteten Weine stammen von der Ostküste (Catawba) und aus Frankreich (Roederer-Champagner und St.-Julien-Bordeaux).

Ce somptueux banquet est préparé par un traiteur local, Keppler & Bro. Les huîtres sont acheminées jusqu'à l'Ohio par la « route de l'huître », puis à bord de péniches le long du canal de l'Erie à partir de 1852. La liste des vins (« sundries », littéralement « divers ») comporte des vins locaux de la côte Est, comme le catawba, ainsi que des crus français (champagne Roederer et bordeaux Saint-Julien).

E PLURIBUS UNUM
1870.
Society of the
ARMY OF THE
CUMBERLAND.
BANQUET.
Friday Evening, November 25
CLEVELAND, OHIO.
ARMY OF THE CUMBERLAND
Lith. by Sanford & Hayward, Cleveland, O.

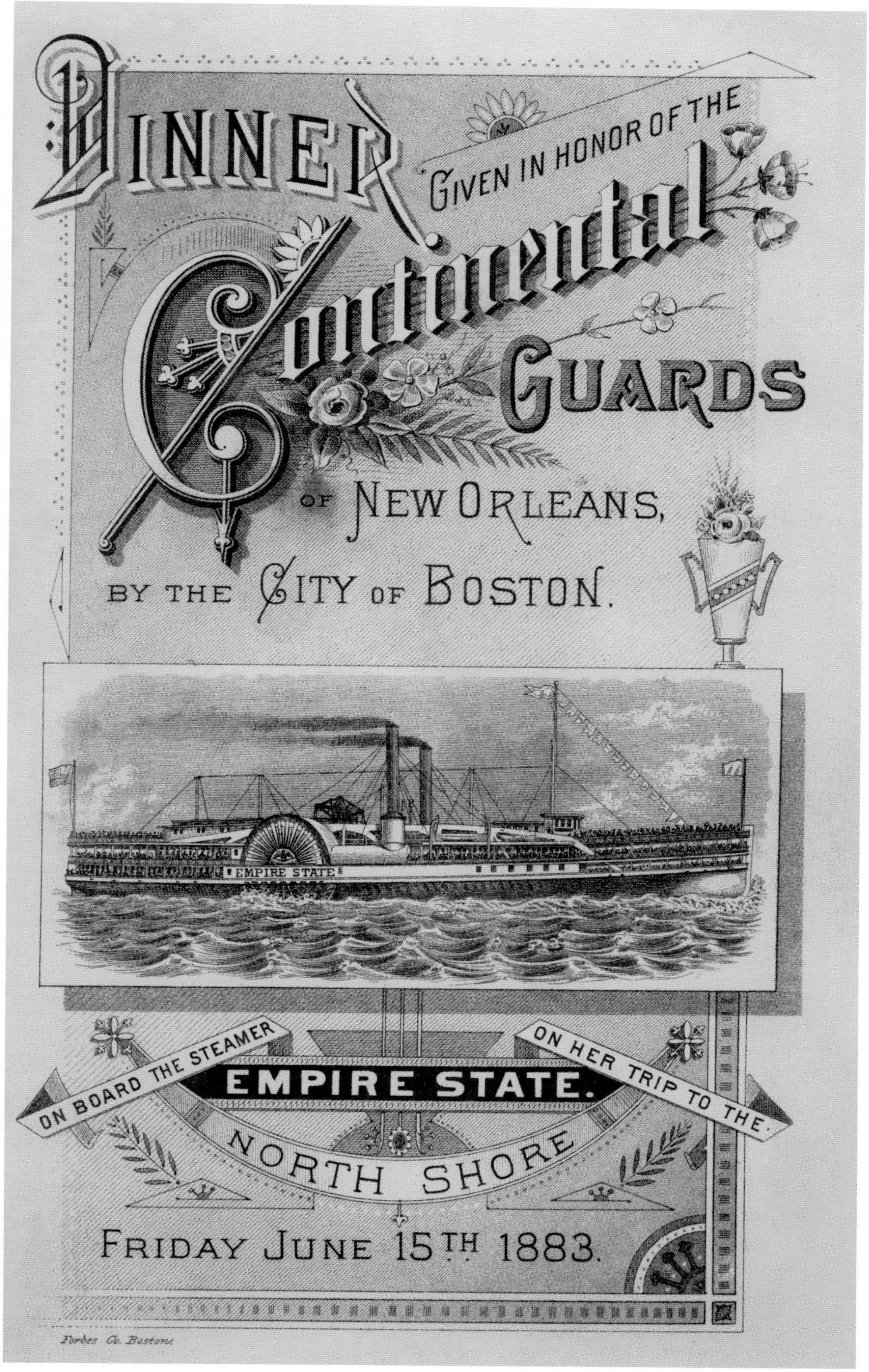

OPPOSITE **Society of the Army of the Cumberland Banquet, 1870, Cleveland, Ohio**

ABOVE **Hotel Nantasket, 1881, Boston, Massachusetts**

DINNER GIVEN IN HONOR OF THE
Continental
GUARDS
OF NEW ORLEANS,
BY THE CITY OF BOSTON.

EMPIRE STATE

ON BOARD THE STEAMER
EMPIRE STATE.
ON HER TRIP TO THE
NORTH SHORE
FRIDAY JUNE 15TH 1883.

Forbes Co. Boston

ABOVE **Dinner Given in Honor of the Continental Guards of New Orleans by the City of Boston, *Empire State*, 1883**

Aboard the steamer *Empire State*, the Continental Guards, a New Orleans Mardi Gras organization, were fêted and later appeared in a Revolutionary War costumed tableaux in Boston at Faneuil Hall.

An Bord des Dampfschiffs *M. S. Empire State* wurden die Continental Guards gefeiert, ein Karnevalsverein vom Mardi Gras in New Orleans, der anschließend in Revolutionskostümen in der Bostoner Faneuil Hall auftrat.

À bord du vapeur *Empire State*, les Continental Guards célébraient le mardi gras comme à La Nouvelle-Orléans. Ils apparaissaient ensuite en costume révolutionnaire dans des tableaux vivants au Faneuil Hall de Boston.

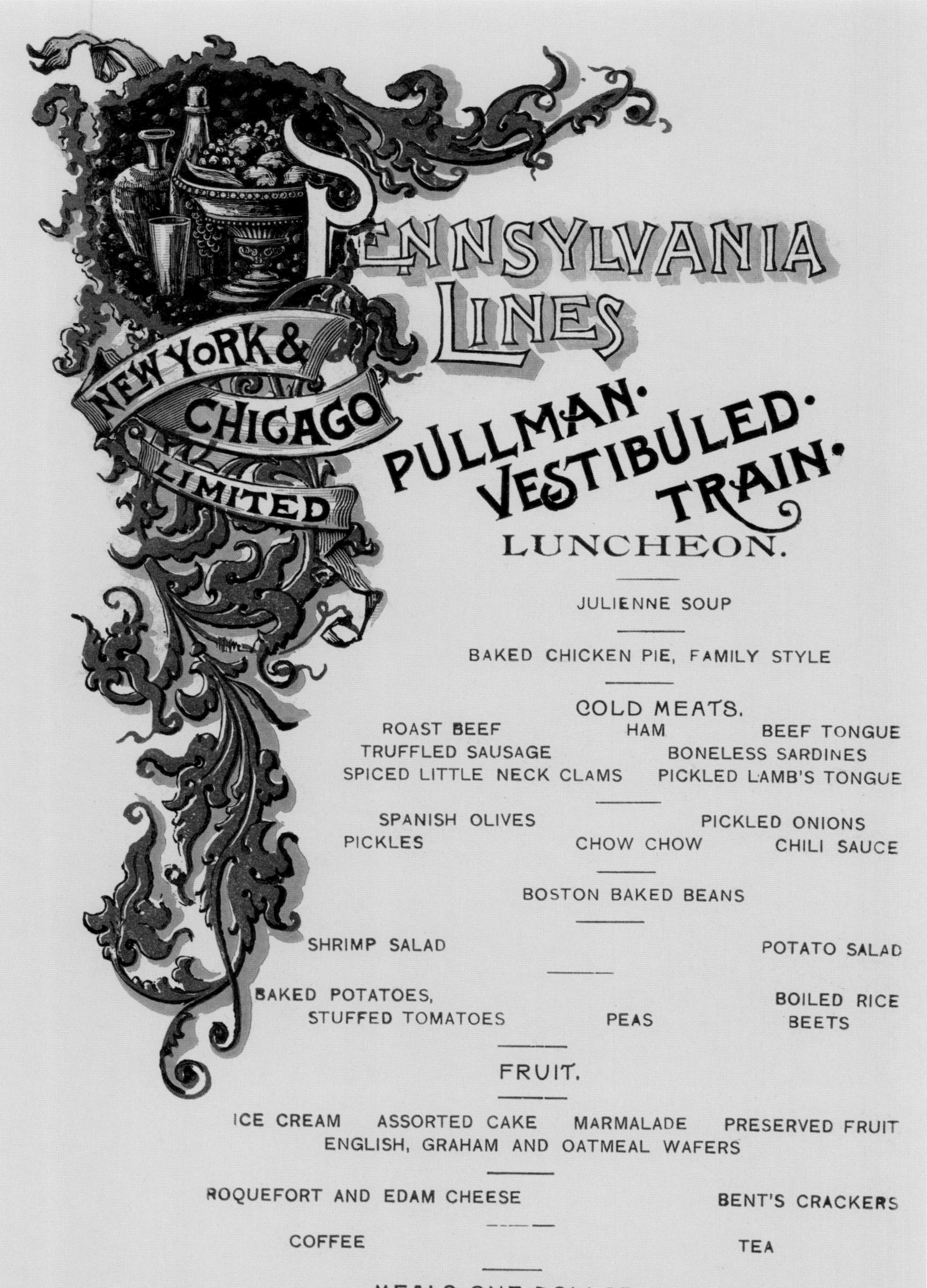

PENNSYLVANIA LINES

NEW YORK & CHICAGO LIMITED

PULLMAN. VESTIBULED. TRAIN.

LUNCHEON.

JULIENNE SOUP

BAKED CHICKEN PIE, FAMILY STYLE

COLD MEATS.

ROAST BEEF HAM BEEF TONGUE
TRUFFLED SAUSAGE BONELESS SARDINES
SPICED LITTLE NECK CLAMS PICKLED LAMB'S TONGUE

SPANISH OLIVES PICKLED ONIONS
PICKLES CHOW CHOW CHILI SAUCE

BOSTON BAKED BEANS

SHRIMP SALAD POTATO SALAD

BAKED POTATOES, BOILED RICE
STUFFED TOMATOES PEAS BEETS

FRUIT.

ICE CREAM ASSORTED CAKE MARMALADE PRESERVED FRUIT
ENGLISH, GRAHAM AND OATMEAL WAFERS

ROQUEFORT AND EDAM CHEESE BENT'S CRACKERS

COFFEE TEA

MEALS ONE DOLLAR.

TABLE WATER FROM THE SILURIAN SPRINGS. WAUKESHA.

PULLMAN DINING CAR "WINDSOR."

BELOW & RIGHT Chicago, Rock Island & Pacific Railroad, c. 1882

The Rock Island Line railroad train carried passengers westward and southward from Chicago. This vest-pocket menu is unusual in that it lists Guinness Stout, which was first exported to the United States after the Civil War.

Die Bahnstrecke der Rock Island Line beförderte Reisende von Chicago Richtung Westen und Süden. Das Ungewöhnliche an dieser Karte im Westentaschenformat ist das Guinness-Bier, das ab den 1870ern in die USA importiert wurde.

Les trains de la Rock Island Line transportent des passagers vers l'ouest et le sud à partir de Chicago. Ce menu de poche est assez rare : on y trouve de la Guinness, bière importée pour la première fois aux États-Unis après la guerre de Sécession.

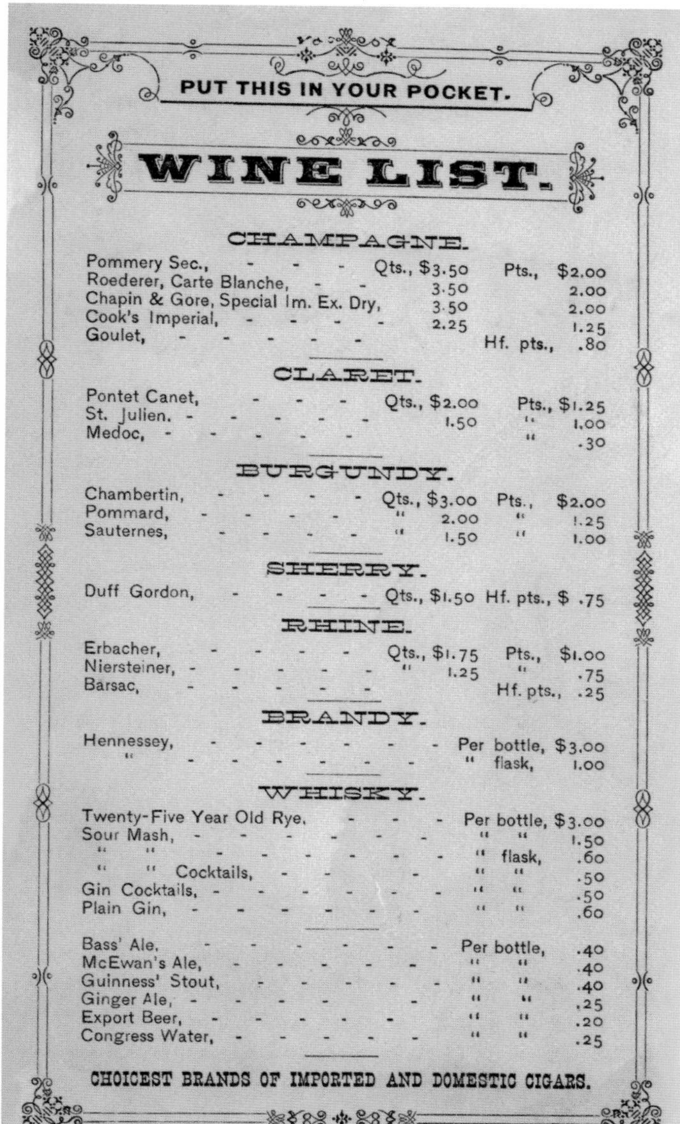

PUT THIS IN YOUR POCKET.

WINE LIST.

CHAMPAGNE.

Pommery Sec., - - - Qts., $3.50 Pts., $2.00
Roederer, Carte Blanche, - - 3.50 2.00
Chapin & Gore, Special Im. Ex. Dry, 3.50 2.00
Cook's Imperial, - - - - 2.25 1.25
Goulet, - - - - - Hf. pts., .80

CLARET.

Pontet Canet, - - - Qts., $2.00 Pts., $1.25
St. Julien. - - - - - 1.50 " 1.00
Medoc, - - - - - " .30

BURGUNDY.

Chambertin, - - - - Qts., $3.00 Pts., $2.00
Pommard, - - - - " 2.00 " 1.25
Sauternes, - - - - - " 1.50 " 1.00

SHERRY.

Duff Gordon, - - - - Qts., $1.50 Hf. pts., $ .75

RHINE.

Erbacher, - - - - Qts., $1.75 Pts., $1.00
Niersteiner, - - - - - " 1.25 " .75
Barsac, - - - - - Hf. pts., .25

BRANDY.

Hennessey, - - - - - - Per bottle, $3.00
" - - - - - - - " flask, 1.00

WHISKY.

Twenty-Five Year Old Rye, - - - Per bottle, $3.00
Sour Mash, - - - - - - " " 1.50
" " - - - - - - " flask, .60
" " Cocktails, - - - " " .50
Gin Cocktails, - - - - - - " " .50
Plain Gin, - - - - - - " " .60

Bass' Ale, - - - - - - Per bottle, .40
McEwan's Ale, - - - - - " " .40
Guinness' Stout, - - - - - " " .40
Ginger Ale, - - - - - " " .25
Export Beer, - - - - - " " .20
Congress Water, - - - - - " " .25

CHOICEST BRANDS OF IMPORTED AND DOMESTIC CIGARS.

OPPOSITE Pennsylvania Lines, 1883

ABOVE LEFT Michigan Central Railroad, 1880

ABOVE Special Dinner for the Washington Correspondents of the Leading Newspapers of the United States to the National Republican Convention, Queen City Hotel, 1884, Cumberland, Maryland

This dinner, prepared by the Queen City Hotel, an affiliate of the Baltimore & Ohio Railroad, whose electrified logo "B&O" adorns this highly stylized menu cover, was for a special Washington newspaper-correspondents dinner on their way to the National Republican Convention in Chicago.

Das Dinner fand im Queen City Hotel statt, das von der Baltimore & Ohio Railroad betrieben wurde. Deren elektrisch zuckendes Logo „B&O" ziert die stark stilisierte Karte dieses Banketts für die Korrespondenten der Washingtoner Zeitungen auf der Reise zum Parteitag der Republikaner in Chicago.

Le dîner préparé au Queen City Hotel, affilié à la compagnie ferroviaire Baltimore & Ohio, dont le logo électrifié illumine le menu très stylisé, est donné en l'honneur des correspondants de presse de Washington se rendant à la convention nationale républicaine à Chicago.

BELOW Fifth Avenue Hotel, 1883, New York, New York

OPPOSITE Centropolis Hotel, 1884, Kansas City, Missouri

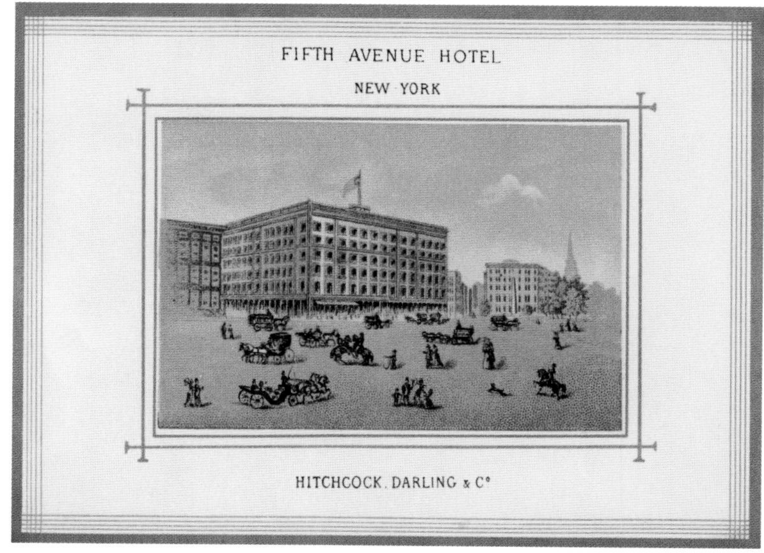

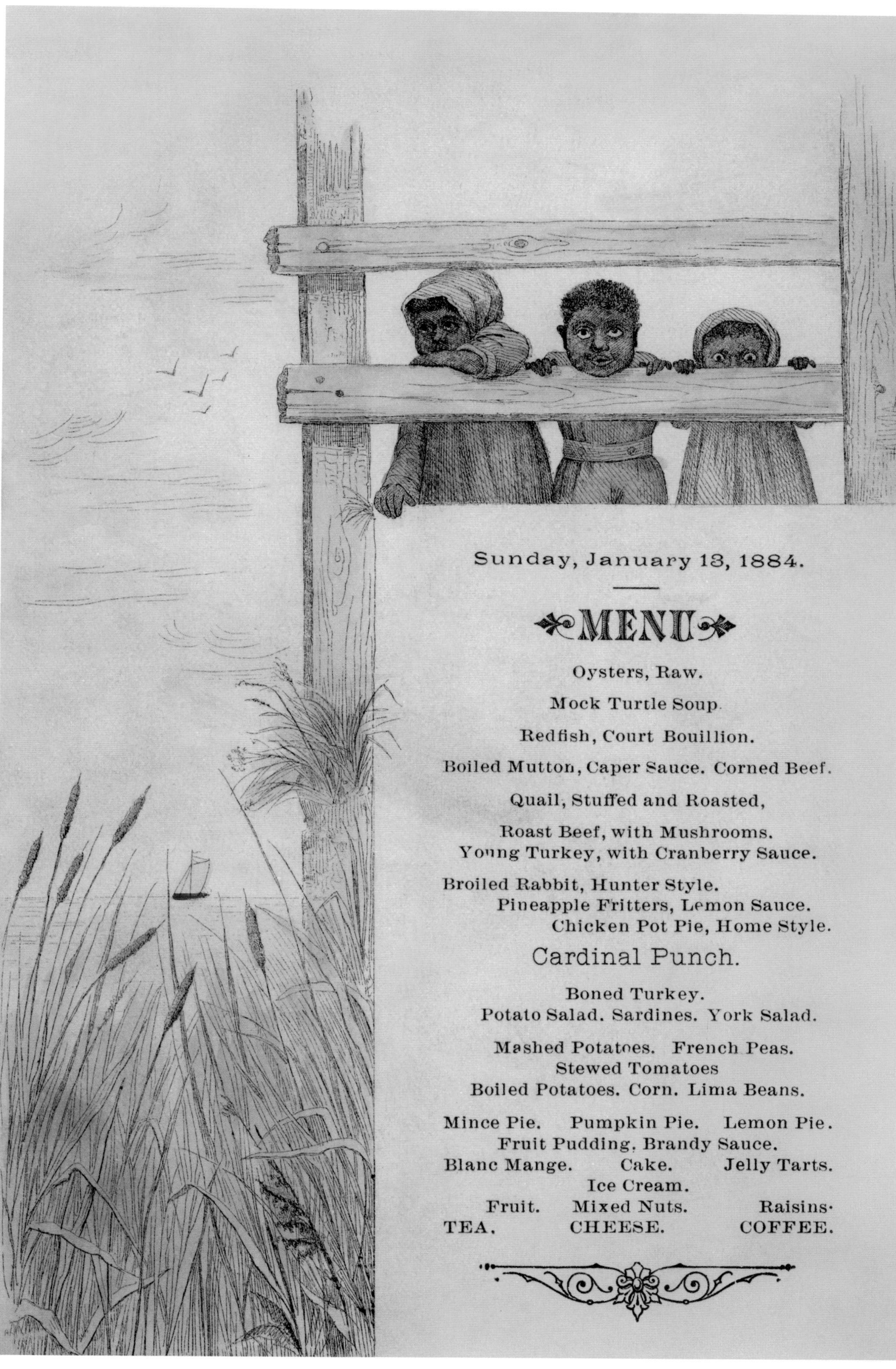

Sunday, January 13, 1884.

MENU

Oysters, Raw.

Mock Turtle Soup.

Redfish, Court Bouillion.

Boiled Mutton, Caper Sauce. Corned Beef.

Quail, Stuffed and Roasted,

Roast Beef, with Mushrooms.
Young Turkey, with Cranberry Sauce.

Broiled Rabbit, Hunter Style.
Pineapple Fritters, Lemon Sauce.
Chicken Pot Pie, Home Style.

Cardinal Punch.

Boned Turkey.
Potato Salad. Sardines. York Salad.

Mashed Potatoes. French Peas.
Stewed Tomatoes
Boiled Potatoes. Corn. Lima Beans.

Mince Pie. Pumpkin Pie. Lemon Pie.
Fruit Pudding, Brandy Sauce.
Blanc Mange. Cake. Jelly Tarts.
Ice Cream.
Fruit. Mixed Nuts. Raisins.
TEA. CHEESE. COFFEE.

ABOVE & OPPOSITE **The Palmer House, 1885, Chicago, Illinois**

RIGHT **The Vendome, 1883, Boston, Massachusetts**

THE
Palmer
THOROUGHLY
FIRE PROOF
MENU
Bluepoints
Anglaise Soup
Kennebec Salmon, a la Hollandaise
SLICED CUCUMBERS
Leg of Mutton, Caper Sauce
Jole and Spinach
Sugar Cured Ham
Roast Beef
Turkey, Cranberry Sauce
Spring Lamb, Mint Sauce
Calf's Head en Tortue
Fried Frogs, a la Crapotine
Small Patties, a la Reine
Sweeetbreads, a la Jardiniere
Timbal of Macaroni
SIBERIAN PUNCH
Roast Mallard Duck
Shrimp Salad
Fresh Lobster
Spiced Oysters
Boned Turkey, with Jelly
Lettuce
Sliced Tomatoes
Currant Jelly
New Boiled Potatoes
New String Beans
Boiled Rice
Asparagus
Mashed Potatoes
New Beets
Stewed Tomatoes
New Green Peas
Fried Oyster Plant
Steamed Plum Pudding, Cognac Sauce
Apple Pie
Cream Meringue Pie
Maderia Wine Jelly
Assorted Cake
Macaroons
Confectionery
Biscuit Glace
STRAWBERRIES AND CREAM
Neufchatel, Roquefort and American Cheese
Fruit
Claret
Raisins
Mixed Nuts
Water Crackers
Coffee
Buttermilk
Chocolate
ONE O'CLOCK
THE PALMER,
CHICAGO.
SUNDAY,
MAY 17. 1885

Bluepoints
Potato Soup — Mutton Broth

Boudin Blanc

Boiled Fresh Cod, Oyster sauce
Baked Lake Trout, Claret sauce

Sugar Cured Ham
Corned Beef and Cabbage — Leg of Mutton Caper sauce
Jowl and Spinach

Roast Beef — Turkey, Cranberry sauce
Loin of Pork, Apple sauce

Calf's Feet a la Vinaigrette
Fricassee of Chicken with Mushrooms
Lamb's Tongue, Tomato sauce
Banana Fritters

Baked Pork and Beans

Peach Sherbet

Roast Mallard Duck

Shrimp Salad — Fresh Lobster — Boned Capon, with Jelly
Spiced Oysters — Cold Roast Beef — Ham — Turkey — Smoked Beef Tongue

Lettuce — Young Onions

Mashed Potatoes — Fried Sweet Potatoes — Boiled Potatoes
Boiled Rice — Cabbage — Pickled Beets
Stewed Onions — Sugar Corn — Fried Oyster Plant
Stewed Tomatoes — Squash

Tapioca Pudding, Hard sauce

Appte Pie — Squash Pie
Jelly Cake — Cream Tartlets — Cerealine Kisses
Maraschino Ice Cream — Swiss Meringues

Fruit — Mixed Nuts — Raisins
CREESE—Roquefort, Neufchatel and Sage
Water Crackers — Coffee — Buttermilk — Chocolate

12.30 O'CLOCK.

Chicago Monday
March 7, 1887.

Union Railroad Ticket Office
in Rotunda of Hotel.

An extra Charge will be made for dishes ordered which are not on the Bill of Fare.

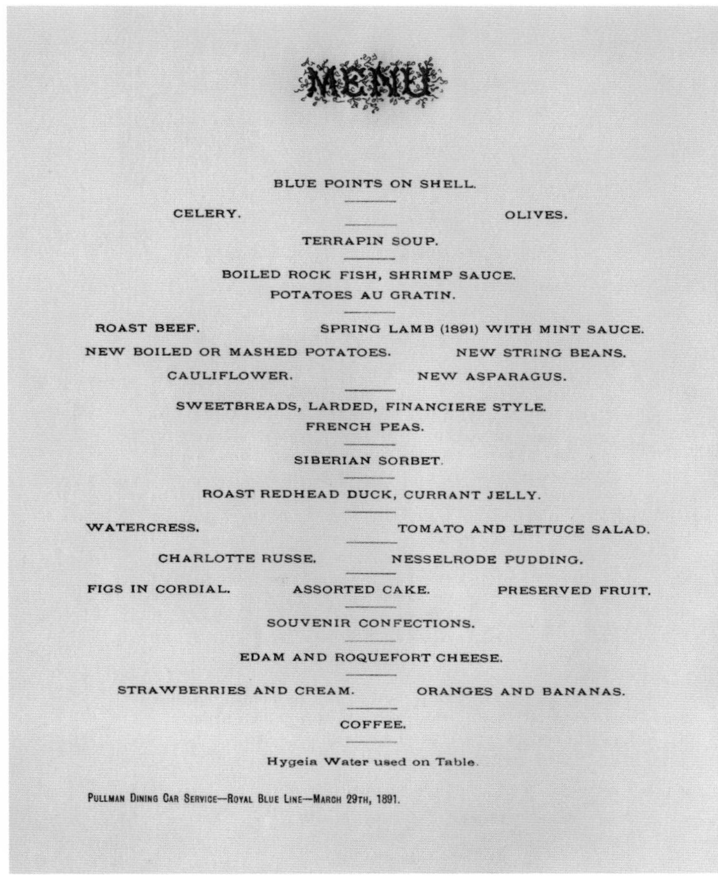

MENU

BLUE POINTS ON SHELL.

CELERY. OLIVES.

TERRAPIN SOUP.

BOILED ROCK FISH, SHRIMP SAUCE.
POTATOES AU GRATIN.

ROAST BEEF. SPRING LAMB (1891) WITH MINT SAUCE.
NEW BOILED OR MASHED POTATOES. NEW STRING BEANS.
CAULIFLOWER. NEW ASPARAGUS.

SWEETBREADS, LARDED, FINANCIERE STYLE.
FRENCH PEAS.

SIBERIAN SORBET.

ROAST REDHEAD DUCK, CURRANT JELLY.

WATERCRESS. TOMATO AND LETTUCE SALAD.

CHARLOTTE RUSSE. NESSELRODE PUDDING.

FIGS IN CORDIAL. ASSORTED CAKE. PRESERVED FRUIT.

SOUVENIR CONFECTIONS.

EDAM AND ROQUEFORT CHEESE.

STRAWBERRIES AND CREAM. ORANGES AND BANANAS.

COFFEE.

Hygeia Water used on Table.

PULLMAN DINING CAR SERVICE—ROYAL BLUE LINE—MARCH 29TH, 1891.

OPPOSITE **Menu, 1887, Chicago, Illinois**

ABOVE **The Royal Blue Line, 1891**

The Royal Blue Line was the ultimate in first-class luxury in the 1890s, and its menu was in the style of the finest land-based restaurants of the era. Terrapin soup was very popular but left American menus during Prohibition because it was laced with sherry. The charlotte russe, originally a French molded dessert of ladyfingers and cream, became, in America, simple sponge cake with whipped cream and maraschino cherries. The bottled Hygeia water came from New York.

Die Royal Blue Line bot in den 1890ern den größten Luxus für Reisende erster Klasse. Die Karte versuchte dem Standard der feinsten Restaurants der Ära zu genügen. Schildkrötensuppe war damals extrem beliebt, verschwand aber mit der Prohibition von amerikanischen Karten, da sie mit Sherry abgeschmeckt wurde. Die Charlotte Russe war ursprünglich ein französisches Dessert aus Sahne und Löffelbiskuits, wurde in Amerika jedoch zum Biskuitkuchen mit Schlagsahne und Maraschinokirschen. In Flaschen abgefülltes Hygeia-Wasser kam aus New York.

La Royal Blue Line est la fine fleur du luxe de première classe dans les années 1890. Son menu s'inspire des plus grands restaurants de l'époque. La soupe de tortue, pourtant très populaire, déserta les menus américains durant la Prohibition, car elle était arrosée de sherry. La charlotte à la russe, dessert français sophistiqué à base de biscuits à la cuiller et de crème Chantilly devient en Amérique une simple génoise, surmontée de crème fouettée et de cerises au marasquin. L'eau en bouteille Hygeia vient de New York.

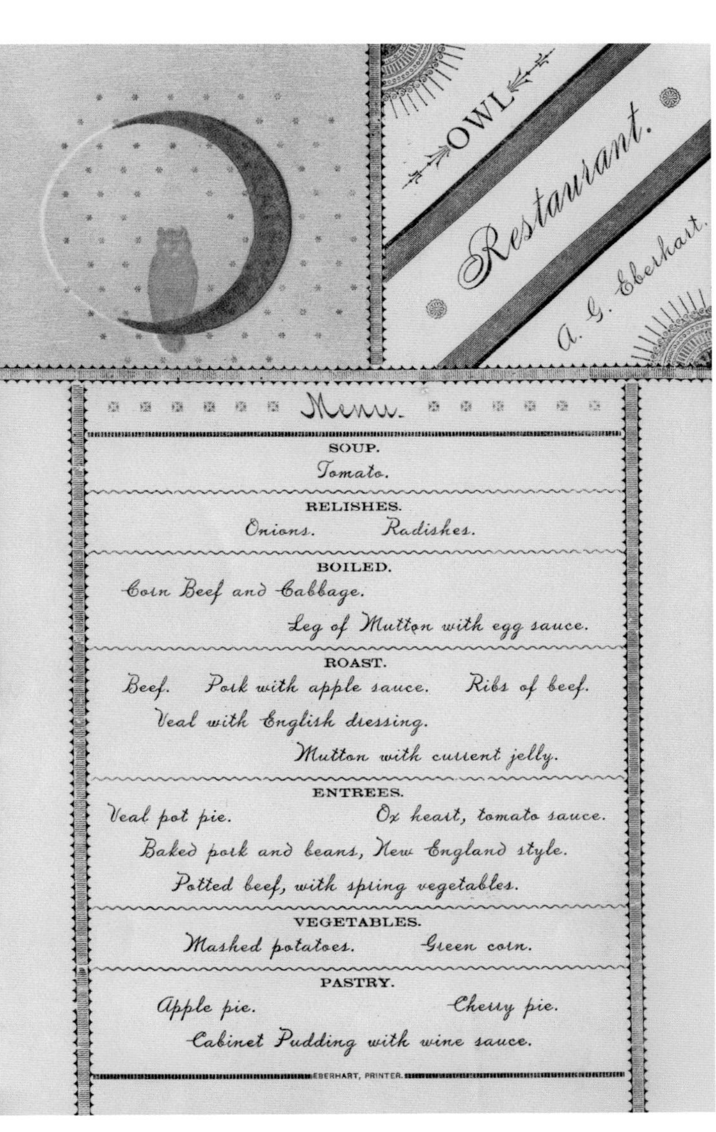

OWL
Restaurant.
A. G. Eberhart.

Menu.

SOUP.
Tomato.

RELISHES.
Onions. Radishes.

BOILED.
Corn Beef and Cabbage.
Leg of Mutton with egg sauce.

ROAST.
Beef. Pork with apple sauce. Ribs of beef.
Veal with English dressing.
Mutton with current jelly.

ENTREES.
Veal pot pie. Ox heart, tomato sauce.
Baked pork and beans, New England style.
Potted beef, with spring vegetables.

VEGETABLES.
Mashed potatoes. Green corn.

PASTRY.
Apple pie. Cherry pie.
Cabinet Pudding with wine sauce.

EBERHART, PRINTER.

RIGHT **Owl Restaurant, c. 1890**

MENU

US

OYSTERS

GREEN TURTLE

PLANKED SHAD — CUCUMBERS

SWEETBREADS
ASPARAGUS TIPS

FILET MIGNON BEARNAISE JARDINIERE
POTATOES PARISIENNE

PUNCH A LA PHILANDER

ROAST SQUAB STUFFED WITH
TRUFFLES AND CHESTNUTS
LETTUCE AND TOMATO

STRAWBERRIES AND ICE CREAM
CAKES

CHEESE — COFFEE

FRUIT
CIGARS

Mess Call

ABOVE Twelfth Annual A. N. V. Reunion, Benevolent Association Headquarters, 1887

RIGHT Christmas, the Ohio, 1884, Erie County, Ohio

BELOW Fourth of July, 1896, Denver, Colorado

OPPOSITE Fifteenth Annual Dinner of the Americus Republican Club of Pittsburgh, P.A., Hotel Scherley, 1901, Pittsburgh, Pennsylvania

This menu for a dinner commemorating Ulysses S. Grant, the 18th president of the United States and commanding general of Union forces in the Civil War, was in the form of an army canteen. The military bugler is blowing the song "Mess Call." The dish "green turtle" refers to soup.

Diese Speisekarte in Form einer Feldflasche erinnert an Ulysses S. Grant, den 18. Präsidenten der USA und Oberbefehlshaber der Nordstaatenarmee im Sezessionskrieg. Geblasen wird das Hornsignal „Mess Call" – „Essen fassen!" Das Gericht „Green Turtle" ist Schildkrötensuppe.

Ce menu créé pour un dîner en l'honneur d'Ulysses S. Grant, 18e président des États-Unis et commandant en chef des armées de l'Union pendant la guerre de Sécession, est en forme de gourde. Le clairon joue *Mess Call* (L'appel au mess). Le plat nommé « green turtle » (tortue verte) est une soupe.

Dinner to
Samuel
Langhorne
Clemens

"Mark Twain"

·Following the Equator· ·Pudd'n-Head Wilson· ·The Jumping Frog· ·Innocents Abroad· ·The Gilded Age· ·Roughing It· ·Huckleberry Finn· ·Tom Sawyer· ·The Prince and the Pauper· ·Life on the Mississippi· ·A Tramp Abroad· ·A Conn. Yankee at King Arthur's Court· ·Mark Twain's Scrap Book· ·Joan of Arc·

by the
Lotos Club
New York
November 10th
1900·

"In the shade of the Lotos flower."

Dan'l W. of Calaveras Co.

OPPOSITE Dinner to Samuel Langhorne Clemens, the Lotos Club, 1900, New York, New York

Founded in 1870, the Lotos Club on East 66th Street was founded by American writers, including Samuel Langhorne Clemens—Mark Twain—who once called it "the Ace of Clubs." The club was named after Tennyson's poem "The Lotos Eaters" (1832). Many of Twain's works are inscribed on the menu illustration of a ship's wheel, and the frog depicts Dan'l Webster, from Twain's 1865 short, "The Celebrated Jumping Frog of Calaveras County."

Der Lotos Club wurde 1870 von amerikanischen Schriftstellern an der East 66th Street eröffnet. Einer von ihnen war Samuel Langhorne Clemens, besser bekannt als Mark Twain, der ihn als „den besten aller Klubs" bezeichnete. Benannt war er nach dem Tennyson-Gedicht „Die Lotos-Esser" (1832). Etliche von Mark Twains Werken sind auf dem Steuerrad auf der Speisekarte verzeichnet, der Frosch ist Dan'l Webster aus seiner Kurzgeschichte „Der berühmte Springfrosch von Calaveras" (1865).

Le Lotos Club sur la 66e rue Est est fondé en 1870 par des écrivains américains, dont Samuel Langhorne Clemens – alias Mark Twain – qui l'a un jour appelé l'« as des clubs ». Son nom vient du poème de Tennyson *The Lotos Eaters* (Les Lotophages) de 1832 et de ses heureux marins échoués. Sur le menu, de nombreuses œuvres de Twain sont inscrites sur une barre de navire et la grenouille n'est autre que Dan'l Webster, d'après *La Célèbre Grenouille sauteuse du comté de Calaveras*, la nouvelle de Twain écrite en 1865.

Chamber of Commerce of the State of New York
131st
Annual Banquet
Tuesday evening, November the twenty-first
1899
Delmonico's

ABOVE Dinner to Mark Twain in honor of his 70th birthday, Delmonico's, 1905, New York, New York

LEFT Chamber of Commerce of the State of New York 131st Annual Banquet, Delmonico's, 1899, New York, New York

The creation of a retired Swiss sea captain named Giovanni Del-Monico and his brothers, Delmonico's was the first true restaurant in America, opening at the foot of Manhattan in the late 1830s and setting the standard for fine dining and menu contents for the next 80 years. While Delmonico's entire menu in the 1890s was vast, this one is relatively modest in its service of a mere 10 courses. Note the Brooklyn Bridge (1883) in the background. The female figure holds the shield of Hermes, god of luck and wealth as well as merchants and thieves.

Der Schweizer Kapitän i. R. Giovanni Del Monico und seine Brüder gründeten das erste echte Restaurant in Amerika. Das Delmonico's machte im Süden Manhattans in den späten 1830ern auf und gab in den nächsten 80 Jahren vor, was feines Essen war. Seine Speisekarte war extrem umfangreich, aber diese hier ist mit nur zehn Gängen relativ bescheiden. Man beachte die 1883 erbaute Brooklyn Bridge im Hintergrund. Die weibliche Figur hält den Schild des Hermes, des Gottes der Händler und Diebe, der Glück und Reichtum bringt.

Premier véritable restaurant américain, le Delmonico ouvre au pied de Manhattan à la fin des années 1830 et fera figure de modèle de la gastronomie américaine pendant quatre-vingts ans. Comparé à l'impressionnant menu des années 1890, celui paraît relativement modeste avec ses dix plats. Le pont de Brooklyn (1883) est en arrière-plan. La figure féminine (Aphrodite) porte le bouclier d'Hermès, dieu de la chance, de la fortune, des marchands et des voleurs.

ABOVE Breakfast for His Royal Highness Prince Henry of Prussia by the Citizens of St. Louis, St. Louis Club, 1902, St. Louis, Missouri

BELOW & OPPOSITE Menus from the Pan-American Exposition, 1901, Buffalo, New York

World's fairs had become popular events in the late 19th and early 20th centuries. The Pan-American Exposition ran from May to November 1901 in Buffalo, New York. These menus illustrate the various exposition buildings called "The Rainbow City" and all offer different dishes. Armour & Company, a meatpacking business out of Chicago, apparently was involved in the catering of the fair.

Die Weltausstellungen wurden im ausgehenden 19. Jahrhundert zu populären Massenveranstaltungen. Die Pan-American Exposition lief von Mai bis November 1901 in Buffalo, New York. Auf diesen Speisekarten sind die verschiedenen Gebäude der „Regenbogenstadt" abgebildet, jeweils mit einem anderen Speisenangebot. Armour & Co. war ein Chicagoer Schlachtereibetrieb, der offensichtlich als Caterer fungierte.

Les expositions universelles deviennent des événements très populaires à la fin du XIXe siècle et au début du XXe. L'Exposition panaméricaine se tient entre mai et novembre 1901 à Buffalo, dans l'État de New York. Ces cartes représentent les pavillons baptisés « Cité arc-en-ciel » et proposent différents plats. Armour & Company est un abattoir de Chicago apparemment impliqué dans la restauration de l'événement.

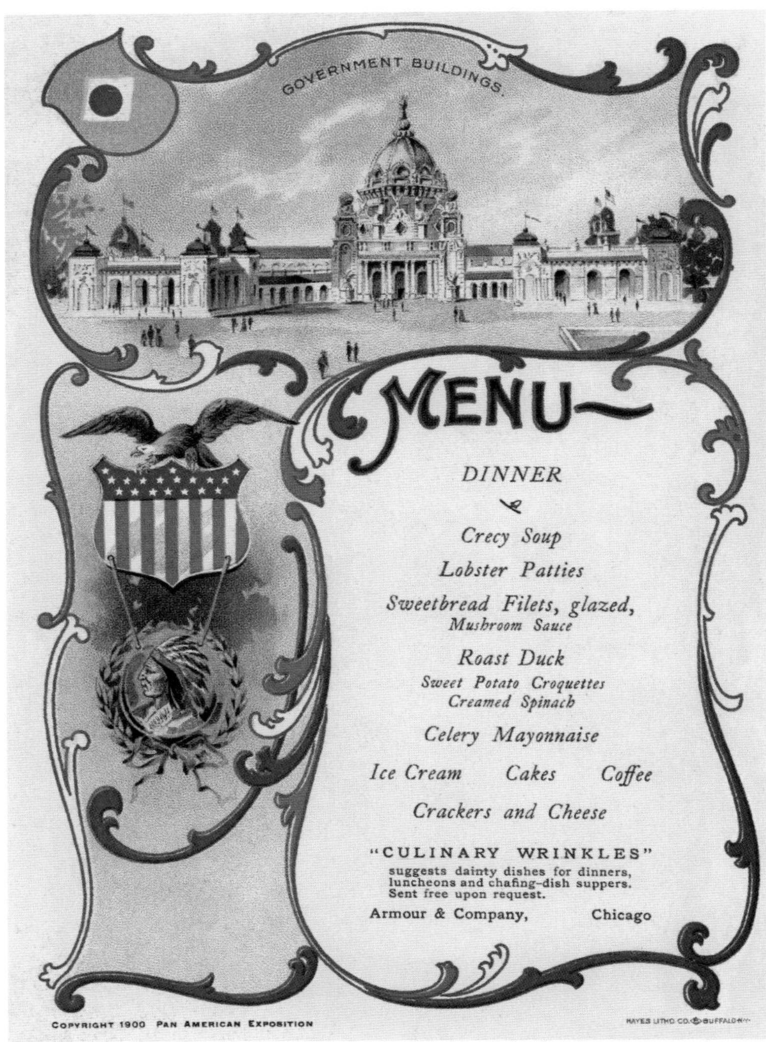

MENU
CHAFING-DISH SUPPER
Grilled Oysters
Deviled Cheese Crackers
Potato Salad
Pate-de-Foie-Gras Sandwiches
Coffee
"CULINARY WRINKLES"
suggests dainty dishes for dinners, luncheons and chafing-dish suppers. Sent free upon request.
Armour & Company, Chicago
ELECTRIC TOWER.
HAYES LITHO. CO. BUFFALO N.Y.
COPYRIGHT 1900 PAN AMERICAN EXPOSITION

OPPOSITE Churchill's, 1913, New York, New York

Opened in 1909 by a former captain of the New York City Police Department, Jim Churchill, this restaurant-cabaret on Broadway and 49th Street sat 1,200 people.

Jim Churchill, ein ehemaliger Hauptkommissar der New Yorker Polizei, eröffnete 1909 ein Restaurant mit Bühne an der Ecke Broadway und 49th Street, in dem 1200 Gäste Platz fanden.

Ouvert en 1909 par un ancien capitaine de la police de New York, Jim Churchill, ce restaurant-cabaret situé au coin de Broadway et de la 49e rue peut accueillir 1 200 personnes.

ABOVE Thanksgiving, the Barbara Worth Hotel, 1918, El Centro, California

RIGHT Thanksgiving, Hotel Leighton, 1905, Los Angeles, California

This Thanksgiving menu for the Hotel Leighton in Los Angeles offered a great deal more than the pictured holiday gobbler, including chow chow, a dish that may have its roots among Chinese workers, many of whom immigrated to California.

Das Hotel Leighton tischte zum Thanksgiving-Festmahl weit mehr als nur den abgebildeten Truthahn auf: Es gab auch „Chow Chow", ein möglicherweise von den chinesischen, in großer Zahl nach Kalifornien eingewanderten Arbeitern übernommenes Gericht.

Ce menu de Thanksgiving de l'hôtel Leighton à Los Angeles offre beaucoup plus de choix que le volatile représenté, en particulier le *chow chow*, un plat qui trouve ses racines chez les nombreux ouvriers chinois émigrés en Californie.

DINNER

LOBSTER OR CRAB MEAT COCKTAIL 50

Blue Points 25 Lynnhavens 40 Little Neck Clams 25

Cape Cods 30 Cotuits 30 Buzzard Bays 30 Smith Island 40 Cherry Stone Clams 30 Cocktail 5c. Extra

APPETIZERS

Beluga Caviar 80 Anchovy Rings 40 Tomato, Surprise 35

Supreme of Grape Fruit 60 Smoked Salmon in Slices 50 Feuille de Laitue, Suédoise 35 Ripe California Olives 25 Hors d'Oeuvres Assortis 50

Radishes 20 Spring Onions 20 New Dill Pickles 15 Celery 25 Grape Fruit Cocktail 50 Lyon Sausage 40

SOUPS (Per Person)

Consommé, Condorcet 25 Cream of Spinach, Scotch Fashion 25 Bisque of Clams, Beaufort 25

Clear Green Turtle 40 Julienne 30 Purée of Tomatoes 30 Potage Mongole 30 Clam Broth 25

Chicken Okra 30 Petite Marmite 35 Chicken Consommé 30 Purée of Peas 30

FISH (Per Person)

BROILED SHAD AND ROE WITH BACON 75 BROILED LIVE LOBSTER 1 50 2 50 FRIED SMELTS, FIGARO SAUCE 60

Scallops, Leonia 60 SOFT SHELL CRABS, TARTAR SAUCE 60 Baked Oysters à la Moderne 60

Chicken Halibut à la Nesle 60 Shad Roe, Maximilienne 75 Filet of Sole, Montebello 50

Long Island Brook Trout Sauté aux Fines Herbes 65 Baked Bluefish en Bordure au Gratin 60

ENTREES (Per Person)

Mignon Tenderloin of Beef, Stanley 75 Minced Sweetbread, Dewey 80 Veal Pot Pie, Country Style 65

Salmis of Guinea Chicken with Fresh Mushrooms 75 Broiled English Mutton Chop, Century Club 80 Venison Steak Sauté, Oporto 1 00

Half Squab Chicken en Casserole, Sardaigne 1 00 Half Red Leg Partridge, Charles XV 1 25

Fresh Mushrooms in Cream under Glass 65 Diamond Back Terrapin, Maryland Club 1 50

ROAST (Per Person)

Half Special Stuffed Baby Duckling, Apple Sauce 1 00

Leg of Spring Lamb, Mint Sauce 65 Stuffed Vermont Turkey, Cranberry Sauce 75 Prime Ribs of Beef 60

Rack of Lamb (25 Minutes) 2 50 Saddle of Lamb (30 Minutes) 2 50 Half Milk-fed Chicken 1 00

Philadelphia Capon, Club Style (45 Minutes) 4 00 Half Boston Duckling, Apple Sauce 1 25 SPECIAL STUFFED ROYAL SQUAB 1 00

POULTRY AND GAME

Guinea Chicken 2 00 Squab Chicken 1 50 Philadelphia Spring Chicken 2 00 Squab Turkey 3 50 Half 2 00

Venison 1 00 Red Leg Partridge 2 50 English Pheasant 3 00 Celery-Fed Duckling 2 00

COLD

Supreme of Chicken, Alexandra 1 00 Terrine, Marie Louise 60 Assorted Cold Meat 75 Squab in Jelly, George Sand 1 00 Galantine of Capon Truffled 50

Pate de Volaille en Croute 50 Boned Squab à la Gelee 1 00 Terrine de Foie-Gras 1 00 Rack of Lamb, Laura 70 Egg, Nevada or Russe (1) 35 Westphalia Ham 70

VEGETABLES (Per Person)

NEW ASPARAGUS 60 Celery au Gratin on Toast 50 Grilled Tomatoes 35 French or German Asparagus 65 New Bermuda Potatoes 25

NEW GREEN PEAS 30 NEW STRING BEANS 35 Spinach with Eggs 25 French Peas 30

Fried Egg Plant 25 Cauliflower au Gratin 35 French Artichokes, Hollandaise Sauce 50 Macaroni au Gratin 35

Stuffed Green Peppers (1) 30 Souflée Potatoes 35 Spaghetti Napolitain 35 Celery Braisé au Jus 35 Stuffed Tomatoes (1) 30

POTATOES: Boiled, Baked, Mashed or French Fried 15 O'Brien 30 Lyonnaise 25 Gaufrette 30 Sarah Bernhardt 30

SWEET POTATOES: Saute or Fried 25 Grilled 30 au Gratin 30 Southern Style 35

SALADS (Per Person)

Endive 40 Heart of Lettuce 30 Cucumber 30 Feodora 40 Kuroki 40 Fruit 50 Tomato 30 Trophy 40

Churchill's 40 Escarole 30 Chicory 30 Romaine 30 Spring 35 Chiffonade 50 My Fancy 40 Saratoga 40 Royal 40

PASTRY

STRAWBERRY SHORT CAKE 50

BAKED APPLE DUMPLING, HARD AND BRANDY SAUCE 25 Cold Rice Pudding 25 OLD-FASHION STRAWBERRY SHORT CAKE 50

PIES-French Apple, Peach, Banana Custard 25 Deep Dish Apple Pie 25 Gateau Java 15 Diplomate Pudding 25 Rice à la Federale 35

Charlotte Russe 35 Cup Custard 20 Assorted Cakes 25 French Pastry 15

FRUIT

STRAWBERRIES WITH CREAM 50 GRAPE FRUIT 40 BAKED APPLE WITH CREAM 25

STEWED FRESH RHUBARB 25 PINEAPPLE (SLICED) 30

ICE CREAM

Peche Bonton 65 Biscuit Glacé Arlesien 40 Coupe Royale 50 Parfait Excelsior 35 Meringue Glacé Pistache 35

Fresh Strawberry Ice Cream 35 Tutti Frutti 35 Strawberry Melba 60 Peach Melba 60

Basket of Strawberries with Maraschino 60 Charlotte Plombiere 40 Orange Water Ice 25

Vanilla, Chocolate, Coffee or Pistache Ice Cream 25 Mixed 30 Lemon Water Ice 25

Biscuit Tortoni 35 Nesselrode Pudding 35 Aeroplane 50 Neapolitan 35 Parisian Hobble Skirt Souvenir 75

Plantation Guava Marmalade 20 Cheese with Deviled Crackers 20 Guava or Bar-le-Duc Jelly 40

CHEESE--Camembert 20 Brie 20 Liederkranz 20 Gervais 20 Cream 20 Roquefort 20

Java Tea 20 Pot of Coffee 20 Demi Tasse 15

PRIVATE DINING ROOMS ACCOMMODATING FROM 15 to 200 NOW READY FOR BOOKING

THIS RESTAURANT OPENS DAILY AT 11 A. M. SPECIAL LUNCHEON SERVED.

MONDAY, APRIL 7, 1913

ROMANOFF CAVIAR 1 25 (PRIVATE STOCK

SNAILS A LA PARSINIENN (6) 60

Menu

DINNER: $1.50

From 6 to 9 o'clock P. M.

25 Cents extra for each Dinner taken without Wine

26th St. & Broadway **Tuesday, October 13, 1903**

Blue Point Oysters

HORS-D'ŒUVRE

Olives Saucisson Radishes
Cœurs d'Artichauts Robespierre

POTAGES

Choice { Cream of Celery
Consommé Sévigné

POISSONS

Choice { Casserolette of Scollops à la Newburg
Cold Lobster à la Châtillon

ENTREES

Choice { Leg of Lamb Dauphinoise
Timbale of Grouse Saint-Hubert

LEGUMES

Choice { Stuffed Lettuce au jus
Spaghetti à l'Italienne

ROTIS

Choice { Roast Beef Broiled Chicken
Truffled Pâté of Game à la gelée

Salad in Season

ENTREMETS

Choice { Profiterole au Chocolat Croquets aux Raisins
Gaufrettes Vanillées Glace à l'Abricot

Cheese Dessert : Assorted Fruits.

Coffee, ½ tasse, 10 c. Special Coffee, 25 c.
Café frappé au Kirsch, 25 c.

Martin Cup (½ Champagne, ½ Claret) . . **$2.50**

Something New! Green Curaçao dry frappé, **25c.**
(From Curaçao, Dutch West Indies.)

Ask for the Key of the Cellar

☛ Patrons will confer a favor by reporting to the management any incivility from the waiter or any inattention in the service.

OPPOSITE Café Martin, 1903, New York, New York

Famed poster artist Alphonse Mucha illustrated the Café Martin menu. It was one of the most popular restaurants with New York society before Prohibition. Opened by Jean Baptiste and Louis Martin in 1899 on Broadway and 26th Street, it introduced banquettes to dining rooms and a dining terrace outside. The French menu, priced at a hefty $1.50, charged 25 cents extra "for each Dinner taken without wine."

Die Illustration der Speisekarte des Café Martin stammt von dem berühmten Jugendstilgrafiker Alphonse Mucha. Das Café Martin war vor der Prohibitionszeit einer der beliebtesten Treffpunkte der New Yorker High Society. 1899 von Jean Baptiste und Louis Martin Ecke Broadway und 26th Street eröffnet, bot es Bankette und eine Terrasse zum Speisen an der frischen Luft. Das französische Menü zum gesalzenen Preis von 1,50 Dollar kostete 25 Cent mehr „für jedes Essen ohne Wein".

Le célèbre affichiste Alphonse Mucha illustre la carte du Café Martin, l'un des restaurants les plus courus de la bonne société new-yorkaise avant la Prohibition. Ouvert par Jean-Baptiste et Louis Martin en 1899 au coin de la Cinquième avenue et de la 26e rue, il introduit les banquettes dans la salle à manger et une terrasse extérieure. Le menu est français et le tarif salé de 1 dollar 50 est surtaxé de 25 cents « pour chaque dîner pris sans vin ».

ABOVE Twenty-Sixth Annual Banquet of the New York City Hotel Association, Delmonico's, 1905, New York, New York

LEFT Delmonico's, Banquet Room, 1902, New York, New York

The extraordinary lavishness of Delmonico's banquet facilities was a fit symbol of the Gilded Age.

Die verschwenderische Pracht des Festsaals im Delmonico's war der Inbegriff des Gilded Age, der amerikanischen Gründerzeit.

L'opulence extraordinaire de la salle de réception du Delmonico qui arbore fièrement le drapeau américain est le symbole même de son âge d'or.

ABOVE Pabst Café, c. 1906, San Francisco, California

The Pabst Café was a San Francisco German beer hall. This menu possibly predates the earthquake of 1906, which destroyed much of the city.

Das Pabst Café war ein deutsches Bierlokal in San Francisco. Diese Speisekarte stammt vermutlich aus der Zeit vor dem großen Erdbeben von 1906, bei dem die Stadt weitgehend zerstört wurde.

Le Pabst Café est un bar à bières allemand de San Francisco. Ce menu date probablement d'avant le séisme de 1906 qui a détruit une grande partie de la ville.

BELOW Murray's, c. 1898, New York, New York

OPPOSITE Pullman Buffet, c. 1901

This menu for Pullman club cars, in American art nouveau-style, offered sit-down dinners and buffets.

Diese Karte aus dem Pullman-Club-Speisewagen im amerikanischen Jugendstil bot Abendessen und Selbstbedienung am Büffet an.

Ce menu Art nouveau américain pour les voitures Pullman propose des dîners assis et des buffets.

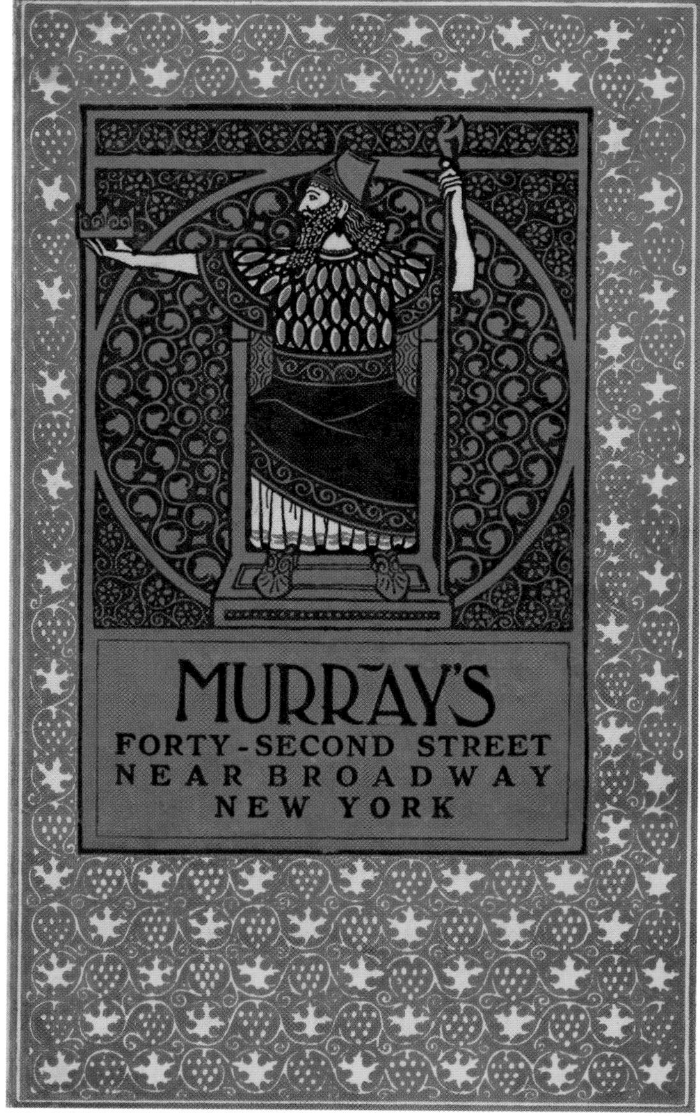

PULLMAN BUFFET
Man, be merie
as Brid on berie
and al
thi Care let away
MENU AND WINES
F.B.S.
1901

Menu

Yaquina Bay Oysters

-

Clear Green Turtle—en tasse

Salted Almonds Celery Ripe Olives

-

Royal Oregon Chinook Salmon—Hollandaise Sauce

Parisian Potatoes

Sliced Cucumbers

-

Calves Sweetbreads—Fresh Mushrooms

-

Roast Milk Fed Spring Chicken

Hearts of Lettuce—Mayonnaise

-

Fresh Strawberries

Glace en Surprise

Roquefort Cheese Camembert Cheese Toasted Crackers

Demi Tasse

Martini Cocktail
Diedesheimer, 1904 E. Leiden
Italian Swiss Colony Tipo Chianti Red
Louis Roederer, Brown Label
XXXXX Waldorf-Astoria Private Stock Brandy
Apollinaris
Turkish Cigarettes
Romeo and Juliet Cigars

ABOVE & LEFT **Dinner to Theodore Roosevelt, Portland Commercial Club, 1911, Portland, Oregon**

OPPOSITE **Pacific Coast Steamship Co., 1911, Frederick Sound, Alaska**

From 1899 to 1917, the Pacific Coast Steamship Co. sailed from San Francisco to Pacific Northwest and Alaskan ports from May to October.

Die Dampfschiffe der Pacific Coast Steamship Co. verbanden von 1899 bis 1917 im Sommer San Francisco mit den Pazifikhäfen in Kanada und Alaska.

De 1899 à 1917, la Pacific Coast Steamship Co. a relié San Francisco au Pacifique nord-ouest et aux ports d'Alaska de mai à octobre.

Alaska Cruises

Steamship
"SPOKANE"

SEASON 1911

LUNCH

CREAM OF NEW
TOMATO

CLAM BROTH
CHANTILLY IN CUP

BROILED ALASKA SALMON
CHICKEN FRICASSEE

FILET OF PORK
WITH APPLE SAUCE

FRIED EGG PLANT

COLD: ROAST BEEF
ROAST CHICKEN
ROAST LAMB
HAM

ASPARAGUS SALAD

WAX BEANS

BOILED AND BAKED
NEW POTATOES

BOILED RICE

SQUASH PIE
GRAPE PIE
COFFEE CAKE

ASSORTED PASTRY

STEWED APRICOTS
ASSORTED JAMS
STEWED PRUNES
PRESERVED APRICOTS

RASPBERRY ICE

FRUITS IN SEASON

CHEESE: SWISS, EDAM,
ROQUEFORT, AMERICAN

TOASTED CRACKERS

TEA, COFFEE,
CHOCOLATE, MILK

Friday, August 4th, 1911.
Wrangell Narrows, Alaska.

FOLD IN CREASE AND STAND UPRIGHT

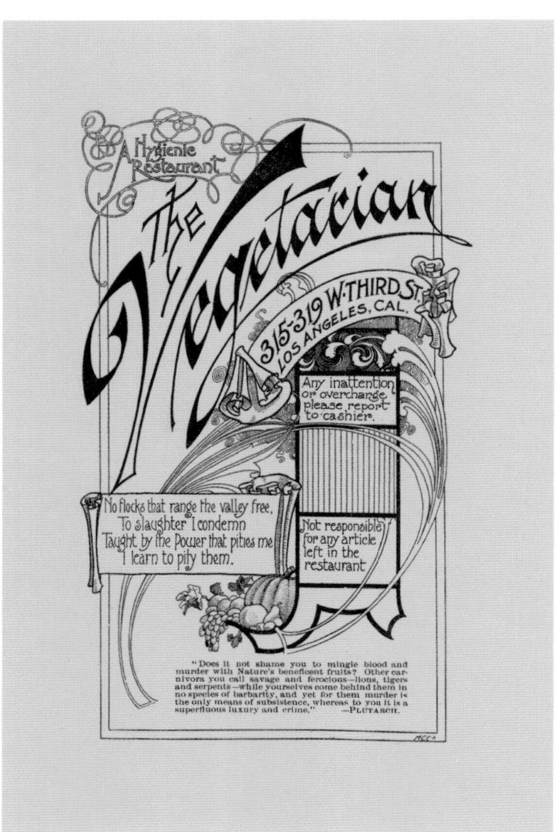

LEFT & BELOW The Vegetarian, 1902, Los Angeles, California

This example of a California vegetarian restaurant, rare at the time, includes "Protose Steak," a meat substitute made from nut and wheat gluten invented in the late 19th century by John Harvey Kellogg of cornflakes fame.

Auf dem Speiseplan dieses damals seltenen vegetarischen Restaurants in Kalifornien steht ein „Protose Steak", ein von John Harvey Kellogg, Erfinder der Corn Flakes, Ende des 19. Jahrhunderts entwickelter Fleischersatz aus Nüssen und Weizengluten.

Cet exemple précoce et rare d'un restaurant végétarien en Californie propose un bifteck de « protose », un substitut de viande composé d'arachide et de gluten, inventé à la fin du XIXe siècle par John Harvey Kellog, le célèbre créateur des corn-flakes éponymes.

Breakfast, 6 to 10. Dinner, 11:30 to 2:30, and 4:45 to 7:30

Breakfast — **MENU** — **Dinner**

Sunday, Aug. 17, 1902

BREAKFAST

COOKED FRUITS

Peach Sauce 5
Pear Sauce 5
Stewed Prunes 5
Apple Sauce 5
Apricot Sauce 5
Blackberry Sauce 5
Sliced Pineapple 10
Baked Apples 5

GRAINS

Germea 5
Rolled Wheat 5
Boiled Rice 5
Granola Mush 5
Gluten Mush 5
Steamed Brown Rice 5
Rolled Oats 5
Grains with Milk 5; Dairy Cream, 10

TOASTS

Pineapple Cream Toast 5
Cream Sauce Toast 5
Fruit Toast 5
Apple Toast 5
Toasted Granose Biscuit 5
Dry Toast with Hot Cream 10
Dairy Cream Toast 10

ENTREES

Egg Plant on Toast 10
Green Pea Omelet 20

VEGETABLES

Baked Potato, with Cream Sauce 5
Sugar Peas 5
Whole Wheat Puffs ....
Stewed Lima Beans 5
Stewed Tomatoes 5
Fruit Bread 5

NUT DISHES

Nut Bromose 5
Fig Bromose 5
Walnuts 5
Almonds 5
Mixed Nuts 5
Mixed Nuts with Raisins 5
Nuttolene with Jelly 10
Protose with Jelly 10
Malted Nuts Dry 10
Shelled Pecans 10

BEVERAGES

Caramel Cereal Coffee, with Cream 5
Lemonade, Hot or Cold 5
Hot Milk 5
Cold Milk 5
Buttermilk 5
Malted Nut Broth 10
Glass ½ Milk ½ Cream 10
Sanitarium Un-fermented Grape Juice... 5

BREADS

Gluten Sticks ....
Zweiback, Unleavened Sticks....
Whole Wheat, Graham, White...
Oatmeal Sticks ....
Graham Sticks ....
Crisps ....
Granose Biscuit 5
Fruit Sticks 5

CEREALS.

Fruit Nuts (Malted) 5
Toasted Wheat Flakes 5
Corn Flakes 5
Granut 5
Granose Flakes 5
Granola 5
Gluten Mush (to order) 5
Granose Flakes with Fruit Juice. 10
Grains with Milk or Nut Cream 5c. With Dairy Cream 10c.

Our bread and other bakery supplies are furnished by our own bakery and guaranteed absolutely pure.

No baking powder, ammonia, cream of tartar, soda or lard are used.

FRESH FRUITS
(Served All Day)

Strawberries 10
Burbank Plumes 5
Blackberries 5
Sliced Peaches 5
Raspberries 5
Muscat Grapes 5

DINNER

SOUPS

Tomato and Rice 5
Lentil and Cream 5

RELISHES AND SALADS

Olives 5
Sliced Tomatoes 5
Sanitarium Baked Beans 10
Lettuce with Lemon 5
Nut Chicken 10

ENTREES COTTAGE CHEESE 5

Protose Steak with Jelly 15
Nut Roast 5
Protose Cutlets on Green Pea Puree 10
Navy Bean Puree 10

VEGETABLES

Baked Sweet Potato 5
Mashed Potato 5
Stewed French Carrots 5
Stewed Lima Beans 5
Breaded Tomatoes 5
Sugar Corn 5 ~~Scalloped Oyster Plant~~ 5

COOKED FRUITS

Pear Sauce 5
Peach Sauce 5
Apricot Sauce 5
Stewed Prunes 5
Apple Sauce 5
Blackberry Sauce 5
Sliced Pineapple 10
Baked Apples 5

CEREALS

Germea with Dates 5
Boiled Rice 5
Steamed Brown Rice 5

DESSERTS

Farina Custard 5
Bread Pudding with Lemon Sauce 5
Sanitarium Un-fermented Grape Juice... 5
Watermelon 5
Cantaloupe 5

EGGS.

Scrambled or Shirred 15
Poached 15
Boiled 15
Eggs on Toast 20
Poached on Granose 20
Poached on Zweiback 20
Gluten Omelet (Orders, 20 minutes)..20
Protose Omelet " " " 25
Omelet Plain " " " 20
All Egg orders include Bread. Butter and one five cent Vegetable.

LIQUID FOODS

Gluten Gruel 5
Pure Olive Oil 5
Pure Maple Syrup 5
Comb Honey 5
Malt Honey 10
Malted Nut Gruel 10
Egg Nog 10
Grape-juice Egg Nog 10

Caramel Cereal Coffee or Milk with 20c Order Free.

Nut or Dairy Butter with Bread Free with 15c Order.

ALMOND BUTTER, 5 CENTS

All Articles named in the lower section of this Menu will be served at every meal.

Please report to the Manager or Cashier any inattention or discourtesy on the part of waiters.

Bread and Butter will be served with all orders unless otherwise specified, and charged for when order is less than 15c.

NO SERVICE LESS THAN 10 CENTS

THE GARFIELD CLUB
COLUMBUS, OHIO.

Menu
Scalloped Oysters
Chicken Croquettes.
Salad. Deviled Eggs
India Relish
Plum Marmelade. Jelly
Soda Biscuit
Pudding & Sauce.
Cake Ice Cream
Coffee.

ABOVE & RIGHT The Garfield Club, c. 1910, Columbus, Ohio

The club had only five original members, including U.S. President and Ohio state Senator James A. Garfield, who died in 1881. It must have enlisted a few others by the time this modest hand written menu appeared around 1910, illustrating early usage of photography on a lunch menu.

Der Klub hatte anfangs nur fünf Mitglieder, darunter der amerikanische Präsident und Senator aus Ohio, James A. Garfield, der 1881 starb. Der Klub muss aber noch ein paar dazugewonnen haben, bis diese bescheidene, handgeschriebene Mittagskarte um 1910 erschien, ein frühes Beispiel für die Verwendung einer Fotografie auf einer Speisekarte.

Le club ne compte que cinq membres à l'origine, dont le président des États-Unis, James A. Garfield, mort en 1881, Quatre ans plus tard, il n'en a plus qu'un seul, mais à l'époque de ce modeste menu manuscrit, il en a manifestement de nouveaux. Voici un exemple précoce de l'emploi d'une photographie en guise d'illustration.

LEFT & BELOW **Annual Banquet of the Chamber of Commerce, 1903, Los Angeles, California**

A unique menu—with a metal cover—which lists a typical wine serving of the time, a sweet "Sauterne" (sic), which was matched with the fish course, followed by a California Chianti from "Swiss Italian Colony."

Diese einzigartige Karte – mit einem aus Metall gestanzten Einband – führt, wie damals üblich, zum Fischgang einen süßen „Sauterne" (Weißwein) auf, gefolgt von kalifornischem Chianti aus „italienisch-schweizerischer Kolonie."

Un menu unique – avec une couverture en métal – qui propose des vins typiques de l'époque, dont un «Sauterne» (sic) liquoreux en accord avec le plat de poisson, suivi par un chianti californien provenant de la «colonie suisse italienne».

OPPOSITE **Electric Grill, Hotel St. Francis, 1908, San Francisco, California**

Menu....

Blue Points on Shell
Celery
Clear Green Turtle, Au Champagne
Olives Salted Almonds
Filet of Sole, en Papillote
Pommes a la Militaire
Sweet Breads, en Casserole
Sorbet a L'Imperial
Supreme of Fowl, aux Truffes
Petits Pois, a la Francaise
Souffle Glace De Volaille
Frozen Nesselrode Pudding
Fruits Raisins Nuts
Cheese Water Wafers
Cafe Noir
Cigars Shasta Water

Old Madera
Corona Blanco Sauterne
Tipo Chianti Swiss Italian Colony
Champagne Mumm's Extra Dry

Toasts...

Toastmaster - - - - - - J. S. SLAUSON

The President of the United States
HON. WILL A. HARRIS

Southern California
SAM T. CLOVER

George Washington
OSCAR LAWLER

Some Ideals of the Citizen
J. H. McBRIDE, M. D.

Music...

1. March - - Hurrah Boys - - - *Lacalle*
2. Forgotten - - - - - - - *Eugene Cowles*
3. Selection - King Do Do - - - *Luders*
4. A Hunting Scene - - - - *Bucalossi*
5. (a) In the Good Old Summer Time - *Chattaway*
   (b) Hiawatha - - - - - - *Moret*
6. Pilgrims Chorus - From Tannhauser - *Wagner*
7. Cavalry Charge - - - - - - *Luders*
8. Patriotic Airs - - - - - - - *Arend*
9. Minuet - - - - - - - *Paderewski*
10. Melodies that Everybody Knows - - *Arend*

Britton & Rey, Lith. S.F.
HOTEL
ST FRANCIS
ELECTRIC
GRILL

LEFT Original Poodle Dog, 1912, San Francisco, California

The Original Poodle Dog, named after a dog, Ami, was a lavish six-story French restaurant. Destroyed in the 1906 earthquake, it was quickly rebuilt but did not survive Prohibition and closed in 1922, because Chef Calixte Lalanne moaned, "great cuisine cannot be served without wine."

Das erste Poodle Dog, nach einem Pudel namens Ami benannt, war ein prunkvolles, sechs Stockwerke hohes französisches Restaurant. Es wurde beim Erdbeben zerstört, aber innerhalb eines Jahres wieder aufgebaut. Die Prohibitionszeit überstand es nicht, da, wie Koch Calixte Lalanne stöhnte, „herausragendes Essen nicht ohne Wein serviert werden kann", und es musste 1922 schließen.

L'Original Poodle Dog (baptisé d'après un «caniche» répondant au nom d'Ami) est un luxueux restaurant français à six étages. Détruit par le séisme de 1906, il est reconstruit mais ne survit pas à la Prohibition et ferme en 1922, car, comme le chef Calixte Lalanne s'en plaignait, «on ne peut servir de grande cuisine sans vin».

BELOW Raisin Day, Bergez-Frank's Old Poodle Dog, 1911, San Francisco, California

OPPOSITE Interior of Bergez-Frank's Old Poodle Dog, c. 1910, San Francisco, California

Eat Raisins Eat Raisins Eat Raisins

Eat Raisins Think Raisins Boost Raisins

Raisin Day
Luncheon

April 29, 1911

Under Auspices of the Transportation Club

COMMITTEE

S. F. BOOTH
F. JACOBS
F. C. HENRI
O. S. NUNTINGTEN
W. F. HITCH
C. H. WEST, Fresno
TOASTMASTER

All Raisin
Boosters

Boost Raisins Think Raisins Eat Raisins

Eat Raisins Eat Raisins Eat Raisins

Eat Raisins Eat Raisins Eat Raisins

Eat Raisins Think Raisins Boost Raisins

.. MENU ..

Hors-d'OEuvres
Shrimp Salad Mayonnaise Dressing with Raisins
Radishes Olives Raisins

Soup
Essence of Chicken Some Raisins

Fish
Filet of Bass Polonaise Fresno Raisins

Entree
Croustade Toulousaine Hanford Raisins

Roast
Roast Spring Chicken au Jus Raisin stuffing

Vegetable
Green Peas French Style Raisins Nix

Dessert
Neapolitan Ice Cream, Raisin Decoration
Petits Fours, Raisin Cakes, Fruits
Raisins, Assorted Cheese
Demi-Tasse

Italian-Swiss Colony *Sauterne* Italian-Swiss Colony *Zinfandel*

Boost Raisins Think Raisins Eat Raisins

Eat Raisins Eat Raisins Eat Raisins

ABOVE **Casa Verdugo, c. 1912, Glendale, California**

BELOW **The Mission Indian Grill, Hotel Alexandria, 1911, Los Angeles, California**

OPPOSITE **Casa Verdugo, 1912, Glendale, California**

An early Mexican restaurant—referred to at the time as Spanish — Casa Verdugo in Glendale, California, was a must-see tourist spot. The fare was an early example of what came to be termed "ethnic foods," as opposed to more available American or French foods of this period.

Einer der allerersten Mexikaner – damals noch spanisches Restaurant genannt – war die Casa Verdugo in Glendale, Kalifornien, eine große Touristenattraktion. Serviert wurden „ethnische Spezialitäten", im Gegensatz zu dem damals überwiegenden amerikanischen oder französischen Essen.

L'un des premiers restaurants mexicains – appelés alors espagnols – de la région de Los Angeles, le Casa Verdugo, devient un site touristique incontournable. Les plats proposés sont l'un des exemples précoces de ce qu'on appelle désormais cuisine « ethnique », par contraste avec la gastronomie française ou américaine, plus courante à l'époque.

CASA VERDUGO

THE OLD SPANISH RESTAURANT

Carta de Hoy

Domingo Septiembre 1 de 1907

Dinner $1.00

Ensalada de Ejotes

" " Tomates

Aceitunas

Sopa de Gallina

" " Albondigas

Pollo en Salsa

Arroz y Macarrones

Enchiladas, Frijoles

Sandia, y Leche Nevada

Cafe Negro

P. S.—IF YOU WISH TO REACH CASA VERDUGO BY AUTOMOBILE TAKE EITHER THE SAN FERNANDO ROAD OR VERMONT AVENUE ROUTE, TURNING NORTH AT TROPICO TO THE FOOTHILLS. TELEPHONE GLENDALE 370 OR 1481

OPPOSITE The National Cigar Leaf Tobacco Association, the Waldorf-Astoria, 1912, New York, New York

This leather menu themed for its hosts, the National Cigar Leaf Tobacco Association, used words such as "fresh" next to "mushrooms" to inform guests they were not from a can.

Dieses Menü zu Ehren der National Cigar Leaf Tobacco Association ist auf Leder gedruckt. Die Betonung von „frisch" neben den Pilzen soll den Gästen deutlich machen, dass diese nicht aus der Dose kommen.

Ce menu à thème a été concocté pour la National Cigar Leaf Tobacco Association. L'emploi de l'adjectif « frais » à côté de « champignons » indique qu'il ne s'agit pas de conserve.

ABOVE & RIGHT United Fruit Company Steamship Service, 1913

Boston-based United Fruit Company owned Caribbean plantations and a steamship company to service the West Indies. The menu is written in English and Spanish, and listed items such as bloater toast, albondigas soup, and broiled bluefish, reflecting regional viands.

Die in Boston ansässige United Fruit Company war Besitzerin von Plantagen in der Karibik und von Dampfschiffen, die die karibischen Inseln anfuhren. Die Speisekarte auf Englisch und Spanisch bietet Exotisches wie „Bloater Toast", „Albondigas Soup" (mexikanische Fleischklößchensuppe) und gebratenen Blaubarsch.

La United Fruit Company, basée à Boston, possédait des plantations aux Caraïbes, en particulier des bananeraies, et une compagnie maritime qui desservait les Antilles. Le menu, écrit en anglais et en espagnol, est un hymne à la gastronomie locale : tartines de hareng saur, soupe d'*albondigas* (boulettes) ou *tassergal* grillé.

Menu

Luncheon
Lyon's Sausage
Smoked Salmon Bloater Toast
SOUPS
Scotch Broth Cold Consommé
HOT DISHES
Broiled Bluefish
Rice, á la Milanaise Beef, á la Mode
Albondigas, Spanish Style
Baked Sweet, and Boiled Potatoes
GRILL ORDERS, (10 Minutes)
Mutton Chops
COLD BUFFET
Roast Beef Roast Mutton Pig's Feet
York Ham Bologna Sausage
SALAD
Waldorf
Tapioca Custard, Lemon Sauce
Blueberry Pie Assorted Pastry
Preserved Peaches
Orange Sherbet
American and Edam Cheese
Cocoa Tea Coffee
Fresh Fruit

Merienda
Salchichon de Lyon
Salmon Ahumado Tostada de Arengues
SOPAS
Caldo Escoces Consommé Frio
PLATOS CALIENTES
Pescado Azul, á la Parrilla
Arroz, á la Milanesa Vaca, á la Moda
Aldondigas, á la Spañola
Boniatos al Horno y Papas Cocida
DE LA PARRILLA, (10 Miuutos)
Costillas de Carnero
FIAMBRES
Carne Asada Carnero Asado Patas de Cerdo
Jamon de York Lengua de Buey
ENSALADA
Waldorf
Tapioca Flan, Salsa de Limon
Pastel de Uva Mora Pasteletes Surtidos
Melocotones en Conservas
Sorbetes de Naranja
Queso Americano y Holandesa
Cacao Té Café
Frutas Frescas

T.S.S. "PASTORES"
H. A. HENSHAW COMMANDER,
Tuesday, August 12th, 1913.

THE
NATIONAL CIGAR LEAF TOBACCO ASSOCIATION
THE WALDORF-ASTORIA, NEW YORK, MAY 14, 1912
MENU
LITTLE NECK CLAMS
SORREL SOUP, PRINTANNIÈRE
RADISHES
OLIVES
CELERY
SALTED ALMONDS
KINGFISH, MEUNIÈRE
CROWN VIRGINIENNE WITH
TOMATOES AND CUCUMBER SALAD
FRESH MUSHROOMS
SADDLE OF SPRING LAMB
COLBERT SAUCE
POTATOES PALESTINE
MACÉDOINE OF FRESH VEGETABLES
NEW ASPARAGUS
HOLLANDAISE SAUCE
SQUAB GUINEA HEN WITH
SAUERKRAUT
EN CASSEROLE
HEARTS OF LETTUCE SALAD
FRENCH DRESSING
ASSORTED CHEESE
MOUSSE OF FRESH
STRAWBERRIES
ASSORTED CAKES
COFFEE
CIGARS
HOYO
DE MONTERREY
POMMERY SEC
APOLLINARIS

TRY A "TAIT'S" COCKTAIL BEFORE DINNER

BEFORE PAYING—SEE THAT YOUR CHECK IS TOTALED AND STAMPED IN FIGURES

MENU
DINNER

FRIDAY JULY 7, 1905

OYSTERS

California Oysters, 35 Blue Points (6) 35 Toke Points (6) 35 Club Selected (6) 35
Little Neck Clams, 35 California Oyster or Clam Cocktail, 25

Fresh Astrachan Caviar, (Our Own Importation) 60

HORS D'OEUVRE

Caviar Canape, 25 Shrimps with Fine Herbs, 30 Anchovy on Toast, 25

SOUPS

Consomme, 15 Consomme Frappe, 15 Clam Juice, 15 Chicken Broth in Cup, 20 Clear Green Turtle, 25
Onion, 15 Green Turtle a L'Americaine, 15

FISH

Boiled Salmon Parsley Sauce, 30 Striped Bass Maitre d'Hotel, 35 Filet of Sole, Mornay, 35
Split Smelts broiled, 25 Lake Tahoe Trout fried in butter, 50 Sand Dabs Meuniere, 30
Bouille a Baisse, 35

ENTREES

English Mutton Chop with new Peas, 50 Pattie a la Reine (1), 30 Marrow Bone on Anchovy toast, 35
Tenderloin Steak with Stuffed Tomatoes, 60
Vol au Vent of Sweetbreads, 50
Curried Oysters with Rice, 50 New England Boiled Dinner, 35 Scalloped Shrimp Bechemel, 40
Baked Crab Pie, 40 Stewed Terrapin with Hominy, $1.00 Boiled Leg of Lamb with Turnips, 35
Chicken Saute Parisienne, 65.

ROASTS

Ribs of Beef, 35 Extra Cut, 70 Turkey, Cranberry Sauce, 60 Lamb, Mint Sauce, 35
Loin of Pork, Apple Sauce, 35

To Order { Rack of Lamb (for 1) 50; (for 2) 1.00; (for 3) 1.50 / Saddle of Lamb (for 4) 2.50; (for 6) 3.00 / Baked Chicken Pie (for each person) 75 } **30 Minutes Notice Required**

GAME AND POULTRY

Squab, 60 Broiled Chicken, 65-1.25 Squab Chicken, 75 Broiled Spring Turkey (for 4 or 6) 3 00

COLD

Ham, 25 Corned Beef, 25 Smoked Tongue, 25 Roast Beef, 35 Turkey, 60
Westphalia or Virginia Ham, 40 Galatine of Capon, 50 Half Spring Chicken, 65 (whole) 1.25

SALADS

Tomato and Onion, 25 Lettuce and Egg, 20 Cold Artichoke, 15 Romain or Lettuce, 15 Crab, 25
Celery, Mayonnaise, 15 Chicken, 25 Celery, Apple and Whipped Cream, 25 Potato Salad, 10
Tomatoes Stuffed with Celery, 25 Shrimp, 25 Cold Canned Asparagus, 25

Alligator Pear, 50

VEGETABLES

Fried Sweet Potatoes, 15 Spaghetti, Italienne, 15 Broiled Tomatoes, 25 Artichoke, Melted Butter (1) 15
Fried Hominy, 15 New Potatoes in Cream, 15 New Peas, 15 Macaroni and Cheese, 15 French Peas, 25
Spinach with Egg, 15 Special Baked Potato, 10 Succotash, 20 Fried Egg Plant, 20 Stewed Tomatoes, 15
Green Corn on Cob, 15 Cauliflower, Cream Sauce, 15 New String Beans, 15 Boiled New Potatoes, 10
Potatoes au Gratin, 20

DESSERT AND ICES

Meringue Glace, 25 Neapolitaine Ice Cream and Cakes, 25 Charlotte Russe, 20 Chocolate Eclair, 10
Omelet with Rum, 40 Roman Punch, 25 Fresh Strawberry Ice Cream and Cake, 25 Pear, Melba, 25
Banana Fritters, Brandy Sauce, 20 Vanilla Ice Cream and Cakes, 25 Biscuit Tortoni, 25 Peach, Melba, 25
Assorted French Pastry, 10 Lemon Water Ice, 20 Frozen Nesselrode Pudding, 25 Biscuit Glace, 25
Apple Pie, 10 Punch, Wellington, 25 Cafe Parfait, 25 Punch Yvette, 25 Strawberries and Ice Cream, 25
Raspberries with Ice Cream, 25 Blackberries with Ice Cream, 25 Apple Pie and Ice Cream, 20
Nutmeg Melon with Ice Cream (½) 25 Pumpkin Pie, 10 Strawberry Pie, 15 **Strawberry Short Cake, 25**

FRUITS

Sliced Fresh Figs and Cream, 25 Raspberries and Cream, 25 Logan Berries and Cream, 25 Grape Fruit, 25
Blackberries and Cream, 25 Sliced Oranges, 15 Sliced Bananas and Cream, 20
Nutmeg Melon, 25 Stewed Prunes, 15 Baked Apples and Cream, 20 Strawberries and Cream, 25
Peaches and Cream, 20 Apricots and Cream, 20 **Sliced Fresh Peaches with Cream, 25**

CHEESE

Sierra, 10 Brie, 15 Camembert, 15 Neufchatel, 15 Oregon Cream, 15 English Stilton, imp., 25 Swiss, 15
American, 10 English Cheddar, imp., 25 Bar le duc Currants, 50 Limburger, 15 Roquefort, 15

Demi Tasse. Cup of Coffee and Cream, 10 Pot of Chocolate or Cocoa, 15 Pot of Coffee and Cream, 15
Turkish Coffee, 25 Pot of Special Coffee and Cream (for two) 50 Glass of Milk, 10 Pot of Tea, 15

BUDWEISER ON DRAUGHT, 10c PER GLASS

Not Responsible For Hats Or Coats Unless Checked.

OVER

GATHERING GRAPES IN THE MONTEBELLO VINEYARDS.

ABOVE **College Inn, 1914, Oakland, California**

RIGHT **Hotel Touraine, 1911, Boston, Massachusetts**

BELOW **Hotel Touraine, 1915, Boston, Massachusetts**

OPPOSITE **Tait's, 1905, San Francisco, California**

Tait's Café had a Pompeian garden with white Roman columns, potted ferns, and grape leaf vines on the ceiling. The menu was huge and eclectic, with both little-neck clams and California oysters.

Das Tait's Café besaß ein pompejisches Gartenrestaurant mit weißen römischen Säulen, Farnen und Weinreben an der Decke. Die Speisekarte war umfangreich und ausgefallen: Es gab Venusmuscheln und kalifornische Austern.

Le Tait's possédait un jardin de style pompéien avec colonnes romaines blanches, fougères en pot et tonnelles où croissait la vigne. L'énorme et éclectique carte propose à la fois des clams et des huîtres de Californie.

PAGE 92 **Mouquin's, 1913, New York, New York**

PAGE 93 **Ye Oregon Grille, c. 1913, Portland, Oregon**

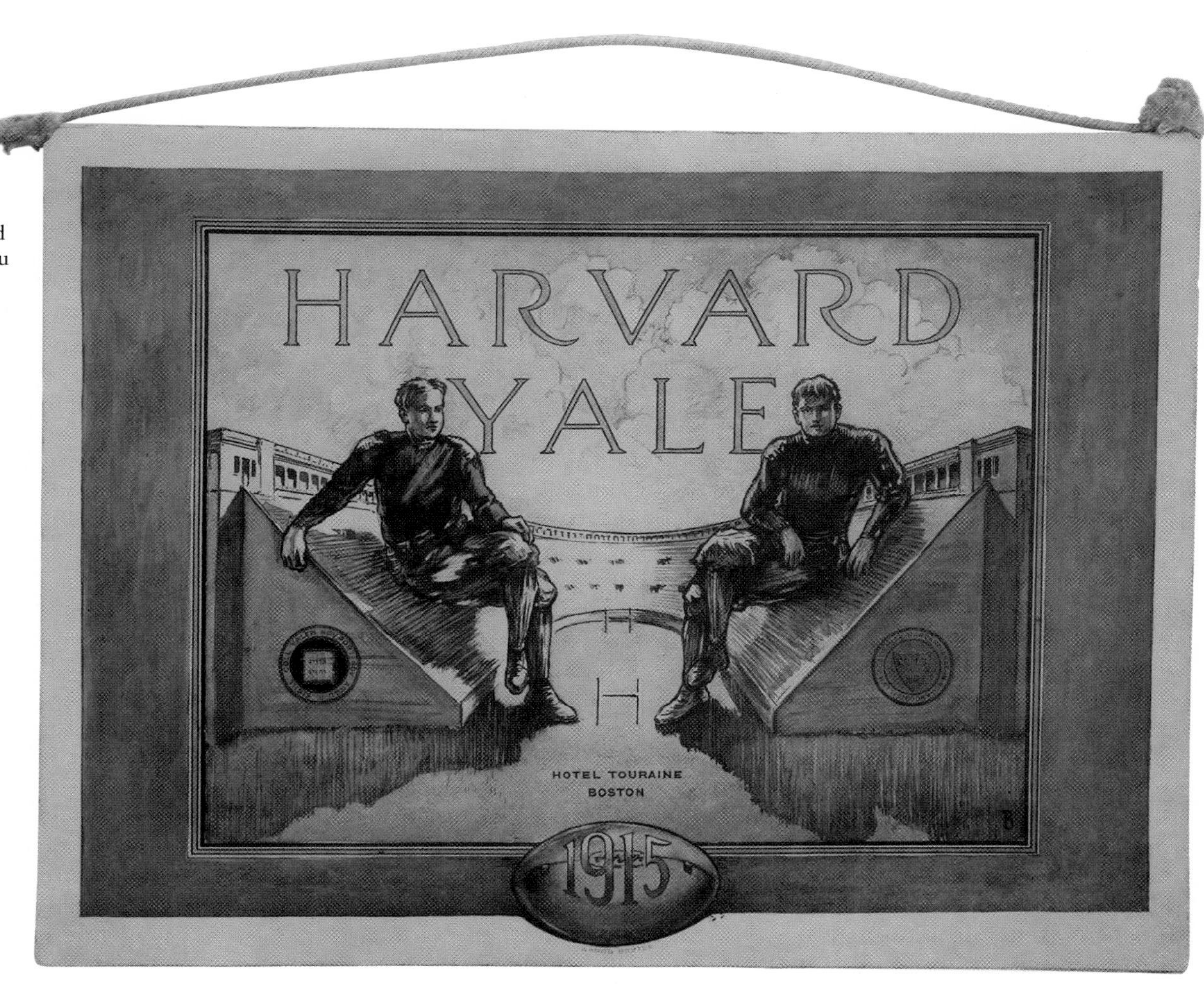

What do you think of this

13

MEN-U

MOUQUIN'S 454 (4+5+4=13) Sixth Avenue

Thursday, Feb. 13, 1913, 6:13 P.M.

Presiding officer—J. Arthur Lehmann, Chief Ruler.

Guest of Honor—Julius Harburger, Sheriff of New York.

Toastmaster and Chairman Dinner Committee--Col. John F. Hobbs.

Treasurer of Dinner Committee and Comptroller—Chas. Huethwohl.

Salutation—Morituri te Salutamus.

1. In Vino Veritas. (Free translation—filled out—Superstitions About Men Telling the Truth When in Their "Cups."

2. Superstitions about the Maison de la Mort, or the House of Death.

Talent— Mouquin's famous quartette and other entertainers there.

Sweeney, Nelson and Ross, the Little Hungary Sensation that is the talk of New York; sent up by fellow-member Max Schwartz, with his compliments.

Other talent—Some of it you know.

The "Assemble Earlies" may line up along the "rail" and tickle the channel with "Patterson" cocktails, et al.

The "Assemble Lates" may kick because the dinner starts on time.

If, in a nervous fit, you break a dish, glass or two, it will be a 13 mishap and a Fondeville incident. Louis Mouquin will explain.

The Eyes of the potatoes have been removed so they can't see the horrors of your tunnel.

Don't fill up too fast, more's coming.

Feel Royal—get Dry and drink Mouquin's "Dry Royal", Champagne.

At the "Smoke"—for which those fine **FATIMA CIGARETTES** have been donated by the proprietors—. Hon. Julius Harburger, Chauncey Depew's suceessor as a "peach" of an after dinner speaker, and the best Sheriff New York ever had, will be introduced.

From that stage on, events will shape themselves

Linger as late as you like; then go home feeling like a remade "Kid."

P. S. If you see any old Stilton cheese walking around loose, report it to the sheriff.

P. S. again. The March Dinner will be at Little Hungary, 255-263 East Houston Street, City; a Railroad Dinner, run by a Railroad Man, 2nd Vice-Ruler P. W. Heroy, General Eastern Passenger Agent Central Railroad of New Jersey.

I — Pamplemousse au madere

II — Essence de Volaille en tasse

III — Celeri en branches, Canape d'Anchois, Olives Mures

IV — Paupiettes de Sole Joinville, Pommes persillade, Graves

V — Poulet de Grain Saute a la Mouquin, Choux de Bruxelles, Rissoles

VI — SORBET ALPIN

VII — Contrefilet do Boeuf pique au jus Medoc

VIII — Salade Chiffonnade

IX — Glace francaise, Petit Fours

X — Fromages assortis

XI — Fruits Mendiants

XII — Cafe

XIII — Fatima Cigarettes

After-Theatre Specialties
Ye
Oregon Grille
Hotel Oregon
Oregon Grille
Seventh and Stark Sts.
Portland, Ore.

BELOW RIGHT & OPPOSITE The Saratoga, c. 1909, Chicago, Illinois

Until the turn of the century the exclusively male Saratoga was notorious for its attic "beefsteak dinners," where patrons ate without silverware on tables made from packing boxes, followed by "old-fashioned dances."

Bis zur Jahrhundertwende stand das Saratoga nur Männern offen. Es war berüchtigt für seine „Beefsteak Dinners auf dem Dachboden", bei denen die Gäste ohne Besteck an Tischen aus Kisten aßen, gefolgt vom „Tanz wie in alten Zeiten".

Le Saratoga reste exclusivement réservé aux hommes jusqu'au tournant du siècle. Sa salle mansardée est célèbre pour ses « beefsteak dinners » où les clients mangent sans argenterie sur des cartons. Le « buffet de biftecks » est ensuite suivi de « danses d'autrefois ».

ABOVE Celebrating New Year's Eve at Rector's, 1905, New York, New York

RIGHT Hotel Rector, 1908, New York, New York

The heraldic griffin, half lion and half eagle of the hotel Rector, which opened in 1899, may have been adopted by hotelier Charles Rector as an emblem for intelligence and strength.

Das Wappentier des 1899 eröffneten Hotel Rector, ein Greif, halb Löwe, halb Adler, hatte sich der Hotelier Charles Rector wahrscheinlich als Symbol seiner eigenen Intelligenz und Stärke zugelegt.

Le griffon héraldique mi-lion, mi-aigle de l'Hotel Rector qui ouvrit en 1899, a peut-être été adopté par l'hôtelier Charles Rector comme symbole d'intelligence et de force.

WATERS, Etc.

		SPLITS.	PTS.	QTS.
85	APOLLINARIS	$ .15	.25	
86.	WHITE ROCK	.15	.25	
87.	BOKERT WATER, Glass	.10		
88.	VICHY (Celestines), Glass	.10	.25	.40
89.	CALWA—Non Alcoholic, Red or White (The juice of California Wine Grapes)	.20		
90.	HUNYADI JANOS, Glass	.10		
91.	RED RAVEN	.15		
92.	CLUB SODA		.25	
93.	C. & G. GINGER ALE		.25	

WHISKIES, BRANDIES.

			DRINK.
96	G. & U. MARQUETTE RYE		.15
97.	CEDAR BROOK		.15
98.	C. & G. OLD RESERVE RYE OR BOURBON		.15
99.	HERMITAGE		.15
100.	CANADIAN CLUB		.20
101.	DEWAR'S WHITE LABEL		.15
102.	SANDERSON'S MOUNTAIN DEW		.15
103.	BLACK AND WHITE		.15
104.	KING WILLIAM		.20
105.	PINCH HAIG & HAIG, SCOTCH	.25	.15
106.	BUSHMILLS		.15
107.	JOHN JAMESON 3 STAR		.15
108.	BLACKBERRY		.15
109.	JAS. HENNESSY'S 3 STAR	.15	.25
110.	OTARD BRANDY	.15	.25
111.	FINEST OLD "CALWA" BRANDY		.15

GINS AND RUMS.

115.	OLD TOM GIN	.15
116.	JOHN DE KUYPER (Holland)	.15
117.	SLOE (Fields)	.15
118.	GORDON	.15
119.	PLYMOUTH	.15
120.	SCHIEDAM (Holland)	.15
121.	OLD MEDFORD	.15
122.	JAMAICA (Old London Dock)	.15

CORDIALS.

125.	ELIXIR D'AUVERS	.15
126.	APRICOT BRANDY	.20
127.	CREME DE MENTHE (Ruby, Green or White)	.20
128.	CHARTREUSE (Green or Yellow)	.20
129.	CREME DE COCOA	.20
130.	CREME DE YVETTE	.20
131.	CURACAO	.20
132.	MARASCHINO	.20
133.	KUMMEL (Gilka)	.20
134.	BENEDICTINE	.20
135.	DUBONNET	.20

WINE
LIST
The Saratoga
CHICAGO

LEFT **Cafe Diable, 1912**

BELOW **The Taft, 1912, New Haven, Connecticut**

In a nod to the growing suffragette movement, the women on these menu covers display joy in inflicting discomfort to the males around them.

Als Anspielung auf die wachsende Sufragettenbewegung sind auf dieser Speisekarte Frauen zu sehen, die den anwesenden Männern mit Freude Unbehagen bereiten.

En signe d'adhésion au mouvement des suffragettes de plus en plus important, les femmes figurant sur ces menus semblent tirer une certaine joie des tourments infligés aux hommes qui les entourent.

OPPOSITE **Annual Dinner of the CC, 1913, New York, New York**

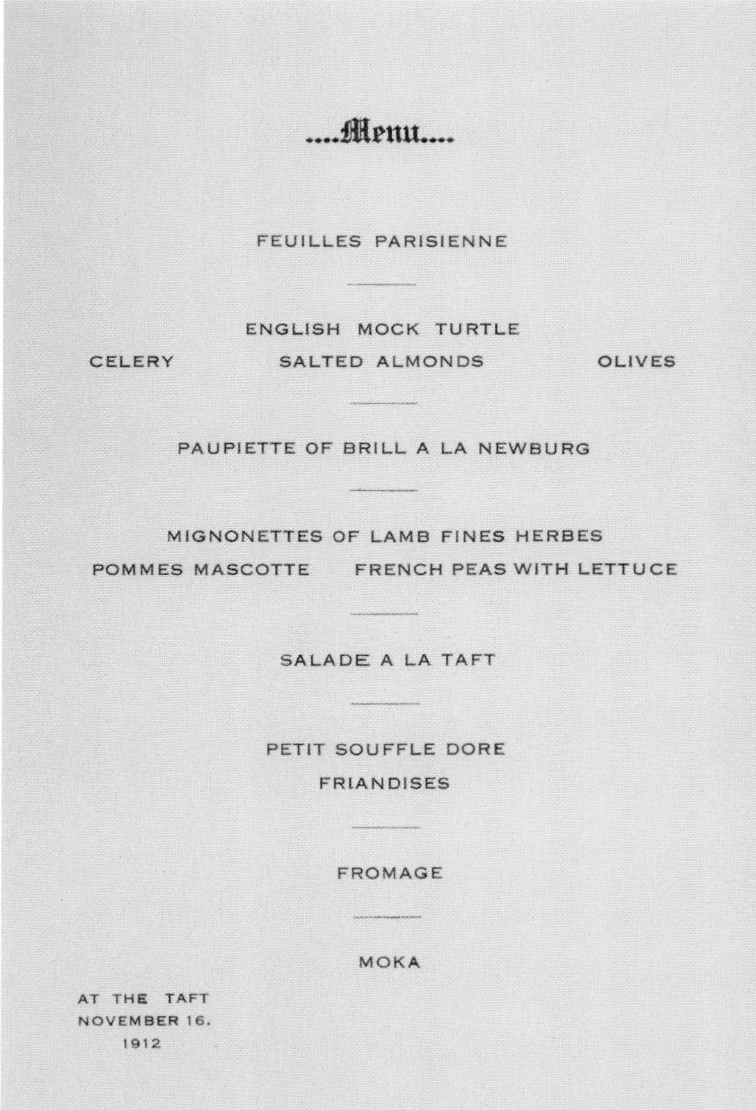

....Menu....

FEUILLES PARISIENNE

ENGLISH MOCK TURTLE

CELERY SALTED ALMONDS OLIVES

PAUPIETTE OF BRILL A LA NEWBURG

MIGNONETTES OF LAMB FINES HERBES

POMMES MASCOTTE FRENCH PEAS WITH LETTUCE

SALADE A LA TAFT

PETIT SOUFFLE DORE

FRIANDISES

FROMAGE

MOKA

AT THE TAFT
NOVEMBER 16.
1912

Annual Dinner of the
CC
1913
Here's Luck To You!

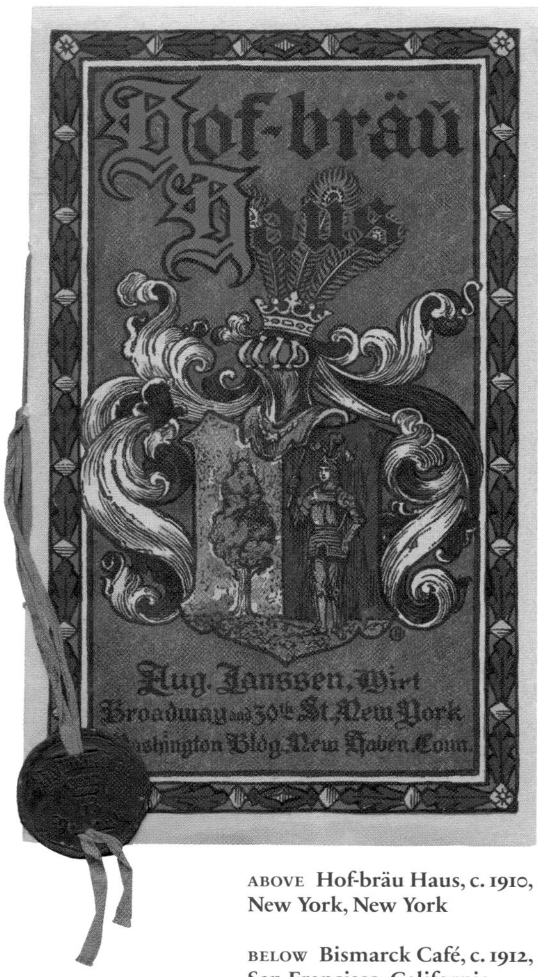

ABOVE Hof-bräu Haus, c. 1910, New York, New York

BELOW Bismarck Café, c. 1912, San Francisco, California

OPPOSITE Hofbräu Haus, 1916, New York, New York

Variations of Hofbräuhaus — the name of a royal brewing company in Munich — were used by many German-American restaurants to distinguish them from less savory beer halls.

Der Name „Hofbräuhaus" – in Anlehnung an das berühmte Wirtshaus in München – wurde von vielen deutsch-amerikanischen Gaststätten benutzt, um sich von Kneipen mit weniger gutem Bier abzusetzen.

Variations sur la Hofbräuhaus – la célèbre brasserie de Munich – utilisées par de nombreux restaurants germano-américains pour se distinguer des bars à bière moins raffinés.

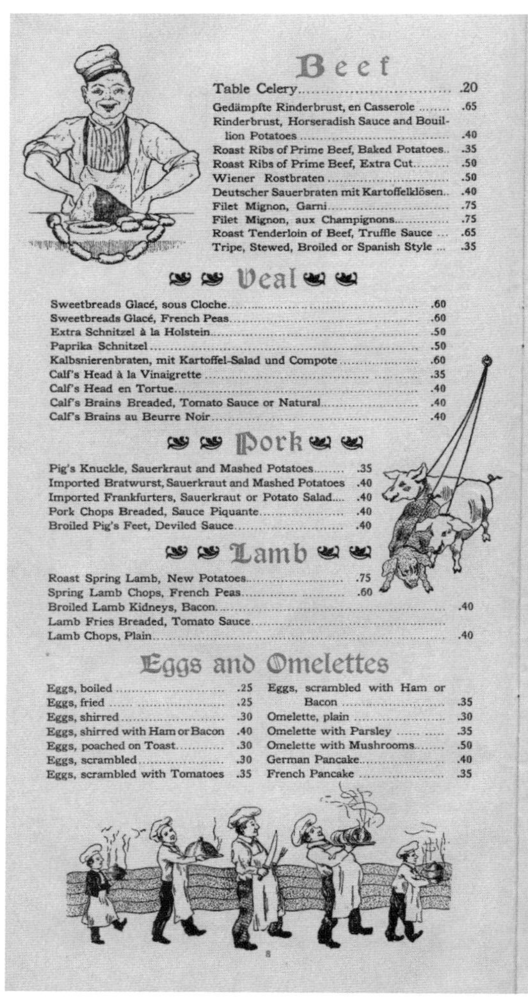

Beef

Table Celery	.20
Gedämpfte Rinderbrust, en Casserole	.65
Rinderbrust, Horseradish Sauce and Bouillion Potatoes	.40
Roast Ribs of Prime Beef, Baked Potatoes	.35
Roast Ribs of Prime Beef, Extra Cut	.50
Wiener Rostbraten	.50
Deutscher Sauerbraten mit Kartoffelklösen	.40
Filet Mignon, Garni	.75
Filet Mignon, aux Champignons	.75
Roast Tenderloin of Beef, Truffle Sauce	.65
Tripe, Stewed, Broiled or Spanish Style	.35

Veal

Sweetbreads Glacé, sous Cloche	.60
Sweetbreads Glacé, French Peas	.60
Extra Schnitzel à la Holstein	.50
Paprika Schnitzel	.50
Kalbsnierenbraten, mit Kartoffel-Salad und Compote	.60
Calf's Head à la Vinaigrette	.35
Calf's Head en Tortue	.40
Calf's Brains Breaded, Tomato Sauce or Natural	.40
Calf's Brains au Beurre Noir	.40

Pork

Pig's Knuckle, Sauerkraut and Mashed Potatoes	.35
Imported Bratwurst, Sauerkraut and Mashed Potatoes	.40
Imported Frankfurters, Sauerkraut or Potato Salad	.40
Pork Chops Breaded, Sauce Piquante	.40
Broiled Pig's Feet, Deviled Sauce	.40

Lamb

Roast Spring Lamb, New Potatoes	.75
Spring Lamb Chops, French Peas	.60
Broiled Lamb Kidneys, Bacon	.40
Lamb Fries Breaded, Tomato Sauce	
Lamb Chops, Plain	.40

Eggs and Omelettes

Eggs, boiled	.25	Eggs, scrambled with Ham or Bacon	.35
Eggs, fried	.25	Omelette, plain	.30
Eggs, shirred	.30	Omelette with Parsley	.35
Eggs, shirred with Ham or Bacon	.40	Omelette with Mushrooms	.50
Eggs, poached on Toast	.30	German Pancake	.40
Eggs, scrambled	.30	French Pancake	.35
Eggs, scrambled with Tomatoes	.35		

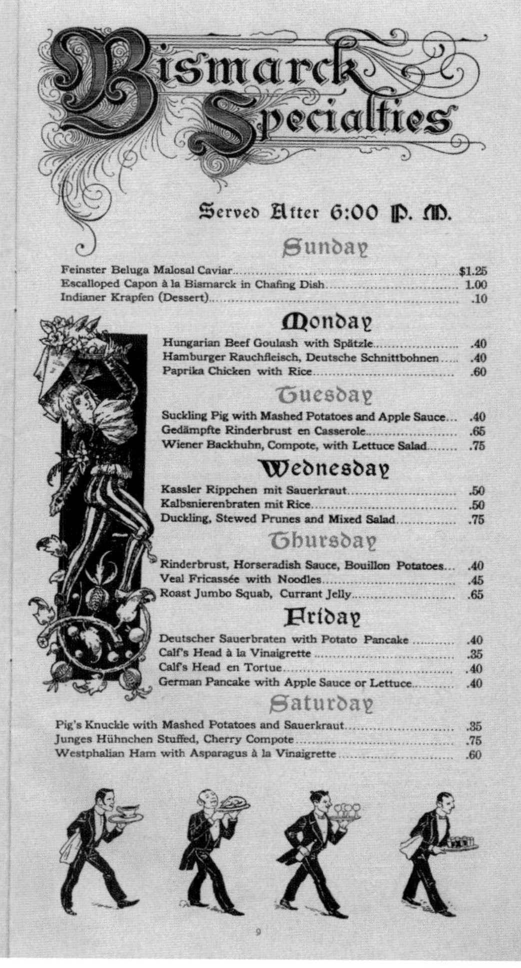

Bismarck Specialties

Served After 6:00 P. M.

Sunday

Feinster Beluga Malosal Caviar	$1.25
Escalloped Capon à la Bismarck in Chafing Dish	1.00
Indianer Krapfen (Dessert)	.10

Monday

Hungarian Beef Goulash with Spätzle	.40
Hamburger Rauchfleisch, Deutsche Schnittbohnen	.40
Paprika Chicken with Rice	.60

Tuesday

Suckling Pig with Mashed Potatoes and Apple Sauce	.40
Gedämpfte Rinderbrust en Casserole	.65
Wiener Backhuhn, Compote, with Lettuce Salad	.75

Wednesday

Kassler Rippchen mit Sauerkraut	.50
Kalbsnierenbraten mit Rice	.50
Duckling, Stewed Prunes and Mixed Salad	.75

Thursday

Rinderbrust, Horseradish Sauce, Bouillon Potatoes	.40
Veal Fricassée with Noodles	.45
Roast Jumbo Squab, Currant Jelly	.65

Friday

Deutscher Sauerbraten with Potato Pancake	.40
Calf's Head à la Vinaigrette	.35
Calf's Head en Tortue	.40
German Pancake with Apple Sauce or Lettuce	.40

Saturday

Pig's Knuckle with Mashed Potatoes and Sauerkraut	.35
Junges Hühnchen Stuffed, Cherry Compote	.75
Westphalian Ham with Asparagus à la Vinaigrette	.60

Hof Bräu
Hof Bräu Haus
Hof Bräu
Haus
Broadway & 30th Street
New York
August Janssen
30th-Street-30th
and Broadway

RIGHT Hofbrau Haus, 1916, New York, New York

After the Civil War, America saw an enormous flood of immigrants from Germany who opened beer halls and restaurants of their own. The menus were as immense as the restaurants.

Nach dem Ende des Sezessionskriegs wanderten wahre Heerscharen von Deutschen in die USA ein, wo sie zahlreiche Bierlokale und deutsche Wirtshäuser eröffneten. Die Speisekarten waren so riesig wie die Gaststätten.

Après la guerre de Sécession, l'Amérique connaît un énorme flot d'immigrants venus d'Allemagne, lesquels ouvrent bars à bière et restaurants. Les menus sont aussi gigantesques que les restaurants.

Our Bread and Rolls are

DINNER

WEDNESDAY, NOV, 8

Relishes

Hors d'Oeuvre, per person .50
Russian Caviar 1.25
Malossol Caviar 2.00
Table Celery 30
Radishes 15
Dill Pickle 10
Sweet Pickles 15
Pickled Beets 15
Senfgurken 20
Queen Olives 15
Ripe Olives 20
Olives, stuffed 25
Chutney 15
Indian Chow Chow 20
Pickled Walnuts 25
Anchovies on Toast 60
Sardines, 50 Box 90
Sardellen with Egg 50
Salami and Cervelatwurst 50
Roll, Bismarck or Mar. Herring 40
Swedish Herring Filets 40
Swedish Appetit Sild 40

Oysters a
Blue Points, Cape Co
Cotuits, Robbins
Lynnhavens
Cocktail
Stew 40 Fr
Steamed 50 Pa
Poulette 60 Pa
Omelet
Baked a la Hofbrau
Little Neck or Cherry
Cocktail
Steamed Soft Clams
Baked Soft Clams a l

Soups

Consomme in Jelly 25
Chicken Okra with Rice 20
Consomme, Lammartine 25
Deutsche Erbsen Suppe mit Wurstschnitten 25
Cream of Tomatoes with Rice, Carmen 25
Deutsche Nudelsuppe 25
Clam Broth with Essence of Celery 30
Puree Mongole 25
Tomato with Rice 25
Petite Marmite 40
Chicken Broth
Onion Soup au gratin
Deutsche Huhner Sup in Bouillon Rice)
Deutsche Kraftbruh Beef in Bouillon)
Green Turtle, clear
Green Turtle, English

Fresh Artichoke, Sauce Hollandaise 50
Fried Egg Plant 25 Casaba Melon 25

SPECIAL TO-NIGHT

Alligat
Franklin
Hard S

Reserve Your Tables Now for Election Night

Cold Kennebec Salmon, Sauce Mayonnaise 75
Eel in Jelly, Cucumber Salad 6

Steamed Soft Clams, Butter Sauce .50
Crab Stuffed and Deviled (1) .50
Boiled Codfish, Egg Sauce .50
Steamed Finnan Haddie, Butter Sauce .50
Boiled Redsnapper, Parsley Sauce, Bouillon Potatoes .60
Baked Sea Trout, Creole .60
Filet of Sole Baked a la Mornay .60
Crab Meat Cocktail .60
Sea Bass Saute, Meuniere .65
Broiled Chicken Halibut, Maitre d'Hotel .65
Broiled Fresh Mackerel, Parsley Butter .60
Broiled Bluefish, Maitre d'Hotel .65

Fried Smelts, Sauce Tartare or Sau
Fried Scallops and Bacon, Sauce T
Filet of Sole, Marguery (15 m.)
Boiled Kennebec Salmon, Hollanda
Lobster Cocktail
Crab Flakes, Maryland (15 m.)
Crab Flakes with Green Peppers and Clams, Frica
Lobster Stuffed and Deviled (1) (15
Fried Frogs' Legs, Sauce Remoula
Live Lobsters Every Day from Main
Lobster Cold, Mayonnaise
Lobster, Newburg in Chafing Dish

Spinach with Bratkartoffeln .40
Nürnberger Würstchen, Sauerkraut, Salat .50
Leipziger Allerlei, Pastete .50
Spinach with Broiled Sardines .50
Frankfurters, Sauerkraut, Mashed Potatoes .50
Hamburger Steak, Smothered Onions, Potatoes .60
Boiled Beef, Horseradish Sauce, Bouillon Potatoes .60
Hungarian Goulash with Spätzle .60
Pig's Knuckle, Sauerkraut, Kartoffelbrei .60
Apfeleierkuchen .60
Calf's Head with Suessauere Pflaumen .65
Beef a la Mode, Potato Pancakes .65
Roast Prime Ribs of Beef, Baked Potato .75
Kalbsnierenbraten, Leipziger Allerlei .75
Broiled Beech-Nut Ham Steak, Asparagus Tips (15 m.) 75
Lamb Chops (2), Mashed Sweet Potatoes, Peas .80
Wiener Schnitzel, Garnirt mit Ei und Sardellen (10 m.) 85
Broiled Pork Tenderloin, Apple Sauce, Sweet Potatoes (10 m.) .85
Paprika Schnitzel with Spätzle (8 m.) .85
Veal Cutlet Breaded, Celery au Gratin .85
Fricassee of Chicken with Rice and Pastete .85
Deutsche Huehner Suppe with Rice .85
Ragout a la Deutsch (8 m.) .85
Sweetbread Patties a la Toulouse .85
Small Steak, Stanley, Potatoes (8 m.) .85

Filet Mignon (1) en Casserole, Garni
Wiener Rostbraten, Merrettig und Zwiebeln
Combination Grill: 1 Loin Lamb C Kidney, Calf's Liver
Brat Ente mit gedaempften Rothkoh Bratkar
Broiled Sweetbreads on Toast, Green Peas
Fresh Mushrooms in Cream on Toa
A King's Dinner: Consisting of Chicken, Swe Mushrooms, Krebsschwanze, Fleurons, S
Royal Squab Broiled, Currant Jelly
Venison Steak, Casserole, Cumberla
Riesen-Taube (Royal Sqaub) im Topf m Gruenen Erbsen, Erdschwaemme und Spa
Squab Chicken a la Paradise (mit F en Casserole (
Whole Broiled Squab Chicken, Irish Ba Served for One Person On
Chicken in Paprika with Noodles (10 m.)
Fried Chicken, Wiener Style, Compote (15 m
Broiled Guinea Chicken, Currant Jelly (15
Roast or Broiled Squab Duckling, Apple Sauce (15 m
Roast Guinea Chicken en Casserole, Jardinie
Broiled Squab Turkey, Sweet Potato Cranberries

Vegetables

Green Peas 25
String Beans 25
Lima Beans 25
Spinach 25
Noodles 20
Baked Noodles 30
Spätzle 20
Baked Spätzle 30
Potato Pancakes with Preiselbeeren 50
Potato Dumplings 20
Sauerkraut 25
Cauliflower, Butter Sauce 30
Cauliflower au Gratin 40
Brussels Sprouts 25
Fresh Artichoke, Sauce Hollandaise 50
Fried Egg Plant 25
Boiled Onions in Cream 25
Stewed Corn 20
Boiled Rice 15
Asparagus 50
Asparagus Tips 40
Macaroni au Gratin 35
Spaghetti a l' Italienne 35
Succotash 20
Deutsche Schnittbohnen 25
Leipziger Allerlei 25

Potat
Boiled Potatoes
Mashed
Baked (1)
Hashed in Cream
German Fried
Lyonnaise
Julienne
French Fried
Au Gratin
Stuffed (1)
Saratoga Chips
Fried Sweet Potatoes
Sweet Potatoes, Souther
Bermuda Potatoes

Salads, Etc.

Vegetable Salad 40
Potato 15
Bermuda Onion 25
Watercress 25
Cold Slaw 35
Lettuce 35
Lettuce with Grapefruit 50
Tomato 35
Cucumber 35
Romaine 35
Imported Knob Celery 35
Celery 30
Chiffonade
Salad Kuroki
Salmon
Chicken
Crabmeat
Lobster

Finest Selection of Domestic and Imported

After Theatre Arrangements for Parties, Dancing, Etc.

Sanitary Bakery in New York: The Franco-American Baking Co.

ıade Pastry
ce Cream

. . . . 20
. . . . 15
. . . . 15
el . . . 25
(Whipped Cream 5c. Extra)

en 10
.... 10
.... 15
.... 10
.... 15
.... 15
.... 15
.... 15
hen mit Zimmet . 60
Confitures ... 50
hum 50
lee 75
ding 15
.... 25
.... 25
.... 25
.... 40
.... 30
e or Panache 30
.... 75
Ice 25
am 25
............25
............25
.... 25
.... 30
.... 30
lding 30

and Compote

. . . . . .15 25
.... 30
.... 15
.... 50
elbeeren 25
.... 15
.... 10
Fruits in Season

heese

............15 25
.... 15 25
.... 15 25
.... 15 25
.... 15 25
.... 15 25
.... 25
............15 25
.... 25
.... 15 25
.... 15 25
ı 15 25
.... 25
on Served for
erson Only

and Tea

ream Cup 15
for one) 20
or Two 35
Caffeine re-
% (for one), Pot.25
ı Coffee (for
hine 60
th Whipped
.... 20 35
.... 15 25
.... 15
.... 15
.... 25

From the Grill: Steaks and Chops

Small Steak, plain	65
Sirloin Steak, plain	85
Sirloin Steak with Onions	1 00
Sirloin Steak with Mushrooms	1 00
Sirloin Steak, Bearnaise	1 00
Sirloin Steak en Casserole	1 25
Sirloin Steak, Hofbrau	1 25
Extra Sirloin Steak, plain	1 75
Extra Sirloin Steak with Onions	2 00
Extra Sirloin Steak with Mushrooms	2 25
Extra Sirloin Steak, Bearnaise	2 25
Extra Sirloin Steak en Casserole	2 50
Extra Sirloin Steak, Hofbrau	2 50
Extra Sirloin Steak, Planked	3 25
Club Steak, plain	2 50
Club Steak with Mushrooms	3 25
Club Steak with Onions	3 00
Club Steak en Casserole	3 25
Club Steak, Planked	4 50
Porterhouse Steak, single	1 75
Porterhouse Steak with Onions	2 00
Porterhouse Steak with Mushrooms	2 25
Porterhouse Steak, Bearnaise	2 25
Filet Mignon, plain (1)	70
Filet Mignon with Mushrooms (1)	90
Filet Mignon, Bearnaise (1)	90
Filet Mignon en Casserole (1)	90
Tenderloin Steak	1 10
Tenderloin Steak with Mushrooms	1 50
Tenderloin Steak, Bearnaise	1 50
Tenderloin Steak en Casserole	1 50
Tenderloin Steak with Sweetbreads en Casserole	2 00
Chateaubriand, plain	2 00
Chateaubriand with Mushrooms	2 75
Chateaubriand, Bearnaise	2.75
Chateaubriand en Casserole	2 75
Chateaubriand, Hofbrau	2 75
French Lamb Chops (3)	90
French Lamb Chops, Jardiniere (3)	1 25
English Mutton Chops, String Beans	80

Poultry

OUR SPECIALTY: Hamburger Kuecken (Squab Chicken) mit geduensteten Fruechten im Topf		1 50
Roast Chicken, 2 lbs.		2 00
Roast Chicken en Casserole, 2 lbs.		2 50
Broiled Chicken, 2 lbs.	1 00	2 00
Chicken, Maryland Style	1 15	2 25
Chicken Saute, Marengo	1 15	2 25
Chicken in Bouillon Rice with Asparagus		85
Squab, Roasted or Broiled, Currant Jelly		1 25
Junge Taube mit Spargel, Morcheln, gruenen Erbsen		1 50

All Our Poultry is of the Highest Class and Received Daily From Our Farm

Eggs and Omelettes

Eggs Boiled	25
Eggs Fried, Scrambled or Poached	30
Eggs Scrambled with Tomatoes	35
Ham and Eggs or Bacon and Eggs	45
Eggs a la Hofbrau	40
Poached Eggs on Anchovy Toast	40
Spiegeleier mit Bratkartoffeln	40
Scotch Woodcock	50
Omelette, plain	30
Omelette with Tomatoes	40
Omelette with Chicken Livers	50
Omelette with Parsley	35
Omelette with Ham	40
Omelette, Spanish	50
Omelette with Asparagus Tips	50
" with Mushrooms	50
Omelette Confitures or au Rhum	50
Omelette Souffles	75
French Pancakes with Jelly	50
German Pancake with Imported Preiselbeeren	50
Apfeleierkuchen	60

Cold Dishes

Lettuce Salad with Two Boiled Eggs	50
Matjes Haring, New String Beans, Potatoes	50
Salamiwurst with Potato Salad	50
Cervelatwurst with Potato Salad	50
Boiled Ham, Potato Salad	50
Smoked Beef Tongue with Potato Salad	50
Westphalian Ham	75
Braunschweiger Leberwurst	50
Geraucherte Schweinerippchen mit Gemischtem Salat	60
Cold Turkey and Virginia Ham	1 00
Pickled Pig's Feet, Bratkartoffeln	45
Pickled Lamb's Tongue, Vegetable Salad	45
Italienischer Salat	50
Crab, Ravigote	50
Corned Beef with Potato Salad	50
Roast Prime Ribs of Beef, Hofbrau Salad	75
Sauerbraten mit Gemuese Salat	65
Eggs (2) a la Russe	75
Illustrierte Gurke	65
Roast Leg of Lamb, String Bean Salad	65
Beech-Nut Ham, Speck Salat	60
Smoked Loin of Pork, Knob Celery	60
Kalter Aufschnitt for one	75
Smoked Sturgeon and Cold Slaw	80
Smoked Salmon with Asparagus	80
Virginia Ham with Asparagus	80
Russisches Vorgericht, Matjes Haring, Caviar, Zwiebeln, Bermuda Kartoffeln	80
Roast L. I. Duckling, Cold Slaw and Compot	1 00
Half Roast Milk-fed Chicken, Sliced Tomatoes	1 00
Schwedische Platte, Bestehend aus Lachs, Caviar mit Ei, Sardinen, Anchovies und Frischen Radieschen	1 50
Delicatessen Aufschnitt for two	1 50
Hofbrau Platte (for 2,) Bestehend aus Frischem Hummer, Raeucher Lachs, Raeucher Stoehr, Caviar mit Ei, Aal in Gelee, Salaten, Kaesesorten und Radieschen	1 75

Sandwiches

Limburger	15
Brie Cheese	15
Swiss Cheese	15
American Cheese	15
Caviar	30
Leberwurst	15
Chicken	25
Blutwurst	15
Club	40
Anchovy	30
Roast Beef	30
Sardine on Toast	30
Westphalian Ham	25
Cervelatwurst	25
Smoked Salmon	30
Boiled Ham	15
Sardine	25
Tongue	20
Sardellen	25
Raw Meat	20
Tartare, Egg and Sardellen	30
Buffetschnittchen	40

On Toast 5c Extra

Recommended

Hofbrau Special	20
Jannsen's Ideal Cocktail	20
Sherry Cobbler	25
New Orleans Fizz	25
Rhine Wine, plain or with Rhenser Water, Glass 15 Half Schoppen 30 Schoppen	60
Oberingelheimer (Red Rhine Wine) Glass 20 Half Schoppen 40 Schoppen	80
Wininger Uhlen, Pints Only	1 40
Trabener, Pints Only	25
Liebfraumilch, Pints Only	1 25

After Theatre Suggestions

Lobster Cocktail		80
Crab Meat Cocktail		60
Mussels, Vinaigrette		50
Soft Clams Baked in Shell, Ancienne		75
Canape Lorenzo		50
Crab Meat au Gratin		80
Cold Lobster, Sauce Mayonnaise	75	1 50
Broiled Lobster, Butter Sauce		1 50
Stuffed Lobster, Flambe with Grilled Sweet Potatoes	1 00	2 00
Ragout Fin en Coquille		70
Chicken Patty a la Reine		75
Breast of Chicken, Eugenie, Sous Cloche		1 25
Eggs, Benedictine		75
Lamb Kidneys Saute, Fresh Mushrooms		75
Pork Tenderloin Saute, Red Cabbage		90
Nuernberger Sausages Broiled, Potato Salad		60
Sweetbread Saute au Madere, New Green Peas		1 00
Brochette of Chicken Livers with Bacon		80
Kalbschnitzel Naturel mit Frischen Schnittbohnen		90
Filet Mignon (1) en Casserole with Bouquet of Dainty Vegetables		1 00
Muenchner Casserole for 2 (Assorted Sausages, Smoked Pork, Sauerkraut, Mashed Potatoes, Onions		1 25
Hamburger Kuecken mit Fruchten, Neuen Erbsen und Wuerfel Kartoffeln in Casserole		1 50
Broiled Squab, Currant Jelly		1 10
Royal Squab en Casserole, Hofbrau		1 35
Fruit Salad, Maraschino Dressing		60

Chafing Dishes

Sea Food, Exquisite	1 25
Finnan Haddie in Cream, Fin de Siecle	1 00
Crab Flakes a la Dewey	1 25
Lobster a la Newburg	1 75
Lobster, Americaine	2 00
Chicken a la King	1 50
Chicken, Marie Stuart	1 75
Frogs' Legs a la Poulette	1 25
Sweetbread with Fresh Mushrooms	1 50
Ragout a la Deutsch	1 00

Rarebits

Welsh Rarebit	35
Long Island Buck	45
Golden Buck	45
Yorkshire Buck	60

Private Rooms for Meetings, Luncheons, Dinners and Beefsteak Parties or Dances

Table d'Hote $1.25
From 6 to 9 P. M.
in Our Grill Room
Sundays from 12 noon to 9 P. M.

Combination Breakfast
or a la Carte from 7 to 11 A. M.

Ladies' Waiting *and* Dressing Rooms on Second Floor, take Elevator

NOT RESPONSIBLE For Hats, Coats or other Valuables Unless Checked

ettes. — Our Hofbrau Haus Cigars are made in Tampa from the Choicest Havana Tobacco

OPPOSITE Une Poule au Pot, 1912, San Francisco, California

A most provocative menu for a private dinner features local sand dabs as well as *Poule au Pot Henri IV* (chicken in the "pot"). King Henry IV (1553–1610) declared this dish to be eaten by Frenchmen every Sunday. The celebrants, Cercle de l'Union, a local dining club, was also known as the French Club and is still active today.

Die höchst frivole Karte eines privaten Vorweihnachtsessens, bei dem kalifornische Flundern und *Poule au Pot Henry IV* („Hühnersuppe Heinrich IV.") serviert wurden. Heinrich IV. (1553–1610) hatte verfügt, dass alle Franzosen dieses Gericht jeden Sonntag im Topf haben sollten. Der Club Cercle de l'Union ist auch als der heute noch aktive French Club bekannt.

Menu pour le moins provocateur d'un dîner privé proposant aussi bien de la limande qu'une « poule au pot Henri IV ». Henri IV (1553-1610) avait décrété que tous les Français devaient pouvoir manger une poule au pot le dimanche. L'association hôte, le Cercle de l'Union, club gastronomique local connu également sous le nom de French Club, est toujours en activité de nos jours.

ABOVE Tait's, James Flood Building, c. 1907, San Francisco, California

RIGHT 142nd Annual Banquet, Chamber of Commerce of the State of New York, the Waldorf-Astoria, 1910, New York, New York

MENU
Huitres Toke Point sur Coquille
Chablis
Potage de Tortue Amontillado
Turban de Sand Dabs Joinville
Lur Saluces
Poule au Pot Henri IV.
Filet de Bœuf Talleyrand-Périgord
Chateau Margaux
Cœurs d'Artichauts Dubarry
Salade
Plum Pudding Edouard VII.
Cordon Rouge
Gâteaux Assortis
Café
Liqueurs
Une Poule au Pot au Cercle de l'Union en l'Honneur de MM. Mérou de Chantreau de Sabla et de Coulon
SAN FRANCISCO,
23 Décembre, 1912

ESTABLISHED 1847.
THE
GEM
127-129 ROYAL STREET,
NEW ORLEANS
Gielle-Egerton Co.

ABOVE Portola-Louvre, 1915, San Francisco, California

OPPOSITE The Gem, c. 1915, New Orleans, Louisiana

RIGHT & BELOW Portola-Louvre, c. 1917, San Francisco, California

Seating 1,500 guests, the Portola-Louvre proudly promoted its gargantuan space and menu. Fresh vegetables were harvested from the hotel's own San Mateo gardens. A true innovation of the day, and, only invented in 1902, was its "refrigerated air ventilation" system "at a cost of $30,000."

Das Portola-Louvre mit Platz für 1500 Gäste war sehr stolz auf seine riesigen Räumlichkeiten und Speisenangebote. Frisches Gemüse wurde in den hoteleigenen Gärten in San Mateo geerntet. Eine wahre technische Sensation war das erst 1902 erfundene „Ventilationssystem für gekühlte Luft", Kostenpunkt 30.000 Dollar.

Baptisé d'après le nom du missionnaire franciscain Gaspar de Portolà et du grand musée parisien, le Portola-Louvre, qui pouvait accueillir 1 500 clients, vantait son espace impressionnant et son menu gargantuesque. Tous les légumes frais provenaient du potager de l'hôtel, à San Mateo. On y trouvait également une véritable innovation (elle date en effet de 1902) : un système de « ventilation à air réfrigéré ayant coûté 30 000 dollars ».

MENU

DINNER—*Tuesday, Dec. 23, 1913*

Hors d'Oeuvres
Boneless Sardine 35 Senfgurken 10
Marinirter or Bismarck Herring 35
Assorted Hors d'Oeuvres (Served for 1 or 2) 50
Ripe, Queen or Manzanilla Olives 15
Caviar 50 Caviar Canape 40
Celery en Branch 25 Anchovy Canape 30
Anchovies in Oil 35 Swedish Anchovies 25
Grape Fruit (half) 15 German Dill Pickles 10

Oysters and Shell Fish
California Oyster Cocktail 30
Celebrated Swan Point Oysters from our own Oyster Beds (6) 40
Shrimp Cocktail 35 Clam Cocktail 30
Little Neck Clams on half shell 40
Stewed Oysters 50 Toke Point (6) 40
Blue Points (6) 40 Half Broiled Live Lobster 65
Half Cold Lobster, Mayonaise 65
Cracked Crab, Mayonnaise 50 Crab, Louis 60

Salads Portola Special (Individual Service) 30
Consisting of Heart of Lettuce, Sliced Tomato, Water Cress, Asparagus Tips, Fresh Lobster and French Dressing
Stuffed Tomato with Celery 25 Lobster 40
Cosmopolitan 35 Chicken 35 Crab 35
Asparagus Tips 35 Combination 35 Shrimp 40
Alligator Pear half 40 whole 75 Tomato 25
Lettuce or Romaine 20 Lettuce and Tomato 25

Soups and Broth
English Beef Broth with Barley 15
Cream of Cauliflower, Duchesse 15
Consomme en Tasse 15 Consomme Frappe 15
Chicken Broth in Cup 25
Clam Juice 20 Green Turtle (in Cup) 25
Mock Turtle a l'Anglaise 25

Fish (to Order 10 to 20 minutes)
Boiled Salmon, Hollandaise Sauce 45
Filet of English Sole au Gratin 40
Broiled Striped Bass, Maitre d'Hotel 50
Broiled Salmon, Maitre d'Hotel 45
English Sole Fried in Butter 40
Filet of Sole, Sauce Remoulade 40
Clams or Mussels, Bordelaise 40
Sand Dabs, Meuniere 50

Special Entrees for Today
Potted Squab Chicken en Casserole 90
Sirloin of Beef Braised a la Mode 40
Chicken Liver Brochette, Sauce Perigueux 45
Grilled Lamb Chops with French Peas 50
Fried Calves Sweetbreads a la Mont-rouge 65
Creamed Fresh Mushrooms under Glass 75
Small Steak, Jardiniere 50
Minced Turkey in Cream with Poached Egg 60
Deviled Crab in Shell, Philadelphia Style 65
Swan Point Oysters Baked a la Rector 60
Fresh Mushrooms any Style 75

Roasts and Poultry
Prime Ribs of Beef 45, Extra Cut 80
Stuffed Turkey, Cranberry Sauce 75
Spring Lamb, Mint Sauce 50
Rack of Lamb (for 1) 20 minutes 75
Rack of Lamb (for 2) 20 minutes 1.40
Broiled Chicken (half) 75 (whole) 1.50
Broiled Squab 75 Whole Squab Chicken Broiled 1.00

Game
Mallard 2.50 Sprig 2.00 Teal 1.25

Cold Dishes
Westphalia Ham 60 Boiled Ham 35
Genuine Virginia Ham 60 Smoked Tongue 40
Prime Roast Beef, Lamb or Pork 45
Kalter Aufschnitt (Assorted Cold Meat) 60
Turkey, Cranberry Sauce 75
Chicken, (half) with Jelly 75 Corned Beef 40
Potato Salad Served Free with Cold Dishes

Fresh California Vegetables
From our own Gardens in San Mateo County, and especially prepared under the supervision of our Chef Monsieur Roumiguere.
Artichoke, Melted Butter, Hot or Cold 25
Cauliflower au Gratin 20 String Beans 20
Cauliflower, Cream Sauce 15 Spinach 15
Fried Eggplant 20

Canned Vegetables
Stewed Tomatoes 15 Sugar Peas 15
Stewed Corn 15 French Peas 25 Okra Saute 25
Clear Lake String Beans 15
French String Beans 25 Asparagus, hot or cold 30

Potatoes
Hashed Brown 15 O'Brien or au Gratin 20
Souffle 30 German Fried or Saute 15
Lyonnaise 15 French Fried 10
Potatoes in Cream 15 Potatoes in Jackets 10
Hashed in Cream 15 Cottage Fried 20
Saratoga Chips 10 Minced 15 Baked Salinas 10
Sweet Potatoes Fried or Baked 15,
Virginia Style 25

BEERS Acme Glass 10c Seidel 15c
Imp. Pilsner, Wuerzburger or Culmbacher, Glass 15c, Double Glass 25c, Half Litre 30c

MENU

Fruits and Desserts
*German Apricot Cake 15
*Peach Pudding 15
*Walnut Custard Pie 15
Individual Pear Pie 15
German Coffee Cake 10
Assorted Nuts and Raisins 15
Hot Mince Pie 15 *Green Apple Pie 10
*Peach Tart 10 Charlotte Russe 25
*French Pastry (1) 10 *Chocolate Eclair 10
English Plum Pudding, Hard and Brandy Sauce 20
Fresh Fruits 15 All Preserved Fruits 15
Baked Apples and Cream 15
Stewed Prunes 15 Sliced Oranges 15
Pie a la Mode 25 Grape Fruit (½) 15
Bananas and Cream 20 Sliced Pineapple 15

Ices
*Vanilla, *Strawberry or *Chocolate Ice Cream 25
*Orange Water Ice 20 *Lemon Water Ice 20
Banana Special 25 Sorbet au Kirsch 25
*Coffee Parfait 25
Strawberry Parfait 25 Cardinal Punch 25
Romaine Punch 25 Meringue Glace 25

Cheese
†Imported Camembert, Individual Jar (for 1 or 2) 40
*Neufchatel 15 *Imported Swiss 20 *Brie 15
Imported Roquefort 25 *Sierra 15
*Limburger or Oregon Cream 15 *Schloss 15
*American or Camembert 15
After Dinner Portion Roquefort 15
After Dinner Portion 10 except those marked †

Coffee, Tea, Etc.
Pot Coffee (1) 15 (2) 25 Coffee, Cup 10
Glass of Milk 10 Pot of Tea 15
Glass of Buttermilk 10
Pot of Cocoa or Chocolate, Whipped Cream 20
Glass of Cream 20 Demi Tasse 5
Special Coffee, Freshly Prepared at Table for 2-4-50c or 6-75c

We recommend:
Expressly bottled for us by the Italian-Swiss Colony

No.		Split	Pt.	Quart
400	Asti Colony (red)	15	25	50
500	Asti Colony (white)	15	25	50

Not Responsible for Hats, Coats, Etc., Lost or Damaged, Unless Checked. No Charge for Checking.
Cigars and Cigarettes to be had from Clerk on Floor of Cafe.
Souvenir Postals to be had for the Asking.

NOTICE: TABLES RESERVED FOR DINNER WILL NOT BE HELD LATER THAN 6:30 P. M.

Lobby, Prince of Wales Hotel
Waterton Lakes
National Park
GREAT
NORTHERN

BELOW RIGHT Opening, Palace Hotel, 1909, San Francisco, California

Inaugural menu for the reopening of the hotel after the San Francisco earthquake of 1906.

Bankett aus Anlass der Wiedereröffnung des Hotels nach dem großen Erdbeben von 1906 in San Francisco.

Menu inaugural à l'occasion de la réouverture de l'hôtel après le séisme de San Francisco de 1906.

OPPOSITE Great Northern, c. 1916

ABOVE Banquet to Washington Delegation Panama-Pacific International Exposition, St. Francis Hotel, 1915, San Francisco, California

ABOVE **Dinner to Good Fellows by J. Rosenberg, Louis Martin's, 1905, New York, New York**

From coffins to devils, a host of unusual and macabre menus illustrates that dining could be infused with humor. The menu for Internal Revenue employees makes light of taxpayers and references the discovery of King Tut's tomb in 1922.

Von Särgen bis Teufeln zeigten viele makabre Speisekarten, dass Essengehen auch humorvoll sein konnte. Die Karte für Mitarbeiter des Finanzamts amüsiert sich über die Steuerzahler und bezieht sich auf die Entdeckung des Grabs von Pharao Tutanchamun 1922.

Ornementées de cercueils ou de démons, des cartes inhabituelles et macabres illustrent l'idée que gastronomie peut rimer avec humour. Ce menu destiné aux employés de l'administration fiscale traite le contribuable à la légère et fait référence à la découverte de la tombe de Toutankhamon en 1922.

RIGHT **Dinner, French Lick Springs Hotel, 1920, French Lick, Indiana**

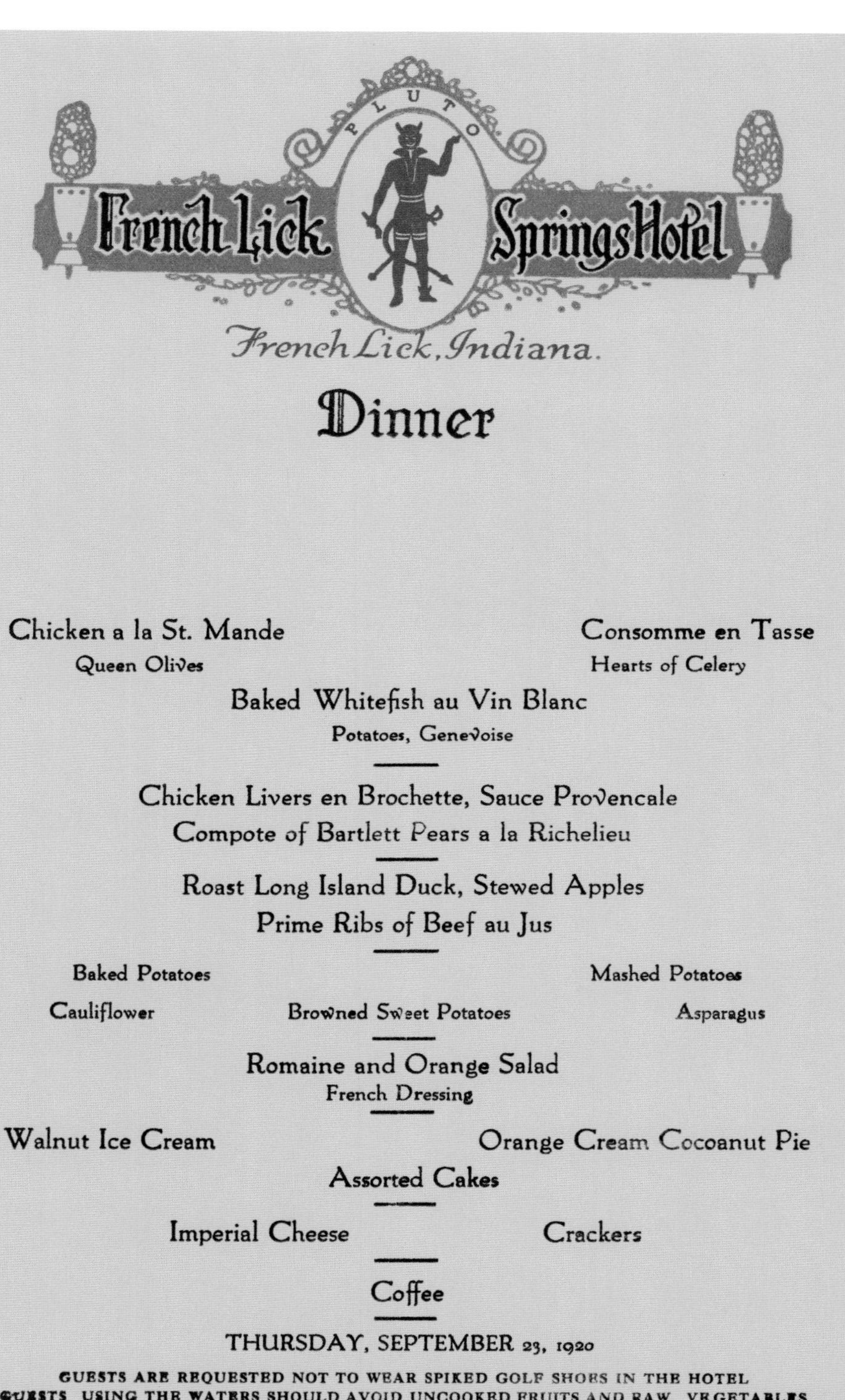

French Lick, Indiana.

Dinner

Chicken a la St. Mande — Queen Olives

Consomme en Tasse — Hearts of Celery

Baked Whitefish au Vin Blanc
Potatoes, Genevoise

Chicken Livers en Brochette, Sauce Provencale
Compote of Bartlett Pears a la Richelieu

Roast Long Island Duck, Stewed Apples
Prime Ribs of Beef au Jus

Baked Potatoes — Mashed Potatoes
Cauliflower — Browned Sweet Potatoes — Asparagus

Romaine and Orange Salad
French Dressing

Walnut Ice Cream — Orange Cream Cocoanut Pie
Assorted Cakes

Imperial Cheese — Crackers

Coffee

THURSDAY, SEPTEMBER 23, 1920

GUESTS ARE REQUESTED NOT TO WEAR SPIKED GOLF SHOES IN THE HOTEL
GUESTS USING THE WATERS SHOULD AVOID UNCOOKED FRUITS AND RAW VEGETABLES

DINNER SERVED FROM 6:30 TO 8:30

ABOVE Maryland State Funeral Directors Ladies Night, Lord Baltimore Hotel, 1932, Baltimore, Maryland

BELOW Annual Banquet and Dance given by the Internal Revenue Employees, 1923, Tacoma, Washington

RIGHT Hotel Stimson, 1913, Athens, Pennsylvania

MAUI HOTEL

Menu

THANKSGIVING DINNER

Eastern Oysters

Olives Celery Pickles

* * * *

Soup

Consomme—Chicken with Rice and Tomatoes

* * * *

Fish

Fried Mullet, Sauce Tartare

* * * *

Entrees

Baked Ham, Champagne Sauce
Frog Legs a la Francaise
Ox Tongue with Spinach

* * * *

Roasts

Prime Ribs of Beef—Young Island Turkey, Cranberry Sauce
Sucking Pig Apple Sauce

* * * *

Vegetables

Brown Sweet Potatoes—Mashed Potatoes
Asparagus—Cauliflower

* * * *

Salad

Crab Salad

* * * *

Dessert

Plum Pudding, Hard Sauce—Mince Pie—Ice Cream
Assorted Cakes—Nuts, Raisins—Fruits
California and Edam Cheese
Tea—Coffee

ABOVE **Thanksgiving Dinner and Wine List, Maui Hotel, 1913, Maui, Hawaii**

An early Hawaiian hotel in Wailuku, Maui, its menu is illustrated by a photo of the "Iao Needle," a 2,250-foot foliage-covered stone pillar. The Thanksgiving menu is traditional American, even with Eastern oysters, while the turkey seems to have been raised on the island itself.

Ein frühes Hotel auf Hawaii in Wailuku, Maui, zeigt auf der Speisekarte die „Iao Needle", eine 685 m hohe, bewachsene Felssäule. Das Mahl zum Thanksgiving-Fest ist traditionell amerikanisch, sogar mit Austern von der Ostküste. Der Truthahn scheint jedoch von der Insel selbst zu stammen.

Un des premiers hôtels d'Hawaii, à Wailuku sur Maui. La carte est illustrée par une photographie de l'« Iao needle », une aiguille rocheuse de 685 mètres couverte de végétation. Le menu de Thanksgiving respecte la tradition américaine, jusqu'aux huîtres de Virginie. En revanche, les dindes semblent avoir été élevées sur l'île.

RIGHT **Hotel St. Francis, 1913, San Francisco, California**

OPPOSITE **Hotel St. Francis, 1920, San Francisco, California**

"THE ORIENT"
ONE OF THE SEVEN FAMOUS MURAL PAINTINGS
BY ALBERT HERTER. IN THE GRILL OF THE
HOTEL ST. FRANCIS, SAN FRANCISCO.

McALPIN
Grill Room

OPPOSITE McAlpin Grill Room, 1916, New York, New York

The McAlpin Hotel was the largest in the world when it opened on New York's Herald Square in 1912.

Als das McAlpin Hotel 1912 am Herald Square in New York seine Tore öffnete, war es das größte Hotel der Welt.

Le McAlpin Hotel de New York est le plus grand hôtel du monde lorsqu'il ouvre à Herald Square en 1912.

LEFT F. M. Howell & Co., c. 1916, Elmira, New York

ABOVE Churchill's, 1918, New York, New York

The menu cover was by Hamilton King, a highly successful artist of the day known for his pastels of young women who came to be called "Hamilton King Girls."

Dieser Einband wurde von Hamilton King gestaltet, einem damals sehr erfolgreichen Künstler, der für seine Pastellzeichnungen junger Frauen berühmt war, die nach ihm „Hamilton King Girls" hießen.

Couverture de Hamilton King, artiste alors réputé pour ses pastels de jeunes femmes, qu'on appellera bientôt les « Hamilton King Girls ».

LEFT New Year's Greeting, Cafe Nat Goodwin, 1915, Santa Monica, California

BELOW New Year's Eve, New Grand Hotel, 1916, North Yakima, Washington

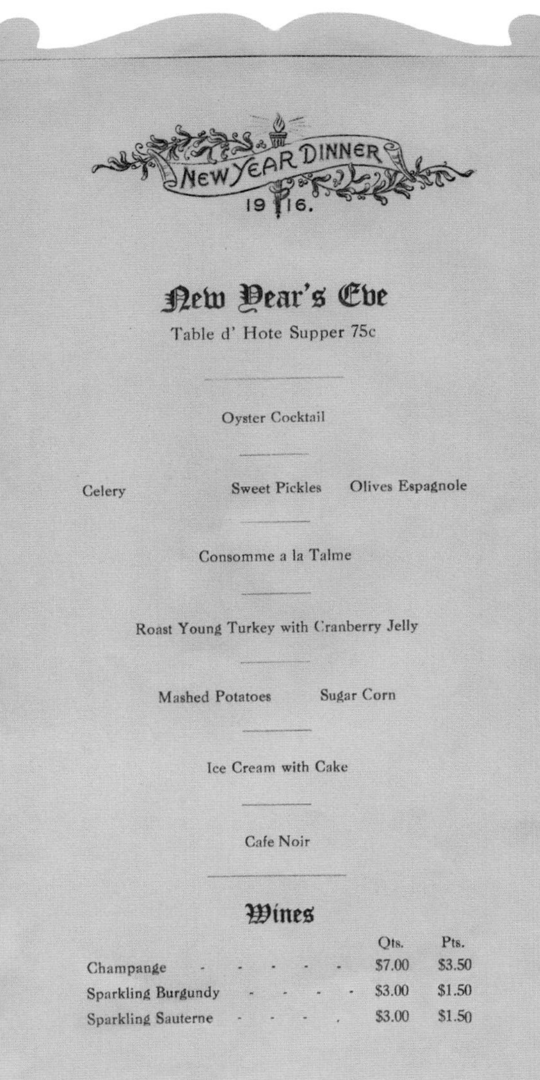

NEW YEAR DINNER
1916.

New Year's Eve

Table d' Hote Supper 75c

Oyster Cocktail

Celery — Sweet Pickles — Olives Espagnole

Consomme a la Talme

Roast Young Turkey with Cranberry Jelly

Mashed Potatoes — Sugar Corn

Ice Cream with Cake

Cafe Noir

Wines

	Qts.	Pts.
Champange	$7.00	$3.50
Sparkling Burgundy	$3.00	$1.50
Sparkling Sauterne	$3.00	$1.50

Hale! Hale! the gang's all here

MENU

Pickled Picas
Fillmore Cocktail
Candied Nonpareils

White Sparrow Bird Seed
Composing Room Turtle Soup aux Matrix Wafers
Consomme—Mailroom Stickum

Buttered Press Rollers with Red Ink
Fricasseed Type Lice
Dross Smothered in Onions
Hashed Press Blankets a la Petticrew
Creamed Curly Want Ads, Indented All Around
Scooped Beats

Long Green Salad with Lambert Dressing
Galley Proof Salad, Van der Cook—with Pure Apple Brinegar

English Prune Whip, whipped by Ottinger
Pi

Tribune Green Mints

Potassium Cyanide, Engravers' Delight

Flor de Fogarty Cigars
Piper Heidsieck

ABOVE *Register* and *Tribune* Banquet, 1917, Des Moines, Iowa

For members of two Des Moines papers, the menu gave dishes names germane to typesetter's lingo, like "Pickled Picas," "Galley Proof Salad," "Fricasseed Type Lice," and "Potassium Cyanide" ("Engravers' Delight"). The menu's cartoon image of a black waiter seems harshly stereotypical today but would not have raised eyebrows in the early 20th century.

Diese Speisekarte wurde aus Anlass eines Banketts für die Mitarbeiter zweier Zeitungen aus Des Moines erstellt. Die Gerichte haben neue Namen aus der Sprache der Schriftsetzer erhalten: „Pickled Picas" („Saure Picas") „Galley Proof Salad" („Druckfahnensalat") und „Fricasseed Type Lice" („Druckfehlerfrikassee"). „Zyankali" („Engravers' Delight") wurde für die Galvanisierung verwendet. Die Karikatur des schwarzen Kellners wirkt heute rassistisch, erregte aber Anfang des 20. Jahrhunderts kein Aufsehen.

Réservé aux journalistes de deux quotidiens de Des Moines, ce dîner propose des plats inspirés du jargon des imprimeurs : « *Cicéro* au vinaigre », « Salade des *placards* » ou « Fricassée de *lézarde* » et « Cyanure de potassium » (ou « Délice des imprimeurs »). Le serveur noir qui apparaît sur le menu peut nous sembler caricatural de nos jours, mais au début du XXe siècle, personne ne s'en offusquait.

RIGHT Ye Liberty, c. 1917, Oakland, California

BELOW LEFT Delmonico's, 1916, New York, New York

The once all-male restaurant Delmonico's, which pioneered the concept of allowing women to dine without men in the 1880s, had by 1916 developed into a place for young members of both sexes to play out the Jazz Age described by F. Scott Fitzgerald in *This Side of Paradise* (1920). The menu depicts a frivolous evening, with women dancing with women, three years before Prohibition crippled Delmonico's business.

Das zunächst nur Männern zugängliche Delmonico's, das aber bereits in den 1880ern als erstes Restaurant Damen das Speisen ohne Herrenbegleitung erlaubte, war 1916 ein beliebtes Lokal für die modernen jungen Leute der Jazz-Ära geworden, wie sie von F. Scott Fitzgerald in *Diesseits vom Paradies* (1920) beschrieben werden. Auf der Karte ist ein frivoles Treiben zu sehen, Frauen tanzen mit Frauen – nur drei Jahre, bevor das Alkoholverbot das Delmonico's ruinierte.

Restaurant autrefois réservé aux hommes, le Delmonico a innové en autorisant les femmes à dîner sans présence masculine dans les années 1880. En 1916, il devient un endroit où les jeunes gens des deux sexes se retrouvent pour vivre l'Ère du jazz, tel que F. Scott Fitzgerald le décrit dans *L'Envers du paradis*, paru en 1920. Le menu dépeint une soirée légère où des femmes dansent ensemble, trois ans avant que la Prohibition ne paralyse les activités du Delmonico.

OPPOSITE Baron Long's Ship Cafe, c. 1918, Venice, California

ABOVE Wolferman's Tiffin Room, c. 1918, Kansas City, Missouri

BELOW RIGHT Roman Gardens, c. 1918, San Francisco, California

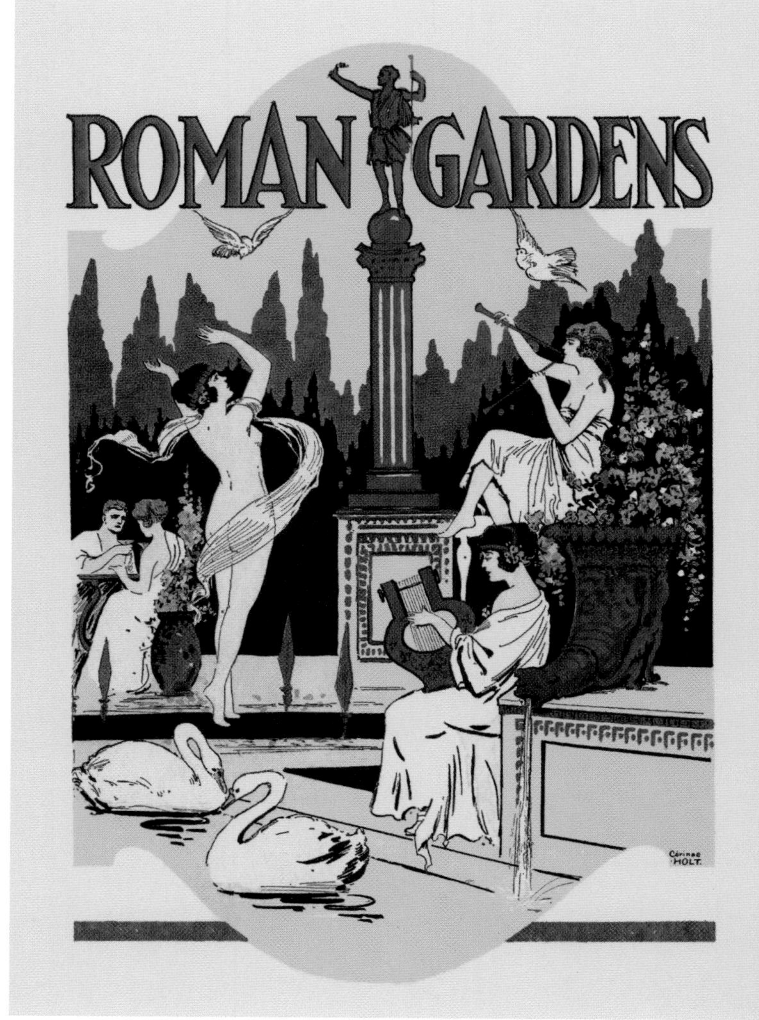

ALMACEN
Menu
Baron Long's
Ship Cafe
VENICE

ABOVE The Friars' Complimentary Dinner and Dance to Miss Mary Pickford and Mr. Douglas Fairbanks, Hotel Astor, 1920, New York, New York

BELOW & OPPOSITE The Friars Complimentary Dinner to Mr. Al Jolson, Hotel Astor, 1918, New York, New York

The show business Friars Club, founded by press agents in 1904 on East 55th Street, was known for its bawdy celebrity "roasts" of entertainment figures such as Mary Pickford and Douglas Fairbanks, two of the most popular movie stars and couples of the day. Vaudevillian Al Jolson, who often performed in black face as indicated by the interior cartoons, was being feted by the host, American playwright Channing Pollock.

Der Friars Club für Gäste aus dem Showbusiness, von Presseagenten 1904 an der East 55th Street gegründet, war für seine zotigen Persiflagen auf berühmte Persönlichkeiten bekannt; hier wurde das Paar Mary Pickford und Douglas Fairbanks, zwei der damals bekanntesten Filmstars der Welt, durch den Kakao gezogen. Der Vaudeville-Komiker Al Jolson, der oft mit schwarzer Schminke, wie auf den Karikaturen zu sehen, auftrat, wurde vom Gastgeber, dem amerikanischen Theaterautor Channing Pollock, mit diesem Essen geehrt.

Le Friars Club, fondé par des agents de publicité en 1904 sur la 55ᵉ rue Est était connu pour ses soirées animées réunissant des célébrités, telles Mary Pickford et Douglas Fairbanks, deux des vedettes les plus populaires du cinéma et couple à la ville. L'acteur de variétés Al Jolson, connu pour ses personnages d'hommes noirs, comme le montre le dessin de couverture, reçoit un hommage festif de la part de son hôte, le dramaturge américain Channing Pollock.

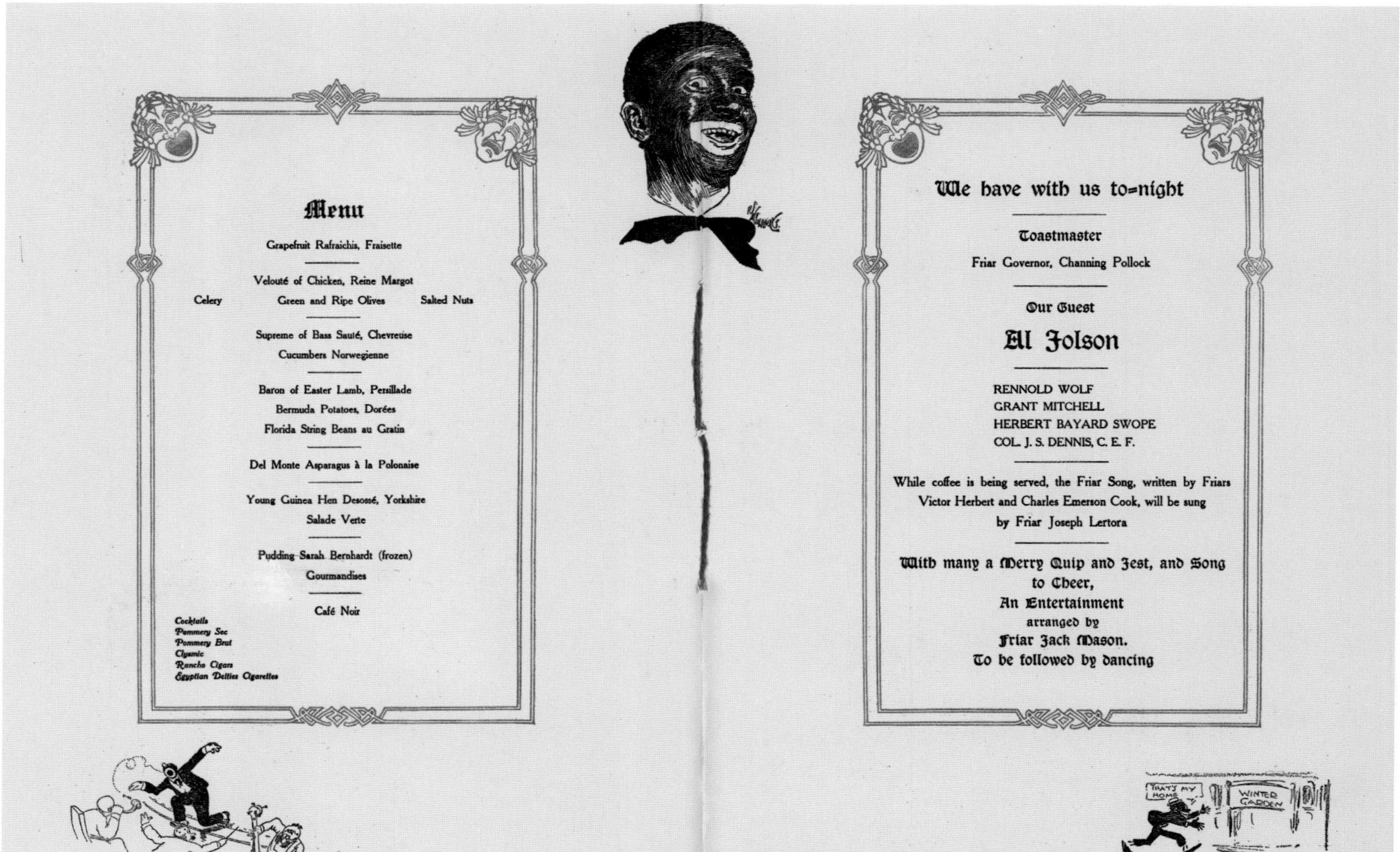

Menu

Grapefruit Rafraichis, Fraisette

Velouté of Chicken, Reine Margot
Celery — Green and Ripe Olives — Salted Nuts

Supreme of Bass Sauté, Chevreuse
Cucumbers Norwegienne

Baron of Easter Lamb, Persillade
Bermuda Potatoes, Dorées
Florida String Beans au Gratin

Del Monte Asparagus à la Polonaise

Young Guinea Hen Desossé, Yorkshire
Salade Verte

Pudding Sarah Bernhardt (frozen)
Gourmandises

Café Noir

Cocktails
Pommery Sec
Pommery Brut
Clysmic
Rancho Cigars
Egyptian Deities Cigarettes

We have with us to-night

Toastmaster
Friar Governor, Channing Pollock

Our Guest
Al Jolson

RENNOLD WOLF
GRANT MITCHELL
HERBERT BAYARD SWOPE
COL. J. S. DENNIS, C. E. F.

While coffee is being served, the Friar Song, written by Friars Victor Herbert and Charles Emerson Cook, will be sung by Friar Joseph Lertora

With many a Merry Quip and Jest, and Song to Cheer,
An Entertainment
arranged by
Friar Jack Mason.
To be followed by dancing

THAT'S MY HOME
WINTER GARDEN

THE FRIARS
COMPLIMENTARY DINNER
TO
MR. AL JOLSON
HOTEL
ASTOR
SUNDAY
MARCH
31st
1918
RYAN WALKER

ABOVE A Good Flare-Up, 1917

A Christmas menu for a meal served "in the field." The flare-up refers to the flaming destruction of an observation balloon by fighter planes.

Kartes eines Weihnachtsessens, das „auf dem Schlachtfeld“ serviert wurde. Mit „A good flare-up!“ ist der Beobachtungsballon gemeint, der nach dem Beschuss durch Kampfflugzeuge in Flammen aufgeht.

Menu de Noël servi sur le « champ d'honneur ». Le Flare-up (embrasement) évoque la destruction d'un ballon par des avions de chasse.

ABOVE RIGHT Hotel Belmont, 1918

EAT PLENTY · EAT WISELY
BUT WITHOUT WASTE

FOOD WILL DECIDE THE WAR

SAVE THE WHEAT - SAVE THE MEATS
SAVE THE FATS - SAVE THE SUGAR
FOR
YOUR SOLDIERS AT THE FRONT
NEED THEM ALL

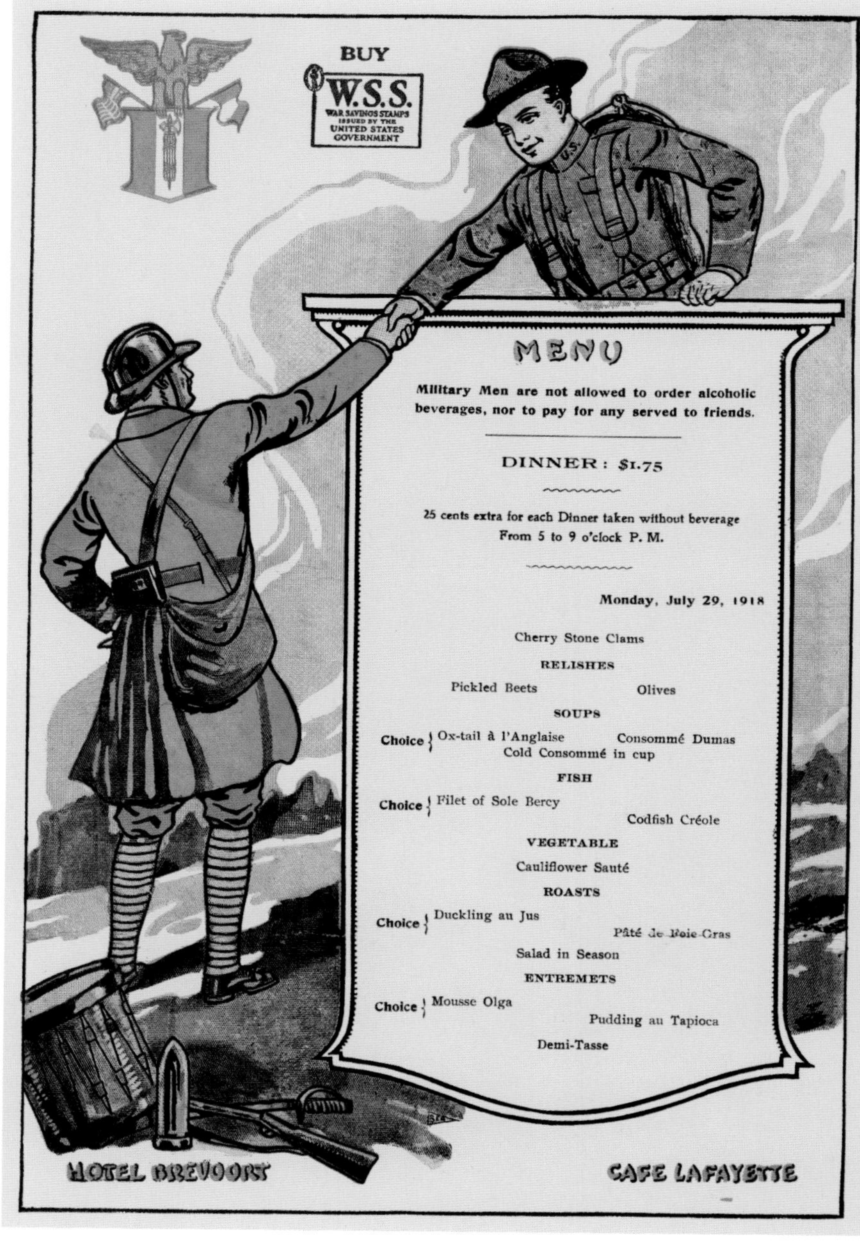

MENU

Military Men are not allowed to order alcoholic beverages, nor to pay for any served to friends.

DINNER: $1.75

25 cents extra for each Dinner taken without beverage
From 5 to 9 o'clock P. M.

Monday, July 29, 1918

Cherry Stone Clams

RELISHES
Pickled Beets — Olives

SOUPS
Choice { Ox-tail à l'Anglaise — Consommé Dumas
Cold Consommé in cup

FISH
Choice { Filet of Sole Bercy — Codfish Créole

VEGETABLE
Cauliflower Sauté

ROASTS
Choice { Duckling au Jus — ~~Pâté de Foie Gras~~
Salad in Season

ENTREMETS
Choice { Mousse Olga — Pudding au Tapioca
Demi-Tasse

OPPOSITE Cafe Lafayette, Hotel Brevoort, 1918, New York, New York

The menu from the famous downstairs café at the Greenwich Village townhouse hotel, the Brevoort, advocates buying War Savings Stamps and prohibits servicemen from buying alcohol.

Diese Speisekarte aus dem berühmten Café im Untergeschoss des kleinen Hotel Brevoort in Greenwich Village in New York wirbt für den Erwerb von Kriegssparmarken und verbietet Soldaten den Alkoholgenuss.

Cette carte créée pour le célèbre café situé au rez-de-chaussée de l'Hotel Brevoort à Greenwich Village, promeut l'achat d'obligations de guerre et met en garde les militaires contre les ravages de l'alcool.

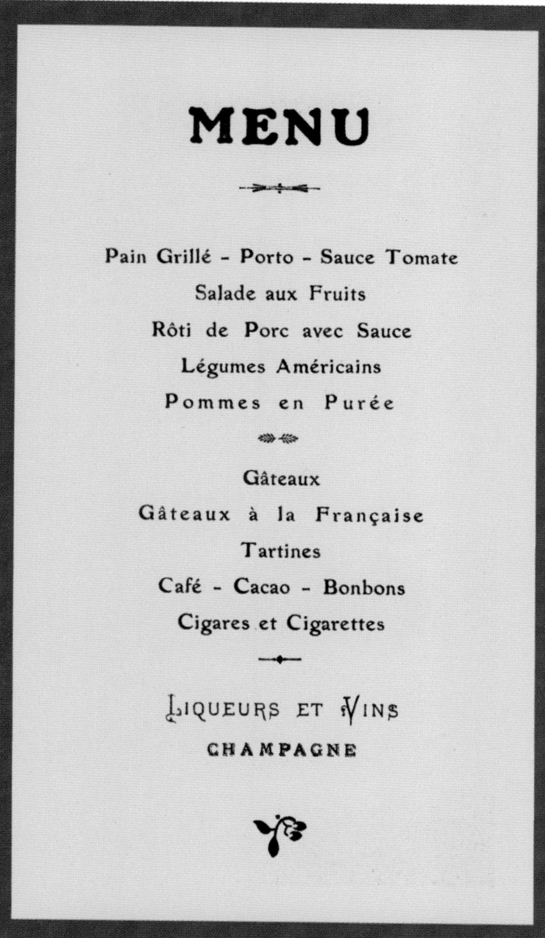

ABOVE Fourth Annual Banquet and Ball, the Showmen's League of America, Congress Hotel, 1918, Chicago, Illinois

LEFT Thanksgiving, 1918, France

The "Hat in the Ring" on the menu cover referred to the 94th Fighter Squadron, America's second-oldest fighter squadron. Its most famous member, "Ace of Aces" Eddie Rickenbacker, was in attendance at the dinner "somewhere in France," an intended reference to a secret location should the menu fall in the hands of the enemy.

Der Zylinder im Ring auf der Speisekarte bezieht sich auf das 94. Jagdgeschwader, das zweitälteste der USA. Das berühmte Fliegerass Eddie Rickenbacker nahm an diesem Essen „irgendwo in Frankreich" teil – der Ort wurde geheim gehalten, falls die Karte dem Feind in die Hände fallen sollte.

Le « haut-de-forme dans un cerceau » qui illustre ce menu fait référence à la 94e escadrille de chasse américaine, la deuxième plus ancienne des États-Unis. Son membre le plus éminent, l'as des as Eddie Rickenbacker assistait à ce dîner « quelque part en France »… dans un endroit gardé secret au cas où ce menu tomberait dans les mains de l'ennemi.

Farewell Dinner to Personal Liberty

Mouquin's Uptown June 19th, 1919

OPPOSITE Farewell Dinner to Personal Liberty, Mouquin's Uptown, 1919, New York, New York

RIGHT & BELOW Bergez-Frank's Old Poodle Dog, 1919, San Francisco, California

With the passing of the Volstead Act in January 1919, soon to outlaw alcohol, these menus reflect the sorry state of things to come, when iced tea would replace wine. The poem echoes some of the lines in *The Rubaiyat of Omar Khayyam*. A "blind pig" referred to a speakeasy. "J. B. Corn" refers to John Barleycorn, a nickname for whiskey.

Mit dem im Januar 1919 verabschiedeten Volstead Act sollte Alkohol in den USA bald illegal werden. Diese Karte weist bereits auf die traurige Zukunft hin, in der in Restaurants wie dem Old Poodle Dog statt Wein Eistee ausgeschenkt würde. Das Gedicht bezieht sich auf Verse aus den Vierzeilern *Rubai'yat* von Omar Khayyam. Mit „blind pig" ist eine Flüsterkneipe gemeint, mit „J. B. Corn" John Barleycorn, ein Deckname für Whiskey.

Ce menu reflète la désolation qui a suivi le vote du Volstead Act, ratifié en janvier 1919, bannissant l'alcool des États-Unis. Le thé glacé remplace le vin. Quelques vers du poème rappellent le *Rubayat* d'Omar Khayyam. Quant à « Blind pig » (« Le cochon aveugle »), il évoque un *speakeasy* (bar clandestin) et J. B. Corn renvoie à John Barleycorn, surnom du whiskey.

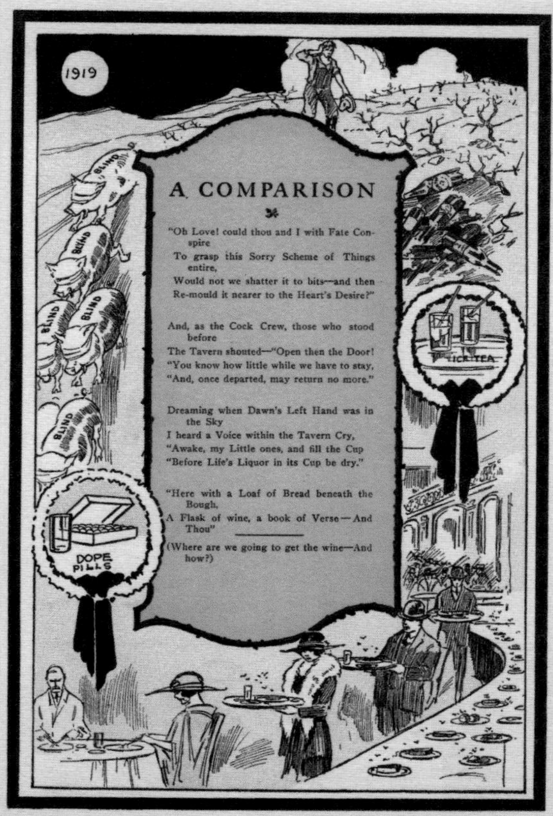

A COMPARISON

"Oh Love! could thou and I with Fate Conspire
To grasp this Sorry Scheme of Things entire,
Would not we shatter it to bits—and then
Re-mould it nearer to the Heart's Desire?"

And, as the Cock Crew, those who stood before
The Tavern shouted—"Open then the Door!
"You know how little while we have to stay,
"And, once departed, may return no more."

Dreaming when Dawn's Left Hand was in the Sky
I heard a Voice within the Tavern Cry,
"Awake, my Little ones, and fill the Cup
"Before Life's Liquor in its Cup be dry."

"Here with a Loaf of Bread beneath the Bough,
A Flask of wine, a book of Verse—And Thou"

(Where are we going to get the wine—And how?)

ON THE OCCASION OF THE UNTIMELY DEMISE OF J. B. CORN, THIS FINAL DINNER IS TENDERED BY MR. CARL A. HENRY TO FRIENDS WHO HAVE ENJOYED A LIBERTY AND SPIRIT THAT IS APPARENTLY DESTINED TO BE CRUSHED

BERGEZ-FRANK'S OLD POODLE DOG
SAN FRANCISCO, CALIFORNIA
JUNE THIRTIETH, NINETEEN NINETEEN

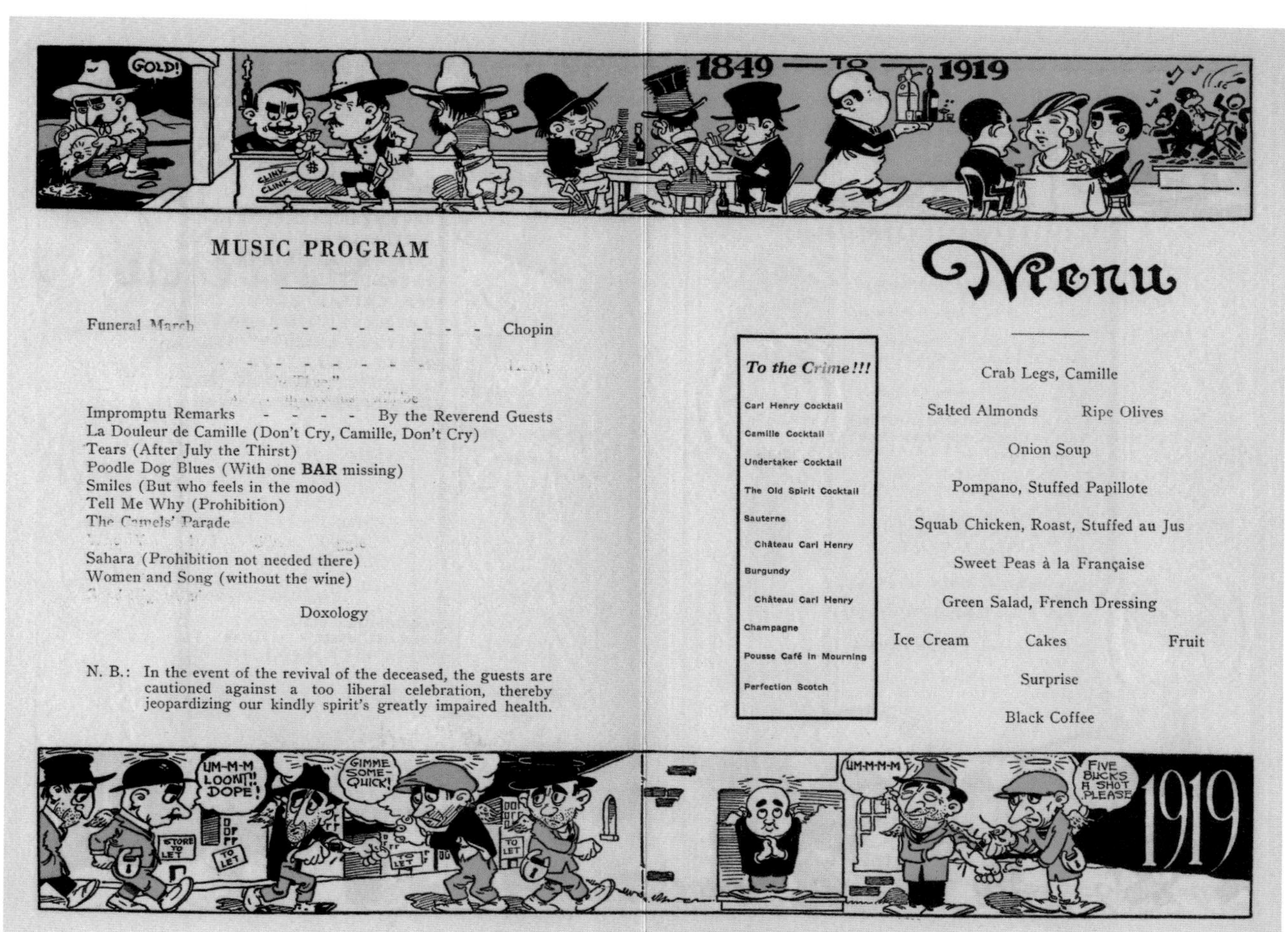

MUSIC PROGRAM

Funeral March - - - - - - - - - - Chopin

Impromptu Remarks - - - - By the Reverend Guests
La Douleur de Camille (Don't Cry, Camille, Don't Cry)
Tears (After July the Thirst)
Poodle Dog Blues (With one **BAR** missing)
Smiles (But who feels in the mood)
Tell Me Why (Prohibition)
The Camels' Parade

Sahara (Prohibition not needed there)
Women and Song (without the wine)

Doxology

N. B.: In the event of the revival of the deceased, the guests are cautioned against a too liberal celebration, thereby jeopardizing our kindly spirit's greatly impaired health.

Menu

To the Crime!!!
Carl Henry Cocktail
Camille Cocktail
Undertaker Cocktail
The Old Spirit Cocktail
Sauterne
Château Carl Henry
Burgundy
Château Carl Henry
Champagne
Pousse Café in Mourning
Perfection Scotch

Crab Legs, Camille
Salted Almonds Ripe Olives
Onion Soup
Pompano, Stuffed Papillote
Squab Chicken, Roast, Stuffed au Jus
Sweet Peas à la Française
Green Salad, French Dressing
Ice Cream Cakes Fruit
Surprise
Black Coffee

FAR LEFT **The Oasis, 1928, Portland, Oregon**

LEFT **Omar Khayyam's, 1940, San Francisco, California**

Armenian immigrant George Mardikian opened Omar Khayyam featuring Middle Eastern cuisine, which was unusual for its day, since few American cities, and certainly not San Francisco, had significant Middle Eastern communities.

Der armenische Einwanderer George Mardikian servierte im Omar Khayyam Gerichte des Vorderen Orients, was damals höchst ungewöhnlich war, da es nur in wenigen amerikanischen Städten und erst recht nicht in San Francisco eine große Bevölkerungsgruppe aus dem Nahen Osten gab.

L'immigrant arménien George Mardikian ouvre le Omar Khayyam, qui propose une gastronomie du Moyen-Orient, peu courante à l'époque, car il n'existe pas de communautés de cette origine dans les villes américaines, et encore moins à San Francisco.

BELOW **Sphinx Cafe, c. 1934, San Francisco, California**

OPPOSITE **The Turkish Village, 1920, Los Angeles, California**

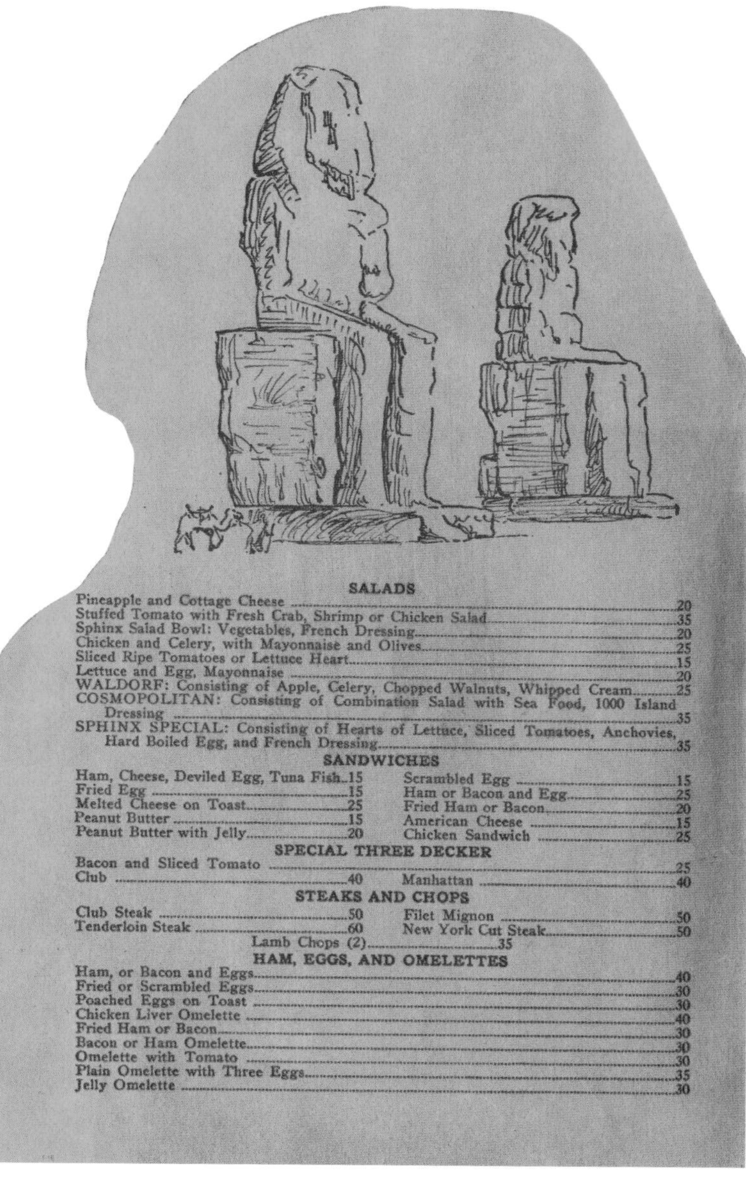

SALADS

Pineapple and Cottage Cheese .20
Stuffed Tomato with Fresh Crab, Shrimp or Chicken Salad .35
Sphinx Salad Bowl: Vegetables, French Dressing .20
Chicken and Celery, with Mayonnaise and Olives .25
Sliced Ripe Tomatoes or Lettuce Heart .15
Lettuce and Egg, Mayonnaise .20
WALDORF: Consisting of Apple, Celery, Chopped Walnuts, Whipped Cream .25
COSMOPOLITAN: Consisting of Combination Salad with Sea Food, 1000 Island Dressing .35
SPHINX SPECIAL: Consisting of Hearts of Lettuce, Sliced Tomatoes, Anchovies, Hard Boiled Egg, and French Dressing .35

SANDWICHES

Ham, Cheese, Deviled Egg, Tuna Fish .15
Fried Egg .15
Melted Cheese on Toast .25
Peanut Butter .15
Peanut Butter with Jelly .20
Scrambled Egg .15
Ham or Bacon and Egg .25
Fried Ham or Bacon .20
American Cheese .15
Chicken Sandwich .25

SPECIAL THREE DECKER

Bacon and Sliced Tomato .25
Club .40
Manhattan .40

STEAKS AND CHOPS

Club Steak .50
Tenderloin Steak .60
Filet Mignon .50
New York Cut Steak .50
Lamb Chops (2) .35

HAM, EGGS, AND OMELETTES

Ham, or Bacon and Eggs .40
Fried or Scrambled Eggs .30
Poached Eggs on Toast .30
Chicken Liver Omelette .40
Fried Ham or Bacon .30
Bacon or Ham Omelette .30
Omelette with Tomato .30
Plain Omelette with Three Eggs .35
Jelly Omelette .30

CAFE

A RESTFUL SPOT FOR LUNCHEON

THE PLANTATION CLUB

— TO QUENCH YOUR THIRST

AND

TO SATISFY YOUR HUNGER

MAMMY'S SUPPER SUGGESTIONS

MAMMY'S CREAM WAFFLES, 75c

Heart of Celery	.40	Jumbo Ripe Olives	.45
Plantation Tenderloin Steak Sandwich	.75	Golden Buck	.90
Welsh Rarebit	.75	Louisiana Shrimp Creole	.90
Virginia Ham and Eggs	1.00	Plantation Special Club Sandwich	.75
Premium Ham and Scrambled Eggs	.75	Carolina Frog Legs, Sauce Tartar	1.25
Plantation Chicken Tamale	.60	Sliced Chicken a la King	1.25

Melted Cheese Toast .50

COVER CHARGE EVERY NITE

from

6 to 9—50 cents :: after 9—~~75 cents~~ 100

Saturdays, Sundays and Holidays

$1.00

OPPOSITE & BELOW The Plantation Club, 1922, Culver City, California

Located along a stretch of Washington Boulevard that was lined with movie studios, the restaurant had a menu, shaped like a watermelon, which played off Southern plantation images.

Der Plantation Club befand sich am Washington Boulevard in direkter Nähe zu den großen Filmstudios. Die Speisekarte mit ihrer Wassermelonenform spielt auf die Südstaatenplantagen an.

Situé sur une partie de Washington boulevard où s'alignaient les studios de cinéma, le restaurant offre une carte en forme de pastèque qui joue sur les références aux plantations du Sud.

RIGHT The Plantation Club, c. 1923, Culver City, California

REFRESHING DRINKS CONCOCTED BY RUFUS

CUPS

Plantation Fruit Cup	$1.75	$3.25
Pure Orange Juice	2.00	4.00
Loganberry Cup	1.75	3.25
Grape Juice	1.75	3.25
Raspberry Cup	1.75	3.25

GINGER ALE and SARSAPARILLA

C. & C. Imported Ginger Ale	$ .75
Cliquot Club Sarsaparilla	.70
Shasta Ginger Ale	.50

JUICES

Grape Juice Nips	$ .50
Loganberry Nips	.50
Glass Orange Juice	.50
Pineapple Juice	.50

SPECIALS

Raspberry Punch	$ .50
Old Fashioned Lemonade	.50
Grape Lemonade	.50
Napa Soda	.50
Egg Soda	.50
California Snow Ball	.50
Grenadine Punch	.50
Grape Float	.50
Fruit Punch	.50
Orangeade	.50
Horlick's Malted Milk, plain	.50
with egg	.60
Coca Cola (glass)	.50
East Side	.50
Budweiser	.50

MINERAL WATERS

White Rock	$ .50
Jackson's Napa Soda	.50
Celestine Vichy	.70
Shasta Water	.50

EGG DRINKS

Egg Frappe	$ .50
Egg Coffee	.50
Egg Phosphate	.50
Egg Chocolate	.50
Egg Flip	.50

FROZEN DRINKS

Mint Freeze	$ .50
Pineapple Freeze	.50
Loganberry Freeze	.50
Lemon Freeze	.50
Orange Freeze	.50
Grape Freeze	.50
Coca Cola Freeze	.50

Ice Cream Sodas, all Flavors ...... $ .50

Please do not embarrass the management by bringing intoxicating liquors into this establishment.

LEFT **Canton Tea Garden, c. 1927, Chicago, Illinois**

Chinese cuisine was introduced to the United States via West Coast Chinese immigrants who came to work on the railroads, often as cooks who served up an amalgam of rice dishes with American ingredients, which was to become Chinese-American cuisine. Their menus offered dishes like egg foo young and chop suey, cuisine unknown in China.

Die chinesischen Einwanderer kamen zuerst an die Westküste der USA, wo sie beim Eisenbahnbau arbeiteten, oft als Köche. Sie brachten die chinesische Küche mit und entwickelten daraus eine Mixtur aus Reisgerichten mit amerikanischen Zutaten, aus denen die chinesisch-amerikanische Küche entstand. Gerichte wie Egg Foo Young und Chop Suey sind in China selbst unbekannt.

La cuisine chinoise est introduite aux États-Unis par les immigrants chinois de la côte Ouest, venus travailler sur les lignes de chemin de fer, le plus souvent comme cuisiniers. Ils servaient un mélange de riz et d'ingrédients américains qui deviendraient plus tard la cuisine sino-américaine. Ces menus proposent par exemple des œufs *foo young* ou des *chop suey*, plats inconnus en Chine.

漢拿魯爐
雜碎樓

HONOLULU CHOP SUI HOUSE

32 HOTEL ST., BET. NUUANU & SMITH

HONOLULU, T. H.

P. O. BOX 1039 PHONE 1713

BILL OF FARE

ABOVE **Honolulu Chop Sui House, c. 1927, Honolulu, Hawaii**

RIGHT **Grand View Garden, c. 1922, Los Angeles, California**

OPPOSITE **Yoengs Restaurant, c. 1922, New York, New York**

Bill of Fare

WRIGHT ACT IS STRICTLY ENFORCED HERE

官廳厲行禁酒 貴客携到飲酒 如被警干涉 概由貴客自理

CHOP SUEY (雜碎)

Tai Hang Chop Suey....$ .30 大行雜
Chinese Mushrooms, Bean Sprouts Onions, Celery, Pork, or Beef

Tai Yat Chop Suey......$ .40 第一雜
Same as Above with Water Chestnut, Extra Fine

Chop Kam Chop Suey..$ .45 什錦雜
Extra Fine Cut Chicken Meat, Broiled Pork and Green Peppers, as Above

Shrimp Chop Suey........$ .45 蝦肉雜

Crab Chop Suey............$ .50 蟹肉雜

Li Hong Chong Chop Suey..............................$ .60 李鴻章
Pork, Chicken Meat, Chinese Mushroom, Bean Sprouts, Onions, Celery, Water Chestnut, Bamboo Shoots

Chicken Chop Suey......$ .80 嫩鷄雜
Same as Above, with Extra Chicken, Broiled Pork and White Mushrooms

Mushroom Chicken Chop Suey..................$1.00 香菇雞雜
Same as Above, Extra Fine

Almond Chicken Chop Suey..............................$1.00 杏仁雞雜
Chicken Chop Suey, Extra Fine, with Almonds

FRIED NOODLES (炒麵)

Canton or Chicago Style

Pork Chow Mein............$ .50 炒肉麵

Chicken Chow Mein......$ .75 雞絲炒麵

Shrimp or Crab Chow Mein..............................$ .75 蝦或蟹炒麵

Fried Fun Tun..............$ .75 炒雲吞

Fried Fresh Shrimp......$ .60 炒鮮蝦球

Almond Duck................$1.25 窩燒鴨

Fried Chicken................$1.25 炸子雞

White Mushroom Chicken.......................$1.25 毛菇雞球

EGGS (蛋)

Chop Suey Dun............$ .40 雜碎蛋
Omelette with Mixture of Meat and Vegetables

Foo Young Dun............$ .35 芙蓉蛋
Omelette with Onion and Bamboo Shoots

Cha Siu Dun..................$ .40 叉燒蛋
Omelette with Broiled Meat

Foyung Ha......................$ .50 芙蓉蝦
Omelette with Shrimps

Foyung Hai....................$ .50 芙蓉蟹
Omelette with Crab

Please Be Careful of Your Things, as We Are Not Responsible for Their Safety

YOENGS RESTAURANT

1607 – 1609 BROADWAY
S.W. COR. BWAY. AND 49TH ST.
NEW YORK CITY

THE
ROYCROFT
INN
R
R

OPPOSITE, BELOW & RIGHT The Roycroft Inn, 1921, Aurora, New York

Opened in 1905 to accommodate visitors who came to the arts and crafts movement community founded by writer-philosopher Elbert Hubbard in East Aurora, the Roycroft Inn is now a national landmark. The menu was standard American fare.

Das Roycroft Inn ist heute eine denkmalgeschützte Sehenswürdigkeit; eröffnet wurde es 1905 für die Besucher der von dem Philosophen Elbert Hubbard in East Aurora gegründeten Künstlergemeinschaft des Arts and Crafts Movement. Auf dem Speiseplan stand amerikanische Durchschnittskost.

Ouvert en 1905 pour accueillir les visiteurs de la communauté fondée par l'écrivain et philosophe Elbert Hubbard à East Aurora et issue du mouvement Arts & Crafts, le Roycroft Inn est devenu un site historique national. Le menu est typiquement américain.

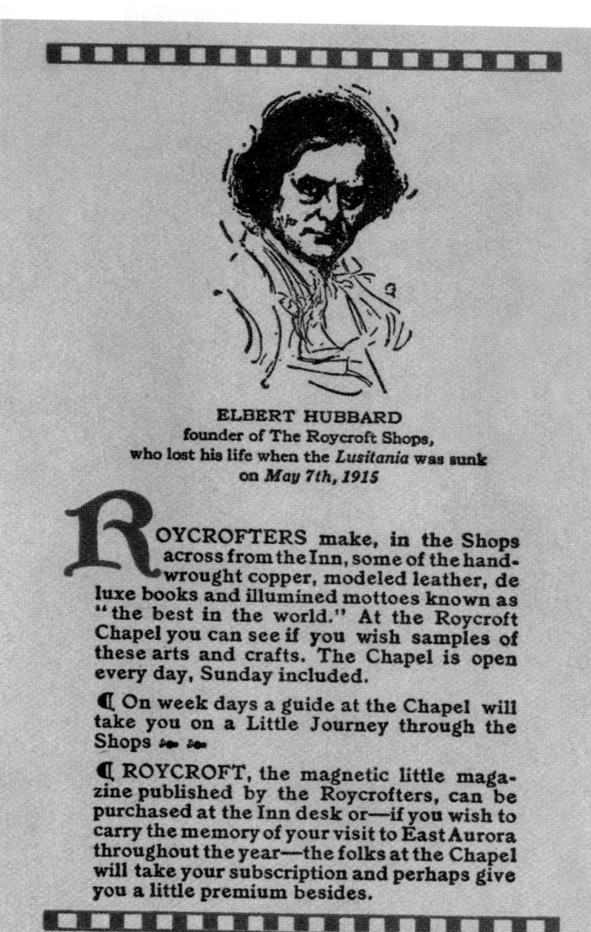

ELBERT HUBBARD
founder of The Roycroft Shops,
who lost his life when the *Lusitania* was sunk
on *May 7th, 1915*

ROYCROFTERS make, in the Shops across from the Inn, some of the hand-wrought copper, modeled leather, de luxe books and illumined mottoes known as "the best in the world." At the Roycroft Chapel you can see if you wish samples of these arts and crafts. The Chapel is open every day, Sunday included.

¶ On week days a guide at the Chapel will take you on a Little Journey through the Shops

¶ ROYCROFT, the magnetic little magazine published by the Roycrofters, can be purchased at the Inn desk or—if you wish to carry the memory of your visit to East Aurora throughout the year—the folks at the Chapel will take your subscription and perhaps give you a little premium besides.

Yes, certainly you may take this Menu with you

The Menu for Today

Monday—July 25, 1921

LUNCHEON 12 to 2

Bouillon with Spaghetti

Catsup · Chili Sauce
Pickled Beets

Apple Butter
Preserves

Minced Ham with Scrambled Eggs
Fricassee Breast of Veal with Rice
Small Steak Saute · Parsley Butter

Cold
Roast Beef · Boiled Ham
Salmon · Pickled Pig's Feet

Potatoes Saute · New Buttered Beets
Cold Slaw

Cottage Pudding · Sauce and Cake

Tea · Coffee · Cocoa · Milk · Postum
Ice Tea

DINNER 6 to 8

Vegetable Soup

Catsup · Chili Sauce
Pickled Beets

Apple Butter
Preserves

Japanaise Crab Meat au Gratin
Tenderloin Tips with Mushrooms
Boiled Star Bacon with New Cabbage
Roast Leg of Veal with Dressing

Cold
Roast Beef · Boiled Ham
Salmon · Pickled Pig's Feet

Mashed Potatoes · Creamed Cauliflower
Lettuce and Cucumbers · French Dressing

Blackberry Pie · Ice Cream and Cake

Tea · Coffee · Cocoa · Milk · Postum
Ice Tea

Truth is a useful idea—Elbert Hubbard

LEFT **Hotel Traymore, 1924, Atlantic City, New Jersey**

OPPOSITE **Investment Bankers Association of America, Southern Pacific Lines, 1922, Del Monte, California**

The style of this cover replicates a woodcut, a popular arts and crafts technique.

Diese Speisekarte ist wie ein Holzschnitt gestaltet, eine in der Arts-and-Crafts-Bewegung beliebte Technik.

Le style de cette couverture imite la sculpture sur bois, un artisanat populaire.

RIGHT **Hotel Cleveland, c. 1922, Cleveland, Ohio**

During Prohibition, tearooms became much more popular, for what had previously been mainly a ladies' afternoon respite became an opportunity to serve alcohol in a teacup. Thus, tearooms that might once have been only in hotels were now popping up around the city as small storefronts.

Während der Prohibitionszeit wurden Teesalons beliebter: Zuvor vornehmlich nachmittäglicher Treffpunkt von Damen, boten sie jetzt Gelegenheit, Alkohol in Teetassen zu servieren. Daher machten nun auf einmal überall in kleinen Ladengeschäften Teestuben auf, etwas, das es vorher nur in Hotels gegeben hatte.

Durant la Prohibition, les salons de thé deviennent beaucoup plus populaires. Refuge féminin autorisant un répit bien mérité au cours de l'après-midi, ils offrent désormais la possibilité de boire de l'alcool caché dans une tasse de thé. Ils essaiment alors dans la ville, au lieu de rester cantonnés dans les hôtels.

EN ROUTE
INVESTMENT
BANKERS
ASSOCIATION
OF AMERICA
TO
DEL MONTE
CALIFORNIA
OCTOBER 9 TO 12
1922

Tea Service De Luxe

From 4 to 5

Orange Marmalade 30 *Quince Jelly 30*
Guava Jelly 30 *Comb Honey 25* *Bar le Duc 25*
Raspberry or Blackberry Jam 30

Tea Waffle Lady Astor 50
Finger Rolls 10 *Cinnamon Toast 15*
Toasted Muffins 25 *Tea Biscuit and Honey 30*

Salads

Bartlett Pear Geisha 60 *Romaine Dixie 60*
Stuffed Avocado Aristocrat 75
Fresh Fruit, El Cortez 60

Dainties

Calavo Sandwich, Lady Cummings 65
Toasted Cheese and Pineapple 50
El Cortez Club 75 *San Diego Sailors 75*
Ice Cream Sandwich, Mikado 50

French Pastry 25 *Petite Four 25* *Macaroons 20*
Danish Pastry 25 *Lady Fingers 15*
Ice Cup, El Cortez 40 *Parfait Point Loma 35*

Tea (all bouquets) 25 *Coffee 25* *Orangeade 35*
Cafe Glace 30 *Malted Milk 30* *Egg Nog 30*

ABOVE Tea Service De Luxe, El Cortez, c. 1926, San Diego, California

OPPOSITE Willard Tea Shop, 1922, New York, New York

Willard Tea Shop
MENU
557 Fifth Avenue
New York

Happy New Year
1924

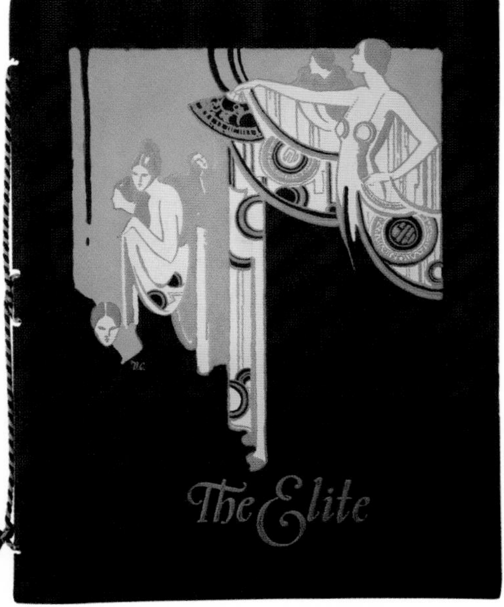

ABOVE The Elite, 1925, Los Angeles

BELOW Candyland, c. 1930, Grinnell, Iowa

OPPOSITE New Year's Eve, Hotel St. Francis, 1924, San Francisco, California

On this risqué art deco cover by F. L. Packer, a satyr and seminude flapper are pictured with what seems to be a firebird.

Ein gewagter Art-déco-Einband von F. L. Packer mit einem Satyr, einem halb bekleideten Flapper und einem Feuervogel darauf.

Sur cette couverture Art déco osée signée F. L. Packer, un satyre et une garçonne dévêtue côtoient ce qui paraît être un phénix.

ABOVE Chicago Trust Club, 1926, Chicago, Illinois

LEFT & BELOW El Cortez, c. 1925, San Diego, California

OPPOSITE Pig 'n' Whistle, c. 1924, Hollywood, California

The first Pig 'n' Whistle candy shop was opened by John H. Gage on South Broadway in Los Angeles in 1908. As a restaurant on Hollywood Boulevard, Pig 'n' Whistle opened July 22, 1927, at a time when movie theaters like Grauman's Chinese Theatre and the Egyptian did not have food concessions. The ice cream and candy counter was up front and a fine-dining room was in the rear.

Die erste Pig-'n'-Whistle-Confiserie wurde 1908 von John H. Gage am South Broadway in Los Angeles eröffnet. Das Restaurant gleichen Namens folgte am 22. Juli 1927 am Hollywood Boulevard. Große Kinos wie das Grauman's Chinese Theatre und das Egyptian hatten damals noch keine Snackbar. Das Pig 'n' Whistle besaß vorn einen Eis- und Süßwarenverkauf und hinten einen eleganten Speisesaal.

La première confiserie Pig 'n' Whistle est créée par John H. Gage sur South Broadway à Los Angeles en 1908. Un restaurant Pig 'n' Whistle, situé sur Hollywood Boulevard, ouvrira le 22 juillet 1927, à une époque où les cinémas tels que le Grauman's Chinese Theatre ou The Egyptian ne proposent pas encore de restauration. Les comptoirs de glace et de bonbons sont placés devant, tandis que la salle est reléguée à l'arrière.

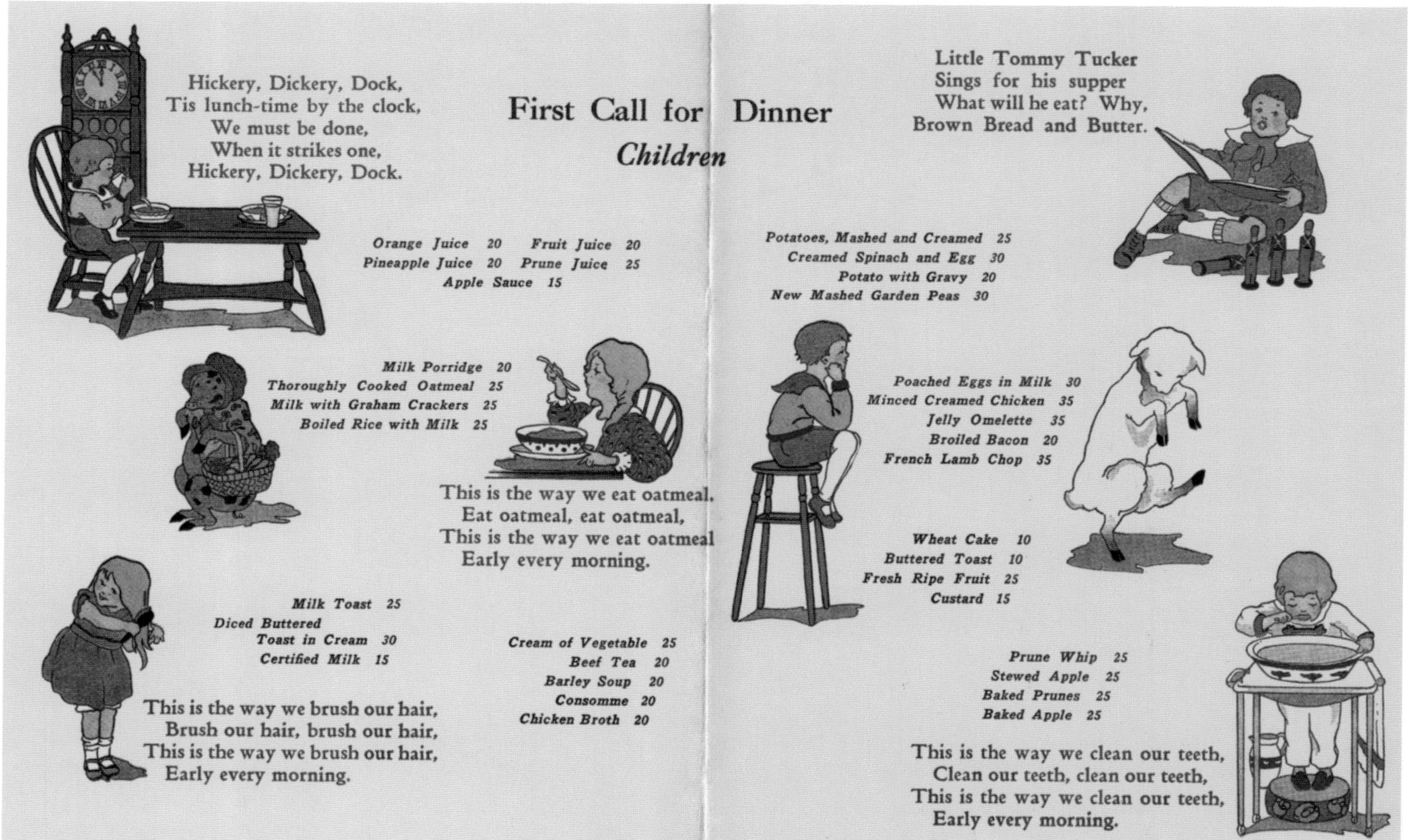

Hickery, Dickery, Dock,
Tis lunch-time by the clock,
We must be done,
When it strikes one,
Hickery, Dickery, Dock.

First Call for Dinner
Children

Little Tommy Tucker
Sings for his supper
What will he eat? Why,
Brown Bread and Butter.

Orange Juice 20 *Fruit Juice 20*
Pineapple Juice 20 *Prune Juice 25*
Apple Sauce 15

Milk Porridge 20
Thoroughly Cooked Oatmeal 25
Milk with Graham Crackers 25
Boiled Rice with Milk 25

This is the way we eat oatmeal,
Eat oatmeal, eat oatmeal,
This is the way we eat oatmeal
Early every morning.

Milk Toast 25
Diced Buttered Toast in Cream 30
Certified Milk 15

Cream of Vegetable 25
Beef Tea 20
Barley Soup 20
Consomme 20
Chicken Broth 20

This is the way we brush our hair,
Brush our hair, brush our hair,
This is the way we brush our hair,
Early every morning.

Potatoes, Mashed and Creamed 25
Creamed Spinach and Egg 30
Potato with Gravy 20
New Mashed Garden Peas 30

Poached Eggs in Milk 30
Minced Creamed Chicken 35
Jelly Omelette 35
Broiled Bacon 20
French Lamb Chop 35

Wheat Cake 10
Buttered Toast 10
Fresh Ripe Fruit 25
Custard 15

Prune Whip 25
Stewed Apple 25
Baked Prunes 25
Baked Apple 25

This is the way we clean our teeth,
Clean our teeth, clean our teeth,
This is the way we clean our teeth,
Early every morning.

Pig'n Whistle
Candies
are made for those
who demand the best

LEFT & OPPOSITE **Roscoe Arbuckle's Plantation Cafe, c. 1928, Culver City, California**

After silent movie comedian Roscoe "Fatty" Arbuckle emerged from a sex scandal that effectively ended his acting career, he opened the Plantation Club in 1928, which was decorated by MGM Studios' art department. Arbuckle himself entertained his Hollywood clientele here, but with the stock market crash a year later, he sold out his interest.

Nachdem ein Sexskandal die Karriere des Stummfilmkomikers Roscoe „Fatty" Arbuckle beendet hatte, eröffnete er 1928 den Plantation Club, der von den Kulissenmalern der MGM Studios gestaltet wurde. Arbuckle empfing seine Gäste aus Hollywood persönlich, aber als der Aktienmarkt im folgenden Jahr zusammenbrach, verkaufte er seinen Anteil.

Sa carrière ayant connu une fin abrupte après un scandale sexuel, Roscoe « Fatty » Arbuckle, vedette du cinéma muet, ouvre le Plantation club en 1928 avec un décor conçu par le département artistique de la MGM. Arbuckle s'occupe lui-même de sa clientèle hollywoodienne, mais en raison de la crise de 29, il doit revendre ses parts.

BELOW **Plantation Cafe, 1928, Culver City, California**

DINNER MENU

$2.00 PER PERSON

&

SEAFOOD OR FRUIT COCKTAIL
CANAPE OF ANCHOVIES
CELERY VICTOR WITH ANCHOVIES
BABY ARTICHOKE, RICHELIEU
CRISP CELERY RIPE COLOSSAL OLIVE

SOUPS
CONSOMME SOUP DU JOUR CHICKEN BROTH

CHOICE
CORN FED CHICKEN PLANTATION, OR A SEC
BROOK TROUT SAUTE, BROWN BUTTER
BROILED SQUAB WITH BACON
FROG LEG SAUTE, FATTY ARBUCKLE SPECIAL
TENDERLOIN OF BEEF GOULASH, A LA DEUTCH
VIRGINIA HAM STEAK, LOUISIANA
LAMB CHOPS, MIXED GRILL
N. Y. CUT SIRLOIN OR FILET MIGNON
HALF BROILED LOBSTER, FRENCH FRIED

VEGETABLE POTATOES
SALAD DU SASON

CHOICE
ASSORTED ICE CREAM SUNDAES PETIT FOURS
HOMEMADE PIES

DEMI TASSE

DRINK LIST

American Dry Ginger Ale, Splits	1.00
Canadian Dry, Splits	1.00
Cantrell & Cochrance C. & C. Splits	1.00
Sarsaparilla C. & C. Splits	1.00
Budweiser, Bottle	1.00
White Rock, Splits	1.00
Poland Water, Splits	1.00
Appolinaris	1.00
French Vichy, Splits	1.00
Perrier Water, Splits	1.00
Pure Orange Juice, Glass	1.25
Pure Lemon Juice, Glass	1.25

• • •

SPECIAL CUPS

Fruit Punch, Quarts	3.50
Grape Juice, Quarts	3.50
Lemonade, Quarts	3.50
Orange Juice, Quarts	5.00

ABOVE **The Cotton Club, c. 1937, New York, New York**

One of the most famous nightclubs of the 1920s and 1930s, the Cotton Club featured all the great African American performers, from Duke Ellington to Cab Calloway. Heavyweight boxer Jack Jackson opened the swank-but-whites-only club at 142nd Street and Lenox Avenue in 1920 as the Club De Luxe. It was soon taken over by bootlegger Owney Madden, who changed its name to the Cotton Club.

Der Cotton Club One war einer der berühmtesten Nachtklubs der 1920er- und 30er-Jahre. Alle großen afroamerikanischen Musiker der Zeit traten dort auf: von Duke Ellington bis Cab Calloway. Den schicken, nur für Weiße offenen Klub eröffnete 1920 der Schwergewichtsboxer Jack Jackson als Club De Luxe an der 142nd Street und Lenox Avenue. Bald übernahm ihn der Alkoholschmuggler Owney Madden, der den Namen in Cotton Club änderte.

L'un des night-clubs les plus célèbres des années 1920 et 1930, le Cotton Club a accueilli tous les grands artistes afro-américains, de Duke Ellington à Cab Calloway. En 1920, le boxeur Jack Jackson ouvre un club chic réservé aux Blancs, le « Club De Luxe », 142ᵉ rue et Lenox Avenue, bientôt repris par le bootlegger Owney Madden et rebaptisé « Cotton Club ».

BELOW Texas Guinan's, c. 1926, New York, New York

Waco-born Mary Louise "Texas" Guinan was a vaudeville singer and chorus girl who opened the speakeasy called the 300 Club on West 54th Street in New York. It was known for its scantily clad dancers and well-heeled clientele. Guinan would greet her guests with the phrase, "Hello, suckers!"

Die in Waco geborene Mary Louise „Texas" Guinan war Vaudevillesängerin und Revuetänzerin und machte die Flüsterkneipe 300 Club an der West 54th Street in New York auf. Der 300 Club war für seine knapp bekleideten Tänzerinnen und wohlhabende Kundschaft bekannt. Mrs. Guinan pflegte ihre Gäste mit „Na, ihr Trottel!" zu begrüßen.

Mary Louise « Texas » Guinan, née à Waco, actrice, chanteuse de variétés et danseuse, ouvre le *speakeasy* baptisé 300 Club sur la 54ᵉ rue Ouest à New York. Il est réputé pour ses danseuses en tenue légère et sa clientèle fortunée. George Gershwin y jouera des concerts improvisés. Guinan accueillait ses clients par cette phrase : « Salut les gogos ! »

ABOVE Connie's Inn, c. 1928, New York, New York

Originally a Harlem-basement whites-only nightclub located at Seventh Avenue and 131st Street, Connie's Inn hosted most of the era's best African American entertainers, including Louis Armstrong, "Moms" Mabley, Fats Waller, and Fletcher Henderson.

Connie's Inn war ursprünglich ein Nachtklub nur für Weiße in einem Keller an der Seventh Avenue und 131st Street in Harlem – viele der besten schwarzen Musiker der Zeit traten dort auf: Louis Armstrong, „Moms" Mabley, Fats Waller und Fletcher Henderson.

D'abord night-club réservé aux Blancs à Harlem, au coin de la Septième avenue et de la 131ᵉ rue, Connie's Inn accueillera à partir de 1923 les plus grands artistes afro-américains dont Louis Armstrong, Moms Mabley, Fats Waller et Fletcher Henderson.

OPPOSITE & BELOW RIGHT “We,” 1927, Wilmington, Delaware

ABOVE Hotel Ambassador, 1927, Paris, France

BELOW LEFT Breakfast in Honor of Charles Lindbergh, Hotel Brevoort, 1927, New York, New York

Lindbergh’s solo flight across the Atlantic from New York to Paris on May 20–21, 1927, was celebrated around the world. These menus show a breakfast menu from June 17 at the Hotel Brevoort in New York, noting the $25,000 prize offered for such a feat by Raymond Orteig; one showing Lindbergh’s plane, *The Spirit of St. Louis*, passing the Eiffel Tower, held at the Hotel Ambassador in Paris; and one given by the city of Wilmington, Delaware, that year, with the word “WE,” which was Lindbergh’s way of referring to himself and his plane. *We* was also the title of Lindbergh’s chronicle of the flight, published in 1927.

Lindberghs Alleinflug von New York nach Paris über den Atlantik am 20./21. Mai 1927 wurde auf der ganzen Welt gefeiert. Die Speisekarten zeigen ein Frühstücksmenü vom 17. Juni im Hotel Brevoort in New York, auf dem der Preis in Höhe von 25 000 Dollar vermerkt ist, der von Raymond Orteig ausgesetzt worden war. Auf einer ist Lindberghs Flugzeug, die *Spirit of St. Louis*, zu sehen, wie sie am Eiffelturm vorbeifliegt. Ein im selben Jahr von der Stadt Wilmington, Delaware, veranstaltetes Festessen trug das Motto „WE“ (wir), wie Lindbergh von sich und seinem Flugzeug zu sprechen pflegte. *We* war auch der Titel des Buches, das Lindbergh 1927 über seinen Flug veröffentlichte.

Le vol transatlantique en solo de Lindbergh entre New York et Paris les 20 et 21 mai 1927 a été célébré dans le monde entier. On voit ici des menus de petits-déjeuners : l’un organisé le 17 juin à l’Hotel Brevoort de New York, avec mention du prix de 25 000 dollars offert par Raymond Orteig pour récompenser l’exploit ; l’autre représentant *The Spirit of St. Louis*, l’avion de Lindbergh, devant la tour Eiffel, à l’Hotel Ambassador de Paris ; et enfin celui du petit-déjeuner donné par la ville de Wilmington, dans le Delaware, illustré du mot « WE » (« NOUS ») par lequel Lindbergh désignait son avion et lui-même. *We* est aussi le titre du récit de son vol publié en 1927.

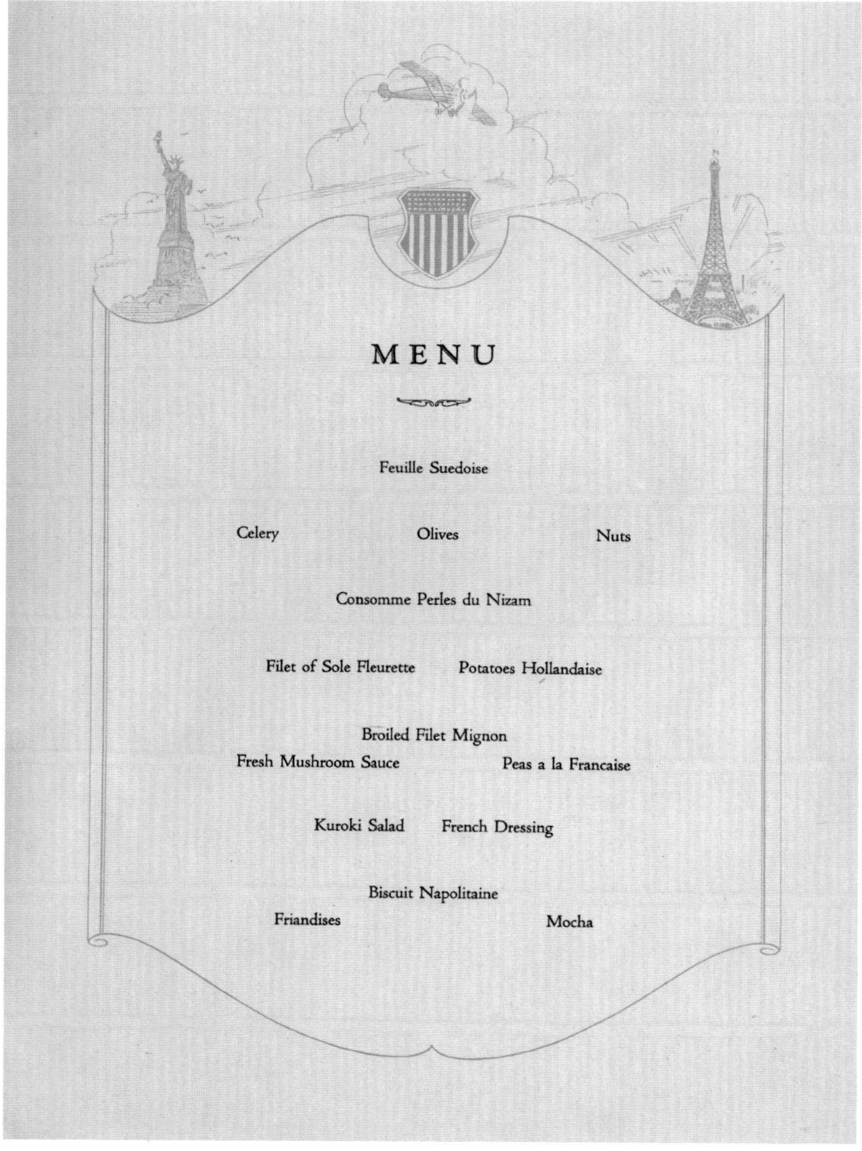
MENU

Feuille Suedoise

Celery Olives Nuts

Consomme Perles du Nizam

Filet of Sole Fleurette Potatoes Hollandaise

Broiled Filet Mignon
Fresh Mushroom Sauce Peas a la Francaise

Kuroki Salad French Dressing

Biscuit Napolitaine
Friandises Mocha

"WE"
BANQUET
In honor of
COLONEL CHARLES A. LINDBERGH
"AMERICA'S AIR AMBASSADOR" — NEW YORK TO PARIS NON-STOP FLIGHT
Given by The City of Wilmington Delaware.
SEAL OF THE CITY OF WILMINGTON
DELAWARE

Jack & Charlie's "21"

DINER

Wednesday, July 30, 1941

CLAMS, ETC.

Cherrystones 45 — Combination Sea Food Cocktail 1 25 — Shrimp Cocktail 90 — Crab Meat Cocktail 90
Little Necks 40 — Clam Juice Cocktail 50 — Tomato Juice Cocktail 50 — Lobster Cocktail 1 35 — Crab Meat Ravigote 1 10
Cocktail Sauce (10c. Extra)

HORS D'OEUVRES

Wild Boar or Prosciutto and Fresh Figs 1 75 — Hors d'Oeuvres Parisienne 1 00 — Snails Bourguignonne 85
Filet of Tunafish 1 00 — Anchovy Salad 1 00 — Marinated Scotch Herring 75 — Prosciutto or Wild Boar Ham 1 50
Smoked Sturgeon 1 35 — Canapé of Anchovies 75
Smoked Nova Scotia Salmon 1 10 — Suprème of Fruit Cocktail 75 — Imported Bismarck Herring 75
Cantaloupe 60 — Honey Dew Melon 60 — Smoked Brook Trout 1 25
Alligator Pear "21" 1 50 — Paté de Foie Gras 1 25 — Tomato Surprise Maison 90
Ripe Olives 40 — Green Olives 40 — Ripe Olives "21" 50 — Celeri 60 — Celeri and Olives 60 — Stuffed Celeri 75
Mackerel in White Wine 75 — Tomato Farcie Walters 1 25 — French Sardines 90 — Smoked Salmon "21" 1 75

POTAGES

Potage Parisienne 50 — Consommé Solange 45 — Cream Andalouse 50
Onion Soup au Gratin 55 — Minestrone Milanaise 50
Petite Marmite Bouchère 65 — Green Turtle Soup au Sherry 75
Cold: Cream Senegales 45 — Cream Vichyssoise 45 — Russian Bortsch 45
Madriléne Jelly 45 — Gumbo en Gelée 45 — Cream Cyrano 45
Clear Ox-tail en Gelée 45

POISSONS (Per Person)

Filet of Lemon Sole Metternich 1 35
Swordfish Steak Marchand de Vin 1 50
Broiled Soft Shell Crabs Hotelière 1 65
Brook Trout aux Court Bouillon 1 30
Shrimps and Lobster Mexicaine 1 45
Frogs' Legs Sauté Fines Herbes 1 35

ENTREES (Ready Per Person)

*Roast Long Island Duckling, French Peas Bonne Femme 1 65 (Ready)
*Sweetbread Brochette Risi-Bisi 1 70 (Ready)
*Filet Mignon Sauté Tosca 2 50 (Ready)
Half Chicken Grain Maryland 2 00
Breaded Lamb Chops, Squash Orientale 1 70
Veal Chop Sauté Delmonico 1 50
Royal Squab Cocotte Chipolata 2 25

BUFFET FROID

Sirloin de Boeuf, Salade Mexicaine 1 75
Carre d'Agneau, Monte Carlo 1 75
Poitrine de Volaille Jeannette 2 00
Pigeon Royal, Desossé Veronique 2 25
Demi Caneton, Bigarade 1 75
Galantine de Capon, Parisienne 1 75
Jambon de Virginie et Volaille, Pointe d'Asperges 1 75
Viande Froide Assortie, Salade de Pomme de Terre 2 00

SALADES

Fruits	75
Chicken	2 50
Escarole	45
Martin	50
Mexicaine	60
Niçoise	60
Chiffonade	50
Lettuce	50
Fresh Vegetable	1 25
Mixed Green	50
Tomato and Lettuce	50
Alligator Pear	75

(Served as Main Course 50c. Extra)
(Roquefort, Lorenzo or Russian Dressing 25c. Extra)

FROMAGES

Cream Cheese with Bar-le-Duc	65
Camembert	45
English Stilton	60
Bel Paese	45
Switzerland Swiss	50
Trappist Oka	45
Roquefort	60
Petite Gruyère	35
Brie	50

CAFE, THES

Café Rico	45
Demi Tasse Rico	30
Café Kirsch	1 00
Coffee with Cream	40
Special Percolated Coffee	50
Orange Pekoe Tea	40
Café Diablé Special	1 00

LEGUMES

Purée of Cauliflower 45
New Corn Sauté 60 — New Corn "21" 65 — Acorn Squash 50 — Broccoli 65
Succotash 60 — Oyster Bay Asparagus 90 — Zucchini 60 — New Beets au Beurre 45
New Peas 50 — Cauliflower 65 — Lima Beans 50 — Braised Celery 60 — French Peas 55; Bonne Femme 65 — String Beans 50
Carrots Vichy 50 — Spinach 50 — Creamed Spinach 60 — Egg Plant, Orientale 55 — Hearts of Palms Mousseline 75

POMMES

Parisienne Persillées 40 — Au Gratin 50 — Anna 50 — Lyonnaise 40 — Sauté 40 — Julienne 40 — Allumette 40 — Baked Idaho 40
Hashed Brown 45 — Hashed in Cream 45 — Candied Sweet Louisiana 50 — New Bermuda Potatoes 50

DESSERTS ET GLACE

Special "21": Coupe Montmorency 65
Fresh Raspberries, Blackberries or Blueberries and Cream 75 — Cranshaw Melon 60 — Strawberries Romanoff 1 25
Blueberries Reisman 1 00 — Sabayon 1 00 — Fruit Rafraichis au Kirsch 1 25
Roulade "21", Saboyan Sauce 65 — Petit Pot de Riz à la Vanille 45 — Compote of Fruit 60 — Baked Alaska (for 2) 2 00
Pot de Crème, Chocolat or Vanille 45 — Caramel Custard 45 — Ice Cream; Vanilla, Chocolate, Banana, Peach, Coffee or Pistachio 50
Pineapple, Raspberry or Lemon Water Ice 40 — Peach Melba 75 — Pear Belle Hélène 75 — Profiterole au Chocolat 75 — Petit Fours 50
Cerises Jubilée 1 25 — Stewed Rhubarb 60 — Baba au Rhum 75 — French Pancake 1 00 — Crepes Suzette 1 50
Macédoine de Fruits au Kirsch 1 00 — Coupe aux Marrons 75 — Coupe St. Jacques 75 — Apple Pancake 90

PRIVATE BAR AND DINING ROOMS AVAILABLE FOR PRIVATE PARTIES

CLOSED SUNDAYS

ABOVE Bartender at the "21" Club, 1933, New York, New York

"21"s clientele ranged from mayors to movie stars, and after Prohibition ended, became a very expensive and exclusive restaurant. Its famous iron gates and jockeys were totems of the restaurant's brownstone location.

Die Kundschaft des „21" reichte von Bürgermeistern bis zu Kinostars, und nachdem die Prohibition zu Ende war, wurde es zu einem sehr teuren und exklusiven Restaurant. Seine berühmten Eisentore und die Jockeystatuen waren Wahrzeichen des erhaltenen historischen Hauses.

La clientèle du « 21 » comptait des maires, des vedettes du cinéma et, après la Prohibition, ce bar clandestin se transforma en un restaurant chic et hors de prix. Les grilles métalliques et les jockeys devinrent emblématiques du bâtiment de grès brun.

OPPOSITE Jack and Charlie's "21," 1941, New York, New York

One of the most famous speakeasies of Prohibition, located at 21 West 52nd Street, "21," opened by Jack Kriendler and Charlie Berns on New Year's Day 1930, was notorious for evading federal agents and hiding its liquor behind a massive cement wall in the cellar. The photo of the bar shows the counter in the background, which emptied booze into chutes if "21" was raided.

Eine der berühmtesten Flüsterkneipen der Prohibitionszeit an der 21 West 52nd Street, das „21", wurde am Neujahrstag 1930 von Jack Kriendler und Charlie Berns aufgemacht und schaffte es immer wieder, Polizeizugriffen zu entgehen: Der Alkohol war hinter einer dicken Betonwand im Keller versteckt. Das Foto der Kneipe zeigt die Theke im Hintergrund, an der der Alkohol in einen Schacht geschüttet wurde, wenn es eine Razzia gab.

Un des plus fameux *speakeasies* de la Prohibition, situé au numéro 21 de la 52ᵉ rue Ouest. Le « 21 » ouvert par Jack Kriendler et Charlie Berns le jour du nouvel an 1930 reste célèbre pour avoir échappé aux agents fédéraux en dissimulant l'alcool derrière un mur en ciment de la cave. La photo du bar montre le comptoir en arrière-plan. L'alcool y était évacué par des canalisations en cas de descente de police.

COPIES OF THIS MENU MAY BE HAD UPON REQUEST

the PIRATES' DEN

8 CHRISTOPHER ST
GREENWICH VILLAGE
N.Y.C.

DESIGNED & PRODUCED by DON DICKERMAN CAPTAIN

COVER CHARGE 50¢

BEEFSTEAK DINNER
DANCING $1.25 DANCING

the FAMOUS COFFIN-NAILS 35¢

GALLEY SPECIALS
BEEFSTEAK SANDWICH 1.00 CHICKEN SALAD 1.25
RAREBIT " .50 TOPSA'L SANDWICH .60
VIRGINIA HAM " .40 CHICKEN " .60
GRUYÈRE (SWISS CHEESE) " .45 HOT DOG .30

OVER the BAR
PIRATE COCKTAIL .60 ORANGEADE .40
BLACK SKULL PUNCH .60 LEMONADE .40
ASSORTED CAKES & COOKIES .40

"THE BUCCANEERS' BIG HIT"
BEST CIDER YOU EVER TASTED 35¢
GINGER ALE .40 SARSAPARILLA .40
BUDWEISER .50 MINERAL WATER .40

BOWL of ICE CREAM .40 BOZO'S DELIGHT .50
TREASURE ISLAND .50 ICE BERG GLACÈ .50

ASSORTED NUTS & RAISINS 1.00

HOT CHOCOLATE 40¢
TEA OR COFFEE 25¢

with DANCE MUSIC UNTIL ONE O'CLOCK BY the ORIGINAL PIRATE BAND SEVEN NIGHTS

ANY COMPLAINTS SHOULD BE REPORTED TO THE OFFICER OF THE MAIN-DECK, WELL-DECK, GUN-DECK, OR HURRICANE DECK OR THE FIRST MATE OFFICER IN COMMAND

DEMAND ITEMIZED CHECK

D. D.

CIDERS

Martinelli's Sparkling .60
Martinelli's Still .45

FANCY MIXED DRINKS

Vermouth Cocktail .35
Mate Vermouth .35
Ambassador Cocktail .40
Ambassador Smile .40
Rose Cocktail .40
London Fog .40
Cocoanut Grove Special .40
Clover Club Cocktail .40
Clover Leaf .40
Orange Blossom .40
June Bug .40
Raspberry Rickey .40
Loganberry Rickey .40
Grenadine Rickey .40
Mint Julep .50

LEFT: **Pirates' Den, c. 1928, New York, New York**

ABOVE **The Cocoanut Grove, the Ambassador Hotel, c. 1927, Los Angeles, California**

The Cocoanut Grove restaurant and nightclub opened four months after the Ambassador Hotel did on New Year's Day 1921. Its décor was, like many others, based on Hollywood movies, with props said to come from Rudolph Valentino's *The Sheik*, palm trees, hanging monkeys galore, and a ceiling painted with twinkling stars. The coconut-shaped menu shows that alcohol was not yet legal.

Das Nachtlokal Cocoanut Grove wurde vier Monate nach dem Ambassador Hotel am Neujahrstag 1921 eröffnet. Die Ausstattung bezog sich wie in vielen anderen Restaurants der Zeit auf Hollywoodfilme, die Dekoration stammte angeblich direkt aus Rudolph Valentinos Film *Der Scheich*: Palmen, durch die sich Affen schwingen, und eine mit blinkenden Sternen bemalte Decke. An der kokosnussförmigen Speisekarte lässt sich ablesen, dass Alkohol noch nicht wieder legalisiert war.

Le Cocoanut Grove, restaurant et night-club, ouvre ses portes quatre mois après l'Ambassador Hotel, inauguré au nouvel an 1921. Comme de nombreux autres établissements, son décor s'inspire d'Hollywood et on raconte que les palmiers, la profusion de singes accrochés un peu partout et le plafond pailleté d'étoiles scintillantes proviennent du film *Le Cheik*, avec Rudolph Valentino. Le menu en forme de noix de coco suggère que l'alcool n'était pas encore légal.

BELOW Forty Famous Cocktails, c. 1928, New York, New York

A booklet for cocktail recipes "in this arid era" of Prohibition. The illustration shows an earlier day when bars were open and served cheese and pretzels as part of the free lunch. The reference to "that master engraver John Held Jr." is to the magazine illustrator of that name, famous for both his cartoons of flappers of the Jazz Age and for his *New Yorker* magazine woodcuts in a 19th-century style.

Ein Heftchen mit Cocktailrezepten für die „Dürrezeit" der Prohibition. Auf dem Bild ist die schöne Vergangenheit zu sehen, als es noch offenen Alkoholausschank an der Theke, mittags mit kostenlosem Käse und Salzgebäck, gab. Mit „that master engraver John Held Jr." ist der Zeitschriftenillustrator John Held gemeint, der für seine Karikaturen von Flappern der Jazzära und für seine Holzschnitte im Stil des 19. Jahrhunderts für das Magazin *New Yorker* berühmt war.

Recueil de recettes de cocktails pendant l'« ère aride » de la Prohibition. L'illustration évoque une époque passée quand les bars étaient ouverts et servaient gratuitement du fromage et des bretzels. La référence au « maître graveur John Held Jr. » évoque le célèbre illustrateur, connu pour ses dessins de garçonnes de l'Ère du jazz, mais aussi pour ses gravures sur bois dans un style XIXe siècle, réalisées pour le magazine *New Yorker*.

MENU
THE ADMIRAL LINE

OPPOSITE The Admiral Line, the Pacific Steamship Lines, 1929

RIGHT Get-Together Dinner, *USS Statendam*, 1931

In the 1930s ship lines competed mightily to serve elegant cuisine, usually an amalgam of French classics, a few dishes from the line's country of origin, and American items favored by a clientele largely from the United States.

In den 1930er-Jahren wetteiferten die Reedereien miteinander darum, wer das exklusivste Essen servierte. Meist gab es an Bord französische Klassiker, einige Gerichte aus dem Herkunftsland des Schiffs und die Lieblingsgerichte der überwiegend amerikanischen Passagiere.

Dans les années 1930, les compagnies maritimes rivalisent pour servir la cuisine la plus raffinée, généralement un mélange de classiques français, de quelques plats du pays d'origine et de spécialités américaines appréciées par une clientèle venue en majorité des États-Unis.

BELOW LEFT *S. S. America*, United States Lines, 1930

BELOW RIGHT *S. S. City of Los Angeles*, Los Angeles Steamship Co., 1931

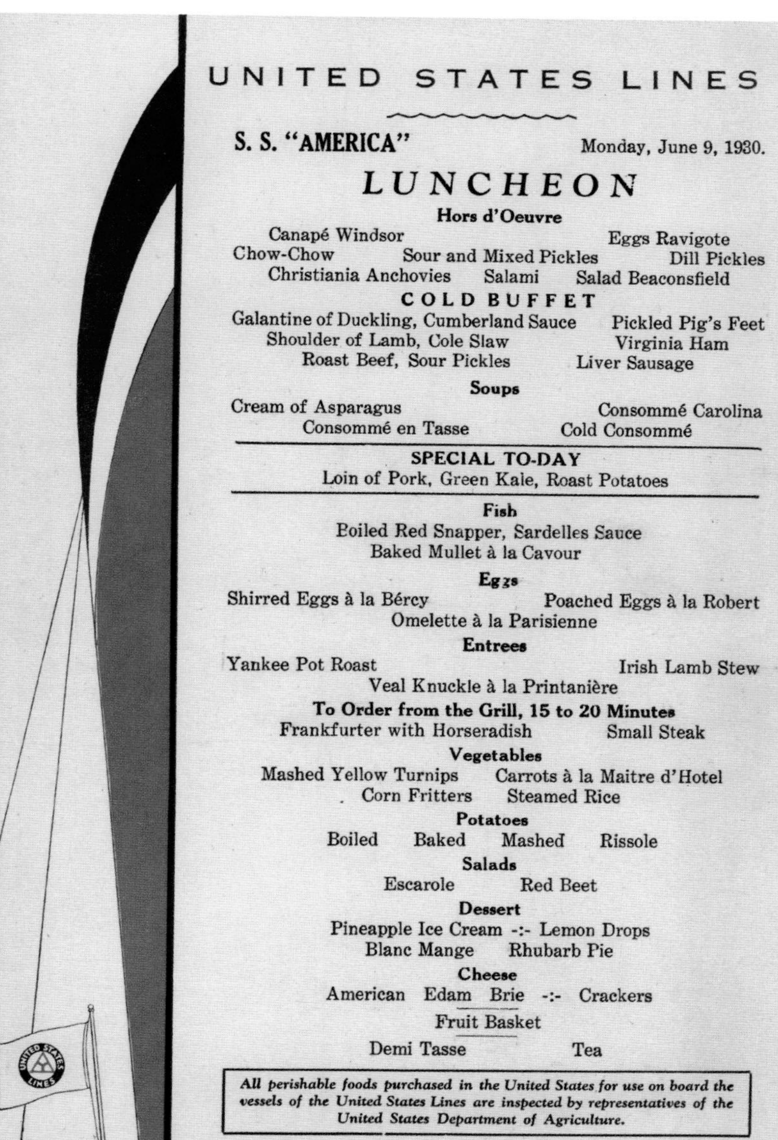

UNITED STATES LINES

S. S. "AMERICA" Monday, June 9, 1930.

LUNCHEON

Hors d'Oeuvre

Canapé Windsor Eggs Ravigote
Chow-Chow Sour and Mixed Pickles Dill Pickles
Christiania Anchovies Salami Salad Beaconsfield

COLD BUFFET

Galantine of Duckling, Cumberland Sauce Pickled Pig's Feet
Shoulder of Lamb, Cole Slaw Virginia Ham
Roast Beef, Sour Pickles Liver Sausage

Soups

Cream of Asparagus Consommé Carolina
Consommé en Tasse Cold Consommé

SPECIAL TO-DAY

Loin of Pork, Green Kale, Roast Potatoes

Fish

Boiled Red Snapper, Sardelles Sauce
Baked Mullet à la Cavour

Eggs

Shirred Eggs à la Bércy Poached Eggs à la Robert
Omelette à la Parisienne

Entrees

Yankee Pot Roast Irish Lamb Stew
Veal Knuckle à la Printanière

To Order from the Grill, 15 to 20 Minutes

Frankfurter with Horseradish Small Steak

Vegetables

Mashed Yellow Turnips Carrots à la Maitre d'Hotel
Corn Fritters Steamed Rice

Potatoes

Boiled Baked Mashed Rissole

Salads

Escarole Red Beet

Dessert

Pineapple Ice Cream -:- Lemon Drops
Blanc Mange Rhubarb Pie

Cheese

American Edam Brie -:- Crackers
Fruit Basket
Demi Tasse Tea

All perishable foods purchased in the United States for use on board the vessels of the United States Lines are inspected by representatives of the United States Department of Agriculture.

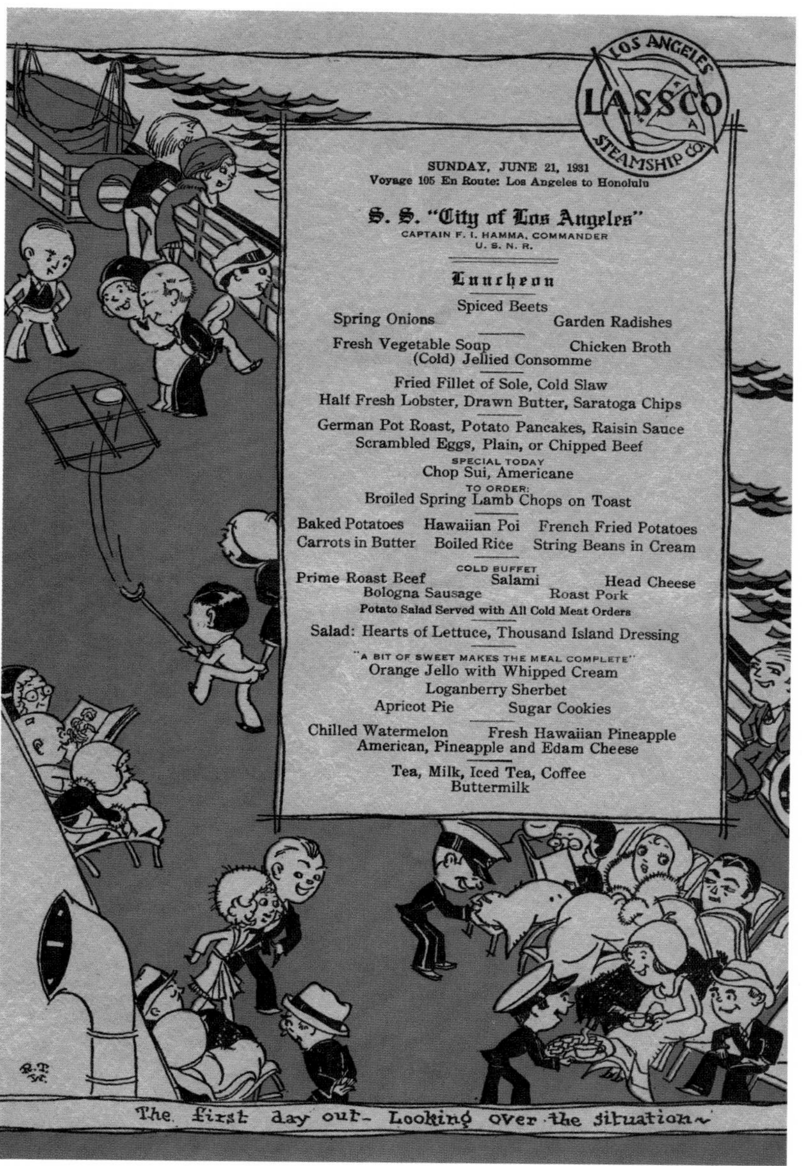

LOS ANGELES STEAMSHIP CO. LASSCO

SUNDAY, JUNE 21, 1931
Voyage 105 En Route: Los Angeles to Honolulu

S. S. "City of Los Angeles"
CAPTAIN F. I. HAMMA, COMMANDER U. S. N. R.

Luncheon

Spiced Beets
Spring Onions Garden Radishes

Fresh Vegetable Soup Chicken Broth
(Cold) Jellied Consomme

Fried Fillet of Sole, Cold Slaw
Half Fresh Lobster, Drawn Butter, Saratoga Chips

German Pot Roast, Potato Pancakes, Raisin Sauce
Scrambled Eggs, Plain, or Chipped Beef

SPECIAL TODAY
Chop Sui, Americane

TO ORDER:
Broiled Spring Lamb Chops on Toast

Baked Potatoes Hawaiian Poi French Fried Potatoes
Carrots in Butter Boiled Rice String Beans in Cream

COLD BUFFET
Prime Roast Beef Salami Head Cheese
Bologna Sausage Roast Pork
Potato Salad Served with All Cold Meat Orders

Salad: Hearts of Lettuce, Thousand Island Dressing

"A BIT OF SWEET MAKES THE MEAL COMPLETE"
Orange Jello with Whipped Cream
Loganberry Sherbet
Apricot Pie Sugar Cookies

Chilled Watermelon Fresh Hawaiian Pineapple
American, Pineapple and Edam Cheese

Tea, Milk, Iced Tea, Coffee
Buttermilk

The first day out- Looking over the situation-

OPPOSITE The Blackhawk Restaurant, c. 1935, Chicago, Illinois

The Blackhawk opened in Chicago's Loop district in 1920 as a nightclub with a jazz orchestra, later broadcast on the Mutual Network, with stars like Chico Marx, Mel Tormé, and Louis Prima. The menu-cover artist, Edouardé, worked very much in the style developed by John Held Jr.

Das Blackhawk eröffnete 1920 im Chicagoer Loop als Nachtklub mit Jazzorchester, späteren Live-Übertragungen im Radio und Stars wie Chico Marx, Mel Tormé und Louis Prima. Der Zeichner des Karteneinbands, Edouardé, bediente sich des von John Held Jr. entwickelten Stils.

Le Blackhawk ouvre dans le Loop district de Chicago en 1920. Il s'agit d'un night-club avec un orchestre de jazz. Plus tard, ce dernier sera diffusé sur les ondes de Mutual Network et présentera des vedettes telles que Chico Marx, Mel Tormé et Louis Prima. Edouardé, l'artiste ayant réalisé la couverture, travaillait dans le style de John Held Jr.

ABOVE Helen Swope, c. 1932, Seattle, Washington

ABOVE CENTER Vassar House, 1932, Chicago, Illinois

RIGHT Club Ballyhoo, c. 1934, Hollywood, California

The
BLACKHAWK
EDOUARDE'
RESTAURANT

SUPPER
HOTEL
PENNSYLVANIA
KLIZ

OPPOSITE Hotel Pennsylvania Roof, c. 1933, New York, New York

The Pennsylvania Railroad built the hotel, designed by McKim, Mead & White, and opened January 25, 1919, at Seventh Avenue and 33rd Street, near Pennsylvania Terminal. The Manhattan Room restaurant was turned into the Roof Garden in summer. Glenn Miller's 1940 hit record "Pennsylvania 6-5000" referred to the hotel's telephone number, the oldest continuing phone number in New York.

Die Pennsylvania Railroad ließ das von McKim, Mead & White entworfene Hotel bauen, das am 25. Januar 1919 Ecke Seventh Avenue und 33rd Street in der Nähe des Bahnhofs Pennsylvania Terminal seine Pforten öffnete. Das Restaurant Manhattan Room wurde im Sommer in einen Dachgarten verwandelt. Glenn Millers Hit „Pennsylvania 6-5000" von 1940 bezieht sich auf die Telefonnummer des Hotels, die älteste, heute noch vergebene Telefonnummer in New York.

Cet hôtel, conçu par McKim, Mead & White, a été bâti par le Pennsylvania Railroad. Il ouvre le 25 janvier 1919, au coin de la Septième avenue et de la 33e rue, près de la gare Pennsylvania Terminal. Cet été-là, le restaurant Manhattan Room devient le Roof Garden. Le tube de 1940 enregistré par Glenn Miller, *Pennsylvania 6-5000*, fait référence au téléphone de l'hôtel (le plus vieux numéro jamais attribué au même usager dans tout New York).

ABOVE Opening, Club New Yorker, 1932, Hollywood, California

LEFT Mark Hopkins Hotel, c. 1933, San Francisco, California

Mark Hopkins, cofounder of the Central Pacific Railroad, built a mansion on Nob Hill that was destroyed in the 1906 earthquake. The Mark Hopkins Hotel opened on the site and is now a national landmark.

Mark Hopkins, Mitbegründer der Central Pacific Railroad, baute sich eine Villa auf dem Nob Hill, die bei dem Erdbeben 1906 zerstört wurde. Das Mark Hopkins Hotel wurde an der gleichen Stelle errichtet und ist heute ein Wahrzeichen San Franciscos.

Mark Hopkins, cofondateur du Central Pacific Railroad, a construit un manoir sur Nob Hill, plus tard détruit par le séisme de 1906. Le Mark Hopkins Hotel a ouvert au même endroit. Il est par la suite devenu un monument historique national.

Visit the

Schwarzwald

(Black Forest)

while at the World's Fair.

Enjoy ice skating in the open no matter how hot the day.

ICH HAB' MEIN HERZ IN HEIDELBERG VERLOREN!

Ich hab' mein Herz in Heidelberg verloren,
In einer lauen Sommernacht;
Ich war verliebt bis ueber beide Ohren
Und wie ein Roeslein hat ihr Mund gelacht.
Und als wir Abschied nahmen vor den Toren,
Beim letzten Kuss, da hab' ich klar erkannt,
Dass ich mein Herz in Heidelberg verloren,
Mein Herz es liegt am Neckarstrand!

PIONEERS in 1871

Even before the days of the great Civil War, word had spread to all states bordering Wisconsin that in Milwaukee a brewer named Blatz was making a beer of exceptionally fine quality.

As the "iron horse" pushed its double line of steel into newer sections of the country, the fame of Blatz-Milwaukee Beer spread to distant states.

Travelers who had been "out west" carried back to thirsty easterners the news of a wonderfully fine beer being made in Milwaukee. Intrepid men going to the west coast also carried the news of the fine beer being brewed by Blatz of Milwaukee.

And thus—as long ago as 1871 Blatz was known from coast to coast as one of the country's leading "shipping brewers."

Spend an Evening at

Old Heidelberg Inn

14-16 Randolph Street

In Chicago's famous loop.

See and hear the Original Bavarian Orchestra under the leadership of George Hessberger.

Under Eitel management

DU, DU LIEGST MIR IM HERZEN

Du, du liegst mir im Herzen, du, du liegst mir im Sinn; —
Du, du machst mir viel Schmerzen, weisst nicht, wie gut ich dir bin.—
Ja, ja, ja, ja, weisst nicht, wie gut ich dir bin.
Ja, ja, ja, ja, weisst nicht, wie gut ich dir bin.

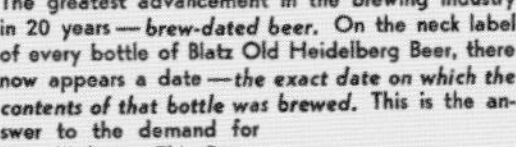

PIONEERS in 1934

Again Blatz pioneers—this time by bringing a positive guarantee as to the exact age of every bottle of Blatz Old Heidelberg Beer—the only beer that is Brew-Dated.

The greatest advancement in the brewing industry in 20 years — *brew-dated beer.* On the neck label of every bottle of Blatz Old Heidelberg Beer, there now appears a date — *the exact date on which the contents of that bottle was brewed.* This is the answer to the demand for "aged" beer. This Brew-Date on every bottle is the Blatz guarantee that every bottle of Blatz Old Heidelberg Beer is *fully-aged.*

REMEMBER — only Blatz Old Heidelberg Beer is Brew-Dated — only Blatz Old Heidelberg Beer *tells its exact age* — by the date on every bottle.

Blatz

MILWAUKEE

Blatz Old Heidelberg BEER

Black Forest Inn

Eitel's

Souvenir

A Century of Progress · Chicago

1934

ABOVE **Eitel's Old Heidelberg Inn, 1934, Chicago, Illinois**

LEFT **Eitel's Black Forest Inn, 1934, Chicago, Illinois**

OPPOSITE **The Swift Bridge, 1934, Chicago, Illinois**

Themed as "A Century of Progress International Exposition," the fair ran from 1933–1934, symbolized by its motto "Science Finds, Industry Applies, Man Conforms." The restaurant concessions offered an array of international cuisines.

Die Weltausstellung „Ein Jahrhundert internationaler Fortschritt" (1933/34) stand unter dem Motto: „Wissenschaft entdeckt, Industrie benutzt, der Mensch passt sich an." Die Lokale auf der Weltausstellung boten Spezialitäten aus aller Welt an.

L'exposition internationale « Un siècle de progrès », symbolisée par sa devise « La science découvre, l'industrie applique, l'homme s'adapte », se déroule de 1933 à 1934. Les restaurants offrent un éventail de gastronomies internationales.

SPLENDID VIEW
THESE ARE NOT
STORM CLOUDS
DON'T BE FRIGHTENED
THE SWIFT BRIDGE
A Century of Progress
The
SWIFT BRIDGE
The World's Fair Chicago 1934
SPLENDID VIEW

"AN - INSTITUTION - BUILT - THRU - MERIT"

GENERAL OFFICE
3614 W. Jefferson Blvd.

Location of Bowls

3012 Crenshaw Boulevard LOS ANGELES	1401 North Atlantic Blvd. LONG BEACH
2228 East Florence Avenue HUNTINGTON PARK	111 North Fairfax HOLLYWOOD
801 North La Brea HOLLYWOOD	4351 South Figueroa Street LOS ANGELES
5061 Whittier Boulevard BELVEDERE	2453 Fletcher Drive LOS ANGELES
3668 Beverly Boulevard LOS ANGELES	1601 East Anaheim WILMINGTON

The Objective to Which We Strive Is—

FAST COURTEOUS SERVICE

We Will Greatly Appreciate Your Reporting to Our Office Any Failure to Live Up to These Principles . . .

CHILI BOWL MENU and GUEST CHECK

ENTREES		SANDWICHES	
Size (Grilled Steak / Chili - Beans)	.25	Cold Ham W	.15
Spaghetti Size (Grilled Steak / Spaghetti)	.35	Fried Ham W	.15
Tamale & Chili	.30	Cheese W	.15
Tamale & Chili Con Carne	.35	Egg W	.15
Tamale-Chili Beans	.40	*Above If Toasted*	.05
Spaghetti	.30	Grillburger Sandwich	.15
Spaghetti Texas Beans	.40	Grillburger Sand. Cheese	.20
Chili Straight (Con Carne)	.25	Melted Cheese W	.20
Chili Beans (Con Carne)	.25	Special Club W	.20
Chili Beans	.20	Ground Steak Sand. W	.25
Chicken Ravioli Special	.35	Ham and Egg Sand. W	.25
Enchilada Special	.35	**DRINKS**	
Grillburger Steak Plain	.25	Coffee Real Cr. per cup	.05
Grillburger Steak Chili	.30	Tea	.10
Grillburger Steak Chili Beans	.35	Hot Chocolate	.10
Egg Royal Plain	.30	Buttermilk	.10
Egg Royal Chili	.35	Milk	.10
Egg Royal Chili Beans	.40	Soda 12 oz. Bottle	.10
Gr. Round Steak Potatoes	.35	Kava Kola (Fountain)	.05
Ham Omelette	.40	Bottled Beer	.10
Cheese Omelette	.40	" "	.15
Plain Omelette	.35	Canned Beer	.20
Ham & Eggs	.40	**DESSERTS**	
2 Eggs Fried or Scrambled	.25	Pie (our own)	.10
Cold-Plate Pot. Salad (Summer Months)	.30	Pie in a Bowl (cream)	.15
EXTRA ITEMS		Tomato Juice	.15
		Soup	.15
		Roll (Franco)	.05
		Roll - Butter	.10

CHECK NO.	WAITER NO.	
00038	A-B-C-D	TOTAL

PLEASE PAY AT YOUR SEAT - THANK YOU

LEFT **Wimpy's Grill, c. 1934, San Francisco, California**

ABOVE **Chili Bowl, c. 1934, Los Angeles, California**

The Chili Bowl chain, founded by Arthur Whizin, was one of the first fast-food chains, long before McDonald's. A "Chili Size" was slang for an open-faced hamburger smothered in chili. "Size" referred to the size of the scoop of chili placed on the burger.

Die Kette Chili Bowl wurde von Arthur Whizin gegründet und war lange vor McDonald's eine der ersten Fast-Food-Ketten. „Chili Size" war der Slangausdruck für einen aufgeklappten Hamburger, der mit Chili con Carne übergossen wird. „Size" bezog sich auf die Chili-Menge, die auf den Hamburger kam.

La chaîne Chili Bowl fondée par Arthur Whizin est l'une des premières chaînes de fast-foods à voir le jour, bien avant McDonald's. Un « Chili Size » désigne en argot un hamburger sans pain sur le dessus et couvert de chili. « Size » se réfère à la quantité de chili placée sur le steak haché.

RIGHT Eddie's Grill, c. 1936, Maui, Hawaii

BELOW Pig Stand, c. 1934, Los Angeles, California

The first Pig Stand barbecue drive-in eatery with "carhops" opened in Dallas, Texas, in 1921. Such places specialized in hog meat slowly smoked over hardwood coals, called, variously, barbecue, barbeque, bar-b-q, and just 'cue.

Der erste Pig Stand Barbecue Drive-in mit Bedienung am Auto eröffnete 1921 in Dallas, Texas. Der Imbiss war auf langsam über Holzkohle geräuchertes Schweinefleisch spezialisiert, das *barbecue, barbeque, bar-b-q* oder einfach nur *'cue* genannt wurde.

Le premier barbecue drive-in Pig Stand et ses « carhops » (serveurs) a ouvert à Dallas au Texas en 1921. Ces restaurants spécialisés dans une viande de porc lentement fumée au charbon de bois, s'appelaient indifféremment « barbecue », « barbeque », « bar-b-q », ou simplement « 'cue ».

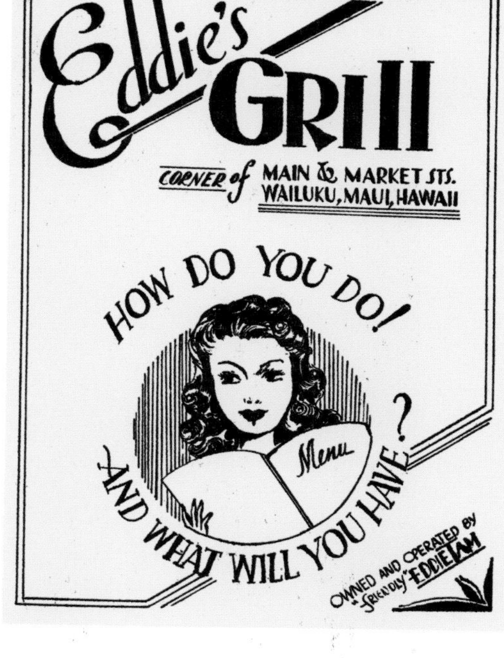

"A Tasty Meal Served at Your Wheel"

SANDWICHES

Pig (barbecued) 20
Beef (barbecued) 20
Ham (barbecued) 20
Pig or Beef (on a bun) . .15
Hamberger . . . . .10 or .15
Cheese and Hamberger Combination 20
Steak 15
Swiss, Amer. Cheese . . .15
Red Hots 10
Tuna Salad 15
Chicken Salad 15
Ham and Egg Comb. . . .25
Chili and Beans 20

Pies

Crust Pies 10
Cream Pies 10

"Look for the Sign of the Pig"

FOUNTAIN SERVICE

Ice Cream Sodas . . .15
Sundaes 15
Frosted Root Beer 15
Root Beer Rochester . . .05
Malted Milks 20
Milk Shakes 15
Coca-Cola 05
Orange Juice (fresh) . . .10
Lime (fresh) 10
Grape Juice (Welch's) . .10
Hot Chocolate (Nestle's) .10
Tea (iced or hot) 10
Tomato Juice 10
Coffee (with pure cream) .05
Beer (Eastside) 10
Milk 10
Ginger Ale 25

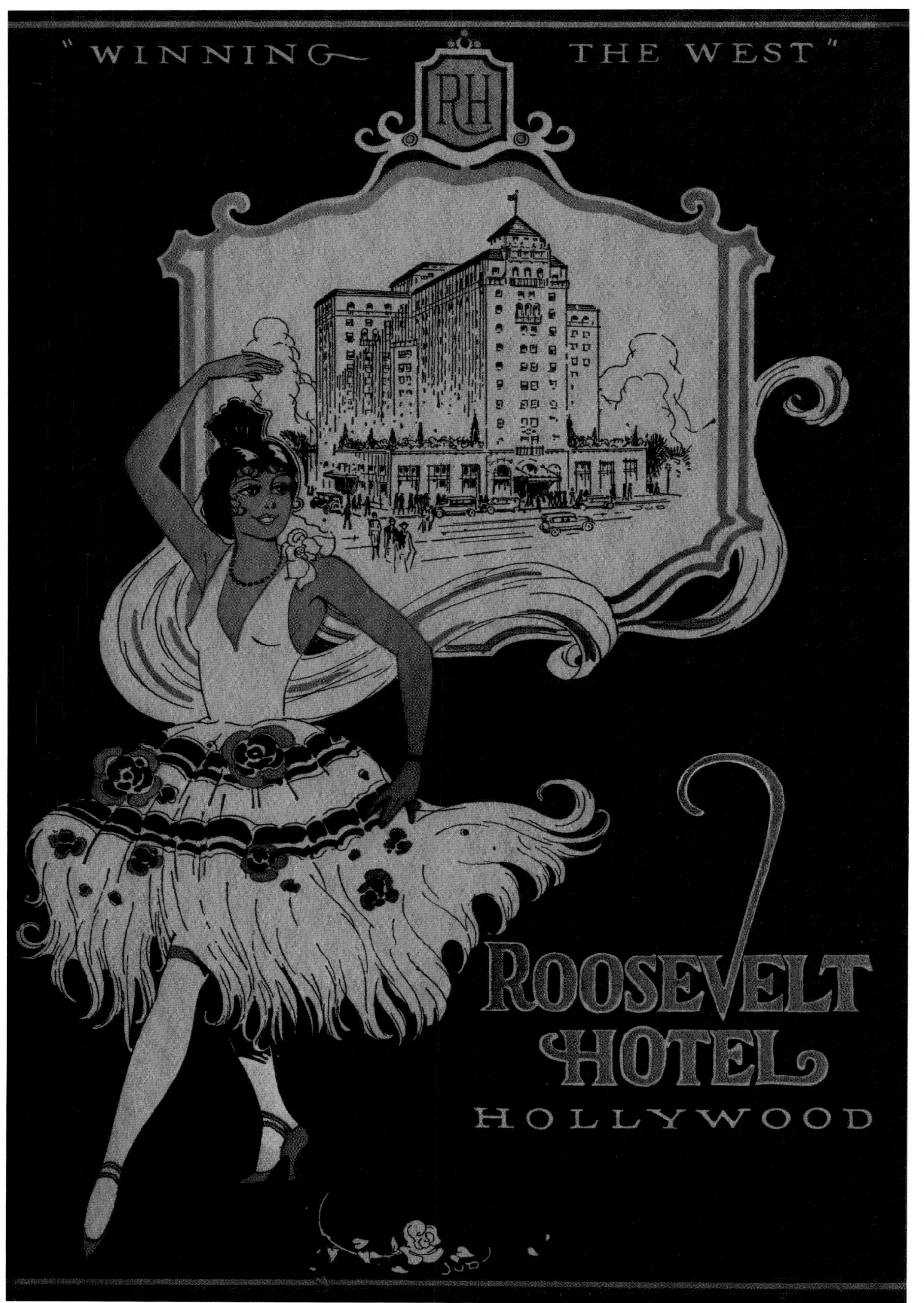
"WINNING THE WEST"
RH
ROOSEVELT HOTEL
HOLLYWOOD

OPPOSITE Roosevelt Hotel, 1929, Hollywood, California.

The Hollywood Roosevelt opened in May 1927 backed by a consortium of celebrities including Douglas Fairbanks, Mary Pickford, and Louis B. Mayer. The Blossom Room at the Roosevelt was the location for the first Academy Awards dinner and ceremony.

Das Hollywood Roosevelt öffnete im Mai 1927 seine Pforten, finanziert von Größen aus der Filmbranche wie Douglas Fairbanks, Mary Pickford und Louis B. Mayer. Im Blossom Room im Roosevelt Hotel fand die erste Oscarverleihung mit Dinner statt.

L'hôtel Roosevelt ouvre à Hollywood en mai 1927. Il est financé par un consortium de célébrités dont Douglas Fairbanks, Mary Pickford et Louis B. Mayer. Le Blossom Room du Roosevelt accueillera la première cérémonie et le premier dîner des Oscars.

ABOVE Roosevelt Inn, 1933, Stockton, California

A Depression-era menu reflects frugal times with its hand-drawn and mimeographed cover.

Diese von Hand gezeichnete und vervielfältigte Speisekarte aus der Weltwirtschaftskrise zeugt von den harten Zeiten.

Cette carte sommaire de 1933, avec sa couverture dessinée à la main et ronéotypée, reflète la crise qui sévit à l'époque de la Grande Dépression de 1929.

LEFT Sandwich Shop, Hotel Roosevelt, c. 1934, Cedar Rapids, Iowa

ABOVE 365 Club, c. 1935, San Francisco, California

RIGHT Colonial Room, Pantlind Hotel, 1936, Grand Rapids, Michigan

OPPOSITE New Year's Eve, the Mayflower, 1937, Washington, D.C.

Here, a New Year's menu from the Mayflower Hotel, opened by Alle E. Walker as the "Grande Dame of Washington" in 1925. It was said to be trimmed with more gold leaf than any building except the Library of Congress. J. Edgar Hoover, director of the FBI, had lunch there daily for 20 years.

Zu sehen ist eine Karte vom Silvesterabend im Mayflower Hotel, das Alle E. Walker 1925 als „Grande Dame Washingtons" konzipiert hatte. Es war angeblich mit mehr Blattgold verziert als alle Regierungsgebäude mit Ausnahme der Library of Congress. J. Edgar Hoover, Leiter des FBI, aß hier 20 Jahre lang täglich zu Mittag.

Menu du nouvel an du Mayflower Hotel, la « Grande Dame de Washington », ouvert par Alle E. Walker en 1925. On prétend que seule la bibliothèque du Congrès contient plus de dorures que ce bâtiment. J. Edgar Hoover, directeur du FBI, y a déjeuné tous les jours pendant vingt ans.

The Mayflower - Washington, D.C.

LEFT Lucca, c. 1937, Los Angeles, California

BELOW Lucca, c. 1935, San Francisco, California

Established in 1930 in San Francisco, owner Bert Rovere opened a Los Angeles outlet several years later. Both locations were Depression-era hits featuring generous portions, dancing, and live operatic radio broadcasts.

Bert Rovere eröffnete das erste Lucca 1930 in San Francisco und ein weiteres einige Jahre später in Los Angeles. Beide waren während der Weltwirtschaftskrise große Hits, da sie deftige Portionen, Tanz und Live-Übertragungen von Opern boten.

Installé dès 1930 à San Francisco, Bert Rovere ouvrira une deuxième enseigne à Los Angeles quelques années plus tard. Ses deux restaurants font florès malgré la crise. Ils offrent des portions généreuses, on peut y danser et ils accueillent des émissions de radio.

ABOVE **Cafe Club Stratosphere, 1935, Everett, Washington**

LEFT **Mike Lyman's Grill, 1936, Hollywood, California**

LEFT **Rubenak's Half-Way House, c. 1935, Everett, Washington**

OPPOSITE **Sutton's Club Lido, c. 1934, Los Angeles, California**

RIGHT **The Cafe des Artistes, c. 1937, New York, New York**

Opened in 1917 on West 67th Street, the Café des Artistes was indeed a draw for theater and music people for 90 years, and was particularly famous for a series of nudes romping in a forest, painted by Howard Chandler Christy, as shown on the menu cover. The café closed in 2009.

Das ab 1917 an der West 67th Street bestehende Café des Artistes war 90 Jahre lang eine Institution für die Theater- und Musikszene. Berühmt waren die von Howard Chandler Christy gemalten nackten Schönheiten, die durch den Wald hüpften und die auch auf der Speisekarte zu sehen waren. Das Café wurde 2009 geschlossen.

Ouvert en 1917 sur la 67ᵉ rue Ouest, le Café des Artistes a attiré comédiens et musiciens pendant 90 ans. Il est particulièrement connu pour sa série de nus s'ébattant dans la forêt, peinte par Howard Chandler Christy, dont on voit un exemple sur la couverture du menu. Le café a fermé en 2009.

MEET ME AT
Sutton's Club Lido
PICO AND WESTERN • LOS ANGELES, CALIF.

ABOVE **Hotel Del Monte, 1937, Monterey, California**

Originally opened in 1886 by railroad tycoons on 7,000 acres, the Hotel del Monte burned to the ground a year later, was rebuilt, and burned down again in 1924. It was then rebuilt again, bigger than ever. In 1952 it became the Naval Postgraduate School. The menus show scenes from California history, drawn by Joseph Jacinto "Jo" Mora, a Uruguayan artist, cartoonist, and author.

Das 1886 von Eisenbahnmagnaten auf 3000 Hektar Land erbaute Hotel del Monte brannte ein Jahr später ab, wurde wieder aufgebaut und brannte 1924 erneut ab. Danach wurde es noch größer wieder aufgebaut. 1952 funktionierte man es zur Postgraduate School der Marine um. Auf den Speisekarten sind Szenen aus der kalifornischen Geschichte zu sehen, gezeichnet von Joseph Jacinto „Jo" Mora, Zeichner und Autor aus Uruguay.

Ouvert d'abord en 1886 par des magnats du chemin de fer, l'Hotel del Monte, qui s'étend sur près de 3 000 hectares, est détruit par un incendie l'année suivante. Rebâti, il brûle à nouveau en 1924. Il est reconstruit derechef, plus grand que jamais. En 1952, il finira par abriter la Naval Postgraduate School. Le menu dessiné par Joseph Jacinto « Jo » Mora, peintre, dessinateur et auteur uruguayen, évoque des scènes de l'histoire californienne.

BELOW **El Sombrero Plaza Tavern, c. 1937**

RIGHT El Coyote Spanish Cafe, c. 1935, Los Angeles, California

Mexican eateries continued to serve a very American-Mexican menu of Texas and Western dishes like chili con carne, along with Spanish rice and french-fried potatoes. Such places were also doing brisk business in take-out foods, an option in almost all ethnic restaurants.

Beim Mexikaner wurde eine amerikanisch-mexikanische Mischung serviert: Gerichte wie Chili con Carne, spanischer Reis und Pommes frites. Gaststätten wie diese waren auch mit ihren Gerichten zum Mitnehmen sehr erfolgreich, was von fast allen ethnischen Restaurants angeboten wurde.

Les restaurants mexicains servent un menu tex-mex composé de plats occidentaux et texans, comme le chili con carne, le riz à l'espagnole ou les frites. Comme dans la plupart des établissements «ethniques», ils proposent également des plats à emporter – un commerce florissant !

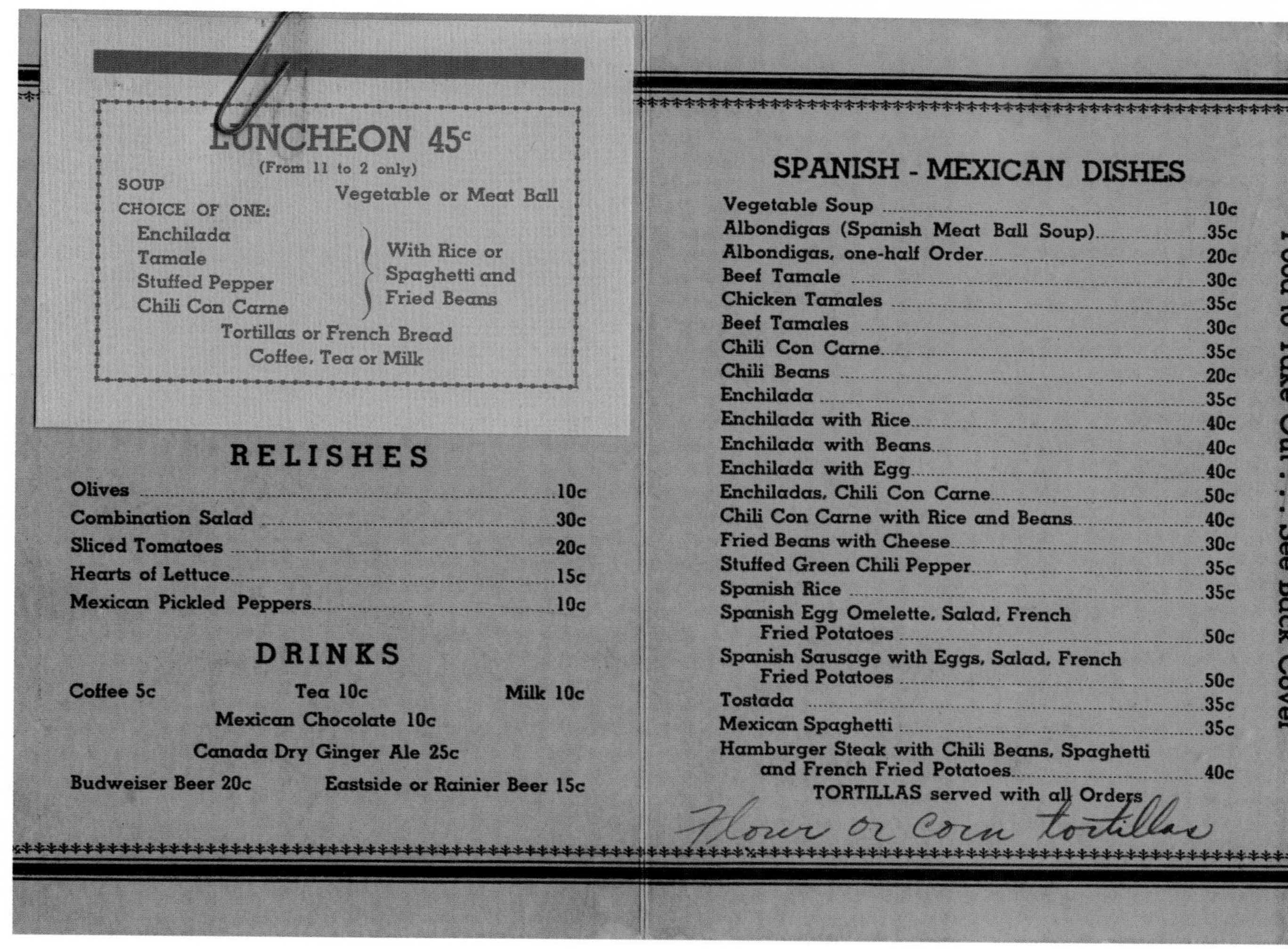

el nuevo
Salón Imperial

OPPOSITE El Nuevo Salon Imperial, Empire Room, the Palmer House, 1933, Chicago, Illinois

The ritzy and elegant Empire Room opened in 1933 at the Palmer House just as Prohibition ended. This menu suggests it was holding an event with a Spanish theme in the "New Imperial Salon."

Der todschicke Empire Room machte 1933 im Palmer House auf, als die Prohibitionszeit vorbei war. Die Speisekarte scheint für einen Abend mit spanischem Motto im „Neuen Imperial Salon" bestimmt gewesen zu sein.

Luxueux et élégant, l'Empire Room ouvre en 1933 dans les murs du Palmer House juste à la fin de la Prohibition. Ce menu indique qu'une réception sur le thème de l'Espagne est donnée dans le « New Imperial Salon ».

ABOVE LEFT Club Zarape, c. 1937, Los Angeles, California

ABOVE Aragon, 1932, Chicago, Illinois

The Aragon Ballroom opened in Chicago in July 1926 in the style of a Moorish castle. Newspaper advertisements for the ballroom described "visions of languorous senoritas and dashing caballeros, of moon-drenched patios and stately turrets gently brushing Mediterranean skies."

Der Aragon Ballroom in Chicago eröffnete im Juli 1926 im Stil eines maurischen Alcazar. In Zeitungsanzeigen wurde der Ballsaal so beschrieben: „Visionen schmachtender Señoritas und stolzer Caballeros, monddurchfluteter Patios und grandioser Türme, die sanft in den Mittelmeerhimmel ragen."

L'Aragon Ballroom ouvre à Chicago en juillet 1926 dans le style d'un palais mauresque. Les publicités parues dans la presse évoquent la salle de réception en ces termes : « Visions de *señoritas* langoureuses et de fringants *caballeros*, patios au clair de lune, majestueuses tourelles caressant des ciels méditerranéens. »

LEFT Foreign Club Cafe, c. 1935, Tijuana, Mexico

Menu
SEA CAVE
SEA FOODS
HK

THE SEA CAVE
Bill of Fare

COCKTAILS
- California Oyster Cocktail 15
- Eastern Oyster Cocktail 20
- Crab or Shrimp Cocktail 15
- Lobster Cocktail 25
- Sea Cave Cocktail 25
- Clam Cocktail 15
- Abalone Cocktail 20
- Combination Cocktail 25
- Scallop Cocktail 25
- Fruit Cocktail 25

COCKTAILS WITH LOUIE SAUCE, 5c EXTRA

SOUPS
- Coney Island Clam Chowder 15
- Clam Broth 15; with Egg 25
- Cream of Tomato 20
- Chicken Broth 15
- Boston Clam Chowder 15

RELISHES
- Russian Caviar 65
- Green Onions or Ripe Olives 15
- Celery en Branche 20
- Sliced Pickles 10 Radishes 15

SALADS
- Special Sea Cave Salad 45
- Combination Salad 40
- Crab Meat Salad 35
- Fresh Lobster Salad 40
- Sliced Tomatoes 20
- Tuna Fish Salad 35
- Fresh Picked Shrimp Salad 35
- Head of Lettuce with Egg 25
- Asparagus Salad 25
- Chicken Salad 35
- Artichoke (hot or cold) 15
- Potato Salad 20
- Fruit Salad with Ice Cream 50
- Sliced Cucumbers 20
- Lettuce and Tomato Salad 25
- Stuffed Tomato with Crab 50
- Stuffed Tomato with Shrimp 50
- Stuffed Tomato with Chicken 50
- Stuffed Tomato with Lobster 65
- Stuffed Tomato with Abalone 50
- Abalone Salad 40
- Lettuce and Green Peppers 25
- Head of Lettuce with Anchovies 30
- Head of Lettuce with Mayonnaise Dressing 15
- Fresh Crab Meat with Mayonnaise Dressing 55
- Picked Shrimps, Mayonnaise Dressing 50
- Fresh Lobster Meat with Mayonnaise 75
- Fresh Crab Legs with Mayonnaise Dressing 65

LOUIE DRESSING, 5c EXTRA WITH ALL SALADS

LOUIE DISHES
- Crab Louie 75; half 45
- Lobster Louie 80; half 50
- Shrimp Louie 70; half 40
- Scallops Louie 75; half 45
- Abalone Louie 75; half 45

FISH
A FACT! Fish caught at 5 a. m. served here the same day

- RAINBOW TROUT 75
- Fried Frog Legs 90
- Fried Crab Legs in Butter, Tartar Sauce 75
- Baked Alaska Black Cod au Gratin 50
- Fried Filet of Sole, Tartar Sauce 40
- Fried English Sole or Fried Sand Dabs 40
- Fried or Broiled Smoked Alaska Black Cod 50
- Boiled Smoked Alaska Black Cod with Boiled Potatoes 50
- Fried White Baits with Tartar Sauce 40
- Fried Shad Roe 65; with Strip of Ham or Bacon or Egg 75
- Boiled Salt Mackerel with Boiled Potato 40
- Steamed Finnan Haddie, Butter Sauce 50
- Barbecued Alaska Cod or Finnan Haddie 50
- Sea Cave Special, Sea Food Cold Plate 75
- Vegetable Plate 40; with Egg 50
- Fried or Broiled Striped Bass 50
- Combination Sea Food Plate 60
- Fried or Broiled Turbot 40
- Fried or Broiled Halibut Steak 45
- Fried or Broiled Salmon Steak 45
- Creamed Tuna on Toast 60
- Fried Boneless Smelts 40
- Fried Cat Fish 40
- Fried or Broiled Rock Cod 40
- Fried or Broiled Barracuda 40
- Fried or Broiled Sea Bass 50
- Fried Herring 40
- Fresh Spanish Mackerel 40
- Baked Halibut au Gratin 50

DEVILED CRAB IN SHELL, 50c

OYSTERS
WE OPEN OUR OYSTERS DAILY

Eastern
- Eastern Oyster Cocktail 20
- Oysters on Half Shell 50
- Raw Oysters on Plate 40
- Fried Oysters (6) 45; (12) 80
- Fried with Strip of Bacon or Ham 55
- Fried with Egg 55
- Fried Oysters (9) 60
- Hangtown Fry 75
- Pan Roast 50
- Fancy Pepper Roast 50
- Broiled with Ham or Bacon 60
- Creamed on Toast 55
- Oysters Kirkpatrick 75
- Oysters a la Poulette 60
- Milk Stew 40
- Cream Stew 50
- Oyster Dry Stew 40
- Six Large Oysters en Brochette with Bacon 60
- Eastern Oyster Omelette 50

California or Olympia
- Oyster Cocktail 15
- Oyster Fry 65
- Raw Oysters on Plate 55
- Fried with Ham or Bacon 70
- Fried with Egg 70
- Hangtown Fry 75
- Pan Roast 65
- Fancy Pepper Roast 65
- Creamed on Toast 65
- Milk Stew 50
- Oysters a la Poulette 60
- Cream Stew 60
- Oyster Dry Stew 50
- Oyster Omelette 55

NO SERVICE LESS THAN 10 CENTS

Our Fish and Meats are Cooked Over a Charcoal Broiler

STEAKS AND CHOPS
- Sea Cave Steak 1.10
- Rib Steak 65
- T-Bone Steak 1
- Top Sirloin Steak 70
- Club Steak 70
- Filet Mignon on Toast 1
- Minced Chicken on Toast 60
- Sirloin Steak 95
- Porterhouse Steak 1.15
- New York Cut 1.10
- Liver, Bacon or Onions 45
- French Lamb Chops 75
- Pork Chops, plain 50
- Pork Chops, breaded 55
- Veal Cutlets, plain 45
- Veal Cutlets, breaded 50
- Hamburger Steak with Onions 45
- Broiled Half Spring Chicken on Toast 75
- Flank Steak with Country Gravy 45
- Pounded Rump Steak, Country Gravy 45

MUSHROOM SAUCE 25 BORDELAISE SAUCE 10
FRIED ONIONS 10

EGGS AND OMELETTES
- Scrambled .. (2) 25; (3) 35
- Shirred Eggs (2) 25; (3) 35
- Fried Eggs .. (2) 25; (3) 35
- Poached Eggs (2) 25; (3) 35
- Ham and Eggs 40
- Bacon and Eggs 40
- Fried Ham or Bacon 40
- Side order of Ham 20
- Side order of Bacon 20
- Ham Omelette 40
- Bacon Omelette 40
- Plain Omelette (2 eggs) 30
- Plain Omelette (3 eggs) 40
- Jelly Omelette 40
- Eastern Oyster Omelette 50
- Calif. Oyster Omelette 55
- Crab Omelette 50
- Shrimp Omelette 45
- Abalone Omelette 50
- Clam Omelette 50
- Lobster Omelette 60
- Onion Omelette 40
- Cheese Omelette 40
- Scallop Omelette 60
- Asparagus Omelette 50
- Spanish Omelette 40

SANDWICHES
- Special Sea Cave 45
- Crab Louie Sandwich 45
- Shrimp Louie Sandwich 45
- Lobster Louie Sandwich 50
- Manhattan Sandwich 45
- Club House Sandwich 45
- Lobster Sandwich 40
- Oyster Sandwich 25
- Tuna Fish Sandwich 25
- Crab Sandwich 25
- Ham and Egg Sandwich 25
- Fried Ham Sandwich 20
- Deviled Egg Sandwich 25
- Fried Bacon Sandwich 20
- Fried Egg Sandwich 15
- Liberty Sandwich 15
- Cold Boiled Ham 20
- Melted Cheese 25
- Abalone Sandwich 30
- Shrimp Sandwich 20
- Sardine Sandwich 25
- Chicken Sandwich 35
- Denver Sandwich 25
- Cheese Sandwich 15
- Scallop Sandwich 35
- Russian Caviar 65
- Hot Roast Beef Sandwich, Brown Gravy and Potatoes 25
- Combination Ham and Cheese Sandwich 30
- Creamed Chicken Sandwich 30

COLD DISHES
- Cold Roast Beef or Cold Roast Pork, Potato Salad 50
- Cold Boiled Ham with Potato Salad 50
- Sardines with Potato Salad 40
- Cold Chicken with Potato Salad 65
- Cold Tuna Fish with Potato Salad 75
- Assorted Cold Meats with Chicken and Potato Salad 75

BREAKFAST DISHES
- Tomato Juice 15
- Shredded Wheat, Cream 15
- Half Grapefruit 15
- Sliced Oranges 15
- Baked Apple and Cream 15
- Oatmeal and Cream 15
- Corn Flakes and Cream 15
- Grapefruit Juice 15
- Pure Orange Juice 20
- Grape-Nuts and Cream 15
- Milk Toast 20
- Dry or Buttered Toast 10
- French Toast with Jelly 30
- Hot Cakes, Maple Syrup 20
- Hot Cakes with Strip of Ham or Bacon 25

PLEASE PROCURE CHECK AND PAY CASHIER

FRESH DEEP SEA CRABS
- CRACKED CRAB (half) 40; (whole) 75
- Fried Crab Legs in Butter, Tartar Sauce 75
- Crab Legs with Mayonnaise Dressing 65
- Crab Cocktail 15
- Crab Meat, Mayonnaise 55
- Crab Louie 75
- Crab a la Newburg 60
- Crab a la King 60
- Crab a la Creole 60
- Creamed Crab on Toast 60
- Deviled Crab in Shell 50
- Crab Stew 40; Cream Stew 50
- Crab Omelette 50

LOBSTERS (In Season)
- Cold Lobster with Mayonnaise Dressing (half) 70; (whole) 1.30
- Broiled Lobster, Melted Butter (half) 75; (whole) 1.40
- Stuffed Half Lobster a la Cardinal 75
- Lobster Louie 80
- Lobster Cocktail 25
- Lobster Creamed on Toast 70
- Lobster Milk Stew 50; Cream 60
- Lobster Omelette 60
- Lobster a la King 70
- Lobster a la Newburg 70
- Creamed Lobster on Toast 70
- Lobster Meat, Mayonnaise 75

MONTEREY ABALONE
- Abalone Cocktail 20
- Abalone Louie 75
- Abalone Salad 40
- Abalone Milk Stew 40
- Abalone Cream Stew 50
- Abalone a la Newburg 65
- Abalone Supreme 60
- Abalone Omelette 50
- Fried Abalone with Tartar Sauce 50
- Fried Abalone Stripped with Ham, Bacon or Egg 60
- Fried Abalone with Bordelaise Sauce 60

SCALLOPS
- Scallops, Louie 75
- Fried Scallops, Tartar Sauce 60
- Scallops a la King 60
- Scallops Poulette en Casserole 60
- Scallops, Hangtown Fry 75
- Scallops, Cream Stew 60
- Scallop Omelette 60
- Scallop Milk Stew 50
- Scallop Cocktail 25; with Louie Dressing 30
- Scallops Saute with Rice, Creole 60
- Fried Scallops, Stripped with Ham, Bacon or Egg 70
- Scallops in Cream au Gratin 60

SCALLOP LOAF, 75c and up

FRESH SHRIMPS
- Shrimp Louie 70
- Fried Shrimps in Butter 50
- Shrimp Omelette 45
- Creamed Shrimps on Toast 50
- Shrimp Sandwich 20
- Shrimps Curry en Rice 50
- Picked Shrimps with Mayonnaise 45

COO COO CLAMS
- Clams on Half Shell 40
- Clam Cocktail 15
- Fried Clams 40
- Clam Dry Stew 35
- Clam Pan Roast 50
- Clam Fancy Pepper Roast 50
- Hangtown Clam Fry 75
- Clam Omelette 50
- Fried Clams Stripped with Bacon, Ham or Egg 50
- Steamed Clams, Plain or Bordelaise 40

VEGETABLES
- Green Peas or String Beans 15
- Stewed Corn 15
- Cold Artichoke, Mayonnaise 15
- Stewed Tomatoes 15
- Spinach 15
- Creamed Spinach 20
- Hot Asparagus in Butter 25
- Sliced Beets 15

POTATOES
- French Fried 10
- Cottage Fried 15
- Lyonnaise 15
- Shoestring 15
- Long Branch 15
- Au Gratin 25
- Hashed Browned 15
- American Fried 10
- O'Brien 25
- French Fried Onions 25

DESSERTS
- Baked Apple and Cream 15
- Sliced Banana and Cream 15
- Sliced Pineapple 20
- Sliced Peaches and Cream 20
- Strawberries and Cream 15
- Stewed Rhubarb 15
- Stewed Prunes 15
- Fruit Jell-O and Cream 15
- Rice Custard Pudding 10
- Cup Custard 15
- Home-made Pies (per cut) 10
- Strawberry Shortcake 25
- Banana Shortcake 20
- Cake, per cut 10
- Fritters of all kinds 25
- Vanilla, Chocolate or Strawberry Ice Cream 15

DRINKS
- Cup of Coffee 05
- Cup of Chocolate 10
- Postum 10
- Glass of Half Cream & Milk 25
- Buttermilk 05
- Milk (glass) 10
- Pot of Tea 10
- Iced Tea 10

BEVERAGES
- BEER ON DRAUGHT 10

Eastern and Local Bottled Beers of all kinds on hand

NOT RESPONSIBLE FOR LOST ARTICLES

OPPOSITE & ABOVE Sea Cave, c. 1931, Oakland, California

RIGHT Sea Cave, c. 1931, Oakland, California

LEFT & BELOW *S. S. Monte Carlo*, c. 1932, **Long Beach, California**

Designed to be pleasure ship casinos, boats like the *S.S. Monte Carlo* and the *City of Panama* avoided Prohibition laws by staying three miles off the California coast. Prices were remarkably low to encourage legal gambling onboard.

Schiffe wie die *S.S. Monte Carlo* und the *City of Panama* waren Vergnügungsdampfer und Kasinos, die das Alkoholverbot dadurch umgingen, dass sie außerhalb der Drei-Meilen-Zone vor der kalifornischen Küste blieben. Damit die Leute zum legalen Glücksspiel an Bord kamen, waren die Preise erstaunlich niedrig.

Conçus comme des casinos flottants entièrement dédiés au plaisir, des navires tels que le *S. S. Monte Carlo* et le *City of Panama* échappaient à la Prohibition en jetant l'ancre à cinq kilomètres des côtes de la Californie. On maintenait des tarifs remarquablement bas afin d'encourager le jeu légal à bord.

SHOWBOAT MONTE CARLO

MENU

Cocktails

Lobster, 50 Shrimp, 50 Fruit, 40 Crab, 50

Hors d'Oeuvres

Stuffed Olives, 35 Green Olives, 25 Celery en Branch, 30
Stuffed Celery, 50 Canape Anchovy, 50 Caviar Tartines, 50
Canape Chicken Livers, 50

Soups

Soup De Jour, 15 Consomme, Hot or Jellied, 20
Chicken Broth, 25 Clam Chowder, Coney Island, 25
Tomato Bouillon, 20 Clam Nectar, 20

Salads

Hearts of Lettuce, 20 Lettuce Tomato, 30 Combination, 35
Sliced Tomato, 20 Chicken, 60 Crab, 60 Shrimp, 50
Sea Food Combination Special, 60
Mayonnaise, Thousand Island or French Dressing
Served with Above Salads

Steaks and Chops

Double Sirloin, 1.75 Tenderloin, $1.00 Top Sirloin, 60
Filet Mignon, Bearnaise Sauce, $1.10 Club Steak, 60
T-Bone, $1.25 Veal Porterhouse, 80 Pork Chops, 50
Veal Chops (2), 50 French Lamb Chops (3 to order), 60
Hamburger Steak, 40 Breaded Veal Cutlets, 50

Eggs and Omelets

Two Eggs (any style), 25 Eggs Vienna, Pure Cream, 60
Ham or Bacon and Eggs, 40 Plain Omelet, 30
Cheese Omelet, 50 Asparagus Tips Omelet, 50
Chicken Liver Omelet, 60 Order Fried Ham, 50
Shirred Eggs with Sausage or Chicken Livers, 50

BEVERAGE LIST

Cocktails

Dry Martini	.35	Clover Club	.35
Manhattan	.35	Whiskey Sour	.35
Old Fashion	.35	Bronx	.35
Bacardi	.35	Gibson Cocktail	.35

Mixed Drinks

Montecarlo Special Fizz .35

Tom Collins	.35	Silver Fizz	.35
Gin Fizz	.35	Golden Fizz	.35
Gin Rickey	.35	Royal Fizz	.35
Hi-Balls	.35	Mint Julep	.35

Straight Drinks

Whiskey, Straight	.25	Bacardi Rum	.35
Whiskey and Soda	.35	Dry Gin	.25

Liqueurs and Cordials

Charcruese	.35	Blackberry Cordial	.35
Curaco	.35	Brandy	.35
Creme de Menthe	.35	Side Car	.35
Creme de Cacao	.35	Benedictine	.35
French Vermouth	.35	Apricot Cordial	.35

Wines

Champagne (Pint) Imported 3.50
Champagne (Pint) Domestic 2.50
Sparkling Burgundy Pint 1.50; Quart 3.00

Dry Wines

	glass	large bottle	small bottle
Chateau Yquem (Tippo)	.25	1.50	75
Sauterne	.25	1.25	65
Burgundy	.25	1.25	65
Riesling	.25	1.25	65

Sweet Wines

	glass	large bottle	small bottle
Port Wine	.25	1.25	65
Sherry Wine	.25	1.25	65
Angelica Wine	.25	1.25	65
Muscatel Wine	.25	1.25	65

Potatoes

Au Gratin, 20 Au Gratin O'Brien, 25 Hashed Brown, 15
Lyonnaise, 20 American Fry, 15 French Fry, 15
Julienne, 20 Long Branch, 15 Shoestring, 20

Vegetables

Green Peas, 20 String Beans, 20 Lima Beans, 20
Stewed Tomatoes, 25 Corn on Cob, 25
Stewed Corn, 20 Asparagus Tips, 35

Sandwiches

Hamburger Sandwich Monte Carlo, 15 Ham, 20 Tongue, 20
Salami, 20 Roast Beef, 25 Egg, 15 Roast Pork, 25
Swiss Cheese, 20 American Cheese, 20 Sardine, 30
Ham and Egg, 25 Chicken, 40 Manhattan, 60 Club, 60
Tenderloin Steak Sandwich, 75 French Dip Sandwich, 15
Denver, 30 Hot Pork Sandwich, 30 Hot Beef Sandwich, 20
Lettuce and Tomato Sandwich, 20

Desserts

Assorted Pies, 15 Layer Cake, 15 Cookies, 10
Orange Ice, 15 Ice Cream, 15 Iced Canteloupe, 15
Watermelon, 20 Preserved Peaches, 20
Individual Preserved Figs, 20 Prunes and Cream, 20
Fresh Fruits and Berries in Season, 25

Drinks

Coffee, 10 Pot, 15 Milk, 10 Tea, 10 Tomato Juice, 15
Iced Tea or Coffee, 10

Fountain Service

Coca Cola, 10 Orange Juice, 15 Plain Sodas, 15
Ice Cream Soda, 20 Frosted Drinks, 20 Plain Sundaes, 25
Nut Sundaes, 30 Green River, 10 Malted Milk with Egg, 35
Milk Shake, 20 Malted Milk, 25 Canada Dry Ginger Ale, 25
Ginger Ale, 20 White Rock Water, 30

ABOVE *S.S. Monte Carlo* Gambling Ship, c. 1931, Los Angeles, California

RIGHT Steamship *City of Panama*, c. 1934, Santa Monica, California

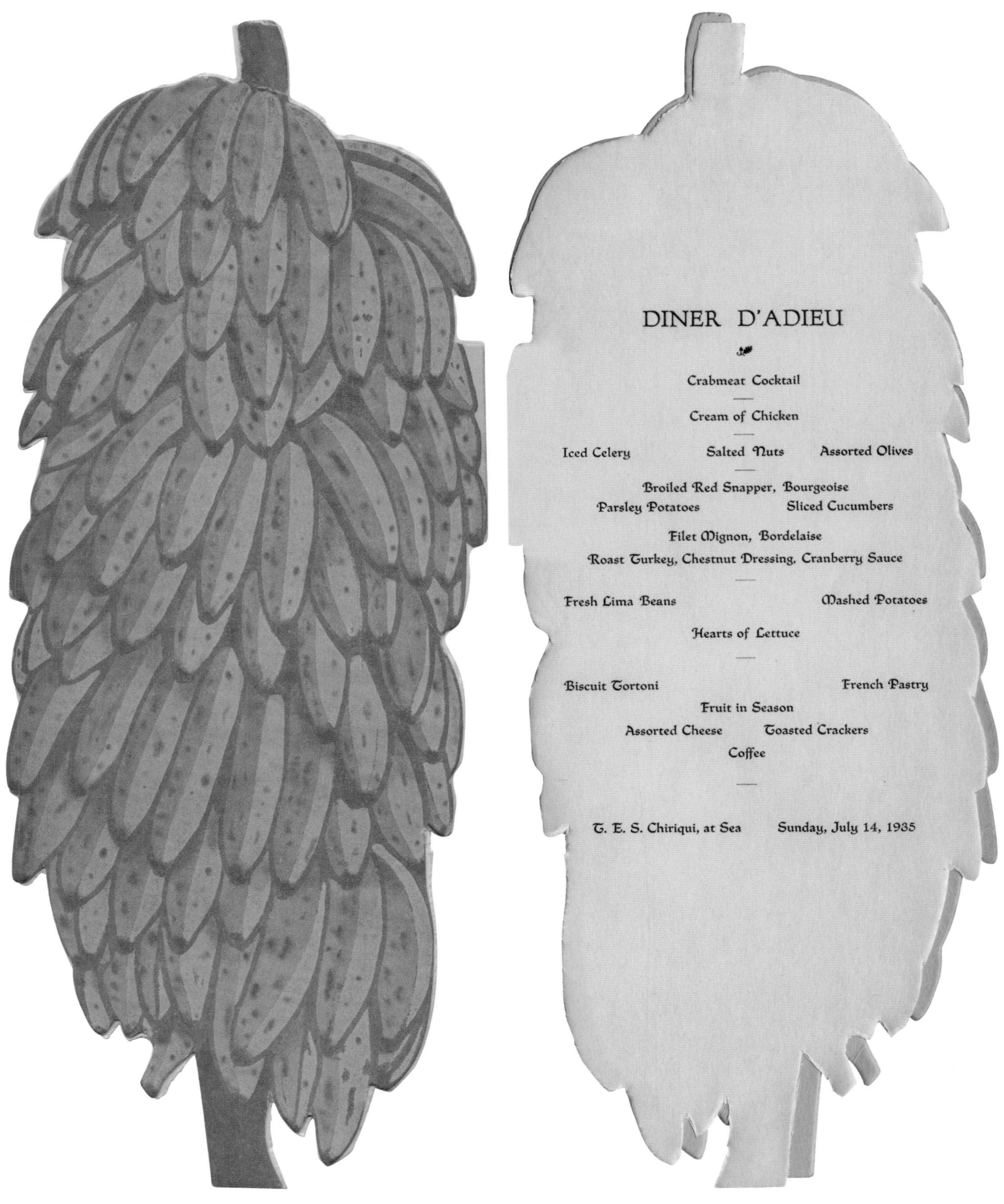

ABOVE **United Fruit Company Steamship Service, 1935**

OPPOSITE **The Cockpit, Grand Central Air Terminal, c. 1935, Glendale, California**

This fanciful cover from the Grand Central Air Terminal is drawn and die-cut like the cylinders from an airplane's rotary engine.

Diese fantasievolle Speisekarte aus dem Grand Central Air Terminal ist wie das Propellertriebwerk eines Flugzeugs gestaltet.

La couverture fantaisie du menu du Grand Central Air Terminal est découpée et dessinée à l'image des cylindres d'un moteur d'avion rotatif.

WINE LIST

COCKTAILS

Tropical .25
Dubbonet .25
Dry Martini .25
Whiskey .30
Old Fashioned .30
Orange Blossom .30
Bronx .30
Mexico .30
Mamie Taylor .30
Pink Lady .35
Bacardi Rum .35
Tequila Manhattan .35
Stinger .35
Sezerac .35
Clover Club .30
Alexander .35
Clover Leaf .35
Side Car .40
Champagne .50
Manhattan .30
Indian .35

MIXED DRINKS

Sherry Flip .30
Imported Sloe Gin Fizz .30
Imported Sloe Gin Rickey .30
Gordon's London Dry Gin Straight .30
New Orleans Fizz .35
Tequila Silver Fizz .40
Gin Fizz .25
Gin Rickey .25
Golden Fizz .35
Royal Fizz .35
Silver Fizz .35
New Orleans Fizz .35
Cream Fizz .35
Whiskey Sour .30
Tom Collins .40
Cordials .35
Claret Lemonade .30

WHISKIES

Bourbon .30
Tequila Highball Jose Cueruo .40
Whiskey Highball .30
Old Scotch Haig and Haig .40
Scotch Highball .35
Bourbon (17 Yrs. Old) .50
Brandy .30

AFTER DINNER DRINKS

Tequila Jose Cueruo, Straight .30
3 Star Hennessy .35
Creme de Menthe .35
Benedictine .35
Cherry Blackberry Peach .35
Apricot Brandy .35
Creme de Cacao .35
Brandy and Benedictine .35
Pousse Cafe .50
Alfonso .35
Peres Chartreux, Yellow or Green .35
Creme de Manderine .35
Gilka Kummel .35
Marie Brizard Maraschino .35
Legendre Heibseint (Absenthe) .50
Contreau .40

BEER

Budweiser .20
Pabst Blue Ribbon .20
Golden Glow .15
Tacoma .15
Imported Guiness Stout .40
Imported Bass Ale .40

ABOVE King's Tropical Inn, c. 1935, Culver City, California

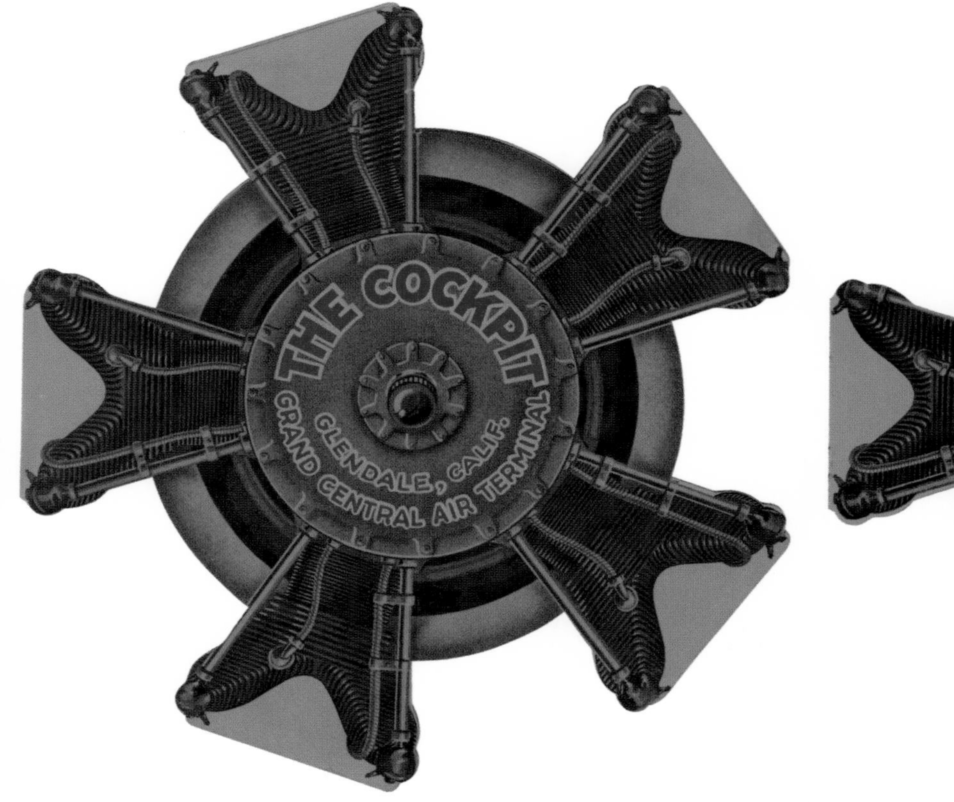

FANCY COCKTAILS

Black-Widow .40
Clover Club .40
Clover Leaf .40
Pink Lady .35
Alexander .35
Blue Moon .35
Bacardi .35
Daiquiri .35
Side Car—Imported .50
Side Car—Domestic .40
Stinger .35
Champagnes .75
Bamboo .35
Green Devil .35
Coffee Cocktail .35
Desert Dream .40
Stingeree .40
Apple Jack .25
Benedictine Cocktail .40
Queen-Elizabeth .40
Rum-Gum-Lime .40
S. O. S. .35
Pernod Drip .55

menu
ALASKA STEAMSHIP CO
A
THE ALASKA LINE
ALASKA STEAMSHIP COMPANY

OPPOSITE *S.S. Alaska*, Alaska Steamship Company, 1934

RIGHT & BELOW *S. S. President Johnson*, Dollar Steamship Lines, 1933

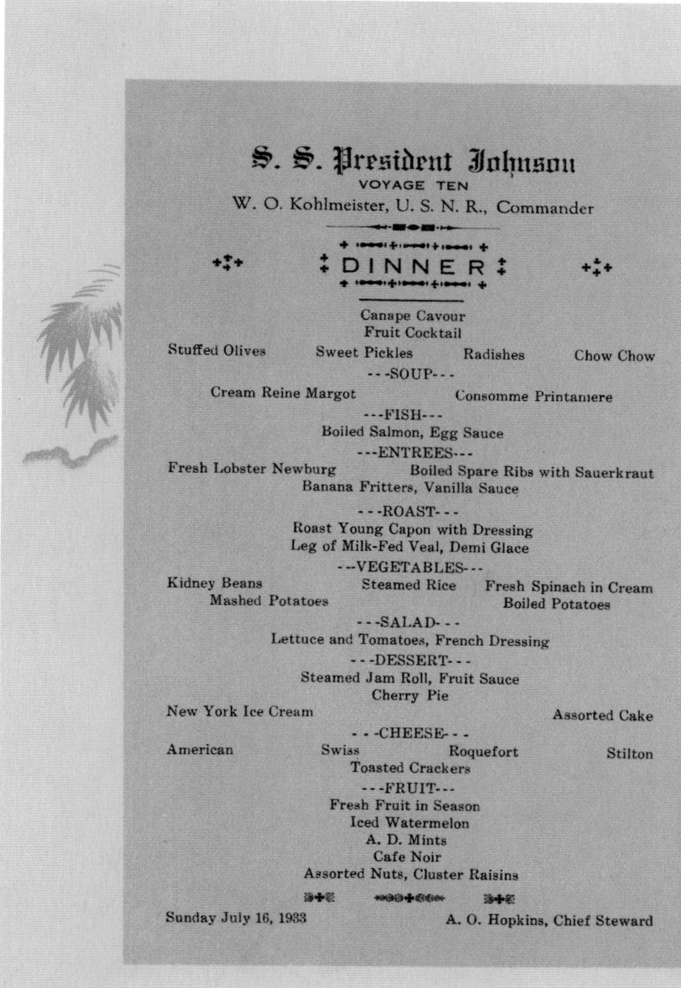

S. S. President Johnson
VOYAGE TEN
W. O. Kohlmeister, U. S. N. R., Commander

DINNER

Canape Cavour
Fruit Cocktail
Stuffed Olives — Sweet Pickles — Radishes — Chow Chow

---SOUP---
Cream Reine Margot — Consomme Printaniere

---FISH---
Boiled Salmon, Egg Sauce

---ENTREES---
Fresh Lobster Newburg — Boiled Spare Ribs with Sauerkraut
Banana Fritters, Vanilla Sauce

---ROAST---
Roast Young Capon with Dressing
Leg of Milk-Fed Veal, Demi Glace

---VEGETABLES---
Kidney Beans — Steamed Rice — Fresh Spinach in Cream
Mashed Potatoes — Boiled Potatoes

---SALAD---
Lettuce and Tomatoes, French Dressing

---DESSERT---
Steamed Jam Roll, Fruit Sauce
Cherry Pie
New York Ice Cream — Assorted Cake

---CHEESE---
American — Swiss — Roquefort — Stilton
Toasted Crackers

---FRUIT---
Fresh Fruit in Season
Iced Watermelon
A. D. Mints
Cafe Noir
Assorted Nuts, Cluster Raisins

Sunday July 16, 1933 — A. O. Hopkins, Chief Steward

SOMEHOW, the achievement of the Panama Canal strikes a responsive chord in us. So smooth and so automatic is the operation of the locks and the handling of our President Liner that we are amazed that such a colossal undertaking could be accomplished by man. The French started work in 1882 and dug intermittently until 1904 when the American engineers took over the project. In the fall of 1914 . . . four hundred and one years after Balboa discovered the Pacific Ocean . . . the canal was opened to the ships of the world. The most unusual fact about the Panama Canal is that the Pacific entrance is twenty-seven miles east of the Atlantic entrance.

LEFT & BELOW New York, New Haven, and Hartford Railroad, 1932

Cartoons by Jazz Age artist John Held Jr. grace this menu for the railroad. Begun in 1872 with runs up the East Coast from New York, it covered 2,131 miles at its peak in 1929. The company went bankrupt in 1935.

Karikaturen des Jazz-Ära-Zeichners John Held Jr. schmücken diese Karte für den Speisewagen. Die Eisenbahngesellschaft fuhr ab 1872 von New York die Ostküste hinauf und deckte zu ihren besten Zeiten 3430 km Strecke ab. 1935 ging die Firma pleite.

Cette couverture de menu, illustrée par une bande dessinée de l'artiste phare de l'Ère du jazz, John Held Jr., est destinée à une compagnie de chemin de fer. Lancée en 1872, celle-ci dessert la côte Est depuis New York. À son apogée, en 1929, elle couvrira 3 430 kilomètres. La société fera faillite en 1935.

OPPOSITE Fountain Room, Statler Hotel, c. 1933

FOUNTAIN
ROOM

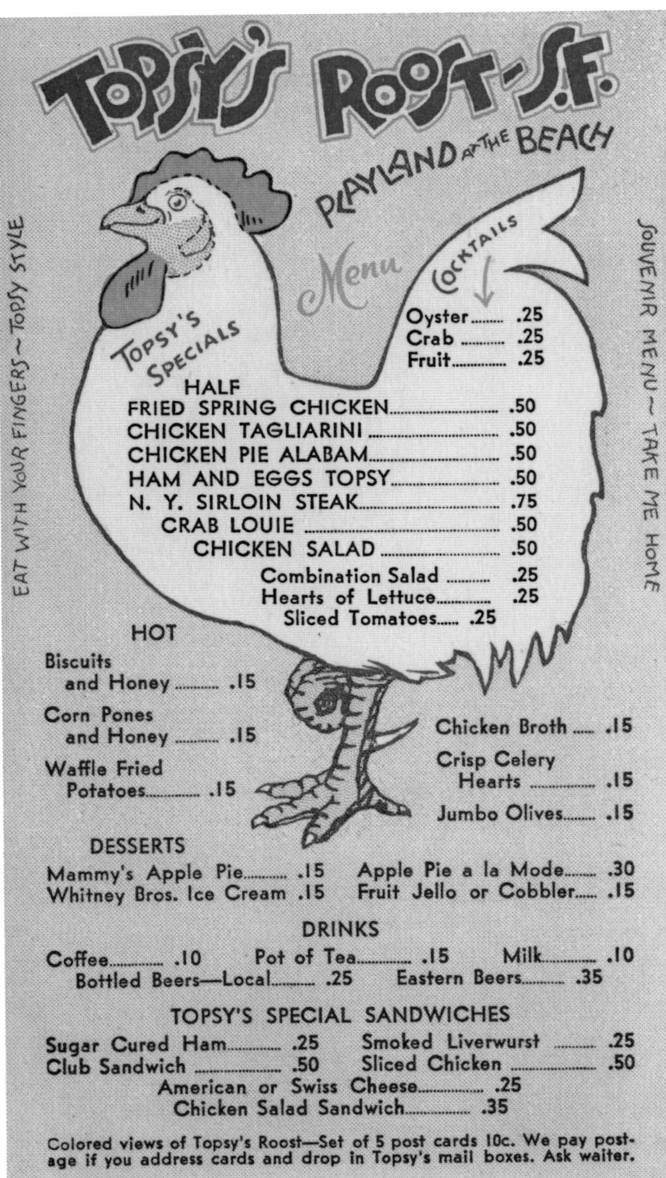

TOPSY'S ROOST-S.F.

PLAYLAND AT THE BEACH

EAT WITH YOUR FINGERS~TOPSY STYLE

SOUVENIR MENU~TAKE ME HOME

Menu

COCKTAILS

Oyster .25
Crab .25
Fruit .25

TOPSY'S SPECIALS

HALF
FRIED SPRING CHICKEN .50
CHICKEN TAGLIARINI .50
CHICKEN PIE ALABAM .50
HAM AND EGGS TOPSY .50
N. Y. SIRLOIN STEAK .75
CRAB LOUIE .50
CHICKEN SALAD .50
Combination Salad .25
Hearts of Lettuce .25
Sliced Tomatoes .25

HOT

Biscuits and Honey .15
Corn Pones and Honey .15
Waffle Fried Potatoes .15
Chicken Broth .15
Crisp Celery Hearts .15
Jumbo Olives .15

DESSERTS

Mammy's Apple Pie .15
Whitney Bros. Ice Cream .15
Apple Pie a la Mode .30
Fruit Jello or Cobbler .15

DRINKS

Coffee .10
Pot of Tea .15
Milk .10
Bottled Beers—Local .25
Eastern Beers .35

TOPSY'S SPECIAL SANDWICHES

Sugar Cured Ham .25
Club Sandwich .50
Smoked Liverwurst .25
Sliced Chicken .50
American or Swiss Cheese .25
Chicken Salad Sandwich .35

Colored views of Topsy's Roost—Set of 5 post cards 10c. We pay postage if you address cards and drop in Topsy's mail boxes. Ask waiter.

ABOVE **Topsy's Roost, c. 1930, San Francisco, California**

LEFT **Topsy's Roost, c. 1934, San Francisco, California**

Topsy's Roost, opened in 1929 at Playland in San Francisco, takes its name from a slave character in the abolitionist novel *Uncle Tom's Cabin*. The menu typically listed food associated with the American South.

Topsy's Roost machte 1929 im Playland in San Francisco auf und bezog seinen Namen von der Figur eines Sklavenjungen aus dem Anti-Sklaverei-Roman *Onkel Toms Hütte*. Auf der Karte stehen Gerichte, die man mit den Südstaaten verbindet.

Le Topsy's Roost ouvre en 1929 au Playland de San Francisco. Il tire son nom d'un personnage d'esclave du roman abolitionniste *La Case de l'oncle Tom*. Les plats évoquent le Sud des États-Unis.

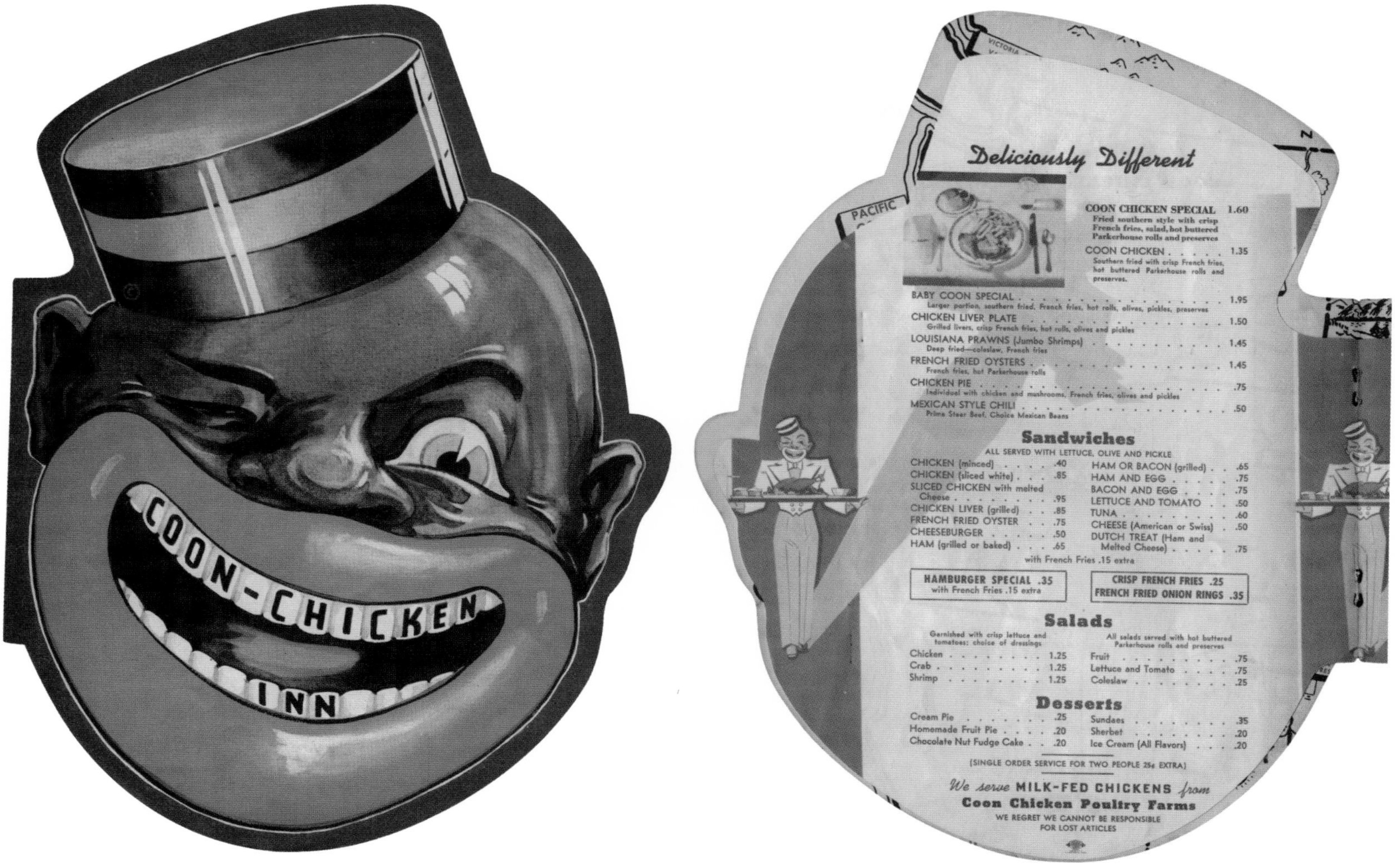

COON-CHICKEN INN

Deliciously Different

COON CHICKEN SPECIAL 1.60
Fried southern style with crisp French fries, salad, hot buttered Parkerhouse rolls and preserves

COON CHICKEN 1.35
Southern fried with crisp French fries, hot buttered Parkerhouse rolls and preserves.

BABY COON SPECIAL . . . 1.95
Larger portion, southern fried, French fries, hot rolls, olives, pickles, preserves

CHICKEN LIVER PLATE . . . 1.50
Grilled livers, crisp French fries, hot rolls, olives and pickles

LOUISIANA PRAWNS (Jumbo Shrimps) . . . 1.45
Deep fried—coleslaw, French fries

FRENCH FRIED OYSTERS . . . 1.45
French fries, hot Parkerhouse rolls

CHICKEN PIE 75
Individual with chicken and mushrooms, French fries, olives and pickles

MEXICAN STYLE CHILI 50
Prime Steer Beef, Choice Mexican Beans

Sandwiches

ALL SERVED WITH LETTUCE, OLIVE AND PICKLE

CHICKEN (minced) 40
CHICKEN (sliced white) 85
SLICED CHICKEN with melted Cheese 95
CHICKEN LIVER (grilled) . . .85
FRENCH FRIED OYSTER . . .75
CHEESEBURGER 50
HAM (grilled or baked) 65
HAM OR BACON (grilled) . . .65
HAM AND EGG 75
BACON AND EGG 75
LETTUCE AND TOMATO . . .50
TUNA 60
CHEESE (American or Swiss) . .50
DUTCH TREAT (Ham and Melted Cheese) 75

with French Fries .15 extra

HAMBURGER SPECIAL .35
with French Fries .15 extra

CRISP FRENCH FRIES .25
FRENCH FRIED ONION RINGS .35

Salads

Garnished with crisp lettuce and tomatoes: choice of dressings

Chicken . . . 1.25
Crab . . . 1.25
Shrimp . . . 1.25

All salads served with hot buttered Parkerhouse rolls and preserves

Fruit 75
Lettuce and Tomato 75
Coleslaw 25

Desserts

Cream Pie 25
Homemade Fruit Pie 20
Chocolate Nut Fudge Cake . . .20
Sundaes 35
Sherbet 20
Ice Cream (All Flavors) 20

(SINGLE ORDER SERVICE FOR TWO PEOPLE 25¢ EXTRA)

We serve MILK-FED CHICKENS from Coon Chicken Poultry Farms

WE REGRET WE CANNOT BE RESPONSIBLE FOR LOST ARTICLES

ABOVE **Coon-Chicken Inn, 1935, Seattle, Washington**

This menu for a fried chicken chain depicts a caricature of a black waiter. The chain apparently saw nothing racist about its name.

Diese Karte einer Hühnerbratereikette hat die Form eines karikierten schwarzen Kellners. Der Namen (Neger-Huhn) erschien offenbar nicht rassistisch.

Créé pour une enseigne proposant du poulet frit, ce menu est illustré par la caricature d'un serveur noir. Apparemment, la direction de la chaîne au nom provocateur («Au poulet nègre») ne voyait rien de raciste dans son nom.

BELOW **Coon-Chicken Inn, 1935, Seattle, Washington**

The James Whitcomb Riley . . . Dining Car Service

A La Carte

APPETIZERS

Celery Hearts 25 — Olives 25
Clam Juice Cocktail 20 — Chilled Tomato Juice 20 — Tomato Juice Cocktail 25
Fruit Cup 25 — V-8 Cocktail 20

SOUPS

Gumbo Creole, Cup 20; Tureen 35
Consomme, Hot or en Gelee 25 — Clam Bouillon 20

ENTREES

Broiled or Sauted Fresh Fish with Potatoes 70
Grilled Lamb Chops (2) with Potatoes 90
Minute Steak Grilled with Potatoes 1.25
Broiled Ham or Bacon 60; Half Portion 30
Broiled Ham or Bacon with Eggs 60
Eggs—Boiled, Fried, Scrambled or Poached 30
Omelettes—Plain 40 — Parsley or Jelly 45 — Chopped Ham or Bacon 50
Oven Baked Beans (Hot or Cold), Brown Bread 40

VEGETABLES

Potatoes French Fried 20 — Parsley Potatoes 15
Fresh Vegetable 25 — Stewed Tomatoes 20

SALADS

Hearts of Lettuce, French Dressing 30 — Lettuce and Tomato 35
Combination 35 — Pineapple Salad 45 — Chicken Salad 50

BREADS

Rolls 10 — Bread 10 — Crackers 10 — Ry-Krisp 10
Toast, Dry or Buttered 15

DESSERTS

Green Apple Pie 15; A la Mode 25 — Rice Pudding with Sultanas 20
N.Y.C. French Vanilla Ice Cream 20
Figs in Syrup 25
Stewed Prunes 25 — Chilled Grape Fruit, Half 25

CHEESE

Camembert 30 — American 15 — Blue 30
(Toasted Hard or Soft Biscuits served with above Cheese orders)
Cream Cheese with Ry-Krisp, Red Currant Jelly 20

BEVERAGES

Coffee, Pot 20; Cup 15 — Tea, Pot 15
Individual Milk 10 — Cocoa, Pot 15
Sanka, Kaffee Hag or Postum, Pot 25

THE
20th CENTURY
SALAD BOWL
Ry-Krisp
(Per Person)
50 Cents

Moselle Wine
¼ Bottle, American 40

Sauterne
¼ Bottle, Imported 1.00
American 40

Claret
¼ Bottle, Imported 1.00
American 40

Riesling
¼ Bottle, American 40

Old Fashioned Cocktail 55

Beer, Club Size .... .20
Bottle .... 20 and 30

MARTINI COCKTAIL 40 — SHERRY WINE 40 — MANHATTAN COCKTAIL 40

Dinner

($1.00)

Wine Pickle — Chilled Celery — Ripe Olives

CHOICE OF:
Gumbo Creole
Hot Clam Bouillon — Chilled Tomato Juice
V-8 Cocktail — Fresh Shrimp Cocktail

CHOICE OF:
Fresh Lake Perch Saute, Meuniere
Salisbury Steak with Mushroom Sauce
Breaded Lamb Chops, Bordelaise
Roast Long Island Duckling, Apple Sauce
Grilled Small Sirloin Steak, Mushroom Sauce 1.75

Garden Vegetable
French Fried Potatoes — Parsley Potatoes

Assorted Rolls

CHOICE OF:
Green Apple Pie
N.Y.C. French Vanilla Ice Cream
Rice Pudding with Sultanas
Camembert or Blue Cheese with Toasted Biscuits

Coffee — Tea — Individual Milk

CORDIALS 60

B. J. Bohlender, Manager Dining Service, New York

ABOVE & LEFT The James Whitcomb Riley, Dining Car Service, c. 1941

Introduced to the railway in 1941, this streamlined train ran between Chicago and Cincinnati. It was named after "Hoosier Poet" James Whitcomb Riley. He was best known for *Little Orphan Annie*.

Dieser stromlinienförmige Zug verkehrte ab 1941 zwischen Chicago und Cincinnati. Benannt war er nach dem „Hoosier-Dichter" James Whitcomb Riley aus Indiana, dessen berühmtestes Werk *Little Orphan Annie* ist.

Inauguré en 1941, ce train aérodynamique reliait Chicago à Cincinnati. Il tire son nom du « Hoosier Poet » (le poète de l'Indiana) James Whitcomb Riley, dont l'œuvre la plus célèbre demeure *Little Orphan Annie*.

BELOW Reception and Dinner Tendered to the Officers and Crew of the New Airship *Hindenburg*, the Waldorf-Astoria Hotel, 1936, New York, New York

One year prior to the disaster that destroyed the airship, this banquet celebrated the *Hindenburg* during one of its 17 crossings in 1936.

Ein Jahr vor dem katastrophalen Ende des Luftschiffs wurde die *Hindenburg* bei einer ihrer 17 Atlantiküberquerungen mit diesem Bankett gefeiert.

En 1936, une année avant le tragique accident du dirigeable, ce banquet célèbre le *Hindenburg* lors d'une de ses dix-sept traversées.

RIGHT *Deutschland*, Hamburg-Amerika Line, 1936

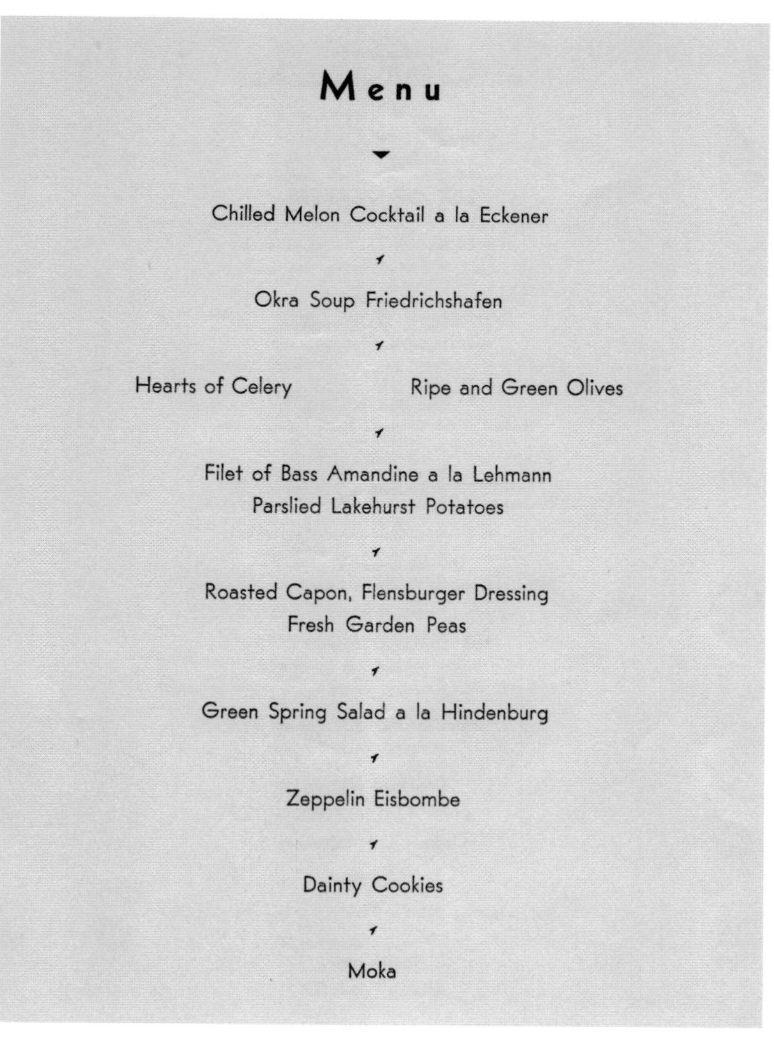

XI·OLYMPIADE
1936
LUDWIG HOHLWEIN
MÜNCHEN
BERLIN u.
GARMISCH-
PARTENKIRCHEN
NORDDEUTSCHER LLOYD BREMEN

OPPOSITE ***S.S. Europa*, Norddeutscher Lloyd Bremen, 1936**

RIGHT Joe Louis promotional photo, 1935, New York, New York

BELOW Testimonial Dinner in Honor of Joe Louis, 1935, New York, New York

A dinner, early in Joe Louis' career, celebrates the success of "the Brown Bomber."

Früh in seiner Karriere wird der „braune Bomber", Boxer Joe Louis, mit diesem Festessen geehrt.

Un dîner en l'honneur de Joe Louis, alias « Brown Bomber », au début de sa carrière à succès.

Testimonial
Dinner
In Honor Of
Joe Louis
Julian Black
John Roxborough

Menu

Hors d'Oeuvres Varies
Fresh Fruit Cocktail
Chicken Consommee in Jelly
Stuffed Fish Roll
Fried Spring Chicken ala Maryland
Corn Fritters Candied Yams
Fresh Green Vegetables
Salad Deon
Ice Cream and Cake
Demi Tasse

ABOVE LEFT Hotel Knickerbocker, c. 1935, Chicago, Illinois

ABOVE Burlington Route, c. 1936

OPPOSITE Statler Hotel, 1936, Boston, Massachusetts

RIGHT Herbert's Cafe, c. 1935, San Francisco, California

FAR RIGHT Baltimore & Ohio Dining Car Service, c. 1935

mixed drinks

ABOVE & RIGHT Great Northern Railway, 1940

This series of menus by German artist Winold Reiss projected the romance of the West in an accurate portrayal of Native Americans.

Diese Serie von Speisekarten von dem deutschen Zeichner Winold Reiss feierte die Romantik des Wilden Westens mit akkuraten Darstellungen von Indianern.

Cette série de menus illustrés par l'artiste allemand Winold Reiss évoque l'aventure du Far West dans des portraits fidèles d'Amérindiens.

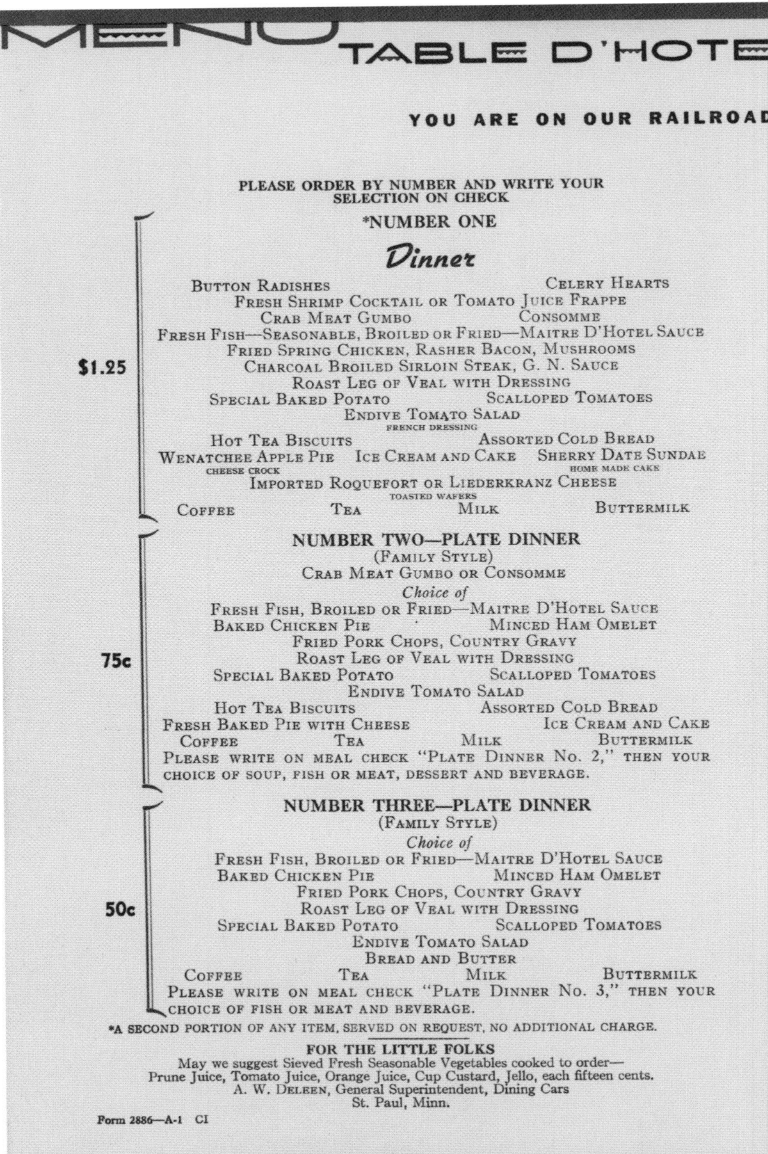

MENU TABLE D'HOTE

YOU ARE ON OUR RAILROAD

PLEASE ORDER BY NUMBER AND WRITE YOUR SELECTION ON CHECK

*NUMBER ONE

Dinner

$1.25

Button Radishes — Celery Hearts
Fresh Shrimp Cocktail or Tomato Juice Frappe
Crab Meat Gumbo — Consomme
Fresh Fish—Seasonable, Broiled or Fried—Maitre D'Hotel Sauce
Fried Spring Chicken, Rasher Bacon, Mushrooms
Charcoal Broiled Sirloin Steak, G. N. Sauce
Roast Leg of Veal with Dressing
Special Baked Potato — Scalloped Tomatoes
Endive Tomato Salad
FRENCH DRESSING
Hot Tea Biscuits — Assorted Cold Bread
Wenatchee Apple Pie — Ice Cream and Cake — Sherry Date Sundae
CHEESE CROCK — HOME MADE CAKE
Imported Roquefort or Liederkranz Cheese
TOASTED WAFERS
Coffee — Tea — Milk — Buttermilk

NUMBER TWO—PLATE DINNER

75c

(Family Style)
Crab Meat Gumbo or Consomme
Choice of
Fresh Fish, Broiled or Fried—Maitre D'Hotel Sauce
Baked Chicken Pie — Minced Ham Omelet
Fried Pork Chops, Country Gravy
Roast Leg of Veal with Dressing
Special Baked Potato — Scalloped Tomatoes
Endive Tomato Salad
Hot Tea Biscuits — Assorted Cold Bread
Fresh Baked Pie with Cheese — Ice Cream and Cake
Coffee — Tea — Milk — Buttermilk
Please write on meal check "Plate Dinner No. 2," then your choice of soup, fish or meat, dessert and beverage.

NUMBER THREE—PLATE DINNER

50c

(Family Style)
Choice of
Fresh Fish, Broiled or Fried—Maitre D'Hotel Sauce
Baked Chicken Pie — Minced Ham Omelet
Fried Pork Chops, Country Gravy
Roast Leg of Veal with Dressing
Special Baked Potato — Scalloped Tomatoes
Endive Tomato Salad
Bread and Butter
Coffee — Tea — Milk — Buttermilk
Please write on meal check "Plate Dinner No. 3," then your choice of fish or meat and beverage.

*A SECOND PORTION OF ANY ITEM, SERVED ON REQUEST, NO ADDITIONAL CHARGE.

FOR THE LITTLE FOLKS
May we suggest Sieved Fresh Seasonable Vegetables cooked to order—
Prune Juice, Tomato Juice, Orange Juice, Cup Custard, Jello, each fifteen cents.
A. W. Deleen, General Superintendent, Dining Cars
St. Paul, Minn.

Form 2886—A-1 CI

NEW YORK CENTRAL LINES
THE WATER LEVEL ROUTE
NEW YORK
CENTRAL
LINES

MENU

★ HOWARD JOHNSON'S ★

delicious food

OPPOSITE Howard Johnson's, 1941

Howard Johnson, starting in Wollaston, Massachusetts, pioneered the franchise system, whereby the same look and menu were repeated in every one of its restaurants, with its famous orange roofs, "Simple Simon and the Pie Man" sign, and dozens of ice cream flavors. Motorists knew Howard Johnson's was dependable and always sanitary.

Howard Johnson startete seine Karriere in Wollaston, Massachusetts, und wurde zum Pionier des Franchisesystems, bei dem derselbe Look und dieselbe Speisekarte in jedem seiner Restaurants zu finden waren. Alle hatten das berühmte orangerote Dach, das Signet „Simple Simon and the Pie Man" und Eis in mehreren Dutzend Geschmacksrichtungen. Die Autoreisenden konnten sich darauf verlassen, dass ein Howard Johnson's verlässlich und immer sauber war.

Howard Johnson, qui ouvre son premier restaurant à Wollaston, dans le Massachusetts, est un pionnier du système de franchise. L'architecture extérieure ainsi que le menu sont les mêmes dans chaque restaurant. On y retrouve son célèbre toit orange, le symbole « Simple Simon and the Pie Man » et l'on y trouve un choix de plusieurs dizaines de parfums de glace. Les routiers savaient qu'ils pouvaient toujours compter sur les Howard Johnson's et leur hygiène impeccable.

BELOW Howard Johnson's restaurant, 1940, New York, New York

ABOVE Greyhound Interstate Restaurant, 1940, Chicago, Illinois

JOHN'S
ISLAND
CAFE
AVALON CATALINA ISLAND

RIGHT El Encanto, c. 1935, Avalon, California

FAR RIGHT Hotel St. Catherine, c. 1935, Avalon, California

LEFT & OPPOSITE **John's Island Cafe, c. 1935, Avalon, California**

The resort island of Catalina off the coast of California, received a unified graphic treatment by artists Dorothy and Otis Sheperd, whose employer, William Wrigley, owned the island and hired them to design all elements of the town of Avalon.

Die Ferieninsel Catalina vor der kalifornischen Küste erhielt ein einheitliches Design von Dorothy und Otis Sheperd, deren Arbeitgeber, William Wrigley, Besitzer der Insel war. Er ließ alles in der Stadt Avalon von den beiden entwerfen.

La publicité pour la station balnéaire insulaire de Catalina au large de la Californie a bénéficié d'un traitement graphique homogène grâce à l'apport des artistes Dorothy et Otis Sheperd, dont l'employeur, William Wrigley, était propriétaire de l'île. Il les avait engagés pour concevoir chaque détail de la ville d'Avalon.

M - E - N - U

Inaugural Dinner of International Casino
Friday, Sept. 17, 1937

International Cocktail

Supreme of Fruit, Casino

Hearts of Kalamazoo Celery
Spanish and California Olives
Salted Nuts and Almonds

Strained Chicken Gumbo, Louisiana

Filet of Sea Bass, Tout Paris

Breast of Capon Souffle, International
New Peas en Croustade, Belle Fermiere
Potato Fondante, Vefour

Salade Moderne

Bombe Surprise Universal
Petits Fours Viennoise — Mignardise de Geneve

Cafe des Princes

ABOVE **International Casino, 1937, New York, New York**

OPPOSITE **The French Casino, c. 1939, New York, New York**

LEFT **Folie Parisienne, French Casino, c. 1938, New York, New York**

The menu for this international dinner was basically French or what became known as Continental cuisine, with dishes that were at once familiar to its clientele and European enough to demonstrate sophistication.

Die Karte dieses internationalen Dinners war im Grunde französisch (bzw. was später als kontinentale Küche bezeichnet wurde), mit Gerichten, die den Gästen einerseits vertraut waren, andererseits aber europäisch genug, um als Edelgastronomie zu gelten.

Ce menu créé à l'occasion d'un dîner international est axé sur la gastronomie française. On connaîtra bientôt ce style sous le nom de « cuisine continentale ». Les plats sont à la fois familiers à la clientèle, mais suffisamment « européens » pour leur paraître raffinés.

THE
French
CASINO
THEATRE RESTAURANT

LOCATED IN THE HEART OF HOLLYWOOD
AN INTERNATIONAL CITY OF SHOPS AND STUDIOS •
CROSS ROADS CAFE
1521 Cross Roads
of the World
Hollywood, California
Telephone
HIllside 9562

OPPOSITE **Cross Roads Cafe, 1939, Hollywood, California**

RIGHT & BELOW **MGM Café, 1939, Culver City, California**

The MGM Studio commissary offered suprisingly modest and predictable fare for such a stellar institution.

Die Kantine im MGM Studio bot für eine von so vielen Filmstars besuchte Einrichtung überraschend bodenständige Hausmannskost an.

Le restaurant du studio MGM propose un menu modeste et sans surprise. Étonnant pour une institution si prestigieuse !

DINING ROOM OPEN FOR DINNER FROM 5 TO 8 P.M.

FROM THE ICED TUREEN

Half of Cracked Jumbo Crab, Mayonnaise Dressing or Chili Sauce .65
Half Dozen Cherry Stone Clams .60
Half Dozen Blue Points on Half Shell .60
Special Salad Bowl .25
Health Salad: Grated Carrots, Cottage Cheese, Raisins, Celery, Fresh Pineapple, Stuffed Dates, Choice of Dressing .45
Bostonian Salad: Chicken Salad Sliced Tomatoes, Sliced Egg, and Mayonnaise Dressing .50
Cold Platter of Half Boiled Lobster, Sliced Tomatoes, and Mayonnaise Dressing .75
Special Sandwich of Baked Ham, Turkey and Tomato on Wheat Toast, (3 High), Cranberry Sauce .50

DU JOUR

M-G-M Special Chicken Broth—(Plain, Cup 15; Plain, Bowl 25) with Noodles or Rice and Chicken 35
Potage Diana 10 Petite Marmite 15
Special Toasted French Cheese Roll 10

Broiled Individual Rock Bass, Cole Slaw .45
Poached Eggs with Shrimps Sauce Newburg .55
Irish Lamb Stew, Steamed Dumplings .50
Braised Brisket of Beef, Bourgeoise .55
Calf Liver Saute with Bacon .55

COCKTAILS

Avocado 35 Oyster 30 Shrimp 35 Lobster 35 Crab Meat 35
Fruit 30 Fresh Fruit 40 Grapefruit Supreme 30
Clam Juice 30 Tomato Juice 10-20 Prune Juice 10
Grapefruit Juice 15-30 Sauerkraut Juice 10

APPETIZERS - RELISHES

Hearts of Celery 15 Utah Celery 25 Stuffed Celery 35
Colossal Ripe Olives 25 Green Olives 20 Stuffed Olives 25
Major Grey's Chutney 25 Sweet Pickles 10 Dill Pickles 10
Mustard Pickles 15 Russian Caviar (Glass or Canape) 90
Pate de Foie Gras 65 Italian Antipasto 65

SEA FOOD (In Season)

Oysters (½ Doz.) Fried 60 Raw on Half Shell 60 Stewed in Milk 50
Half and Half 65 Cream 75 Pepper Pan Roast 55
Shad Roe with Bacon 90 Lobster (½) Broiled 75
Half Dozen Cherry Stone Clams on Half Shell 60
Lobster (½) Cold Boiled 75 Lobster a la Newburg 90
Brook Trout Saute (2) 75 Plate of Iced Fresh Shrimps 60
Half of Cracked Jumbo Crab 75

POTATOES - VEGETABLES

French Fried 15 Hashed in Cream 20 Long Branch 20
Lyonnaise 20 Cottage Fried 20 Au Gratin 20
O'Brien 25 Julienne 20 American Fried 15
French Fried Onions 35 Giant Asparagus 40 Corn on Cob 10
Mammoth White Asparagus 40 Golden Bantam Corn 10
Asparagus Style String Beans 15 Asparagus Tips 25
Hearts of Artichoke 15 Hollandaise Sauce 15
Fresh Artichokes 20 Creamed Spinach 15; with Egg 25

PRESERVES

Individual Preserves 15 Preserved Figs 25
Individual Orange Marmalade 25

81a—L. 92D—3

Thursday, Jan. 19, 1939

SPECIAL NOON LUNCHEON 55c

Choice of:
Tomato Juice Waldorf Salad Pickled Frankfurters
Potage Diana or Petite Marmite

Choice of:
Broiled Individual Rock Bass, Cole Slaw
Poached Eggs with Shrimps Sauce Newburg
Irish Lamb Stew, Steamed Dumplings
Braised Brisket of Beef, Bourgeoise
Calf Liver Saute with Bacon
Carrots Vichy Mashed Potatoes

Frosted Blackberry Pie Chocolate Malted Milk Layer Cake
Pineapple Souffle Pudding, Lemon Sauce
Ice Cream Green Apple Pie Sherbet
Choice of Coffee, Milk or Tea

35c PLATE LUNCH

Special Salad Bowl OR
Little Berkshire Sausages on Toast, Sauce Colbert
Mashed Potatoes

Pineapple Souffle Pudding Frosted Blackberry Pie
Choice of Coffee or Milk—Tea 5c Extra

FOUNTAIN SPECIALS

Rainbow Ice Cream .10
Strawberry Sundae .15
Heinekins Beer .50
Pabst Beer in Can .15
Ballantines Ale .25
Budweiser 20 Rainier Ale 15
Piel's Light .20
Carta Blanca Beer .30
Rainier, Schlitz (in cans) .15
Miller's High Life Beer .20
Pure Juices: Grapefruit, Orange and Apple .10

DESSERTS

Fresh Apple Pie 10; with Cheese 15
All Fruits in Season .25
Frosted Blackberry Pie .10
Pineapple Souffle Pudding, Lemon Sauce .10
Chocolate Malted Milk Layer Cake .10
Cocoanut Custard Pie .15
Raspberry Tart, Whipped Cream .15
Danish Apple Slice, Whipped Cream .15
Chocolate Brownies .15

STEAKS, CHOPS, CHICKEN, ETC.

Eastern New York Sirloin 1.00 Special 1.50 Filet Mignon 90
Eastern Tenderloin 1.25 Eastern Top Sirloin 65 Chicken Fried Steak 55
Minute Steak 85 Special Minute 1.25 Lamb Chops (2) 55
French Lamb Chops (2) 75 Breaded Veal Cutlet 60 Ham Steak 75
Broiled Ham or Bacon 45 Pork Chops (2) 60 Broiled ½ Spring Chicken 75
Chicken Maryland 90 Chicken a la King 75 Chicken Jerusalem 90
Special Davis N. Y. Steak 2.75

GARNITURES

Smothered Onions 15 French Fried Onions 25 Fresh Mushrooms 40
Mushroom Sauce 25 Bearnaise Sauce 20 Bordelaise Sauce 15

CHEESE (with Crackers or Rye Toast)

Swiss Imported 25 Domestic 15 Camembert 20 Roquefort 25
Edam 20 Cottage 15 Jack 15 American 15
Philadelphia Cream 1[illegible]; with Bar le Duc 40

CHEF'S SPECIAL
60c

English Spinach Smoked Beef Tongue Parsley Potatoes

DIRECTOR'S SPECIAL

Fricassee of Chicken with Matzo Dumplings
New Peas
85c

SANDWICHES

Boiled Ham 15 Domestic Cheese 15 Imported Cheese 25
Egg—Deviled, Hard Boiled or Fried 15 Denver 30 Tongue 20
Ham or Bacon and Egg 30 Cold Sausage 20 Sardine 25
Special M-G-M Steak 55 Special Hamburger 20
Lettuce and Tomato 20 Half Reuben 45
Corned Beef 25 Prime Rib, Pork, Lamb or Veal 25 Manhattan 50
Monte Cristo 75 Club House 60 Tuna 30 Tuna Salad 20
Chicken 35 Chicken Salad 25 Minced Olive on Toast 25
Melted Cheese on Toast 30 Avocado 25; with Chicken 55
Fried or Minced Ham or Bacon 20; with Egg 30
No Extra Charge for Toasted Sandwiches

EGGS - OMELETTES

Eggs (2) Boiled, Fried or Scrambled 25; with Ham or Bacon 45
With Sausage 50 Eggs Vienna 65 Shirred 30
Poached, Plain 25; on Toast 30 Eggs Benedictine 75
Omelettes, Plain 30 Ham or Bacon 50 Cheese 40 Jelly 40
Tomato 40 Spanish 45 Asparagus Tips 50 Oyster 55
Fresh Mushroom 60 Fresh Fruit 50 Chicken Livers 60
White Meat of Turkey and Eggs, Country Style 90

SALADS

Chicken, Fresh Shrimp, Lobster or Crab Meat Salad 50
Fruit Salad 30 Egg 40 Lettuce and Egg 30
Pineapple, Peach, Pear or Apricot with Cottage Cheese 30; Half 20
Combination 35; Half 25 Half Imperial 35 Waldorf 35
Asparagus Tips with Mayonnaise 30 Tuna 35
Chef's Salad 50 Crawford 60
Grated Carrots and Cottage Cheese, Mayonnaise 35

COLD MEATS

(With Cole Slaw or Potato Salad)
Ham, Boiled 45 Baked 60 Sliced Chicken 75 Smoked Sprats 45
All Domestic Sausages 40 Assorted Cold Meats 60
Portugaise Sardines 55 Individual Can Tuna 40
Tongue, Smoked or Pickled 50 Cold Prime Rib 65

BEVERAGES

Coffee (Cup) 5; Pot 10 Hot Chocolate 10 Glass Half and Half 15
Iced Tea 10 Iced Coffee 10 Buttermilk 10 Postum 10
Certified Milk (Pint) 15 Small Milk 5 Hot Tea 10
Pot of Sanka 15 Pot of Ovaltine 15

Room Service 25c per Tray

ABOVE **The Brown Derby, 1940, Hollywood, California**

The Brown Derby, shaped like a derby hat, first opened in 1926 across from the Cocoanut Grove. The better-known version, where the Cobb salad was invented, opened in 1929 in Hollywood.

Das Brown Derby hatte die Form einer Melone, eines Herrenhuts, und wurde 1926 gegenüber vom Cocoanut Grove eröffnet. Die bekanntere Version des Brown Derby machte 1929 in Hollywood auf, wo auch der Cobb Salad erfunden wurde, ein gemischter Salat.

Le premier restaurant de la chaîne Brown Derby, à l'architecture en forme de chapeau melon, ouvre en 1926 en face du Cocoanut Grove. L'enseigne la plus connue, où fut inventée la salade Cobb, est inaugurée en 1929 à Hollywood.

RIGHT **The Broadmoor, 1940, Colorado Springs, Colorado**

LEFT The Summit Hotel, c. 1939

RED BURGUNDY—*continued*

No.		*Vintage*	*Half Bottle*	*Bottle*
*165	**BEAUNE GREVES** *Estate Bottling of Louis Voiret.* Beaune is the name of a township; Grèves is the name of a vineyard (incidentally the best in the township of Beaune). A pleasant mellow wine, of a great year.	1934	$1.75	$3.00
*166	**CHARMES MAZYS CHAMBERTIN** *Estate Bottling of Général Rébourseau.* From a vineyard which adjoins Grand Chambertin — a robust and distinguished Burgundy, produced and bottled by one of the best growers of the region.	1934	$1.75	$3.35
161	**CORTON, CHATEAU GRANCEY** *Estate Bottling of Louis Latour.* M. Latour is the largest vineyard owner of the township of Corton, and this wine, fuller-bodied than most of the '34s, is just beginning to come into its own.	1934		$3.50
162	**BONNES MARES** *Estate Bottling of Comte de Vogüé.* Soft, remarkable for its bouquet, a fine wine from an impeccable producer.	1934		$4.00
168	**CLOS DE VOUGEOT** *Estate Bottling of Charles Noëllat.* Vougeot is among the great names of Burgundy, and here is a lovely wine of unusual finesse and charm.	1934		$4.00
*167	**POMMARD RUGIENS** *Estate Bottling of de Chavigné et de Lavoreille.* In addition to the generic name Pommard, this wine carries the name of the little ten-acre vineyard which produced it. In our opinion, one of the finest Pommards ever offered on the American market.	1934		$4.25
*169	**CLOS DE VOUGEOT** *Estate Bottling of Edouard Jayer.* Old M. Jayer is the Mayor of the village of Vosne Romanée, which adjoins Vougeot on the south and this is an altogether exceptional wine.	1934		$5.00
163	**LE MUSIGNY** *Estate Bottling of Comte de Vogüé.* The Comte de Vogüé is one of the most justly famous vineyard owners of the Côte d'Or. This Musigny is his finest wine of the great '34 vintage.	1934		$5.00
*170	**LE MUSIGNY** *Estate Bottling of Frédéric Mugnier.* They say that if Romanée Conti is the queen of Burgundies, Musigny is the dauphin and this exquisite, gracious, delicate wine is certainly worthy of royal rank.	1934		$5.75
*171	**LE CHAMBERTIN** *Estate Bottling of the Domaine Marion Frères.* 1934 was a very great vintage indeed but its wines are velvety rather than heavy — more remarkable for their finesse than for their body. This Chambertin is a typical and beautiful 1934.	1934		$5.75
*172	**ROMANEE CONTI** *Estate Bottling of the Domaine de la Romanée Conti.* Acknowledged the greatest vineyard of Burgundy, Romanée Conti produced in 1934 one of its best wines.	1934		$9.00

**A Frank Schoonmaker Selection.*

[12]

LEFT & ABOVE **Antoine's, 1940, New Orleans, Louisiana**

Antoine Alciatore opened one of the first true restaurants in the United States Managed to this day by his descendants, Antoine's has served French cuisine with a New Orleans "Creole" touch, like its signature Oysters Rockefeller.

Antoine's war nach dem Delmonico's eines der ersten echten Restaurants in den USA. Eröffnet wurde es von Antoine Alciatore, und bis heute wird es von seinen Nachfahren betrieben. Antoine's hat immer französische Küche mit dem für New Orleans typischen „Creole"-Einschlag serviert. Berühmt sind z. B. die „Oysters Rockefeller".

Antoine Alciatore ouvre l'un des premiers vrais restaurants des États-Unis. Encore dirigé de nos jours par ses descendants, Antoine's a toujours servi une cuisine française mâtinée d'une touche créole, comme les huîtres à la Rockefeller, la spécialité de la maison.

LEFT Sea Lion Cafe, Playland at the Beach, c. 1933, San Francisco, California

BELOW Whitney Bros. Pie Shop, Playland at the Beach, c. 1933, San Francisco, California

OPPOSITE The Hot House, Playland at the Beach, c. 1936, San Francisco, California

Originally called Chutes at the Beach in 1913, the 10-acre amusement park had in the mid-1930s 14 rides and five restaurants, including Topsy's, the Hot House, Whitney Bros. Pie Shop, and Sea Lion Café.

Der Rummelplatz am Ocean Beach hieß, als er 1913 aufmachte, Chutes at the Beach. Er bot Mitte der 1930er-Jahre auf vier Hektar 14 Fahrgeschäfte und fünf Gaststätten, darunter Topsy's, The Hot House, Whitney Bros. Pie Shop und das Sea Lion Café.

D'abord appelé « Chutes at the Beach » en 1913, le parc de 4 hectares possédait quatorze attractions et cinq restaurants au milieu des années 1930, dont le Topsy's, le Hot House, le Whitney Bros. Pie Shop et le Sea Lion Café.

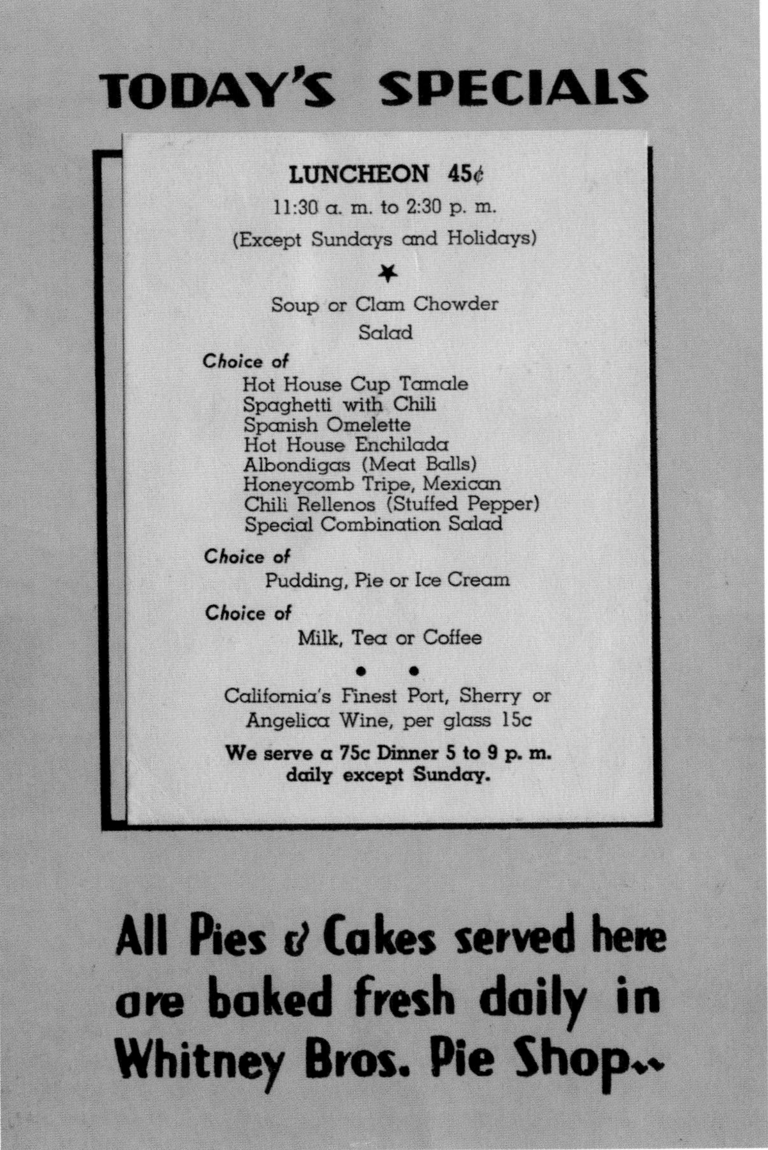

The
HOT
HOUSE
PLAYLAND AT THE BEACH
SAN FRANCISCO
WHITNEY BROS.

LEFT Red Sails Inn, c. 1933, San Diego, California

BELOW Red Sails Inn, 1943, San Diego, California

A graphic gem, the Red Sails menu reflects the rationing policies of World War II. Closing on Tuesdays was a response to "meatless Tuesdays," enacted in World War I and reinstated for the war effort in the 1940s.

Die Speisekarte des Red Sails Inn ist ein Juwel grafischer Gestaltung. Die Rationierungen des Zweiten Weltkriegs zeigen ihre Auswirkungen. Dienstags war Ruhetag, weil im Ersten Weltkrieg und dann wieder in den 1940er-Jahren der „fleischlose Dienstag" vorgeschrieben war.

Bijou de graphisme, la carte du Red Sails reflète la politique de rationnement de la Seconde Guerre mondiale. Le restaurant est fermé le mardi pour respecter les « Mardis sans viande » édictés pendant la Première Guerre mondiale et rétablis durant les années 1940 pour soutenir l'effort de guerre.

OPPOSITE Adams-Sheetz Drive-In, c. 1939, Los Angeles, California

RED SAILS INN
RED SAILS INN
An Eating Place that is Really DIFFERENT
ARTIST'S SKETCH OF ENTRANCE
RED SAILS
Red Sails Inn
"ON FISHERMAN'S WHARF"
FOOT OF G STREET
654 HARBOR DRIVE ★ SAN DIEGO, CALIF.

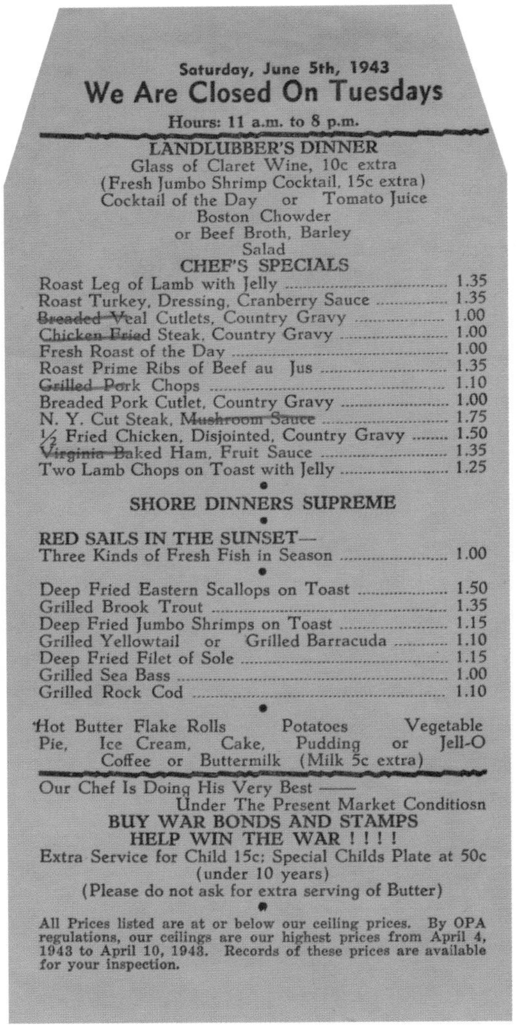

Saturday, June 5th, 1943

We Are Closed On Tuesdays

Hours: 11 a.m. to 8 p.m.

LANDLUBBER'S DINNER

Glass of Claret Wine, 10c extra
(Fresh Jumbo Shrimp Cocktail, 15c extra)
Cocktail of the Day or Tomato Juice
Boston Chowder
or Beef Broth, Barley
Salad

CHEF'S SPECIALS

Roast Leg of Lamb with Jelly	1.35
Roast Turkey, Dressing, Cranberry Sauce	1.35
~~Breaded V~~eal Cutlets, Country Gravy	1.00
~~Chicken Fried~~ Steak, Country Gravy	1.00
Fresh Roast of the Day	1.00
Roast Prime Ribs of Beef au Jus	1.35
~~Grilled Po~~rk Chops	1.10
Breaded Pork Cutlet, Country Gravy	1.00
N. Y. Cut Steak, ~~Mushroom Sauce~~	1.75
½ Fried Chicken, Disjointed, Country Gravy	1.50
~~Virginia Ba~~ked Ham, Fruit Sauce	1.35
Two Lamb Chops on Toast with Jelly	1.25

SHORE DINNERS SUPREME

RED SAILS IN THE SUNSET—

Three Kinds of Fresh Fish in Season	1.00
Deep Fried Eastern Scallops on Toast	1.50
Grilled Brook Trout	1.35
Deep Fried Jumbo Shrimps on Toast	1.15
Grilled Yellowtail or Grilled Barracuda	1.10
Deep Fried Filet of Sole	1.15
Grilled Sea Bass	1.00
Grilled Rock Cod	1.10

Hot Butter Flake Rolls Potatoes Vegetable
Pie, Ice Cream, Cake, Pudding or Jell-O
Coffee or Buttermilk (Milk 5c extra)

Our Chef Is Doing His Very Best —
Under The Present Market Conditiosn

BUY WAR BONDS AND STAMPS
HELP WIN THE WAR ! ! ! !

Extra Service for Child 15c; Special Childs Plate at 50c
(under 10 years)
(Please do not ask for extra serving of Butter)

All Prices listed are at or below our ceiling prices. By OPA regulations, our ceilings are our highest prices from April 4, 1943 to April 10, 1943. Records of these prices are available for your inspection.

ADAMS-SHEETZ
ADAMS-SHEETZ
Drive-In
3653 Cahuenga
Florence and Vermont
Market at Redondo
321 E. 8th, Downtown

The WICH STAND
SANTA BARBARA AND FIGUEROA
4500 WEST SLAUSON AT OVERHILL DRIVE

OPPOSITE The Wich Stand, c. 1933, Los Angeles, California

Drive-in restaurants hit their stride in the 1930s and '40s, producing some of the most satisfying graphics. Most dominant along the Sunbelt, the ubiquitous drive-in could be found in most American towns.

In den 1930er- und 40er-Jahren wurden in den USA Drive-ins populär; aus dieser Zeit gibt es sehr ansprechende Grafiken. Am häufigsten waren die Autoimbisse in den Südstaaten zu finden, aber auch in den meisten anderen amerikanischen Städten gab es sie.

Les restaurants drive-in trouvent leur vitesse de croisière dans les années 1930 et 1940 et sont à l'origine d'illustrations remarquables. Très répandus au Sud, on les trouve cependant sous diverses formes dans la plupart des villes américaines.

ABOVE Katson's Drive-In, c. 1938, Albuquerque, New Mexico

BELOW Harry Carpenter's Sandwich Stands, c. 1938, Los Angeles, California

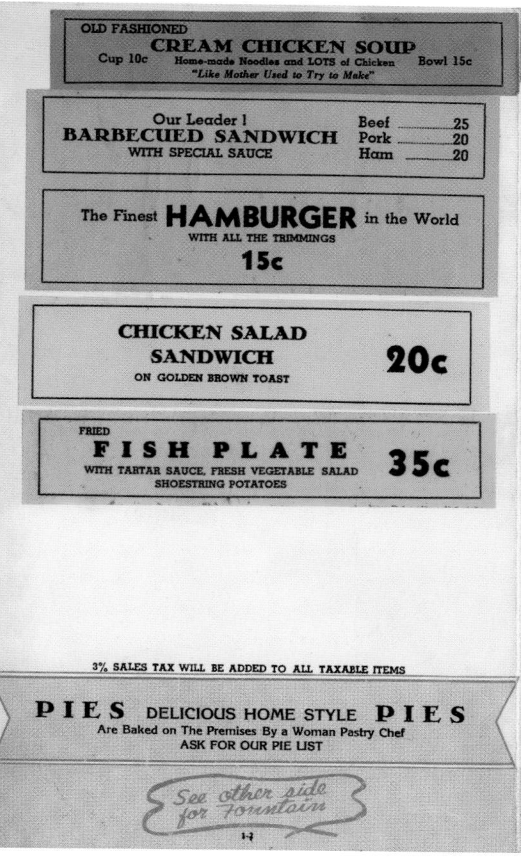

HOTEL DEL MONTE
CALIFORNIA

HOTEL DEL MONTE
CALIFORNIA

HOTEL DEL MONTE
CALIFORNIA

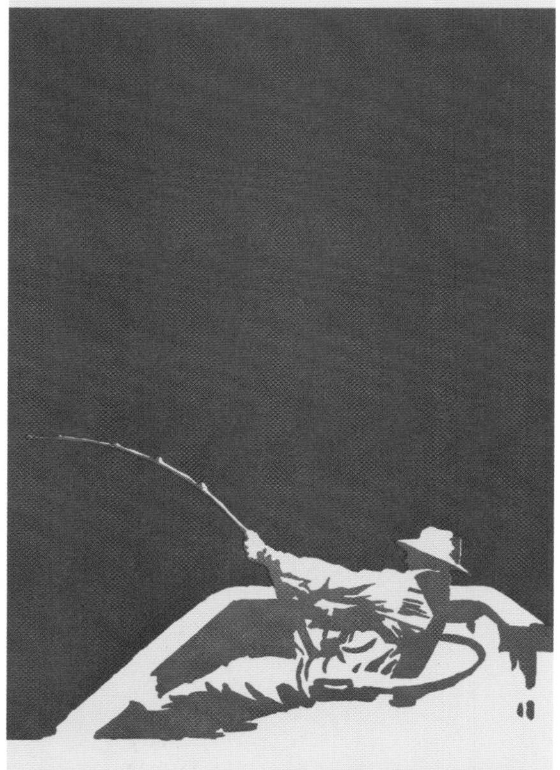
HOTEL DEL MONTE
CALIFORNIA

OPPOSITE Hotel Del Monte, 1940, Del Monte, California

Graphic simplicity highlights this set of menus, which was designed to be given out on consecutive days, a frequent practice during a stay at select resorts and hotels.

Die reduzierten Grafiken zeichnen diese Serie von Speisekarten aus, die den Gästen an aufeinanderfolgenden Tagen vorgelegt wurden, eine verbreitete Sitte in exklusiven Hotels.

La simplicité graphique met en valeur cette série de menus, conçus pour chaque jour de la semaine, une pratique fréquente pour les séjours en hôtel ou en résidence hôtelière de luxe.

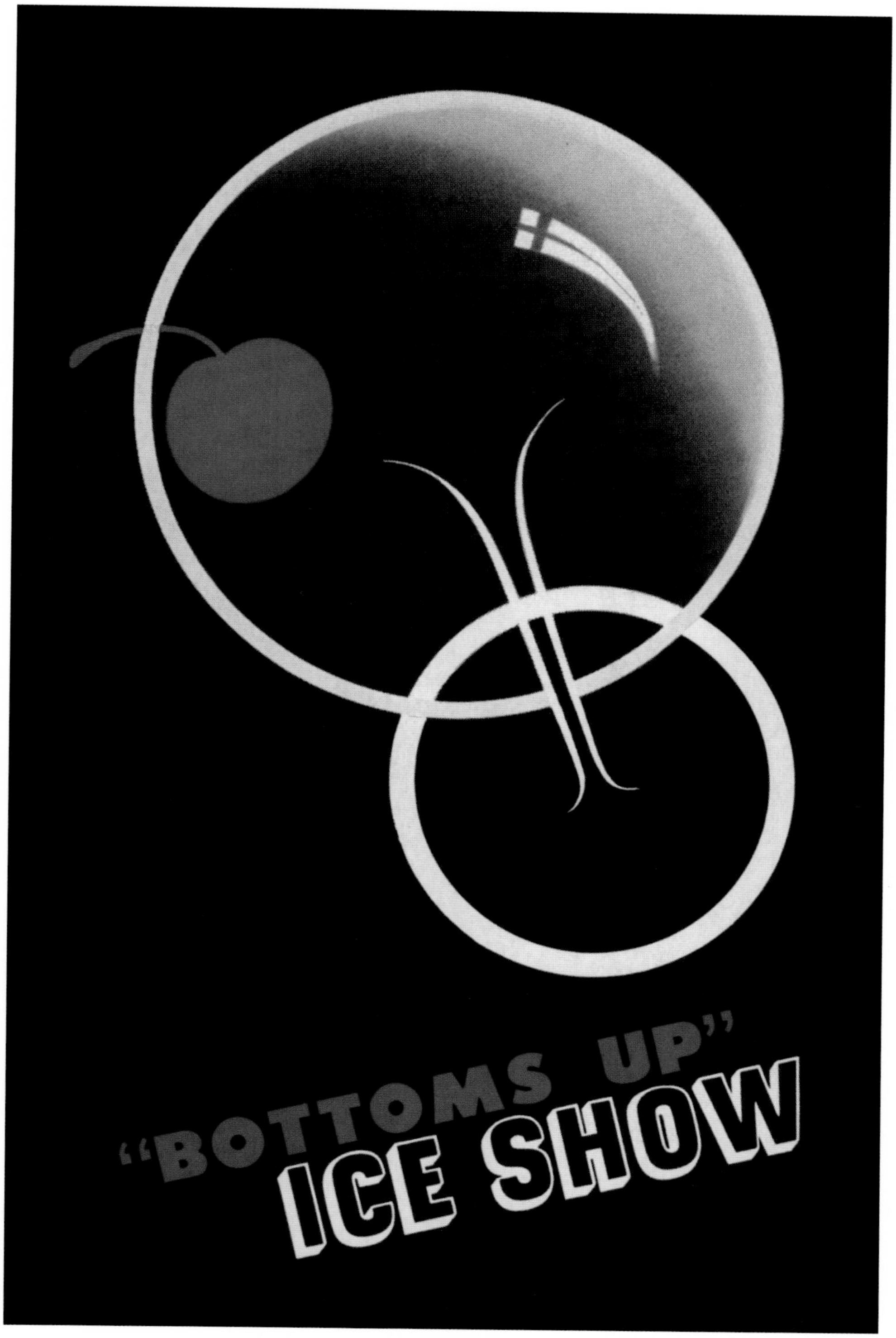

"BOTTOMS UP"
ICE SHOW

LEFT Hotel Astor, c. 1936, New York, New York

ABOVE "Bottoms Up" Ice Show, Terrace Room, Hotel New Yorker, c. 1937, New York, New York

LEFT **Houston Welcomes Howard Hughes, Rice Hotel, 1938, Houston, Texas**

The Rice Hotel, opened in 1912, was known as much for its rice pudding in its downstairs cafeteria as for its illustrious guests, which included honoree Howard Hughes.

Das ab 1912 bestehende Rice Hotel war für seinen Reispudding in der Cafeteria im Erdgeschoss ebenso berühmt wie für seine erlesenen Gäste. Einer davon war der hier geehrte Howard Hughes.

Le Rice Hotel, ouvert en 1912, était aussi connu pour son riz au lait servi dans la cafétéria du rez-de-chaussée que pour ses illustres clients, parmi lesquels Howard Hughes.

BELOW **Rainbow Grill, Rockefeller Center, c. 1936, New York, New York**

OPPOSITE **The Waldorf-Astoria, 1939, New York, New York**

SUPPER A LA CARTE

Served from 10:30 P.M. to 2 A.M., on Saturdays to 3 A.M.
A couvert of $1.50 is charged after 10:30 P.M.

HORS D'OEUVRES

Beluga Caviar 2.25
Buffet Russe 1.25
Virginia Ham Cornets 1.00
Tomato Alexandra .70
Smoked Salmon .80
Hors d'Oeuvres Varies 1.50
Celery .40
Stuffed Celery .75
Queen and Ripe Olives .40

SHELL FISH AND CUPS

Crab Flake Ravigotte 1.00
Steamed Clams 1.00
Melon in Season .60
Shrimps Sauce Mignonette 1.00
Oysters on Half Shell .60
Fresh Lobster Cocktail 1.25
Clams on Half Shell .50
Fresh Fruit Cup .75
Supreme of Pineapple Coral Gables .75

SOUPS

Essence of Tomato Xavier .50
Green Turtle aux Vieux Madere .60
Boula in Cup .50

CHAFING DISHES

Capon a la King 1.50
Crab Meat au Gratin or Newburg 1.25
Lobster Newburg 1.50
Snails Chablisienne 1.00
Frog Legs and Oysters Poulette 1.25
Oyster Stew in Cream .75
Chicken and Sweet Bread Bordelaise 1.50

ENTREES, ETC.

Loin of Lamb Chop Helder 1.50
Squab Chicken en Casserole Grand Mere 1.75
Steak a la Minute aux Chives 1.50
Planked Steak Garnie p.p. 2.25
Filet Mignon aux Priemeur 2.00
Lobster Thermidor (Half) 1.75
Whole Broiled Lobster 2.50
Scrambled Eggs with Irish Bacon .90
Shirred Eggs with Kidneys .90

COLD BUFFET

Supreme of Chicken Jeannette 1.25
Mousse of Virginia Ham Lucullus 1.25
Eggs Mephisto .75
Half Lobster Mayonnaise 1.50
Chicken, White Meat, Salad 1.50
Lobster Salad 1.75
Shrimp Salad 1.25
Crab Flake Salad 1.25

SANDWICHES AND RAREBITS

Sirloin Steak 1.25
Club 1.00
Chicken .75
Tongue .65
Imported Ham .60
Combination .75
Imported Swiss Cheese .60
Toasted Cheese and Bacon .50
Caviar on Toast 1.25
Welsh Rarebit .75
Long Island .80
Golden Buck .80
Yorkshire Buck .90
Cheese Souffle for 2 1.60

DESSERTS

Assorted Pies .40
French or Vienna Pastry .35
Surprise Tangerine .75
Cup St. Jaques .75
Pear Flambe .75
Cherries Jubilee .75
Baked Alaska p.p. 1.25
Assorted Fruit Compote .75
Souffle Citron for 2 1.60
Souffle aux Liquors for 2 1.75
Crepes Suzette p.p. 1.50
Petit Fours Glace .45
Assorted Ice Creams .50
Assorted Sherbets .45

CHEESE

Port du Salut .50
Iowa Roquefort .50
Bel Paese .50
Imported Swiss .50
English Stilton .70
Camembert .60
Gorgonzola .50

BEVERAGES

Coffee .25
Tea .25
Cocoa .30
Chocolate .35
Acidophilus Milk .25

9
193
The
WALDORF-ASTORIA
NEW YORK

LEFT **White Star Restaurant, Golden Gate International Exposition, 1939, San Francisco, California**

BELOW **Le Restaurant Français, 1940, New York, New York**

With France at war with Germany, restaurants like Le Restaurant Français in New York shored up their allegiance to their American protectors by eschewing the racy images of the past in favor of red-white-and-blue banners.

Da Frankreich Krieg gegen Deutschland führte, betonten Häuser wie das Le Restaurant Français in New York ihre Allianz mit der amerikanischen Schutzmacht und tauschten die gewagten Illustrationen aus der Vergangenheit gegen rot-weiß-blaue Banner ein.

La France est en guerre contre l'Allemagne et les établissements tels que Le Restaurant Français à New York renforcent leur allégeance au protecteur américain en oubliant les images lestes du passé au profit de bannières bleu, blanc, rouge.

OPPOSITE **Cafe Lafayette, Golden Gate International Exposition, 1939, San Francisco, California**

Le Restaurant Français

Caviar Frais 3.00
Melon Glacé .... .80
Saumon Fumé .... .90
Demi Grapefruit Nature 45
Demi Grapefruit Avec Liqueurs 55
Jambon de Bayonne 1.25

POTAGES –

Crême Sultane .... .50
Saint Germain .... .50
Crême Froide Pavillon .... .50
Petite Marmite .... .90
Consommé Froid Niçoise .... .50
Madrilène en Gelée .... .50

POISSONS –

Filets de Sole Adrienne 1.80
Homard Archiduc 2.00
Grenouilles Bordelaise 1.80
Truite de Rivière Belle Meunière 1.60
Pompano Grillé Sauce Choron 1.70
Suprême de Barbue Mornay 1.50
Merlan au Gratin 1.25
Délices de Sea Bass au Porto 1.50
Saumon Froid Sauce Verte 1.50
Homard du Maine Froid Parisienne 1.80
Darne de Saumon au Moët 1.70

PLATS DU JOUR –

POULARDE EN COCOTTE ARMENONVILLE 2.25
PIGEON AUX OLIVES 2.25
Noisette de Pré Salé Jussieux 2.00
Tournedos Blanchette 2.75
Ris de Veau des Gourmets 2.00
Pintadon aux Primeurs (pour deux) 4.50
Pilaff de Volaille à la Serbe 1.80
Poussin Grillé Floriant 2.25
Caneton Nantais Bigarrade (le demi pour deux) 4.50
Mignonettes d'Agneau Grillées aux Petits Pois 1.90

ROTIS –

Poularde
Caneton
Poulet de Grain
Pintade
Poussin
Selle et Carré d'Agneau
Pigeon

(Selon Grosseur)

CAFE LAFAYETTE
AMADO GONZALEZ
CARTE DES VINS

RAILROADS
CHILDS
Childs BAR
CHILDS

OPPOSITE **Childs Bar, Railroad Exhibit Building, New York World's Fair, 1940, New York, New York**

ABOVE, FROM LEFT TO RIGHT **Gas Industries Building and Court of Flame Restaurant; the Railroad Building; the Aviation Building; Constitution Mall, New York World's Fair, 1930–40, New York, New York**

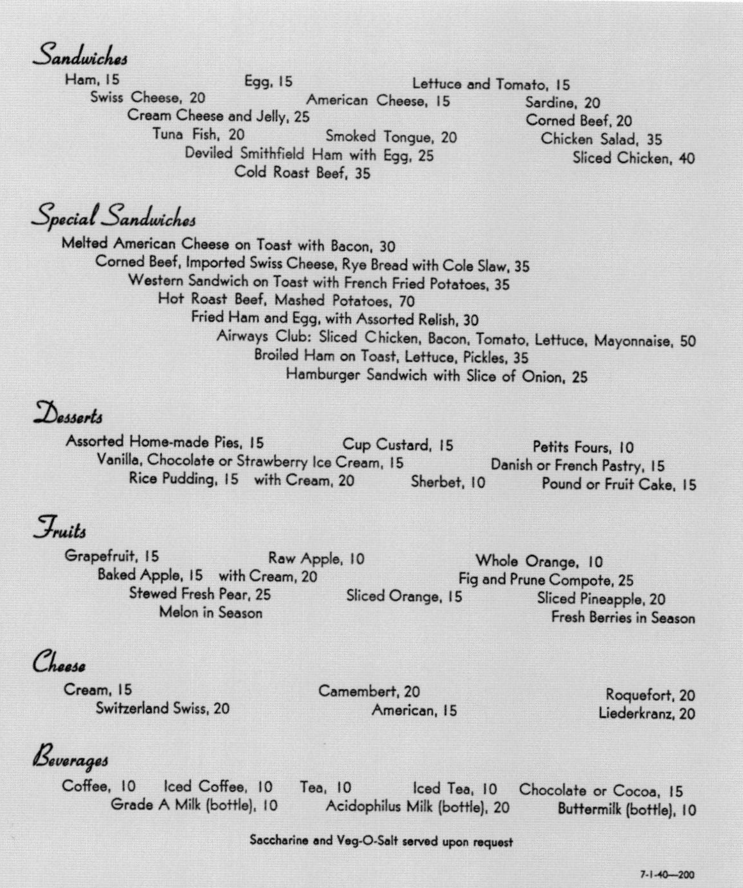

Sandwiches

Ham, 15 · Egg, 15 · Lettuce and Tomato, 15
Swiss Cheese, 20 · American Cheese, 15 · Sardine, 20
Cream Cheese and Jelly, 25 · Corned Beef, 20
Tuna Fish, 20 · Smoked Tongue, 20 · Chicken Salad, 35
Deviled Smithfield Ham with Egg, 25 · Sliced Chicken, 40
Cold Roast Beef, 35

Special Sandwiches

Melted American Cheese on Toast with Bacon, 30
Corned Beef, Imported Swiss Cheese, Rye Bread with Cole Slaw, 35
Western Sandwich on Toast with French Fried Potatoes, 35
Hot Roast Beef, Mashed Potatoes, 70
Fried Ham and Egg, with Assorted Relish, 30
Airways Club: Sliced Chicken, Bacon, Tomato, Lettuce, Mayonnaise, 50
Broiled Ham on Toast, Lettuce, Pickles, 35
Hamburger Sandwich with Slice of Onion, 25

Desserts

Assorted Home-made Pies, 15 · Cup Custard, 15 · Petits Fours, 10
Vanilla, Chocolate or Strawberry Ice Cream, 15 · Danish or French Pastry, 15
Rice Pudding, 15 with Cream, 20 · Sherbet, 10 · Pound or Fruit Cake, 15

Fruits

Grapefruit, 15 · Raw Apple, 10 · Whole Orange, 10
Baked Apple, 15 with Cream, 20 · Fig and Prune Compote, 25
Stewed Fresh Pear, 25 · Sliced Orange, 15 · Sliced Pineapple, 20
Melon in Season · Fresh Berries in Season

Cheese

Cream, 15 · Camembert, 20 · Roquefort, 20
Switzerland Swiss, 20 · American, 15 · Liederkranz, 20

Beverages

Coffee, 10 · Iced Coffee, 10 · Tea, 10 · Iced Tea, 10 · Chocolate or Cocoa, 15
Grade A Milk (bottle), 10 · Acidophilus Milk (bottle), 20 · Buttermilk (bottle), 10

Saccharine and Veg-O-Salt served upon request

7-1-40—200

LA GUARDIA FIELD *New York*

LEFT **The Aviation Building, New York World's Fair, 1940, New York, New York**

LEFT **Jack Dempsey, Vanderbilt Hotel, 1938, Miami Beach, Florida**

BELOW **Jack Dempsey's, 1935, New York, New York**

OPPOSITE **Dempsey's Corner, 1936, New York, New York**

"The House That Jack Built" was ex-heavyweight boxer Jack Dempsey's restaurant at 50th Street and Eighth Avenue. It opened in 1935 and then moved to larger quarters on Times Square. Dempsey, "the Manassah Mauler," was known for greeting patrons nightly, along with his passel of celebrity friends.

„The House That Jack Built" war das Restaurant des Exschwergewichtsboxers Jack Dempsey an der Ecke 50th Street und Eighth Avenue. 1935 eröffnet, zog es bald in größere Lokalitäten am Times Square um. Dempsey, genannt der „Schläger aus Manassa", war, zusammen mit seiner Clique berühmter Freunde, jeden Abend im Restaurant, um die Gäste zu begrüßen.

« La maison bâtie par Jack » est le restaurant fondé par l'ancien boxeur poids lourd Jack Dempsey au coin de la 50e rue et de la Huitième avenue. Ouvert en 1935, il déménage plus tard pour un espace plus vaste sur Times Square. Dempsey « le tueur de Manassa » accueillait les clients tous les soirs, lui-même, parmi une ribambelle d'amis célèbres.

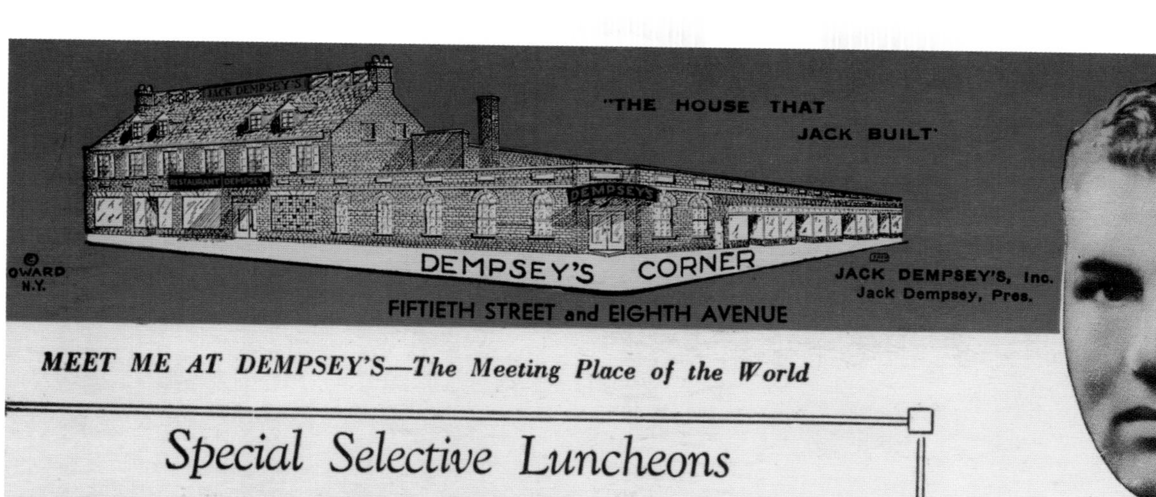

MEET ME AT DEMPSEY'S—The Meeting Place of the World

Special Selective Luncheons

Price of Entree Includes, Appetizer, Soup, Choice of Dessert, Coffee, Tea or Milk

(Choice of)

Blue Point Oysters or Little Neck Clams (25 Cents Additional)
Casaba Melon   Honey Dew Melon   Chopped Chicken Livers
Tomato with Anchovies   Swedish Appetizer   Sauerkraut Juice
Tomato Juice Cocktail   Gefuelter Fish   Shrimps with Russian Dressing

CHOICE OF

CHICKEN OKRA LOUISIANA   **CONSOMME ITALIENNE**

ENTREES

1—**BROILED BLUEFISH,** Maitre d'Hotel, Escarole Farmerette, New Potatoes 90
2—**FRIED L. I. SCALLOPS** and Cape Cod Oysters, Mexican Slaw 1 35
3—**OMELETTE** with Chicken Livers and Mushrooms, Julienne Potatoes 1 10
4—**CUTLET OF CAPON,** Sauce Fleurette, Young Carrots and Peas .. 65
5—**TENDERLOIN RAGOUT** with Fresh Mushrooms en Casserole Parisienne 1 10
6—**CHICKEN AND MUSHROOM PATTY** with New Peas 1 00
7 **ROAST LEG OF YOUNG LAMB,** Brussels Sprouts Polonaise, Rissolee Potatoes 1 10
8 **BRAISED BEEF** a la Mode, Macaroni Au Gratin 85
9 **HALF BROILED SPRING CHICKEN,** French Fried Potatoes .. 1 25
10—**ROAST VERMONT TURKEY,** Cranberry Sauce, Sweet Potatoes Nassau 1 50

DESSERTS

BLUEBERRY PIE WITH ICE CREAM
BOSTON CREAM PIE   **CHERRY PUDDING**
Apple Pie with Ice Cream   Rice Pudding   Fruit Jell-o
Meringue Glace   Compote of Fruit   Cup Custard   Biscuit Tortoni
Vanilla, Coffee or Chocolate Ice Cream   Frozen Eclair, Chocolate Sauce
French or Danish Pastry   Stewed Fresh Pear   Cheese and Crackers

—o—

Coffee, Tea or Milk

(Iced Tea or Coffee 10 Cents Additional)

A la Carte

OYSTERS, CLAMS and APPETIZERS

BLUE POINT OYSTERS .... .35
CAPE COD OYSTERS .... .45
CHERRYSTONE CLAMS .... .40
LITTLE NECK CLAMS .... .35
BISMARCK HERRING .... .40
GRAPEFRUIT (HALF) .... .30
TOMATO JUICE .... .15
CELERY .... .35   QUEEN OLIVES .... .25

SOUPS

Chicken Okra Louisiana .... .25
Consomme Italienne .... .25

SPECIALTIES TO ORDER

LONG ISLAND BROOK TROUT (1) Saute in Butter with Julienne Potatoes .... .75
FROGS' LEGS Fried, Tartar Sauce, Waffle Potatoes 1 35
FRIED SOFT SHELL CRABS, Sauce Tartare, Julienne Potatoes .... .75
JACK'S DELIGHT (Just a Little Different), Virginia Ham and Eggs with Pure Cream, Raw Fried Idaho Potatoes 1 10
GENUINE SMITHFIELD VIRGINIA HAM Glaced on Creamed Spinach, Currant Jelly Wine Sauce, Bermuda Potato 1 35
WHOLE BROILED BABY CHICKEN in Sizzling Platter, String Beans and Julienne Potatoes 1 25
LAMB CHOP, Lady Hannah, Pineapple, Sweet Potato 1 10
CALF'S LIVER, Beech-Nut Bacon, Fried Potatoes 90
HAMBURGER STEAK, French Fried Onions, O'Brien Potatoes 1 00
SIRLOIN STEAK, Minute with O'Brien Potatoes 1 25
FRIED L. I. SCALLOPS, Sauce Tartare, Beech-Nut Bacon, Mexican Slaw 90

SPECIAL SANDWICHES

Dempsey's Club Sandwich .... .85
Nova Scotia Salmon .... .75
Lake Sturgeon .... .85
Chicken and Lettuce .... .60
Genuine Smithfield Virginia Ham .. .65

Smoked Beef Tongue .... .50
Ham .... .40
Steak Tartare .... .85
Brisket Corned Beef .... .40
Combination Ham, Swiss Cheese .. .50
Sliced Egg .... .35

Western Sandwich .... .40
Imported Swiss Cheese .... .40
Cold Roast Beef .... .60
Turkey and Virginia Ham .... .75
Lettuce and Tomato, Mayonnaise .. .35

DESSERTS

Boston Cream Pie .... .25
Blueberry Pie with Ice Cream ..... .25
Cherry Pudding .... .25

RICE PUDDING .... .25
STEWED BARTLETT PEAR .... .35
FRUIT JELLO .... .25
CUP CUSTARD .... .25
FRENCH PASTRY .... .25

COMPOT OF FRUIT .... .40
DANISH PASTRY .... .20
FRENCH ICE CREAM .... .35
PETIT FOURS .... .30
PRESERVED FIGS WITH CREAM .... .35

COFFEE, TEA, Etc.

OUR OWN BLEND OF COFFEE (PER POT) .. .15
CHOCOLATE OR COCOA (PER POT) ...... .25

ORANGE PEKOE OR OOLONG TEA (POT) .. .25
DEMI TASSE .... .10
ICED TEA OR COFFEE .... .25

GRADE "A" MILK (HALF PINT) .... .15
BUTTERMILK CHURNED .... .15
GLASS OF HALF MILK AND CREAM .... .35

Single Portion Served Per Person Only

Sunday, October 4, 1936

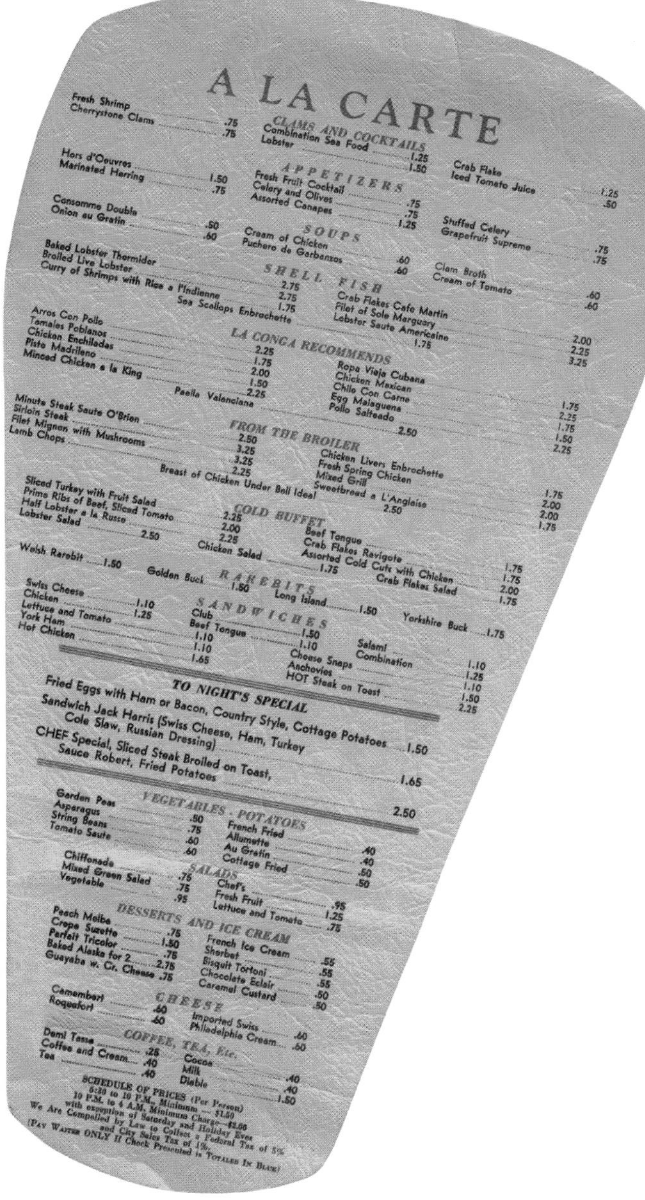

A LA CARTE

CLAMS AND COCKTAILS

Fresh Shrimp .75
Cherrystone Clams .75
Combination Sea Food 1.25
Lobster 1.50
Crab Flake 1.25
Iced Tomato Juice .50

APPETIZERS

Hors d'Oeuvres 1.50
Marinated Herring .75
Fresh Fruit Cocktail .75
Celery and Olives .75
Assorted Canapes 1.25
Stuffed Celery .75
Grapefruit Supreme .75

SOUPS

Consomme Double .50
Onion au Gratin .60
Cream of Chicken .60
Puchero de Garbanzos .60
Clam Broth .60
Cream of Tomato .60

SHELL FISH

Baked Lobster Thermidor 2.75
Broiled Live Lobster 2.75
Curry of Shrimps with Rice a l'Indienne 1.75
Sea Scallops Enbrochette 1.75
Crab Flakes Cafe Martin 2.00
Filet of Sole Marguery 2.25
Lobster Saute Americaine 3.25

LA CONGA RECOMMENDS

Arros Con Pollo 2.25
Tamales Poblanos 1.75
Chicken Enchiladas 2.00
Pisto Madrileno 1.50
Minced Chicken a la King 2.25
Paella Valenciana 2.50
Ropa Vieja Cubana 1.75
Chicken Mexican 2.25
Chile Con Carne 1.75
Egg Malaguena 1.50
Pollo Salteado 2.25

FROM THE BROILER

Minute Steak Saute O'Brien 2.50
Sirloin Steak 3.25
Filet Mignon with Mushrooms 3.25
Lamb Chops 2.25
Breast of Chicken Under Bell Ideal 2.50
Chicken Livers Enbrochette 1.75
Fresh Spring Chicken 2.00
Mixed Grill 2.00
Sweetbread a L'Anglaise 1.75

COLD BUFFET

Sliced Turkey with Fruit Salad 2.25
Prime Ribs of Beef, Sliced Tomato 2.00
Half Lobster a la Russe 2.25
Lobster Salad 2.50
Chicken Salad 1.75
Beef Tongue 1.75
Crab Flakes Ravigote 1.75
Assorted Cold Cuts with Chicken 2.00
Crab Flakes Salad 1.75

RAREBITS

Welsh Rarebit 1.50
Golden Buck 1.50
Long Island 1.50
Yorkshire Buck 1.75

SANDWICHES

Swiss Cheese 1.10
Chicken 1.25
Lettuce and Tomato 1.10
York Ham 1.10
Hot Chicken 1.65
Club 1.50
Beef Tongue 1.10
Salami 1.10
Combination 1.25
Cheese Snaps 1.10
Anchovies 1.50
HOT Steak on Toast 2.25

TO NIGHT'S SPECIAL

Fried Eggs with Ham or Bacon, Country Style, Cottage Potatoes 1.50
Sandwich Jack Harris (Swiss Cheese, Ham, Turkey Cole Slaw, Russian Dressing) 1.65
CHEF Special, Sliced Steak Broiled on Toast, Sauce Robert, Fried Potatoes 2.50

VEGETABLES - POTATOES

Garden Peas .50
Asparagus .75
String Beans .60
Tomato Saute .60
French Fried .40
Allumette .40
Au Gratin .50
Cottage Fried .50

SALADS

Chiffonade .75
Mixed Green Salad .75
Vegetable .95
Chef's .95
Fresh Fruit 1.25
Lettuce and Tomato .75

DESSERTS AND ICE CREAM

Peach Melba .75
Crepe Suzette 1.50
Perfait Tricolor .75
Baked Alaska for 2 2.75
Guayaba w. Cr. Cheese .75
French Ice Cream .55
Sherbet .55
Bisquit Tortoni .55
Chocolate Eclair .50
Caramel Custard .50

CHEESE

Camembert .60
Roquefort .60
Imported Swiss .60
Philadelphia Cream .60

COFFEE, TEA, Etc.

Demi Tasse .25
Coffee and Cream .40
Tea .40
Cocoa .40
Milk .40
Diable 1.50

SCHEDULE OF PRICES (Per Person)
6:30 to 10 P.M., Minimum — $1.50
10 P.M. to 4 A.M. Minimum Charge—$2.00
with exception of Saturday and Holiday Eves
We Are Compelled by Law to Collect a Federal Tax of 5%
and City Sales Tax of 1%.
(Pay Waiter ONLY If Check Presented is Totaled In Black)

OPPOSITE ABOVE La Conga, c. 1937, New York, New York

OPPOSITE BELOW La Conga, c. 1937, New York, New York

Broadway nightclub La Conga was Cuban-themed, with a conga orchestra, though its menu was a mishmash of Continental and American dishes—with sandwich specials of the night—and a dozen or so vaguely Spanish items prepared by Cuban-born chefs who had emigrated to the United States after the Spanish-American War.

Der kubanische Broadway-Nachtklub La Conga hatte ein Conga-Orchester, doch auf der Karte standen eine Mischung europäischer und amerikanischer Gerichte und jeden Abend Sandwich-Angebote. Ein Dutzend spanisch angehauchter Gerichte wurden von den kubanischen Köchen zubereitet, die nach dem Spanisch-Amerikanischen Krieg in die USA gekommen waren.

Night-club de Broadway, La Conga propose un thème cubain, avec orchestre de congas, malgré un méli-mélo de plats européens et américains (dont un sandwich spécial chaque soir) et une dizaine de recettes vaguement espagnoles préparées par des chefs nés à Cuba, puis émigrés aux États-Unis après la guerre hispano-américaine.

ABOVE Harlem Uproar House, 1937, New York, New York

Mimicking the true Harlem nightclubs of the day, the Ubangi Club and the Harlem Uproar House were known for their good bands and scantily clad female performers.

Der Ubangi Club und das Harlem Uproar House waren Kopien der echten Nachtklubs in Harlem und bekannt für ihre guten Bands und spärlich bekleideten Revuetänzerinnen.

Pastiche des vrais night-clubs de Harlem, l'Ubangi Club et le Harlem Uproar House sont réputés pour leurs orchestres et leurs chanteuses court-vêtues.

LEFT Ubangi Club, c. 1940, New York, New York

LEFT Frederic at Baltimore's Oasis Cabaret, c. 1935, Baltimore, Maryland

BELOW LEFT French Casino, c. 1938, New York, New York

BELOW CENTER Bal Tabarin, c. 1937, San Francisco, California

BELOW RIGHT Paris Inn, c. 1935, Los Angeles, California

OPPOSITE Billy Rose's Casa Mañana, c. 1939, New York, New York

Billy Rose's
CASA
MAÑANA

TRADER Vic

OPPOSITE, RIGHT & BELOW Trader Vic's, c. 1942, Oakland, California

Victor Jules Bergeron Jr. began his Trader Vic's Polynesian-themed restaurant chain—famous for its signature mai tai cocktail—as Hinky Dink's bar in Oakland. Eventually there were 25 restaurants worldwide, all with the same tiki décor and menus loosely based on foods from Hawaii and the Pacific. From the start he got away with showing bare-breasted maidens on his menus because it was considered native dress. As the dessert menu notes, "In order not to cause embarrassment to yourselves and us, please do not bring children under sixteen years of age."

Angefangen hatte Victor Jules Bergeron Jr. mit Hinky Dink's Bar in Oakland, bevor er seine Kette von Trader Vic's Restaurants im polynesischen Stil – berühmt für ihre Mai-Tai-Cocktails – eröffnete. Schließlich besaß er 25 Restaurants in aller Welt, alle mit derselben Tiki-Dekoration und von Hawaii und Südsee inspirierten Gerichten. Er konnte es sich von Anfang an herausnehmen, barbusige Maiden auf seinen Speisekarten abzubilden, weil das als lokale Südseetracht galt. Auf der Dessertkarte ist vermerkt: „Es wird gebeten, keine Kinder unter 16 Jahren mitzubringen, um uns und Ihnen Peinlichkeiten zu ersparen."

Victor Jules Bergeron Jr. inaugure sa chaîne d'inspiration polynésienne Trader Vic's – rendue célèbre par l'invention du cocktail Mai Tai – en ouvrant le Hinky Dink's à Oakland. Finalement, la chaîne comptera 25 établissements dans le monde entier, avec le même décor de style tiki et des menus librement inspirés de recettes de Hawaii ou du Pacifique. Il échappe à la censure des femmes aux seins nus de ses menus en proclamant qu'il s'agit d'un costume traditionnel. Comme indiqué sur la carte des desserts : « Afin d'éviter toute gêne aux clients ou à la direction, nous vous prions de ne pas venir accompagnés d'enfants de moins de seize ans. »

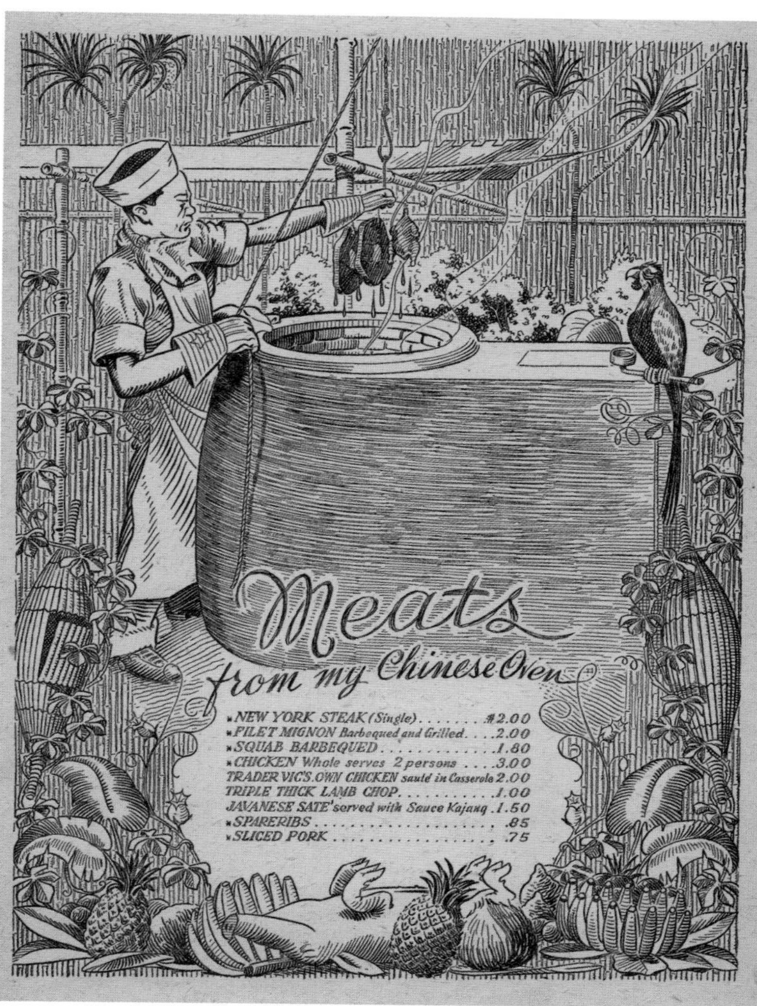

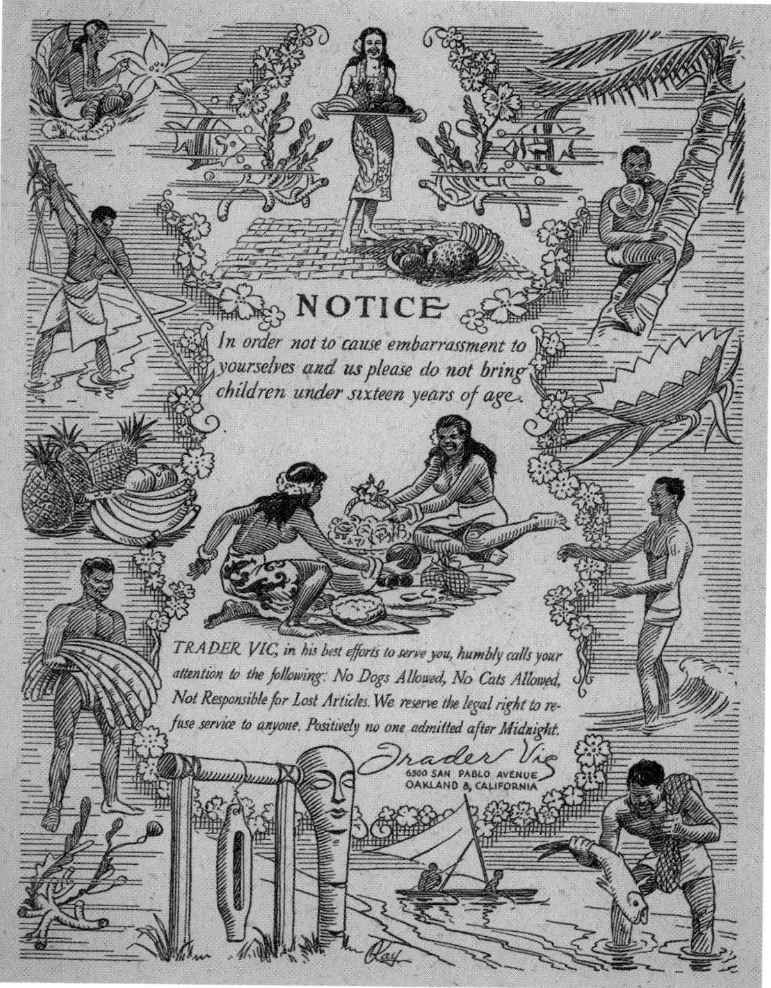

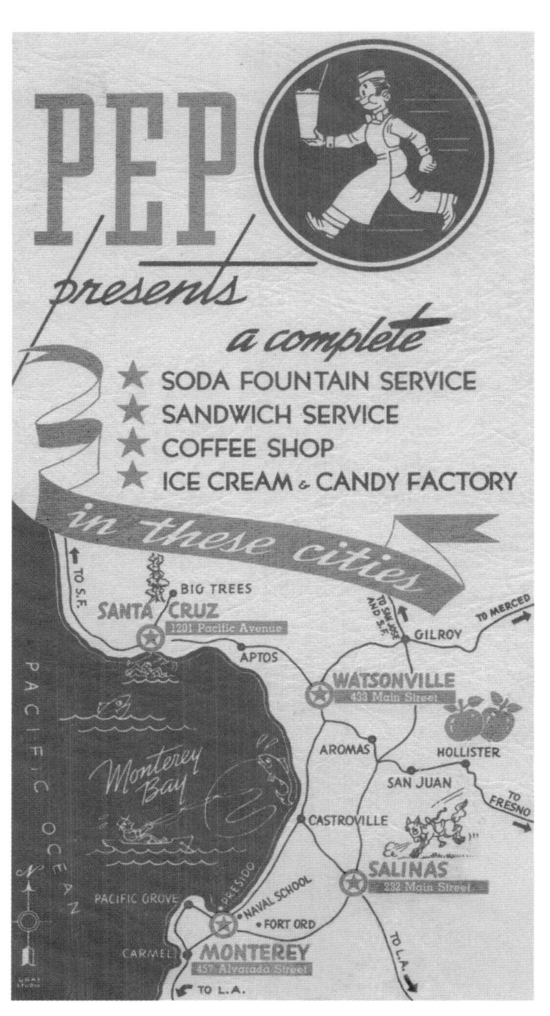

LEFT & BELOW Pep, c. 1942, Santa Cruz, California

True to its name the interior of Pep's menu is loaded with snappy graphics to entice the customer.

Die grafische Gestaltung dieser Speisekarte hat Pepp und lässt den Kunden das Wasser im Mund zusammenlaufen.

L'intérieur de la carte du Pep, fidèle à son nom, propose un graphisme plein d'énergie pour allécher le client.

ABOVE Goldenmoon Products, c. 1943

OPPOSITE Majestic Malted Milk Shop, 1942

Majestic
MALTED MILK SHOP

"El Morocco"

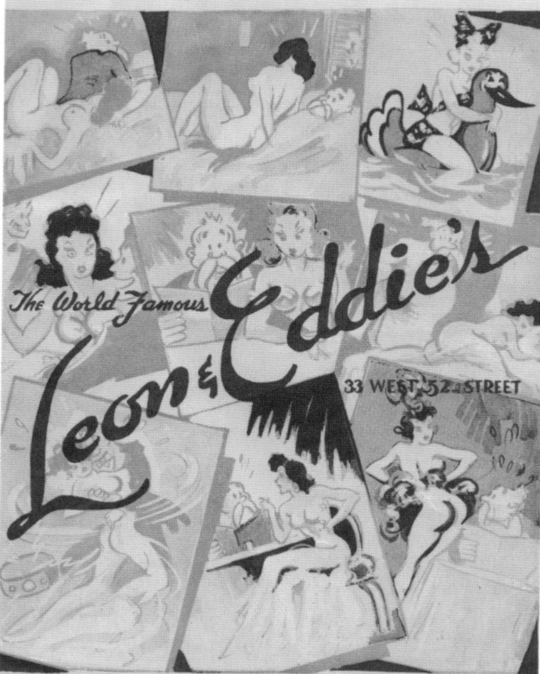

FAR LEFT Coq Rouge, 1940, New York, New York

LEFT Leon & Eddie's Stork Club, 1940, New York, New York

BELOW Cafe Society, 1942, New York, New York

OPPOSITE El Morocco, 1944, New York, New York

One of the most famous nightclubs of its day, El Morocco—nicknamed "Elmo's"—was opened in 1931 by John Perona as a speakeasy on East 54th Street. When Prohibition ended it became a restaurant and club known for its parade of celebrities and its blue-and-white zebra-striped banquettes.

Einer der berühmtesten Nachtklubs seiner Zeit war das El Morocco – Spitzname „Elmo's" –, 1931 von John Perona als Flüsterkneipe an der East 54th Street eröffnet. Als der Alkoholausschank wieder erlaubt war, wurde sie zum Restaurant und Klub, der für seine illustren Gäste und die Sitzbänke mit den blau-weißen Zebrastreifen berühmt war.

L'un des plus célèbres night-clubs de l'époque, El Morocco – surnommé « Elmo's » – est ouvert en 1931 par John Perona. Il s'agit alors d'un *speakeasy* situé sur la 54e rue Est. À la fin de la Prohibition, il devient un club-restaurant connu pour son défilé de célébrités et pour ses banquettes zébrées bleu et blanc.

OPPOSITE Casa Mañana, c. 1940, New York, New York

Entrepreneur and producer Billy Rose opened the dinner theater Casa Mañana as a showcase for striptease dancer Sally Rand.

Der Unternehmer und Produzent Billy Rose eröffnete das Dinnertheater Casa Mañana als Auftrittsort für die Stripteasetänzerin Sally Rand.

L'entrepreneur et producteur Billy Rose ouvre le Casa Mañana, à la fois restaurant et cabaret, avec pour vedette la strip-teaseuse Sally Rand.

ABOVE Billy Rose's Diamond Horseshoe, c. 1939, New York, New York

RIGHT Minsky's Follies, Colonial Inn, c. 1942, Hallandale, Florida

Food was at least third down the list of attractions at risqué nightclubs like Billy Rose's Diamond Horseshoe and Minsky's Follies — the setting for several Hollywood backstage movies in the 1930s and 1940s. First on the list would be the gorgeous showgirls, second the cocktails. Obvioulsy, where one was seated also mattered.

Eigentlich kam man nicht des Essens wegen in anrüchige Nachtklubs wie Billy Rose's Diamond Horseshoe oder Minsky's Follies, in dessen Kulissen mehrere Hollywoodfilme der 1930er- und 40er-Jahre gedreht wurden. Wichtiger waren die hinreißenden Showgirls und die Cocktails, auch wo man saß, spielte natürlich eine Rolle.

La nourriture arrive en troisième position sur la liste des attractions des night-clubs libertins comme le Diamond Horseshoe et le Minsky's Follies de Billy Rose, qui ont servi de décors pour de nombreux films hollywoodiens des années 1930 et 1940. En tête, on trouve bien entendu des filles somptueuses, et ensuite les cocktails. Évidemment, le choix du placement dans la salle était également crucial.

CASA
MANANA
Menu
MENU

COCKTAILS
Alexander
Martini .40
Stinger .30
Bronx .45
Clover Leaf .30
Dubonnet .40
Manhattan .30
Sidecar .35
Old Fashioned .40
Bacardi .35
Pink Lady .40
Orange Blossom .40
Sazerac .30
Brandy .40
Daiquiri .40
Rum Old Fashioned .40
Champagne .35
Brandy Float .75
.45
WHISKIES
American Whiskies .35
American Whiskies Bonded .40
Hi-balls 5c Extra
CANADIAN WHISKIES
Canadian Club .40
Seagram's V O Rye .40
Seagram's Ancient .40
G. & W. Gold Label .40
Hi-balls 5c Extra
SCOTCH WHISKIES
Haig & Haig Pinch Bottle .50
Teacher's Highland Cream .45
Vat 69 .45
White Horse .45
Black and White .45
Old Angus .40
CATACOMBS
CAVERNS
SPRING AND HIGH, COLUMBUS, O.

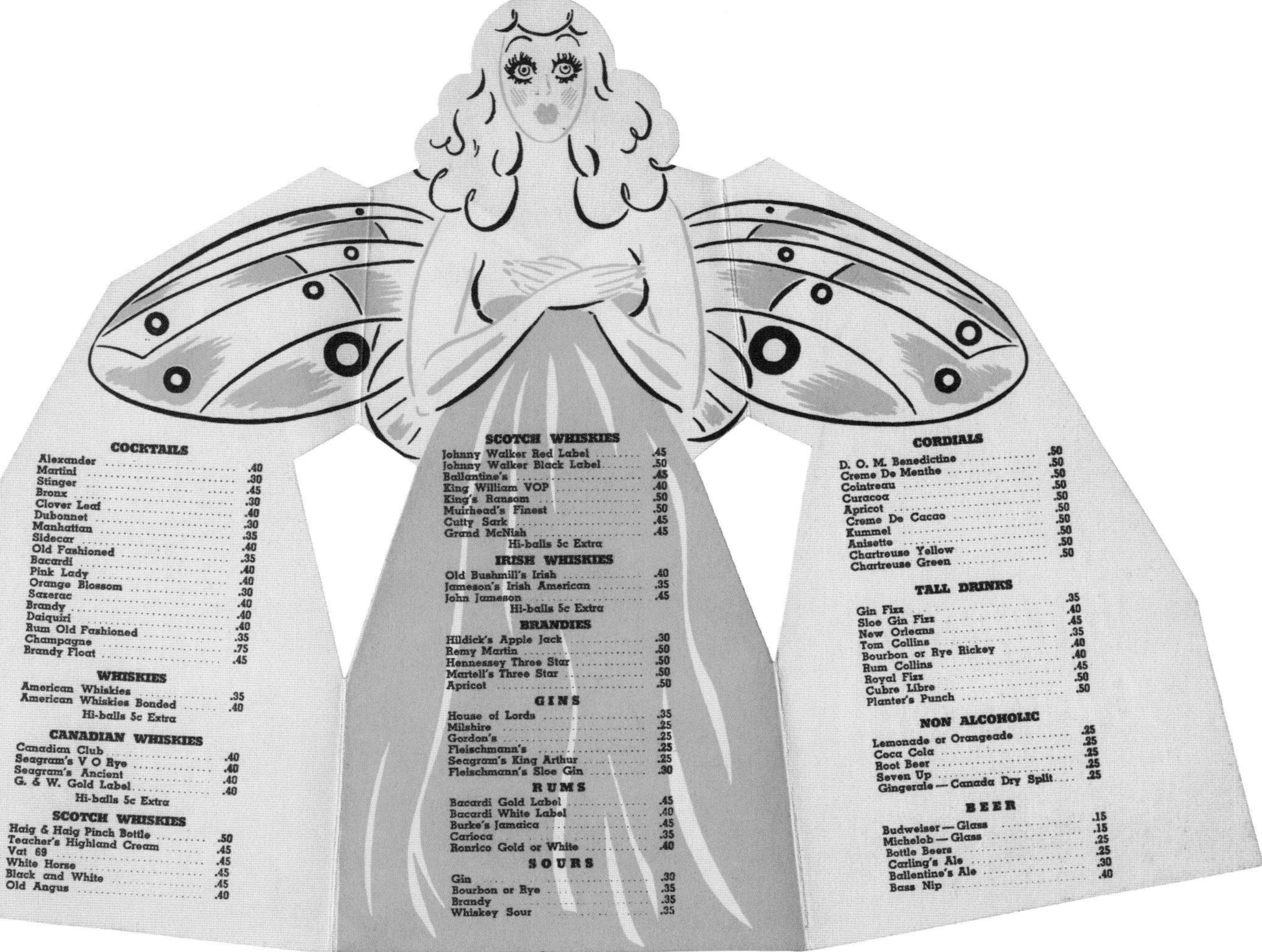
COCKTAILS
Alexander
Martini .40
Stinger .30
Bronx .45
Clover Leaf .30
Dubonnet .40
Manhattan .30
Sidecar .35
Old Fashioned .40
Bacardi .35
Pink Lady .40
Orange Blossom .40
Sazerac .30
Brandy .40
Daiquiri .40
Rum Old Fashioned .40
Champagne .35
Brandy Float .75
.45
WHISKIES
American Whiskies .35
American Whiskies Bonded .40
Hi-balls 5c Extra
CANADIAN WHISKIES
Canadian Club .40
Seagram's V O Rye .40
Seagram's Ancient .40
G. & W. Gold Label .40
Hi-balls 5c Extra
SCOTCH WHISKIES
Haig & Haig Pinch Bottle .50
Teacher's Highland Cream .45
Vat 69 .45
White Horse .45
Black and White .45
Old Angus .40
SCOTCH WHISKIES
Johnny Walker Red Label .45
Johnny Walker Black Label .50
Ballantine's .45
King William VOP .40
King's Ransom .50
Muirhead's Finest .50
Cutty Sark .45
Grand McNish .45
Hi-balls 5c Extra
IRISH WHISKIES
Old Bushmill's Irish .40
Jameson's Irish American .35
John Jameson .45
Hi-balls 5c Extra
BRANDIES
Hildick's Apple Jack .30
Remy Martin .50
Hennessey Three Star .50
Martell's Three Star .50
Apricot .50
GINS
House of Lords .35
Milshire .25
Gordon's .25
Fleischmann's .25
Seagram's King Arthur .25
Fleischmann's Sloe Gin .30
RUMS
Bacardi Gold Label .45
Bacardi White Label .40
Burke's Jamaica .45
Carioca .35
Ronrico Gold or White .40
SOURS
Gin .30
Bourbon or Rye .35
Brandy .35
Whiskey Sour .35
CORDIALS
.50
D. O. M. Benedictine .50
Creme De Menthe .50
Cointreau .50
Curacoa .50
Apricot .50
Creme De Cacao .50
Kummel .50
Anisette .50
Chartreuse Yellow .50
Chartreuse Green
TALL DRINKS
.35
Gin Fizz .40
Sloe Gin Fizz .45
New Orleans .35
Tom Collins .40
Bourbon or Rye Rickey .40
Rum Collins .45
Royal Fizz .50
Cubre Libre .50
Planter's Punch
NON ALCOHOLIC
.25
Lemonade or Orangeade .25
Coca Cola .25
Root Beer .25
Seven Up .25
Gingerale — Canada Dry Split
BEER
.15
Budweiser — Glass .15
Michelob — Glass .25
Bottle Beers .25
Carling's Ale .30
Ballentine's Ale .40
Bass Nip

OPPOSITE Catacombs Caverns, c. 1942, Columbus, Ohio

ABOVE McDonnell's, c. 1939, Los Angeles, California

ABOVE **"It" Cafe, 1938, Hollywood, California**

LEFT **Romanoffs, 1949, Los Angeles, California**

OPPOSITE **Mocambo, c. 1945, Hollywood, California**

RIGHT **Earl Carroll Hollywood, 1941, Hollywood, California**

Backed by movie star and mogul investors, New York impresario Earl Carroll opened his Hollywood theater on Sunset Boulevard on December 26, 1938, as a supper club with the motto, "Through these portals pass the most beautiful girls in the world."

Der New Yorker Impresario Earl Carroll eröffnete sein von Filmstars und Millionären finanziertes Hollywood-Revuetheater am Sunset Boulevard am 26. Dezember 1938 als Supper Club unter dem Motto: „Durch diese Pforte schreiten die schönsten Mädchen der Welt."

Soutenu par des vedettes du cinéma et des grandes fortunes, l'imprésario newyorkais Earl Carroll ouvre son Hollywood Theater sur Sunset Boulevard le 26 décembre 1938, un club-restaurant arborant la devise « Sous ces portes passent les plus belles filles du monde ».

Mocambo

BELOW Sugie's Original Tropics, c. 1942, Beverly Hills, California

Opened by London-born Harry "Sugie" Sugarman on Rodeo Drive, this was a tropics-themed Hollywood restaurant. Sugarman named cocktails after contemporary stars like Dorothy Lamour, Errol Flynn, and Bette Davis. Its wine list was unusual in that it noted the region in California where the wines were from.

Dieses Hollywoodrestaurant mit Tropenambiente wurde von dem gebürtigen Londoner Harry „Sugie" Sugarman am Rodeo Drive eröffnet. Sugarman benannte seine Cocktails nach damaligen Stars wie Dorothy Lamour, Errol Flynn und Bette Davis. Die Weinliste war ungewöhnlich, weil sie die Anbaugebiete Kaliforniens aufführte, aus denen der Wein stammte.

Créé par le Londonien de naissance Harry « Sugie » Sugarman sur Rodeo Drive, ce restaurant hollywoodien avait pour thème les tropiques. Sugarman donnait à ses cocktails le nom des vedettes du moment, comme Dorothy Lamour, Errol Flynn et Bette Davis. La carte des vins est inhabituelle : sont en effet mentionnées les régions de Californie d'où proviennent les crus.

OPPOSITE Panther Room, Hotel Sherman, 1943, Chicago, Illinois

LUNCHEON
PANTHER ROOM
HOTEL SHERMAN
CHICAGO

LEFT **Pete's Bar, c. 1942, Chicago, Illinois**

BELOW **Monte Carlo Bar, c. 1937, Chicago, Illinois**

OPPOSITE **Russell's, c. 1942, Chicago, Illinois**

ABOVE **The College Inn, the Hotel Sherman, 1943, Chicago, Illinois**

The Hotel Sherman opened in 1837 as the City Hall, then in 1844 was renamed in honor of Chicago Mayor Francis Cornwall Sherman. Rebuilt after the 1871 Chicago fire and added onto later, the hotel had several dining venues, including the College Inn and the Panther Room, with live music and waiters dressed in turbans who served skewered kebabs.

Das Hotel Sherman hieß, als es 1837 eröffnet wurde, „City Hall“ und wurde 1844 zu Ehren des Chicagoer Bürgermeisters Francis Cornwall Sherman umbenannt. Nach dem großen Brand von 1871 wieder aufgebaut und später erweitert, besaß es mehrere Speisesäle, darunter das College Inn und den Panther Room, in dem es Live-Musik und mit Turbanen ausstaffierte Kellner gab, die Kebabs am Spieß servierten.

L'Hotel Sherman ouvre en 1837 sous le nom de City Hall, puis en 1844, il est rebaptisé en l'honneur du maire de Chicago, Francis Cornwall Sherman. Reconstruit après le grand incendie de la ville en 1871, puis agrandi, l'établissement dispose de plusieurs restaurants avec orchestre, dont le College Inn et le Panther Room, et des serveurs affublés de turbans y proposent des chiches-kebabs.

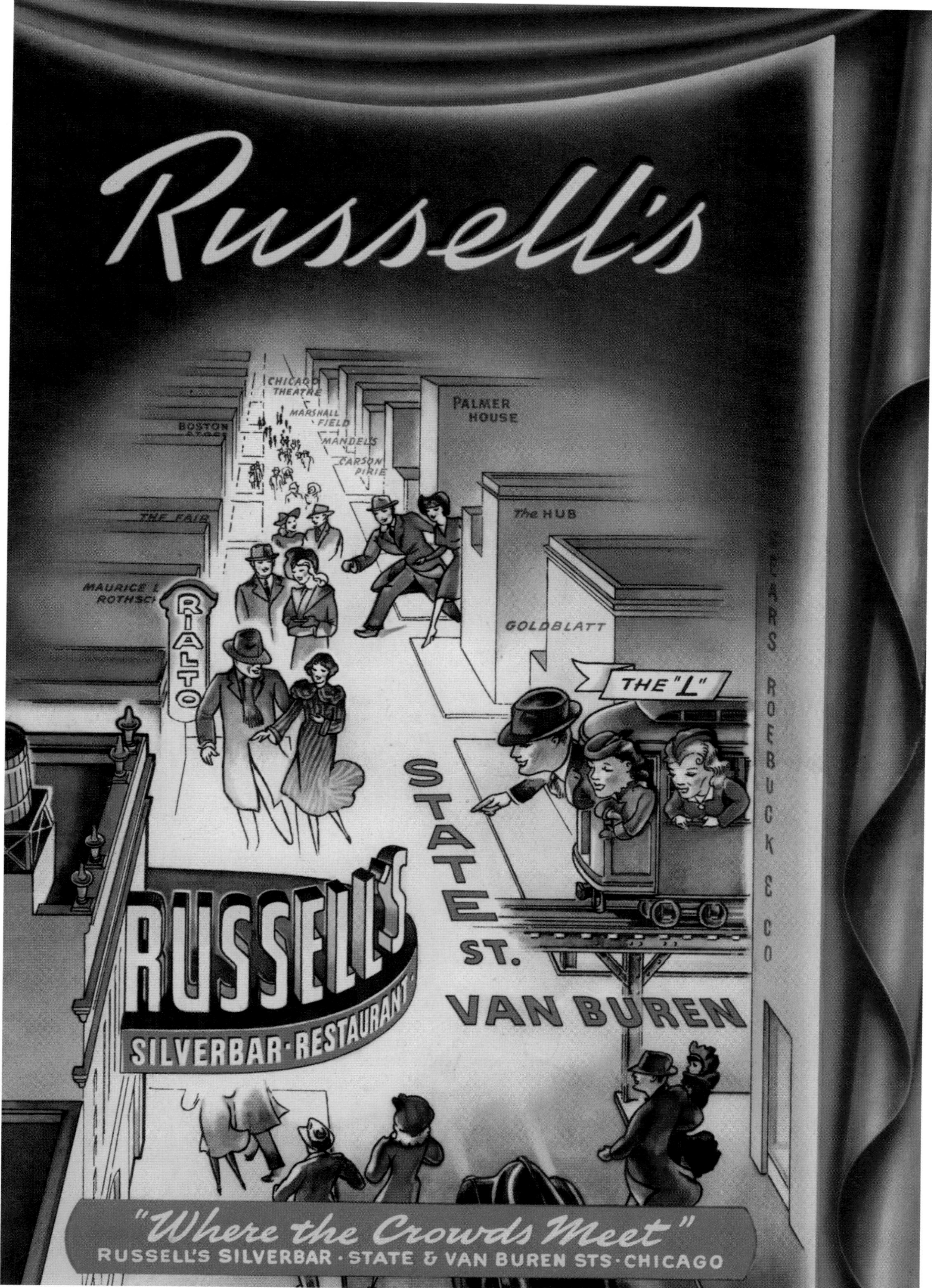
Russell's
CHICAGO THEATRE
MARSHALL FIELD
MANDELS
CARSON PIRIE
PALMER HOUSE
BOSTON
THE FAIR
The HUB
GOLDBLATT
RIALTO
THE "L"
SEARS ROEBUCK & CO
STATE ST.
VAN BUREN
RUSSELL'S
SILVERBAR·RESTAURANT·
"Where the Crowds Meet"
RUSSELL'S SILVERBAR · STATE & VAN BUREN STS · CHICAGO

LEFT & BELOW **The Flamingo Hotel, c. 1950, Las Vegas, Nevada**

Mobster Bugsy Siegel opened the $6 million Flamingo Hotel (allegedly named after his girlfriend Virginia "Flamingo" Hill) on December 26, 1946, with just 105 rooms.

Mafiaboss Bugsy Siegel ließ für 6 Mio. Dollar das Flamingo Hotel (angeblich nach seiner Freundin Virginia „Flamingo" Hill benannt) erbauen, das am 26. Dezember 1946 mit nur 105 Zimmern aufmachte.

Le 26 décembre 1946, le gangster Bugsy Siegel ouvre un hôtel à six millions de dollars, le Flamingo Hotel (peut-être en l'honneur de sa compagne Virginia «Flamingo» Hill). Il possède alors 105 chambres.

OPPOSITE **Hotel El Rancho, c. 1942, Las Vegas, Nevada**

THE Flamingo HOTEL

Featuring . . .

EASTERN PRIME BEEF, AGED TO PERFECTION

All Our Steaks and Chops Are Broiled Over Charcoal

New York Sirloin Steak
4.50

Filet Mignon
4.75

T-Bone Steak
5.00

Club Steak with Onions
3.50

Chateaubriand for 2 or more
5.50 per person

Double Thick French Lamb Chops
3.75

Extra Cut Prime Ribs of Beef
3.75

Served with French Fried or Baked Idaho Potato and Flamingo Toast or Hot Rolls and Butter

For the finest in Food and Entertainment . . .
"IT'S ALWAYS *The Flamingo!*"

HOTEL
El Rancho
VEGAS
El
RANCHO
VEGAS
WESTERN AMERICA'S FINEST

NO DANCING
STORK CLUB

OPPOSITE & BELOW The Stork Club, 1944, New York, New York

This photo of the main dining room and bar shows the elegant lunchtime atmosphere of the Stork Club, which opened in 1929 and then moved after Prohibition to 3 East 53rd Street. Gossip journalist Walter Winchell called it "New York's New Yorkiest place."

Dieses Foto vom großen Speisesaal und der Bar zeigt die mondäne Atmosphäre im Stork Club zur Mittagszeit; 1929 eröffnet, zog er nach der Prohibitionszeit an die 3 East 53rd Street. Der Klatschkolumnist Walter Winchell nannte ihn „New York's New Yorkiest place".

Cette photo de la salle principale et du bar révèle l'atmosphère élégante qui règne à l'heure du déjeuner au Stork Club. Ouvert en 1929, il emménage à la fin de la Prohibition au n° 3 de la 53ᵉ rue Est. L'échotier Walter Winchell le baptisera « l'endroit le plus new-yorkais de New York ».

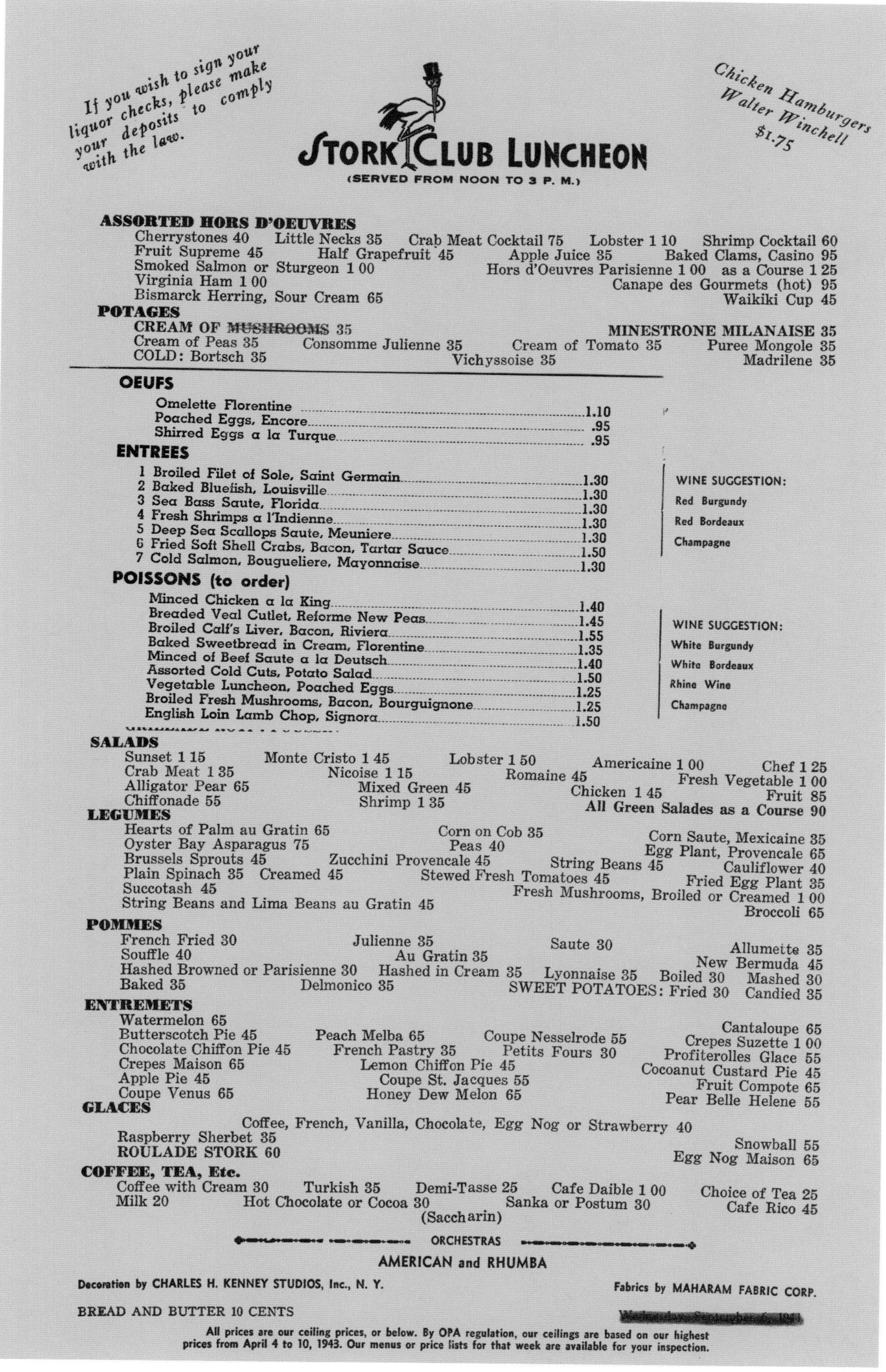

If you wish to sign your liquor checks, please make your deposits to comply with the law.

Chicken Hamburgers Walter Winchell $1.75

STORK CLUB LUNCHEON

(SERVED FROM NOON TO 3 P. M.)

ASSORTED HORS D'OEUVRES

Cherrystones 40 — Little Necks 35 — Crab Meat Cocktail 75 — Lobster 1 10 — Shrimp Cocktail 60
Fruit Supreme 45 — Half Grapefruit 45 — Apple Juice 35 — Baked Clams, Casino 95
Smoked Salmon or Sturgeon 1 00 — Hors d'Oeuvres Parisienne 1 00 as a Course 1 25
Virginia Ham 1 00 — Canape des Gourmets (hot) 95
Bismarck Herring, Sour Cream 65 — Waikiki Cup 45

POTAGES

CREAM OF ~~MUSHROOMS~~ 35 — MINESTRONE MILANAISE 35
Cream of Peas 35 — Consomme Julienne 35 — Cream of Tomato 35 — Puree Mongole 35
COLD: Bortsch 35 — Vichyssoise 35 — Madrilene 35

OEUFS

Omelette Florentine 1.10
Poached Eggs, Encore .... .95
Shirred Eggs a la Turque .... .95

ENTREES

1 Broiled Filet of Sole, Saint Germain 1.30
2 Baked Bluefish, Louisville 1.30
3 Sea Bass Saute, Florida 1.30
4 Fresh Shrimps a l'Indienne 1.30
5 Deep Sea Scallops Saute, Meuniere 1.30
6 Fried Soft Shell Crabs, Bacon, Tartar Sauce 1.50
7 Cold Salmon, Bouguelière, Mayonnaise 1.30

WINE SUGGESTION:
Red Burgundy
Red Bordeaux
Champagne

POISSONS (to order)

Minced Chicken a la King 1.40
Breaded Veal Cutlet, Reforme New Peas 1.45
Broiled Calf's Liver, Bacon, Riviera 1.55
Baked Sweetbread in Cream, Florentine 1.35
Minced of Beef Saute a la Deutsch 1.40
Assorted Cold Cuts, Potato Salad 1.50
Vegetable Luncheon, Poached Eggs 1.25
Broiled Fresh Mushrooms, Bacon, Bourguignone 1.25
English Loin Lamb Chop, Signora 1.50

WINE SUGGESTION:
White Burgundy
White Bordeaux
Rhine Wine
Champagne

SALADS

Sunset 1 15 — Monte Cristo 1 45 — Lobster 1 50 — Americaine 1 00 — Chef 1 25
Crab Meat 1 35 — Nicoise 1 15 — Romaine 45 — Fresh Vegetable 1 00
Alligator Pear 65 — Mixed Green 45 — Chicken 1 45 — Fruit 85
Chiffonade 55 — Shrimp 1 35 — All Green Salades as a Course 90

LEGUMES

Hearts of Palm au Gratin 65 — Corn on Cob 35 — Corn Saute, Mexicaine 35
Oyster Bay Asparagus 75 — Peas 40 — Egg Plant, Provencale 65
Brussels Sprouts 45 — Zucchini Provencale 45 — String Beans 45 — Cauliflower 40
Plain Spinach 35 Creamed 45 — Stewed Fresh Tomatoes 45 — Fried Egg Plant 35
Succotash 45 — Fresh Mushrooms, Broiled or Creamed 1 00
String Beans and Lima Beans au Gratin 45 — Broccoli 65

POMMES

French Fried 30 — Julienne 35 — Saute 30 — Allumette 35
Souffle 40 — Au Gratin 35 — New Bermuda 45
Hashed Browned or Parisienne 30 — Hashed in Cream 35 — Lyonnaise 35 — Boiled 30 — Mashed 30
Baked 35 — Delmonico 35 — SWEET POTATOES: Fried 30 Candied 35

ENTREMETS

Watermelon 65 — Cantaloupe 65
Butterscotch Pie 45 — Peach Melba 65 — Coupe Nesselrode 55 — Crepes Suzette 1 00
Chocolate Chiffon Pie 45 — French Pastry 35 — Petits Fours 30 — Profiterolles Glace 55
Crepes Maison 65 — Lemon Chiffon Pie 45 — Cocoanut Custard Pie 45
Apple Pie 45 — Coupe St. Jacques 55 — Fruit Compote 65
Coupe Venus 65 — Honey Dew Melon 65 — Pear Belle Helene 55

GLACES

Coffee, French, Vanilla, Chocolate, Egg Nog or Strawberry 40
Raspberry Sherbet 35 — Snowball 55
ROULADE STORK 60 — Egg Nog Maison 65

COFFEE, TEA, Etc.

Coffee with Cream 30 — Turkish 35 — Demi-Tasse 25 — Cafe Daible 1 00 — Choice of Tea 25
Milk 20 — Hot Chocolate or Cocoa 30 — Sanka or Postum 30 — Cafe Rico 45
(Saccharin)

ORCHESTRAS

AMERICAN and RHUMBA

Decoration by CHARLES H. KENNEY STUDIOS, Inc., N. Y. — Fabrics by MAHARAM FABRIC CORP.

BREAD AND BUTTER 10 CENTS

All prices are our ceiling prices, or below. By OPA regulation, our ceilings are based on our highest prices from April 4 to 10, 1943. Our menus or price lists for that week are available for your inspection.

HEADQUARTERS

108 WEST 49TH STREET · N. Y. C.

We Serve—ROYAL BANQUET—The Aristocrat of Blended Scotch-Type Whisky

Dinner

APPETIZERS

Iced Cantaloupe or Honey Dew Melon	45
Tomato Juice	20
Half Grapefruit	25
Filet of Maatjes Herring	35
Bismarck Herring	35
Marty's Fillets of Herring in Cream	40
Chopped Egg with Onions and Chicken Fat	40
Fruit Cup	45
Celery and Olives	45
Chopped Chicken Livers	45
Gefuelte Fish	50
Nova Scotia Salmon	65
Imported Sardines	75
Lake Sturgeon	75
Crab Meat Cocktail	75
Shrimp Cocktail	55
Lobster Cocktail	85
Hors d'Oeuvres Variees	85
Sea Food Cocktail	1.00
Crab Meat, Louis	1.25
Cherrystone Clams	50
Little Neck Clams	50

SOUPS

Cream of Asparagus	35
Chicken Consomme with Noodles	35
Cold Vichyssoise	40
Chilled Jellied Consomme	35
Onion Soup au Gratin	50
Clam Stew in Milk	65
Clam Stew in Cream	75

FISH

Broiled Halibut Steak, au Beurre	1.35
Broiled Fresh Weakfish, Maitre d'Hotel	1.35
Fried Soft Shell Crabs, Tartar Sauce, Cole Slaw	1.60
Broiled Kennebec Salmon Steak	1.50
Scallops Saute in Butter	1.45
Fried Jumbo Shrimps, Tartar Sauce, Cole Slaw	1.50
Whole Broiled Live Lobster (according to size)	
Lobster a la Newburgh	2.15

Above items served with Potatoes

For That After Theater Snack - HQ!

Headquarters will be closed on Sundays during the Summer

OPPOSITE Headquarters, c. 1945, New York, New York

As head service man for the headquarters of General Dwight Eisenhower during World War II, Sergeant John Schwarz catered to the military and civilian elite in the European theatre. After the war he used his experience as planner and culinary organizer to open a fine dining restaurant called Headquarters with partner Chas Fodor.

Sergeant John Schwarz war während des Zweiten Weltkriegs für das leibliche Wohl der militärischen und zivilen Elite im europäischen Hauptquartier von General Dwight Eisenhower zuständig. Nach dem Krieg nutzte er seine Kenntnisse als kulinarischer Organisator und eröffnete zusammen mit seinem Partner Chas Fodor das elegante Restaurant Headquarters.

Responsable du QG du général Dwight Eisenhower au cours de la Seconde Guerre mondiale, le sergent John Schwarz a cuisiné pour l'élite militaire et civile en Europe. Après-guerre, il a mis à profit son expérience de l'organisation et de la planification culinaires pour ouvrir avec Chas Fodor un restaurant gastronomique baptisé le Headquarters (le «QG»).

ABOVE Bruce's Blackout Cafe, 1943, Honolulu, Hawaii

LEFT Super Grouper Dooper, 335th Bomb Group, c. 1944, Barksdale Field, Louisiana

BELOW The Liberty Room, the Plaza, c. 1944, New York, New York

OPPOSITE New York Central System, c. 1943

ABOVE The French Room, Hotel William Penn, 1946, Philadelphia, Pennsylvania

ABOVE RIGHT Hotel Astor, c. 1943, New York, New York

Patriotic symbolism abounded on menus during World War II, and some restaurants were given patriotic names, like the Liberty Room. The Hotel Astor's menu shows the motif of Uncle Sam being thrown into the ring of conflict.

Patriotische Symbole fanden sich während des Zweiten Weltkriegs überall auf Speisekarten, und manche Restaurants erhielten sogar patriotische Namen wie Liberty Room. Auf der Karte des Hotel Astor wird Uncle Sam in den Konflikt hineingezogen.

Le symbolisme patriotique abonde dans les menus au cours de la Seconde Guerre mondiale. Certains restaurants portent des noms idoines, tels que le Liberty Room. Oncle Sam projeté au cœur du conflit illustre cette carte de l'Hotel Astor.

V
NEW YORK
CENTRAL
SYSTEM

CHEF'S
MIXED GREEN
SALAD BOWL
30c
½ ORDER 15c

DINNERS

BUY DEFENSE BONDS AND STAMPS

OUR OLD SOUTHERN BARBECUE DINNER

Barbecued Spareribs	.80
Barbecued Shortribs	.80
Barbecued Beef	.80
Barbecued Pork	.80
Barbecued Ham	1.00
Barbecued Chicken	1.15

SERVED WITH ABOVE
Salad with Special Dressing,
French Fries, Barbecued Beans,
Sour Dough French Bread and Butter
Sweet Potato or Apple Pie, Ice Cream or Sherbet
Coffee, Tea or Milk
All the Barbecue Sauce You Want

"OLD DIXIE"
SPECIAL BARBECUED DINNER
INCLUDES
Beef, Ham, Pork and Spareribs,
French Fries and Salad
Barbecued Beans and Sweet Potato or Apple Pie,
French Bread and Fresh Creamery Butter,
Choice of Coffee, Tea or Buttermilk
All the Barbecue Sauce You Wish
$1.00

Try Our
BRANDY AND SODA
for Dinner

OPPOSITE **The Cotton Club, c. 1937, New York, New York**

After a race riot in 1935, the Harlem club closed the following year, then reopened on Broadway and 48th Street, eventually shutting its doors for good in 1940.

Nach Rassenunruhen 1935 schloss der Klub in Harlem, machte dann an Broadway und 48th Street wieder auf und schloss 1940 endgültig seine Pforten.

À la suite d'une émeute raciale en 1935, le club de Harlem ferme, puis rouvre au coin de Broadway et de la 48e rue. Il fermera définitivement en 1940.

ABOVE **Old Dixie Southern Barbeque, c. 1941, Los Angeles, California**

A black "mammy" figure was common to Southern-style menus, dating back to minstrel show figures and the song "Old Aunt Jemima" (1875).

Eine schwarze „Mammy"-Figur war auf den Speisekarten in den Südstaaten keine Seltenheit. Die Figur entstammt den Minstrel Shows und dem Lied „Old Aunt Jemima" (1875).

Une nourrice noire apparaît souvent sur les menus qui puisent leur inspiration dans le Sud des États-Unis et renvoie à l'époque des spectacles où des Blancs se déguisaient en Noirs. Elle rappelle également la chanson *Old Aunt Jemima* (1875).

THE WORLD FAMOUS
COTTON CLUB

Menu
PABST BLUE RIBBON BEER

OPPOSITE Harv's Cafe, 1938

RIGHT Budweiser, c. 1940

BELOW Acme Ale, the Oakwood Barbecue, 1938, Treasure Island, San Francisco, California

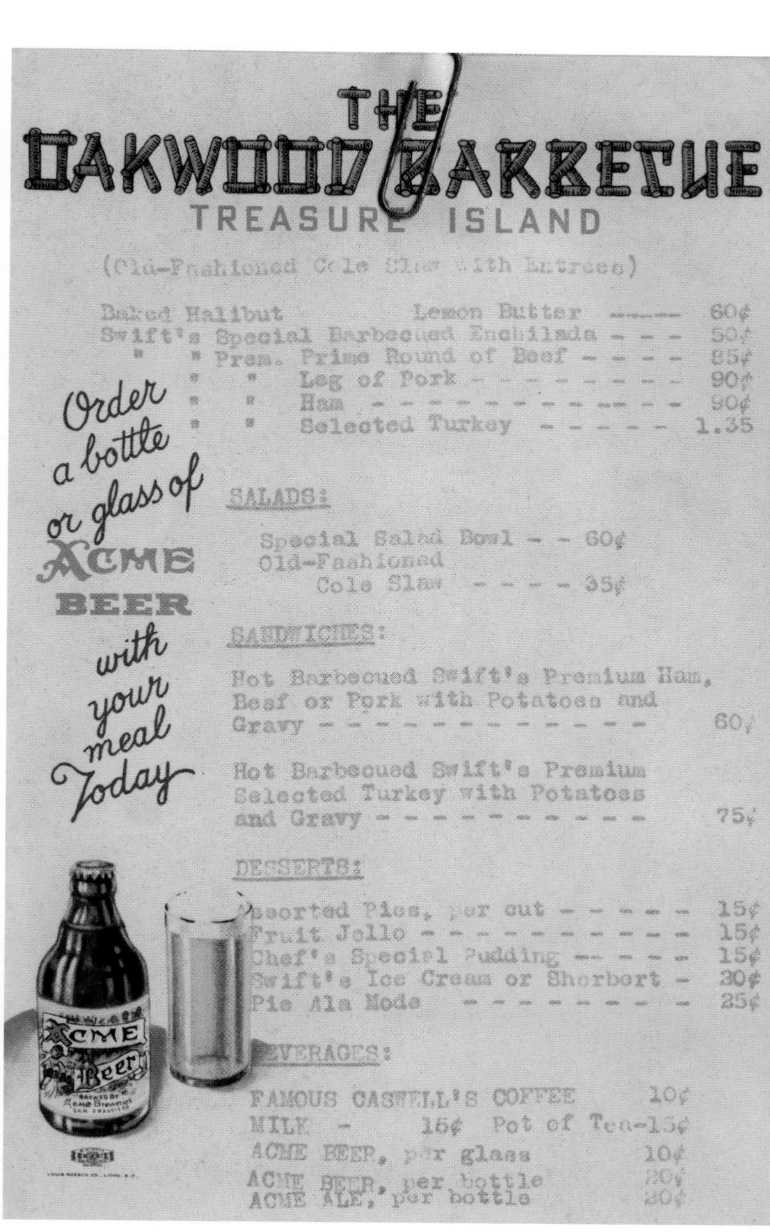

THE OAKWOOD BARBECUE
TREASURE ISLAND

(Old-Fashioned Cole Slaw with Entrees)

Baked Halibut Lemon Butter ---- 60¢
Swift's Special Barbecued Enchilada - - - 50¢
" " Prem. Prime Round of Beef - - - - 85¢
" " Leg of Pork - - - - - - - - 90¢
" " Ham - - - - - - - - - - - - 90¢
" " Selected Turkey - - - - - 1.35

Order a bottle or glass of ACME BEER with your meal Today

SALADS:

Special Salad Bowl - - 60¢
Old-Fashioned
Cole Slaw - - - - 35¢

SANDWICHES:

Hot Barbecued Swift's Premium Ham, Beef or Pork with Potatoes and Gravy - - - - - - - - - - - - 60¢

Hot Barbecued Swift's Premium Selected Turkey with Potatoes and Gravy - - - - - - - - - - 75¢

DESSERTS:

Assorted Pies, per cut - - - - - 15¢
Fruit Jello - - - - - - - - - - 15¢
Chef's Special Pudding -- - - - 15¢
Swift's Ice Cream or Sherbert - 30¢
Pie Ala Mode - - - - - - - - 25¢

BEVERAGES:

FAMOUS CASWELL'S COFFEE 10¢
MILK - 15¢ Pot of Tea-15¢
ACME BEER, per glass 10¢
ACME BEER, per bottle 20¢
ACME ALE, per bottle 20¢

THIS PAGE Pump Room, Ambassador East Hotel, 1945, Chicago, Illinois

The Pump Room opened in 1938 by hotelier Ernest Lessing Byfield. The service was famous for cooking and serving many dishes on flaming swords. "We flame everything," Byfield once said, "but it doesn't seem to hurt the food much."

Der 1938 von Hotelier Ernest Lessing Byfield eröffnete Pump Room war berühmt für seine Küche und servierte viele Gerichte flambiert und aufgespießt auf Säbeln. „Wir flambieren alles, aber es scheint dem Essen nicht viel auszumachen", sagte Byfield einmal.

Ernest Lessing Byfield ouvre le Pump Room en 1938, un restaurant réputé pour la préparation et le service de nombreux plats sur des épées enflammées. « Nous flambons tout, déclara Byfield, mais la nourriture ne semble pas s'en plaindre. »

OPPOSITE Armando, 1939, New York, New York

Cream Soups & Conſommés.

Potage Portugueſe 30 *Conſomme Princeſs 30*
Eſſence of Black Muſhrooms au Chablis 40
Cold Creme Vichyſſoiſe 35 *Chicken Cuban, Carola 35*

Freſh from the Lakes & Seas.

Boneleſs Baby Pike, Split and Broiled, Tomato with Cucumbers 1.35
Filets of Lake Trout Saute Meuniere, Perſillade Potato 1.35
Broiled Live Lobſter, Potatoes 2.75 Baked Devilled Giant Crab 1.65
Baked Stuffed Lobſter, Thermidor 2.75 Lake Superior Jumbo Whitefiſh 1.75
Crepes Louiſe, Freſh Crabmeat in Madeira Sauce 1.65
Fried Filets of Flounder, Tartar Sauce, Cole Slaw, Potato 1.35

Sandwiches.

Salmon Salad with Diced Sweet Pickles and Egg on Toaſt 75
Fried Egg on Toaſt, French Fried Potatoes and Slice Tomato 75
Pump Room Chicken Haſh Sandwich 1.35 *Bal Tabarin 1.25* *Chicken 90*
Chicken Salad on Toaſt 90 Freſh Lobſter Club 1.35 Pump Room Club 1.00
Ariſtocrat: Sliced Chicken, Roquefort Cheeſe au Gratin 1.35 *Chef's Special 1.25*
Toaſted Sardines, Houſe of Parliamant 90

Criſp Salads, Stuffed Avacados & Tomatoes

Kentucky Limeſtone Lettuce with Heart of Artichoke and Egg 70
Tomato Stuffed with Chicken Salad 1.10 *Freſh Fruit Plate with Cottage Cheese 95*
Avocado Filled with Freſh Crabmeat or Shrimps 1.25 Hollywood Bowl 1.35
Criſp Hearts of Lettuce 55 *Pump Room Bowl 55 (on wagon)* *Chiffonade Salad 55*
Crabmeat Salad 1.75 Shrimp Salad 1.65
Freſh Fruit, Pump Room Dreſſing 1.10 *Freſh Vegetable Salad 1.00* *Lorenza Salad 65*
Chicken Salad 1.75 Chicken and Vegetable 1.65
Aſparagus Vinaigrette 1.00 *Half Avocado Pear 55*
Dreſſings: Lorenzo 25; Thouſand Iſland 25; Roquefort 35
Perrymead Pear Vinegar uſed in all dreſſings

Chafing Diſh & Skillet.

Chicken Saute Ambaſſador, Hearts of Artichoke and Muſhrooms, Wine Sauce 2.00
Chicken Tetrazzini 1.75
Creamed Capon on Buttered Noodles 1.85 *Shrimps Louiſiana 1.65*
Capon and Lobſter Madeira, Rice 2.25 Crabflakes Narraganſette 1.85
Chicken a la King 1.85 *Freſh Lobſter, Newburg 2.75*

Curries from India.

Rijſttafel: Lobſter, Shrimps or Crabmeat 1.85 Half Chicken Unjointed, Calcutta 2.00
Curry of Capon Flakes a l'Indienne 1.85 *Pilaff of Chicken, Minaret 1.85*
Freſh Shrimps and Rice 1.75 Curried Hard Boiled Eggs and Avocado Pear 1.50
Kabab with Rice 1.65

All prices are our ceiling prices, or below. By OPA regulation, our ceilings are based on our highest prices from April 4 to 10, 1943. Our menus or price lists for that week are available for your inspection

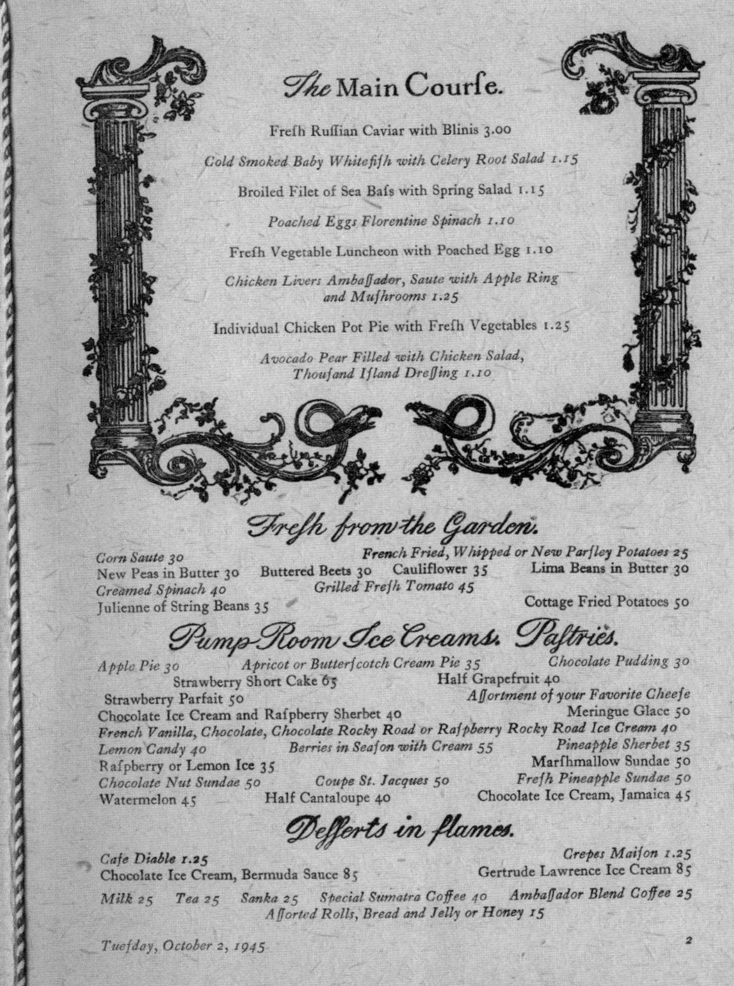

The Main Courſe.

Freſh Ruſſian Caviar with Blinis 3.00
Cold Smoked Baby Whitefiſh with Celery Root Salad 1.15
Broiled Filet of Sea Baſs with Spring Salad 1.15
Poached Eggs Florentine Spinach 1.10
Freſh Vegetable Luncheon with Poached Egg 1.10
Chicken Livers Ambaſſador, Saute with Apple Ring and Muſhrooms 1.25
Individual Chicken Pot Pie with Freſh Vegetables 1.25
Avocado Pear Filled with Chicken Salad, Thouſand Iſland Dreſſing 1.10

Freſh from the Garden.

Corn Saute 30 *French Fried, Whipped or New Parſley Potatoes 25*
New Peas in Butter 30 Buttered Beets 30 Cauliflower 35 Lima Beans in Butter 30
Creamed Spinach 40 *Grilled Freſh Tomato 45*
Julienne of String Beans 35 Cottage Fried Potatoes 50

Pump Room Ice Creams. Paſtries.

Apple Pie 30 *Apricot or Butterſcotch Cream Pie 35* *Chocolate Pudding 30*
Strawberry Short Cake 65 Half Grapefruit 40
Strawberry Parfait 50 *Aſſortment of your Favorite Cheeſe*
Chocolate Ice Cream and Raſpberry Sherbet 40 Meringue Glace 50
French Vanilla, Chocolate, Chocolate Rocky Road or Raſpberry Rocky Road Ice Cream 40
Lemon Candy 40 *Berries in Seaſon with Cream 55* *Pineapple Sherbet 35*
Raſpberry or Lemon Ice 35 Marſhmallow Sundae 50
Chocolate Nut Sundae 50 *Coupe St. Jacques 50* *Freſh Pineapple Sundae 50*
Watermelon 45 Half Cantaloupe 40 Chocolate Ice Cream, Jamaica 45

Deſſerts in flames.

Cafe Diable 1.25 *Crepes Maiſon 1.25*
Chocolate Ice Cream, Bermuda Sauce 85 Gertrude Lawrence Ice Cream 85
Milk 25 *Tea 25* *Sanka 25* *Special Sumatra Coffee 40* *Ambaſſador Blend Coffee 25*
Aſſorted Rolls, Bread and Jelly or Honey 15

Tueſday, October 2, 1945 2

Franklin Hughes
A

OPPOSITE The Colony, 1940, New York, New York

ABOVE & RIGHT The Colony, 1954, New York, New York

Vying with Le Pavillon for New York's fine-dining crowd, the Colony, at 667 Madison Avenue, originated under Joe Pani as a bistro serving booze to gamblers in the back. After Prohibition, new owners turned it into a society restaurant on East 62nd Street, where, said *Vogue* magazine, "it was harder to get a good table at the Colony than to join the Junior League."

The Colony und Le Pavillon lagen nach dem Krieg im Wettstreit als New Yorks feinste Adressen zum Speisen. Ursprünglich war das Restaurant an der 667 Madison Avenue eine Kaschemme, deren Besitzer Joe Pani den Kartenspielern im Hinterzimmer Alkohol ausschenkte. Nach der Prohibitionszeit verwandelten neue Besitzer das Lokal in einen gesellschaftlichen Treffpunkt an der East 62nd Street, wo es laut *Vogue Magazine* „schwieriger war, einen Tisch zu bekommen als Mitglied der Junior League zu werden".

Rivalisant dans l'après-guerre avec Le Pavillon pour attirer les fins gourmets de New York, The Colony est à l'origine un tripot ouvert par Joe Pani au n° 667 de Madison Avenue, où l'on sert de l'alcool aux joueurs dans l'arrière-salle. À la fin de la Prohibition, les nouveaux propriétaires transforment l'établissement en un restaurant de la bonne société donnant sur la 62ᵉ rue Est. Le magazine *Vogue* affirme qu'« il y est plus difficile d'obtenir une table que d'entrer dans la Junior League ».

Dejeuner

Les Hors d'Oeuvres

Suprême de Fruits 1.00 Melon Rafraichi 1.00 Paté Maison 2.00
B. & B. et Celeris .75 Canapé Colony 1.75 Saumon Fumé 1.75
Truite Fumée Sauce Raifort 1.75 Anguille au Vin Blanc 1.75
Tomate Surprise 1.75 Whitefish Fumé 1.75 Chair de Crabe 1.75
Poire Avocado Colony 2.00 Crevettes à la Russe 1.75
Blue Points 1.00 Sea Cress 1.00 Canadian 1.00 Cherrystones .90

Potages

Le Potage Minestrone .90 Le Consommé Vert Pré .90
La Crème Germiny .90 La Soupe à l'Oignon Gratinée 1.00
Froid: Madrilène .90 Bortch .90 Waterbury .90 Vichyssoise .90

Oeufs

Pochés Florentine 1.90 Omelette Fines herbes 2.00
Sur le Plat Bercy 1.90 Benedict 1.90

Poissons

Les Suprêmes de Sole Anglaise Cancalaise 3.00 La Bass de Mer Rayée Grillée Casino 3.00
Les Goujeonettes de Flounder Frites Tartare 3.00 Le Swordfish Sauté Bretonne 3.00
Les Scallops du L. Island Marinière 3.00 Les Crevettes Rosées Newburg 3.00

Entrees

Le Boeuf Bouilli Assorti 3.50
Le Vol-au-Vent de Volaille à la Reine 3.00
Escalope de Veau Grillée aux Champignons 3.25
La Brochette de Rognons d'Agneau Vert Pré 3.00
Les Bitokes de Veau à la Russe Sauce Smitane 3.50
Les Macaronis au Gratin 2.25 La Côte d'Agneau à l'Anglaise au Cresson 3.50
Le Pied de Porc Sainte Menehould Pommes Mousseline 3.00

Vin en Carafe, Blanc et Rouge, La Carafe $2.00; La Demie 1.00

Legumes

Broccolis Hollandaise 1.20 Celeris Braisés 1.20 Corn Colony 1.00
Choux de Bruxelles .95 Carottes Vichy .95 Haricots de Lima .95
Haricots Verts .95 Courgettes .95 Petits Pois .95 Pommes de Terre .95

Salades

Laitue .85 Romaine .85 Escarole .85 Endives 1.10
Poire Avocado 1.35 Chiffonade 1.10

Entremets

Petits Fours .75 Compote de Fruits 1.00 Crêpes Suzette 2.00
Beignets Soufflés Sauce Sabayon 1.35 Poire Sicilienne 1.75
Meringue Glacée 1.30 Profiterolles au Chocolat 1.30

Glaces

Vanille .95 Chocolat .95 Café .95 Fraise .95 Pistachio .95
Ananas .95 Framboise .95 Citron .95 Orange .95

9/30/1954.

SHEFFER
PAN AMERICAN ROOM

LEFT **New Year's Eve, Hotel Taft, 1939, New York, New York**

BELOW **New Year's Eve, Illinois Athletic Club, 1938, Chicago, Illinois**

OPPOSITE **Pan American Room, La Salle Hotel, 1944, Chicago, Illinois**

ABOVE **New Year's Eve, Embassy Cafe, 1938, San Francisco, California**

A carnival-like reverie and commedia dell'arte figures are shown celebrating the New Year in front of San Francisco's Ferry Building terminal on the Embarcadero. It opened in 1898 and survived the 1906 earthquake.

Fröhliche Clowns und Figuren aus der Commedia dell'arte feiern vor dem Ferry Building am Embarcadero in San Francisco Silvester. Das Hafengebäude wurde 1898 eingeweiht und überstand das Erdbeben 1906.

Dans une sorte de rêverie carnavalesque, des personnages de la commedia dell'arte célèbrent le nouvel an devant le terminal du ferry de San Francisco, sur l'Embarcadero. Ouvert en 1898, il survivra au séisme de 1906.

LEFT & BELOW New Year's Eve, Hotel Del Monte, 1940, Monterey, California

OPPOSITE New Year's Eve, the Congress, 1924, Chicago, Illinois

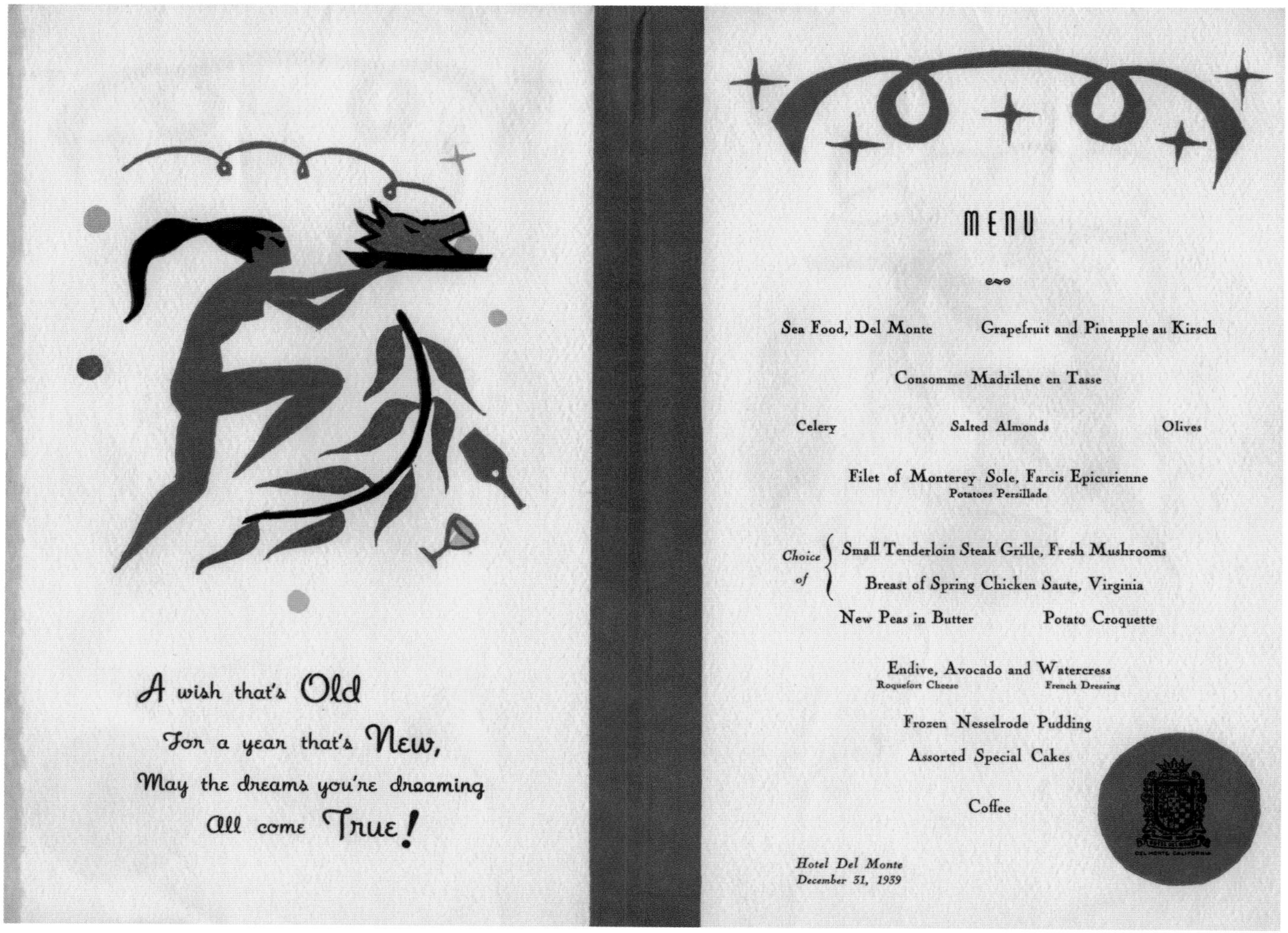

A wish that's Old
For a year that's New,
May the dreams you're dreaming
All come True!

MENU

Sea Food, Del Monte — Grapefruit and Pineapple au Kirsch

Consomme Madrilene en Tasse

Celery — Salted Almonds — Olives

Filet of Monterey Sole, Farcis Epicurienne
Potatoes Persillade

Choice of:
- Small Tenderloin Steak Grille, Fresh Mushrooms
- Breast of Spring Chicken Saute, Virginia

New Peas in Butter — Potato Croquette

Endive, Avocado and Watercress
Roquefort Cheese — French Dressing

Frozen Nesselrode Pudding

Assorted Special Cakes

Coffee

Hotel Del Monte
December 31, 1939

New Year's Eve
at the Congress
BRI

NEW YEAR'S
EVE
The Lotus

OPPOSITE New Year's Eve, the Lotus, 1945

LEFT Zamboanga, c. 1943, Los Angeles, California

RIGHT & BELOW The Nut Club, 1944, Richmond, California

COCKTAILS

Martini	60
Manhattan	60
Alexander	75
Bacardi	65
Daiquiri	65
Clover Club	65
Pink Lady	65
Pink Rose	60
Honolulu	65
Havana	65
Mary Pickford	65
Presidente	70
Orange Blossom	65
La Florida	75
Old Fashioned	60
Sazerac	70
Dubonnet	60
Svissesse	75
Stinger	75
Paradise	70
Side Car	75
Ward 8	70
Coffee	75
Champagne	1.00

WHISKEYS and Mixed Drinks

Bourbon	50
Call	60
Bottled in Bond	65
Balfours — 8 yrs. old	65
Call Scotch — 8 yrs. old	65
Balfours Scotch — 15 yrs. old	75
Call Scotch — 12 yrs. old	75
Rum	50
Brandy	50
Gin	50
Christian Bros. Brandy	60
Singapore Sling	75
Zombie	1.50
Mint Julep	1.50
Nut Club Cooler	1.75

Watch Your Step—2 to a Customer

SNAX

Victory (Baked Virginia Ham, Lettuce, Tomato)	50
Sensation (Roast Turkey, Lettuce, Tomato)	75
Nut Club (Sliced Chicken Club Double Decker)	1.00

Potatoe Chips & Olives Served with Our SNAX

ABOVE House of Murphy, c. 1942, Los Angeles, California

BELOW Walt Disney's Studio Restaurant, c. 1942, Burbank, California

Movie studio restaurants served laborers and stars with economical prices to keep them from straying off the lot.

Die Kantinen der Filmstudios boten allen, von Bühnenarbeitern bis Filmstars, preisgünstiges Essen an, damit in den Pausen niemand das Filmgelände verließ.

Les restaurants des studios de cinéma servaient à manger pour un prix modique à l'ensemble du personnel – des ouvriers jusqu'aux plus grandes vedettes – afin de lui éviter de s'éloigner des plateaux de tournage.

OPPOSITE Florentine Gardens, c. 1944, Hollywood, California

Florentine Gardens opened in 1938 attempting to rival Earl Carroll's but with more of a middle-class tourist clientele.

Das Florentine Gardens bemühte sich ab 1938, für ein gutbürgerliches und touristisches Publikum so berühmt wie das Earl Carroll's zu werden.

Le Florentine Gardens ouvre ses portes en 1938 pour rivaliser avec le restaurant de l'Earl Carroll Theater. La clientèle touristique, cependant, appartient plutôt à la classe moyenne.

FRUITS

Baked Apple with Cream 15
Sliced Bananas with Cream 15
Berries in Season 15
Half Grapefruit 10
Sliced Oranges 10
Sliced Pineapple 10
Stewed Prunes 10
Melons in Season 15

FRUIT JUICES

Orange Juice 10 · Grapefruit Juice 10 · Tomato Juice 10
Pineapple Juice 10 · Grape Juice 15

POST'S CEREALS

All Cereals Served with Cream
Hot Cereal 15 · Grape-Nuts 15 · Grape-Nut Flakes 15
Whole Bran Shreds 15 · Post Toasties 15
Post Bran Flakes 15 · Huskies 15

EGGS, OMELETTES, ETC.

Two Eggs: Fried, Scrambled, Boiled or Poached 25; with Ham, Bacon, or Sausage 40
Shirred Eggs (2) 25 · Plain Omelette 25 · French Toast 25
Fried Ham 25 · Rasher of Bacon 20 · Link Sausages 25
French Lamb Chops 50 · Corned Beef Hash 25; with Poached Egg 30
Toast and Potatoes with Above

HOT CAKES AND WAFFLES

Wheat, Corn, or Buckwheat Cakes with Syrup and Butter 15
Cream Waffle 20
Waffle or Cakes with Ham, Sausage, Bacon or Two Eggs 35

TOAST AND ROLLS

Toast with Jelly 10 · Milk Toast 20 · Cinnamon Toast 15
Hot Rolls with Jely 10 · Pound Cake 10 · Hot Muffins, each 05
Coffee Cake 10 · Doughnuts, each 05 · Sweet Rolls 10
Strawberry Preserves 10 · Orange Marmalade 10

BEVERAGES

Coffee 05 · Tea 10 · Postum 10 · Sanka 10
Milk 10 · Chocolate 10 · Buttermilk 05

3% Sales Tax will be added to all taxable items

Hollywood / Hollywood

Les Comiques
AMERICA'S HAPPIEST INSTITUTION
HOLLYWOOD PLAZA HOTEL
YA ALMOST HAD 'IM WHEN HE WAS AGAINST TH' ROPES -- LISSEN-- CAREFUL NOW -- AS SOON AS HE COMES OUT---
OKAY.
THIS IS ORFUL SUDDING, GIVE ME 30 SECONDS TO THINK IT OVER-- YA MUSTN' MOVE
TIME IN THE FUTURE- THIS AFTER-NOON
MAKE IT 20 SECONDS
KNOW YOU, MR. BOGGS!
MOMENTS LATER, THE MAN OF TOMORROW IS ZOOMING CROSS-COUNTRY AT INCREDIBLE SPEED—
700 MILES IN 1:03:27... IT'S THIS STORM THAT'S SLOWING ME UP!
NOW, THE PROBLUM IS – IS HE ALIVE OR HAIN'T HE? – AN' DO HE COUNT FO' AS MUCH IN ONE CONDISHUN AS IN TH' OTHER? – AN EF SO, HOW M-MUCH?
HERE, BLACKIE, YOU HOLD THE BABY, WHILE I TELEPHONE TO FIND OUT WHERE IT CAME FROM!
-THE CHILDREN AREN'T GOING TO BE JUDGED FOR THEIR BEAUTY, YOU KNOW
WELL, WELL! IMAGINE HEARING FROM THE OLD GIRL, HERSELF! I WONDER WHAT'S UP -- SHE NEVER DID LIKE ME!
DROP THAT GIN RUMMY GAME, COOKIE, AND RUSH HOME! I GOTTA BIG SURPRISE FOR YOU - IT'S THE HOTTEST THING YOU EVER LAMPED!
PARTY LION
WIF ALL THAT TIED UP IN HER, NOW, CAIN'T EVEN GIVE HER AWAY!!
OW
MY EARS ARE RINGIN' LIKE A BUZZ-SAW! I'LL WAGER TH' VARMINT WHUT'S MAKIN' DEROGGERY REMARKS ABAAT ME HAIN'T GOT A PENNY IN HIS STOCKIN'.
I'D SAY TH' WOMEN GET A TOUGH DEAL, JAKE!
UND DEN GOLDIE-LOCKS SAID TO DER MIDDLE-SIZED BEAR---

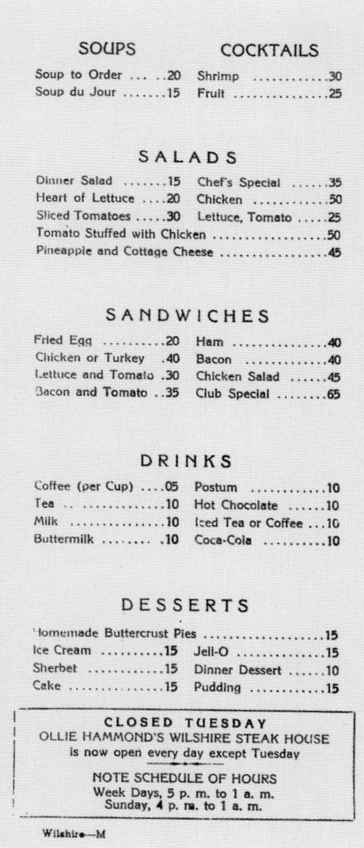

SOUPS

Soup to Order .... .20
Soup du Jour .... .15

COCKTAILS

Shrimp .... .30
Fruit .... .25

SALADS

Dinner Salad .... .15
Heart of Lettuce .... .20
Sliced Tomatoes ..... .30
Chef's Special ...... .35
Chicken .... .50
Lettuce, Tomato ..... .25
Tomato Stuffed with Chicken .... .50
Pineapple and Cottage Cheese .... .45

SANDWICHES

Fried Egg .... .20
Chicken or Turkey ... .40
Lettuce and Tomato . .30
Bacon and Tomato .. .35
Ham .... .40
Bacon .... .40
Chicken Salad ..... .45
Club Special .... .65

DRINKS

Coffee (per Cup) .... .05
Tea .... .10
Milk .... .10
Buttermilk .... .10
Postum .... .10
Hot Chocolate ..... .10
Iced Tea or Coffee ... .10
Coca-Cola .... .10

DESSERTS

Homemade Buttercrust Pies .... .15
Ice Cream .... .15
Sherbet .... .15
Cake .... .15
Jell-O .... .15
Dinner Dessert ..... .10
Pudding .... .15

CLOSED TUESDAY
OLLIE HAMMOND'S WILSHIRE STEAK HOUSE
is now open every day except Tuesday
NOTE SCHEDULE OF HOURS
Week Days, 5 p. m. to 1 a. m.
Sunday, 4 p. m. to 1 a. m.

Wilshire—M

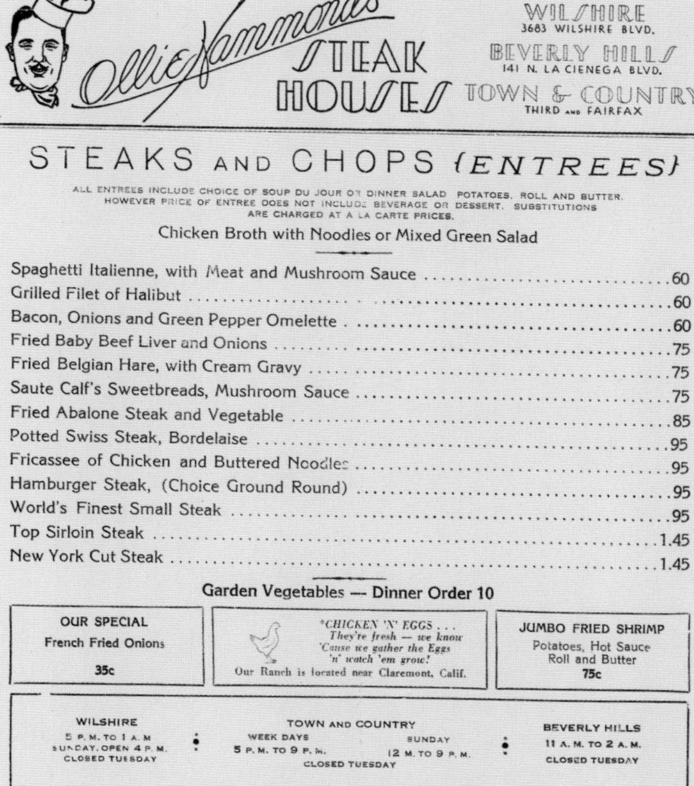

Ollie Hammond's STEAK HOUSES

WILSHIRE 3683 WILSHIRE BLVD.
BEVERLY HILLS 141 N. LA CIENEGA BLVD.
TOWN & COUNTRY THIRD AND FAIRFAX

STEAKS AND CHOPS (ENTREES)

ALL ENTREES INCLUDE CHOICE OF SOUP DU JOUR OR DINNER SALAD POTATOES, ROLL AND BUTTER. HOWEVER PRICE OF ENTREE DOES NOT INCLUDE BEVERAGE OR DESSERT. SUBSTITUTIONS ARE CHARGED AT A LA CARTE PRICES.

Chicken Broth with Noodles or Mixed Green Salad

Spaghetti Italienne, with Meat and Mushroom Sauce .... .60
Grilled Filet of Halibut .... .60
Bacon, Onions and Green Pepper Omelette .... .60
Fried Baby Beef Liver and Onions .... .75
Fried Belgian Hare, with Cream Gravy .... .75
Saute Calf's Sweetbreads, Mushroom Sauce .... .75
Fried Abalone Steak and Vegetable .... .85
Potted Swiss Steak, Bordelaise .... .95
Fricassee of Chicken and Buttered Noodles .... .95
Hamburger Steak, (Choice Ground Round) .... .95
World's Finest Small Steak .... .95
Top Sirloin Steak 1.45
New York Cut Steak 1.45

Garden Vegetables — Dinner Order 10

OUR SPECIAL
French Fried Onions
35c

"CHICKEN 'N' EGGS ...
They're fresh — we know
'Cause we gather the Eggs
'n' watch 'em grow!
Our Ranch is located near Claremont, Calif.

JUMBO FRIED SHRIMP
Potatoes, Hot Sauce
Roll and Butter
75c

WILSHIRE
5 P. M. TO 1 A. M.
SUNDAY, OPEN 4 P. M.
CLOSED TUESDAY

TOWN AND COUNTRY
WEEK DAYS 5 P. M. TO 9 P. M.
SUNDAY 12 M. TO 9 P. M.
CLOSED TUESDAY

BEVERLY HILLS
11 A. M. TO 2 A. M.
CLOSED TUESDAY

All prices listed are at or below our ceiling prices. By O. P. A. regulation, our ceiling prices are our highest prices from April 4th to April 10th, 1943. Records of these prices are available for your inspection.

SPECIALTIES

SMALL STEAK SANDWICH
With Potatoes, Lettuce, Tomato, Steak Sauce and Grilled Onion .... .55

HAMBURGER SANDWICH
With Lettuce, Mayonnaise, Steak Sauce and Potato Chips .... .25

CHILI AND BEANS
Our Original, Exclusive Recipe, Made Fresh Daily 25

LITTLE THIN HOT CAKES
With Butter and Maple Syrup .... .25

MAIN STREETS
With Butter and Maple Syrup .... .35

FRENCH TOAST
With Powdered Sugar, Jelly or Syrup .... .45

BREAKFAST SUGGESTIONS
SERVICE INCLUDES POTATOES, TOAST, JELLY AND COFFEE

Two Eggs .... .40
Bacon and Eggs .... .65
Sausage and Eggs ... .70
Ham and Eggs ...... .75
Plain Omelette ...... .45
Ham Omelette ...... .55
Spanish Omelette ... .55
Creamed Scrambled Eggs and Tomatoes .75

SIDE ORDERS

Ham .... .35
Bacon .... .25
Toast and Jelly ..... .15
Sausage .... .30
One Egg .... .15
Milk Toast .... .30

IF DESIRED . . .
A COMPLIMENTARY COPY OF THIS MENU
MAY BE OBTAINED FROM THE CASHIER

Sunday, September 2, 1945

OPPOSITE Les Comiques, Hollywood Plaza Hotel, c. 1944, Hollywood, California

Using the French name for a populist American art form was an interesting twist calculated to upgrade the image of a hotel restaurant with a mainly adult clientele.

Durch die französische Schreibweise der populären amerikanischen Kunstform sollte vermutlich das Image des Hotelrestaurants mit seiner vorwiegend erwachsenen Kundschaft aufpoliert werden.

L'utilisation du nom francisé d'une forme d'art populaire américain est une astuce pour améliorer l'image de marque d'un restaurant d'hôtel à la clientèle principalement adulte.

ABOVE Ollie Hammond's Steak Houses, 1945, Los Angeles, California

Views aboard the Ship that never goes to Sea

Promenade Deck—On this spacious deck there exists the true atmosphere of the ocean-going cruiser. The bonhomie of the sea is evident everywhere, and all hands are ever eager to please.

Promenade Bridge—Here the voyager has the opportunity to become part of the ship's family as he observes the officers and crew make their log entries and plot their courses regularly.

The Boat "Nellie"—A snug little craft typical of the many that have cast anchor in the waters of the Ship-Ahoy. No sailor would be blamed for wanting to spend his leave with "Nellie".

NELLIE

Torpedo Room—The Ship-Ahoy fleet also includes a submarine, the "Nautilus", built exactly to scale. The torpedoes here are always ready to ensure the absolute safety of the passengers.

Launch Deck—Abaft midships of the launch a comfortable retreat for those who wish to dine in time is always accessible. Close to the galley, the launch deck is provided with the same fine fare excellently served.

Flagship of the Fleet — Situated squarely in the center of the extensive fleet is the Flagship, the fore-runner of all the other vessels. From the deck of the flagship are controlled all the implements that create the voyage atmosphere.

Waves on the Waves—Just as the able-bodied seaman enjoys his liberty on a small boat, so do his patriotic female counterparts. There is always a race for space here, and sometimes the WAVES lose to the SPARS and WACS.

The Gangplank—The vital passageway that serves as the main traffic artery for the ship's crew cannot be overlooked. Passengers take great delight in waving hello to friends from here.

Eyes of the Submarine—The periscope is poised to keep the "Nautilus" clear of dangerous shoals. All that the passenger sees, however are sailing ships on a rolling sea, observed through the portholes.

Supplies—Here one of our many trucks is about to start out for supplies. Captain Mike, always with an eye out for the weather, dispatches his crew for the best of everything at the most opportune time.

-HOY SEA FOOD

MIKE'S SHIP-A-HOY

FISH GROTTO

OPPOSITE Mike's Ship-a-Hoy, c. 1945, New York, New York

Nautical themes became increasingly popular in the 1940s and through the 1960s. At Mike's Ship-a-Hoy the gimmick was to have diners sit in various faux nautical environments.

Nautische Themen waren von den 1940er- bis in die 1960er-Jahre sehr beliebt. Das Besondere an Mike's Ship-A-Hoy waren die nautisch gestalteten Sitzgelegenheiten.

Les thèmes nautiques deviennent de plus en plus populaires entre les années 1940 et 1960. Au Mike's Ship-a-Hoy, les clients dînent dans divers décors nautiques factices.

ABOVE LEFT Spenger's Fish Grotto, c. 1949, Berkeley, California

ABOVE RIGHT Tick Tock Restaurants, c. 1954, Hollywood, California

LEFT & PAGES 266-267 Famous Seafood House Inc., c. 1951

A graphic nightmare, this menu has been amended with so many attachments that the original is almost illegible.

Diese Speisekarte ist ein grafischer Albtraum. Es wurden so viele Ergänzungen auf die Karte geheftet, dass sie kaum noch zu entziffern ist.

Véritable cauchemar graphique, cette carte a connu tellement de modifications qu'elle en est devenue presque illisible.

Try our Fillet of Flounder today! You'll find it's all that it should be. It's fresh! It's crusty! It's tender and sweet! It's *FILLET OF FLOUNDER SAUTE* served with butter sauce and French fried potatoes that are crisp and golden brown, and tasty cole slaw for zest. There are crisp rolls, and creamery butter. **$1.25**

REAL
CRAB GUMBO
NEW ORLEANS STYLE
Made from fresh hard shell crabs, okra, onions, fresh tomatoes, green peppers and served with rice.
Cup 50c Bowl 1.00

Special
Green Turtle Soup
Cup 50c Bowl $1.00

Special
Green Turtle Steak
Saute in Sweet Butter
FRENCH FRYS
COLE SLAW
HOT BISCUITS 2.25

Special
TOMATO Stuffed with Baby Lobster Meat
MAYONNAISE
COLE SLAW
HOT BISCUITS 1.75

Special
BOILED PIKE
COLE SLAW
HOT BISCUITS
BOILED POTATO 1.60

CASSEROLE
LOBSTER a la King
FRENCH FRYS
COLE SLAW
HOT BISCUITS 2.25

OUR MOST DELICIOUS
OYSTER BALTIMORE
STYLE SAUTE
Served with Barbecue Sauce
FRENCH FRYS
COLE SLAW
HOT BISCUITS 1.35

Our *BROILED FRESH SALMON TROUT* with parsley butter is so fresh, so full of delicate flavor, so hot from the glowing grill, you'll surely agree we're not boasting when we say it's delicious. With French fried potatoes, a delicious relish, fresh rolls, or bread, and creamery butter, it's a fisherman's dream. And it's only $1.65

ar 2.25
.... .60
kraut, Fresh Picked .... .90
Cocktail .... .65
ing .... .45
sels .... .45
res .... .40
ery, Roquefort Cheese .... .95
Jumbo .... .40
.... .40
.... .40
Chutney .... .25

and Soups . . .

Bowl .... .60
.... .30
r Manhattan, Bowl .... .40
.... .20
er Boston, Bowl .... .40
.... .20
Cup .... .30
owl .... .40 Cup .... .20
Bowl .... 1.00 Cup .... .50
New England, Bowl .... .40
.... .20
, Cup .... .40
Order
d Butter extra .... .15

(IN SEASON)

Oyster Cocktail .... .60
ster Cocktail .... .60
cktail (6) .... .50
cktail (6) .... .50
ole Slaw 1.25
d in Crumbs 1.35
Newburg 1.35
Milk .... .60
d Half .... .75
atin 1.35
.... 1.35
nore 1.35
o 1.35

Special
SOFT SHELL CRABS
FRIED
ON TOAST TARTAR SAUCE
FRENCH FRYS
COLE SLAW
HOT BISCUITS 1.75

Clam Fry in Butter ....
Clams Casino ....

Soft Shell Clams . . .

Soft Clams, Steamed, Butter S
Soft Clam Fry ....
Soft Clam Fry in Butter ....
Soft Clams a la Casino ....
Soft Clam Stew ....

Scallops . . .

Deep Sea Scallops . . . $1.25
Long Island Bay Scallops $1.50
In Saute, Sweet Butter 2.25
Broiled 2.25

Crabs . . .

Imperial Crab 1.20
Deviled Crab 1.10
Crab Meat Cocktail .... .65
Crab Meat au Gratin 1.45
Crab Meat Salad 1.60
Crab Meat a la Newburg 1.75
Crab Cakes (2) 1.45
Crab Meat Saute 1.75

Shrimps . . .

Shrimps, Creole 1.45
Shrimps Curry with Steamed Rice 1.45
Fried Shrimps 1.35
Shrimps, Newburg 1.75
Shrimp Cocktail .... .60
Shrimps Sauted in Butter 1.75
Shrimp Salad 1.60

TO-DAY'S SPECIAL
Fresh New Orleans Prawns Platter
Fresh New Orleans Prawns Fried in Sweet Butter Sauce Tartar, Cole Slaw, Russian Dressing, French Frys, Hot Biscuits **$1.45**

Salad Bowls

THE SEA ....
Tomatoes, Cucumbers, Radishes, Celery, Ch
Chopped Egg, Dressing
WHITE MEAT TUNAFISH SALAD
ed Egg, Russian Dressing
JUMBO FLORIDA SHRIMP SALA
Crisp Lettuce, Tomatoes and Dr
MARYLAND CRAB MEAT

CREME DE-MINT PARFAIT

Southern Comfort MANHATTAN
• SOUTHERN COMFORT
• DRY VERMOUTH or DRY SHERRY
• DASH ANGOSTURA BITTERS
65c

TRY OUR SPECIAL FOR DINNER
SPARKLING BURGUNDY
85¢

RTINI .60 HARVEY BRISTOL CREAM SHERRY .85

Impor
J. &
JU
PALL M

OBSTERS RE
T RECEI

CIAL SAL
PLATTER
Lake Superior Sal
Steamed with Holla
Sauce, Boiled Potato
Slaw Hot Biscuits . $

POACHED HAL
STEAK
With Lobster Sauce e
ly poached into a
tantalizing morsel, H
steak is embellished
Lobster Sauce. French
Cole Slaw and Hot B
$

COMBINATION
FOOD A LA
NEWBURG
Oysters, Clams, Lo
Scallops and Crab M
served in Newburg
$

Just Arrived from
DENVER, COL
LARGE RAINB
TROUT
Saute in Sweet Bu
French Frys, Cole
Hot Biscuits .... $

HOT SE
No. 1 — Consisting
Lobster, Shrimps, File
Fried Clams, Scallops
Frys, Cole Slaw, Hot

Home Made PICKL

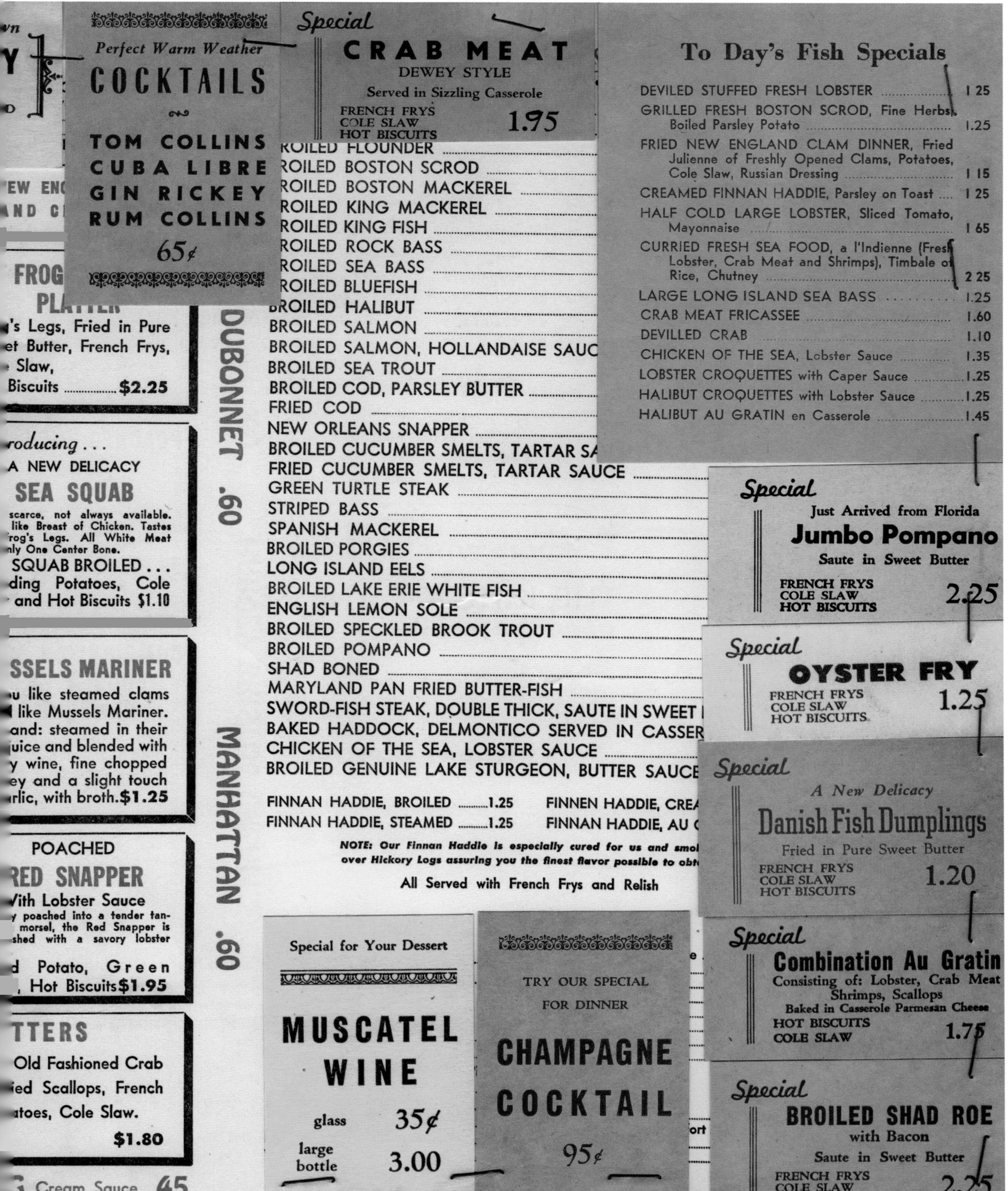

Perfect Warm Weather
COCKTAILS
TOM COLLINS
CUBA LIBRE
GIN RICKEY
RUM COLLINS
65¢
Special
CRAB MEAT
DEWEY STYLE
Served in Sizzling Casserole
FRENCH FRYS
COLE SLAW
HOT BISCUITS
1.95
To Day's Fish Specials
DEVILED STUFFED FRESH LOBSTER 1 25
GRILLED FRESH BOSTON SCROD, Fine Herbs, Boiled Parsley Potato 1.25
FRIED NEW ENGLAND CLAM DINNER, Fried Julienne of Freshly Opened Clams, Potatoes, Cole Slaw, Russian Dressing 1 15
CREAMED FINNAN HADDIE, Parsley on Toast 1 25
HALF COLD LARGE LOBSTER, Sliced Tomato, Mayonnaise 1 65
CURRIED FRESH SEA FOOD, a l'Indienne (Fresh Lobster, Crab Meat and Shrimps), Timbale of Rice, Chutney 2 25
LARGE LONG ISLAND SEA BASS 1.25
CRAB MEAT FRICASSEE 1.60
DEVILLED CRAB 1.10
CHICKEN OF THE SEA, Lobster Sauce 1.35
LOBSTER CROQUETTES with Caper Sauce 1.25
HALIBUT CROQUETTES with Lobster Sauce 1.25
HALIBUT AU GRATIN en Casserole 1.45
ROILED BOSTON SCROD
ROILED BOSTON MACKEREL
ROILED KING MACKEREL
ROILED KING FISH
ROILED ROCK BASS
ROILED SEA BASS
ROILED BLUEFISH
BROILED HALIBUT
BROILED SALMON
BROILED SALMON, HOLLANDAISE SAUC
BROILED SEA TROUT
BROILED COD, PARSLEY BUTTER
FRIED COD
NEW ORLEANS SNAPPER
BROILED CUCUMBER SMELTS, TARTAR SA
FRIED CUCUMBER SMELTS, TARTAR SAUCE
GREEN TURTLE STEAK
STRIPED BASS
SPANISH MACKEREL
BROILED PORGIES
LONG ISLAND EELS
BROILED LAKE ERIE WHITE FISH
ENGLISH LEMON SOLE
BROILED SPECKLED BROOK TROUT
BROILED POMPANO
SHAD BONED
MARYLAND PAN FRIED BUTTER-FISH
SWORD-FISH STEAK, DOUBLE THICK, SAUTE IN SWEET
BAKED HADDOCK, DELMONTICO SERVED IN CASSER
CHICKEN OF THE SEA, LOBSTER SAUCE
BROILED GENUINE LAKE STURGEON, BUTTER SAUCE
FINNAN HADDIE, BROILED 1.25
FINNEN HADDIE, CRE
FINNAN HADDIE, STEAMED 1.25
FINNAN HADDIE, AU
NOTE: Our Finnan Haddie is especially cured for us and smo over Hickory Logs assuring you the finest flavor possible to obt
All Served with French Frys and Relish
DUBONNET .60
MANHATTAN .60
FROG
's Legs, Fried in Pure
et Butter, French Frys,
Slaw,
Biscuits $2.25
roducing . . .
A NEW DELICACY
SEA SQUAB
scarce, not always available. like Breast of Chicken. Tastes rog's Legs. All White Meat nly One Center Bone.
SQUAB BROILED . . .
ding Potatoes, Cole and Hot Biscuits $1.10
SSELS MARINER
u like steamed clams like Mussels Mariner. and: steamed in their juice and blended with y wine, fine chopped ey and a slight touch rlic, with broth. $1.25
POACHED
RED SNAPPER
With Lobster Sauce
d Potato, Green , Hot Biscuits $1.95
TTERS
Old Fashioned Crab
ied Scallops, French
atoes, Cole Slaw.
$1.80
Cream Sauce .45
Special
Just Arrived from Florida
Jumbo Pompano
Saute in Sweet Butter
FRENCH FRYS
COLE SLAW
HOT BISCUITS
2.25
Special
OYSTER FRY
FRENCH FRYS
COLE SLAW
HOT BISCUITS
1.25
Special
A New Delicacy
Danish Fish Dumplings
Fried in Pure Sweet Butter
FRENCH FRYS
COLE SLAW
HOT BISCUITS
1.20
Special
Combination Au Gratin
Consisting of: Lobster, Crab Meat Shrimps, Scallops
Baked in Casserole Parmesan Cheese
HOT BISCUITS
COLE SLAW
1.75
Special
BROILED SHAD ROE
with Bacon
Saute in Sweet Butter
FRENCH FRYS
COLE SLAW
HOT BISCUITS
2.25
Special for Your Dessert
MUSCATEL WINE
glass 35¢
large bottle 3.00
TRY OUR SPECIAL FOR DINNER
CHAMPAGNE COCKTAIL
95¢

LEFT & BELOW **McHuron's Toed Inn, c. 1944, Los Angeles, California**

OPPOSITE TOP **Toad in the Hole, c. 1943, Hollywood, California**

Even in 1943, Toad in the Hole's filet mignon dinner for a dollar might make customers wonder about the kitchen's food costs and quality of ingredients.

Selbst 1943 war ein Dollar für einen ganzen Filet-Mignon-Teller sehr günstig und mag Zweifel an der Qualität der Zutaten im Toad in the Hole geweckt haben.

Même en 1943, le filet mignon à un dollar du Toad in the Hole devait conduire les consommateurs à s'interroger sur la qualité des ingrédients et de la cuisine.

A LA CARTE
½ FRIED CHICKEN
French Fried Potatoes, Cole Slaw and Toasted Bun
$1.65

Table d' Hote Dinners

Served from 5 P. M. to 9 P. M.

CHOICE OF ONE: Soup du Jour or Tomato Juice
CHOICE OF ONE: Our Famous Cole Slaw or Mixed Green Salad

BARBECUED DINNERS

Barbecued Beef	1.30
Barbecued Ham	1.40
Barbecued Pork	1.40
Chicken Fried Steak	1.30
Hamburger Steak with Mushroom Sauce	1.30
Breaded Cutlet with Mushroom Sauce	1.40
Grilled Baby Beef Liver with Bacon or Onions	1.45
Ground Sirloin Steak Smothered in Onions	1.45
Two Loin Lamb Chops	1.65
Two Choice Pork Chops	1.45

Served with French Fries or Mashed Potatoes — Hot Vegetable
DESSERT: Ice Cream, Sherbet or Jell-O
DRINK: Coffee, Tea or Buttermilk (Milk 5c Extra)

SALADS A LA CARTE

Fresh Shrimp Salad	95
Stuffed Tomato with Chicken Salad	85
Mixed Green Salad Bowl	65
Lettuce and Tomato	60
Cottage Cheese and Pineapple	65
Fresh Shrimp Cocktail	50

HOT SPECIALS

We Make Our Own Chili Fresh Daily

Chili, Straight	45
Chili and Beans	40
Chili and Spaghetti	55
Hamburger Size	55

Not Responsible for Lost or Stolen Articles
Sales Tax will be added to retail price on all taxable items

SEA FOOD DINNERS

Served From 5 P. M. to 9 P. M.
CHOICE OF ONE: Soup du Jour or Tomato Juice
CHOICE OF ONE: Our Famous Cole Slaw or Mixed Green Salad

French Fried Shrimp	1.40
Fried Scallops	1.40
Filet of Sole	1.30
Grilled Salmon Steak	1.40
Grilled Halibut Steak	1.45
Grilled White Sea Bass	1.45
Grilled Swordfish Steak	1.45
Shore Dinner (Combination of Shrimp, Scallops and Filet of Sole)	1.60
Eastern Lobster Tails	1.85

Ice Cream, Sherbet or Jell-O — Coffee, Tea or Buttermilk (Milk 5c Extra)

A LA CARTE
THICK, KANSAS CITY
STEAKS
Served on
SIZZLING
Platter

Porterhouse Steak	2.60
Top Sirloin Steak	2.75
K. C. New York Cut	2.70
K. C. Filet Mignon	2.90

SPECIAL
T-BONE STEAK
$2.25

Chef's Salad, French Fries and Toasted Bun Served with Above Orders

A LA CARTE SPECIAL
Barbecued Spareribs Plate
with French Fried Potatoes, Cole Slaw and Toasted Bun
$1.60

Genuine Louisiana
Fresh Frog Legs
Cole Slaw and French Fries
$1.75

May We Suggest
Italian Spaghetti
Served with GROUND ROUND
95c

Sandwiches

HOT BEEF SANDWICH with Potatoes and Gravy 65

Ham and Egg	60	Bacon and Egg	50
Pork	55	Sliced Turkey	65
Baked Ham	55	Melted Cheese	35
Cheese	35	Bacon, Melted Cheese	50
Peanut Butter and Jelly	30	Fried Egg	25
Deviled Egg	30	Bacon, Lettuce and Tomato	50
Lettuce and Tomato	40	Fried Ham or Bacon	50
Corned Beef on Rye	50	Sliced Chicken	65
Tuna	35	Chicken Salad	55

STEAK SANDWICH
TOASTED
Served with Cole Slaw and French Fries
85c

BAR-B-Q SANDWICHES
Beef - Pork - Ham
55c

BURGERS

Cheeseburger	40
Hamburger	35
Chiliburger	50

Our Hamburger is Ground Fresh Daily

WAFFLE 35c
Served with Butter and Maple Syrup

French Fried Onion Rings	45
French Fries	30
Cole Slaw (Side Order)	25
Homemade Soups	25

HOT DRINKS

Coffee	10
Tea	10
Hot Chocolate	15
Milk	10

Soft Drinks 10c

EASTERN BEER 35c

LOCAL BEER 30c

DESSERTS

Assorted Pies	15
French Cream Pie	25
Ice Cream	10
Pie a la Mode	25
Cheese Cake	25
Jell-O	15

HOT APPLE PIE
with Rum Sauce
25c

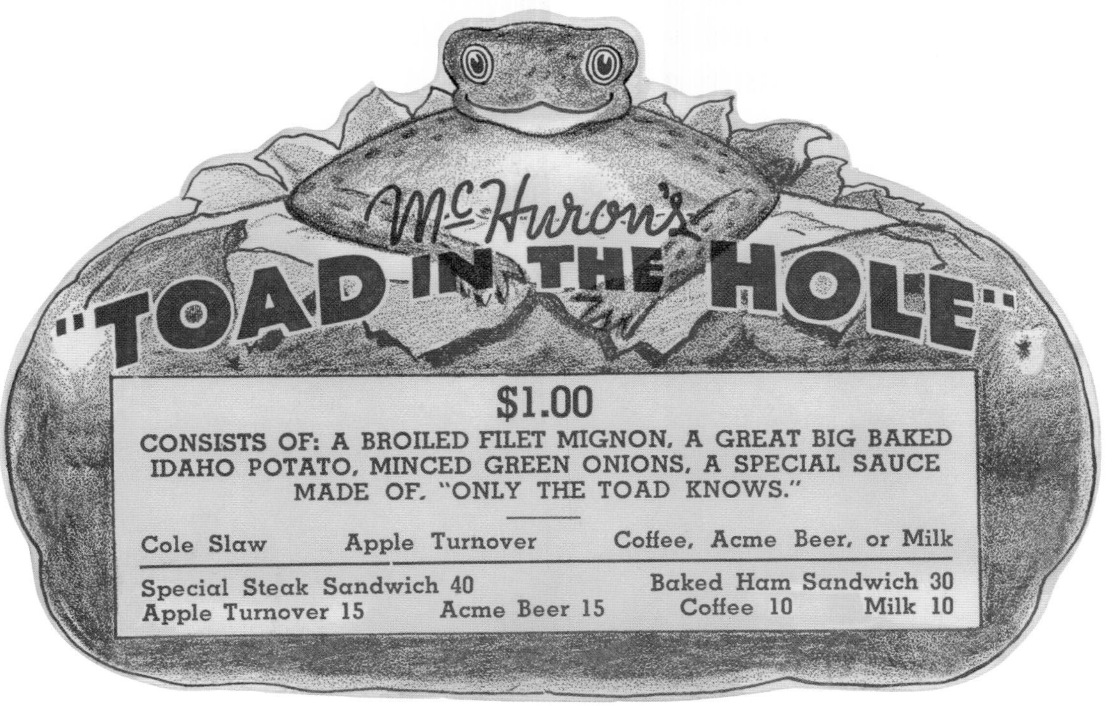

BELOW Ho-Tei, c. 1944, Long Beach, California

LEFT El Navajo Dining Room, Franciscan Hotel, c. 1936, Albuquerque, New Mexico

Built in 1922 in the adobe style, the Franciscan Hotel used a Navajo motif throughout its El Navajo Dining Room.

Im 1922 im Adobe-Stil erbauten Franciscan Hotel war der gesamte El Navajo Dining Room mit Navajo-Motiven ausgestattet.

Construit en 1922 en imitation pisé, le Franciscan Hotel exploite le thème navajo, notamment dans sa grande salle « El Navajo Dining Room ».

BELOW Indian Grill, 1950, Colorado Springs, Colorado

OPPOSITE Trans World Airlines, c. 1948

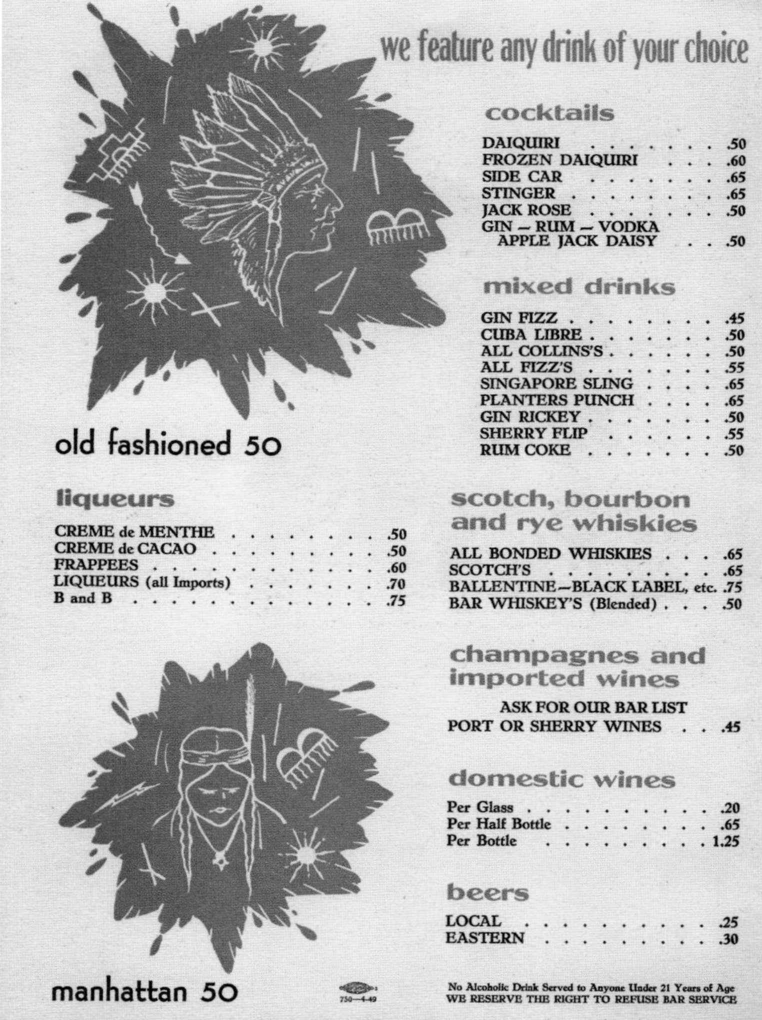

we feature any drink of your choice

cocktails

DAIQUIRI	.50
FROZEN DAIQUIRI	.60
SIDE CAR	.65
STINGER	.65
JACK ROSE	.50
GIN – RUM – VODKA APPLE JACK DAISY	.50

mixed drinks

GIN FIZZ	.45
CUBA LIBRE	.50
ALL COLLINS'S	.50
ALL FIZZ'S	.55
SINGAPORE SLING	.65
PLANTERS PUNCH	.65
GIN RICKEY	.50
SHERRY FLIP	.55
RUM COKE	.50

old fashioned 50

liqueurs

CREME de MENTHE	.50
CREME de CACAO	.50
FRAPPEES	.60
LIQUEURS (all Imports)	.70
B and B	.75

scotch, bourbon and rye whiskies

ALL BONDED WHISKIES	.65
SCOTCH'S	.65
BALLENTINE—BLACK LABEL, etc.	.75
BAR WHISKEY'S (Blended)	.50

champagnes and imported wines

ASK FOR OUR BAR LIST

PORT OR SHERRY WINES	.45

domestic wines

Per Glass	.20
Per Half Bottle	.65
Per Bottle	1.25

beers

LOCAL	.25
EASTERN	.30

manhattan 50

No Alcoholic Drink Served to Anyone Under 21 Years of Age
WE RESERVE THE RIGHT TO REFUSE BAR SERVICE

Friday 16th SPECIAL DINNERS June 1950
Price of Entree Determines Cost

LOBSTER COCKTAIL 50¢ SHRIMP COCKTAIL 40¢ OLIVES & CELERY 20¢ BEERS 25¢-30¢

Choice of Appetizer: Seafood Cocktail; Bismarck Herring Cutlets, Wine Sauce; Anchovy or Caviar Canape; Cantaloupe; Tomato or Grapefruit Juice; Orange or Grape Punch; Clam Chowder; Cold Jellied Consomme; Italian Spaghetti
Chicken Broth Noodles

Fish Entrees
Fresh Broiled Columbia River Salmon, Lemon and Butter $1.60
Whole Broiled Eastern Live Lobster, Melted Butter $2.00
Fried Fresh Eastern Scallops, Tartar Sauce $1.65
Colorado Mountain Trout, Saute Meuniere $2.00
Jumbo Fried Shrimp, Saute in Butter $1.80
Broiled Fresh Shad Roe with Bacon $1.75
Whole Florida Pompano, Lemon and Butter $2.10
Fresh Halibut Steak, Saute in Butter $1.60
Hard Shell Crab, Lemon Butter $1.85

Enjoy Wine with Your Dinner: Sauterne or Burgundy 65¢ Half Bottle -- Sauterne, Sherry, Burgundy or Port $1.25 Full Bottle -- Glass of Dry Wine 20¢ ---- Creme de Cocoa 50¢

Meat Entrees
DOUBLE SIZZLING STEAK FOR TWO $5.50
Grilled Sirloin Steak $2.50 -- Broiled Filet Mignon $2.60
Club Steak $2.15 -- Roast Prime Rib of Cornfed Beef au Jus $2.00
Homemade Ravioli al Sugo or Half and Half $1.30 *Broiled Sweetbreads on Toast $1.40*
Braised Short Ribs of Beef $1.50 -- Spaghetti, Italian Style $1.30
Chicken a la Caccintori $2.10 -- Omelette with Mushrooms $1.30
Broiled Frankfurters with Hot Potato Salad $1.35
Grilled Spring Lamb Chops with Currant Jelly $2.25
Half Milkfed Spring Chicken, Broiled or Fried $2.00
Whole Broiled Jumbo Squab $2.10 *Irish Lamb Stew with Vegetables $1.25*

Vegetables: Cauliflower - Beets
Potatoes: Mashed - French Fried - Parsley Broiled after 5 p.m.
Salad: Indian Grill - Cottage Cheese with Peaches

Choice of Dessert: Fresh Apricot or Banana Cream Pie; Chocolate Cottage Pudding; Vanilla, Chocolate, Peppermint Stick or Sweetheart Ice Cream; Orange Sherbet; Vino Rossi or Chocolate Ice Cream; Swiss, Liederkranz, Roquefort, American or Camembert Cheese

COFFEE .... TEA .... MILK .... BUTTERMILK
HOME OF THE FAMOUS INDIAN GRILL SALAD DRESSING 41¢ PER BOTTLE
Children's Dinner $1.00 (No Substitutions) Hot Chocolate 10¢ Extra

HAM AND EGG	.65
CLUB (THREE DECKER)	1.00
HAMBURGER	.55
CHICKEN OR TURKEY	.90
BACON – LETTUCE – TOMATO	.65

desserts

ASSORTED CHEESES	.25
ASSORTED ICE CREAMS	.15
ASSORTED PIES	.15
COFFEE – TEA – MILK	.10
ICED COFFEE OR ICED TEA	.15

whiskey sour 55

MANAGEMENT NOT RESPONSIBLE FOR ARTICLES LOST — STOLEN OR EXCHANGED.

Taos Pueblo, New Mexico
David Klein

Vogue Room
HOTEL HOLLENDEN • CLEVELAND

OPPOSITE Vogue Room, Hotel Hollenden, 1950, Cleveland, Ohio

BELOW Hotel Mayflower Coffee Shop, 1947, Akron, Ohio

As a hotel dining room, the Mayflower had to offer something for everyone, night and day, hence the inclusion of everything from corn flakes to (canned) foie gras.

Das Mayflower war ein Speisesaal in einem Hotel und bot für jeden etwas an, Tag und Nacht, alles von Cornflakes bis zu Gänseleberpastete (aus der Dose).

En tant que restaurant d'hôtel, le Mayflower se devait de proposer des collations à tout type de clientèle et à toute heure du jour ou de la nuit. Sur sa carte, on remarque des corn-flakes, mais aussi une conserve de foie gras.

ABOVE Netherland Plaza, 1950, Cincinnati, Ohio

Choice of Soups (in cup) Choice of Juices
GOOSELIVER SANDWICH ON TOAST
DILL PICKLE & POTATO CHIPS **65**
Milk Coffee Tea

Appetizers - Soups

Blue Points on the Half Shell - -	.50
Fresh Shrimp Cocktail - - -	.50
Iced Tomato or Apple Juice - -	.15
Half Grapefruit Maraschino - -	.25
Oyster Stew .75 Half and Half .85 with Cream	.95
Fresh Fruit Cup Maraschino - - -	.35
Chopped Poultry Liver Canape on Toast	.30
Old fashion navy bean soup Cup .15 Bowl	.25
Consomme with egg dumpling Cup .15 Bowl	.25

Salads

Sliced Tomato -	.20	Tossed Up Garden	.15
Cole Slaw -	.15	Combination -	.20

Entrees

ENTREE PRICE INCLUDES CHOICE OF TWO VEGETABLES

GRILLED FRESH BOSTON COD FISH WITH PARSIEY BUTTER	.85
SCRAMBLED EGGS WITH FRESH DICED MUSHROOMS	.90
BOILED BRISKET OF CORN BEEF & CABBAGE	1.00
CHOPPED ROUND STEAK WITH ONION SAUCE	1.00
POTATO PANCAKES WITH BACON & MAPLE SYRUP	.85
FRESH SEA FOOD NEWBURG ON TOAST EN CASSEROLE	.85
CHEF'S SALAD IN BOWL with h. b. egg, tomato & julienne of swiss cheese	.80
ASSORTED COLD CUTS WITH POTATO SALAD	1.00

Mashed Rutabagas or Buttered Green Peas
Parsley Boiled or Mashed Potatoes

Coffee .10 Tea .10 Milk .10 Postum .15 Chocolate .15

Choice of Soups (in cup) Choice of Juices
Creamed Ham & Macaroni au gratin en casserole, buttered green peas & cole slaw. Apple Pie Rolls, Butter **95**
Milk Coffee Tea

Choice of Soups (in cup) Choice of Juices
Mayflower Special Fruit Plate with creamed cotttge cheese & corn flakes
Marble Cake Rolls, Butter **80**
Milk Coffee Tea

Sandwiches

Junior Club -	.75	Bacon, Lettuce, Tom.	.50
Chicken -	.70	Toasted Cheese -	.50
Egg Salad -	.40	Baked Ham - -	.75

Hamburger on toasted bun with Sweet Relish .30
Mayflower Cannibal Sandwich Garnished 1.35
Gooseliver on toast with onions .50
Club Steak with potato chips .90
Old fashion Dixie .45

Desserts - Ice Cream

Apple Pie .15 Stewed Rhubarb .15
Sour Cherry Cobbler .15
Diplomat Pudding .15
Marble Cake .20
Frozen Chocolate Eclair .30
Vanilla, Chocolate or Peppermint Candy Ice Cream or Orange Sherbet .15

Cheese

Leiderkranz, Bleu, American, Swiss and Camembert .25

Coffee Shop HOTEL MAYFLOWER · AKRON · GEORGE THOMAS CULLEN MANAGER

MONDAY, NOVEMBER 17, 1947

LEFT Hotel Hollenden, 1948, Cleveland, Ohio

BELOW Flemish Room, Hotel Hollenden, 1948, Cleveland, Ohio

OPPOSITE The Empire Room, the Palmer House, c. 1948, Chicago, Illinois

ABOVE Café Pierre, c. 1949, New York, New York

The Pierre hotel, opened in 1930 at Fifth Avenue and East 61st Street, by Corsican-born Charles Pierre Casalasco, went bankrupt and was taken over by oil tycoon J. Paul Getty in 1938. Its Café Pierre was a swank restaurant and nightclub until replaced by Le Caprice in 2009.

Das Hotel Pierre eröffnete 1930 an der Ecke Fifth Avenue und East 61st Street. Der erste, korsische Besitzer Charles Pierre Casalasco ging Pleite, Ölmagnat J. Paul Getty übernahm es 1938. Das Café Pierre war ein mondänes Speise- und Tanzlokal, das erst 2009 vom Le Caprice ersetzt wurde.

L'hôtel Pierre ouvre en 1930 au coin de la Cinquième Avenue et de la 61e rue Est. Établi par Charles Pierre Casalasco, natif de Corse, il fait faillite avant d'être repris par le magnat du pétrole J. Paul Getty en 1938. Le Café Pierre, le restaurant m'as-tu-vu de l'hôtel, fait également office de night-club. Il sera remplacé par Le Caprice en 2009.

Flemish Room

CASSEROLE SPECIAL

CHICKEN POT PIE
(Boneless Chicken Stew with Vegetables baked in Golden Crust)
Lettuce and Tomato Salad, French Dressing
including Rolls and Butter
Cup of Coffee, Tea or Milk
1.25

DAIRY LUNCHEON

ALL BRAN CEREAL with Fresh Blue Berries
Pitcher of Half and Half
70c

Bowl of Hominy Grits with Hot Milk
and Stewed Figs
Cup of Coffee, Tea or Milk
80c

SALAD SPECIALS

Lettuce, Pineapple Ring, Cottage Cheese, Grapes, French Dressing	75
Hollenden Fruit Salad with Melon Balls and Sherbet Center	75
Fresh Vegetables Bouquetiere in Lettuce Cup, Sour Cream Dressing	70
Chef's Salad, plain .... 50 with Julienne of Chicken	75

Including Cup of Coffee, Tea or Milk, Saltine Wafers or Ry Krisp
(Melba Toast 10c Extra)

SANDWICH SPECIALS

Including Cup of Coffee, Tea or Milk

Toasted Cheese and Bacon, Cole Slaw and Pickle	65
Lettuce, Thousand Island Dressing, Sliced Turkey, Tomato, Stuffed Olives	80
Hamburger on Toasted Bun, French Fried Potatoes, Chopped Relish	70
Peanut Butter and Jelly on Raisin Bread, Spiced Peaches	60

VEGETABLES & POTATOES

Corn on Cob 25 Fresh Spinach 25 Fresh String Beans 25
Cauliflower in Cream 25 New Peas 30 Buttered Beets 25
Boiled 20 Mashed 20 French Fried 25 Cottage Fried 30 Hashed Brown 30

FRESH FRUITS

Half Avacado Pear, French Dressing 55 Sliced Bananas with Cream 25
Watermelon 50 *Black or Blueberries* 55 Cantaloupe 40
Honey Dew Melon 55 Sliced Peaches with Cream 55 Persian Melon 55

FRUITS IN SYRUP
Italian Prunes, Peaches, Apricots, Pineapple or Royal Ann Cherries 30
Brandied Peaches 85 Brandied Figs 85 Brandied Bing Cherries 85

The Empire Room
P

ABOVE **Famous Hamburger Frank, c. 1945, Los Angeles, California**

BELOW **Keith's, c. 1945, Studio City, California**

Rare is the American restaurant that makes only negative remarks about its own food, although Keith's did throughout its menu, promising tough steaks, indigestion, and terrible service.

Amerikanische Gaststätten, die nur Schlechtes über ihr eigenes Essen zu sagen haben, sind selten, aber Keith's versprach zähe Steaks, Verdauungsstörungen und miserable Bedienung.

Rares sont les établissements américains qui se fendent de commentaires négatifs sur leur propre cuisine. Pourtant, chez Keith's, c'est le cas tout au long du menu. Il promet des «steaks durs», des «indigestions» et même un «service exécrable».

It Ain't Easy . . .

to take a beautiful grade AA Steak and toughen it the way we do! In fact, it has taken our chef years of practice and still, every once in a while, she slips and serves a TENDER one. However, as they say, "Practice Makes Perfect," so we sincerely hope that the day will come when we can unconditionally guarantee each Steak to be tougher than the one before. Now for our DULL KNIFES—well, they're not really so DULL, if you cut with the handle.

If exercise will eliminate fat, how in the world does one get a double chin eating Tough Steaks? . . . It ain't easy!

The Four Hinges of Life

CHEATING . . . STEALING . . . LYING . . . DRINKING

If you must cheat — CHEAT for your country.
If you must steal — STEAL away fro[illegible] ad company.
If you must lie — LIE for a pretty woman.
If you must drink — DRINK with US!

So-o-o

DRINK TO YOUR FRIENDS' HEALTH AND RUIN YOUR OWN WITH OUR **BUM BOOZE**

Chuck and Bettye Hawley

ALL PRICES ARE OUR O.P.S. CEILING PRICES OR LOWER. A LIST SHOWING OUR CEILING PRICE FOR EACH ITEM IS AVAILABLE FOR YOUR INSPECTION. . . NOT RESPONSIBLE FOR LOST OR STOLEN ARTICLES.

WE KNOW THE SERVICE IS TERRIBLE . . .
BUT . . . PEOPLE DON'T MIND WAITING
. . . . BECAUSE THE FOOD IS WORSE!

SHRIMP COCKTAIL
THE SAUCE IS EXCEPTIONALLY GOOD —BUT—THE SHRIMP TASTES LIKE FISH
.85

WE KNOW OUR
GRAVY IS TENDER
BECAUSE WE RUN IT THROUGH A MEAT GRINDER

From the Broiler

Our Steaks are so tough we sprinkle fresh mushrooms over them to try to make them taste like beef . . .

TIRED T-BONE—25 Cents—WITH MEAT 2.25
TOUGH TOP SIRLOIN STEAK—For Whom the Bull Toils 2.75
MISERABLE NEW YORK CUT 2.90
UNCHEWABLE FILET MIGNON 2.90
INDIGESTIBLE PORK CHOPS—with Applesauce 2.50
DISAGREEABLE FRENCH LAMB CHOPS—Wee Wee 2.90

Above orders served with baked potato, our famous tossed green salad bowl, roquefort dressing, hot roll, butter and coffee.

—Confidentially—

For TWENTY-FIVE CENTS you can find the little woman in the dark by having an order of garlic toast — For another TWO-BITS you can dress your baked potato first class with sour cream and chives — They say a dollar is only worth fifty cents these days — That makes fifty cents worth nothing — so what can you lose.

FROG LEGS 2.25
Served with Tartar Sauce, Lemon and Green Salad
MOST PEOPLE CONSIDER FROG LEGS A DELICACY . . . MR. FROG CONSIDERS THEM A NECESSITY!

For the Not-So-Hungry

STEAK SANDWICH — HAWLEYWOOD STYLE 1.35
Served on Toast — with Fresh Mushrooms — Green Salad
Indigestion Follows Immediately — No Waiting Until 3:00 A. M.

TOSSED GREEN SALAD BOWL 1.00
(Tossed from the Crate to the Plate)
CRISP GREENS TOSSED WITH OUR FAMOUS ROQUEFORT DRESSING
(Tried the dressing out in a small town of 300 once and received 1,000 complimentary votes on it --- Must Be Good!)

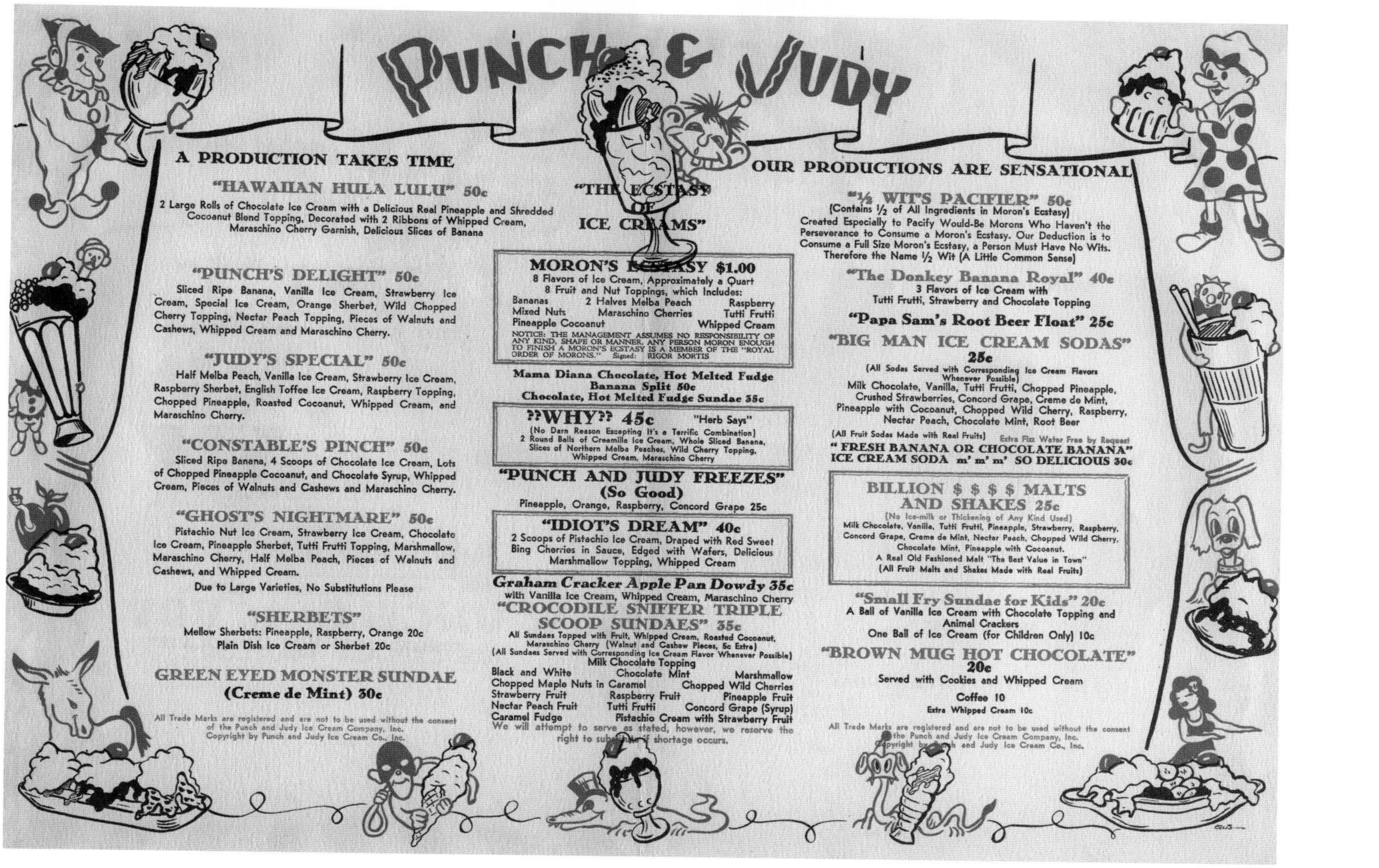

PUNCH & JUDY

A PRODUCTION TAKES TIME

"HAWAIIAN HULA LULU" 50c
2 Large Rolls of Chocolate Ice Cream with a Delicious Real Pineapple and Shredded Cocoanut Blend Topping, Decorated with 2 Ribbons of Whipped Cream, Maraschino Cherry Garnish, Delicious Slices of Banana

"PUNCH'S DELIGHT" 50c
Sliced Ripe Banana, Vanilla Ice Cream, Strawberry Ice Cream, Special Ice Cream, Orange Sherbet, Wild Chopped Cherry Topping, Nectar Peach Topping, Pieces of Walnuts and Cashews, Whipped Cream and Maraschino Cherry.

"JUDY'S SPECIAL" 50c
Half Melba Peach, Vanilla Ice Cream, Strawberry Ice Cream, Raspberry Sherbet, English Toffee Ice Cream, Raspberry Topping, Chopped Pineapple, Roasted Cocoanut, Whipped Cream, and Maraschino Cherry.

"CONSTABLE'S PINCH" 50c
Sliced Ripe Banana, 4 Scoops of Chocolate Ice Cream, Lots of Chopped Pineapple Cocoanut, and Chocolate Syrup, Whipped Cream, Pieces of Walnuts and Cashews and Maraschino Cherry.

"GHOST'S NIGHTMARE" 50c
Pistachio Nut Ice Cream, Strawberry Ice Cream, Chocolate Ice Cream, Pineapple Sherbet, Tutti Frutti Topping, Marshmallow, Maraschino Cherry, Half Melba Peach, Pieces of Walnuts and Cashews, and Whipped Cream.
Due to Large Varieties, No Substitutions Please

"SHERBETS"
Mellow Sherbets: Pineapple, Raspberry, Orange 20c
Plain Dish Ice Cream or Sherbet 20c

GREEN EYED MONSTER SUNDAE
(Creme de Mint) 30c

All Trade Marks are registered and are not to be used without the consent of the Punch and Judy Ice Cream Company, Inc.
Copyright by Punch and Judy Ice Cream Co., Inc.

"THE ECSTASY OF ICE CREAMS"

MORON'S ECSTASY $1.00
8 Flavors of Ice Cream, Approximately a Quart
8 Fruit and Nut Toppings, which Includes:
Bananas — 2 Halves Melba Peach — Raspberry
Mixed Nuts — Maraschino Cherries — Tutti Frutti
Pineapple Cocoanut — Whipped Cream
NOTICE: THE MANAGEMENT ASSUMES NO RESPONSIBILITY OF ANY KIND, SHAPE OR MANNER. ANY PERSON MORON ENOUGH TO FINISH A MORON'S ECSTASY IS A MEMBER OF THE "ROYAL ORDER OF MORONS." Signed: RIGOR MORTIS

Mama Diana Chocolate, Hot Melted Fudge
Banana Split 50c
Chocolate, Hot Melted Fudge Sundae 35c

??WHY?? 45c "Herb Says"
(No Darn Reason Excepting It's a Terrific Combination)
2 Round Balls of Creamilla Ice Cream, Whole Sliced Banana, Slices of Northern Melba Peaches, Wild Cherry Topping, Whipped Cream, Maraschino Cherry

"PUNCH AND JUDY FREEZES"
(So Good)
Pineapple, Orange, Raspberry, Concord Grape 25c

"IDIOT'S DREAM" 40c
2 Scoops of Pistachio Ice Cream, Draped with Red Sweet Bing Cherries in Sauce, Edged with Wafers, Delicious Marshmallow Topping, Whipped Cream

Graham Cracker Apple Pan Dowdy 35c
with Vanilla Ice Cream, Whipped Cream, Maraschino Cherry

"CROCODILE SNIFFER TRIPLE SCOOP SUNDAES" 35c
All Sundaes Topped with Fruit, Whipped Cream, Roasted Cocoanut, Maraschino Cherry (Walnut and Cashew Pieces, 5c Extra)
(All Sundaes Served with Corresponding Ice Cream Flavor Whenever Possible)
Milk Chocolate Topping
Black and White — Chocolate Mint — Marshmallow
Chopped Maple Nuts in Caramel — Chopped Wild Cherries
Strawberry Fruit — Raspberry Fruit — Pineapple Fruit
Nectar Peach Fruit — Tutti Frutti — Concord Grape (Syrup)
Caramel Fudge — Pistachio Cream with Strawberry Fruit
We will attempt to serve as stated, however, we reserve the right to substitute if shortage occurs.

OUR PRODUCTIONS ARE SENSATIONAL

"½ WIT'S PACIFIER" 50c
(Contains ½ of All Ingredients in Moron's Ecstasy)
Created Especially to Pacify Would-Be Morons Who Haven't the Perseverance to Consume a Moron's Ecstasy. Our Deduction is to Consume a Full Size Moron's Ecstasy, a Person Must Have No Wits. Therefore the Name ½ Wit (A Little Common Sense)

"The Donkey Banana Royal" 40c
3 Flavors of Ice Cream with
Tutti Frutti, Strawberry and Chocolate Topping

"Papa Sam's Root Beer Float" 25c

"BIG MAN ICE CREAM SODAS"
25c
(All Sodas Served with Corresponding Ice Cream Flavors Whenever Possible)
Milk Chocolate, Vanilla, Tutti Frutti, Chopped Pineapple, Crushed Strawberries, Concord Grape, Creme de Mint, Pineapple with Cocoanut, Chopped Wild Cherry, Raspberry, Nectar Peach, Chocolate Mint, Root Beer
(All Fruit Sodas Made with Real Fruits) Extra Fizz Water Free by Request

" FRESH BANANA OR CHOCOLATE BANANA" ICE CREAM SODA m' m' m' SO DELICIOUS 30c

BILLION $ $ $ $ MALTS AND SHAKES 25c
(No Ice-milk or Thickening of Any Kind Used)
Milk Chocolate, Vanilla, Tutti Frutti, Pineapple, Strawberry, Raspberry, Concord Grape, Creme de Mint, Nectar Peach, Chopped Wild Cherry, Chocolate Mint, Pineapple with Cocoanut.
A Real Old Fashioned Malt "The Best Value in Town"
(All Fruit Malts and Shakes Made with Real Fruits)

"Small Fry Sundae for Kids" 20c
A Ball of Vanilla Ice Cream with Chocolate Topping and Animal Crackers
One Ball of Ice Cream (for Children Only) 10c

"BROWN MUG HOT CHOCOLATE"
20c
Served with Cookies and Whipped Cream

Coffee 10
Extra Whipped Cream 10c

All Trade Marks are registered and are not to be used without the consent of the Punch and Judy Ice Cream Company, Inc.
Copyright by Punch and Judy Ice Cream Co., Inc.

ABOVE & RIGHT Punch & Judy Ice Cream Parlors, 1947, Los Angeles, California

Arthur Whizin formerly owned the Chili Bowl chain and opened these ice cream parlors in bowl-shaped buildings after World War II. They were featured in *Life* magazine, especially the "Moron's Ecstasy." Whizin was a public relations master and this concept of an outrageous ice cream parlor was an instant hit.

Arthur Whizin, ehemaliger Besitzer der Chili-Bowl-Kette, machte nach dem Zweiten Weltkrieg diese Eiscafé-Kette in eisbecherförmigen Gebäuden auf. Sogar das *Life Magazine* berichtete über verrückte Eisbecher wie „Moron's Ecstasy" („Ekstase des Irren"). Das Konzept der verrückten Eisdiele war sofort ein Hit.

Arthur Whizin est d'abord le propriétaire de la chaîne Chili Bowl. Il ouvre ses glaciers en forme de rotonde après la Seconde Guerre mondiale. Ses fameuses recettes, comme le « Moron's Ecstasy » (« délice du crétin »), sont publiées dans le magazine *Life*. Whizin est un maître des relations publiques et son concept de glacier extravagant connaît un succès immédiat.

ABOVE **McDonnell's, c. 1946, Los Angeles, California**

OPPOSITE **California Zephyr Dining Car, c. 1947**

BELOW **Santa Fe Dining Car, c. 1949**

As families with children traveled more after World War II, restaurants had to cater to kids with special menus that had enough color and illustrations to keep them entertained. Cartoon characters and nursery rhymes, here tied to food items, were key to this railroad train menu.

Nach dem Zweiten Weltkrieg waren mehr Familien mit Kindern auf Reisen, und Restaurants mussten ihre kleinen Gäste mit Speisekarten bei Laune halten, die bunt und voller Bilder waren. Comicfiguren und Kinderverse, die alle etwas mit dem Essen zu tun haben, stehen im Mittelpunkt dieser Speisewagenkarte.

Après la Seconde Guerre mondiale, les Américains voyagent plus souvent en famille et les restaurants proposent désormais des menus pour enfants spécialement illustrés et colorés à leur intention. Personnages de bandes dessinées et comptines, ici en rapport avec les plats proposés, sont essentiels sur cette carte de wagon-restaurant.

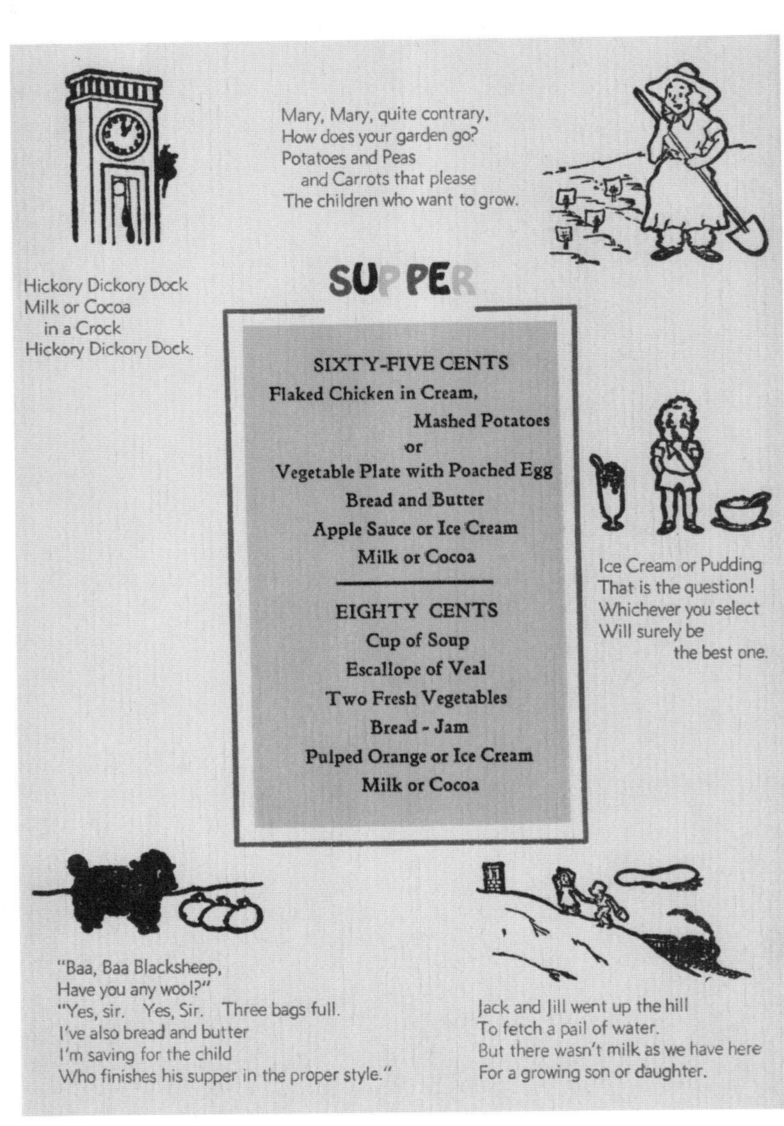

Mary, Mary, quite contrary,
How does your garden go?
Potatoes and Peas
and Carrots that please
The children who want to grow.

Hickory Dickory Dock
Milk or Cocoa
in a Crock
Hickory Dickory Dock.

SUPPER

SIXTY-FIVE CENTS
Flaked Chicken in Cream,
Mashed Potatoes
or
Vegetable Plate with Poached Egg
Bread and Butter
Apple Sauce or Ice Cream
Milk or Cocoa

EIGHTY CENTS
Cup of Soup
Escallope of Veal
Two Fresh Vegetables
Bread - Jam
Pulped Orange or Ice Cream
Milk or Cocoa

Ice Cream or Pudding
That is the question!
Whichever you select
Will surely be
the best one.

"Baa, Baa Blacksheep,
Have you any wool?"
"Yes, sir. Yes, Sir. Three bags full.
I've also bread and butter
I'm saving for the child
Who finishes his supper in the proper style."

Jack and Jill went up the hill
To fetch a pail of water.
But there wasn't milk as we have here
For a growing son or daughter.

CHILDREN'S
MENU
California
Zephyr

LEFT *S.S. Lurline*, Matson Lines, c. 1941

OPPOSITE & ABOVE ***S.S. Lurline*, Matson Lines, 1951**

Matson Lines was famous for its graphic art in the 1940s. John Kelly, Frank MacIntosh, and Eugene Savage were among those on the cruise company's menu-design roster. Savage's covers above were designed to form a mural when the individual menus, issued daily on board, were lined up.

Die Reederei Matson Lines war in den 40er-Jahren berühmt für ihre Illustrationen; zum Designteam des Kreuzfahrtveranstalters gehörten John Kelly, Frank MacIntosh und Eugene Savage. Die abgebildeten, von Savage gestalteten, täglich wechselnden Bordkarten bildeten nebeneinandergehängt ein Wandbild.

La Matson Lines est réputée pour ses signatures artistiques des années 1940 : John Kelly, Frank MacIntosh et Eugene Savage font partie des artistes employés par cette compagnie maritime pour créer ses menus. Les couvertures de Savage (ci-dessus) sont conçues pour former une fresque lorsque les menus distribués à bord chaque jour sont affichés côte à côte.

RIGHT **Aloha Dinner, *S.S. Lurline*, Matson Lines, 1948**

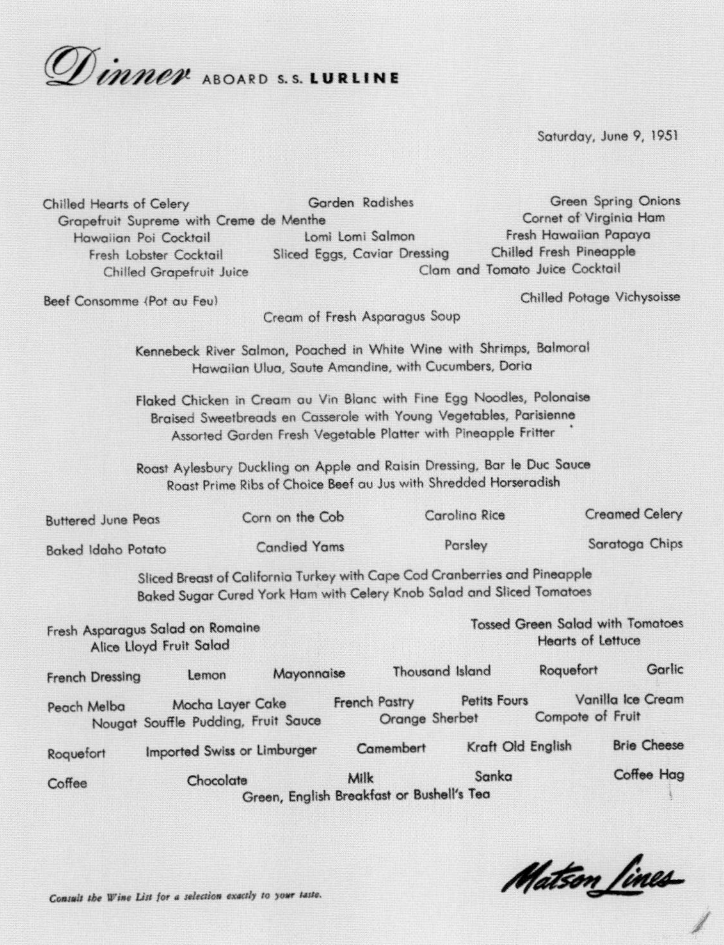

Dinner ABOARD S. S. **LURLINE**

Saturday, June 9, 1951

Chilled Hearts of Celery   Garden Radishes   Green Spring Onions
Grapefruit Supreme with Creme de Menthe   Cornet of Virginia Ham
Hawaiian Poi Cocktail   Lomi Lomi Salmon   Fresh Hawaiian Papaya
Fresh Lobster Cocktail   Sliced Eggs, Caviar Dressing   Chilled Fresh Pineapple
Chilled Grapefruit Juice   Clam and Tomato Juice Cocktail

Beef Consomme (Pot au Feu)   Chilled Potage Vichysoisse
Cream of Fresh Asparagus Soup

Kennebeck River Salmon, Poached in White Wine with Shrimps, Balmoral
Hawaiian Ulua, Saute Amandine, with Cucumbers, Doria

Flaked Chicken in Cream au Vin Blanc with Fine Egg Noodles, Polonaise
Braised Sweetbreads en Casserole with Young Vegetables, Parisienne
Assorted Garden Fresh Vegetable Platter with Pineapple Fritter

Roast Aylesbury Duckling on Apple and Raisin Dressing, Bar le Duc Sauce
Roast Prime Ribs of Choice Beef au Jus with Shredded Horseradish

Buttered June Peas   Corn on the Cob   Carolina Rice   Creamed Celery
Baked Idaho Potato   Candied Yams   Parsley   Saratoga Chips

Sliced Breast of California Turkey with Cape Cod Cranberries and Pineapple
Baked Sugar Cured York Ham with Celery Knob Salad and Sliced Tomatoes

Fresh Asparagus Salad on Romaine   Tossed Green Salad with Tomatoes
Alice Lloyd Fruit Salad   Hearts of Lettuce

French Dressing   Lemon   Mayonnaise   Thousand Island   Roquefort   Garlic

Peach Melba   Mocha Layer Cake   French Pastry   Petits Fours   Vanilla Ice Cream
Nougat Souffle Pudding, Fruit Sauce   Orange Sherbet   Compote of Fruit

Roquefort   Imported Swiss or Limburger   Camembert   Kraft Old English   Brie Cheese

Coffee   Chocolate   Milk   Sanka   Coffee Hag
Green, English Breakfast or Bushell's Tea

Consult the Wine List for a selection exactly to your taste.

Matson Lines

LEFT The DC7 Statesman, American Airlines, 1953

With no cooking possible while in flight, airlines competed to showcase their first-class offerings, while in coach class the food was basic and crafted for a largely American family trade. The meals for both classes were prepared and cooked at airport commissary kitchens, to be reheated onboard. Airlines also made a major effort to have fine restaurants in their terminals so that passengers could arrive hours before flight time and eat before boarding.

Während des Flugs konnte nicht gekocht werden, doch die Fluggesellschaften wetteiferten in der ersten Klasse mit Luxusessen. In der Touristenklasse servierte man weitgehend amerikanische Hausmannskost. Die Mahlzeiten wurden in Flughafenküchen zubereitet und an Bord aufgewärmt. Die Fluggesellschaften bemühten sich auch sehr darum, gute Restaurants in die Flughäfen zu locken, damit die Fluggäste mehrere Stunden vor dem Abflug kommen und essen konnten.

Sans la possibilité de cuisiner en vol, les compagnies aériennes rivalisent d'ingéniosité pour présenter leurs menus de première classe, tandis qu'en classe économique, les repas conçus pour une clientèle américaine familiale restent basiques. Dans les deux cas, les repas sont préparés et cuisinés dans les cuisines des aéroports avant d'être réchauffés dans l'avion. Les compagnies s'évertuent également à proposer des restaurants gastronomiques dans leur terminal afin que les voyageurs prennent le temps de se restaurer avant l'embarquement.

BELOW Skyview Dining Room, Philadelphia International Airport, 1956, Philadelphia, Pennsylvania

OPPOSITE Bond Fifth Avenue, Flight Deck Restaurant, 1948, New York, New York

Skyview

SPECIAL PLATTER LUNCHEONS

SERVED FROM NOON UNTIL 2:30 P.M. WEDNESDAY, NOVEMBER 14, 1956

APPETIZERS

Chilled Grapefruit Juice .... .25
V-8 Cocktail .... .25 Chilled Tomato Juice .... .25
Marinated Herring, Sour Cream.. .50 Shrimps Lamaze or Cocktail Sauce 1.00
Fresh Fruit Supreme .... .50 Backfin Crabmeat Cocktail 1.00

SOUP

Philadelphia Pepper Pot Cup .25; Bowl .40 Consomme Alphabet
Berlo Famous Snapper Soup, Roll and Butter .60 —.40

PLATTERS

1—Braised Swiss Steak, with Mushrooms en Casserole 1.65
2—Hot Roast Turkey Sandwich, Giblet Gravy, Cranberry Jelly........ 1.40
3—Broiled Ocean Fresh Blue Fish with Chive Butter 1.40
4—Virginia Ham and Turkey a la King on Crisp Noodles 1.35
5*Baked Italian La Sagna, Ravioli Style, with Meat Balls, Salad Bowl 1.50
6—*Fresh Fruit Salad Bowl with Cottage Cheese, Melba Toast 1.10
7—Fluffy Omelette with Currant Jelly 1.25
8—Fresh Calf's Liver Saute with Bacon Strip (to order) 2.75

(Served with Rolls and Butter) * Items Do Not Include Vegetables

CHOICE OF TWO

Mashed Yellow Turnips
Whipped Potatoes
Mixed Garden Salad
Fresh String Beans
French Fried Potatoes

DELAWARE VALLEY, U. S. A.

SPECIAL LUNCHEON FROM THE VALLEY

Philadelphia Pepper Pot
BAKED CHESTER COUNTY SAUSAGE CAKES
Fried Montgomery County Apples
Baked Burlington County Potato All Valley Tossed Salad
Philadelphia Cream Cheese with Toasted Crackers
Hot Corn and All Bran Muffins
Coffee Tea Homogenized Milk

$1.40

DESSERTS

Frozen Chocolate Eclair .... .50 French Pastry .... .50
Assorted Pies .... .30 Gelatin with Whipped Cream ...... .35
Layer Cake .... .30 Ice Cream .... .35
Rice Pudding .... .25 Sundaes .... .50
Delicious Baked Apple with Cream .... .40

BEVERAGES

Coffee .... .15 Homogenized Milk .... .15
Tea .... .15 Buttermilk .... .15
Chocolate Milk .... .15

(We Regret that We Cannot be Responsible for Personal Property)

Bond
FIFTH AVENUE
FLIGHT DECK RESTAURANT

1947
New Years' Eve
THE WALDORF-ASTORIA

OPPOSITE New Year's Eve, the Waldorf-Astoria, 1947, New York, New York

ABOVE The Waldorf-Astoria, 1950, New York, New York

Dinner de Luxe

Selection of Entrée Indicates Price of Complete Dinner

CHOICE OF

Cherrystone Clams on the Shell
Sea Food Cocktail Fruit Supreme
Chilled Tomato Juice

CHOICE OF

Consommé with Noodles
Manhattan Clam Chowder
Chicken Gumbo in Jelly

Celery Ripe Large Olives

CHOICE OF

Fried Filet of Sole, Tartar Sauce............2.25
Broiled Lobster, Melted Butter (Half)...3.00
Curried Shrimps with Rice....................2.85
Casserole of Chicken, Virginia Ham, Mushrooms, Newburg 2.75
Braised Leg of Lamb, Pan Gravy, Mint Jelly 2.75
Pounded Club Steak, Bordelaise............3.00
Breast of Capon Under Glass, Eugènie 3.25
Veal Cutlette Sauté, Bércy with Shredded Mushrooms, Red Peppers and Artichokes...........3.00
Brook Trout Sauté, Amandine...............3.50
Roast Young Turkey, Giblet Gravy...3.25
~~Charcoal Broiled Tenderloin Steak,~~ Maître d'Hôtel 4.25

Potatoes Rissolée Navy Beans, Bretonne
Fresh String Beans

Salad Beaudry, French Dressing

CHOICE OF

Prune Cheese Cake
Pumpkin Pie Strawberry Parfait
Mixed Stewed Fruit, Sponge Cake
Coupe Ambassador
Sultana Ice Cream Roll
Ice Cream Sherbet

Demi-Tasse

COUVERT CHARGE AFTER 9:00 P.M., $1.00
EXCEPT SATURDAYS AND HOLIDAYS, $1.50

Cocoanut Grove
Los Angeles Ambassador

RELISHES AND APPETIZERS

Blue Point Oysters, Shell.. .90 · Olympia Oysters.........1.00 · Antipasto.............. .80 · Fresh Caviar............3.00 · Fresh Shrimp Cocktail....1.00 · Celery.. .45 Stuffed.. .80
Crab Cocktail..........1.00 · Smoked Salmon......... .90 · Canape of Anchovies... .90 · Herring............... .70 · Olives, Jumbo or Queen. .45 · Avocado Cocktail...... .80
Fruit Cocktail.......... .80 · Radishes.............. .40 · Grapefruit Supreme.... .80 · Salami................ .75 · Tomato Juice Cocktail .. .40 · Sardines..............1.00
Lobster Cocktail........1.25 · Clam Juice Cocktail.... .55
Mixed Fresh Sea Food Cocktail....1.10 · Ambassador Assorted Hors d' Oeuvres....1.25

SOUPS

***Consommé with Noodles..... .35** ***Manhattan Clam Chowder..... .35**
Specia Chicken Noodle.. .65 Chicken Broth in Cup.. .50 Chicken Gumbo, Creole .55
Cream of Puree of Tomatoes or Peas..... .50 Onion Soup au Gratin................ .65
COLD SOUP IN CUP: Tomato.... .45 Chicken Broth.... .50 Consomme.... .40
Green Turtle with Sherry. .70 Strained Gumbo....... .50 Fresh Open Oyster Stew 1.10

FISH

***Filet of Flounder, Bonne Femme, Potatoes Parisienne..............1.00**
Broiled Barracuda, Lemon Butter, Waffle Potatoes............ .95
Brook Trout Sauté with Almonds Butter............1.50
Boneless Smelts Sauté, Fines Herbes with Egg Plant.............. .95
Baked Sea Bass, Spanish Style with Rice.............. .95
Brook Trout, Broiled or Meuniere.......1.35 Filet of Sand-dabs...................1.30
Sand-dabs, Sauté or Broiled............1.10 Filet of Sole, Fried or Sauté...........1.10

TODAY'S SPECIAL SUGGESTIONS AND ROASTS

***Braised Leg of Lamb with Navy Beans, Bretonne..................1.25**
***Casserole of Chicken and Virginia Ham, Newburg with Fresh Mushrooms, New Peas..................1.35**
***Broiled Salisbury Steak, Sauce Piquante, Demi-French Fried Potatoes.. .95**
***Veal Cutlette Sauté, Bércy with Shredded Fresh Mushrooms, Red Peppers and Artichokes, Spinach..............1.25**
Curried Gulf Shrimp with Rice..................1.40
Broiled Live Lobster with Melted Butter Demi-French Fried Potatoes (Half)..........1.45
Breast of Capon Under Glass, Mushrooms, Asparagus Tips, Eugènie...1.75
Filet Mignon Sauté, Bouquetière with Fresh Mushrooms Sauce........3.00
***Roast Prime Rib of Beef, au Jus..................1.35**
***Roast Lamb with Mint Sauce..................1.35**
***Roast Turkey with Cranberry Sauce..................1.50**

FROM THE BROILER

Sirloin Steak............3.25 · Rump Steak............2.25 · Steak Minute...........2.50 · Filet Mignon............3.25
Lamb Chops...........1.40 · Special Lamb Chop....1.40 · Baby Lamb Chops......1.45 · Porterhouse Steak, p.p. 3.25
Tenderloin Steak......3.25 · English Mutton Chop...1.50 · Broiled Chicken 3.30; ½1.65 · Squab Chicken........1.75
Broiled Squab, Currant Jelly........1.90

POTATOES

Mashed, Boiled or French Fried 40 Sauté, Hash Browned or Lyonnaise 45
Cottage Fried 55 Au Gratin 50 Hashed in Cream 45 Saratoga or Julienne 40
Boiled New Potatoes, Parsley Butter or Cream 40 Souffle 55 Baked 45
SWEET POTATOES: Baked 45 Candied 50 Fried 50 Grilled 50 Southern Style 60

VEGETABLES

Corn Saute in Butter 60 Stewed Corn 50 Fresh Asparagus, Butter Sauce or Hollandaise 90
Fresh String Beans 55 Boiled Onions 50 Cauliflower 55 Stewed Tomatoes 50 Peas 50
Turnips 50 Boiled Rice 50 French Fried Zucchini 60
Fresh Vegetable Selection with Poached Egg 1.25 Buttered Beets 50 Fresh Artichokes 65
Carrots, Puree or Sauté 50 Broiled or Fried Tomatoes 65 Whole Spinach 50; Creamed 55
Fresh Mushrooms Saute 1.10

SALADS: Cole Slaw, Julienne of Chicken, Ham, Tongue, Charley 1.50
Combination 90 Mixed Green Salad, Shredded Chicken 1.50
Watercress 55 Waldorf 70 Cucumbers 60 Chicory and Beets 50
Los Angeles 75 Fresh Asparagus, Mayonnaise or Vinaigrette 90
Ambassador Cooks 80 Avocado 85 Pineapple-Cottage Cheese 65
Fresh Vegetable 95 Chicken 1.65 Fresh Crab 1.60 Fruit 85
Ambassador Fruit Special 95 Romaine 50 Hearts of Lettuce 50
Lettuce and Tomato 50 Mixed Green Salad 75 Shrimp 1.50
Lobster 1.65

DRESSINGS: Mayonnaise, Cream or Egg 35 Russian Dressing 70
Lorenzo 40 Blue Cheese or 1000 Island 40
Dressings Made with Pure Olive Oil or Non-Fattening Salad Oil.

COLD: Roast Chicken, Half 1.65 Pressed Chicken and Virginia Ham 1.25
Virginia Ham 1.40 Roas Beef 1.40 Sliced Chicken, Virginia Ham 1.75
Tongue 1.10 Ham 1.25 Pressed Corned Beef 95 Roast Turkey 1.65
Assorted Cold Meats with Chicken 1.75 Rack of Lamb 1.40
Crab Louie 1.60 All Cold Meats Served with Potato Salad or Cold Slaw
Half Lobster 1.65 Cracked Crab 1.35

DESSERTS: Pumpkin Pie 35 Blueberry Pie 35 Fresh Apple Pie 30 Mixed Stewed Fruit, Sponge Cake 35
Prune Cheese Cake 35 Sultana Ice Cream Roll 45 Coupe Ambassador 50 Strawberry Parfait 45

Pound Cake 45 Fruit Jell-O 40 Fresh Stewed Fruit 60 Cup Custard 40
Fresh Strawberry Tart 40 Rice Pudding with Cream 45 Petits Fours 50
Strawberry Short Cake 60

Crepes Suzette with Liquor 1.50 French Pastry 35 Pie a la Mode 60
Ambassador Fruit Cake 50 Vienna Apple Cake 40 Assorted Cakes 50
Green Apple Pie 35

ICE CREAMS AND ICES: Vanilla, Chocolate, Coffe or Pistachio 50
Meringue Glacé 65 Strawberry 55 Sherbets 45
Nesselrode Pudding 65 Parfaits 65

FRUITS: Grapefruit ½ 45 Strawberries 65 Fresh Pineapple 55
Grapes 45 Orange 30 Apple 30 Fresh Pear 30 Casaba Melon 55
Persian Melon 55

TEA: English, Ceylon, Orange Pekoe, Black, Mingcha or Oolong 30

CHEESE: Camembert 50 Philadelphia Cream 45 Gruyere 60
Pimiento 45 Blue Cheese 50 Swiss 60 Liederkranz 50 Cottage 50

BEVERAGES: Pot of Coffee 30 Sanka Coffe 50 Silex Coffe 50
Turkish Coffee 75 Demi-Tasse 20 Postum 30
Certified Milk 30 Buttermilk 25
Ice Tea, Coffee or Chocolate 35

COUVERT CHARGE AFTER 9:00 P.M., $1.00. EXCEPT SATURDAYS AND HOLIDAYS, $1.50

* DISHES MARKED WITH STAR READY TO SERVE PORTIONS SERVED FOR ONE PERSON ONLY

Service charge 15c per person. No service charge with food orders of $1.00 or more.

Not responsible for coats, wraps or other personal property that is not checked.

Jan. 22

Cocoanut Grove

OPPOSITE & ABOVE Cocoanut Grove, the Ambassador Hotel, 1945, Los Angeles, California

ABOVE & BELOW Brown Derby, 1947, Hollywood, California

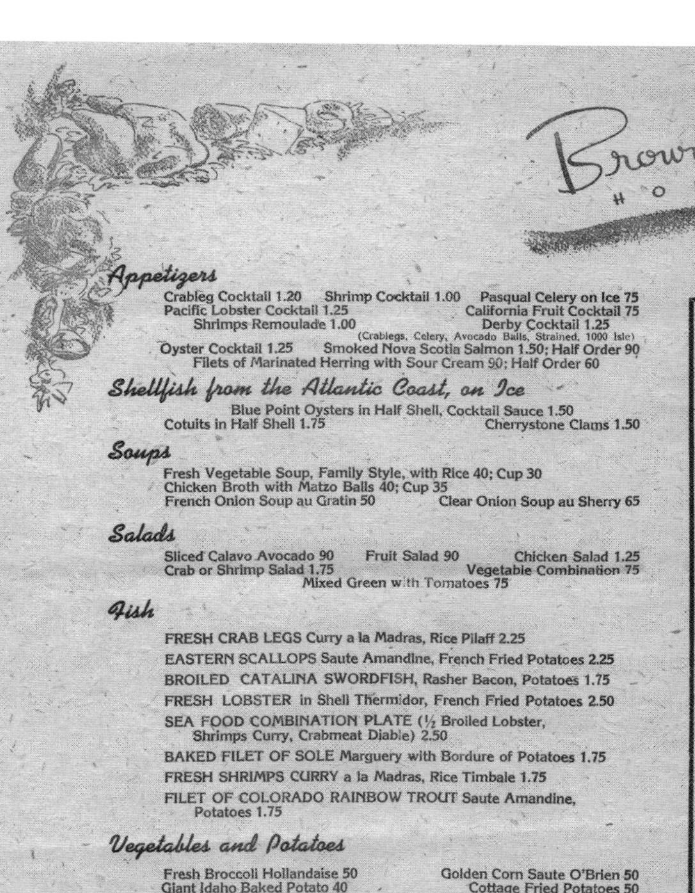

Brown Derby
HOLLYWOOD

Appetizers

Crableg Cocktail 1.20 — Shrimp Cocktail 1.00 — Pasqual Celery on Ice 75
Pacific Lobster Cocktail 1.25 — California Fruit Cocktail 75
Shrimps Remoulade 1.00 — Derby Cocktail 1.25
(Crablegs, Celery, Avocado Balls, Strained, 1000 Isle)
Oyster Cocktail 1.25 — Smoked Nova Scotia Salmon 1.50; Half Order 90
Filets of Marinated Herring with Sour Cream 90; Half Order 60

Shellfish from the Atlantic Coast, on Ice

Blue Point Oysters in Half Shell, Cocktail Sauce 1.50
Cotuits in Half Shell 1.75 — Cherrystone Clams 1.50

Soups

Fresh Vegetable Soup, Family Style, with Rice 40; Cup 30
Chicken Broth with Matzo Balls 40; Cup 35
French Onion Soup au Gratin 50 — Clear Onion Soup au Sherry 65

Salads

Sliced Calavo Avocado 90 — Fruit Salad 90 — Chicken Salad 1.25
Crab or Shrimp Salad 1.75 — Vegetable Combination 75
Mixed Green with Tomatoes 75

Fish

FRESH CRAB LEGS Curry a la Madras, Rice Pilaff 2.25
EASTERN SCALLOPS Saute Amandine, French Fried Potatoes 2.25
BROILED CATALINA SWORDFISH, Rasher Bacon, Potatoes 1.75
FRESH LOBSTER in Shell Thermidor, French Fried Potatoes 2.50
SEA FOOD COMBINATION PLATE (½ Broiled Lobster, Shrimps Curry, Crabmeat Diable) 2.50
BAKED FILET OF SOLE Marguery with Bordure of Potatoes 1.75
FRESH SHRIMPS CURRY a la Madras, Rice Timbale 1.75
FILET OF COLORADO RAINBOW TROUT Saute Amandine, Potatoes 1.75

Vegetables and Potatoes

Fresh Broccoli Hollandaise 50 — Golden Corn Saute O'Brien 50
Giant Idaho Baked Potato 40 — Cottage Fried Potatoes 50
Julienne of String Beans 40 — Hashed in Cream Potatoes 55
Hot Artichoke, Sauce Hollandaise 50
Fresh Jumbo Asparagus, Sauce Hollandaise 75

NO HALF PORTIONS SERVED

Brown Derby No. 2 (Dinner)—2 — Tuesday, April 22, 1947

Visit Our Liquor Store at 1632 No. Vine For Your Requirements in SCOTCH BONDED BOURBON or Other SPIRITS and WINES We Deliver

Specialties

SPAGHETTI DERBY: Italian Spaghetti, Fresh Tomatoes, Mushrooms and Meat Sauce 1.10
MEXICAN TAMALE (Old Fashioned Mexican Maize Chicken Tamale, Fresh Daily) 90
CREAMED TURKEY DERBY (All White Meat, Served in Toasted Crouton, with Cranberry Jelly) 2.25
PAN FRIED CORNED BEEF HASH 1.00; with Poached Egg 1.25
STEAK HAMBURGER DE LUXE (Ground Sirloin Steak) with or without Onions, Potatoes 1.85
DE LUXE CHICKEN ENCHILADAS with Chili Con Carne and Frijoles 1.50
FILET MIGNON TID-BITS with Sliced Mushrooms, Chef's Special, Risotto 1.85
SCALLOPED CHICKEN a la King, Patty Shell, Peas in Butter 1.25

Entrees

ROAST PRIME RIB OF BEEF au Jus, Giant Idaho Baked Potato 2.50
SCALLOPED BREAST OF CHICKEN Niceoise in Chafing Dish 2.50
OLD FASHIONED POT ROAST, Potato Pancakes, Creamed Spinach 1.50
RAGOUT OF FILET BEEF a la Deutch in Casserole 2.00
~~BARBECUED BREAST OF LAMB, Mashed Potatoes 1.35~~
BROILED CENTER CUT HAM STEAK, Candied Yams, Pickled Pear 2.25
BREADED FILET OF PORK a la Mornay, Fresh Asparagus Tips 1.65
FRESH MUSHROOMS SAUTE Ber [illegible] Fried Ham, English Muffin 2.00
PAPRIKA VEAL CUTLET, Egg Noodles Polonaise 1.65
SPRING CHICKEN Saute in Butter, Peas in Butter, French Fried Potatoes 2.50
BROILED FRESH CALF'S LIVER, Egg Plant, Tomato, Bacon 1.50

Pastry Specials

Cherry Pie 40 — Banana Shortcake 40
Assorted Parisian Pastries 40 — Rice or Chocolate Pudding 35

Desserts

Ice Cream 40 — Sherbet 40 — Fresh Fruit Compote 50
Baked Fresh Rhubarb 50 — Parfait 50 — Coupe St. Jacques 50
Meringue Glace 75 — Cherry Flambe 2.00 — Crepe Suzette 2.00

BEVERAGES AS LISTED ON A LA CARTE MENU

Sales Tax will be added on all taxable items in accordance with the rulings issued under the Sales and Use Tax Law

Sorry we cannot be responsible for lost articles

LEFT & BELOW The Players, 1940, Hollywood, California

Playwright, screenwriter, and director Preston Sturges (The Miracle of Morgan's Creek, Hail the Conquering Hero, The Lady Eve, and others) founded and invested in the Players, an unsuccessful 1940s nightclub-restaurant that drew fellow directors like Ernst Lubitsch and Billy Wilder. It closed in 1953.

Autor und Regisseur Preston Sturges (*Sensation in Morgan's Creek, Heil dem siegreichen Helden, Die Falschspielerin* u. a. m.) investierte in den 1940er-Jahren in das Players. Das Nachtlokal zog zwar Regiekollegen wie Ernst Lubitsch und Billy Wilder an, wurde aber schon 1953 wieder geschlossen.

En 1940, l'auteur, scénariste et réalisateur Preston Sturges (*Miracle au village, Hail the Conquering Hero, Un cœur pris au piège, etc.*) crée et finance The Players, un night-club et restaurant qui attire des cinéastes comme Ernst Lubitsch et Billy Wilder. Il connaîtra un succès relatif et fermera en 1953.

OPPOSITE La Rue Restaurant, c. 1946, Hollywood, California

Billy Wilkerson, of Ciro's and Trocadero fame, opened the French restaurant La Rue in 1944.

Billy Wilkerson, bereits durch Ciro's and Trocadero berühmt, machte 1944 das französische Restaurant La Rue auf.

Billy Wilkerson, connu pour le Ciro's et le Trocadero, ouvre le restaurant français La Rue en 1944.

Hors D'Oeuvres

Caviar
Prosciutto 2.25
Smoked Salmon 2.25
Escargots 2.25
Terrine de Foie Gras Truffé 3.50
Crèpes Farcies, Colony 2.25
Blue Points, Cherrystone 2.25
Chicken Livers Maison 1.50
Shrimps LA RUE 2.25
Marinated Herrings ... 1.50
Coupe au Fruit 1.00
Cracked Crab 2.50

COCKTAILS, Lobster, Shrimps ...... 1.60 Louisiana Fresh Crab Meat Lumps 1.75

Potages

Petite Marmite Henry IV ... 1.50
Consommé Double au Sherry .90
FROID: Vichyssoise ...... .80
Green Turtle au Xérès 1.25
Soupe a l'Oignon Gratinèe. 1.00
Madrilène en Gelée ...... .90
Boula Boula LA RUE 1.50
Saint Germain 1.00
Waterburry .... .90

Poissons

Dover Sole Grillée à l'Anglaise 4.25
Lobster Grillée au Beurre Foundu 4.50
Filets of Boston Sole Belle Meunière 3.75
Sea Food Newburg 4.00
Shrimps a l'Indienne 4.00
Deviled Crab Meat, New Orleans Style 4.00
Filets of Trout, Caprice du Chef 4.25
Grenouilles Provençale 4.25
Goujonette of Sole, Sauce Tartare 3.75
Pompano Veronique 4.25

Grillades

New York Steak 5.50
French Minute 5.50
Lamb Chops 4.25
Calf's Liver 3.75
Filet Mignon 5.50
Royal Squab 4.25
Chicken, Cressonière 3.75
Côtes de Porc 3.75
Minute Steak 5.00
Squab Chicken 4.00
Lamb Kidney 3.75
Sauce Béarnaise .... .50

Rotis

Faisan Reine Grain Poussin Canard
Carré d'Agneau Pigeon Selle d'Agneau Rock Cornish Game Hen

Legumes

Fresh Asparagus 1.25
Petits Pois Française ..... .90
Hearts of Celery, Madère .. 1.00
Cauliflower Gratiné 1.00
French Endives 1.25
Broccoli .... .90
Artichoke 1.00
Zucchini 1.00
Spinach à la Crème ...... .90
Egg Plant, Orientale 1.00
Fresh String Beans ...... .90
Sauce Hollandaise .... .50

Pommes Soufflées 1.50 Mousseline .85 Baked .75 Frites .75 Sautées .85 Cottage Fried 1.25

Salades

Boston Lettuce Maison 1.25
Bibb Lettuce 1.25
Romaine .... .90
Endives Belge 1.25
Cressonière 1.00
Tomato .... .90
Hearts of Palm 1.50
Verte Melangée .... .90
Italienne 1.25

Entremets

Macedoine de Fruits 1.75
Mousse au Chocolat 1.00
Meringue Glacée 1.00
Crèpes Suzette 2.50
Coupe aux Marrons 1.50
Peach Melba 1.50
Zabaglione 1.75
French Pastry .... .75
Dobos .... .90
Pear Hélène 1.50
Cherries Jubilées 1.75
Cômpote de Fruit 1.25
Almond Cake .... .90
Ananas au Kirsh 1.75
Strawberries Flambées ... 1.75

GLACES
Vanille, Chocolat, Moka, Citron, Pineapple, Raspberries .... .75

Coffee .40 Tea .40 Sanka .40 Postum .40 Espresso .50 Iced Tea .50 B & B .25

Nos Plats Choisis

La Poitrine de Faisan á la Fine, Palace 7.00
Le Tournedos á la Mode de Strasbourg 6.50
La Suprème de Volaille, Parisienne 4.50
Le Pigeonneau en Cocotte, Montmorency 4.50
Le Medaillon de Ris de Veau aux Fruits de Perigourd 4.25
Le Coq au Vin du Vieux Pays 4.25
Le Rognon de Veau Sauté au Chambertin 4.25
La Poularde de Choix, Souvaroff 15.00
La Noisette d'Agneau, Archiduc 4.75
Le Caneton a l'Orange 4.75
La Côte de Veau aux Petits Pois, Clamart 4.75
Le Poulet de Grain en Casserolle, LA RUE 10.00
La Côte de Pauillac, Villeroy 5.00

RESTAURANT
La Rue
HOLLYWOOD

FORBIDDEN-PALACE
CHINESE FOOD AT ITS BEST
團
和
頤
Choice Savory Foods
Refined Atmosphere
Courteous Service
Popular Prices
451 Gin Ling Way (New Chinatown) VAndike 5229

OPPOSITE Forbidden Palace, c. 1939, Los Angeles, California

BELOW Maxey's Singapore Spa, c. 1938, Hollywood, California

Chinese restaurants like Maxey's Singapore Spa played off Oriental stereotypes of Fu Manchu-like figures and the word "den," to conjure the image of an opium den.

Chinarestaurants wie das Maxey's Singapore Spa bezogen sich auf Klischeedarstellungen wie diese Fu-Manchu-Figur und nannten sich gerne „Den" („Höhle"), eine Anspielung auf Opiumhöhlen.

Les restaurants chinois comme le Maxey's Singapore Spa jouent sur les stéréotypes orientaux avec des silhouettes à la Fu Manchu et le mot anglais « den » (tanière) évoquant les fumeries d'opium.

ABOVE Lamps of China, c. 1949, San Francisco, California

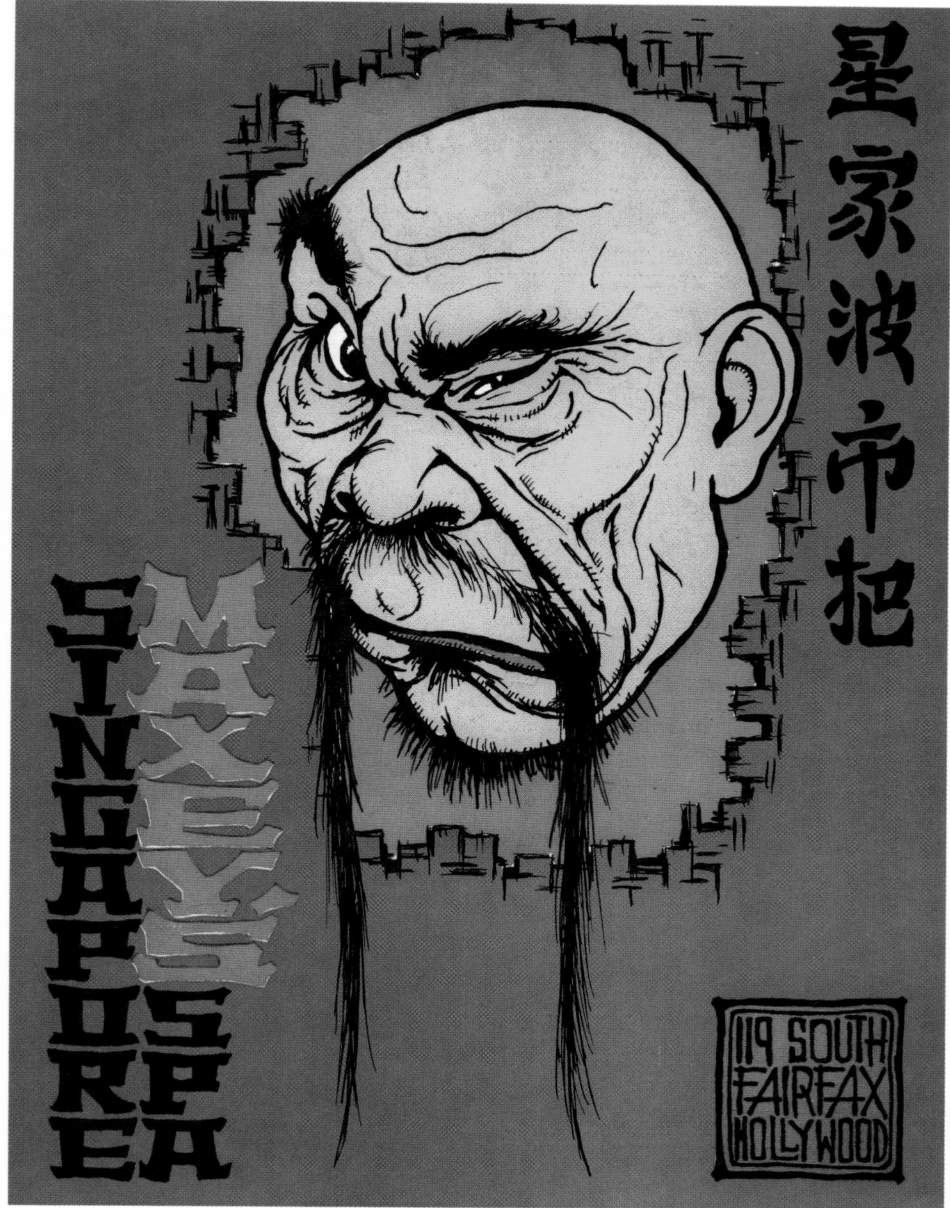

LEFT Ruby Foo's Den, c. 1939, Boston, Massachusetts

BELOW & OPPOSITE Frank's 806, 1944, Sacramento, California

CHINESE MENU

GAI (CHICKEN)

No My Gai (whole boned chicken, stuffed with sweet rice) 4.50
Hung Ngon Gai Ding (diced chicken with almonds) .... .85
Hop Tow Gai Ding (diced chicken with walnuts) .... .85
Chow Gai Peen (chicken filled with mushrooms and vegetables) .... .85
Moo Goo Gai Kow (boneless chicken with white mushrooms) 1.00
Lon Dow Gai Kow (Chinese sugar peas with chicken) .... .90
Ho Yow Bow Yee Gai Kow (abalone with chicken and oyster sauce) 1.00
Bo Low Gai Kow (boned chicken with pineapple) .... .95

APP (DUCK)

Wor Sui App (braised duck with almond) 1.10

BOK OPP (SQUAB)

Hoong Siew Bok Opp (soyo squab deep fried) 1.25
Chow Bok Opp Peen (boneless squab cooked with mushroom and bamboo shoot) 1.50

PAI QWAT (SPARERIBS)

Teem Seen Pai Qwat (sweet and sour spare ribs) .... .50
Gon Jow Pai Qwat (dry fried spare ribs) .... .60
Siew Pai Qwat (barbecued spareribs) .... .90
Bor Lor Pai Qwat (spare ribs with pineapple) .... .60

CHOP SUEY

Gee Yuke Chop Suey (with tender pork) .... .40
Ngow Yuke Chop Suey (with beef) .... .50
Lee Hong Chong Chop Suey (Chop Suey a la King) .... .50

NOT RESPONSIBLE FOR LOST OR EXCHANGED ARTICLES

CHINESE MENU

CHOW MEIN (FRIED NOODLES)

(Please mention crisp or pan fried)

Sang Gai Chow Mein (with fresh boneless chicken) .... .75
Har Yuke Chow Mein (with crab meat) .... .65
Hah Yuke Chow Mein (with prawns) .... .65
Fon Ker Ngon Yuke Chow Mein (with tomato and beef) .... .55
Hung Ngon Gai Chow Mein (with toasted almond and chicken) .... .90
Sub Gum Chow Mein (with almond and pork) .... .65
Cha Siew Chow Mein (with barbecued pork) .... .50

WOR MEIN (BOILED NOODLES IN SOUP)

Young Chew Wor Mein (with fowl and seafood) .... .65

SUEY MEIN (PLAIN BOILED NOODLES)

Gai See Suey Mein (with shredded chicken) .... .40
Cha Siew Suey Mein (with barbecued pork) .... .30

JOW WON TON

(CHINESE RAVIOLI, DEEP FRIED CRISP)

Teem Seen Jow Won Ton (with sweet and sour sauce) .... .75

WOR WON TON

(CHINESE RAVIOLI IN SOUP)

Young Chew Wor Won Ton (with fowl and seafood) .... .65
Cha Siew Won Ton (with barbecued pork) .... .35
Jop Suey Won Ton (with mixed vegetables and meat) .... .45

YEE HAH (SEA FOOD)

Jow Hah Kow (Fried Prawns) .... .85
Fon Ker Hah Kow .... .75
Sub Gum Hah Kow .... .75

NOT RESPONSIBLE FOR LOST OR EXCHANGED ARTICLES

FRANK'S
806
生發酒家

張鵬一之家
HOUSE OF P. Y. CHONG
Me-P. Y. Chong say: These 4 stlong peoples must stick together for keep peace in world always!
GOOD FOOD ALL TAMS
Charcoal bloiled steaks, chickens, ducks, oysters, sea foods . . . Me-P. Y. Chong serve them any tam can get same. Also usee plenty island growed vegebles, fluits for cooking when same on market.
This tam no more ala carte style in my restaulant. Ala carte only for take home. Spacial dinna must order before tam.
Please you no bling liquor my place—no come drunk my place. You bling liquor, Me-P. Y. must check same. You come drunk, Me-P. Y. no can allow you come in. Too muchee tlouble. You please excusee me and thank you vely muchee.
Me-P. Y. Chong
We takee care spacial banquet dinnas but can only takee limit numbas. First come first serve, you please placee order early for no disappoint.
Sometams fliends make appointmans. When come, place full no room. Vely sorry. You please wait little while.
Fliends sometams make appointmans but no keep. Me-P. Y. then must give nother peoples chance. You please excusee me.
Me-P. Y. Chong

OPPOSITE & BELOW House of P.Y. Chong, c. 1944, Honolulu, Hawaii

The pidgin English on this menu, parodying of the way Chinese people spoke American English, from House of P.Y. Chong in Honolulu was a clever marketing tool by its owner to capitalize on a regional and racial stereotype.

Das Pidginenglisch auf dieser Speisekarte parodierte den Akzent, mit dem viele Chinesen Englisch sprachen. Das House of P. Y. Chong in Honolulu machte sich die rassistischen Klischees clever als Werbegag zunutze.

Sur ce menu, le texte en pidgin parodie la façon dont les Chinois sont censés s'exprimer en anglais. Cette carte du House of P. Y. Chong à Honolulu est un outil marketing astucieux imaginé par son propriétaire pour jouer sur les stéréotypes régionaux et ethniques.

RIGHT Golden Pagoda, c. 1948, Los Angeles, California

HOUSE OF P.Y. CHONG

Story about Me-P. Y. vely intelest. I tell you in no too longwind way. After blitzquick Me-P. Y. start restaulant business again on April 4, 1942, flom sclatch. No got too muchee money. Get up dark in morning, go downtown shop, do cook, sometams wait tables. Slow way build business. Many fliends help P. Y., come eat dinna, tell fliends about good food. Me-P. Y. vely thankful.

* * *

First tam only Chinesee food, later add steak dinna. Plepare spacial Me-P. Y. saucee seclet way numba one good taste. Steaks go likee hot cakes, now vely famous.

* * *

Business pick up. Me-P. Y. buy Housee P. Y. Chong ploperty more than 100,000 square feets ocean side. No only talk-talk, must cost plenty money. But can do becausee fliends help.

* * *

Bimeby save more money for buy farm, plant fluits, vegebles, raisee chickens, ducks, goosee, etc. Part for myself usee; what no can usee sell away. Good for evelybody. This only plan inside head, bimeby some more talk-talk.

* * *

Me-P. Y. feel bad many tams becausee fliends all same soldiers, sailors, marines come eat—no more room left. So, soon when I can get material for remodel for make my placee more big. Me-P. Y. likee makee quick, if can. No have to send fliends away any more.

Me-P. Y.'s third son, Jackie Hok Pang, holding tlophy plesented Me-P. Y. by HHD for good work in sell War Bond. First son, Harrison Hok Nyeu, not in picture, in Army.

HOUSE OF P.Y. CHONG

P. Y. STEAK DINNER

FOUR PERSON SIX COURSE CHINESE DINNER

RIGHT Frederick & Nelson, c. 1945, Seattle, Washington

BELOW Melrod's, c. 1950, Los Angeles, California

BELOW The Pie Shop, c. 1946, San Francisco, California

OPPOSITE The Keg, c. 1950, North Hollywood, California

PHONE: SUnset 3-7912
The KEG
11002 VENTURA BLVD. - COR VINELAND, NORTH HOLLYWOOD
YOUR HOSTS — Mary and Bill
ITALY AT ITS BEST!
SPAGHETTI with our own SPECIAL MEAT SAUCE PARMESAN CHEESE & GARLIC TOAST
70c
"FAMOUS AMERICAN PARTNERS"
HAM OR BACON & Fresh RANCH EGGS fried in butter POTATOES BUTTERED TOAST & JELLY
85c
BEER ON TAP
JUMBO and GOLDEN LOUISIANA SHRIMP Fried in a perfect batter! POTATOES - COLE SLAW
Enuf said!
80c
"Bit-O'-England" FISH and CHIPS Served with COLE SLAW & TARTER SAUCE
60c
FROM THE DEEP, BLUE SEA! Fried EASTERN SCALLOPS COLE SLAW POTATOES TARTER SAUCE
75c
"MAMMY" Fried 1/2 DISJOINTED CHICKEN with FRENCH FRIES, COLE SLAW, HOT BISCUITS & HONEY
"Then you'll be sittin - sittin on top of the world"
$1.25
A KNOCK-OUT! I.M. BARBECUED - referee "KID PORK" vs "JUICY BEEF" 8 BITES TO A FINISH! on French Roll EVEN MONEY BET - TAKE YOUR "CHERCE"
40c
BARGAIN! ONE DOLLAR -Size HOT CAKES & A PITCHER OF MELTED GOLDEN BUTTER with SYRUP
35c
For the JITTERS "GRAVEYARD STEW" (MILK TOAST TO YOU)
30c
GRILLED AMERICAN CHEESE SANDWICH with POTATOES
35c
FOOD TO TAKE OUT
HOURS - 10:30 AM - 3:00 AM CLOSED SUNDAY

BIMBO'S
365
Club
JACK MARSHAL
HOCTOR AND BYRD
DORBEN DANCERS
365

OPPOSITE **New Year's, Bimbo's 365 Club, 1957, San Francisco, California**

ABOVE **Bimbo's 365 Club, 1963, San Francisco, California**

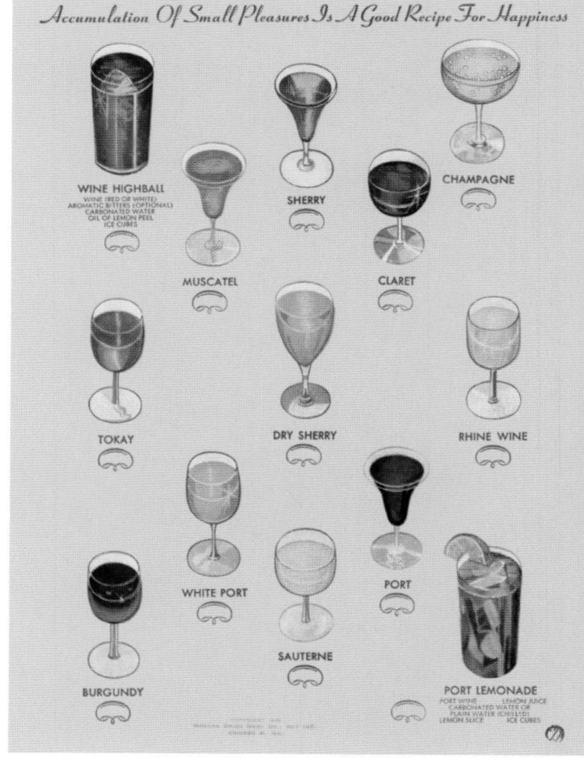

ABOVE **Heaven City Hotel, c. 1946, Mukwonago, Wisconsin**

By the mid-1940s most classic American cocktails were part of every bartender's repertoire, from the old-fashioned and sidecar to the Singapore sling and mint julep. These menus are proof of a fully developed cocktail culture.

Mitte der 1940er-Jahre beherrschte jeder Bartender die klassischen amerikanischen Cocktails, vom altmodischen Sidecar bis zum Singapore Sling und Mint Julep. Diese Speisekarten sind der Beweis für eine bereits voll entwickelte Cocktailkultur.

Dès le milieu des années 1940, les cocktails américains les plus classiques font partie du répertoire de chaque barman, de l'Old Fashioned au Side-Car, du Singapore Sling au Mint Julep. Ces cartes sont la preuve de l'existence d'une culture du cocktail bien établie.

ABOVE RIGHT & RIGHT **Lander's Restaurant and Cocktail Lounge, 1949, Chicago, Illinois**

Pagan 1.25
mild and satisfying

Ryan's Downfall
it can happen to you! 1.50

Green Dragon 1.25
beautiful, but beware

Bambisie for 2
nectar for lovers 3.00

Hurricane 1.10
no let-down here

Gold Cup 1.25
like small packages

Dr. Enoch 1.25
often deadly

Fog Cutter 1.75
your own risk

Vicious Wahine
careful of this one! 1.25

Typhoon 2.00
2 to a person

Pi Aye 2.00
served in fresh pineapple

Witches Brew 1.75
not recommended for the cardiac

Planter's Punch
greatest rum punch!
1.50

Coconga 1.00
coconut sensation

Navy Grog 1.60
limit of 3 to a person

Zombie 2.00
our own, without comparison

Scorpion
for 2, 3.00

Tabu 3.00
limit of one!

Head Hunter 2.00
the coconut is yours!

STATE and Local Taxes included in price. FEDERAL EXCISE TAX, 20%, for entertainment will be added.

ABOVE South Pacific Room, El Mirador Hotel, c. 1955, Las Vegas, Nevada

RIGHT Tonga Room, the Fairmont Hotel, c. 1945, San Francisco, California

TONGA ROOM
TROPICAL DRINK RECIPES
The Fairmont Hotel

Tonga Tabu (FOR 4 PERSONS)
1 oz. lemon juice, ½ lime; drop in ½ oz. cherry juice, ½ oz. papaya syrup, ½ oz. Curacao, 3 ozs. Coca-Cola, 3 ozs. rum • Fill bowl with shaved ice; decorate with cherries, sliced orange and gardenia; serve in fish-bowl glass. 2.50

Tonga Punch (FOR 2 PERSONS)
2 ozs. lemon juice, 2 ozs. orange juice, 1 dash Grenadine, 2½ ozs. light rum, ½ oz. Curacao • Top with Creme de Menthe, green; serve in 16-oz. Zombie glass; decorate with orange and cherry. 1.50

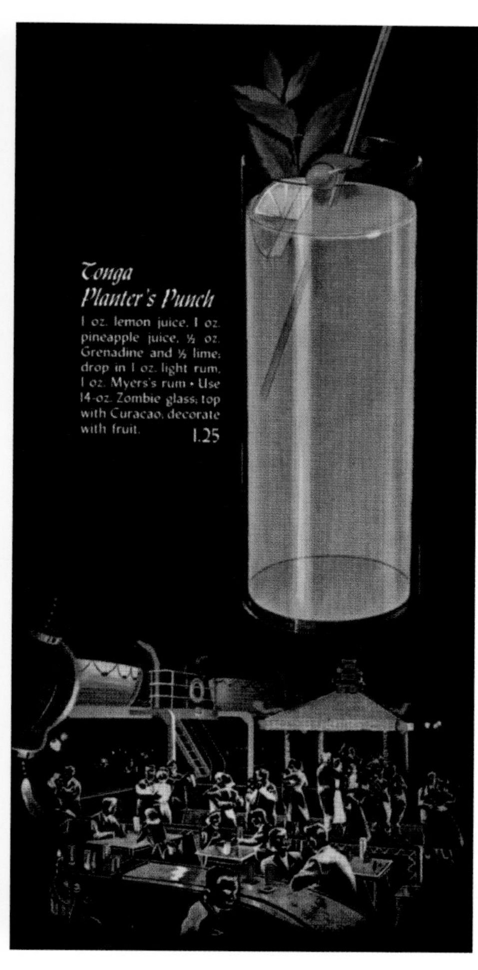

Tonga Planter's Punch
1 oz. lemon juice, 1 oz. pineapple juice, ½ oz. Grenadine and ½ lime; drop in 1 oz. light rum, 1 oz. Myers's rum • Use 14-oz. Zombie glass; top with Curacao; decorate with fruit. 1.25

LEFT & BELOW **Tiny's, 1944, Oakland, California**

A casual dining spot, Tiny's cleverly described certain items—a hamburger and milk shake became "Steak An' A Shake," Sausage Cakes were sausage patties—to elevate common food items. Regional dishes such as abalone steak were also featured.

Tiny's war ein zwangloses Lokal, das seine Besucher mit ungewöhnlichen Wortschöpfungen umgarnte: Ein Hamburger mit Milkshake war ein „Steak An' A Shake", „Wurstkuchen" wurde „Sausage Patty" genannt, damit er raffinierter klang. Auch regionale Spezialitäten wie gebratenes Meerohr wurden serviert.

Restaurant décontracté, le Tiny's présente certains plats d'une façon astucieuse : un hamburger et un milk-shake deviennent un « Steak An' A Shake ». Les « Sausages Cakes » sont des petits pâtés de chair à saucisse. L'objectif est d'anoblir les plats les plus simples. On trouve également des plats régionaux, comme le steak d'ormeau.

ABOVE **La Joya, c. 1945, Houston, Texas**

OPPOSITE **El Charro Cafe, c. 1952, Tucson, Arizona**

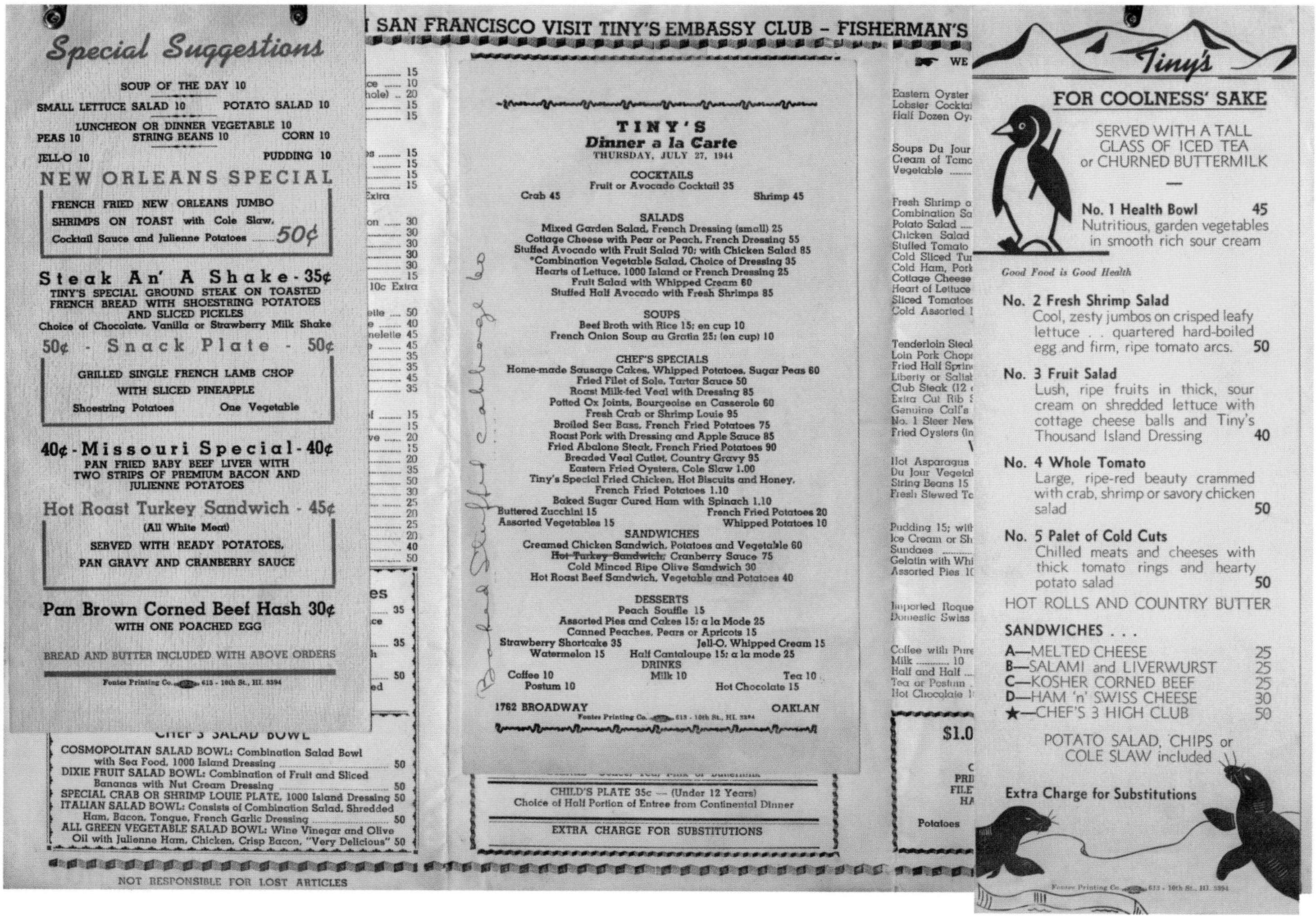

SAN FRANCISCO VISIT TINY'S EMBASSY CLUB – FISHERMAN'S

Special Suggestions

SOUP OF THE DAY 10
SMALL LETTUCE SALAD 10 POTATO SALAD 10
LUNCHEON OR DINNER VEGETABLE 10
PEAS 10 STRING BEANS 10 CORN 10
JELL-O 10 PUDDING 10

NEW ORLEANS SPECIAL
FRENCH FRIED NEW ORLEANS JUMBO SHRIMPS ON TOAST with Cole Slaw, Cocktail Sauce and Julienne Potatoes ...... 50¢

Steak An' A Shake - 35¢
TINY'S SPECIAL GROUND STEAK ON TOASTED FRENCH BREAD WITH SHOESTRING POTATOES AND SLICED PICKLES
Choice of Chocolate, Vanilla or Strawberry Milk Shake

50¢ - Snack Plate - 50¢
GRILLED SINGLE FRENCH LAMB CHOP WITH SLICED PINEAPPLE
Shoestring Potatoes One Vegetable

40¢ - Missouri Special - 40¢
PAN FRIED BABY BEEF LIVER WITH TWO STRIPS OF PREMIUM BACON AND JULIENNE POTATOES

Hot Roast Turkey Sandwich - 45¢
(All White Meat)
SERVED WITH READY POTATOES, PAN GRAVY AND CRANBERRY SAUCE

Pan Brown Corned Beef Hash 30¢
WITH ONE POACHED EGG

BREAD AND BUTTER INCLUDED WITH ABOVE ORDERS

Fontes Printing Co. 613 - 10th St., HI. 3394

CHEF'S SALAD BOWL
COSMOPOLITAN SALAD BOWL: Combination Salad Bowl with Sea Food, 1000 Island Dressing 50
DIXIE FRUIT SALAD BOWL: Combination of Fruit and Sliced Bananas with Nut Cream Dressing 50
SPECIAL CRAB OR SHRIMP LOUIE PLATE, 1000 Island Dressing 50
ITALIAN SALAD BOWL: Consists of Combination Salad, Shredded Ham, Bacon, Tongue, French Garlic Dressing 50
ALL GREEN VEGETABLE SALAD BOWL: Wine Vinegar and Olive Oil with Julienne Ham, Chicken, Crisp Bacon, "Very Delicious" 50

NOT RESPONSIBLE FOR LOST ARTICLES

TINY'S
Dinner a la Carte
THURSDAY, JULY 27, 1944

COCKTAILS
Fruit or Avocado Cocktail 35
Crab 45 Shrimp 45

SALADS
Mixed Garden Salad, French Dressing (small) 25
Cottage Cheese with Pear or Peach, French Dressing 55
Stuffed Avocado with Fruit Salad 70; with Chicken Salad 85
*Combination Vegetable Salad, Choice of Dressing 35
Hearts of Lettuce, 1000 Island or French Dressing 25
Fruit Salad with Whipped Cream 60
Stuffed Half Avocado with Fresh Shrimps 85

SOUPS
Beef Broth with Rice 15; en cup 10
French Onion Soup au Gratin 25; (en cup) 10

CHEF'S SPECIALS
Home-made Sausage Cakes, Whipped Potatoes, Sugar Peas 60
Fried Filet of Sole, Tartar Sauce 50
Roast Milk-fed Veal with Dressing 85
Potted Ox Joints, Bourgeoise en Casserole 60
Fresh Crab or Shrimp Louie 95
Broiled Sea Bass, French Fried Potatoes 75
Roast Pork with Dressing and Apple Sauce 85
Fried Abalone Steak, French Fried Potatoes 90
Breaded Veal Cutlet, Country Gravy 95
Eastern Fried Oysters, Cole Slaw 1.00
Tiny's Special Fried Chicken, Hot Biscuits and Honey, French Fried Potatoes 1.10
Baked Sugar Cured Ham with Spinach 1.10
Buttered Zucchini 15 French Fried Potatoes 20
Assorted Vegetables 15 Whipped Potatoes 10

SANDWICHES
Creamed Chicken Sandwich, Potatoes and Vegetable 60
~~Hot Turkey Sandwich~~, Cranberry Sauce 75
Cold Minced Ripe Olive Sandwich 30
Hot Roast Beef Sandwich, Vegetable and Potatoes 40

DESSERTS
Peach Souffle 15
Assorted Pies and Cakes 15; a la Mode 25
Canned Peaches, Pears or Apricots 15
Strawberry Shortcake 35 Jell-O, Whipped Cream 15
Watermelon 15 Half Cantaloupe 15; a la mode 25

DRINKS
Coffee 10 Milk 10 Tea 10
Postum 10 Hot Chocolate 15

1762 BROADWAY OAKLAN

Fontes Printing Co. 613 - 10th St., HI. 3394

Baked Stuffed cabbage 60

CHILD'S PLATE 35c — (Under 12 Years)
Choice of Half Portion of Entree from Continental Dinner

EXTRA CHARGE FOR SUBSTITUTIONS

Tiny's

FOR COOLNESS' SAKE

SERVED WITH A TALL GLASS OF ICED TEA or CHURNED BUTTERMILK

No. 1 Health Bowl 45
Nutritious, garden vegetables in smooth rich sour cream

Good Food is Good Health

No. 2 Fresh Shrimp Salad
Cool, zesty jumbos on crisped leafy lettuce . . quartered hard-boiled egg and firm, ripe tomato arcs. 50

No. 3 Fruit Salad
Lush, ripe fruits in thick, sour cream on shredded lettuce with cottage cheese balls and Tiny's Thousand Island Dressing 40

No. 4 Whole Tomato
Large, ripe-red beauty crammed with crab, shrimp or savory chicken salad 50

No. 5 Palet of Cold Cuts
Chilled meats and cheeses with thick tomato rings and hearty potato salad 50

HOT ROLLS AND COUNTRY BUTTER

SANDWICHES . . .
A—MELTED CHEESE 25
B—SALAMI and LIVERWURST 25
C—KOSHER CORNED BEEF 25
D—HAM 'n' SWISS CHEESE 30
★—CHEF'S 3 HIGH CLUB 50

POTATO SALAD, CHIPS or COLE SLAW included

Extra Charge for Substitutions

Fontes Printing Co. 613 - 10th St., HI. 3394

MENU

The definition of the word "Charro" is "a name given to the peasants of the province of Salamanca". This word was adapted in 1857 and applied in Mexico to good, able horsemen, recognized by the costume or uniform they wear, especially the high-crowned, wide-brimmed hat.

140 W. BROADWAY

ORDERS TO TAKE OUT RESERVATIONS

CALL 4197

140 W. BROADWAY
Call 4197
TUCSON, ARIZONA

El Charro Cafe

ORDERS TO TAKE OUT
RESERVATIONS

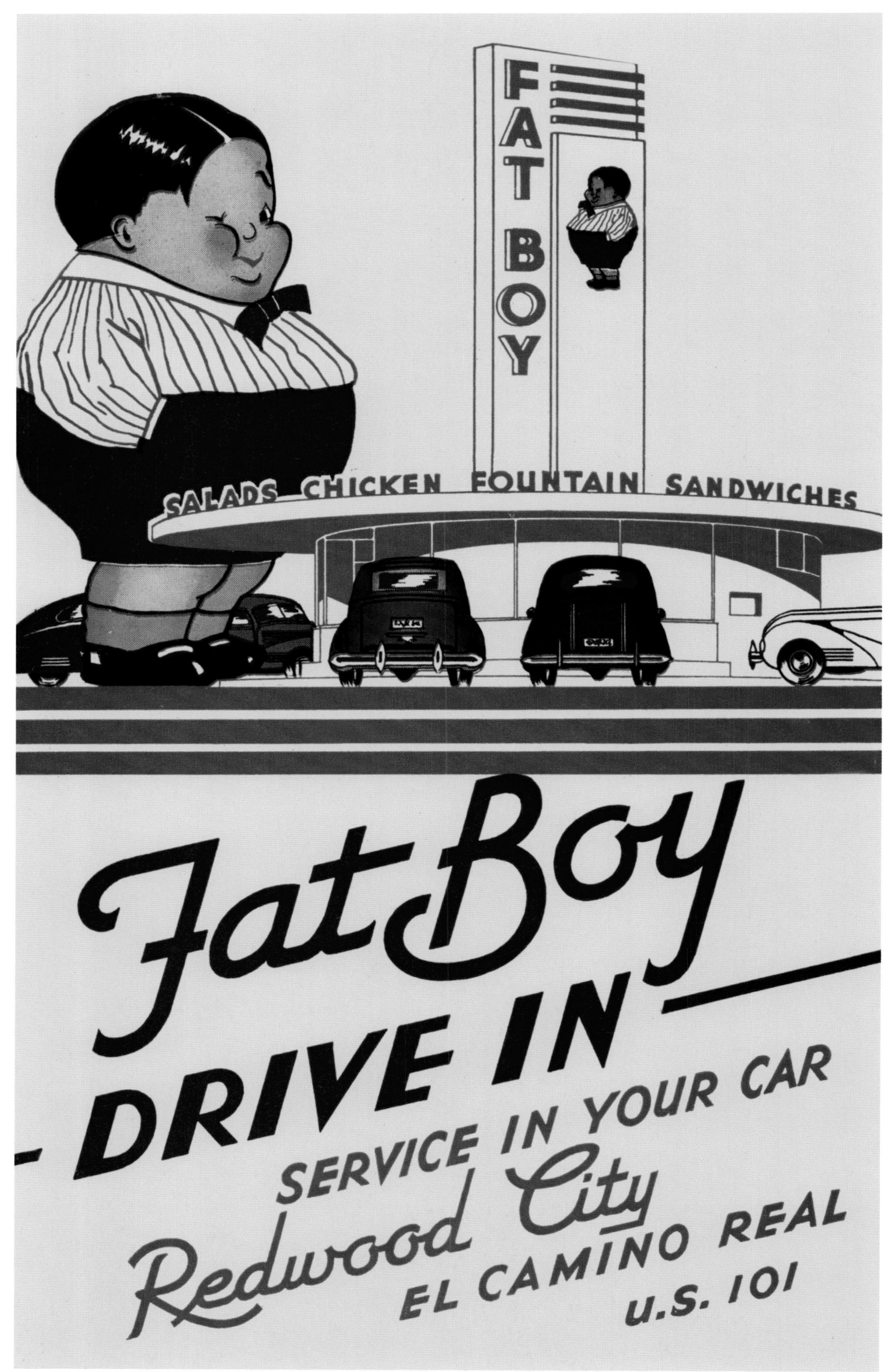
FAT BOY
SALADS CHICKEN FOUNTAIN SANDWICHES
Fat Boy
DRIVE IN
SERVICE IN YOUR CAR
Redwood City
EL CAMINO REAL
U.S. 101

OPPOSITE Fat Boy Drive In, c. 1944, Redwood City, California

RIGHT & BELOW Bob's Big Boy, 1949, Los Angeles, California

Big Boy's trademark was a chubby little boy in checkered overalls, and its double-decker burgers were conceived to distinguish the brand, founded by Bob Wian and Arnold Peterson in 1936 in Glendale, California. The image would be imitated by Fat Boy Drive In in Redwood City. In 1949 a branch designed by architect Wayne McAllister signaled the new post-war streamlined California drive-in, horizontal in style with a circular driveway.

Das Markenzeichen von Big Boy, das in jeder Filiale dieser Hamburgerkette zu finden war: ein kleiner dicker Junge im karierten Overall. Die Doubledecker-Burger wurden in der von Bob Wian and Arnold Peterson 1936 in Glendale, Kalifornien, gründeten Kette erfunden. Deren Image wurde vom Fat Boy Drive In in Redwood City nachgeahmt. 1949 baute der Architekt Wayne McAllister eine neue Filiale im hochmodernen, stromlinienförmigen Stil mit geschwungener Auffahrt.

Big Boy, un garçon rondouillard portant une combinaison à damier, ainsi que les hamburgers à deux étages, ont été créés pour symboliser l'enseigne fondée par Bob Wian et Arnold Peterson en 1936 à Glendale, en Californie. Ce personnage sera imité par le Fat Boy Drive In de Redwood City. En 1949, une franchise conçue par l'architecte Wayne McAllister inaugure la nouvelle mode des drive-in de l'après-guerre en Californie : des lignes épurées horizontales et une allée circulaire.

THE Big Boy HAMBURGER

Made as Only We Know How . . Two Patties of Freshly Ground Hamburger on a Special Baked Sesame Seed Toasted Bun with Mayonnaise Lettuce, Cheese and Topped with Our Own Relish . . . .

45c

THE Big Boy COMBINATION PLATE

By Popular Demand!

A Delicious BIG BOY HAMBURGER with French Fries and Hearts of Lettuce with 1000 Island Dressing

65c

Bob's SALAD DRESSINGS

Bob's FRIED SHRIMP HEAT AND SERVE

Bob's MOCHA BOY COFFEE

Bob's Yummy Boy DOUGHNUTS

Salads

Each Made with the Freshest of Ingredients and a Meal in Itself

CHILLED PINEAPPLE AND DAIRY-FRESH COTTAGE CHEESE 60
Dairy-Fresh Cottage Cheese on Crisp Lettuce, Chilled Pineapple with Toasted Buttered Bun.

CHEF'S SPECIAL SALAD BOWL . . .60
Hearts of Lettuce, Tomato, Avocado, Fresh Baby Alaskan Shrimp and a Really Delicious Chef's Salad Dressing, Served with Toasted Buttered Bun.

DICED HAM AND CHEESE SALAD 60
Large Bowl of Crisp Fresh Lettuce and Diced Ham, Cheese, Tomato, French Dressing, and Served in a Chilled Salad Bowl with Toasted Buttered Bun.

Sandwiches

SHRIMP SANDWICH 65
Jumbo Southern Fried Shrimp Served Open-Face, Heart of Crisp Lettuce with 1000 Island Dressing and French Fried Potatoes

SPECIAL STEAK SANDWICH. 65
Tasty, Tender and Tempting Spencer Steak Served American Sandwich Style with Crisp Lettuce, Tomato, Fresh Mayonnaise, French Fries

TOASTED SANDWICHES

Tuna Sandwich 35
Lettuce and Tomato 30
Melted Cheese 30
Ham .45
Ham or Bacon and Melted Cheese 45
Bacon with Tomato or Avocado 40
Bacon or Ham and Egg 50

(Above Sandwiches Served on Toasted Bread, French Fried Potatoes)

ORDER OF FRENCH FRIED POTATOES 20

Dinners

BOB'S SPECIAL SPENCER STEAK 1.40
(Over 7 oz. top quality Steer Beef, Grilled to a turn and served with French Fries, Heart of Crisp Lettuce with 1000 Island Dressing and Toasted Buttered Bun.)

THE HALF POUND O'GROUND ROUND 1.00
(One-Half pound Freshly Ground, from Finest Quality Steer Beef, Grilled to Your Desire, Served with French Fries, Heart of Lettuce, 1000 Isle Dressing, Toasted Buttered Bun.)

HAM STEAK 1.10
(Generous Center Cut, Eastern Corn-Fed Ham with Grilled Pineapple, Served with French Fries, Heart of Lettuce with 1000 Isle Dressing and Toasted Buttered Bun.)

FRIED SHRIMP 1.20
(Jumbo Shrimp from the Blue Waters of the Gulf of Calif., Deep Fried to a Golden Brown, Served with French Fries, Heart of Lettuce, 1000 Isle Dressing and Toasted Buttered Bun.)

HAM OR BACON AND RANCH-FRESH EGGS 80
(America's Favorite All-Day Meal, with Ranch-Fresh Eggs, Grilled in Butter and Generous Portion of Ham or Bacon, Served with Potatoes, Buttered Toast and Jelly.)

Old Fashioned Golden Brown Pancakes . . .30
Grilled to a Golden Brown, Served with Plenty of Butter and Hot Maple Syrup
Served with Ham, Bacon or Two Fried Eggs 60c

Sales Tax Will Be Added to Retail Price on All Taxable Items

We Reserve the Right to Refuse Service to Anyone

Chili Dishes

Chili and Beans 35
Chili, Straight 40
(Above Served with Crisp Crackers)

Spaghetti & Chili (Spanish) . . .55
(Served with Melted Cheese, Plenty of Fresh Raw Onions)

Chili Size (Beans or Spaghetti) 70
Tamale and Chili 70
(Above Served with Toasted Buttered Bun)

DRINKS

Mocha Boy Coffee, Tea, Milk, Hot Chocolate, Ice Tea, Buttermilk, Tomato Juice, Coca-Cola, Nesbitt Orange Drink, Hires Root Beer, Lemonade

EACH 10c

Any Item Not Meeting Your Complete Satisfaction Cheerfully Exchanged

Fountain

Bob's Super Thick MILK SHAKE 30c
Topped with Whipped Cream and a Cherry
So Thick You Eat It with a Spoon
Chocolate - Vanilla - Strawberry

Bob's Special HOT FUDGE SUNDAE 35c
Two Scoops of Ice Cream, Hot Chocolate Fudge, Toasted Almonds, Whipped Cream

DESSERTS

SUNDAES 30
(Chocolate, Pineapple, Strawberry)
PIE 15; CREAM PIE 25
PIE A LA MODE OR WHIPPED CREAM 25

LORD PRINTING CO., L.A. – MENUS

To Take Home

Bob's Fried Shrimp, Heat 'n Serve 69
Bob's Yummy Boy Doughnuts (1 doz.) . . .60

DRESSINGS & RELISHES
Garlic 'n Oil 35
Tomato & Spice .35
1000 Isle 35
Shrimp Sauce . .35
Steak Relish 35
(Package of Four 35c Items $1.20)

Big Boy Carries a Complete Line of High Quality Baby Food for the Little Ones

OPPOSITE Casa D'Amore, c. 1946, Hollywood, California

New Yorker Patsy D'Amore brought pizza to Hollywood in 1939, popularizing a dish inspired by the memories of World War II veterans who savored this Neapolitan "pie." D'Amore later opened Villa Capri, a favored restaurant of Frank Sinatra and James Dean.

Die New Yorkerin Patsy D'Amore führte 1939 die Pizza in Hollywood ein. Nach dem Zweiten Weltkrieg, als Soldaten gute Erinnerungen an den neapolitanische „Kuchen" mit nach Hause brachten, nahm die Beliebtheit von Pizza schnell zu. D'Amore machte später das Villa Capri auf, in das Frank Sinatra und James Dean gern kamen.

Le New-Yorkais Patsy D'Amore fait découvrir les pizzas à Hollywood en 1939. Les anciens combattants de la Seconde Guerre mondiale, qui rapporteront des souvenirs émus de cette « tarte napolitaine » achèveront de la populariser. Plus tard, D'Amore ouvrira la Villa Capri, le restaurant préféré de Frank Sinatra et James Dean.

ABOVE Barney's Market Club, c. 1949, Chicago, Illinois

RIGHT DiMaggio's, c. 1949, San Francisco, California

Baseball star Joe DiMaggio and his brothers Dom and Vince, who also played, owned this Fisherman's Wharf restaurant in the 1930s.

Baseballstar Joe DiMaggio und seine Brüder Dom and Vince, die ebenfalls Baseball spielten, waren in den 1930ern Besitzer dieses Restaurants an der Fisherman's Wharf.

La vedette du baseball Joe DiMaggio et ses frères Dom et Vince, également joueurs, possédaient ce restaurant sur le Fisherman's Wharf dans les années 1930.

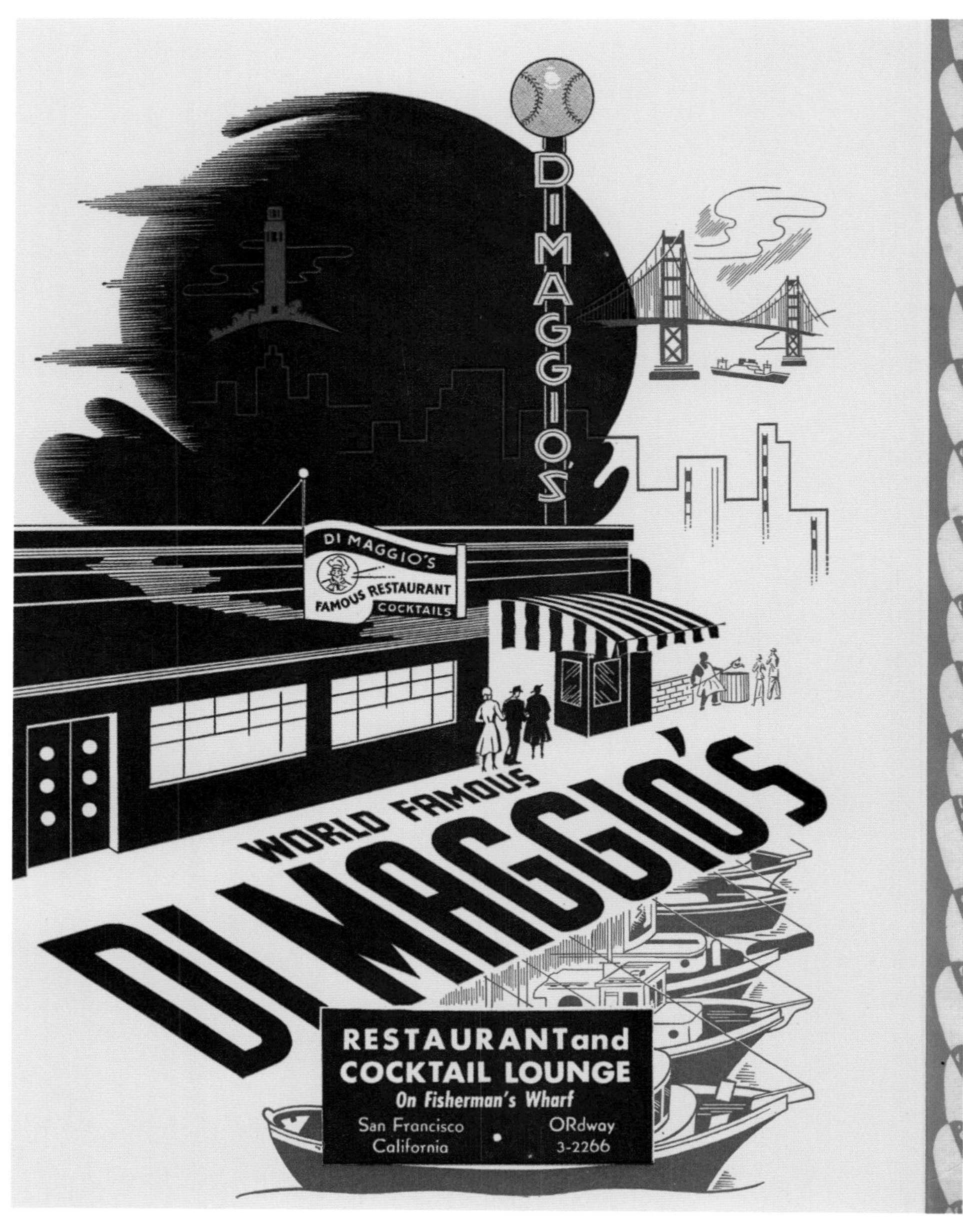

Try Our Specialty . . . Pizza

PIZZA MARINARA	.85 & 1.25
PIZZA WITH CHEESE	.85 & 1.25
PIZZA WITH MUSHROOMS	1.30 & 2.00
PIZZA WITH ANCHOVIES	.90 & 1.50
LARGE PATSY SPECIAL PIZZA	2.50
SPECIAL	1.20 & 1.65
MIXED OR HALF AND HALF	1.00 & 1.50
CALZONE IMBOTTITO	1.75 & 3.00
CHEESE AND SAUSAGES	1.40 & 2.00

Special Combination Plates

LARGE NEW YORK CUT, WITH FRENCH FRIED POTATOES AND MIXED GREEN SALAD 3.25

SMALL NEW YORK CUT, WITH SIDE ORDER OF SPAGHETTI, MEAT SAUCE 2.75

BROILED LAMB CHOPS (2), FRENCH FRIED POTATOES AND MIXED GREEN SALAD 2.00

Chef's Specials

VEAL SCALOPPINE FRANCESE WITH SIDE OF SPAGHETTI, MEAT SAUCE	1.50
YOUNG MILK FED CHICKEN A LA MARSALA, WITH RAVIOLI, MEAT SAUCE AND MIXED GREEN SALAD	1.75
FILET A LA PARISIENNE	2.75
ROLLATINI A LA MARGHERITA	2.25
SPEDINO A LA ROMANA	1.25
FILETTO A LA FINANZIERA	2.75
FILET MIGNON WITH MUSHROOMS	3.25
SALTIMBOCCA A LA ROMANA	2.25

BACON AND EGGS
HAM AND EGGS
French Fried Potatoes
90c

California Wines

PER GLASS

CALIMPO BURGUNDY	.20	SHERRY	.25
CALIMPO SAUTERNE	.20	PORT	.25
MUSCATEL	.25	TOKAY	.25
IMPORTED VERMOUTH COCKTAIL			.35

PER BOTTLE

	Small	Large
ECKERT NAPA VALLEY SAUTERNE	1.10	2.00
I. V. C. SAUTERNE	1.10	2.00
I. V. C. RED	1.10	2.00
B. V. SAUTERNE OR BURGUNDY		2.25
AMBASSADOR NAPA COUNTY BURGUNDY	1.10	2.00

IMPORTED CHIANTI AND OTHER CHOICE WINES ON REQUEST

DOMESTIC AND EASTERN BEER

LEFT Fleur de Lis Room, Fontainebleau, 1956, Miami Beach, Florida

The extravagant design of the Fountainebleau Hotel by Morris Lapidus helped to bring Miami Beach out of its postwar doldrums. Its over-the-top faux luxury was such an attraction that the hotel charged tourists a fee to tour it. Of his 1954 design Lapidus said, "I designed what I did for them.... When they walk in they do feel, 'This is what we've dreamed of, this is what we saw in the movies.'"

Das Hotel Fontainebleu mit dem extravaganten Design von Morris Lapidus katapultierte Miami Beach aus dem Dornröschenschlaf der Nachkriegszeit. Der verschwenderische Luxus war eine solche Touristenattraktion, dass das Hotel Eintrittsgeld für Besichtigungen verlangte. Lapidus sagte zu seinem Entwurf von 1954: „Ich habe es so entworfen, dass man beim Hereinkommen sofort sagt: ‚Das ist genau wie im Film, genau, wie ich's mir immer erträumt habe.'"

Le design extravagant de l'hôtel Fontainebleau de Morris Lapidus va aider Miami Beach à sortir du marasme de l'après-guerre. Son luxe de pacotille outrancier devient une telle attraction touristique que l'établissement organise des visites payantes. En 1954, à propos de son décor, Lapidus expliquera : « C'est un concept... Quand on arrive, on se dit vraiment "J'en ai rêvé... C'est ce que j'ai vu dans les films". »

BELOW Fountainebleau Cafe, 1954, Miami Beach, Florida

ABOVE **The Camellia House, the Drake Hotel, c. 1941, Chicago, Illinois**

RIGHT **The Camellia House, the Drake Hotel, 1950, Chicago, Illinois**

Interior designer Dorothy Draper, famous for her pink and green colors and lavish use of chintz fabrics, did Chicago's Camelia House in typically posh style, with a bit more Midwestern swagger than in her effusively sunny Florida décors.

Die Innenarchitektin Dorothy Draper, berühmt für ihre Farbpalette in Grün und Pink und verschwenderische Mengen von Chintz, richtete das Camellia House in Chicago im gewohnt üppigen Stil, aber mit etwas mehr mittelwestlichem Pomp als bei ihren überschwänglich sonnigen Floridadekors ein.

L'architecte d'intérieur Dorothy Draper, réputée pour l'utilisation du chintz et le recours aux couleurs rose et vert, réalise The Camellia House à Chicago dans son style typique, avec toutefois une touche de chic Midwest plus prononcée que pour ses intérieurs solaire et lumineux de Floride.

ABOVE Boca Raton Hotel and Club, 1954, Boca Raton, Florida

Opened on February 6, 1926, as the Ritz-Carlton Cloister Inn, a members-only club, the rambling resort was designed by Addison Mizner during the Florida land boom.

Der bei seiner Eröffnung am 6. Februar 1926 Ritz-Carlton Cloister Inn genannte Privatklub war eine riesige, von Addison Mizner entworfene Anlage, die während des ersten Baubooms in Florida errichtet wurde.

Ouvert le 6 février 1926 sous le nom de Ritz-Carlton Cloister Inn, un club réservé à ses membres, ce vaste complexe hôtelier a été conçu par Addison Mizner pendant le boom immobilier de Floride.

BELOW Balinese Room, the Blackstone Hotel, c. 1949, Chicago, Illinois

OPPOSITE Halekulani Hotel, 1951, Waikiki, Hawaii

Post-war interest in Hawaii grew enormously, and rooms at good hotels could be had for $6 to $14. The Halekulani ("House Befitting Heaven") opened as a small hotel in 1917, the Hau Tree, later expanding into 37 bungalows.

Nach dem Krieg wuchs das Interesse an Hawaii enorm, und Zimmer in einem guten Hotel kosteten nicht mehr als 6 bis 14 Dollar. Das Halekulani („Himmlisches Haus") eröffnete 1917 als die kleine Pension Hau Tree und wurde später auf 37 Bungalows erweitert.

Dans l'après-guerre, l'intérêt porté à Hawaii croît considérablement. On peut y louer une chambre dans un bon hôtel pour un tarif oscillant entre 6 et 14 dollars. Le Halekulani (« La maison du paradis ») ouvre en 1917. Le Hau Tree comptera jusqu'à 37 bungalows.

PAGES 312 & 313 The Banyan Lanai, Moana Hotel, 1951, Honolulu, Hawaii

Menu
HALEKULANI HOTEL · WAIKIKI

the Banyan Lanai
Moana Hotel ... ON THE BEACH AT Waikiki IN HONOLULU

DINNER

WEDNESDAY, OCTOBER 31, 1951 — SERVED FROM 6 to 9 P. M.

Selection of Entrees Determines Price of Dinner

Appetizers — CHOICE OF ONE

Iced Fresh Hawaiian Fruit Cocktail en Supreme Glass

Chilled Pineapple, Papaya, Guava, Tomato or V-8 Juice

Soup du Jour - Poi Cocktail - Hot or Cold Consomme

Iced Jellied Chicken Broth - Iced Jellied Tomato Broth

Salads

Our Famous Salad Bowl, Special Dressing

Heart of Lettuce, French Dressing

Entrees (*Served with Vegetables and Special Potatoes*)

Fresh Mahimahi Saute in Butter, Tartar Sauce	2.25
Fried Jumbo Gulf of Mexico Shrimps, Dipping Sauce	2.25
Rogout of Wyoming Spring Baby Lamb, Jardiniere of Vegetables	2.50
Pork Tenderloin Saute, Country Style, Apple Ring	2.50

Desserts

Fresh Baked Pie - Home-made Layer Cake - - Sliced Pineapple

Coconut Ice Cream - Guava Sherbet - Hawaiian Snowball - Fruit Jell-o

Camembert, Swiss, Roquefort, Phil. Cream or Edam Cheese with Crackers

Coffee - Hot or Cold Tea or Coffee - Milk or Buttermilk

Special Continental Dinner - $1.65

CHOICE OF

Iced Tropical Fruit Cocktail en Supreme Glass

Salad ***Soup du Jour***

ENTREE

Fried Deep Sea Eastern Scallops, Tartar Sauce

Salisbury Steak Saute Bordelaise

DESSERTS

Fresh Hawaiian Pineapple ***Fresh Solo Papaya***

Ice Cream (choice of 8 flavors) ***Fruit Sherbet (choice of 6 flavors)***

Fruit Jell-o with Whipped Cream

Coffee ***Hot or Iced Tea*** ***Buttermilk***

Children's Dinner -- Half the price of the dinner selected plus fifty cents.
Room Service --- Additional charge of fifty cents per person.
For special parties, cocktails, banquets, etc., call or see your Headwaiter.

SHADOWS
JULIUS' CASTLE
MARIO'S
PIZZA
HOUSE
NEW TIVOLI
NEW PISA
OTT'S
365
TRADER VICS
ITALIAN VILLAGE
BOCCE BALL
SINALOA
BEIGE ROOM
JOHN'S
RENDEVOUS
EL MATADOR
FIOR D'ITALIA
VANESSI'S
FINOCCHIO'S
3 LITTLE SWISS
NEW JOE'S
HOUSE OF PISCO
VELTRI'S
LARRY'S
VIENI VIENI
1224
COLUMBUS
GRANT
BROADWAY
HUNGRY I
POT
XOCHIMILCO
JAI ALAI
NORMANDIE
WAMSLEY

RIGHT & BELOW New Year's Eve Gala, Cumberland Hotel, 1954

The exciting possibilities of space travel and postwar rocketry caught the fancy of popular artists, and this menu trades the traditional images of Father Time and the New Year baby or nude women in champagne glasses for an image that might have come from the pages of a science-fiction magazine.

Die aufregenden Möglichkeiten von Raumfahrt und Raketen beschäftigten viele Zeichner. Auf dieser Speisekarte sind traditionelle Silvestermotive wie Vater Zeit mit dem neuen Jahr als Baby oder nackte Damen in Sektkelchen durch ein Bild ersetzt, das auch einem Science-Fiction-Heft hätte entstammen können.

Les fascinantes perspectives de la conquête spatiale et de l'astronautique de l'après-guerre inspirent les artistes populaires, et les menus troquent les images traditionnelles (le Père Temps, le Bébé du nouvel an, les femmes nues dans des coupes de champagne…) pour des illustrations dignes d'un magazine de science-fiction.

OPPOSITE Mario's Pizza House, 1954, San Francisco, California

TICKETS
W.C.M.
The Union News Company
ESTABLISHED 1864
SERVING THE TRAVELING PUBLIC FOR OVER 80 YEARS

OPPOSITE The Union News Company, c. 1953, New York, New York

BELOW The Night Hawk Grill Room, c. 1953, Austin, Texas

ABOVE **Panza's Lazy Susan, c. 1952, Hollywood, California**

Early-1950s Los Angeles graphic art took on the whimsy of abstraction and Miró-like colors, exemplified by animation studios such as UPA.

In den frühen 1950er-Jahren ließ sich die Druckgrafik in Los Angeles von verspielten Abstraktionen und Mirós Farben inspirieren, die in Zeichentrickstudios wie UPA absolut en vogue waren.

À Los Angeles, l'art graphique du début des années 1950 se tourne vers l'abstraction fantasque et s'empare des couleurs à la Miró, comme dans les dessins animés de l'UPA.

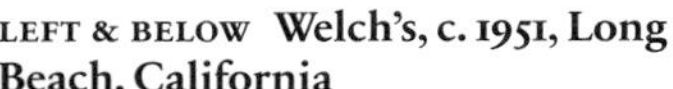

LEFT & BELOW Welch's, c. 1951, Long Beach, California

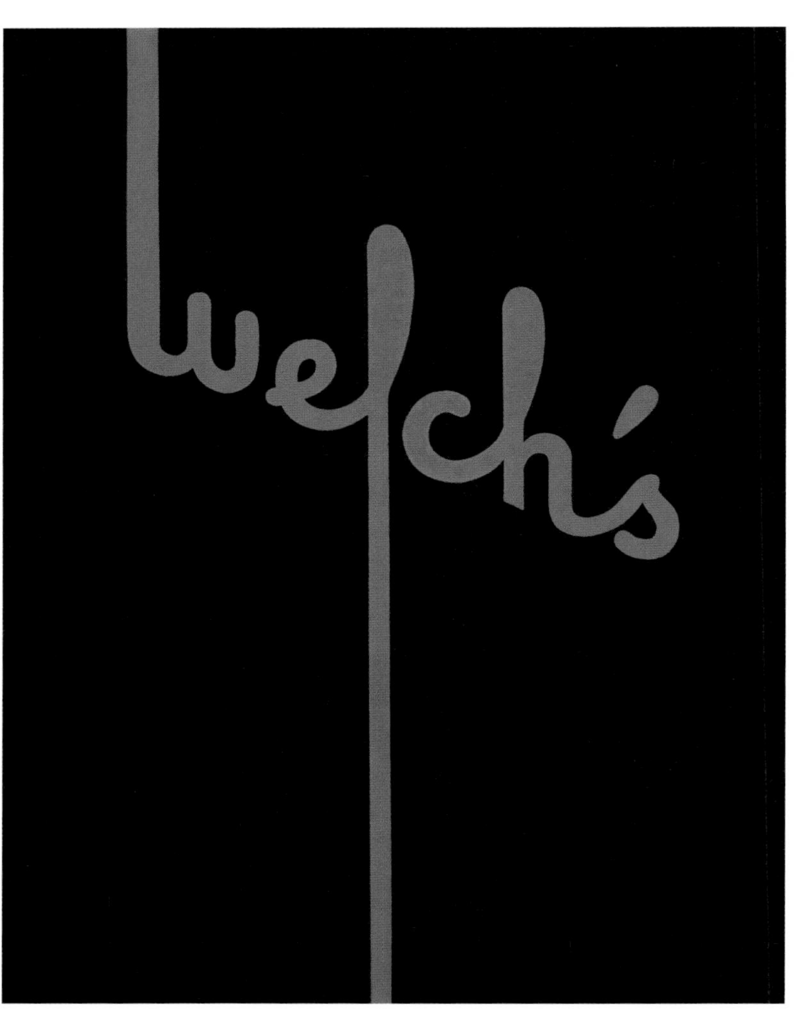

From the Sea Food Bar

Shrimp Cocktail - - .50
Crabmeat Cocktail - - .60
Lobster Cocktail - - .60
Oyster Cocktail - - .60
Cherrystone Clam Cocktail .60
Tuna & Avocado Cocktail .50
Fresh Eastern Bluepoint Oysters on the Half Shell - .75
Fresh Long Island Cherrystone Clams on the Half Shell .75

From the Salad Bowl

Tossed Green Salad with Roquefort Dressing - .50
Fresh Crab Louie - - 1.50
Fresh Lobster Louie - 1.50
Jumbo Shrimp Louie - - - 1.50

Soups

Green Turtle with Sherry - .50
Chicken Royal - - - .40
Green Split Pea St. Germain .30

Vegetables

Garden Fresh Vegetables prepared with butter .25

Desserts

Individual Hot Blueberry Pie .25
French Vanilla Ice Cream .20
Individual Fresh Lemon Pie .25
Sherbet - - - - .20
Parfaits - .40

Beverages

Coffee - .10
Iced Coffee .15
Milk - - .10
Tea (per pot) .15
Iced Tea - .15

Children's Dinners — One Dollar

For that Sunday Family Treat

WELCH'S FRIED CHICKEN
Served with Garden Fresh Vegetables, Whipped Potatoes, Creamed Gravy, and Hot Biscuits
SERVED SUNDAYS ONLY

Dining Rooms available for Luncheons, Teas and Private Parties

For Reservations Call 2-8225

NOT RESPONSIBLE FOR LOST ARTICLES
2½% SALES TAX IN ADDITION TO PRICES LISTED
WE ARE CLOSED ON TUESDAYS

ROAST PRIME RIBS of BEEF au jus - - $1.75

From the Rotary Broiler

Filet Mignon - 2.50 New York Cut Sirloin - 2.50
Plank Chopped Sirloin - 1.50

Shad Roe - Pan-Fried in Butter, Crisp Bacon - 2.25
Seafood Grill - Welch's - - - - - 1.75
Deviled Fresh Northern Crab - - 1.50
Fried Jumbo Shrimps - Hot Sauce - - 1.50
Boston Scallops, with Crisp Bacon - - 1.50
Long Island Oysters, Fried - - 1.50
Newburgs - Shrimp, Lobster or Crab - - 1.50

Tossed Green Salad Bowl — Hot Rolls — Idaho Potato
Coffee — Tea — Milk
Served with the above entrees

BELOW The Pan Lad, c. 1952, Los Angeles, California

RIGHT Hotel Mapes, 1955, Reno, Nevada

OPPOSITE Well of the Sea, Sherman House, c. 1958, Chicago, Illinois

The modern art of this cover evokes the contemporary paintings of Swiss artist Paul Klee and mobile sculptor Alexander Calder.

Die moderne Kunst auf diesem Umschlag erinnert an die zeitgenössischen Gemälde Paul Klees und die Mobiles von Alexander Calder.

Le style contemporain de cette couverture évoque les tableaux du Suisse Paul Klee ou les mobiles d'Alexander Calder.

ABOVE The White Sands of La Jolla, c. 1952, La Jolla, California

RIGHT South Seas, c. 1953, San Diego, California

The risqué illustration plays off the work of Renaissance artist Giuseppe Arcimboldo, who entwined fruits and vegetables into portraits of human beings.

Diese erotische Illustration ist eine Anspielung auf den Renaissancemaler Giuseppe Arcimboldo, der aus Früchten und Gemüsen zusammengesetzte menschliche Gesichter malte.

Cette illustration osée rappelle l'œuvre du peintre de la Renaissance Giuseppe Arcimboldo qui entremêlait fruits et légumes pour créer des silhouettes humaines.

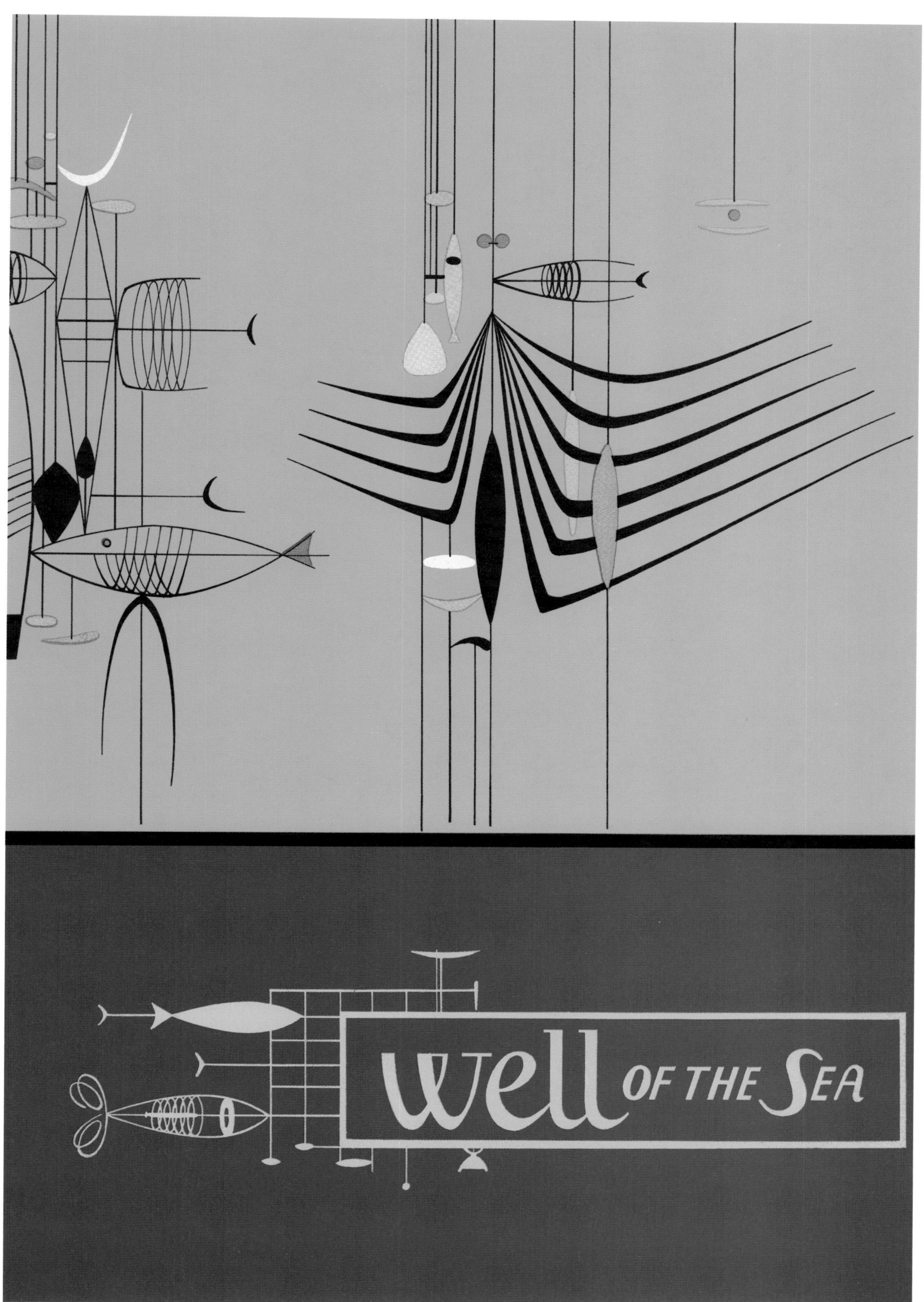
Well of the Sea

ABOVE & RIGHT **The Ahwahnee Hotel, 1941–1954, Yosemite National Parks, California**

The Ahwahnee Hotel was built by the National Parks Service, close to Yosemite's primary sites. They were featured on this series of covers by Ansel Adams, America's great nature photographer.

Das Ahwahnee Hotel wurde vom National Park Service in direkter Nähe zu den größten Sehenswürdigkeiten des Yosemite National Park erbaut. Diese sind auf der Serie von Speisekartenumschlägen des großen amerikanischen Naturfotografen Ansel Adams zu sehen.

L'Ahwahnee Hotel est construit par le National Park Service, près des plus importants sites du parc du Yosemite, dont les paysages grandioses sont représentés sur ces couvertures d'Ansel Adams, l'un des plus grands photographes naturalistes américains.

OPPOSITE ABOVE **Painted Desert Room, Wilbur Clark's Desert Inn, 1952, Las Vegas, Nevada**

OPPOSITE BELOW **Stouffer's, 1951–52, Chicago, Illinois**

THE AHWAHNEE YOSEMITE NATIONAL PARK

LUNCHEON

Monday, July 31, 1950

Chilled grape juice

Indian relish Young onions Red radishes
Crisp carrot sticks

Leek and potato soup

Grilled swordfish steak, Maitre d'hotel
with Julienne potatoes
Creamed chicken and mushrooms on hot biscuits
Sliced tenderloin tips saute a la Deutsch
Breaded pork chop with Country gravy
Chef's Special crab salad bowl

Leaf spinach French carrots Baked potato

Mexican cole slaw salad

Assorted hot luncheon rolls

Fruit jello, Chantilly Chilled watermelon
Hazelnut toffee ice cream, cookies Apricot pie

Coffee Tea Milk Buttermilk Iced tea

Breakfast, 7:30 to 9 Luncheon, 11:45 to 1:30
Dinner, 6:30 to 8

Afternoon Tea is served in the Lounge from 5 to 5:30

Please order box lunches from Dining Room Manager the night before needed.

Wildflowers used in decoration are grown in our own gardens or outside the Park.

Painted Desert Room
Wilbur Clark's
DESERT INN
LAS VEGAS, NEVADA

Painted Desert Room
Wilbur Clark's
DESERT INN
LAS VEGAS, NEVADA

Stouffer's

Stouffer's

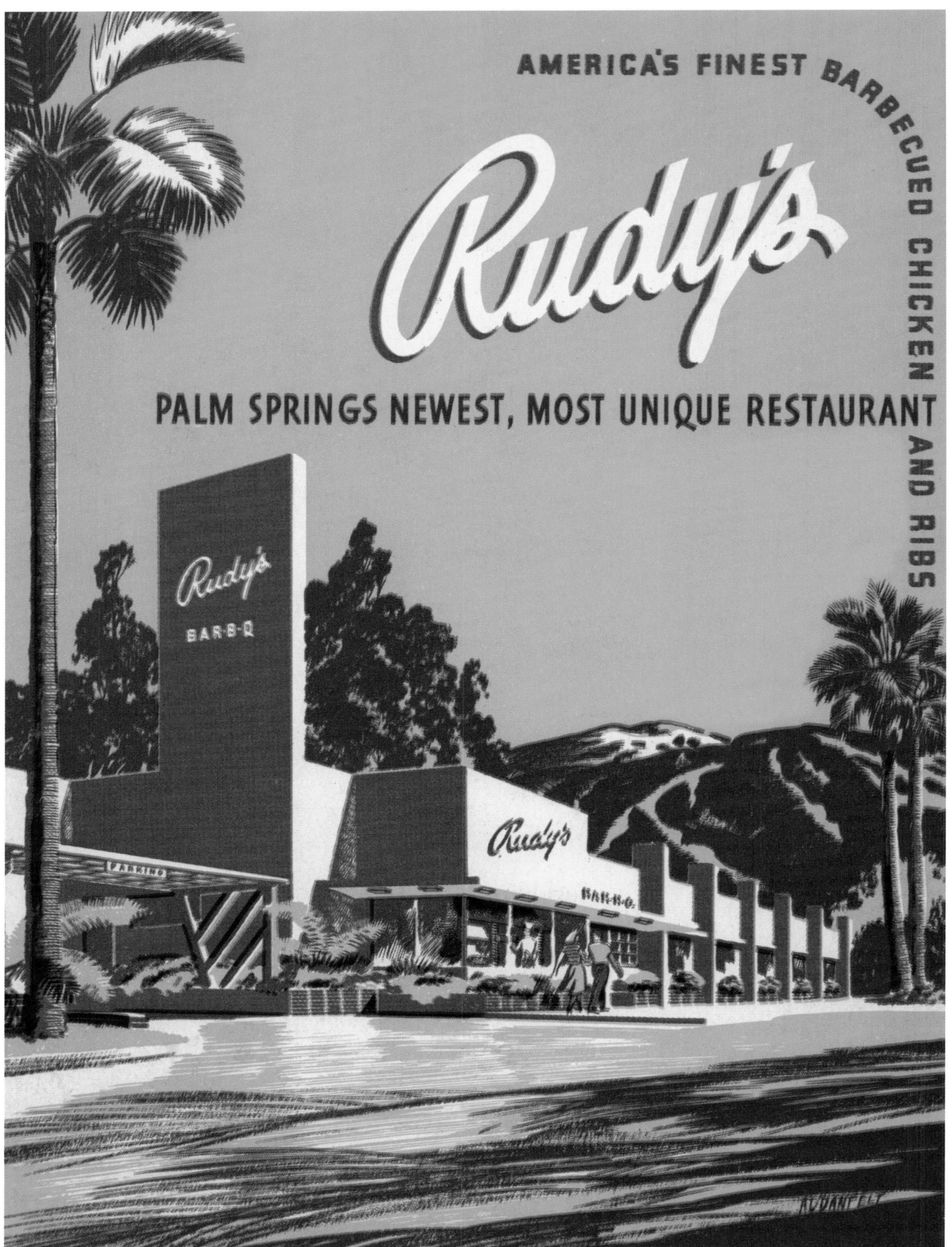
AMERICA'S FINEST BARBECUED CHICKEN AND RIBS
Rudy's
PALM SPRINGS NEWEST, MOST UNIQUE RESTAURANT
Rudy's
BAR-B-Q
PARKING
Rudy's
BAR-B-Q

OPPOSITE & BELOW Rudy's, c. 1953, Palm Springs, California

Rudy's standard fare is spiced up with a "Karnotzel Steak," four small tenderloins from "an old Romanian recipe."

Die Durchschnittskost des Rudy's wird durch ein „Karnotzel Steak" aufgepeppt, vier kleine Lendchen nach „altem rumänischem Rezept".

Le menu classique du Rudy's est relevé par un « Karnotzel Steak », un plat composé de quatre petits filets et inspiré d'une « vieille recette roumaine ».

ABOVE Nickodell, 1952, Hollywood, California

ABOVE Lou's Village, c. 1953, San Jose, California

Karnotzel Steak

CHARCOAL-BROILED

4 individual little steaks — made from chopped choice tenderloin

An old Rumanian receipe for something different in taste and flavor.

DINNER COMPLETE *2.75*

Barbecued Ham or Beef

COMPLETE DINNER *2.35*

Chicken-Livers en brochet

Charcoal Broiled on a skewer!
From our own milk-corn fed Friers

COMPLETE DINNER *2.95*

Filet en brochet

Seven Little Steaks on a skewer
Charcoal Broiled to perfection *3.75*

Barbecued Spare Ribs

We are as proud of our Ribs as we are of our Chicken. Only the choice grade of BABY RIBS are purchased without regard for market prices.

Served piping hot and Golden Brown.

A TASTE THRILL!

COMPLETE DINNER *2.50*

Barbecued Chicken

From milk and corn fed friers grown on our own ranch. One-half portion prepared in our open-view Rotisserie, well basted and deliciously tender.

This is our Pride and Joy!

DINNER COMPLETE *3.25*

Rudy's **DINNER DELUXE**

INCLUDES

Soup du-jour or Tomato Juice, Tossed Green Salad-French or Sour Cream Dressing, French Fried or Baked Potato, Home made Hot Biscuits, Butter, Boysenberry Jam Beverage, Dessert

New York or Filet Mignon Steak

CHARCOAL BROILED

DINNER COMPLETE *4.25*

Your Favorite Brand of *Beer* *.35*

Karnotzel Steak Sandwich

CHARCOAL-BROILED

Served on golden brown toast with crisp French Fried Potatoes Salad & Beverage *1.35*

Barbecued Beef or Ham Sandwich

SALAD
FRENCH FRIES *.95*
BEVERAGE

Good Morning!
NORTHERN HOTEL

OPPOSITE Northern Hotel, c. 1951, Billings, Montana

This appetite-inducing menu cover seems a precursor to the happy-face image created by artist Richard Ball in 1963 and popularized in the 1970s.

Dieses appetitanregende Deckblatt scheint das von dem Zeichner Richard Ball 1963 geschaffene Smileygesicht, das in den 1970er-Jahren so populär wurde, vorwegzunehmen.

Ce menu appétissant semble préfigurer le « smiley » créé par l'artiste Richard Ball en 1963 et popularisé dans les années 1970.

ABOVE Furnace Creek Ranch, c. 1950, Death Valley, California

LEFT Daffodil Room, Hotel Winthrop, c. 1954, Tacoma, Washington

LEFT **Operation Cue, 1955, Yucca Flats, Nevada**

A commemorative menu for military personnel and dignitaries attending the detonation of an atomic bomb test near Las Vegas.

Eine als Andenken gestaltete Speisekarte für Militärs und offizielle Würdenträger, die bei der Testzündung einer Atombombe bei Las Vegas anwesend waren.

Menu commémoratif pour le personnel militaire et les personnalités venus assister au premier essai nucléaire près de Las Vegas.

BELOW **The Copa Room, the Sands, c. 1953, Las Vegas, Nevada**

As one of the most famous entertainment venues in Las Vegas in the 1950s, the Copa Room at the Sands, which opened in 1952, featured the biggest stars such as Jimmy Durante, Dean Martin and Jerry Lewis, and Frank Sinatra's famed "Rat Pack".

Der 1952 eröffnete Copa Room im Sands war eines der berühmtesten Vergnügungslokale in Las Vegas, in dem die größten Stars der Zeit wie Jimmy Durante, Dean Martin, Jerry Lewis und Frank Sinatra mit dem „Rat Pack" auftraten.

Une des plus célèbres salles de spectacles de Las Vegas dans les années 1950, le Copa Room de l'hôtel Sands, inauguré en 1952, présente les plus grandes vedettes du moment : Jimmy Durante, Dean Martin et Jerry Lewis, mais aussi le fameux « Rat Pack » de Frank Sinatra.

OPPOSITE **Congo Room, Hotel Sahara, 1954, Las Vegas, Nevada**

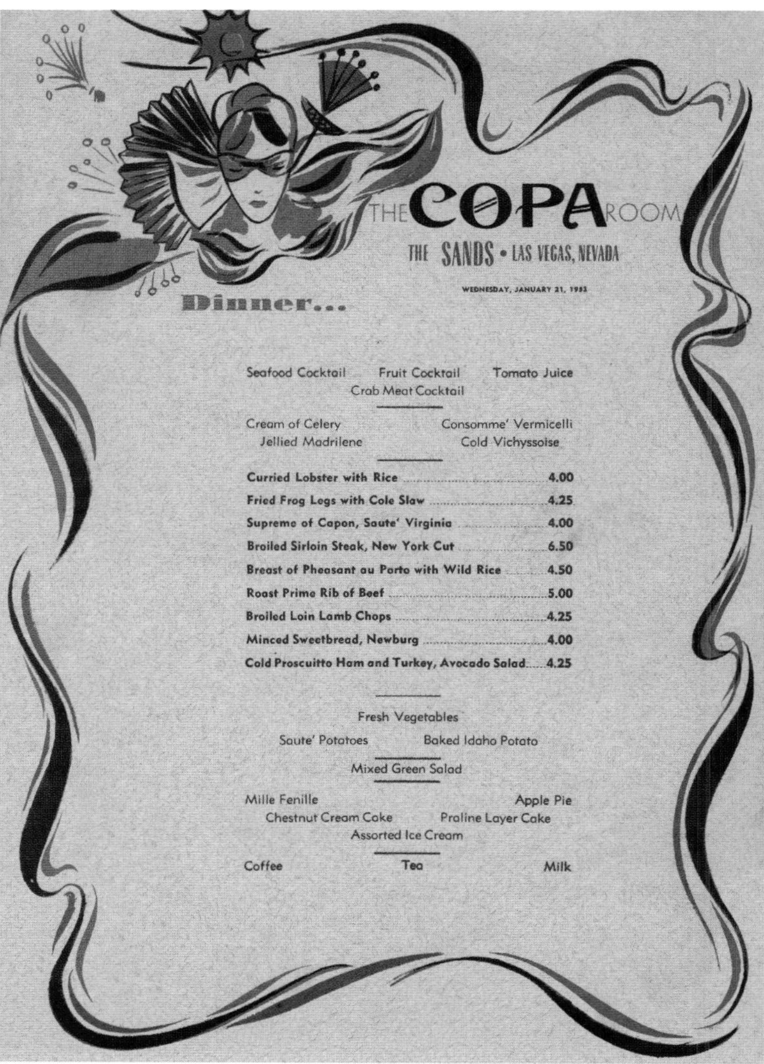
THE COPA ROOM
THE SANDS • LAS VEGAS, NEVADA

WEDNESDAY, JANUARY 21, 1953

Dinner...

Seafood Cocktail — Fruit Cocktail — Tomato Juice
Crab Meat Cocktail

Cream of Celery — Consomme' Vermicelli
Jellied Madrilene — Cold Vichyssoise

Curried Lobster with Rice	**4.00**
Fried Frog Legs with Cole Slaw	**4.25**
Supreme of Capon, Saute' Virginia	**4.00**
Broiled Sirloin Steak, New York Cut	**6.50**
Breast of Pheasant au Porto with Wild Rice	**4.50**
Roast Prime Rib of Beef	**5.00**
Broiled Loin Lamb Chops	**4.25**
Minced Sweetbread, Newburg	**4.00**
Cold Proscuitto Ham and Turkey, Avocado Salad	**4.25**

Fresh Vegetables
Saute' Potatoes — Baked Idaho Potato

Mixed Green Salad

Mille Fenille — Apple Pie
Chestnut Cream Cake — Praline Layer Cake
Assorted Ice Cream

Coffee — Tea — Milk

HOTEL
SAHARA
LAS VEGAS NEVADA
congo room

BAY of NAPLES
49
GORDONS PASS
EL
Naples Beach Hotel
MENU
for Today

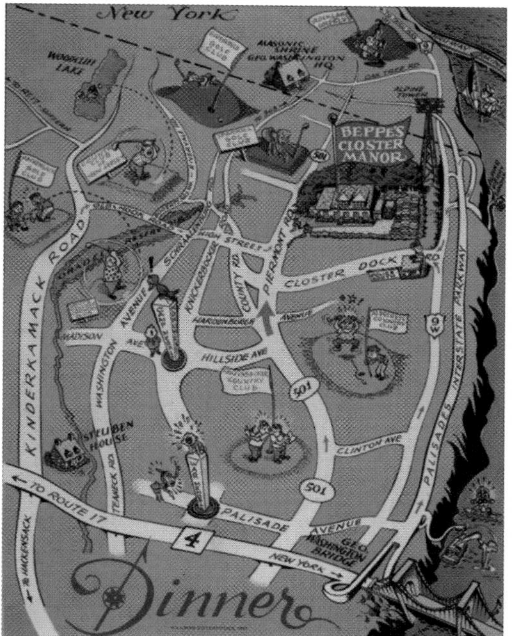

OPPOSITE **Naples Beach Hotel, c. 1955, Naples, Florida**

ABOVE **Beppe's Closter Manor, c. 1956, New York, New York**

ABOVE **The Friendship House, 1960, Biloxi, Mississippi**

Maps and bird's-eye views of a restaurant's locale became popular in the 1950s and 1960s, especially for tourist destinations, providing information on other area attractions.

Ein Blick aus der Vogelperspektive auf die Region, in der ein Restaurant lag, wurde in den 1950ern und 1960ern besonders in Touristenorten sehr beliebt und bot den Besuchern Informationen über die örtlichen Attraktionen.

Cartes et vues générales de la situation du restaurant deviennent populaires dans les années 1950 et 1960, en particulier dans les régions touristiques. Elles fournissent en outre des informations sur les autres attractions à proximité de l'établissement.

OPPOSITE April in Paris Ball, the Waldorf-Astoria, c. 1958, New York, New York

Banquets and benefits provided the framework for elegant oversized menus. These alluded to French sophistication. The cuisine for April in Paris offered dish and wine pairings rivaled by the best New York restaurants. This menu is also aptly illustrated by Bernard Lamotte.

Bankett- und Benefizveranstaltungen boten oft Anlass für elegante, übergroße Speisekarten, die französische Eleganz suggerieren sollten. Serviert wurden aus Anlass von „April in Paris" jeweils mit einem eigenen Wein kombinierte Gerichte, die mit den besten New Yorker Gourmettempeln konkurrieren konnten. Die geschmackvollen Illustrationen stammen von Bernard Lamotte.

Les cartes à la fois élégantes et de grandes dimensions créées à l'occasion des banquets et des soirées de bienfaisance soulignent le raffinement à la française. La cuisine du restaurant April in Paris propose des mariages de mets et de vins dignes des plus grandes adresses new-yorkaises. Ce menu est habilement illustré par Bernard Lamotte.

ABOVE & RIGHT April in Paris Ball, the Waldorf-Astoria, 1957, New York, New York

The menu shows Paris's Place de la Concorde, by French artist Bernard Lamotte, a bon vivant who moved to New York in 1935 and was known for his street scenes of Paris as well as for the bohemian salon he held in his apartment above La Grenouille restaurant on East 52nd Street, where he entertained Greta Garbo, Charlie Chaplin, and Marlene Dietrich.

Auf der Speisekarte ist der Place de la Concorde in Paris in einer Zeichnung des Franzosen Bernard Lamotte zu sehen. Lamotte zog 1935 nach New York und war für seine Pariser Straßenszenen und für den Künstlersalon bekannt, der in seiner Wohnung über dem Restaurant La Grenouille an der East 52nd Street abgehalten wurde und in dem Greta Garbo, Charlie Chaplin und Marlene Dietrich zu Gast waren.

La place de la Concorde à Paris, représentée par l'artiste français Bernard Lamotte. Bon vivant émigré à New York en 1935, il est connu pour ses scènes de rue et pour le salon à l'esprit bohème qu'il tient dans son appartement situé au-dessus du restaurant La Grenouille sur la 52e rue Est, où viennent se divertir Greta Garbo, Charlie Chaplin et Marlene Dietrich.

Le Dîner

Les Amuse-Bouche

Les Champagnes de France

La Procession Royale des Brioches au Fromage,
Dartois aux Lucines, Croûtes au Jambon,
Crustacés en Beignets,
Pomponettes à la Reine,
Petits Feuillants de Volaille,
Petits Croissants La Fayette.

Le Menu

1 ere Assiette

LE POTAGE À L'OSEILLE DU PRINTEMPS
LES CROUSTILLANTS DU PAYSAN

Riesling de Bergheim
1953
Jules Muller

2 ème Assiette

LA TRUITE AU VIN DE CHAMPAGNE
ACCOMPAGNÉE DES PETITES CREVETTES
DES CÔTES DE BRETAGNE

Château Lafite
1954
Château Margaux
1954

3 ème Assiette

LE SUPRÊME DE CANARD AU CHAMBERTIN
AVEC LES CULS D'ARTICHAUTS EN ESTOUFFADE
ET LES PETITS POIS A LA FRANÇAISE

Château Haut-Brion
1954

4 ème Assiette

LE PÂTÉ DE LAPEREAU EN SA CROÛTE DORÉE
AVEC UNE SALADE CRUE À L'HUILE

Château
Beychevelle
1954
Château Latour
1954

Dorure

LES FROMAGES DE FRANCE

Château d'Yquem
1950

Apotheose

LA TOURTE ROYALE D'ABRICOTS
DES CÔTES DE PROVENCE

Château de Marsan
Armagnac
Courvoisier
Marie Brizard Liqueurs

LE CAFÉ DE HAÏTI

MORET
april in paris

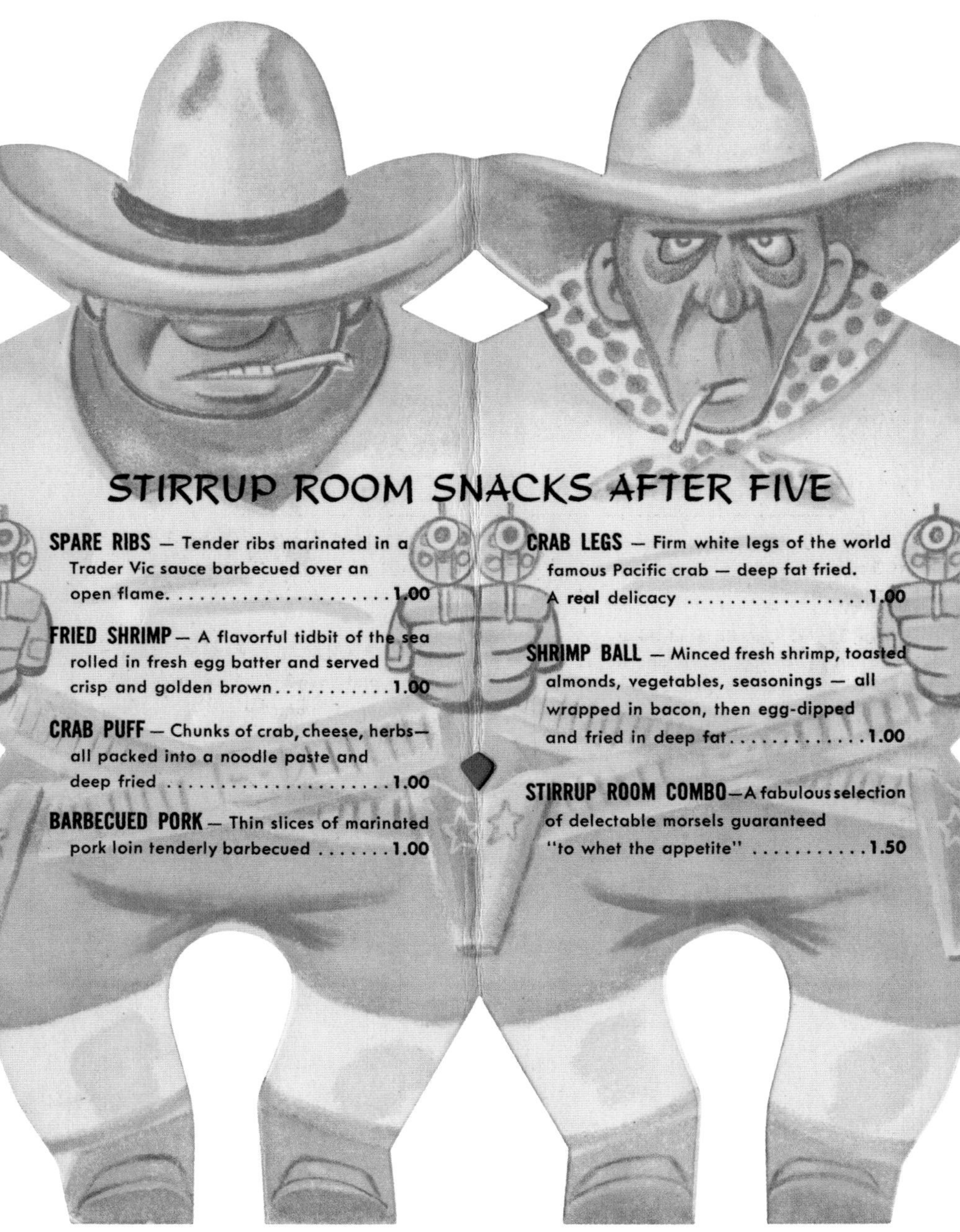

LEFT Buz Dyer's Chuck Wagon, c. 1955, El Cerrito, California

BELOW The Stirrup Room, Hotel Multnomah, c. 1955, Portland, Oregon

Mileage From THE DIAMOND HORSESHOE Laramie, Wyoming

To—
Albuquerque—591
Boise—730
Casper—191
Cheyenne—50
Chicago—1038
Colorado Springs—204
Denver—131
Des Moines—690
Elko, Nev.—655
Evanston—330
Grand Island—406
Idaho Falls—480
Jackson, Wyo.—402
Kansas City—720
Kearney—365
Kemmerer—309
Lander—243
Lincoln, Nebr.—500
Little America—255
Los Angeles—1138
North Platte—269
Ogden—409
Omaha—550
Pocatello—490
Rawlins—115
Reno—948
Rock Springs—224
Salt Lake City—421
San Francisco—1187
Sidney—150
Sun Valley—679
Twin Falls—605
Yellowstone—457

W
30
DIAMOND HORSESHOE
LARAMIE
30
E

The Diamond Horseshoe

- MOTEL
- DINING ROOM
- BAR, LOUNGE & PACKAGE GOODS
- 24 HOUR COFFEE SHOP
- 24 HOUR SERVICE STATION

Howdy

WYOMING

1½ MILES NORTH HIGHWAY 30-80-287

DIAMOND HORSESHOE INC.

LARAMIE, WYO.

ABOVE **The Diamond Horseshoe, c. 1955, Laramie, Wyoming**

RIGHT **The Desert Inn, c. 1955, Lancaster, California**

Cowboy movies and TV Westerns were booming in popularity in the mid-1950s, so restaurants, especially in the West, picked up on the theme with images of cowboys, chuck wagons, and horseshoes.

Mitte der 1950er gab es einen wahren Westernboom in Film und Fernsehen. Deshalb schmückten sich besonders im Westen der USA viele Lokale mit Bildern von Cowboys, Planwagen und Hufeisen.

La popularité des films et des séries télévisées mettant en scène des cow-boys grimpe en flèche dans les années 1950. Les restaurants, surtout dans l'Ouest, s'emparent de ce thème avec des illustrations de cow-boys, de chariots et de fers à cheval.

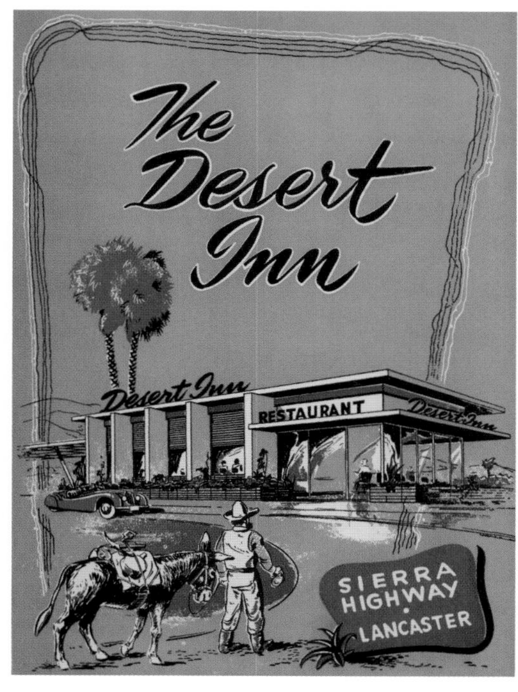

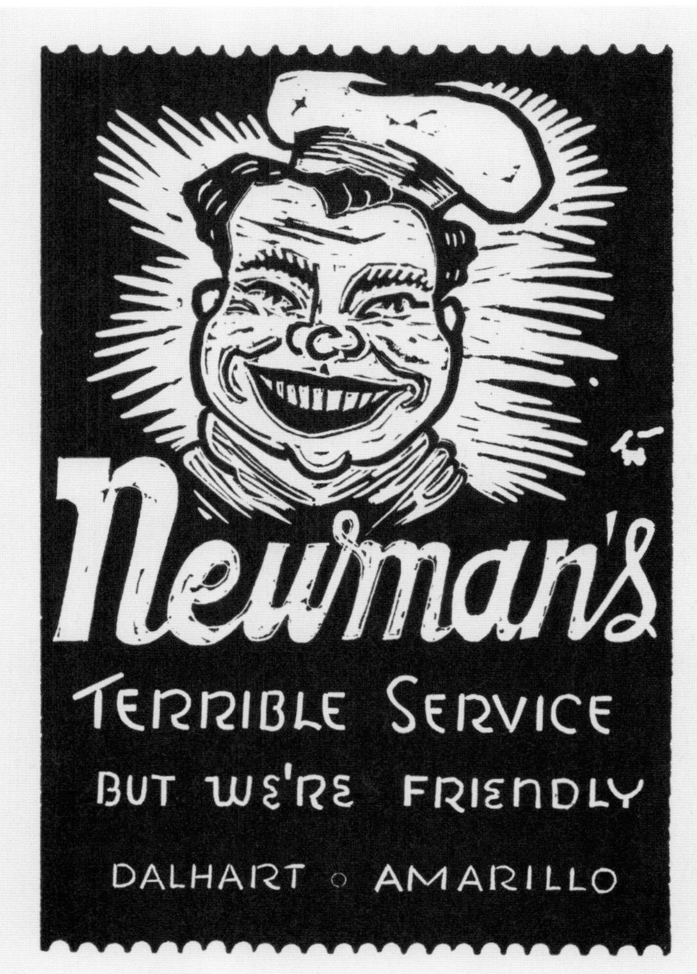

LEFT & BELOW Newman's, c. 1955, Amarillo, Texas

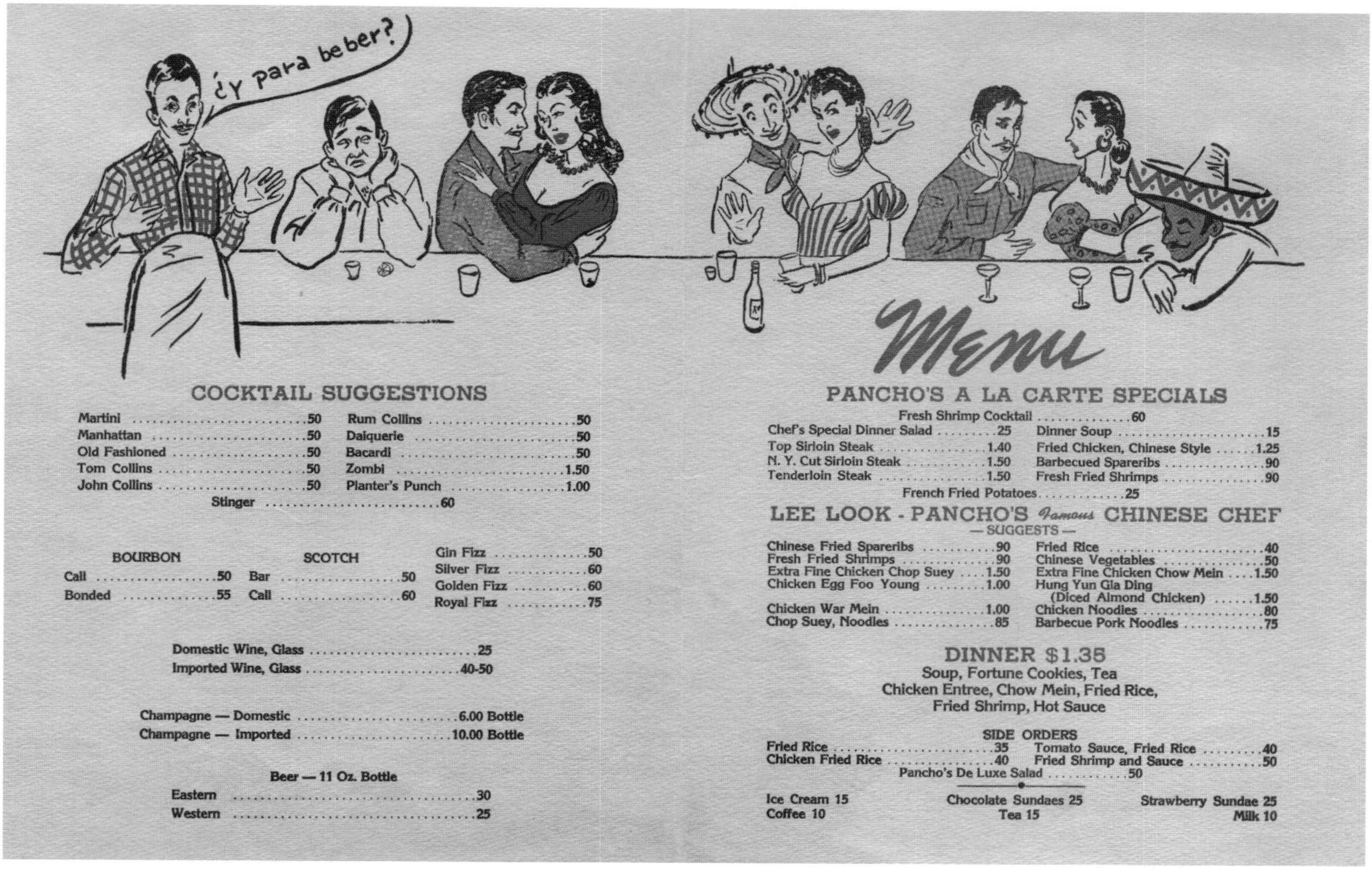

¿Y para beber?

COCKTAIL SUGGESTIONS

Martini .50
Manhattan .50
Old Fashioned .50
Tom Collins .50
John Collins .50
Rum Collins .50
Daiquerie .50
Bacardi .50
Zombi 1.50
Planter's Punch 1.00
Stinger .60

BOURBON		SCOTCH	
Call	.50	Bar	.50
Bonded	.55	Call	.60

Gin Fizz .50
Silver Fizz .60
Golden Fizz .60
Royal Fizz .75

Domestic Wine, Glass .25
Imported Wine, Glass 40-50

Champagne — Domestic 6.00 Bottle
Champagne — Imported 10.00 Bottle

Beer — 11 Oz. Bottle
Eastern .30
Western .25

Menu

PANCHO'S A LA CARTE SPECIALS

Fresh Shrimp Cocktail .60
Chef's Special Dinner Salad .25
Top Sirloin Steak 1.40
N. Y. Cut Sirloin Steak 1.50
Tenderloin Steak 1.50
Dinner Soup .15
Fried Chicken, Chinese Style 1.25
Barbecued Spareribs .90
Fresh Fried Shrimps .90
French Fried Potatoes .25

LEE LOOK - PANCHO'S *Famous* CHINESE CHEF
— SUGGESTS —

Chinese Fried Spareribs .90
Fresh Fried Shrimps .90
Extra Fine Chicken Chop Suey 1.50
Chicken Egg Foo Young 1.00
Chicken War Mein 1.00
Chop Suey, Noodles .85
Fried Rice .40
Chinese Vegetables .50
Extra Fine Chicken Chow Mein 1.50
Hung Yun Gia Ding (Diced Almond Chicken) 1.50
Chicken Noodles .80
Barbecue Pork Noodles .75

DINNER $1.35

Soup, Fortune Cookies, Tea
Chicken Entree, Chow Mein, Fried Rice,
Fried Shrimp, Hot Sauce

SIDE ORDERS
Fried Rice .35
Chicken Fried Rice .40
Tomato Sauce, Fried Rice .40
Fried Shrimp and Sauce .50
Pancho's De Luxe Salad .50

Ice Cream 15
Coffee 10
Chocolate Sundaes 25
Tea 15
Strawberry Sundae 25
Milk 10

OPPOSITE RIGHT Piccaninny Bar-B-Q, c. 1951

The use of racial stereotypes persisted well into the 1950s, as this "Piccaninny" menu cover shows. Note the phrase, "Endorsed by Drunken Hines," a pun on a widely used restaurant guide by Duncan Hines entitled *Adventures in Good Eating*, which first came out in 1935.

Noch in den 1950ern waren rassistische Darstellungen weit verbreitet, wie auf dieser „Piccaninny"-Speisekarte. Man beachte den Satz „Endorsed by Drunken Hines" („Empfohlen vom betrunkenen Hines"), eine Anspielung auf den beliebten Restaurantführer von Duncan Hines, der unter dem Namen *Adventures in Good Eating* 1935 auf den Markt kam.

L'usage de stéréotypes raciaux persiste dans les années 1950, comme le montre le menu du « Piccaninny » (« Au négrillon »). On notera la phrase « Endorsed by Drunken Hines » (« Recommandé par l'ivrogne Hines »), jeu de mots obtenu en déformant le prénom de Duncan Hines, auteur d'un guide à succès *Adventures in Good Eating*, publié pour la première fois en 1935.

ABOVE & RIGHT Pancho's, c. 1954, Manhattan Beach, California

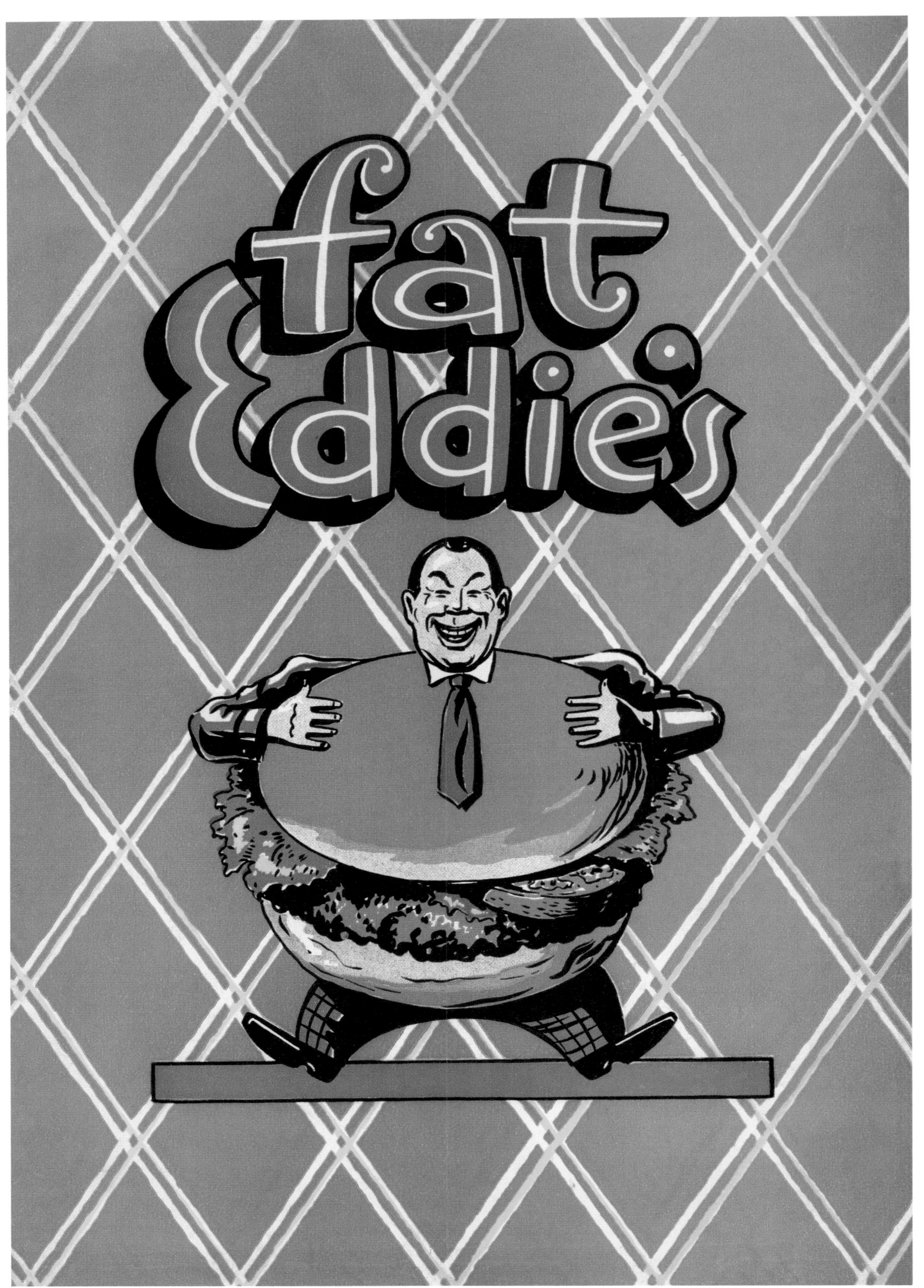
fat
Eddie's

OPPOSITE **Fat Eddie's, c. 1956, Los Angeles, California**

BELOW & RIGHT **Romeo's Times Square, 1956, Los Angeles, California**

The California coffee shop evolved into more of a family restaurant, with far more appealing décor and higher hygiene than lower-end diners and burger stands. Romeo's was typical of a friendly Southern California appeal that quickly spread throughout the United States in the 1960s.

Der kalifornische Coffeeshop entwickelte sich zum Restaurant für die ganze Familie; die Einrichtung war hübscher, und es war sauberer als in Diners und Imbissbuden. Romeo's war typisch für ein freundliches südkalifornisches Ambiente, das sich in den 1960ern schnell in den gesamten USA ausbreitete.

La cafétéria californienne évolue vers un restaurant familial avec un décor plus élégant et une hygiène beaucoup plus stricte que dans les *diners* (gargotes) et les snacks. Le Romeo's Times Square est typique de l'atmosphère amicale de la Californie du Sud qui va se répandre rapidement aux États-Unis durant les années 1960.

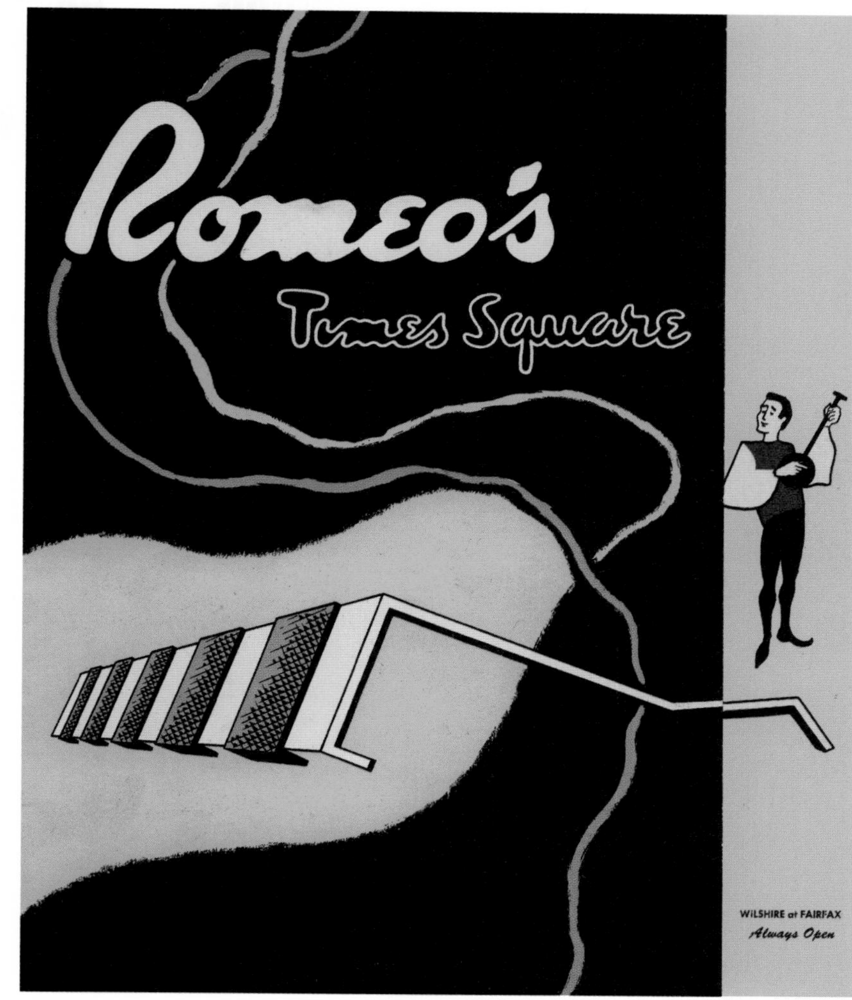

Salads

CHOICE OF ROQUEFORT, FRENCH OR THOUSAND ISLAND DRESSING

ANTIPASTO .85
Italian salami, anchovies, sliced egg, pimento, olives, pickled beets, chickory, celery, sweet pickles, little hot peppers and Provolone cheese.

CHEF'S SPECIAL .95
Julienne ham, chicken and cheese with crisp green salad garnished with tomato and hard boiled egg.

FRUIT EXTRAVAGANZA 1.25
Cottage cheese, fruit gelatine and cranberry sherbet served on a bed of crisp lettuce amidst Elberta peach, Bartlett pear, Hawaiian pineapple, quartered banana, sliced apple, garnished with Mandarin orange slices, Santa Clara prunes, Kadota figs and topped with a maraschino cherry.

TUNA DE LUXE .95
An individual tin of Chicken of the Sea with chopped celery, chopped onions, chopped apples and mayonnaise on the side. You can mix it yourself on the companion bed of crisp lettuce surrounded by tomato wedges or, if you prefer, one of our juliets will be happy to assist.

COTTAGE CHEESE with Elberta Peaches, Bartlett Pears, or Hawaiian Pineapple .75
A generous portion of cottage cheese, garnished with Mandarin orange slices, served on a bed of crisp lettuce with your one favorite fruit as selected.

LETTUCE AND TOMATO .60
MIXED GREEN .30
COLE SLAW .25

Sandwiches

ROMEOBURGER .55
One-quarter pound of our own grind U. S. choice beef, charbroiled and served on a toasted sesame seed bun.

CHEESEBURGER .65
TUNA SALAD .60
BACON AND TOMATO .65
LETTUCE AND TOMATO .45
HAM OR BACON AND EGG .75
FRIED HAM .65
SWISS CHEESE .55
HAM AND SWISS CHEESE .80
TOP SIRLOIN STEAK CHARBROILED 1.75

35¢ minimum service per person at booths and tables

Your Juliet would love to dine with you at Romeo's

Times Square Specialties

.25 MINESTRONE
.65 SPAGHETTI with Tomato Sauce
.75 SPAGHETTI with Meat, Marinara or Butter Sauce
.80 SPAGHETTI with Mushroom Sauce
.90 MEAT RAVIOLI with Tomato, Meat or Marinara Sauce
.90 CHEESE RAVIOLI with Tomato, Meat or Marinara Sauce
1.00 SPAGHETTI with MEAT BALLS
1.20 LASAGNA A LA ROMEO
Long flat pasta arranged in layers with meat and Ricotta cheese, garnished with our famous sauce and then baked.
1.25 EGGPLANT PARMIGANA
Four slices of eggplant dipped into egg batter. Ricotta cheese is sandwiched between the pieces and then all is smothered with our famous sauce, topped with Mozzarella cheese and baked.
1.25 RAVIOLI PARMIGANA
Paste stuffed with beef, plus our famous sauce, smothered with Mozzarella cheese, baked and served in casserole.
1.35 SAUSAGE with SPAGHETTI
Homemade Italian sausage with a generous portion of our spaghetti and famous sauce.
1.50 VEAL CUTLET with SPAGHETTI
A large tender slice of Wisconsin veal dipped into egg batter, covered with bread crumbs, and then fried with lightning speed.
1.85 VEAL PARMIGANA
The cutlet placed in casserole, garnished with our famous sauce, topped with slices of Mozzarella cheese and then baked.
1.95 CHICKEN CACCIATORA
Large pieces of chicken with mushrooms, onions and our famous sauce, blended by roasting over a slow flame.

Pizza

SERVED FROM 6:30 P.M. TO 4:00 A.M.
(Please order by number)

1.25 1. MOZZARELLA CHEESE
1.50 2. GREEN PEPPER
1.50 3. SALAMI
1.50 4. ANCHOVY
1.50 5. MEAT BALL
1.50 6. ITALIAN SAUSAGE
1.50 7. MUSHROOM

"Cooking is the noblest of all the arts
Because it makes so many people happy every day."
ROMEO

Romeo's Big 4

SOUTHERN FRIED CHICKEN 1.85
With French fries and cranberry sauce.
CENTER CUT HAM STEAK 1.85
With pineapple ring and French fries.
HAMBURGER STEAK 1.40
With French fries.
TOP SIRLOIN STEAK 2.95
With French fries or our famous spaghetti and sauce.
ALL ABOVE MEATS EASTERN U. S. GRADED CHOICE
Served with Salad

SIDE ORDER FRENCH FRIED POTATOES .20
SIDE ORDER FRENCH FRIED ONION RINGS .30
SIDE ORDER SPAGHETTI WITH SAUCE .45

Desserts

HOME MADE INDIVIDUAL PIES .40
FRUIT PIES .25
ROMEO'S EXTRA THICK CHEESE CAKE .45
DE LUXE LAYER CAKE .30
DANISH PASTRY .20
FRUIT GELATINE with whipped cream .25
SPUMONI .30

Beverages

COFFEE .10
POT OF TEA .15
MILK .15
BUTTERMILK .15
HOT CHOCOLATE, whipped cream .20
ICED TEA OR COFFEE .15
WESTERN BEER .35
EASTERN BEER .45
WINES Please ask for wine list

If you or your Juliet appear to be of tender age, this Romeo must request proper identification before he can serve wine or beer. We do not want our tale to end, as Shakespeare's:
"For never was a story of more woe
Than this of Juliet and Romeo."

Entire contents and design copyrighted 1956 by Harold S. Ahrens

Your Juliet would love to dine with you at Romeo's

WILSHIRE at FAIRFAX
Always Open

LEFT & BELOW Huddle, 1956, Los Angeles, California

ABOVE Nixon's, 1957, Whittier, California

Sandwiches

HUDDLE-BURGER 85c
Char-Broiled
DELICIOUS IN ANY LANGUAGE
It's the biggest and best sandwich anywhere. Created for a big appetite, the Huddle-Burger is loaded with one-half pound of U. S. choice beef, ground daily in our own kitchen. Served on a huge special protein-rich bun, with melted cheese, red-ripe tomato, onion slice, crisp lettuce, pickles and our own special relish. TRY ONE NOW, then tell your friends.

¼ LB. BURGER 50c
Char-Broiled
U. S. choice beef ground fresh daily in our own kitchen to maintain our high standards of quality. Served with lettuce, carrot curls, pickles, butter patty and our own relish.
with Cheese 60c

Our Famous
PATTY MELT 65c
A TASTE TREAT
¼ lb. ground choice beef. Served with grilled cheese on home style rye bread sprinkled with chopped onions, with lettuce, carrot curls, Kosher pickle and our own special relish.

Sirloin Steak Sandwich 1.35
TENDER AND DELICIOUS U. S. CHOICE
Served on toast, red ripe tomato slice, carrot curls, pickle chips, butter patty and French fries.

TUNA SANDWICH
Sno-White Tender Tuna from the deep blue waters of the Pacific 45
BACON OR FRIED HAM AND CHEESE
Smoke-cured bacon or Premium ham with our special Dairy-Rich cheese 65
GRILLED PREMIUM HAM
We use only the finest 50
PAN-FRIED EGG
Large AA fresh. Our eggs are officially date-graded by U. S. Dept. of Agriculture 35
LETTUCE AND TOMATO
Crisp green lettuce and red-ripe tomatoes, with butter and mayonnaise 35
BACON AND TOMATO
Smoke-cured Premium bacon and red-ripe tomato, served on lettuce bed 50
GRILLED AMERICAN CHEESE
The finest in the land 35
GRILLED NIPPY CHEESE
"It's just the right flavor" 40
PEANUT BUTTER AND JELLY
Served old fashioned home style 35

Denver Sandwich
Prepared with chopped Premium ham, green peppers, onions, and fresh ranch eggs. Served open-face with Hawaiian pineapple ring garnish. **65c**

huddle

Soup

SOUP OF THE DAY
Cup 15; Bowl 25

Salads

Served with Melba Toast or Hot Roll
Choice of Dressing: Louie, French or Roquefort Cheese

OUR FAMOUS CHEF'S SALAD .... .90
FRUIT SALAD BOWL, Topped with Whipped Cream or Ice Cream .... .85
SNO-WHITE TUNA SALAD .... .75
COTTAGE CHEESE with Peach or Pineapple .... .75
LETTUCE AND TOMATO .... .60
SMALL GREEN SALAD, Diced Shrimp (with Melba Toast and Saltines) .... .45
COLE SLAW (with Saltines) .... .25
SHRIMP LOUIE 1.45

HUDDLE MIXED GREEN SALAD WITH SHRIMP .... .85
SERVED WITH MELBA TOAST OR HOT ROLL
CHOICE OF DRESSING: ROQUEFORT, LOUIE OR FRENCH
Small Portion (with Saltines) .... .45

Vegetables Potatoes

BAKED POTATO, Sour Cream and Chives .... .35
HASHED BROWN POTATOES .... .20
FRENCH FRIED ONION RINGS .... .40
FRENCH FRIED POTATOES 20 SLICED TOMATOES .... .35

Fountain

Prepared with Delicious CARNATION Ice Cream and Sherbet

FRESH STRAWBERRY SUNDAE .... .40
OLD FASHIONED DOUBLE DIP SODAS .... .35
HOT FUDGE SUNDAE ...... .40 SHERBET DISH .... .20
CHOCOLATE SUNDAE ..... .35 MALTS AND SHAKES ..... .35
PINEAPPLE SUNDAE ...... .35 FROSTY ROOT BEER ...... .10
RAINBOW PARFAIT .... .45 COCA-COLA .... .10
ICE CREAM DISH .... .25 BANANA SPLIT .... .55

All our sodas, sundaes, malts and shakes are served with 30% butterfat whipped cream, and cherry on sundaes.

CADETS
12 Years and Under
Soup or Salad
Choice of French or Louie Dressing
HUDDLE CLUB STEAK 1.55
JUMBO SHRIMP or HALIBUT FINGERS .... .95
HUDDLE GROUND STEAK 1.25
FRESH FRUIT SALAD with Cottage Cheese .... .95
Hot Roll and Butter Dairy Fresh Milk
Ice Cream or Sherbet

COCKTAILS AND LEISURELY DINING
in the Beautiful
SKYROOM

YES—COFFEE SHOP TOO!

VISIT THE PETITE ROOM
See the Can-Can Girls in a quiet corner of OLD PARIS

ENJOY THE HEATHER ROOM
a bit of Scotland for dining under the stars

SPECIAL ARRANGEMENTS
for
Banquets—Parties—Conferences

From Our Char-Broiler

Served with Soup or Crisp Green Salad, Choice of Dressing, Onion Rings, Large Idaho Baked Potato, Roll and Butter

HUDDLE SPECIAL TOP SIRLOIN U. S. Top Choice Eastern Beef 2.55
NEW YORK CUT STEAK Top U. S. Choice, Tasty and Tender 2.85
FILET MIGNON STEAK Served Continental Style, all fat removed, charcoal broiled to seal in the juices and tender goodness. Cuts like butter. 2.95
CENTER CUT PORK LOIN CHOPS Real Iowa Corn-Fed Pork, fresh and tender. Served with tart smooth Apple Sauce. 1.85
HUDDLE GROUND STEAK One-half pound of our Fresh Ground U. S. Choice Beef, Char-Broiled to your taste. 1.40
THICK CENTER CUT OF PREMIUM HAM STEAK 1.75
Choice and tender. Served with Hawaiian pineapple ring. You'll like it!

From Our Sea Food Bar

Shrimp Cocktail 75 Lobster Cocktail 85 Cracked Crab Cocktail 75 Sea Food Cocktail 75 Oyster Cocktail (in Season) 85

Sea Food Specialties

Served with Cole Slaw, French Fries, Tartar Sauce, Lemon, Roll and Butter

JUMBO SHRIMP, FRENCH FRIED Fresh from Mexican waters—Louisiana sauce. 1.25
MAINE SCALLOPS We use the best of the frozen to assure supply and our uniform quality. 1.25
NORTHERN SWORDFISH Center cut, Char-Broiled. In the mood for fish? This is it. 1.65
NORTHERN HALIBUT FINGERS Crisp, golden brown and tasty. 1.15
COMBINATION SEA FOOD PLATE Shrimp, Scallops, Halibut Fingers 1.45
BROILED CHINOOK SALMON STEAK Broiled to Perfection 1.55

Desserts

OUR SPECIALTY:
Huddle Homemade Individual Pies .... .35
Fresh Boysenberry and Fresh Strawberry
Served with Whipped Cream or Ice Cream

ASSORTED CONTINENTIAL PASTRIES .... .40
PIES, PER CUT .... .25
with Whipped or Ice Cream 5c Extra
FRESH STRAWBERRY SHORTCAKE .... .45
DE LUXE 3-LAYER CAKE .... .20

Drinks

COFFEE (Apffel's) 10
POT OF TEA ...... .15
MILK .... .15
BUTTERMILK ...... .15
HOT CHOCOLATE .. .20
ICED TEA .... .15
ICED COFFEE ...... .15
SANKA OR POSTUM 15

Our Chef's Specials

Our Famous Spicy Chili and Beans 50c
Loaded with Choice Beef.
Served with toasted bun, garnished.

HUDDLE SIZE 85c
¼ lb. of Choice Beef Burger. Smothered with our Special Spicy Chili and Beans and chopped onions. Served with toasted bun, garnished.

DELICIOUS OYSTER STEW 75c
Pacific oysters from deep blue waters. The most nutritious of foods. Floating islands of butter. Salted crackers.

POOR BOY SANDWICH 80c
¼ lb. of Burger topped with Cheese, Chili and Beans, salad, Kosher dill pickle, carrot curl, lettuce and tomato. Coffee or tea.

ABOVE **Ships Coffee Shop, c. 1958, Los Angeles, California**

The three locations of Ships, opened by restaurateur Emmett Shipman between 1956 and 1967, exemplified the Googie architectural style and the infatuation with Space Age design.

Die drei Filialen von Ships Coffee Shop, die Emmett Shipman zwischen 1956 und 1967 aufmachte, waren Inbegriff des futuristischen „Googie"-Architekturstils und der Begeisterung für Raumfahrt-Design.

Les trois adresses de l'enseigne Ships, ouvertes par le restaurateur Emmett Shipman entre 1956 et 1967, illustrent l'engouement pour les styles « googie » (courant architectural futuriste) et « conquête de l'espace ».

LEFT **The Ebbtide, c. 1959, Los Angeles, California**

LEFT & BELOW Jack's Drive-Ins, c. 1956, Los Angeles, California

Drive-in fare altered slightly over the decades. These menus offer virtually similar fare as their counterparts 20 years earlier. The inclusion of a children's menu reflects the postwar baby boom.

Die Angebote der Drive-in-Restaurants änderten sich im Lauf der Jahrzehnte nur wenig. Auf diesen Speisekarten steht praktisch dasselbe wie 20 Jahre zuvor. Dass es jetzt auch eine Kinderkarte gibt, zeugt vom Babyboom nach dem Krieg.

Les menus des drive-in n'évoluent que très légèrement au cours des années. Ils n'ont pratiquement pas changé depuis vingt ans. L'ajout d'un menu enfant rappelle le baby-boom de l'après-guerre.

OPPOSITE Stan's, c. 1956, Various, California

Big Jack

THE JUICIEST YOU EVER TASTED

Big Jack is made as only we know how. TWO Patties freshly ground U. S. Graded Steer Beef, served on sesame seed bun with slice of cheese, mayonnaise, our special relish, sliced tomatoes, crisp lettuce.

50c
with Chili
10c Extra

JACK JR.
BARBECUED HAMBURGER
Cur Own Special Sauce
40c

OUR FAMOUS BURGER IN A BASKET . . . 60
Served with Cheese, Pickle, Lettuce, Tomato and Mayonnaise, Toasted Bun, on a Nest of Shoestrings
(Our Famous Smoke Relish and Onions on Request)

FAT EDDIE BURGER .40
Served with Pickle and Mayonnaise on a Toasted Bun, Onions at Your Request
(Our Famous Smoke Relish and Onions on Request)
Cheeseburger 45c

Sandwiches

Denver Sandwich . . . 60 Tuna Salad . . . . . 40 Egg Salad 40
Ham and Egg . . . . . 65 Chicken Salad . . . . 40 Fried Egg 30
Sliced Turkey . . . . . . 70 Grilled Cheese . . . . . 35 Fried Ham 60
Bacon and Tomato . . . . 50 Avocado and Tomato 45
HOT BEEF OR HAM, Brown Gravy, Potatoes 80
BAR-B-Q MEAT LOAF 45
CHICKEN, BACON, TOMATO CLUB 95
AVOCADO, BACON AND TOMATO CLUB 75
Grilled Cheese with Ham or Bacon 60

Shoestring Potatoes 25 Onion Rings 35
Cole Slaw 25 Potato Salad 25

FRENCH DIP BEEF SANDWICH 70c
U. S. Graded Beef au Jus, Heaping Portion of Shoestring Potatoes, Cole Slaw

FRIED CHICKEN $1.35
½ of a Colored Fryer, Southern Fried
Served with Shoestring Potatoes, Cole Slaw, Hot Biscuits and Honey
HORSESHOE CUT HAM AND EGGS $1.05
BACON OR SAUSAGE AND EGGS 95c
Fresh Premium Large Ranch Eggs, Fried in Butter with a Generous Portion of Meat, Hashed Browned Potatoes, Toast or Hot Biscuits
GRILLED IN AA BUTTER

Luncheon and Dinner Specials

FRESH GROUND HAMBURGER STEAK, U.S. Graded Meat (8-oz.) 95
(Ground Daily in Our Own Commissary)
Vegetable, Shoestring Potatoes, Salad, Hot Rolls
HOMEMADE CHICKEN POT PIE 85
Served with Green Salad and Hot Roll and Butter
JACK'S THICK STEAK, U. S. Graded New York . . 1.65
Golden Brown French Fried Potatoes, Vegetable, Salad with French Dressing, Hot Biscuits
BREADED VEAL CUTLET 1.25
Green Salad, Potatoes, Garden Vegetable
CHICKEN FRIED STEAK 95
Green Salad, Potatoes, Garden Vegetable
MEAT LOAF PLATE 95
Green Salad, Potatoes, Garden Vegetable
JUMBO FRIED SHRIMP 1.10
Cole Slaw, Shoestrings and Hot Roll
SCALLOPS, Deep Fried 95
Cole Slaw, Shoestrings and Hot Roll
SEA FOOD PLATE (Shrimp, Halibut, Scallops) . . 1.25
Cole Slaw, Shoestrings and Hot Roll

STEAK SANDWICH, BARBECUE SAUCE 70c
WITH SHOESTRING POTATOES
BARBECUED BEEF OR HAM SANDWICH 60c
Cooked in Our Own Barbecue Pits with Real Barbecue Wood — Try It!

FISH AND CHIPS 85c
Served with Cole Slaw and Hot Roll
HOT TURKEY SANDWICH 85c
Real Homemade Gravy, Cranberries, Dressing and Potatoes

KRAZY DOG 30c
GRILLED IN PURE CREAMERY BUTTER
Frankfurter Prepared by Our Secret Formula on a Toasted Bun with Mustard and Relish

Soups

Homemade Soup . . . . Cup 15; Bowl 25
Clam Chowder on Friday . . . . Cup 15; Bowl 25

Salads

Choice of French or 1000 Isle Dressing
CHEF'S SPECIAL SALAD BOWL, Topped with Hard Boiled Egg, Diced Ham and Cheese, Quartered Tomatoes 60
Tuna Salad . . . . 70 Chicken Salad 75
Pineapple and Cottage Cheese 65
JACK'S SPECIAL SALAD with Fresh Gulf Shrimp 95
EDDIE'S CALIFORNIA FRUIT SALAD, Choice of Sherbet, Ice Cream or Whipped Cream 75
Fresh Shrimp Salad 1.00
Fresh Shrimp with Avocado Salad 1.15
Crisp Green Salad 30

SPANISH SPECIALTIES

HOMEMADE CHILI AND BEANS . . . 45
Made from Freshly Ground U. S. Beef Only
SPAGHETTI with Meat Sauce . . . 70 HAMBURGER SIZE 80
SPAGHETTI with Chili . . . . 75 CHICKEN TAMALE with Chili . . 70

Drinks

Tomato Juice . . . . 15-25 Buttermilk 15
Fresh Orange Juice . . . 15-25 Iced Coffee 15
Coca-Cola . . . 15 Iced Tea . . . . . 15 Hot Tea 15
Root Beer . . . . 15 Coffee . . . . . . 10 Milk 15
Old Fashioned Lemon or Limeade 20
Pineapple or Grapefruit Juice 15-25
Hot Chocolate with Milk, Pure Whipped Cream 20

CHILDREN'S DINNERS
Fresh Ground Beef Patty or Roast Beef 50
Roast Tom Turkey 65
Served with Whipped Potatoes, Fresh Vegetable Bread and Butter

1000-11-55 LORD PRINTING CO., L.A.—MENUS

COCKTAILS
Stan's
★ PIT ★ BAR-B-Q
★ SANDWICHES & FOUNTAIN
★ LUNCH ★ DINNER
LOCATIONS
OF STAN'S DRIVE INS
LOS ANGELES
*Wilshire & Hoover
*Wilshire & Western
Figueroa & Exposition
*Sunset & Vine
Sunset & Highland
Sunset & Virgil
Olympic & Soto
Washington & Grand
SOUTH PASADENA
5 Pasadena Ave.
BELL
*Atlantic & Florence
EAST LOS ANGELES
Whittier & Atlantic
EL MONTE
*5 Points
*These Locations Have Cocktail Bars
For Your Pleasure

RIGHT & BELOW Eleda, c. 1954, Los Angeles, California

By the mid-1950s what would later be called the "baby boomer generation" was being spoiled by the happy prosperity of the era, and novelty restaurants were part of the allure of going out to dinner with the family. Menus would reflect that appeal with comic characters and animals, and, as Eleda's menu shows, dishes were named after children's cartoon and pop culture favorites like the Jet Pilot, Ferdinand the Bull, and Humpty Dumpty.

Mitte der 50er-Jahre wurde die kleine Babyboomer-Generation dank des neuen Wohlstands verwöhnt. Man ging gern mit der ganzen Familie in fantasievoll ausgestattete Themenrestaurants. Auch die Speisekarten sprachen mit Comicfiguren und Tieren besonders die kleinen Gäste an. Die Gerichte wurden wie hier im Eleda's nach beliebten Figuren wie Jet Pilot, Ferdinand dem Stier und Humpty Dumpty benannt.

Au milieu des années 1950, ceux qu'on appellera plus tard les baby-boomers vivent dans la prospérité et les restaurants fantaisie séduisent les familles désireuses de s'offrir un repas à l'extérieur. Les menus reflètent cet attrait en présentant des personnages de bandes dessinées ou des animaux. Cette carte créée pour l'Eleda montre des plats qui portent le nom de héros d'enfants et de la culture pop : Jet Pilot, Ferdinand le taureau, Humpty-Dumpty.

OPPOSITE ABOVE Holiday Inn, c. 1957, Bakersfield, California

OPPOSITE BELOW Eaton's Restaurants, c. 1954, Los Angeles, California

Children's SOUVENIR MENU

Eleda
4296 CRENSHAW BLVD.
LOS ANGELES, CALIFORNIA

Humpty-Dumpty 75c
Soup
SPAGHETTI & MEAT SAUCE
Vegetable
Bread and Butter
Choice of Milk, Hot Chocolate or Chocolate Milk
Choice of Jello or Pudding

Bronco Buster 85c
Soup
STEERBURGER PATTIE
Vegetable, Potatoes
Bread and Butter
Choice of Milk, Hot Chocolate or Chocolate Milk
Choice of Jello or Pudding

Bring the Family!
EVERY SUNDAY
4—5 p.m.
CHILDREN'S HOUR
Broadcast from the Eleda over KFVD 10:20 K.C.
Starring your child
Interviews — Prizes
Stunts — Favors
BOB MOON, M.C.

Ferdinand the Bull $1.25
Soup
POUNDED STEAK
French Fries, Vegetable
Bread and Butter
Choice of Milk, Hot Chocolate or Chocolate Milk
Choice of Jello or Pudding

Mermaid 75c
Soup
FILET OF SOLE
Vegetable, Potatoes
Bread and Butter
Choice of Milk, Hot Chocolate or Chocolate Milk
Choice of Jello or Pudding

Jet Pilot 90c
Soup
FRENCH FRIED SHRIMP
French Fried Potatoes
Bread and Butter
Choice of Milk, Hot Chocolate or Chocolate Milk
Choice of Jello or Pudding

Strong Man $1.25
Soup
GRILLED LAMB CHOP
Vegetables, Potatoes
Bread and Butter
Choice of Milk, Hot Chocolate or Chocolate Milk
Choice of Jello or Pudding

Indian Chief $1.25
Soup
TURKEY
Candied Yams
Bread and Butter
Choice of Milk, Hot Chocolate or Chocolate Milk
Choice of Jello or Pudding

Holiday Inn
©
Eaton's

ABOVE The Traders, 1957, Chicago, Illinois

Spurred by the early success of Trader Vic's, Polynesian restaurants, often called tiki restaurants because of their reference to the South Seas, became a very popular theme in the late 1950s and early 1960s, evoking Pacific island totems, thatched roofs, and exotic rum cocktails.

Angefeuert vom frühen Erfolg des Trader Vic's wurden Südseelokale, meist „Tiki-Restaurants" genannt, Ende der 1950er-, Anfang der 60er sehr beliebt in den USA. Allgegenwärtige Tiki-Symbole waren geschnitzte Masken, Palmwedeldächer und exotische Rumcocktails.

Encouragés par le succès rapide du Trader Vic's, les restaurants polynésiens, souvent appelés « restaurants tikis » en raison de leur référence aux mers du Sud, deviennent un thème très populaire à la fin des années 1950 et au début des années 1960. On y retrouve des évocations des totems du Pacifique, des toits en feuilles de palme et des cocktails exotiques à base de rhum.

BELOW Tonga Room, the Fairmont Hotel, c. 1960, San Francisco, California

OPPOSITE Ale Ale Kai, Hawaiian Village Hotel, c. 1960, Waikiki, Hawaii

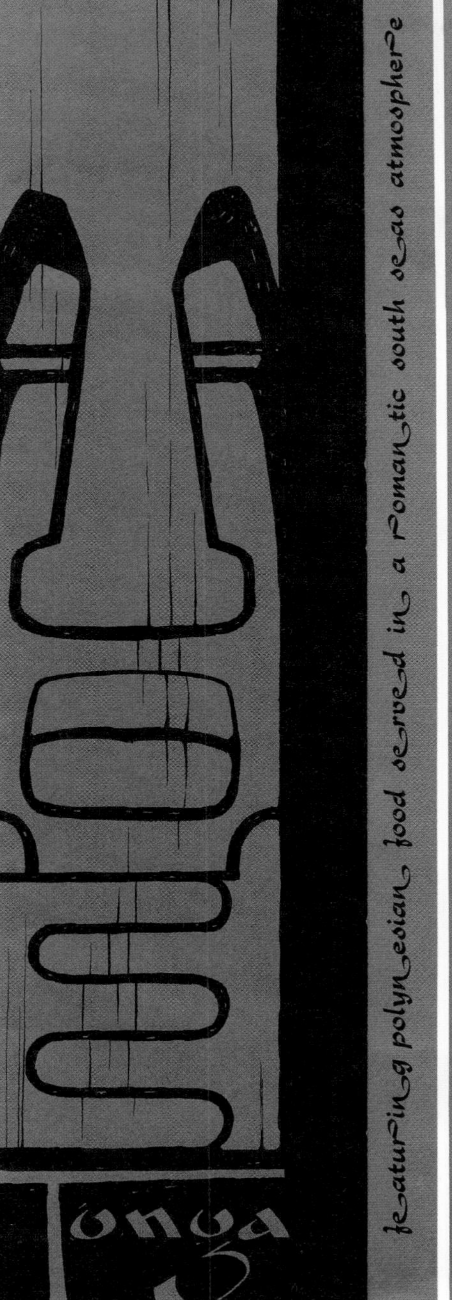

Chow Mein

Crisp French fried or pan fried.

Beef or Pork Chow Mein	2.25
Crab or Shrimp Chow Mein	2.65
Chicken Chow Mein	2.50
Tonga Chow Mein With prawns and chicken.	2.90
Almond Chicken Chow Mein	2.95
Chef's Special Chow Mein Shredded vegetables mixed with pan-fried noodles, chicken and Virginia ham.	3.10
Mon Yee Mein Same as Chef's chow mein but noodles are specially prepared.	3.10
Beef Tomato Chow Mein	2.40
Tau Ban Mein Chop Suey on top of noodles, Hoi-Sin sauce.	2.90

Chop Suey

Served with steamed rice, water chestnuts, bamboo shoots, onions, celery, pea pods, bean sprouts.

Beef or Pork Chop Suey	2.25
Crab or Shrimp Chop Suey	2.65
Chicken Chop Suey	2.50
Pineapple Chicken Chop Suey	2.75
Li Hang Chung Chop Suey With sliced chicken and ham on top.	2.65
Gar Choy Chop Suey Vegetables only.	2.25
Sub Gum Chop Suey Diced bamboo shoots, water chestnuts, bell peppers, chicken, imported mushrooms, garden peas.	2.55

Noodles & Won Ton

Pork Noodles	1.30
Chicken Noodles	1.40
Chop Suey Noodles Chop Suey on top of noodles.	1.70
Beef Noodles or Won Ton Beef sauteed on top of noodles.	1.90
Gai Gong Yee Mein Noodles are specially prepared.	2.90
Pork Won Ton	1.40
Chicken Won Ton	1.70
Jow Won Ton and Sauce	2.25
Wor Won Ton Chinese ravioli cooked with chicken, pea pods, vegetables, topped with Chai Sui.	1.95

Jasmine Tea served with all Chinese foods.

ALE ALE KAI
HAWAIIAN VILLAGE HOTEL - WAIKIKI
WESTERN HOTEL

Le Pavillon

MENU

Déjeuner

Jambon de Bayonne 2.50 | Melon 1.50 | Grapefruit 1.10
Caviar Malossol | Foie Gras Truffé 6.00
Saumon Fumé 3.50 | Cherrystones 1.50 | Anguille Fumée 2.75
Cocktails: Lobster 6.00 | Shrimps 3.50 | Crab Meat 4.50

Oeufs

Omelette à l'Espagnole 3.50 | Cocotte Princesse 3.00 | Plat Meyerbeer 3.25
Poché Bénédictine 3.50 | Frit Américaine 3.00 | Froids à la Gelée 1.75
Timbale à l'Indienne 3.25 | Brouillés aux Champignons 3.25 | Mollet aux Epinards 3.25

Poissons

Filets de Sole Bréval 4.75 | Homard Thermidor 7.50 | Crab Meat Nantua 5.00
Suprême de Striped Bass Jean=Bart 4.75 | Grenouilles aux Fines Herbes 5.00
Goujonnette de Sole 4.25 | Moules du Pêcheur 3.75 | Truite de Rivière Arlésienne 4.50
Spécialités: Homard 8.00 | Sole Anglaise | Moules 3.75

Plats du Jour

SELLE D'AGNEAU ROTIE, PERSILLEE 6.75 | **FRICASSEE DE VOLAILLE AU CHAMPAGNE 6.50**
Grenadin de Veau Maintenon 5.50 | Foies de Volaille Algérienne 4.25 | Rognons Sautés au Chablis 4.75
Cervelles Beurre Noisette 4.50 | Jambon Madère aux Epinards 4.25 | Emincé de Volaille St. Germain 5.00
Foie de Veau au Bacon 4.75 | Sauté de Filet de Boeuf Bercy 5.50 | Ris de Veau Meunière 5.00
Spécialités: Châteaubriand (Pour 2) 10.00 P.P. | Volaille (selon grosseur) | Ris de Veau 6.00

Grillades

Châteaubriand, Sauce Béarnaise (Pour 2) 10.00 P.P. | Côte d'Agneau aux Haricots=Verts 7.00
Rognons d'Agneau Vert=Pré 4.75 | Poulet de Grain Diablé, (Pour 2) 6.50 p.p. | Pigeon en Crapaudine 6.00
Côte de Veau Colbert 7.00 | Entrecôte Minute Pavillon 7.75

Plats Froids

Poularde à la Gelée 5.00 | Langue Givrée 3.25 | Boeuf Mode à la Gelée 4.50
Terrine de Canard 4.50 | Jambon d'York 3.50 | Terrine de Volaille 4.50

Légumes

Haricots Verts Ménagère 2.00 | Courgette Sautée 2.00 | Petits Pois Paysanne 2.00 | Laitue au Jus 2.00
Aubergine Provençale 2.00 | Céleris au Beurre 2.00 | Artichaut Vinaigrette 2.00
Choux=Fleurs au Gratin 2.25 | Epinards au Velouté 2.00 | Champignons au Porto 2.50

Entremets

Patisserie Pavillon 2.50 | Crèpes Pavillon 3.00
Poire Hélène 2.75 | Soufflés Tous Parfums 3.50 | Désir de Roi 2.25
Coupe aux Marrons 2.25 | Pêche Melba 2.50 | Macedoine de Fruits aux Liqueurs 2.50
Glaces: Vanille 1.00 | Chocolat 1.00 | Framboise 1.00 | Moka 1.00 | Citron 1.00 | Fraise 1.00
Cáfé .75 | Demi=Tasse .65 | Bread and Butter 1.00

OPPOSITE & RIGHT Le Pavillon, c. 1959, New York, New York

Le Pavillon, opened by director Henri Soulé for the French Pavilion at the 1939 New York World's Fair, evolved into the most influential classic French restaurant in America, attracting the rich and famous to its carefully regimented tables. Its décor and menu were almost slavishly copied by graduates of Soulé's kitchen and waitstaff, who opened similar restaurants throughout the 1950s and 1960s.

Das von Henri Soulé im französischen Pavillon auf der Weltausstellung 1939 in New York eröffnete Le Pavillon entwickelte sich zum einflussreichsten französischen Restaurant in Amerika, dessen Plätze stets mit handverlesenen Reichen und Berühmten gefüllt waren. Einrichtung und Karte wurden später fast sklavisch genau von Soulés Angestellten kopiert, die in den 50er- und 60er-Jahren viele ähnliche Gourmettempel eröffneten.

Le Pavillon, ouvert par Henri Soulé, directeur du pavillon français de l'Exposition universelle de New York en 1939, s'affirme comme l'un des restaurants français classiques les plus influents des États-Unis. Il attire les nantis et les personnalités à sa table particulièrement guindée. Décor et menu seront copiés sans aucune originalité par les différents membres du personnel de Soulé, qui ouvriront des restaurants similaires durant les années 1950 et 1960.

BELOW Le Pavillon, 1962, New York, New York

ABOVE, RIGHT & OPPOSITE The Four Seasons, c. 1960, New York, New York

Opened in 1959 in the Mies van der Rohe-designed Seagram Building, the Four Seasons was revolutionary in its own international-style design by young architect Philip Johnson. With a Picasso opera curtain dramatically dividing the two dining areas, and a pool in the main dining room, this was the most refined of the restaurants opened by Restaurant Associates, which also built the Forum of the Twelve Caesars, Fonda del Sol, and Zum Zum.

Das Four Seasons, das 1959 im von Mies van der Rohe gebauten Seagram Building aufmachte, hatte eine revolutionär moderne, von dem jungen Architekten Philip Johnson gestaltete Innenausstattung. Ein von Picasso handgemalter Vorhang unterteilte die beiden Sitzbereiche dramatisch, im Speisesaal gab es ein Wasserbecken: Dieses Restaurant war die schickste Adresse der Restaurant Associates, die außerdem das Forum of the Twelve Caesars, das Fonda del Sol und das Zum Zum bauten.

Ouvert en 1959 dans le Seagram Building conçu par Mies van der Rohe, le Four Seasons est révolutionnaire par son design proposé par le jeune architecte Philip Johnson, adepte du Style international. Un rideau d'opéra dessiné par Picasso scinde l'espace en deux et un bassin de marbre trône dans la salle à manger principale. Il s'agit de l'établissement le plus raffiné inauguré par Restaurant Associates, qui ouvrit également le Forum of the Twelve Caesars, le Fonda del Sol et le Zum Zum.

Dinner at The Four Seasons

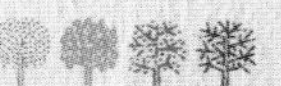

ICED BROCHETTE OF SHRIMP 2.25 PERIWINKLES *Mignonette* 1.65
LOBSTER CHUNKS *with Sorrel* 3.25 *Small Clams with Green Onions and* TRUFFLES 1.65
YOUNG SALMON OR STURGEON, *Our Smokehouse* 2.95
VITTELLO TONNATO — PICCOLO 1.75 SUMMER *Hors d'Oeuvre, A Sampling* 2.50
Today's Melon .95 A TUREEN OF *September Fruit* .95
Ham Mousse in Whole Peach, VIRGINIA 1.50

Hot Appetizers

Crisped Shrimp Filled with MUSTARD FRUITS 1.95
CALF'S BRAINS *en Brioche* 1.85 BEEF MARROW *in Bouillon or Cream* 1.85
Field Mushrooms and PROSCIUTTO EN CROUSTADE 2.25
TINY SHRIMPS *in Shoyu—French Fried* 2.50 THE FOUR SEASONS *Mousse of Trout* 2.50
SNAILS *in Their Shells*, DIJONAISE 1.85

Cream of Broccoli 1.10 A SEPTEMBER *Vegetable Soup* 1.10
Consommé with Herb Royale 1.25
COLD: *Beet and Onion Madrilène* .95 *Carrot Vichyssoise* 1.10

Sea and Fresh Water Fish

Planked Silver SALMON STEAK 5.50 RED CURRY OF ROCKFISH, *Mango Rice* 4.85
Broiled MAINE LOBSTER 6.50; *Filled with* CRABMEAT 7.85 *The* CLASSIC *Truite au Bleu* 5.50
STEAMED LOBSTER *in Court-Boullion* 6.75 *Summer Sole*, FOUR SEASONS 4.95

Red Snapper STEAK, *Grenobloise* 5.50 *Tournedos of* BEEF, *Tyrolienne* 6.50
Poached YOUNG CHICKEN, *Waterzoi* 5.75

A Variety of Seasonals

CALF'S LIVER AND PROSCIUTTO, *Venetian Style* 5.25 RARE FILET STROGONOFF 6.50
ROAST RACK OF LAMB *Persillé with Robust Herbs, for Two* 14.00
THE QUEEN'S GROUSE, *Blackberry Beignets* 8.50 *Braised* BONELESS SQUAB, *Farci Suprême* 6.50

BROILED OVER CHARCOAL *
Amish Ham Steak, Apricot Dumpling 4.85 *Calf's Liver*-THICK, *Sage Butter* 5.25
* * * * * * *
Sirloin VINTNERS STYLE 7.75 SKILLET STEAK *with Smothered Onions* 7.50
Beefsteak SCANDINAVIAN 7.75 *Filet of Beef* POIVRE, *Flambé* 8.00
Butterfly Steak Paillard, FOUR SEASONS 6.75
SPIT ROASTED WITH HERBS *
FARMHOUSE DUCKLING, *Brandied Apricots, for Two* 13.00
BROCHETTE OF MARINATED LAMB, *Turkish Pilaff* 5.25

Summer Salads

* * * * * * *
Bouillabaisse Salad 4.75 *Mousse of Gaspé Salmon* 5.65
JULEP OF CRABMEAT *in Sweet Pepperoni* 5.50 *Buffet of Sliced Meats*, DUTCH POTATO SALAD 5.85
AS A DINNER ACCOMPANIMENT *
COOKED CARROTS, *Minted Dressing* 1.25 *Beefsteak Tomato*, CARVED AT TABLE 1.25
Beets and RIPE OLIVE .85 *Early Summer Greens* .95
OUR FIELD GREENS ARE SELECTED EACH MORNING AND WILL VARY DAILY

SEASONAL GATHERINGS MAY BE VIEWED IN THEIR BASKETS ZUCCHINI *with Walnuts* .95
Leaf Spinach, ELIZABETH .95 BOUQUET PLATTER, *per Person* 1.50
MANGETOUTS 1.25 *Cracked Wheat, Forestière* .95
* * * *
POTATOES: *French Fried* .95 *Roesti* .95 *Mashed in Cream* .95

Cold Appetizers

THE NEW AMSTERDAM HERRING, *Pommes Vapeur* 2.25 MINTED *Lobster Parfait* 2.50
Tidewater BLUE CRAB *Lump* 2.95 SMOKED NATIVE BROOK TROUT, *Spiced Cream* 2.65
SUMMER COUNTRY TERRINE 2.25 *Cherrystones in* PEPPER VINAIGRETTE 1.50
PROSCIUTTO *with Ripe Figs or Melon* 2.75 *Caviar, per Serving* 7.50
Little Neck or Cherrystone Clams 1.50 MOUSSE *of Chicken Livers* 2.25
Egg in TARRAGON ASPIC, *Strasbourg Toast* 1.75

LOBSTER QUICHE, *Savory* 1.50 CRÊPES OF CRABMEAT, *Imperial* 2.45
Smoked SALMON SOUFFLÉ, *Onion Sauce* 2.65
Mussels in POTS 2.25 CLAM AND TOMATO CRÊPES 1.65
Cocotte of SWEETBREADS *with Madeira* 1.65
Our Coquille Saint-Jacques 2.25

Soups and Broths

Chicken Cream with NEW OATS 1.35 *Double Consommé with Sorrel* 1.25
Onion Soup with PORT, *Gratinée* 1.25
Danish Plum Soup 1.25 *Gazpacho* 1.25 *Watercress* VICHYSSOISE 1.10

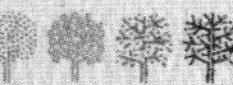

BARQUETTE OF FLOUNDER *with Glazed Fruits* 4.95 *Crabmeat Casanova* FLAMBÉ 5.75
Sea Bass—GRILLED 4.65 LOBSTER AROMATIC *Prepared Tableside* 6.50
Frog's Legs PROVENÇALE *or Sautéed with Moselle* 5.25

This Evening's Entrees

Casserole of LAMB CHOPS, *Boulangère* 5.85
Escalopes of VEAL, *Viennoise* 5.75

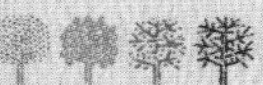

CRISPED DUCKLING *with Peaches, Sauce Cassis* 5.95 MEADOW VEAL CUTLET *with Morels* 5.75
Baby Pheasant in Golden Sauce—NUTTED WILD RICE 6.25
Sweetbreads in Mustard Crumbs, DIABLOTINE 5.50 *Atelier of* TWO QUAIL 6.75

Steaks, Chops, and Birds

* * * * * * *
Jersey Poularde 4.50 *Three French Lamb Chops* 5.95
* * * * * * *
SIRLOIN STEAK OR FILET MIGNON *Served for One* 7.50; *for Two* 15.00
Côte de Boeuf, Bordelaise, for Two 18.00 *Entrecôte à la Moëlle* 7.75
Twin Tournedos with WOODLAND MUSHROOMS 7.00
* * * * * * *
Baby Lamb: MINT ROASTED EPAULET, *for Two* 11.00; OREGANO ROASTED LEG, *for Three* 17.00
THE HEART OF THE PRIME RIB 5.75

* AS A MAIN COURSE
LOBSTER AND SHRIMP *in Zucchini, Sauce Vincent* 6.00 AVOCADO *with Scallops Seviche* 5.25
ROASTED CHICKEN, *Green Bean Salad* 5.75 BEEF IN BURGUNDY ASPIC 4.75
* * * * * * *
NASTURTIUM *Leaves* 1.50 WILTED SPINACH *and Bacon* 1.35
Raw Mushrooms, MALABAR DRESSING 1.75
Salad Dressing with Roquefort or Feta Cheese .50 additional

Vegetables and Potatoes

The YOUNGEST CARROTS *in Butter* 1.25 BEIGNETS VARIES 1.35 ONIONS *in Onions* .95
BROCCOLI FLOWERS, *Hollandaise* 1.95 LANCASTER *Corn Kernels, Tableside* 1.50
NUTTED *Wild Rice* 1.65 SOUFFLÉ OF SPINACH, *for Two* 3.85
* * * *
New Potatoes with DILL .95 *Baked in Jacket* .95

136

ABOVE Dinner in Honor of President John F. Kennedy, Given by the Ancient and Honorable Artillery Co., the Sheraton Plaza Hotel, 1961, Boston, Massachusetts

BELOW L. B. J. Ranch, 1963, Johnson City, Texas

President Lyndon Baines Johnson proudly proclaimed his Texas heritage and used any opportunity to leave the White House to spend time at his ranch. This menu reflects Johnson's simple tastes for American food, including Texas beef and pecan pie.

Präsident Lyndon Baines Johnson war sehr stolz auf seine texanische Herkunft und nutzte jede Gelegenheit, um das Weiße Haus zu verlassen und sich auf seiner Ranch aufzuhalten. An der Menüfolge lässt sich Johnsons Vorliebe für bodenständiges amerikanisches Essen ablesen: texanisches Rinderfilet und Pekannusskuchen.

Le président américain Lyndon Baines Johnson assumait fièrement son héritage texan et profitait de chaque occasion pour quitter la Maison-Blanche et passer du temps dans son ranch. Ce menu rappelle les goûts simples de Johnson et sa prédilection pour une nourriture typiquement américaine, dont le bœuf texan et la tarte aux noix de pécan.

OPPOSITE Luncheon in Honor of Astronaut L. Gordon Cooper Jr., James E. Webb, Administration of NASA, and the Mercury Team, the Waldorf-Astoria, 1963, New York, New York

The Apollo astronauts were fêted many times in formal dinners, this one given at the Waldorf-Astoria by Mayor Robert Wagner to honor astronauts Webb and Cooper, who only a week before had soared into space in a Mercury capsule.

Die Apollo-Astronauten wurden mit unendlich vielen formellen Banketten geehrt, so auch mit diesem von Bürgermeister Robert Wagner zu Ehren der Astronauten Webb und Cooper veranstalteten Mittagessen im Waldorf-Astoria – nur eine Woche vor ihrem Flug ins All mit der Mercury-Raumkapsel.

De nombreux dîners seront organisés en l'honneur des astronautes d'Apollo. Celui-ci est donné au Waldorf-Astoria par le maire de New York, Robert Wagner, en l'honneur de Webb et Cooper, qui, une semaine plus tôt, s'étaient envolés à bord d'une capsule Mercury.

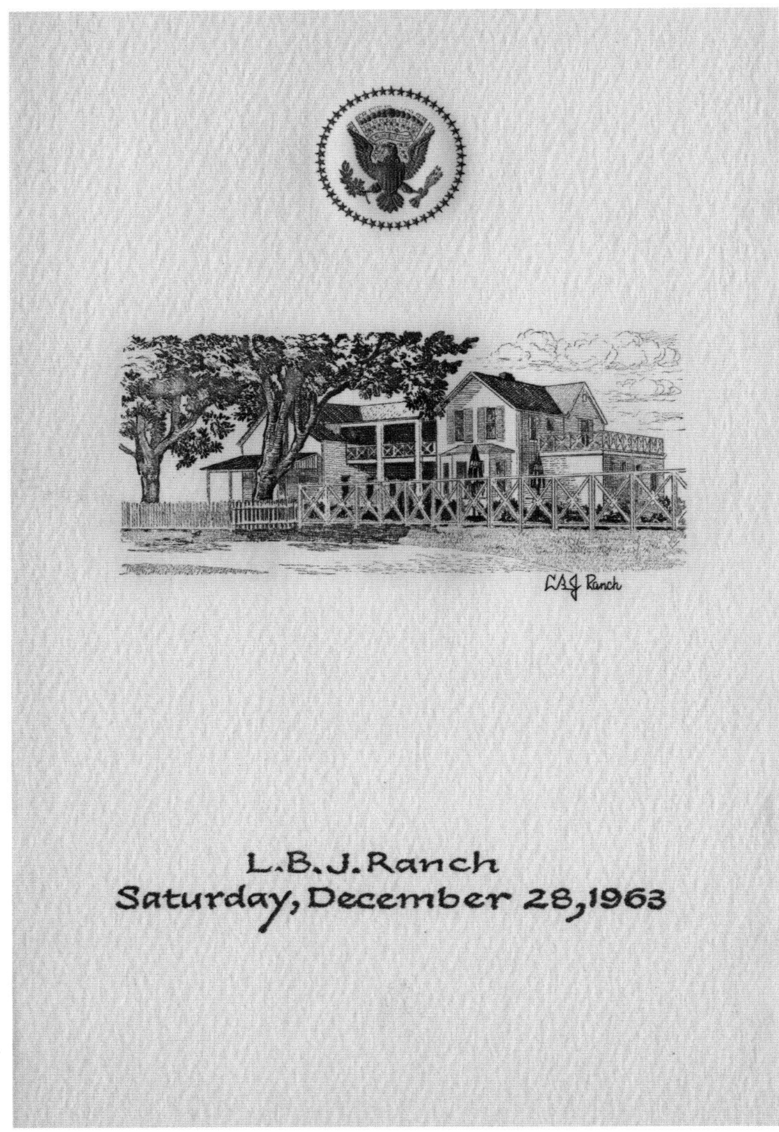

DINNER

Piesporter Treppchen Spätlese 1959 — Shrimp Mousse

Beaulieu Vineyard Beaumont Burgundy — Filet of Beef Texana
Potato Puffs
Creamed Spinach

Green Salad
Brie Cheese

Dom Pérignon 1955 — Pecan Pie

Demi-tasse

Luncheon

in honor of

Astronaut L. Gordon Cooper, Jr.

James E. Webb

Administrator of NASA

and The Mercury Team

given by

The Honorable Robert F. Wagner

Mayor of the City of New York

Menu

Tomato Surprise

Pinot Noir
Buena Vista

Spring Lamb

Asparagus

New Potatoes

Crown of Vanilla Glacé

Macaroons

Coffee

The Waldorf-Astoria Wednesday, May 22, 1963

EARLE DUFF
CENTURY
21
EXPOSITION

OPPOSITE Century 21 Exposition, 1962, Seattle, Washington

The Century 21 Exposition (also known as the Seattle World's Fair) was held from April 21, 1962, to October 21, 1962, and it' Space Needle icon and monorail are shown on the menu at a time when Space Age design coincided with President John F. Kennedy's promise to put a man on the moon by decade's end.

Die Century 21 Exposition, die Weltausstellung in Seattle, dauerte vom 21. April bis zum 21. Oktober 1962. Ihre Ikonen, die Space Needle und die Einschienenbahn, wurden zu einem Zeitpunkt auf der Speisekarte abgebildet, als Präsident Kennedy versprach, dass die Amerikaner noch vor Ende des Jahrzehnts auf dem Mond landen würden.

L'Exposition universelle de Seattle (connue aussi sous le nom de « Century 21 Exposition ») se tient entre le 21 avril et le 21 octobre. Sa tour d'observation Space Needle et son monorail sont reproduits sur le menu, à une époque où le style « conquête de l'espace » coïncide avec la promesse du président Kennedy d'envoyer un homme sur la lune avant la fin de la décennie.

BELOW Lava Pit, New York World's Fair, 1964, Flushing Meadows, New York

ABOVE Caribbean Pavilion, New York World's Fair, 1964, Flushing Meadows, New York

The 1964 World's Fair featured more state-of-the-art food services than any fair before it, most created and run by Restaurant Associates, a NY-based firm that also created the Four Seasons restaurant.

Die Weltausstellung von 1964 prunkte mit den modernsten gastronomischen Dienstleistungen, die es je auf einer Weltausstellung gegeben hatte. Verantwortlich zeichnete die New Yorker Firma Restaurant Associates, die auch das Restaurant Four Seasons betrieb.

L'Exposition universelle de 1964 propose davantage de services de restauration que les précédentes, la plupart proposés et gérés par Restaurant Associates, une société de New York qui a également ouvert le restaurant Four Seasons.

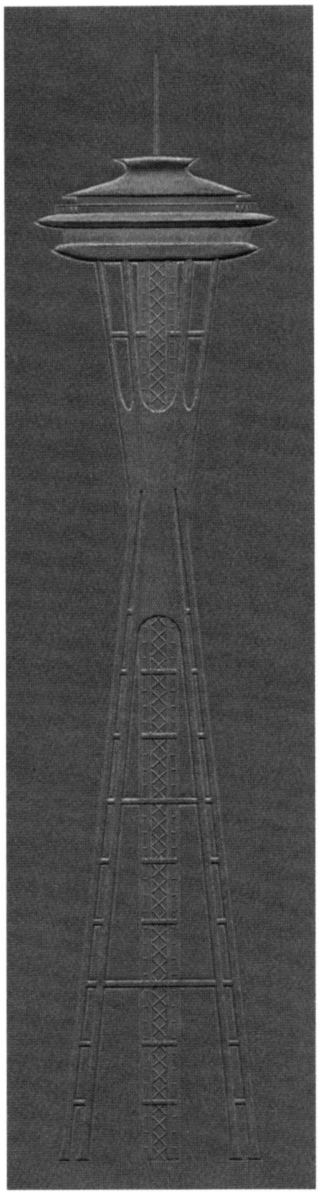

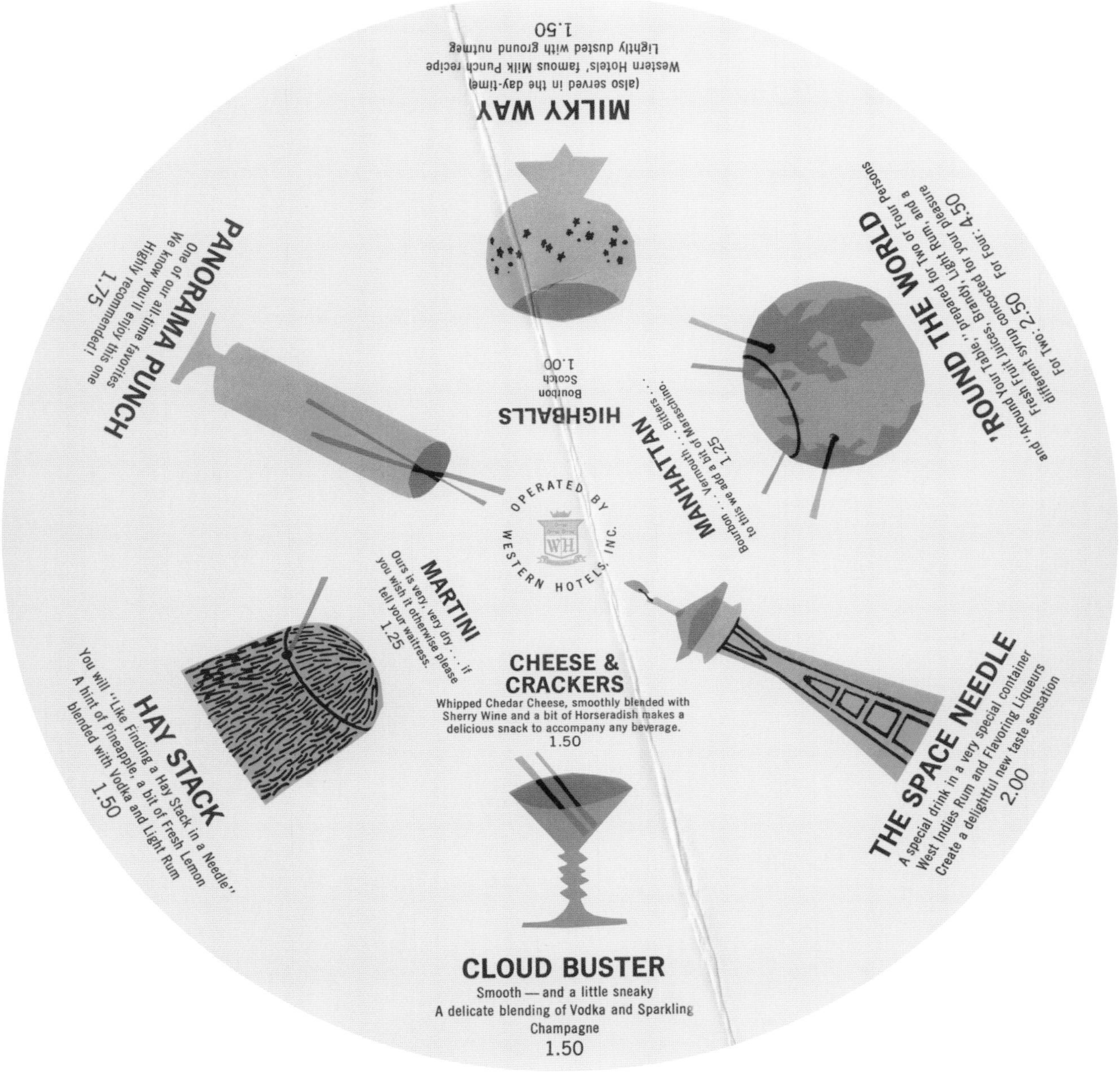

MILKY WAY
(also served in the day-time)
Western Hotels' famous Milk Punch recipe
Lightly dusted with ground nutmeg
1.50

'ROUND THE WORLD
and "Around Your Table," Prepared for Two or Four Persons
Fresh Fruit Juices, Brandy, Light Rum, and a
different syrup concocted for your pleasure
For Two: 2.50 For Four: 4.50

PANORAMA PUNCH
One of our all-time favorites
We know you'll enjoy this one
Highly recommended!
1.75

HIGHBALLS
Bourbon
Scotch
1.00

MANHATTAN
Bourbon . . . Vermouth . . . Bitters . . .
to this we add a bit of Maraschino.
1.25

OPERATED BY WESTERN HOTELS, INC.

MARTINI
Ours is very, very dry . . . if
you wish it otherwise please
tell your waitress.
1.25

CHEESE & CRACKERS
Whipped Chedar Cheese, smoothly blended with
Sherry Wine and a bit of Horseradish makes a
delicious snack to accompany any beverage.
1.50

HAY STACK
You will "Like Finding a Hay Stack in a Needle".
A hint of Pineapple, a bit of Fresh Lemon
blended with Vodka and Light Rum
1.50

THE SPACE NEEDLE
A special drink in a very special container
West Indies Rum and Flavoring Liqueurs
Create a delightful new taste sensation
2.00

CLOUD BUSTER
Smooth — and a little sneaky
A delicate blending of Vodka and Sparkling
Champagne
1.50

ABOVE **The Space Needle Restaurant, c. 1962, Seattle, Washington**

ABOVE RIGHT **The Eye of the Needle, Seattle World's Fair c. 1962, Seattle, Washington**

RIGHT **The Glass Tower Restaurant, 1964, New York, New York**

RIGHT Kentucky Fried Chicken, c. 1964

Although fried-chicken dinner eateries were nothing new in America, a white-suited, goateed Southerner named Colonel Harland Sanders opened the first of what would be thousands of Kentucky Fried Chicken franchises. The units' red-and-white striped circus-like peaks were as identifiable as McDonald's' golden arches.

Auch wenn Gaststätten, die gebratenes Hähnchen servierten, nichts Neues in Amerika darstellten, eröffnete Colonel Harland Sander, ein Südstaatler mit Ziegenbärtchen und weißem Anzug, das erste von später Tausenden von Franchise-Lokalen. Die rot-weiß gestreiften, an ein Zirkuszelt erinnernden Dächer der Schnellrestaurantkette haben einen genauso großen Wiedererkennungswert wie die goldenen Bögen von McDonald's.

Bien que les restaurants de poulet frit ne soient pas une nouveauté en Amérique, un Sudiste à bouc et portant un costume blanc dénommé Colonel Harland Sanders ouvre le premier Kentucky Fried Chicken. La franchise compte aujourd'hui des milliers de succursales à travers le monde. Les chapiteaux rouges et blancs deviendront vite des symboles aussi connus que les arches dorées de McDonald's.

BELOW Aunt Emma's Pancakes, c. 1959, San Diego, California

HOT COFFEES

Espresso (Twist of Lemon on Request) .65
Freshly ground black Italian coffee made by forcing steam through specially roasted coffee beans.

Cappuccino Royal .85
Italian coffee with chocolate, brandy flavor and whipped cream.

Espresso Royal .85
Italian coffee in a large cup with whipped cream.

Mocha .85
A delicious brew of hot coffee and hot cocoa, topped with a mound of whipped cream.

Anisette Royal .85
A tall cup of Caffe Anisette topped with whipped cream.

Russian Coffee .75
An unusual taste of hot black coffee and pure hot chocolate served in a mug.

Turkish Coffee .75
An ibrik of the delightfully sweet thick coffee of the Near East

Cafe O' Rum .70
The flavor of rum goes well with Espresso

Cafe Wien .75
Like old Vienna. A romantic glass of black coffee with a mound of whipped cream.

Insomniac 1.00
This coffee is recommended only to those who seek adventure. We can't tell any more because the recipe is a treasured secret.

Cafe Campana .90
Double (Hot) Espesso montaged with a large scoop of Ice Cream.

TEAS & OTHER HOT DRINKS

Imported Teas served in individual pots .70
Darjeeling Earl Gray Jasmine

Hot Cider .70
Served with cinnamon stick and cloves.

Cioccolatta .75
Sweet imported chocolate with steamed milk and whipped cream.

Cioccolatta Orgeat .80
Hot chocolate blended with almond flavoring and topped with whipped cream.

Mexicàn Chocolate .75

SANDWICHES

Served on Russian Rye or Pumpernickel.

Cold Roast Turkey — 1.25
Italian Salami
Swiss Cheese
Polish Ham
German Liver Sausage — 1.00
Cream Cheese on Date Nut Bread — .75

PASTRIES

French, Italian and Viennese, served from the tray
Italian Cheese Cake (Rum or Pineapple) .60
Baklava (Turkish)

One Drink Minimum per Show

ICED COFFEES

Espresso .75
Iced black coffee, served with cream and sugar on request.

Cappuccino .85
Foamy iced Cappuccino topped with a mound of whipped cream.

Ambrosia .85
Famous love potion of the ancient Greeks.

Mocha Frosted .85
Coffee, chocolate and ice cream combined to make this smooth cooling drink.

Frosted Egg Nog .85
A delicious blend of egg nog ice cream and brandy flavor.

TROPICAL NECTARS & JUICES

Imported from Puerto Rica, contain no artificial flavorings or preservatives.

Papaya .75
Very rich in vitamins A, B, C and G widely used as a digestive aid.

Guanabana .75
Exotic tropical passion fruit

Guava .75
Guava is the highest known natural source of vitamin C.

Pineapple .75
The fantastic flavor of fresh "La Famosa" pineapple

Tigers Milk .85
A salute to health, over 53% protein.

SPECIAL & IMPORTED COLD DRINKS

Iced Tea — .60

Cold Cider
Orgeat
Maraschino
Anisette — .75
Creme de Menthe
Grenadine
Tamarindo
Blackberry

FRUTTA FARCITA

Fresh Fruits of the Season Blended and Frozen in Their Natural Shells

Cedro Rosato (Pink Grapefruit)
Ananas (Pineapple)
Arancino (Orange) .80
Limone (Lemon)
Melone (Cantaloup)
Coconut 1.00

Price of Menu 50 cents

South Bay's First European Coffee House

FEATURING THE FINEST ENTERTAINMENT IN SOUTHERN CALIFORNIA
INTERMISSION'S FEATURE
Silent Movies and Art Films

Visit the International Artists Cooperative Gallery Selling Framed Original Works from both Europe and the United States.

53 Pier Avenue...Hermosa Beach
FRontier 4-9388

South Bay's largest Book and Art Fair over 10,000 Books and LP Records.

Specializing in the Rare and unusual

Open from 10:00 A.M. till 2:30 A.M.

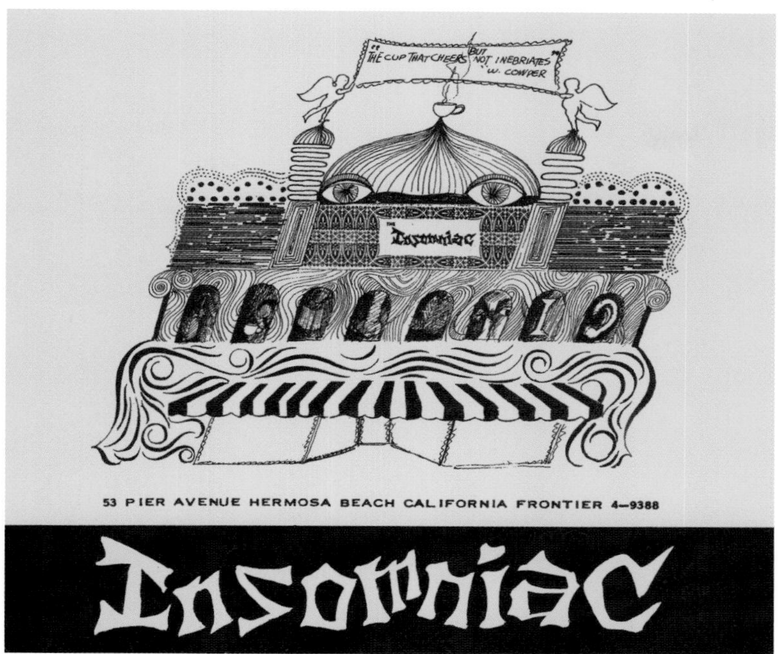

ABOVE & OPPOSITE Insomniac, c. 1958, Hermosa Beach, California

The 1950s was an era when the jazz, dance, art and poetry of the beatniks was ascendant, and their style and graphics poured over into eateries that evoked the kinds of places where bohemians gathered.

Die 1950er-Jahre waren die Ära, als Jazz, Tanz, Kunst und Dichtung der Beatniks aufkamen. Dieser hippe Stil machte sich auch in den Grafiken von Speisekarten bemerkbar und sollte das Flair von Bohemelokalen heraufbeschwören.

Dans des années 1950, le jazz, la danse, l'art et la poésie du mouvement beatnik sont à leur apogée. Le style et le graphisme qui lui sont associés vont se répandre dans les restaurants comme signe de ralliement de la bohème.

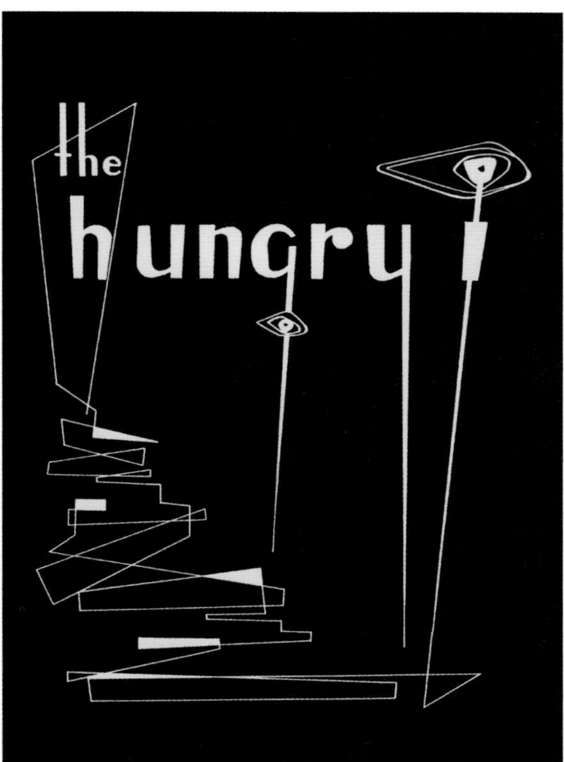

LEFT The Hungry I, c. 1961, San Francisco, California

Throughout the 1960s this San Francisco hipster coffee house was a showcase for talents like the Kingston Trio and comedians Bill Cosby and Mort Sahl. Few came for the coffee or the food, which was minimal.

Dieser Beatnik-Schuppen in San Francisco präsentierte in den 1960er-Jahren junge Talente wie das Kingston Trio oder Komiker wie Bill Cosby und Mort Sahl. Kaffee und das minimale Speisenangebot waren zweitrangig.

Pendant toutes les années 1960, ce café branché de San Francisco présente de jeunes talents comme le Kingston Trio ou des comiques tels Bill Cosby ou Mort Sahl. Rares sont les clients qui venaient pour un simple café ou pour la nourriture austère.

RIGHT Pupu Bar, Hawaiian Village Hotel, c. 1958, Honolulu, Hawaii

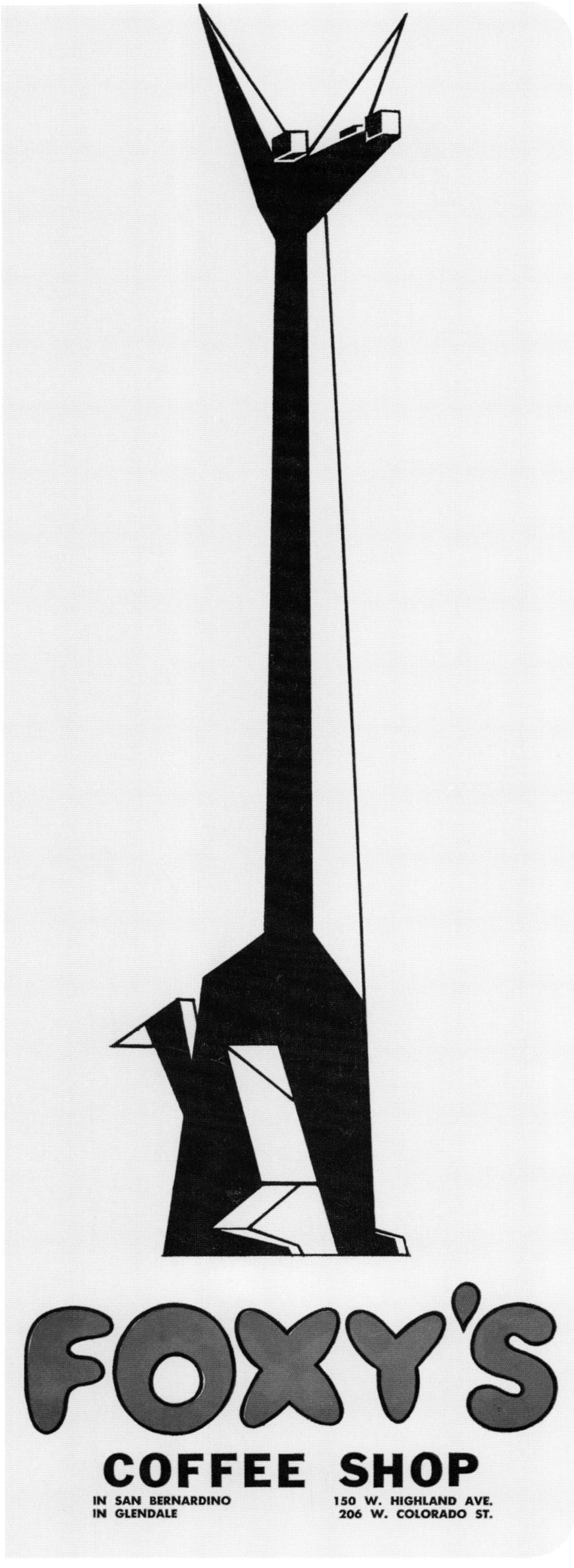

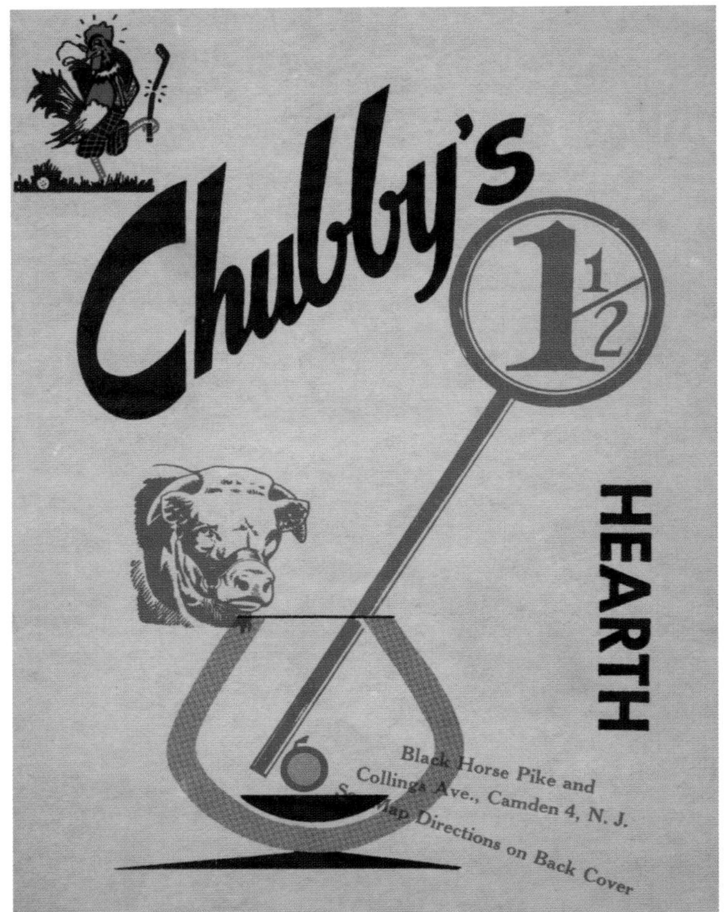

LEFT Foxy's Coffee Shop, c. 1958, San Bernadino, California

ABOVE Chubby's I 1/2 Hearth, c. 1955, Camden, New Jersey

OPPOSITE Hawaiian Village Hotel, c. 1956, Waikiki, Hawaii

PAGES 362 & 363 Islander, c. 1963, Los Angeles, California

islander

PUU PUUS (Appetizers)

HAWAIIAN HONEY LOIN RIBS 1.85
(Prime loin ribs marinated in Islander sauce and barbecued in island imu oven)

RUMAKE 1.50
(Fresh spiced chicken livers and water chestnuts wrapped in crisp bacon and fried to a golden brown)

IMU BARBECUED SQUAB OR CHICKEN 2.50
(Disjointed and barbecued in island imu oven and served with reef seaweed salt and wild plum sauce)

BALI BALI SATI OVER FLAMING HIBACHI 1.75
(Strips of prime tenderloin on bamboo shoots, marinated in balinese herbs and sauces)

TIKI TIKI CHICKEN IN PARCHMENT 1.85
(Sliced, tender baby chicken marinated in special sauces and herbs and barbecued in parchment)

BENGALESE TIM SAM EGG ROLL 1.50
(Shredded chicken, chinese mushrooms, celery, bamboo shoots, water chestnuts)

EASTER ISLAND OPAKE 1.65
(Shrimp and fresh spiced chicken livers wrapped in crisp bacon)

PUA PUA 1.85
(Barbecued tenderloin pork slices served with wild plum sauce)

MANDARIN FRIED SHRIMP 1.75
(Giant shrimp crisp cooked in peanut oil and served with hot coral sauce)

SHANGHAI WON TON 1.50
(Delicately crisped and served with sauce of fresh tomatoes, green peppers and onions)

NA MEA AI PUU PUUS 2.25
(Combination of Rumake, Fried Shrimp and Egg Roll)

LEFT & BELOW The Polynesian, c. 1961, Torrance, California

OPPOSITE Moon Islander, c. 1958, South Titusville, Florida

Welcome to The Polynesian

Aloha Talofa Iaorana

HAWAII
MARQUESAS ISLANDS
SAMOA
FIJI
TONGA
COOK ISLANDS
TAHITI
TUAMOTU
ARCHIPELAGO
AUSTRAL ISLANDS
EASTER ISLAND
POLYNESIA
NEW ZEALAND

SOUTH SEAS Culinary Art has developed through the past two centuries as a result of the interfusion of the Asiatic and European culture into the basic Polynesian methods of utilizing their native foods. The effect is an exotic cuisine, comparable only to the inimitable beauty and graceful figures derived from the intermarriage of these same racial peoples.

THE POLYNESIAN endeavors to bring the epitome of this Island art of cooking to you in its finest form. Our staff is highly trained in this superior method of cooking and in the serving of these authentic foods. If some of the names of the foods seem strange to you, please do not hesitate to ask for an explanation. We will be exceedingly happy to assist you in selections that will assure a satisfying dinner for you and your guests.

Appetizers

RUMAKI (8) 1.35
Marinated Chicken Livers and Water Chestnuts Wrapped in Bacon and Deep Fried

BULA MAKA (4) 1.40
Tenderloin of Beef Broiled with Our Own Spiced Ginger Sauce and Served on a Bamboo Spear

BARBECUED RIBS (6) 1.50
Choice Lean Back Ribs Marinated in Our Own Special Sauce and Barbecued to a Succulent Golden Brown

GOLDEN FRIED SHRIMP (6) 1.50
Jumbo Peeled Guaymas Shrimp Deep Fried Cantonese Style

CHICKEN EGG ROLL (8) 1.35
Select Chicken Meat Blended with Slivers of Chinese Vegetables and Bamboo Shoots, and Fried in a Delicious Egg Batter

CHA SIU 1.65
Sliced Tenderloin of Pork, Barbecued Slowly in Our Own Chinese Oven

BARBECUED CHICKEN 2.00
Cooked with a Special Barbecue Sauce in the Chinese Oven

TAHITIAN DRUMS (6) 1.50
Barbecued Chicken Drum Stick, Flavored with Sauce Made from a Secret Recipe

DIAMOND PORK 1.50
Slices of Diamond-Cut Pork Loin, Barbecued in Our Own Special Barbecue Sauce

COMBINATION PLATE (Taste Teasers for Two) 2.40
An Assortment of Golden Fried Shrimp, Barbecued Ribs, Chicken Egg Roll, Rumaki and Bula Maka

Soups and Broths

(All of Our Soups are Prepared with Chicken Broth)

CHICKEN RICE .... .65
Diced Chicken and Long-Grain Indian Rice

WON TON .... .85
Miniature Cantonese Ravioli, with Pork Filling

SEA WEED .... .65
The Natural Seasoning of the Polynesians is Employed to Produce the Full Flavor of this Exotic Soup

EGG FLOWER .... .65
Chopped Chicken, Water Chestnuts and Eggs, Blended with Sherry Wine

CONTAN .... .85
Miniature Spiced Chinese Meat Balls (Contan) in a Tangy Soup

Salads

POLYNESIAN 1.00
Artichoke Hearts and Hearts of Greens, Intermingled with Chicory and Romaine, and Blended with Our Own Polynesian Dressing

KALANI FRUIT SALAD 1.50
Pineapple Shell Basket Filled with Tropical Fruit and Topped with Our Own Arii (Royal) Dressing

WATERCRESS .... .75
A Tangy Salad, Mixed with Garden Greens, and a Choice of Dressings

KAMEHAMEHA (For Two) 1.50
Our Own Version of the Caesar Salad
HALF ORDER FOR ONE .... .75

HINA VAHINE .... .85
Reminiscent of the Famed Green Goddess Salad
WITH CRAB, SHRIMP OR LOBSTER 1.75

LOMI LOMI SALMON .... .85
The Native Luau Salad of the Hawaiian Islands, Consisting of Diced Salted Salmon, Tomatoes, and Green Onions, Served on a Bed of Romaine

MILLIONAIRE LOTUS EATER (for Two) 2.00
Hearts of Palm (Each Palm Tree Dies to Surrender Its Heart for This Delicacy) Nestled in a Bed of Young Romaine Buds. Arranged with Edible Young Orchids and Tantalizingly Accented with a Rare Dressing of Oriental Origin

20% FEDERAL AMUSEMENT TAX WILL BE ADDED AFTER 9 P.M.

AT THE BEGINNING CANTONESE SPECIALTIES AT THE END

MOON
ISLANDER

KON-TIKI SPECIALS

TONGA-TABU PORK 3.25
Hickory smoked, sugar cured and broiled then served with banana.

MEAAI MALUNA NIU (Served in a Coconut)
With Chicken . **3.50** With Lobster . **3.75**
With Shrimp . **3.50** With Crabmeat **3.25**

CHICKEN AND LONG RICE 2.25
Silvery strands of rice noodles cooked with slices of chicken breast.

KON-TIKI CHICKEN 3.00
Sliced breast of chicken, Virginia ham, and imported black mushrooms.

CHICKEN LONG HUT 3.00
Thinly sliced breast of chicken, dipped in batter and served with button mushrooms, mixed greens and oyster sauce.

BARBECUED CHICKEN 2.50
The Polynesian interpretation.

HAM AND EGGS HAWAIIAN . . . 2.75
Our version of this favourite dish served with pineapple and banana.

SAMOA SATE *(Meat on the stick)* **. . 2.75**
Marinated cubes of pork interlaced with green pepper and pineapple, barbecued with an Island sauce, served with Kumquats on a bed of rice.

COMMUNAL DISHES FOR A FESTIVE OCCASION
These dishes require a minimum number of 20 persons and 48 hours advance notice.

BABY SUCKLING PIG 5.00 ea.
A festive table is always graced with a native prepared suckling pig.

CAPONETTE TIKI-TIKI . . . . 4.25 ea.
Caponette boned and stuffed with lotus nuts, water chestnuts minced meats and exotic spices.

CORNISH GAME HEN AKU-AKU . 4.00 ea.
Game hen roasted Easter Island fashion in native baking clay.

OPPOSITE & BELOW Kon Tiki, Sheraton Cleveland Hotel, c. 1958, Cleveland, Ohio

RIGHT Tahitian Village, c. 1960, Los Angeles, California

Steinberg
ROOM SERVICE
HILTON HAWAIIAN VILLAGE—WAIKIKI

OPPOSITE **Room Service, Hilton Hawaiian Village Hotel, c. 1959, Waikiki, Hawaii**

RIGHT **Tapa Room, Hawaiian Village Hotel, c. 1959, Honolulu, Hawaii**

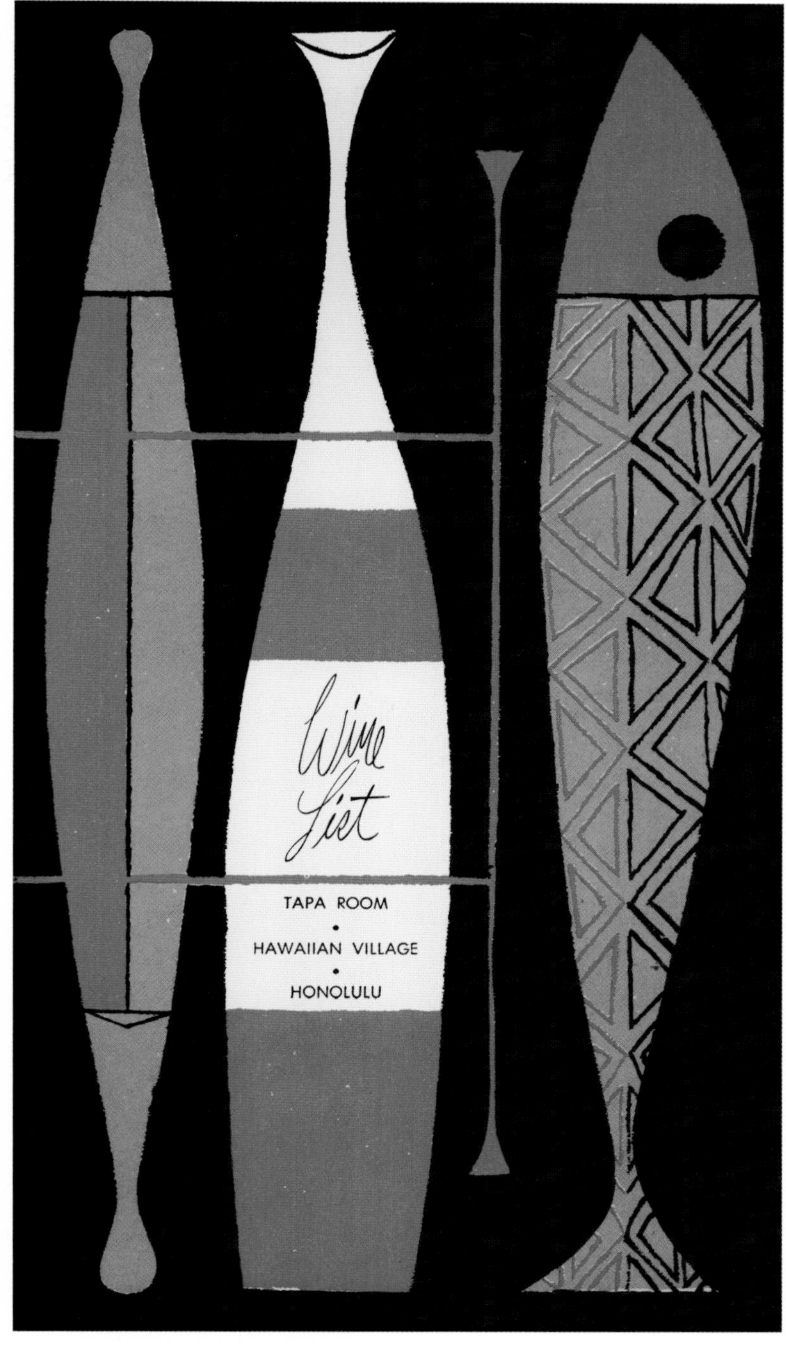

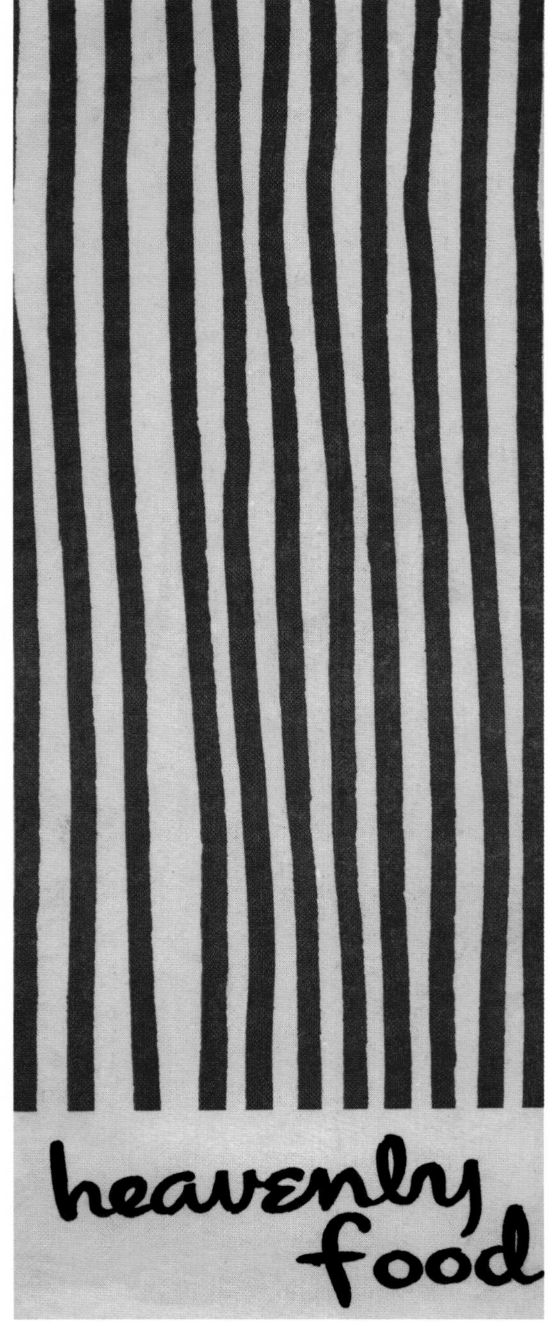

LEFT **Wil Wright's, c. 1961, Hollywood, California**

Capitalizing on nostalgia and a generous selection of ice cream flavors, Wil Wright's drew crowds to its numerous ice cream parlors throughout Southern California. Celebrities were known to have their chauffeurs pick up their favorite confection.

Wil Wright's war eine in Südkalifornien ungemein beliebte Eisdielenkette, die mit Nostalgie und einer Riesenauswahl an Eissorten die Kunden scharenweise anzog. Promis ließen sich ihre Lieblingssorten von ihren Chauffeuren holen.

En misant sur la nostalgie et un choix généreux de parfums, la chaîne Wil Wright's attire les foules dans ses nombreux glaciers répartis dans toute la Californie du Sud. Certaines célébrités y envoyaient leurs chauffeurs chercher leur glace préférée.

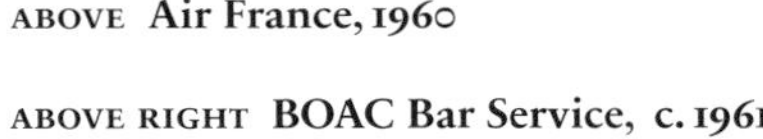

ABOVE Air France, 1960

ABOVE RIGHT BOAC Bar Service, c. 1961

BELOW The Airport Roof Restaurant, Miami International Airport Hotel, 1960, Miami, Florida

OPPOSITE Venus Room, New Frontier Hotel, c. 1956, Las Vegas, Nevada

OUT OF THIS WORLD!
MENU
NEW FRONTIER HOTEL
LAS VEGAS
DESIGNED BY SAUL BASS
VENUS ROOM

ABOVE & RIGHT **Le Cirque, c. 1969, New York, New York**

Former "the Colony" maitre d' Sirio Maccioni picked up New York's society clientele at his own restaurant, Le Cirque, on East 65th Street. Its décor of cavorting monkeys became as famous as the regulars from the theater and Hollywood crowd who came to see and be seen and to dine on simple but exclusive French and Italian cuisine.

Der ehemalige Oberkellner des Colony, Sirio Maccioni, nahm dessen Klientel aus der New Yorker Hautevolee in sein Restaurant Le Cirque an der East 65th Street mit. Das Restaurant war genauso berühmt für das Affenmotiv in der Ausstattung wie für seine Stammgäste aus Theater und Film, die hier sehen und gesehen werden und einfach, aber exklusiv französisch und italienisch speisen wollten.

L'ancien maître d'hôtel de The Colony, Sirio Maccioni, attire la bonne société de New York dans son propre restaurant, Le Cirque, situé sur la 65ᵉ rue Est. Tapisseries murales et céramiques représentant des singes deviennent aussi connues que les célébrités du théâtre et les vedettes hollywoodiennes qui le fréquentent. On venait pour voir et pour être vu et, bien entendu, pour déguster une cuisine française ou italienne simple mais raffinée.

Dejeuner

Specialites de la Maison

Les Crepes Farcies Le Cirque 5.25
Gougeonnettes de Sole Frites Sauce Moutarde 5.25
Carpaccio Toscane 4.75
Supreme de Volaille Gismonda 6.25
Cote de Veau Milanaise 8.75
Entrecote (2) au Poivre Vert au Vinaigre de Bourgogne 22.00

Buffet Froid

Boeuf a la Mode
Roulade de Veau
Contrefilet Roti
Poulet Diable or Roti
Emince de Volaille au Curry
Pipperade
Maquereaux au Vin Blanc
Seviche
Homard Froid
Saumon Froid
Emince de Volaille a la King

Special from the Charcoal Broiler

Cote de Veau Aplatie 9.00
Entrecote Minute Aplatie 9.50
Poulet Diable 6.50
La Selle d'Agneau Desossee 9.25
La Brochette de Rognon de Veau aux Herbes 6.25
Le Dindonneau au Bacon (2) 17.00

Vin en Carafe

Blanc, Rouge, Rose
La Carafe 7.50 La Demi 4.00

BELOW & RIGHT The Forum of the Twelve Caesars, c. 1963, New York, New York

The Forum was built around the acquisition of 12 portraits of Roman emperors by 17th-century artist Camillo Procaccini.

Mittelpunkt des Forums waren zwölf Porträts römischer Cäsaren des Malers Camillo Procaccini aus dem 17. Jahrhundert.

Le Forum est conçu autour de 12 portraits d'empereurs romains, peints par Camillo Procaccini, un artiste du XVIIe siècle.

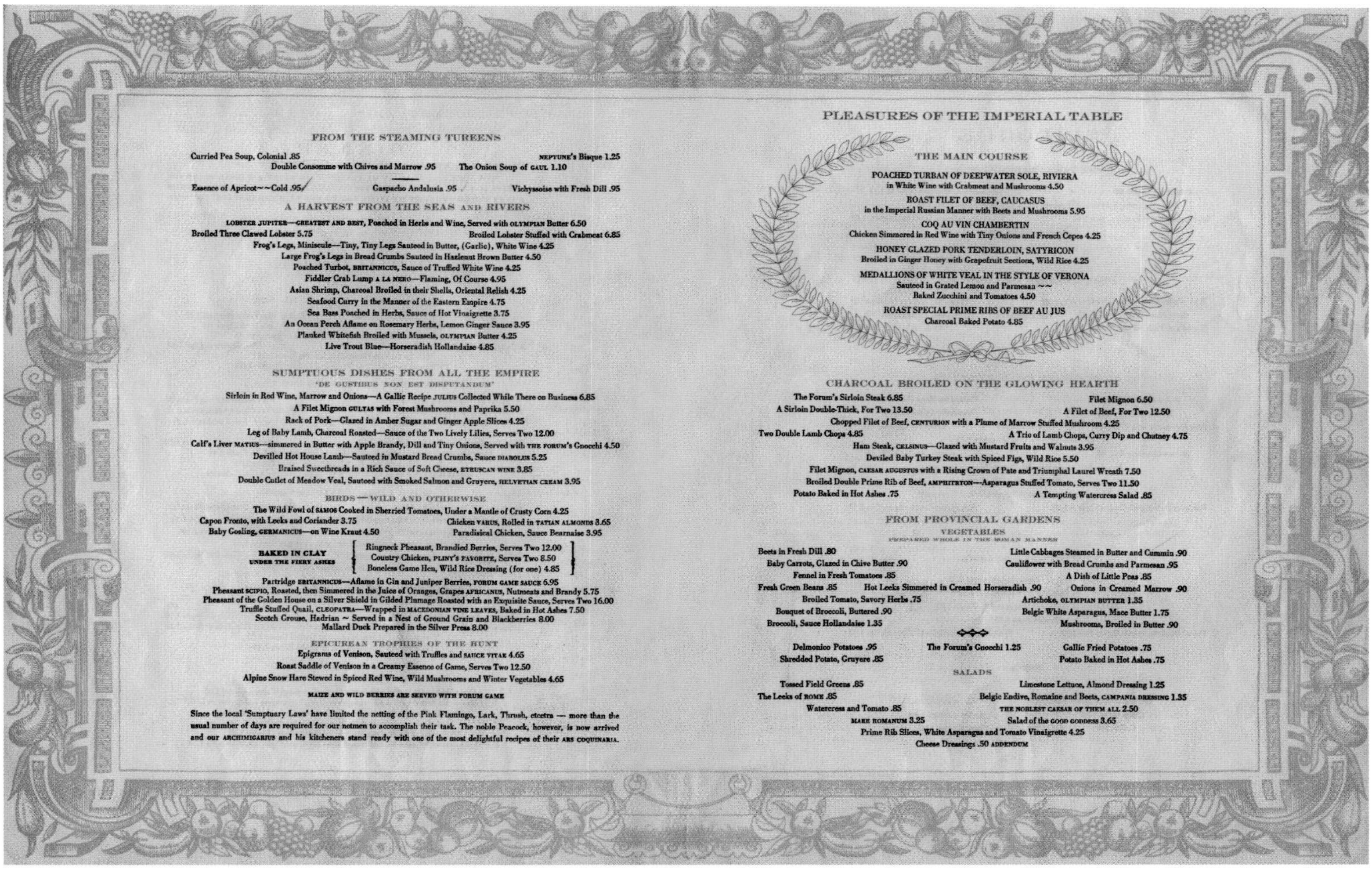

FROM THE STEAMING TUREENS

Curried Pea Soup, Colonial .85
NEPTUNE's Bisque 1.25
Double Consomme with Chives and Marrow .95
The Onion Soup of GAUL 1.10
Essence of Apricot~~Cold .95
Gaspacho Andalusia .95
Vichyssoise with Fresh Dill .95

A HARVEST FROM THE SEAS AND RIVERS

LOBSTER JUPITER—GREATEST AND BEST, Poached in Herbs and Wine, Served with OLYMPIAN Butter 6.50
Broiled Three Clawed Lobster 5.75
Broiled Lobster Stuffed with Crabmeat 6.85
Frog's Legs, Miniscule—Tiny, Tiny Legs Sauteed in Butter, (Garlic), White Wine 4.25
Large Frog's Legs in Bread Crumbs Sauteed in Hazlenut Brown Butter 4.50
Poached Turbot, BRITANNICUS, Sauce of Truffled White Wine 4.25
Fiddler Crab Lump A LA NERO—Flaming, Of Course 4.95
Asian Shrimp, Charcoal Broiled in their Shells, Oriental Relish 4.25
Seafood Curry in the Manner of the Eastern Empire 4.75
Sea Bass Poached in Herbs, Sauce of Hot Vinaigrette 3.75
An Ocean Perch Aflame on Rosemary Herbs, Lemon Ginger Sauce 3.95
Planked Whitefish Broiled with Mussels, OLYMPIAN Butter 4.25
Live Trout Blue—Horseradish Hollandaise 4.85

SUMPTUOUS DISHES FROM ALL THE EMPIRE
'DE GUSTIBUS NON EST DISPUTANDUM'

Sirloin in Red Wine, Marrow and Onions—A Gallic Recipe JULIUS Collected While There on Business 6.85
A Filet Mignon GULYAS with Forest Mushrooms and Paprika 5.50
Rack of Pork—Glazed in Amber Sugar and Ginger Apple Slices 4.25
Leg of Baby Lamb, Charcoal Roasted—Sauce of the Two Lively Lilies, Serves Two 12.00
Calf's Liver MATIUS—simmered in Butter with Apple Brandy, Dill and Tiny Onions, Served with THE FORUM's Gnocchi 4.50
Devilled Hot House Lamb—Sauteed in Mustard Bread Crumbs, Sauce DIABOLUS 5.25
Braised Sweetbreads in a Rich Sauce of Soft Cheese, ETRUSCAN WINE 3.85
Double Cutlet of Meadow Veal, Sauteed with Smoked Salmon and Gruyere, HELVETIAN CREAM 3.95

BIRDS—WILD AND OTHERWISE

The Wild Fowl of SAMOS Cooked in Sherried Tomatoes, Under a Mantle of Crusty Corn 4.25
Capon Fronto, with Leeks and Coriander 3.75
Chicken VARUS, Rolled in TATIAN ALMONDS 3.65
Baby Gosling, GERMANICUS—on Wine Kraut 4.50
Paradisical Chicken, Sauce Bearnaise 3.95

BAKED IN CLAY UNDER THE FIERY ASHES
Ringneck Pheasant, Brandied Berries, Serves Two 12.00
Country Chicken, PLINY'S FAVORITE, Serves Two 8.50
Boneless Game Hen, Wild Rice Dressing (for one) 4.85

Partridge BRITANNICUS—Aflame in Gin and Juniper Berries, FORUM GAME SAUCE 6.95
Pheasant SCIPIO, Roasted, then Simmered in the Juice of Oranges, Grapes AFRICANUS, Nutmeats and Brandy 5.75
Pheasant of the Golden House on a Silver Shield in Gilded Plumage Roasted with an Exquisite Sauce, Serves Two 16.00
Truffle Stuffed Quail, CLEOPATRA—Wrapped in MACEDONIAN VINE LEAVES, Baked in Hot Ashes 7.50
Scotch Grouse, Hadrian ~ Served in a Nest of Ground Grain and Blackberries 8.00
Mallard Duck Prepared in the Silver Press 8.00

EPICUREAN TROPHIES OF THE HUNT

Epigrams of Venison, Sauteed with Truffles and SAUCE VITAE 4.65
Roast Saddle of Venison in a Creamy Essence of Game, Serves Two 12.50
Alpine Snow Hare Stewed in Spiced Red Wine, Wild Mushrooms and Winter Vegetables 4.65

MAIZE AND WILD BERRIES ARE SERVED WITH FORUM GAME

Since the local 'Sumptuary Laws' have limited the netting of the Pink Flamingo, Lark, Thrush, etcetra — more than the usual number of days are required for our netmen to accomplish their task. The noble Peacock, however, is now arrived and our ARCHIMAGARIUS and his kitcheners stand ready with one of the most delightful recipes of their ARS COQUINARIA.

PLEASURES OF THE IMPERIAL TABLE

THE MAIN COURSE

POACHED TURBAN OF DEEPWATER SOLE, RIVIERA
in White Wine with Crabmeat and Mushrooms 4.50
ROAST FILET OF BEEF, CAUCASUS
in the Imperial Russian Manner with Beets and Mushrooms 5.95
COQ AU VIN CHAMBERTIN
Chicken Simmered in Red Wine with Tiny Onions and French Cepes 4.25
HONEY GLAZED PORK TENDERLOIN, SATYRICON
Broiled in Ginger Honey with Grapefruit Sections, Wild Rice 4.25
MEDALLIONS OF WHITE VEAL IN THE STYLE OF VERONA
Sauteed in Grated Lemon and Parmesan ~~
Baked Zucchini and Tomatoes 4.50
ROAST SPECIAL PRIME RIBS OF BEEF AU JUS
Charcoal Baked Potato 4.85

CHARCOAL BROILED ON THE GLOWING HEARTH

The Forum's Sirloin Steak 6.85
Filet Mignon 6.50
A Sirloin Double-Thick, For Two 13.50
A Filet of Beef, For Two 12.50
Chopped Filet of Beef, CENTURION with a Plume of Marrow Stuffed Mushroom 4.25
Two Double Lamb Chops 4.85
A Trio of Lamb Chops, Curry Dip and Chutney 4.75
Ham Steak, CELSINUS—Glazed with Mustard Fruits and Walnuts 3.95
Deviled Baby Turkey Steak with Spiced Figs, Wild Rice 5.50
Filet Mignon, CAESAR AUGUSTUS with a Rising Crown of Pate and Triumphal Laurel Wreath 7.50
Broiled Double Prime Rib of Beef, AMPHITRYON—Asparagus Stuffed Tomato, Serves Two 11.50
Potato Baked in Hot Ashes .75
A Tempting Watercress Salad .85

FROM PROVINCIAL GARDENS
VEGETABLES
PREPARED WHOLE IN THE ROMAN MANNER

Beets in Fresh Dill .80
Little Cabbages Steamed in Butter and Cummin .90
Baby Carrots, Glazed in Chive Butter .90
Cauliflower with Bread Crumbs and Parmesan .95
Fennel in Fresh Tomatoes .85
A Dish of Little Peas .85
Fresh Green Beans .85
Hot Leeks Simmered in Creamed Horseradish .90
Onions in Creamed Marrow .90
Broiled Tomato, Savory Herbs .75
Artichoke, OLYMPIAN BUTTER 1.35
Bouquet of Broccoli, Buttered .90
Belgic White Asparagus, Mace Butter 1.75
Broccoli, Sauce Hollandaise 1.35
Mushrooms, Broiled in Butter .90

Delmonico Potatoes .95
The Forum's Gnocchi 1.25
Gallic Fried Potatoes .75
Shredded Potato, Gruyere .85
Potato Baked in Hot Ashes .75

SALADS

Tossed Field Greens .85
Limestone Lettuce, Almond Dressing 1.25
The Leeks of ROME .85
Belgic Endive, Romaine and Beets, CAMPANIA DRESSING 1.35
Watercress and Tomato .85
THE NOBLEST CAESAR OF THEM ALL 2.50
MARE ROMANUM 3.25
Salad of the GOOD GODDESS 3.65
Prime Rib Slices, White Asparagus and Tomato Vinaigrette 4.25
Cheese Dressings .50 ADDENDUM

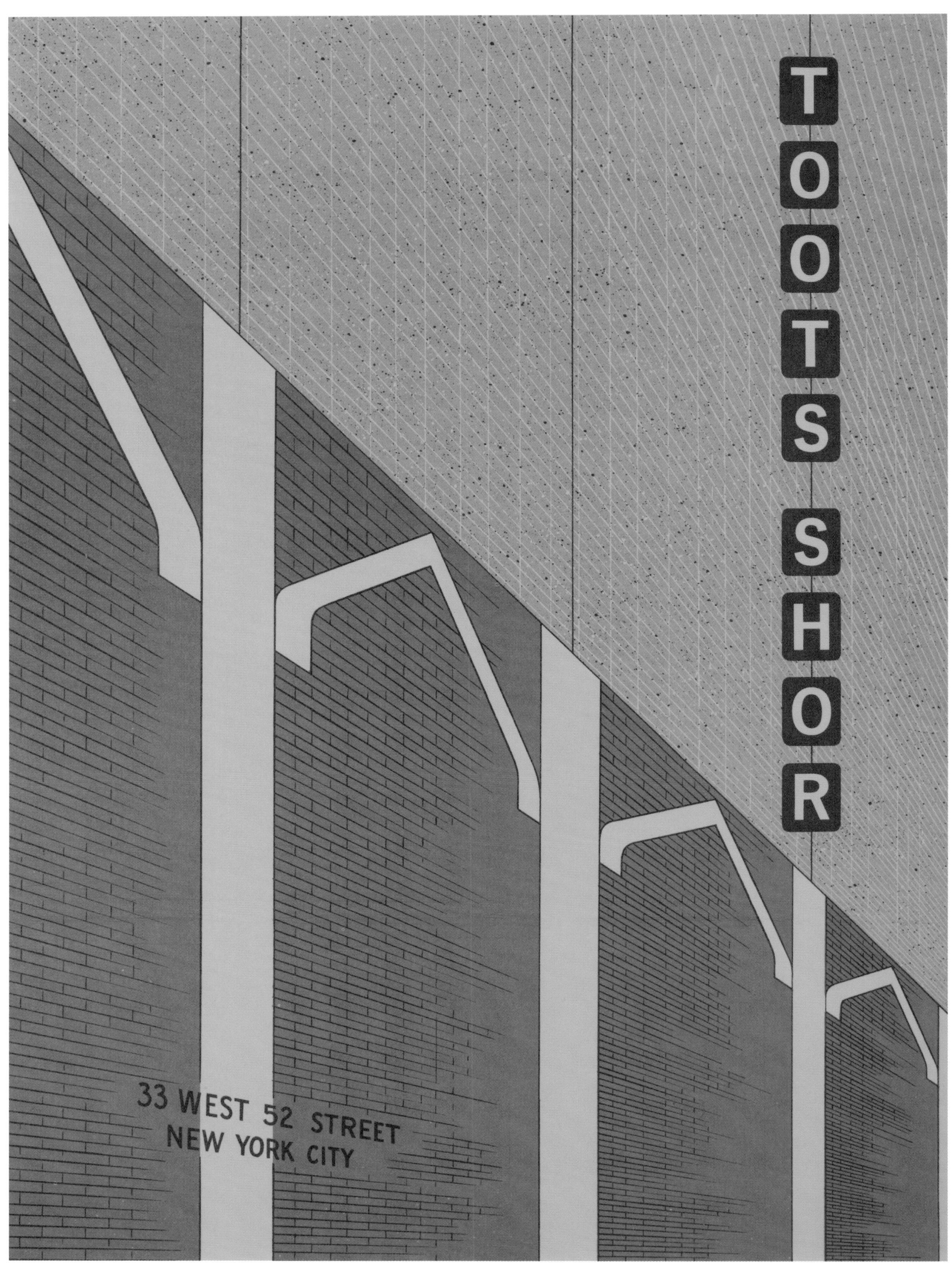
TOOTS SHOR
33 WEST 52 STREET
NEW YORK CITY

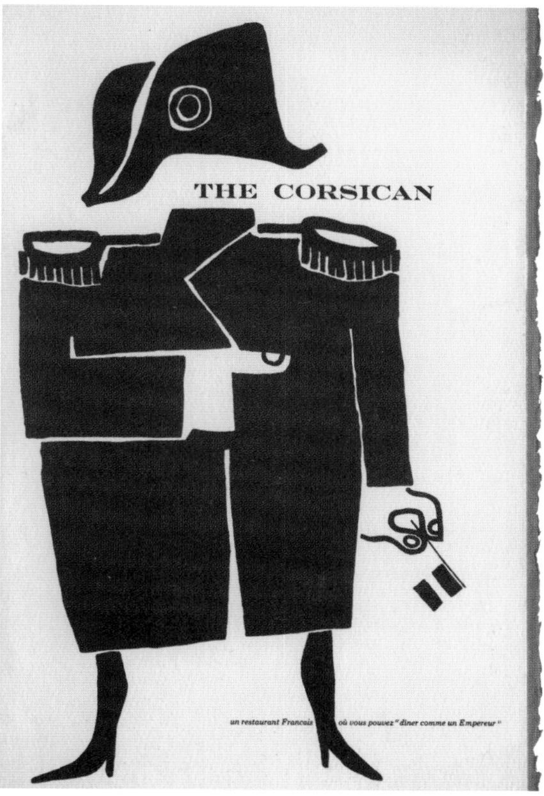

OPPOSITE Toots Shor, 1961, New York, New York

ABOVE Cafe Rouge, Statler Hotel, c. 1960, New York, New York

RIGHT The Corsican, c. 1964, Hollywood, California

BELOW Lisbon Lounge, c. 1961

ABOVE & RIGHT L'Escoffier, c. 1969, Beverly Hills, California

In the 1950s a few Los Angeles restaurants began to take food and haute cuisine more seriously. One of the earliest, L'Escoffier opened in 1955 at the Beverly Hilton Hotel. In the early 1960s it was dubbed the West Coast White House because President John F. Kennedy spent so much time there.

In den 1950er-Jahren gab es die ersten Restaurants in Los Angeles, die die feine Küche ernster nahmen. Eines der ältesten, das L'Escoffier, öffnete 1955 im Beverly Hilton Hotel. Anfang der 1960er wurde es „das Weiße Haus der Westküste" genannt, weil Präsident John F. Kennedy dort so häufig zu Gast war.

Dans les années 1950, quelques restaurants de Los Angeles commencent à considérer plus sérieusement la gastronomie. L'un des premiers, L'Escoffier, ouvre en 1955 au Beverly Hilton Hotel. Au début des années 1960, on le surnomme la « Maison-Blanche de la côte Ouest », car le président John F. Kennedy y passe beaucoup de temps.

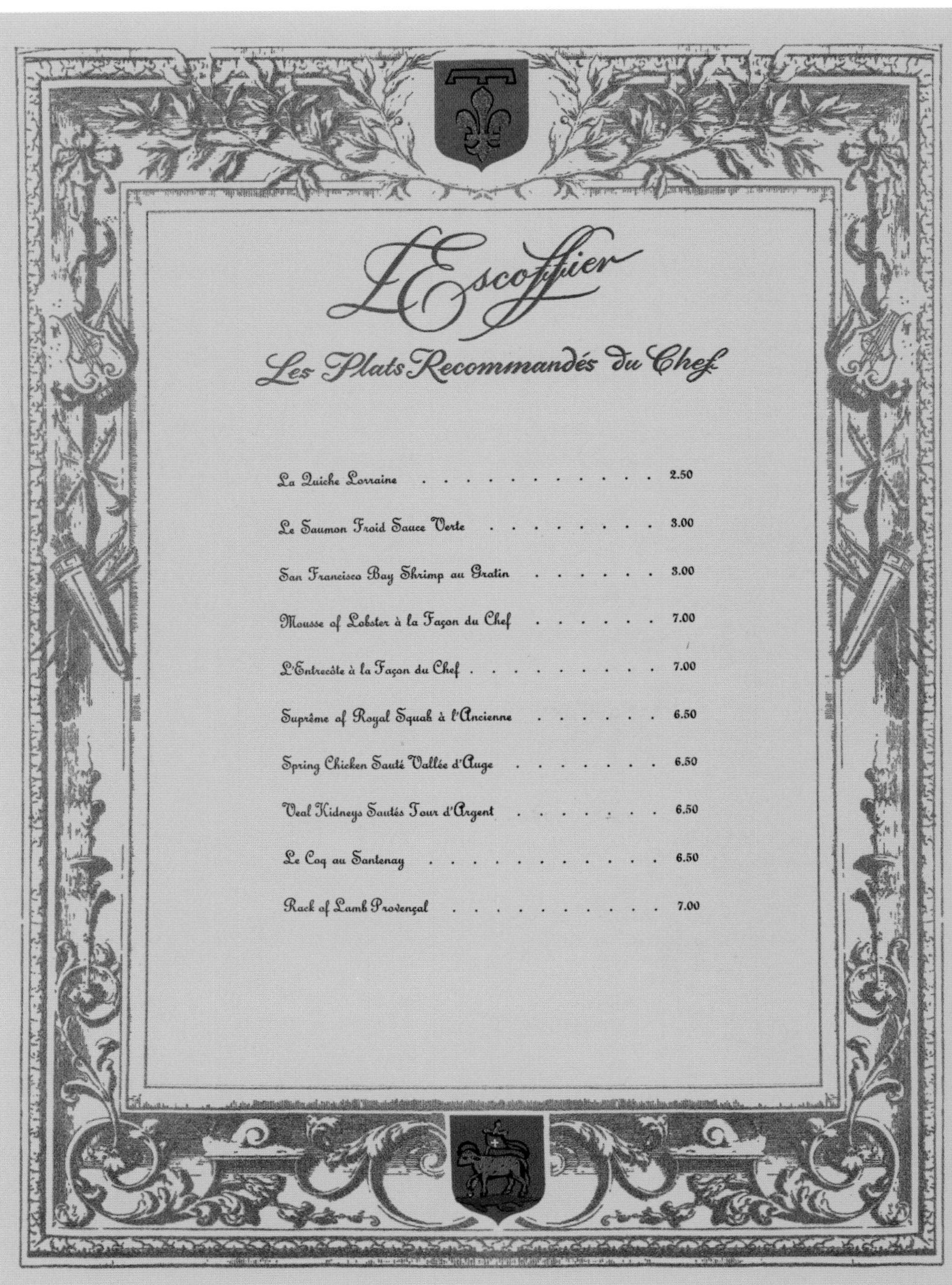

BELOW La Grenouille, c. 1965, New York, New York

Following the same pattern for décor, menu, and haughtiness toward clientele as Le Pavillon, La Grenouille was opened by Charles Masson in 1962 and immediately drew New York society and the fashion crowd for its rarely changing menu of classic French cuisine. It was nicknamed "the Frog Pond" by the press and its regulars.

La Grenouille stand in Ausstattung, Speisekarte und Hochnäsigkeit gegenüber den Gästen dem Le Pavillon nicht nach. La Grenouille wurde 1962 von Charles Masson eröffnet und sofort zum Treffpunkt der New Yorker High Society und Modeszene. Das Angebot klassischer französischer Gerichte auf der Karte änderte sich fast nie. Presse und Stammgäste nannten es „den Froschteich“.

La Grenouille, fondé par Charles Masson en 1962, suit l'exemple du restaurant Le Pavillon pour son décor, son menu et sa façon hautaine de traiter la clientèle. Il attire immédiatement la bonne société new-yorkaise avec un menu immuable qui fait honneur à la gastronomie française. Il sera surnommé « The Frog Pond » (« La mare aux grenouilles » – ou « … aux Français ») par la presse et ses clients les plus réguliers.

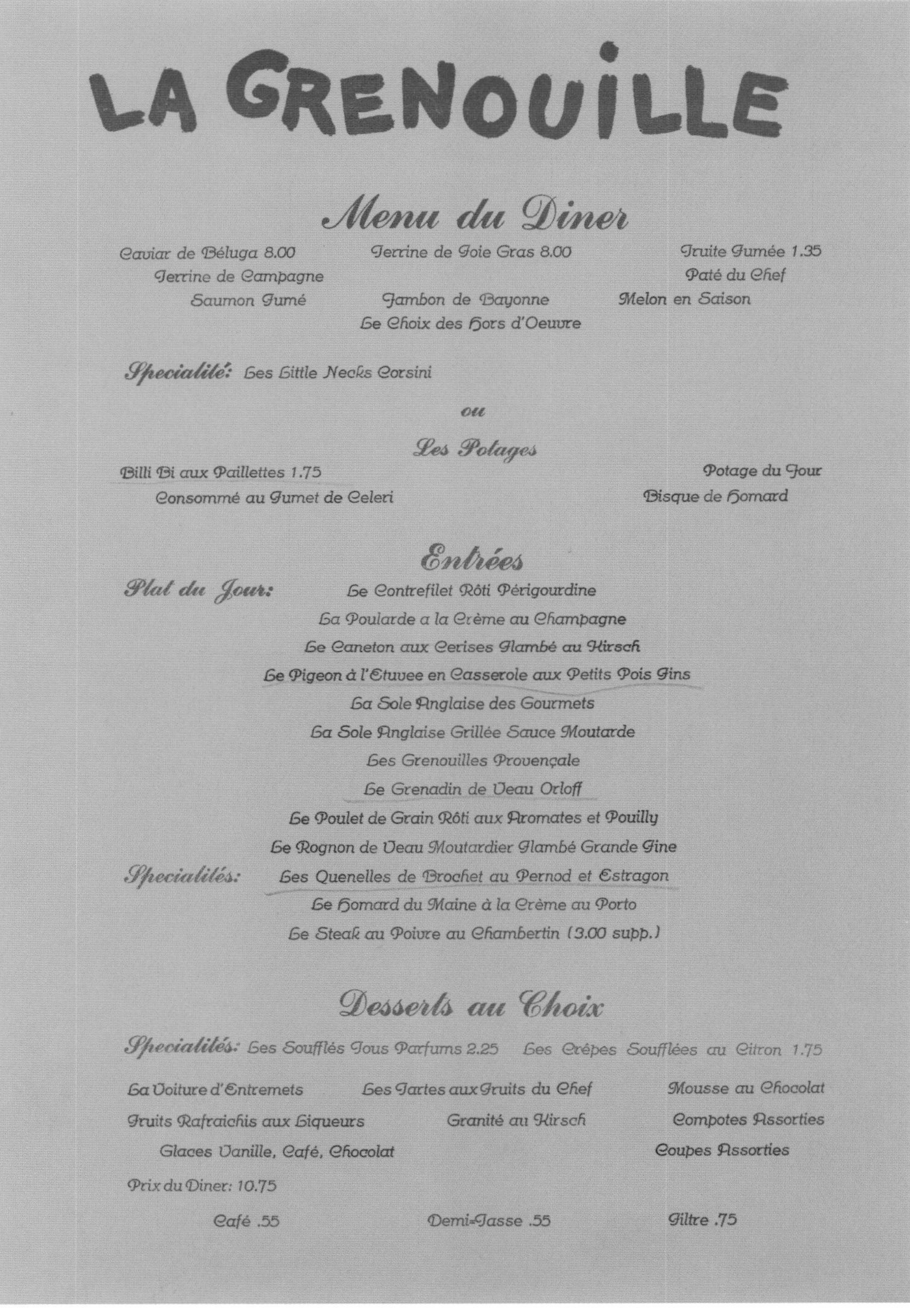

LA GRENOUILLE

Menu du Diner

Caviar de Béluga 8.00 — Terrine de Foie Gras 8.00 — Truite Fumée 1.35
Terrine de Campagne — Paté du Chef
Saumon Fumé — Jambon de Bayonne — Melon en Saison
Le Choix des Hors d'Oeuvre

Specialité: Les Little Necks Corsini

ou

Les Potages

Billi Bi aux Paillettes 1.75 — Potage du Jour
Consommé au Fumet de Celeri — Bisque de Homard

Entrées

Plat du Jour: Le Contrefilet Rôti Périgourdine
La Poularde a la Crème au Champagne
Le Caneton aux Cerises Flambé au Kirsch
Le Pigeon à l'Etuvee en Casserole aux Petits Pois Fins
La Sole Anglaise des Gourmets
La Sole Anglaise Grillée Sauce Moutarde
Les Grenouilles Provençale
Le Grenadin de Veau Orloff
Le Poulet de Grain Rôti aux Aromates et Pouilly
Le Rognon de Veau Moutardier Flambé Grande Fine
Specialités: Les Quenelles de Brochet au Pernod et Estragon
Le Homard du Maine à la Crème au Porto
Le Steak au Poivre au Chambertin (3.00 supp.)

Desserts au Choix

Specialités: Les Soufflés Tous Parfums 2.25 — Les Crêpes Soufflées au Citron 1.75

La Voiture d'Entremets — Les Tartes aux Fruits du Chef — Mousse au Chocolat
Fruits Rafraichis aux Liqueurs — Granité au Kirsch — Compotes Assorties
Glaces Vanille, Café, Chocolat — Coupes Assorties

Prix du Diner: 10.75

Café .55 — Demi-Tasse .55 — Filtre .75

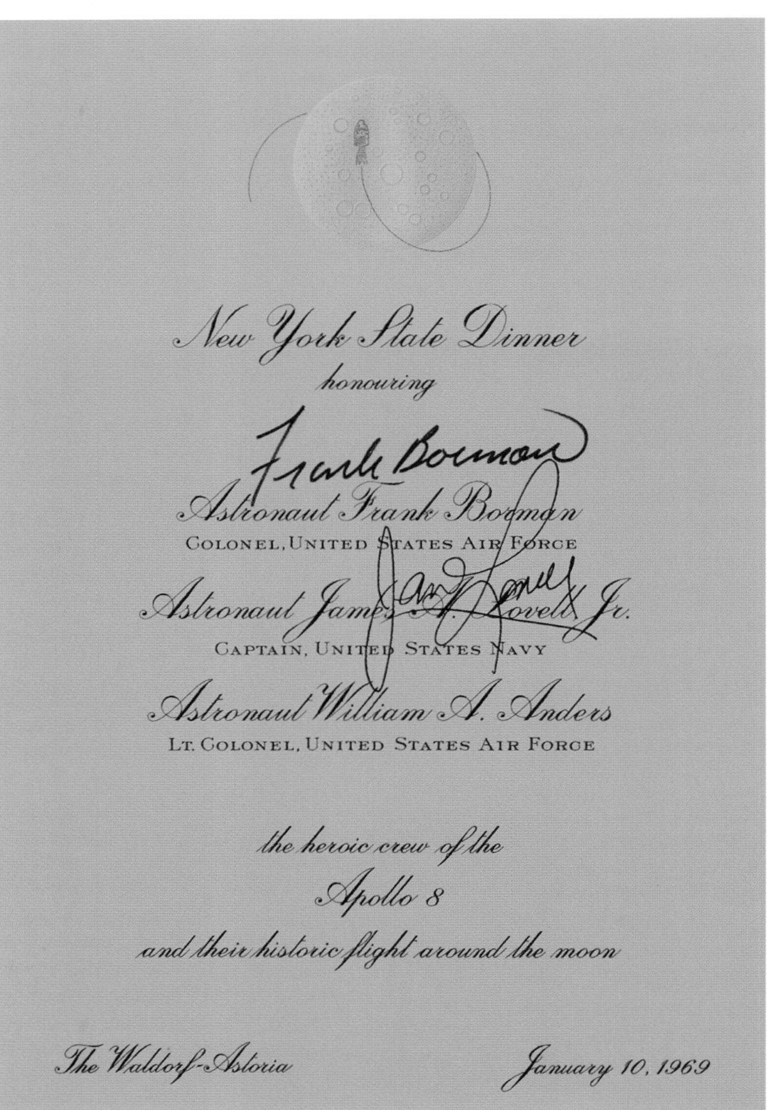

Menu

Melon Glace

*

Veloute Reine-Margot

*

Roast Prime Ribs of Beef

New York State Stringbeans Forestiere

Endive Polonaise

*

Creme a la Glace

Petits Fours

*

Coffee

ABOVE **New York State Dinner, the Waldorf-Astoria, 1969, New York, New York**

LEFT **Delegates Dining Room, the United Nations, 1966, New York, New York**

PAGE 380 The Whale Organic Restaurant, c. 1968, Mill Valley, California

PAGE 381 Trident, c. 1967, Sausalito, California

Psychedelic art of the 1960s, popularized by San Francisco's antiestablishment hippie movement, seemed appropriate to use on menu covers featuring the new "organic" and health foods.

Die psychedelischen Grafiken der Sixties, die von der Hippiebewegung in San Francisco populär gemacht wurden, passten zu Speisekarten, die die neue „organische" Gesundheitskost anboten.

Il paraît naturel de retrouver l'art psychédélique, popularisé par le mouvement contestataire hippie de San Francisco, sur des menus proposant une nouveauté : une nourriture saine et « biologique ».

ABOVE & RIGHT La Côte Basque, c. 1972, New York, New York

Henri Soulé opened La Côte Basque as a "bargain priced" Le Pavillon, but it attracted much the same wealthy clientele and had a very similar menu. The name of the restaurant, made famous in the title of a Truman Capote story featured in *Esquire* magazine, evoked the Basque coast of France, here illustrated by Bernard Lamotte, who did the menu cover for the Waldorf-Astoria.

Henri Soulé eröffnete La Côte Basque als „preiswerte" Alternative zum Le Pavillon, doch die sehr ähnliche Karte zog dasselbe wohlhabende Publikum an. Das Restaurant wurde durch eine in der Zeitschrift Esquire veröffentlichte Kurzgeschichte von Truman Capote berühmt; der Name bezieht sich auf die französische Baskenlandküste, hier von Bernard Lamotte dargestellt, der auch die Speisekarte des Waldorf-Astoria illustrierte.

Henri Soulé ouvre La Côte Basque comme alternative « bon marché » au Pavillon. Toutefois, il attire la même clientèle fortunée et propose une carte assez similaire. Le nom du restaurant est rendu célèbre grâce à une nouvelle éponyme de Truman Capote parue dans le magazine *Esquire*. L'illustration de Bernard Lamotte, concepteur de la couverture du menu du Waldorf-Astoria, évoque le pays basque.

La Côte Basque

Déjeuner

Menu

Caviar Malossol 24.00 Hors d'Oeuvre Terrine Côte Basque
Jambon de Bayonne Saumon Fumé Anguille Fumée
Melon Grapefruit Shrimps Cocktail Coupe de Fruits
Cherrystones Oysters in Season Little Necks
Saucisson Chaud Franc-comtoise Jus de Tomate
Artichaut Vinaigrette Jambon Persillé Oeuf en Gelée
Foie Gras Frais des Landes en Brioche Vielle France 12.00
Foie Gras Frais Prestige des Landes à la Gelée 12.00

Plats du Jour

FILET DE BOEUF FINANCIÈRE
BLANQUETTE DE VEAU À L'ANCIENNE
CERVELLE AU BEURRE NOIR
JAMBON MADÈRE AUX ÉPINARDS
OMELETTE CÔTE BASQUE
POULARDE POÊLÉE BEAU SÉJOUR
DÉLICES DE SOLE VÉRONIQUE
STRIPED BASS BRETONNE

Les Desserts Côte Basque

Ou Les Fromages

Les Soufflés Tous Arômes 4.50

Café 1.00 Demi Tasse 1.00 Filtre 1.00

Prix du Déjeuner $15.75

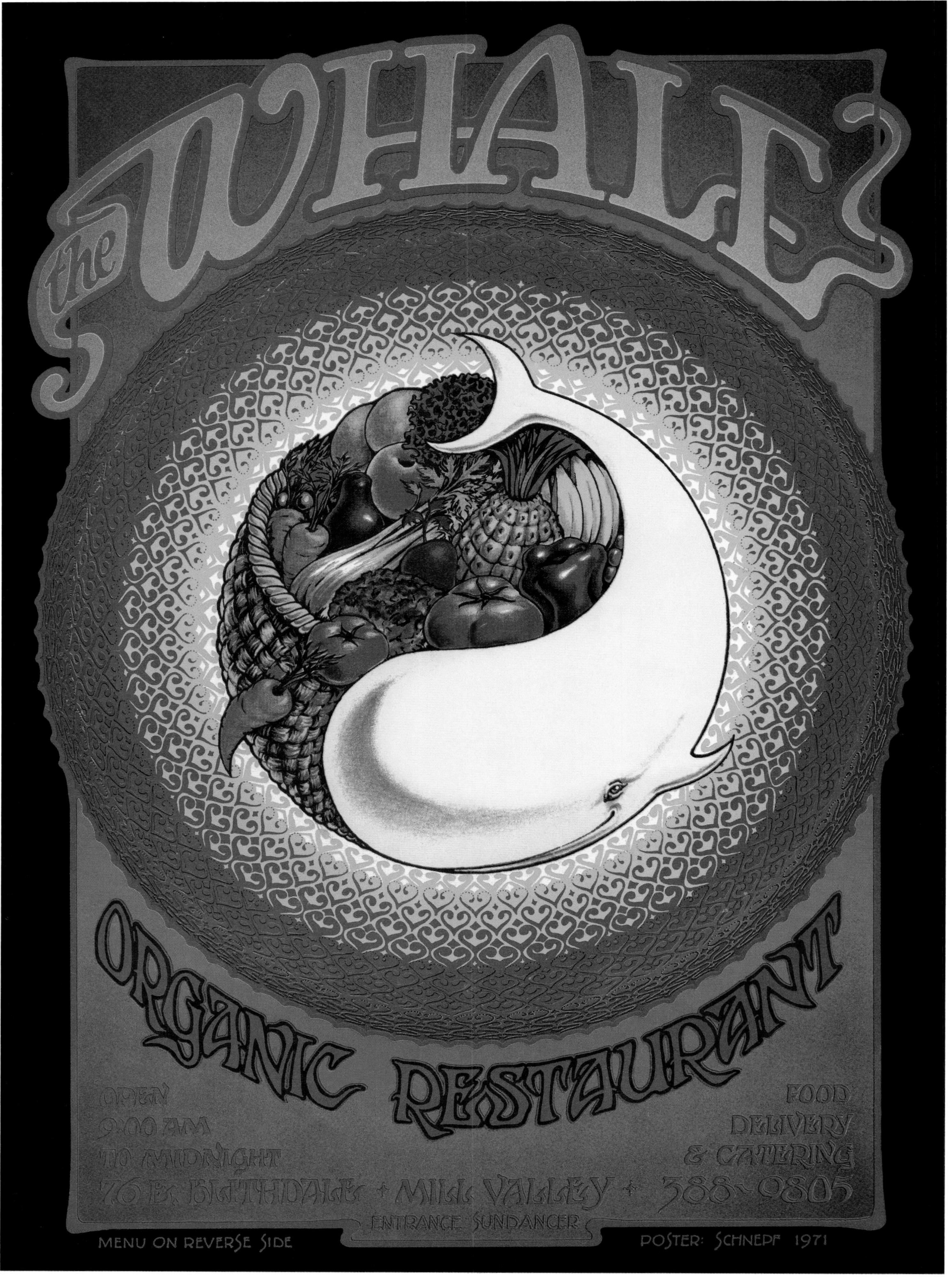
the WHALE
ORGANIC RESTAURANT
OPEN
9:00 AM
TO MIDNIGHT
FOOD
DELIVERY
& CATERING
76 E. BLITHDALE + MILL VALLEY + 388-9805
ENTRANCE SUNDANCER
MENU ON REVERSE SIDE
POSTER: SCHNEPF 1971

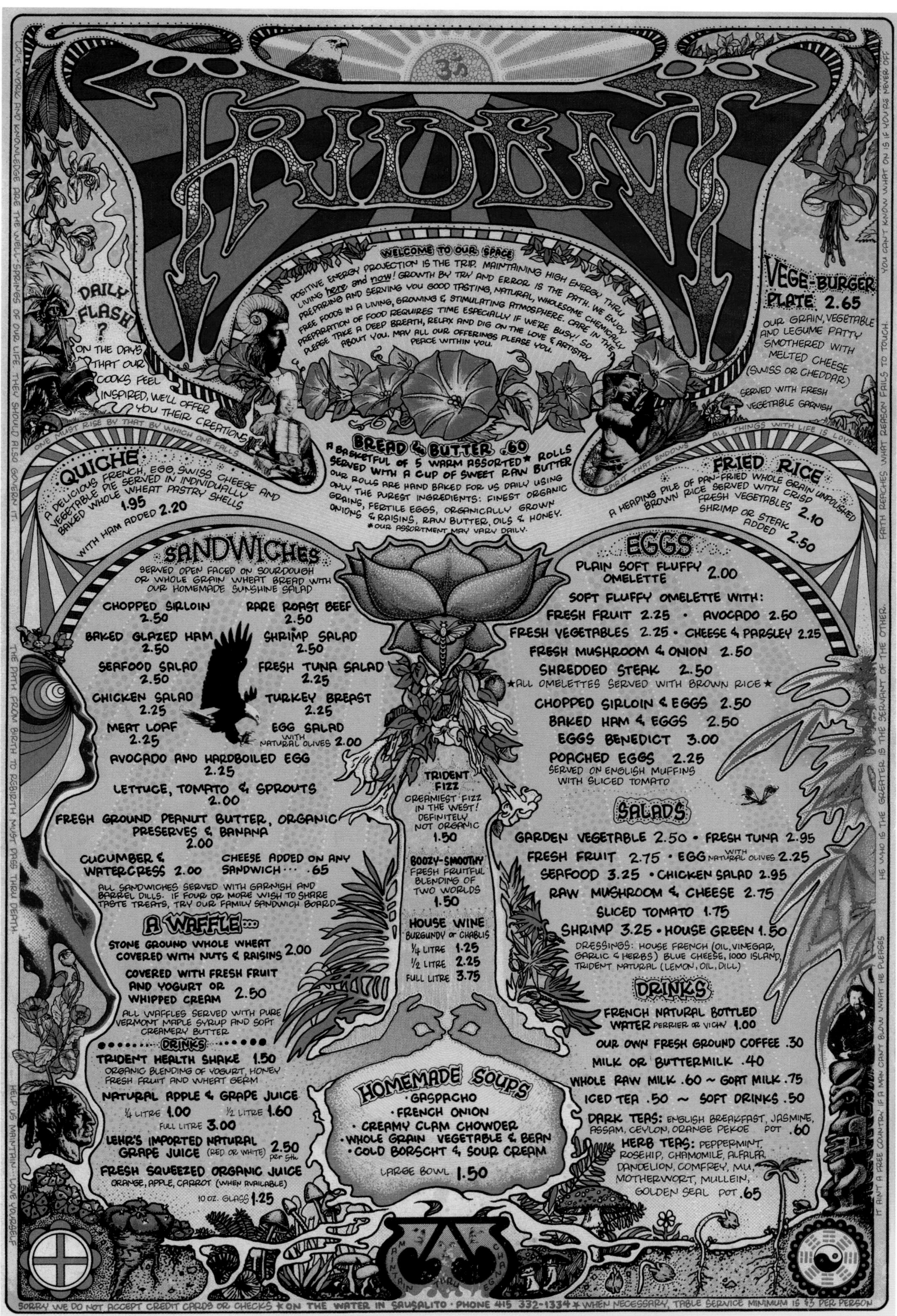
TRIDENT
WELCOME TO OUR SPACE
POSITIVE ENERGY PROJECTION IS THE TRIP. MAINTAINING HIGH ENERGY THRU LIVING here and now! GROWTH BY TRY AND ERROR IS THE PATH. WE ENJOY PREPARING AND SERVING YOU GOOD TASTING, NATURAL, WHOLESOME CHEMICALLY FREE FOODS IN A LIVING, GROWING & STIMULATING ATMOSPHERE. CARE IN THE PREPARATION OF FOOD REQUIRES TIME ESPECIALLY IF WE'RE BUSY! SO PLEASE TAKE A DEEP BREATH, RELAX AND DIG ON THE LOVE & ARTISTRY ABOUT YOU. MAY ALL OUR OFFERINGS PLEASE YOU. PEACE WITHIN YOU.
DAILY FLASH ? ON THE DAYS THAT OUR COOKS FEEL INSPIRED, WE'LL OFFER YOU THEIR CREATIONS
VEGE-BURGER PLATE 2.65
OUR GRAIN, VEGETABLE AND LEGUME PATTY SMOTHERED WITH MELTED CHEESE (SWISS OR CHEDDAR)
SERVED WITH FRESH VEGETABLE GARNISH
ONE MUST RISE BY THAT BY WHICH ONE FALLS
QUICHE
A DELICIOUS FRENCH, EGG, SWISS CHEESE AND VEGETABLE PIE SERVED IN INDIVIDUALLY BAKED WHOLE WHEAT PASTRY SHELLS 1.95
WITH HAM ADDED 2.20
BREAD & BUTTER .60
A BASKETFUL OF 5 WARM ASSORTED★ ROLLS SERVED WITH A CUP OF SWEET RAW BUTTER
OUR ROLLS ARE HAND BAKED FOR US DAILY USING ONLY THE PUREST INGREDIENTS: FINEST ORGANIC GRAINS, FERTILE EGGS, ORGANICALLY GROWN ONIONS & RAISINS, RAW BUTTER, OILS & HONEY.
★OUR ASSORTMENT MAY VARY DAILY.
THE SPIRIT THAT ENDOWS ALL THINGS WITH LIFE IS LOVE
FRIED RICE
A HEAPING PILE OF PAN-FRIED WHOLE GRAIN UNPOLISHED BROWN RICE SERVED WITH CRISP FRESH VEGETABLES 2.10
SHRIMP OR STEAK ADDED 2.50
SANDWICHES
SERVED OPEN FACED ON SOURDOUGH OR WHOLE GRAIN WHEAT BREAD WITH OUR HOMEMADE SUNSHINE SALAD
CHOPPED SIRLOIN 2.50
RARE ROAST BEEF 2.50
BAKED GLAZED HAM 2.50
SHRIMP SALAD 2.50
SEAFOOD SALAD 2.50
FRESH TUNA SALAD 2.25
CHICKEN SALAD 2.25
TURKEY BREAST 2.25
MEAT LOAF 2.25
EGG SALAD WITH NATURAL OLIVES 2.00
AVOCADO AND HARDBOILED EGG 2.25
LETTUCE, TOMATO & SPROUTS 2.00
FRESH GROUND PEANUT BUTTER, ORGANIC PRESERVES & BANANA 2.00
CUCUMBER & WATERCRESS 2.00
CHEESE ADDED ON ANY SANDWICH ... .65
ALL SANDWICHES SERVED WITH GARNISH AND BARREL DILLS. IF FOUR OR MORE WISH TO SHARE TASTE TREATS, TRY OUR FAMILY SANDWICH BOARD.
A WAFFLE...
STONE GROUND WHOLE WHEAT COVERED WITH NUTS & RAISINS 2.00
COVERED WITH FRESH FRUIT AND YOGURT OR WHIPPED CREAM 2.50
ALL WAFFLES SERVED WITH PURE VERMONT MAPLE SYRUP AND SOFT CREAMERY BUTTER
DRINKS
TRIDENT HEALTH SHAKE 1.50
ORGANIC BLENDING OF YOGURT, HONEY FRESH FRUIT AND WHEAT GERM
NATURAL APPLE & GRAPE JUICE
1/4 LITRE 1.00
1/2 LITRE 1.60
FULL LITRE 3.00
LEHR'S IMPORTED NATURAL GRAPE JUICE (RED OR WHITE) 2.50 per 5th
FRESH SQUEEZED ORGANIC JUICE
ORANGE, APPLE, CARROT (WHEN AVAILABLE)
10 OZ. GLASS 1.25
EGGS
PLAIN SOFT FLUFFY OMELETTE 2.00
SOFT FLUFFY OMELETTE WITH:
FRESH FRUIT 2.25 • AVOCADO 2.50
FRESH VEGETABLES 2.25 • CHEESE & PARSLEY 2.25
FRESH MUSHROOM & ONION 2.50
SHREDDED STEAK 2.50
★ALL OMELETTES SERVED WITH BROWN RICE★
CHOPPED SIRLOIN & EGGS 2.50
BAKED HAM & EGGS 2.50
EGGS BENEDICT 3.00
POACHED EGGS 2.25
SERVED ON ENGLISH MUFFINS WITH SLICED TOMATO
TRIDENT FIZZ
CREAMIEST FIZZ IN THE WEST! DEFINITELY NOT ORGANIC 1.50
BOOZY-SMOOTHY
FRESH FRUITFUL BLENDING OF TWO WORLDS 1.50
HOUSE WINE
BURGUNDY or CHABLIS
1/4 LITRE 1.25
1/2 LITRE 2.25
FULL LITRE 3.75
SALADS
GARDEN VEGETABLE 2.50 • FRESH TUNA 2.95
FRESH FRUIT 2.75 • EGG WITH NATURAL OLIVES 2.25
SEAFOOD 3.25 • CHICKEN SALAD 2.95
RAW MUSHROOM & CHEESE 2.75
SLICED TOMATO 1.75
SHRIMP 3.25 • HOUSE GREEN 1.50
DRESSINGS: HOUSE FRENCH (OIL, VINEGAR, GARLIC & HERBS) BLUE CHEESE, 1000 ISLAND, TRIDENT NATURAL (LEMON, OIL, DILL)
DRINKS
FRENCH NATURAL BOTTLED WATER PERRIER OR VICHY 1.00
OUR OWN FRESH GROUND COFFEE .30
MILK OR BUTTERMILK .40
WHOLE RAW MILK .60 ~ GOAT MILK .75
ICED TEA .50 ~ SOFT DRINKS .50
DARK TEAS: ENGLISH BREAKFAST, JASMINE, ASSAM, CEYLON, ORANGE PEKOE POT .60
HERB TEAS: PEPPERMINT, ROSEHIP, CHAMOMILE, ALFALFA, DANDELION, COMFREY, MU, MOTHERWORT, MULLEIN, GOLDEN SEAL POT .65
HOMEMADE SOUPS
• GASPACHO
• FRENCH ONION
• CREAMY CLAM CHOWDER
• WHOLE GRAIN VEGETABLE & BEAN
• COLD BORSCHT & SOUR CREAM
LARGE BOWL 1.50
MAINTAIN THRU CHANGE
LOVE WORK AND KNOWLEDGE ARE THE WELL-SPRINGS OF OUR LIFE. THEY SHOULD ALSO GOVERN IT.
THE PATH FROM BIRTH TO REBIRTH MUST PASS THRU DEATH.
HELP US MAINTAIN · LOVE YOURSELF
YOU CAN'T KNOW WHAT ON IS IF YOU'RE NEVER OFF
FAITH REACHES WHAT REASON FAILS TO TOUCH.
HE WHO IS THE GREATER IS THE SERVANT OF THE OTHER.
IT AIN'T A FREE COUNTRY IF A MAN CAN'T BLOW WHAT HE PLEASES
SORRY WE DO NOT ACCEPT CREDIT CARDS OR CHECKS ★ ON THE WATER IN SAUSALITO • PHONE 415 332-1334 ★ WHEN NECESSARY, TABLE SERVICE MINIMUM IS $3 PER PERSON

LEFT Trans World Service, c. 1973

This Trans World Airlines menu shows New York landmarks by famed illustrator Bob Peak. Trans World Airlines popularized postwar commercial intercontinental air service in the 1940s with a New York–Paris flight.

Diese Karte der Trans World Airlines mit den Wahrzeichen New Yorks stammt von dem namhaften Zeichner Bob Peak. Die Trans World Airlines machten nach dem Krieg in den 1940ern mit ihrer Route New York–Paris Transkontinentalflüge populär.

Cette carte de la Trans World Airlines évoque des symboles new-yorkais illustrés par Bob Peak. À la fin des années 1940, la TWA a popularisé les vols intercontinentaux en inaugurant un vol New York–Paris.

BELOW Continental Airlines, c. 1970

Tropical Bounty

LAMA HO'OHUIHUI 'IA
Proud Bird Cocktail
Beachcomber Chi Chi
Tahitian Coffee • Rum • Scotch • Bourbon
Canadian • Beachcomber Mai Tai • Vodka
Gin • Vermouth • Sherry • Mixes • Beer
Champagne

"ALOHA KAKAHIAKA"

LAMA HO'OHUIHUI 'IA
Tahitian Coffee
Bloody Mary
Screwdriver
Champagne

WAI A ME HUA'AI
Chilled Tomato or
Kauai Guava Juice
Kula Breakfast Fruit

'AI A MA'ONA
Eggs Benedict on Iania English Muffin
Tenderloin Steak, Ulupalakua

PALAOA
Freshly heated Croissants
and Assorted Muffins, Maika'i
Butter, Momona

MEA INU
Kona Coffee • Tea • Sanka
Coca-Cola • Sprite • Fresca
Canada Dry • Quinine • Club Soda

ABOVE American Airlines, 1971

This first-class lounge cabin located in the bulging space atop the main fuselage of a Boeing 747 was a nod to the growing luxury of in-flight casual dining in the 1970s.

Auf diesem Foto ist die Erste-Klasse-Lounge oben im Buckel der Boeing 747 zu sehen. In den 1970ern leistete man sich immer häufiger den Luxus entspannten Speisens während des Flugs.

Cette photo montre la cabine de première classe placée dans le renflement du fuselage du Boeing 747, témoin du luxe croissant de la restauration en vol dans les années 1970.

RIGHT The Russian Tea Room, 1971, New York, New York

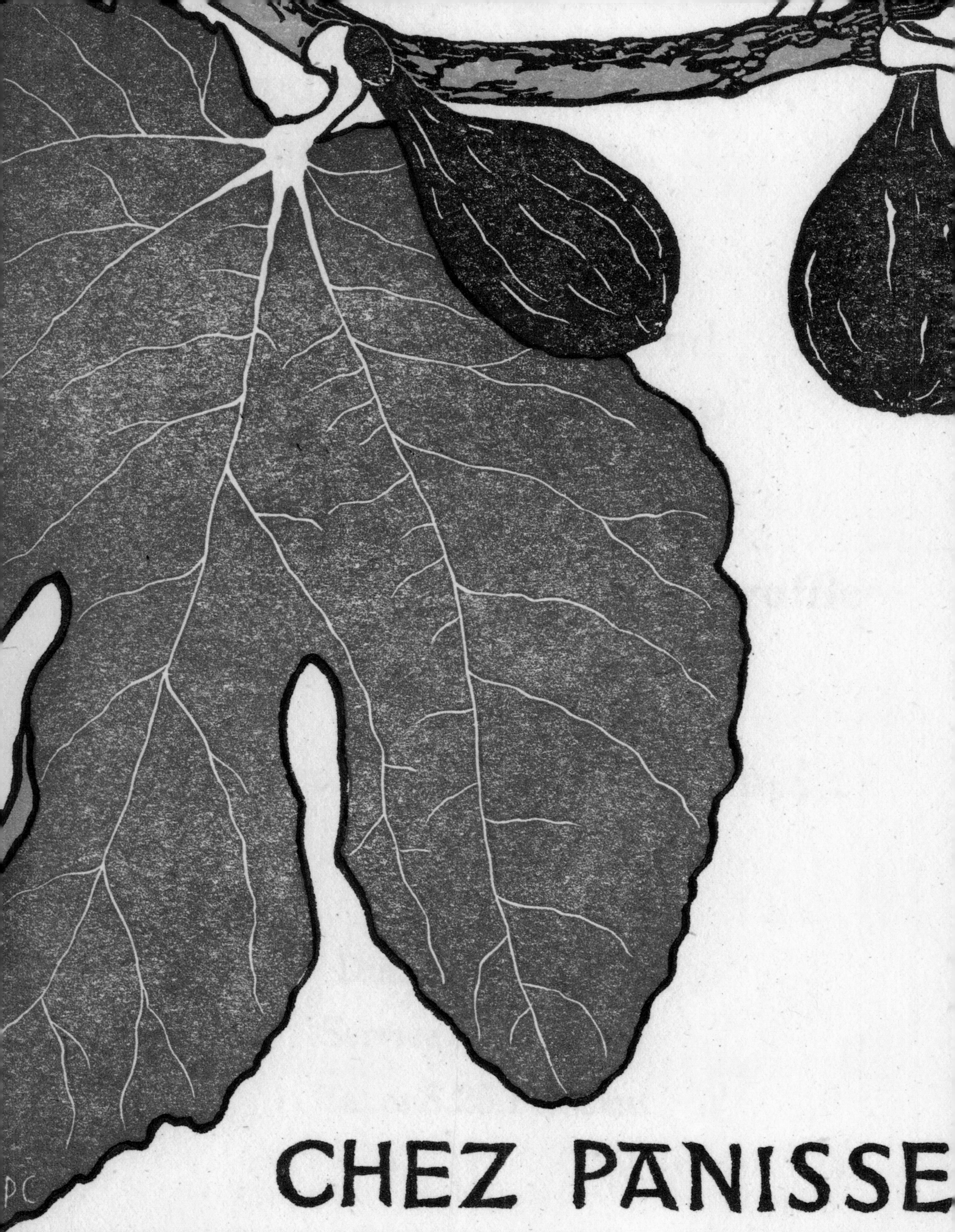
CHEZ PANISSE
PC

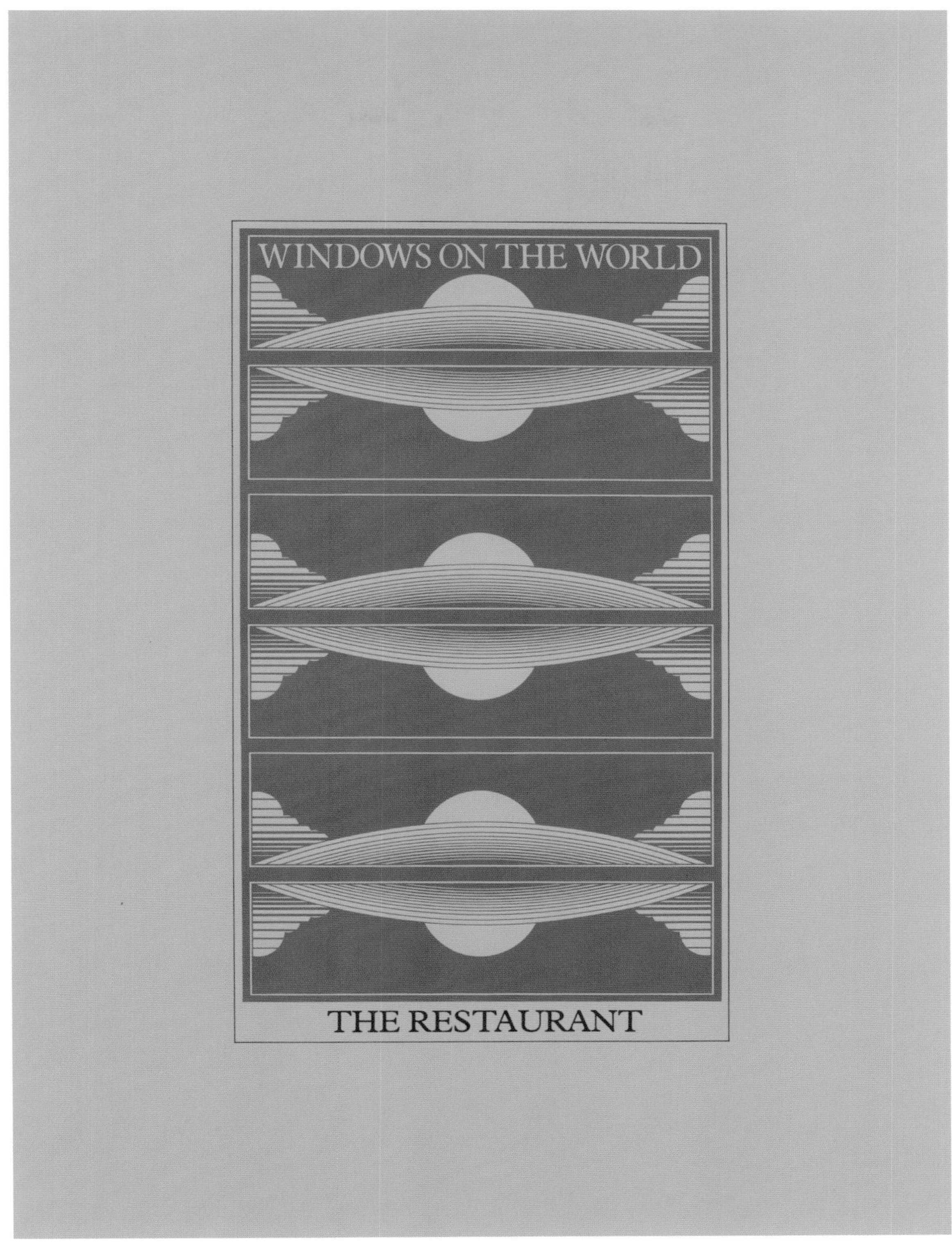

OPPOSITE Chez Panisse, c. 1985, Berkeley, California

Alice Waters first cooked vegetarian food for members of the Berkeley counterculture, and later opened Chez Panisse, a restaurant based on French Provençal models. It had a set menu at a fixed price with no choices, created each day based on the then-revolutionary idea that food should be as fresh and seasonal as possible. This concept was heralded by a quickly developing American "foodie" movement and forged what became known as New American Cuisine.

Anfangs kochte Alice Waters vegetarisches Essen für Hippies in Berkeley, dann eröffnete sie das Chez Panisse, dem die Küche der Provence in Südfrankreich als Vorbild diente. Serviert wurde ein Menü zum Fixpreis ohne Wahlmöglichkeiten. Es war jeden Tag anders, gemäß der damals revolutionären Idee, dass gutes Essen so frisch und saisonal wie möglich sein sollte. Dieses Konzept schrieb sich die amerikanische „Foodie"-Bewegung auf die Fahnen, die den Anfang der New American Cuisine bildete.

Alice Waters cuisine ses premiers plats végétariens pour les adeptes de la contre-culture de Berkeley. Plus tard, elle ouvre Chez Panisse, un restaurant aux influences provençales. Le menu fixe est renouvelé tous les jours selon l'idée, à l'époque révolutionnaire, que le produit doit être à la fois frais et de saison. Ce concept a été porté par le mouvement « foodie » aux États-Unis et s'est rapidement constitué en « nouvelle cuisine américaine ».

ABOVE Windows on the World Restaurant, 1976, New York, New York

When the World Trade Center opened in the 1970s, its restaurants were to be as spectacular. Its food was modern American and European, and its popularity with tourists enduring. The buildings were destroyed in the terrorist attack of Sept. 11, 2001.

Als das World Trade Center in den 1970er-Jahren eröffnet wurde, sollten seine Restaurants so spektakulär sein wie die Bauten. Serviert wurde modernes amerikanisches und europäisches Essen, das bei Touristen ungemein beliebt war. Die Gebäude wurden beim Terroranschlag vom 11. September 2001 zerstört.

À l'ouverture du World Trade Center dans les années 1970, ses restaurants sont spectaculaires. La cuisine y est moderne, américaine ou européenne, et sa popularité internationale. Jusqu'à un certain 11 septembre 2001…

LEFT **Mr. Chow's matchbox, c. 1971**

BELOW **Mr. Chow's, c. 1983, Beverly Hills, California**

Mr. Chow elevated Chinese food to stellar proportions, garnering a celebrity clientele at his original London location, which opened in 1968, and later at his restaurant in Beverly Hills.

Mr. Chow verwandelte chinesisches Essen in eine kulinarische Sensation, was ihm im 1968 in London eröffneten Mr. Chow's und später genauso in Beverly Hills ein prominentes Stammpublikum einbrachte.

Mr. Chow porte la cuisine chinoise à des sommets. Il accueillera une clientèle de célébrités, d'abord à Londres, où il ouvre un établissement en 1968, puis à Beverly Hills.

KOREAN MEAT

If you order this dish, make sure everybody at your table eats some too, as it is highly spiced with garlic and other seasonings. It is sliced pork served almost cold.

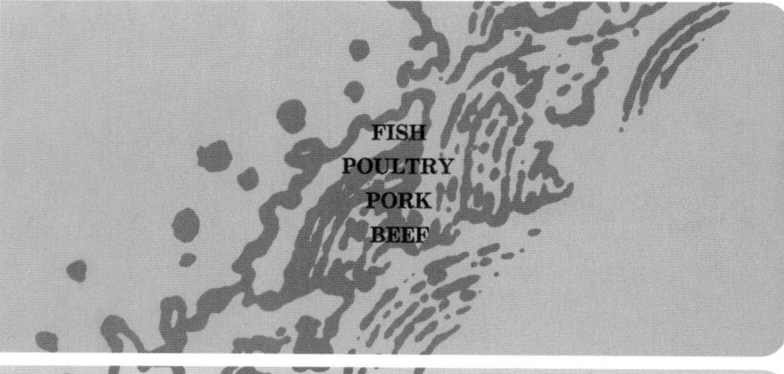

MR. CHOW'S PEKING CHICKEN

The flavour of this chicken dish which comes from the yellow bean sauce is truly Chinese. The breast of the chicken is cubed, seasoned and swiftly sauteed in a mixture of oil and white of egg. The sauce is added at the last moment.

ORANGE CURAÇAO

Whole peeled oranges, steeped in a caramel sauce, topped by shredded orange peel and flavoured with a generous soaking of orange curaçao liqueur.

ABOVE Circus Maximus, Caesar's Palace, c. 1975, Las Vegas, Nevada

LEFT & BELOW Atomic, c. 1979, Los Angeles, California

DINNERS

HALF SPRING CHICKEN............3.20
T-BONE STEAK........................3.50
CHICKEN FRIED STEAK............2.95
GROUND ROUND STEAK..........2.95
SALISBURY STEAK..................2.80
BREADED VEAL CUTLETS........2.95
LIVER AND ONIONS.................2.50
PORTUGUESE RICE 2.95
WEINER AND RICE 2.50
GO GO CHICKEN......................3.20
STEAK DINNER 4.90
BEEF STEW RICE 2.60
PORK CHOP.............................2.90

NOODLES
(Best in town)

PORK NOODLE........................1.85
CHICKEN NOODLE...................1.85
KAMABOKO NOODLE...............1.85
CHOYAN NOODLE.... ....1.95
BEEF NOODLE 2.55
NAMATAMAGO NOODLE...........1.90

JAPANESE DISHES

BEEF TERIYAKI.......................3.20
PORK TERIYAKI......................3.00
BEEF/PORK NIKUYASAI...........3.10
CHICKEN TERIYAKI.................3.10
WEINER TERIYAKI 2.85
SAKANA TERIYAKI..................2.90
BEEF NIKUABE.........................3.20
PORK NIKUABE........................3.20
BUTA TOFU (Beef)....................2.90

FISH

SASHIMI.................................season
YAKISAKANA...........................2.90
TEMPURA................................4.50

ATOMIC SPECIALS

HAMBURGER GACHA................2.50
WEINER GACHA.......................2.50
CHA SHU GACHA......................2.50

CHINESE DISHES

SWEET AND SOUR SPARERIBS...2.70
CHA SHU...............................2.70

CHOW MEIN

PORK/BEEF CHOW MEIN,Chicago..2.90
SHRIMP CHOW MEIN,Chicago....2.95
CHICKEN CHOW MEIN,Chicago...2.90
PORK/BEEF CHOW MEIN,Canton...2.90
SHRIMP CHOW MEIN,Canton......2.95
CHICKEN CHOW MEIN,Canton... 2.90

CHOP SUEY

PORK CHOP SUEY....................2.60
BEEF CHOP SUEY.....................2.60
SHRIMP CHOP SUEY.................2.65
CHICKEN CHOP SUEY...............2.60

FOO YOUNG

EGG FOO YOUNG......................2.70
PORK, BEEF, OR SHRIMP FOO YOUNG 2.80
CHICKEN FOO YOUNG...............2.80

FRIED RICE

PORK OR HAM FRIED RICE........2.60
CHICKEN FRIED RICE...............2.60
SHRIMP FRIED RICE.................2.65
WEINER FRIED RICE................2.60
CHA SHU FRIED RICE...............2.60

BREAKFAST

TWO FRIED EGGS w/potatoes/rice...1.25
HAM, BACON, WEINER, SAUSAGE, BOLOGNA OR HAMBURGER & TWO EGGS w/potatoes or rice......2.50
ORDER OF HAM AND RICE...........2.50
BACON, HAM OR SHRIMP OMELETTE with potatoes or rice.................2.50
BOLOGNA AND RICE...................2.50
BOLOGNA AND EGGS w/rice........2.50
PORTUGUESE SAUSAGE & EGGS with potatoes or rice..................2.60
PORTUGUESE SAUSAGE OMELETTE..2.60

DRINKS

COCA COLA.............................. .30
ORANGE JUICE.......................... .50
MILK.. .45
HOT MILK................................. .50
COFFEE..................................... .35
ICED COFFEE............................ .40
HOT TEA................................... .35
ICED TEA.................................. .40
HOT CHOCOLATE........................ .50

cresc.

HOT SANDWICHES

BEEF OR PORK.......................... 1.80
TURKEY.................................... 1.80

SALADS

CHICKEN - SHRIMPS - TUNA..........1.85
LETTUCE AND TOMATO................1.85

SANDWICHES

CHA SHU................................. 1.35
HAM OR BACON AND EGG............1.45
HAMBURGER 1.00
CHEESEBURGER........................1.20
WEINER................................... .95
LETTUCE AND TOMATO..... .... .95
TUNA.......................................1.00
CHEESE.................................... .95
FRIED HAM................................1.20
BACON AND TOMATO..................1.30
STEAK......................................1.90
CHICKEN...................................1.20
COLD BEEF................................1.20
COLD PORK................................1.20
COLD TURKEY.............................1.20
HAM AND CHEESE.......................1.40
GRILLED CHEESE.......................1.30
GRILLED HAM AND CHEESE.......1.50

SIDE DISHES

CHA SHU...................................1.00
KAMABOKO................................1.00
TOFU..1.00
WEINER.....................................1.00
HAM..1.00
BACON.......................................1.00
BOLOGNA...................................1.00
FRENCH FRIED POTATOES..........1.00

DESSERTS

PIE.. .50
CAKE...... .... .55
ICE CREAM................................ .35

We reserve the right to refuse service to anyone
Sales tax will be added to all taxable items
Not responsible for lost or stolen articles
See you later...Science Holiday Menu Co.

PAGES 388 & 389 Spago, 1981, Los Angeles, California

When Austrian-born chef Wolfgang Puck opened Spago ("string" in Italian) in 1980 as a casual restaurant off Sunset Boulevard, he had no idea he was pioneering what would be called "California cuisine," based on his open-grill kitchen and his "gourmet pizzas," like the one topped with smoked salmon, sour cream, and caviar.

Als der in Österreich geborene Koch Wolfgang Puck 1980 das legere Restaurant Spago (italienisch „Schnur") in der Nähe des Sunset Boulevard eröffnete, ahnte er nicht, dass er zum Pionier der „California Cuisine" werden würde. Mittelpunkt seiner Küche waren der offene Grill und seine „Gourmetpizze", wie die mit Räucherlachs, saurer Sahne und Kaviar.

Le chef autrichien Wolfgang Puck ouvre le Spago (« ficelle » en italien) en 1980, un restaurant décontracté près de Sunset Boulevard. Il ne se doute pas encore qu'il va devenir le pionnier de la « cuisine californienne », basée sur des grillades et des « pizzas gastronomiques » dont l'une recouverte de saumon fumé, crème aigre et caviar.

Basil
Shrimps
Basil
Tomatoe
Vinaigrette
Spago
California Cuisine
Pears
Caramel Sauce
Puffpastry
Watercress
Vegetables
Baby Lamb
Wolfgang Puck 1981

LISA STALVEY—CHEF

APPETIZERS

Marinated fresh tuna with avocado, kaiware and sweet onions	9.50
Fresh asparagus with watercress vinaigrette	8.50
Salad of field greens with goat cheese sauteed in olive oil	8.50
Cream of wild mushrooms	6.00
Sauteed Pacific oysters with spicy salsa	8.50
Marinated salmon with dill, golden caviar and toasted brioche	11.00
Grilled baby chicken salad with red leaves, mache, walnut oil and aged Italian vinegar	9.50
Sauteed foie gras with arugula and chanterelle mushrooms	12.50
Cold lobster salad with sour cream, tarragon and mint sauce	12.50
Spicy rare beef salad with ginger mandarin vinaigrette	9.50

PASTAS

Lobster ravioli with chardonnay dill butter and julienne of vegetables	11.00
Angel hair noodles with goat cheese, broccoli and basil	9.50
Pink & black peppercorn fettuccini with smoked duck breast	10.50
Wild mushroom ravioli with sauteed chanterelles and cabernet butter	9.50
Black angel hair pasta with shrimp, lobster butter and garden vegetables	11.00

PIZZAS

Pizza with prosciutto, goat cheese, sweet peppers, double blanched garlic and red onions	11.00
Pizza with smoked shrimps, tomatoes, artichokes, basil and garlic	12.00
Pizza with duck sausage, tomatoes, mozzarella, fresh oregano and garlic	10.50
Pizza with artichokes, wild mushrooms, leeks, sweet onions, eggplant and fresh herbs	9.50
Pizza with lamb sausage, coriander, wild mushrooms, garlic and zucchini	9.50
Calzone with goat cheese, wild mushrooms, scallions and sun dried tomatoes	11.00

ENTREES

Grilled tuna with tomato basil vinaigrette	17.50
Grilled free-range chicken with garlic and fresh herbs	16.50
Composition of grilled fish with two vinaigrettes	18.50
Crispy sauteed sweetbreads with turnip greens and pancetta	17.50
Grilled John Dory with eggplant caviar and ginger vinaigrette	17.50
Grilled Alaskan salmon with tomatillos, jalapeno and garlic cream	17.50
Roasted Sonoma baby lamb with lime pesto butter	18.50
Grilled squab with foie gras and vinegar butter	17.50
Roasted Chinese duck with honey and mustard sauce	17.50
Grilled calf's liver with red onion marmalade and mustard seeds	16.50
Grilled veal chop with balsamic vinegar, cilantro butter and roasted radicchio	19.50
Whole fish of the day	

DESSERTS

Marjolaine with raspberry sauce	5.50
Creme brulee with fresh berries	5.50
Apple pie with caramel ice cream	5.50
Pecan pie with banana ice cream	5.50
Parfait of three chocolates and bitter chocolate sauce	5.50
Assortment of homemade ice cream and cookies	5.50
Warm puff pastry with raspberries and caramel sauce	5.50

BEVERAGES

Coffee	2.00
Tea	2.00
Fresh mint tea	2.00
Espresso	2.00

Split 2.00

BARBARA LAZAROFF—Interior design and decor, kitchen and lighting design

Index

MÉDAILLE D'ARGENT, VILLE DE PARIS

MAITRES CUISINIERS DE FRANCE

TRADITIONS ET QUALITE

ROUTE DU BONHEUR

CORDONS BLEUS DE FRANCE

CHEVALIERS DU TASTEVIN

COMPAGNONS DU BEAUJOLAIS

TOURING CLUB DE FRANCE

RESTAURANTS DE TOURISME

CHAINE DES ROTISSEURS

Thanks to Benedikt Taschen who wholeheartedly supported this volume and continues to exhibit his prescience in the book world.

Special thanks to the institutions and collectors who made material and research for this book available including: Jeff Carr, Henry Voigt, and an anonymous contributor who graciously opened his collection with "no strings attached." Thanks for the hospitality and the wine.

A special mention goes to "the best dealer around," Dan De Palma, who, for over twenty years, provided me with thousands of items of ephemera and some of the best menus in my collection. His friendship and the conversations we had in his garage warehouse will be sorely missed.

The TASCHEN team: Victoria Birch, as always the consummate professional, Josh Baker, Jennifer Patrick, Kathrin Murr, Will Wasson, Mallory Farrugia, David Martinez, Jessica Sappenfield, and the inimitable Nina Wiener made the elongated process of pulling a book together seamless. And last but not least, a big thanks to my archivist, Ryan Mungia for organizing and cataloging thousands of menus and more importantly for his friendship and our ability to sustain each others' idiosyncrasies.

Additional thanks to Christine Crawford-Oppenheimer, Culinary Institute of America; Michelle Press and Joelle Sedlmeyer, Getty Images; Richard Gutman and Erin Williams, Johnson and Wales University Culinary Arts Museum; Kathryn Kanjo, Museum Of Contemporary Art, San Diego; Kristin Morris, San Francisco Historical Society; Su Kim Chung and Peter Michel, University of Nevada, Las Vegas; New York Historical Society; New York Public Library; University of California, Santa Barbara.

—Jim Heimann, Executive Editor, TASCHEN America

Collectors note: *While the menus in this book retain their original character and integrity, some of the menus have been altered for production and design considerations.*

All images are from the collection of Jim Heimann unless otherwise noted. Any omissions for copy or credit will be given in future editions if such copyright holders contact the publisher. Additional images were provided courtesy of the following individuals and institutions: The Culinary Arts Museum at Johnson & Wales University: 16, 55, 132. The Culinary Institute of America, Conrad N. Hilton Library: 177, 210, 348, 355, 356, 372, 374, 376, 377, 379, 383. © The Granger Collection: 69, 94. Jim Heiman Collection / Whittington Studio: 140. Library of Congress / Gottscho-Schleisner Collection: 308. Library of Congress / Panoramic Photographs collection: 75. Pierre Odier: 175. Private Collection: 8, 10, 12, 14, 18, 21, 22, 24, 25, 26, 30, 32, 36, 40, 43, 46, 47, 48, 49, 50, 51, 52, 53, 54, 55, 56, 57, 58, 59, 60, 61, 62, 63, 64, 65, 66, 67, 68, 69, 70, 71, 72, 73, 74, 75, 79, 82, 89, 91, 96, 97, 102, 106, 107, 109, 116, 118, 119, 120, 121, 133, 136, 137, 142, 144, 145, 146, 154, 180, 184, 185, 186, 187, 210, 211, 216, 219, 226, 247, 284, 285, 352, 353, 359, 378, 385. James R. Smith: 182. Time & Life Pictures/Getty Images: 147, 193, 240, 253, 349. Track 16 Gallery: 183. Carleton Varney: 309. UNLV Special Collections, Bohn-Bettoni Collection: 67, 76, 77, 94, 257.

ISBN: 978-3-8365-2662-3

Hohenzollernring 53, D–50672 Köln
www.taschen.com

To stay informed about upcoming TASCHEN titles, please request our magazine at www.taschen.com/magazine or write to TASCHEN, Hohenzollernring 53, D-50672 Cologne, Germany; contact@taschen.com; Fax: +49-221-254919. We will be happy to send you a free copy of our magazine, which is filled with information about all of our books.

Design: Josh Baker, Los Angeles
Editorial coordination: Victoria Birch, Los Angeles, Florian Kobler, and Kathrin Murr, Cologne
Production: Jennifer Patrick, Los Angeles
Layout: Will Wasson and Rachel Maximo, Los Angeles
German translation: Anke Caroline Burger, Berlin
French translation: Guillaume Marlière, Conches-en-Ouche, France
Collaboration: Jessica Sappenfield, Los Angeles and Arnaud Briand, Paris

Printed in China

The Royal Blue Line

ALE ALE KAI

RECTOR'S

JOHN'S CAFE
AVALON
SANTA CATALINA ISLAND

The Oasis
TLAND, OREGON
pecializing
a Carte Service

Cafe Society

RICE BOWL
THE OUTSTANDING ORIENTAL CAFE
COCKTAIL
DINE
DANCE
MUSIC
大華酒家
949 SUN MUN WAY
NEW CHINATOWN, LOS ANGELES CAL.

ROMANOFFS

rinks

Menu
Baron Long's
Ship Café
VENICE

The Friars
COMPLIMENTARY DINNER AND DANCE
to
Miss Mary Pickford
and
Mr. Douglas Fairbanks
HOTEL ASTOR
AUGUST 1, 1920

THIS IS THE ORIGINAL FRIENDSHIP HOUSE — WE HAVE NO OTHER AFFILIATIONS
FRIENDSHIP HOUSE
The Home of Southern Hospitality
MIDWAY BETWEEN BILOXI AND GULFPORT, MISSISSIPPI, ON HIGHWAY 90
EXTRA CUT
BONELESS SIRLOIN
STRIP STEAK or FILET MIGNON
French Fried Potatoes, Bread and Butter $5.75
LOIN STEAK
Prepared the Friendship House Way
CHOPPED—
BROILED ON PLANK
Mushroom Sauce and Mashed Potatoes, Green Beans and Garden Peas, Bread & Butter $1.65
VEAL CUTLET
BREADED, TOMATO SAUCE
French Fried Onions and Potatoes, Sliced Tomato or Spring Garden Salad, Choice of Dressing, Bread and Butter $1.95
MAMMY
STYLE FRIED CHICKEN
OR SMOTHERED COUNTRY STYLE
French Fried Potatoes, Bread and Butter $1.75
Steak Plate
Grilled Tenderloin Steak
Lettuce and Tomato Salad
French Fried Potatoes
Asparagus
Bread and Butter
$2.45
Turkey Poulet
Sliced Breast of Turkey
Crisp Bacon on Toast with
Mushrooms—Wined
Creamed Sauce—Grated Cheese
$2.35
Chicken Plate
Fried Chicken
Creamed Potatoes
Garden Peas
Spring Garden Salad
Bread and Butter
$1.65
Old Fashion
BEAN SOUP .40
Small size .30
Sliced Prime
ROAST BEEF PLATE
With or Without Dressing
Potatoes and 1 Vegetable
$1.85
Sliced TURKEY PLATE
All White Meat
With or Without Dressing
Potatoes and 1 Vegetable
$1.95
Sliced TURKEY PLATE
All Dark Meat
With or Without Dressing
Potatoes and 1 Vegetable
$1.45
Home Made
VEGETABLE SOUP
Small size .30
SWISS STEAK
WINE GRAVY
Bread and Butter
$1.75
SHORT RIB
OF BEEF
with Rice or Potatoes
$1.35
SPAGHETTI
with Real Italian
Meat Sauce
$1.25
CREAMED
CHICKEN
with Rice or Dressing, in Casserole, Bread & Butter
$1.25
BEEF STEW
with
Vegetable, in Casserole
Bread and Butter
$1.25
STEAKS
FRIENDSHIP HOUSE DELIGHT - World's Best Hamburger Steak, Spaghetti, Brown Gravy 1.65
FILET MIGNON, Thick, all sinew cut out 3.40
BONELESS SIRLOIN STRIP, Thick 3.65
T. BONE and known as PORTERHOUSE 3.55
HAM, Broiled or Fried - F. F. Onions 2.15
PORK LOIN BARBECUE SAUCE, Vegetable 1.75
ROAST PORK Loin, S. Potatoes, Dressing 1.75
BAKED Ham Friendship House raisin sauce 1.75
HOT BISCUITS
FRIED CHICKEN (½) F. Fried Potatoes 1.65
GRILLED Pork Chop (1) F. Fried Potatoes .95
GRILLED Pork Chops (2) F. Fried Potatoes 1.55
CALF LIVER, Broiled or Fried, Onion Gravy 1.60
CHICKEN, A la Creole in Casserole 1.35
LAMB CHOPS, Loin Cut (2) Broiled or Fried 1.95
CHICKEN Gizzards, Mushroom Gravy 1.15
CHICKEN Livers on toast (when available) 1.75
COLD Plate, Astd. meats, cheese, pot. salad 1.75
WE WILL GLADLY MAKE A
Child's Plate
FROM MOST ITEMS ON THE MENU

SUBWAY CAFE 507
SUBWAY
CAFE
507
NORTH WABASH AVE
LONGEST BAR IN THE WORLD!

Menu
Mousse de jambon en Aspic
Potage Creme Palestine Consomme Sevigne
Cheese Sticks
Pickled Walnuts Spiced Pickles Chow Chow
Broiled Columbia River Salmon, Sauce Colbert
Pommes Dauphines
Cucumbers Mission Olives Tomatoes
Supreme of Capon, a l'Imperiale
Grenadins of Veal, a la Trianon Larded Sweetbreads, Parisienne
Roast Ribs of Beef, Garni a la Renaissance
Rice a la Malta
Stuffed Young Turkey, Cranberry Jelly
Roast Suckling Pig, Sweet Potatoes
Boiled Potatoes Mashed Potatoes
New Garden Peas Asparagus, Sauce Mousseline
Punch a la Leighton
Waldorf Salad
Broiled Squab, au Cresson
English Plum Pudding, Hard and Cognac Sauce
Hot Mince Pie Pumpkin Pie
Champagne Jelly
Bisque Ice Cream Assorted Cake
Assorted Fruits Mixed Nuts and Raisins
American, Roquefort and
Neufchatel Cheese
Crackers Wafers
Coffee
1905

The
BUNG
HOLE

Hotel Cleveland
A La Carte
Menu
Good Things to Eat

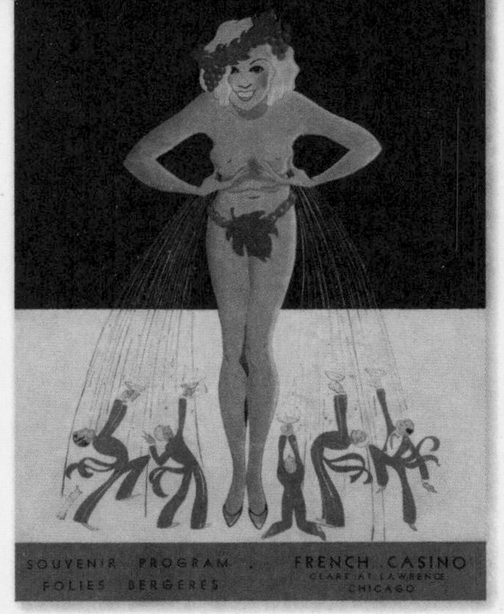
SOUVENIR PROGRAM
FOLIES BERGERES
FRENCH CASINO
CHICAGO

Balinese Room
The Blackstone

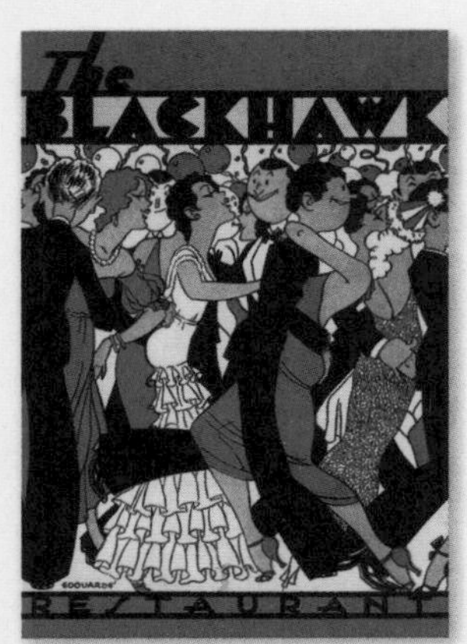
The
BLACKHAWK
RESTAURANT

BILL OF FARE
St. Louis, Cairo, Memphis & New-Orleans Passenger Packet
M. S. MEPHAM
Breakfast from 7½ to 9 A.M.
Dinner from 1 to 2½ P.M.
Supper at 6 P.M.
JAMES ABBEY Steward

LIBERTY
CAFE
COCKTAIL LOUNGE
Albuquerque
NEW MEXICO
105 West Central
Established 1915

The Gulf's Finest Food Fish
THAT GOOD OLD
WOP SALAD
WHOLE
Broiled Lobster
OUR FAMOUS
Sea Food Gumbo
$2.35
FRIED
FLOUNDER PLATE
$1.85
Hush Puppies with Seafood on request 15c per order
Sea Food Platter Deluxe
GULF COAST PLATE
$1.85
FROG LEGS
"JUMBO" SOFT SHELL CRAB
STUFFED DEVILED CRABS
SHRIMP
WHOLE FLOUNDER
All Our Foods Prepared With Fresh Creamery Butter

Zebra
Room

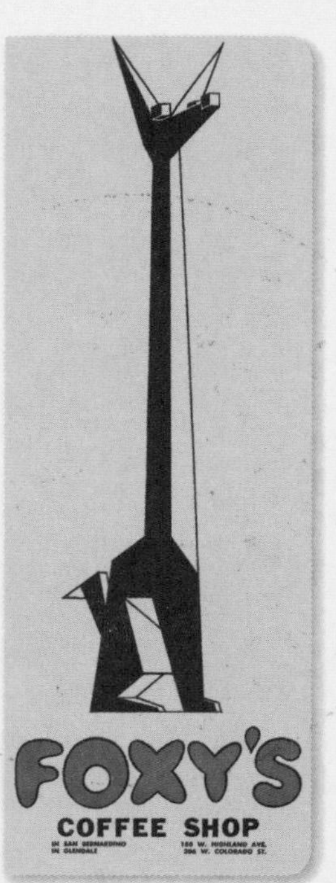
FOXY'S
COFFEE SHOP

TOOTS SHOR

TRADER VIC'S
XXX RUM

TROPICANA